The Limits to Capital

The Limits
to
Capital

DAVID HARVEY

VERSO

London • New York

This edition first published by Verso 1999
© David Harvey 1999
First published by Basil Blackwell, Oxford, 1982
© David Harvey 1982
All rights reserved

The moral rights of the author have been asserted

Verso
UK: 6 Meard Street, London W1V 3HR
US: 180 Varick Street, New York, NY 10014–4606

Verso is the imprint of New Left Books

ISBN 1–85984–714–5
ISBN 1–85984–209–7 (pbk)

British Library Cataloguing in Publication Data
A catalogue record for this book is available from the British Library

Library of Congress Cataloging-in-Publication Data
A catalog record for this book is available from the Library of Congress

Printed by Biddles Ltd, Guildford and King's Lynn

Contents

Introduction to the Verso Edition

The welcome reissue of *The Limits to Capital* in a Verso edition prompts some reflections on the peculiar fortunes of Marxian thinking and practices over the past three decades. My own immediate view of that history rests on the simple fact that I have run either a reading group or a course on Marx's *Capital* (volume 1) every year (except one) since 1971. This has given me a rare insight into how Marx's thought has been received in a particular place (mainly an elite university) over a period of time.

In the early years there was great political enthusiasm for it. Marx seemed to speak to those of us (always a minority, of course) who were seeking a theoretical basis to understand the chaos and political disruptions surrounding us at the time (the imperialist war in Vietnam, the strikes and urban unrest, the civil rights movement, the student movements of 1968 that shook the world from Paris to Mexico City, the Czech 'spring' and its subsequent repression by the Soviets, the war in the Middle East – just to name a few of the signal events that made it seem as if the world as we knew it was falling apart). So, faculty and graduate students gathered together to wrestle with Marx's arguments in the hope of making sense of all these political problems. *Capital* was not an easy text to decipher. But for those of us in universities, the intellectual difficulty was a normal challenge. As my understanding and appreciation of the text grew, I found myself teaching it well beyond the confines of the university: in the community (with activists, teachers, unionists) and even in the Maryland penitentiary (though not very successfully). Undergraduate student activists, on the other hand, often thought it too conventional to ask that they read and understand such a long and tortuous book. They paid no mind to Marx's injunction 'there is no royal road to science'. They were carried forward on a cresting wave of intuitions and bruised emotions (not, I hasten to add, necessarily a bad thing).

The situation is different now. I teach *Capital* as a respectable regular course in the university, and there is no demand for it outside. I rarely – if ever – see any faculty members, and the graduate student audience has largely disappeared. Marx is largely written off in self-styled 'radical' circles as the weaver of an impossibly huge and monolithic master narrative of history, an advocate of some totally impossible historical transformation that has in any case been proven by events (the collapse of the Wall) to be just as fallacious politically and practically as it always was theoretically. To pretend there is anything interesting about Marx after 1989 is to sound more and more like an all-but-extinct dinosaur whimpering its own last rites. Free-market capitalism rides triumphantly across the globe, slaying all such old dinosaurs in its path. The end of history is at hand.

Teaching *Capital* in such an atmosphere feels odd, to say the least. But some undergraduates still take the course. The fear of communism has largely dissipated. The course has a good reputation. Some students are curious to see what Marxism was all about (much as they might be interested in dinosaurs more generally). And a minority (now happily increasing) still have some radical instincts left to which they feel Marx might add an extra insight or two. So – depending on their timetable and their requirements – some undergraduates end up in Marx's *Capital* rather than in Aristotle's *Ethics* or Plato's *Republic*.

But there is another tale to be told that makes matters rather more confusing. In the early 1970s it was hard to find the direct relevance of *Capital* to the political issues that dominated the day. We needed Lenin to get us from Marx to an understanding of the imperialist war in Vietnam. We needed a theory of civil society (Gramsci at least) to get us from Marx to civil rights, and a theory of the state (such as Miliband or Poulantzas) to get us to a critique of state repressions and welfare state expenditures manipulated to requirements of capital accumulation. We needed the Frankfurt School to understand questions of legitimacy, technological rationality, bureaucracy and the environment. We needed, in short, many mediators to get from Marx's *Capital* to the political issues that concerned us.

That, however, has changed. *Capital* teems with ideas on how to explain our current state. There is the fetish of the market that caught out that TV personality and lover of children Kathy Lee Gifford when she was told that the line of clothing she was selling through Wal-Mart was made either by thirteen-year-olds in Honduras paid a mere pittance, or by sweated women workers in New York who had not been paid for weeks (to her credit, she then joined the anti-sweatshop campaign in the United States). There is the savage history of downsizing (prominently reported in the press), the scandals over child labour in Pakistan in the manufacture of carpets and soccer balls (a scandal that was forced upon the attention of the International Federation of Football Associations), and Michael Jordan's $30 million retainer for Nike, set against press accounts of the appalling conditions of Nike workers in Indonesia and Vietnam. There are the billion or so workers in the world struggling to make do on less than a dollar a day. The press is full of complaints about how technological change is destroying employment opportunities, weakening the institutions of organized labour and increasing rather than lightening the intensity and hours of labour (all central themes of Marx's chapter on 'Machinery and Modern Industry'). And then there is the whole question of how an 'industrial reserve army' of labour has been produced, sustained and manipulated in the interests of capital accumulation these last decades, including the public admission by Alan Budd, an erstwhile adviser to Margaret Thatcher, that the fight against inflation in the early 1980s was a cover for raising unemployment and reducing the strength of the working class. 'What was engineered,' he said, 'in Marxist terms – was a crisis in capitalism which re-created a reserve army of labour, and has allowed the capitalists to make high profits ever since' (Brooks, 1992). The rapidly increasing social inequalities (the 358 billionaires in the world who, according to recent UN estimates, command assets equivalent to 2.3 billion of the world's poorest population) obscenely demonstrate the truth of Marx's contention that freedoms of the market inevitably produce 'accumulation of wealth at one pole' and 'accumulation of misery, agony of toil, slavery, ignorance, brutality, mental degradation, at the opposite pole' (*Capital*, vol 1. p. 645).

It is now all too easy to connect the text of *Capital* to daily life. Students who stray into the course very soon feel the heat of a devastating critique of free-market capitalism. For their final paper I give them bundles of cuttings from the *New York Times* and the *Guardian*, and ask them to answer an imaginary letter from a parent/relative/friend which suggests that Marx, however relevant he may have been to the nineteenth century, is outmoded today 'because we have learned to do things differently'. The students write illuminating and stunningly critical (as well as well-documented) letters in reply. Few finish the course without having their views disrupted by the sheer power of a text that sheds such light on the conditions around us.

So here is the paradox. Marx's text was much sought after and studied in radical circles at a time when it had little direct relationship to daily life. But as *Capital* becomes more pertinent, fewer students and academics deign to consider, let alone study it. Unfortunately, this paradox is not confined to the university. It permeates much of civil society.

There are, however, signs of a turnaround. Labour activism, though patchy, is reviving (see, for example, Moody, 1997), and other kinds of oppositional movements to free-market capitalism are popping up all over the place. The connection between universities and a more activist labour movement is being revived in several countries (the USA and France being exemplary). At my own university students have campaigned, with some limited success, to make it a 'living wage' institution. In coalition with churches and other interested parties, they have raised the stakes as to what the 'moral element' (as Marx termed it) in wage determination might be all about. Students elsewhere have demonstrated against the use of sweatshop labour to make college sportswear (big business in the United States). An international anti-sweatshop campaign, mobilized through the unions, the churches, and other social movement groupings, has emerged, putting pressure (again, with some success) on firms like Nike to change their labour practices. International solidarity campaigns around labour issues are burgeoning on the Internet. There is even talk about the idea of a global living wage, and discussion as to what it might mean.

Much of this might have passed unnoticed were it not also for the sudden stalling out of the neo-liberal version of capitalism that formerly held such supremacy. Margaret Thatcher, Ronald Reagan, and Newt Gingrich now appear as somewhat ghostly figures from some strange era when they held unchallenged power and influence. Of course, much of what they stood for – freedoms of the market, privatization, diminution of state power with respect to capital (though not, of course, with respect to labour markets) – still holds sway. But critics now abound. George Soros (1998), a wealthy speculator financier (credited with forcing Britain out of the European Monetary System by his operations), voices strong criticism of the destabilizing threats of an unregulated and unbridled capitalism. John Gray (1998), an eminent conservative political theorist and no friend of socialism, opines that the utopianism of neo-liberalism will kill far more people in the next century than misguided socialist utopianism did in the twentieth. The capitalist way produces disastrous consequences in the ex-Soviet Union. By 1996, the organizers of the Davos Symposium (the global think-tank of neo-liberalism) worried that free-market globalization was a 'brakeless train wreaking havoc', and that the 'mounting backlash against its effects' was threatening to disrupt economic activity and social stability in many countries, promoting a mood of 'helplessness and anxiety' in the industrial democracies that could all too easily 'turn into revolt' (Friedman, 1996). By 1999 they considered it an urgent matter to 'demonstrate that globalization is not just a code word for an exclusive focus on shareholder value at the expense of any other considerations; that the free flow of goods and capital does not develop to the detriment of the most vulnerable segments of the population and of some accepted social and human standards' (Schwab and Smadja, 1999). Interestingly, the rhetoric here bears an uncanny resemblance to that of the Zapatistas who launched their rebellion in Chiapas on the day that NAFTA (the North Atlantic Free Trade Association) came into effect. Instead of humanity – the Zapatistas declared via the Internet – neo-liberalism 'offers us stock market value indexes, instead of dignity it offers us globalization of misery, instead of hope it offers us emptiness, instead of life it offers us the international of terror'.

Then came the bad news from the Far East in 1998: the collapse of currencies and whole economies, the sudden submergence of one of the engines of capitalist growth (most importantly, Japan) under a tidal wave of bankruptcies and plant closures, which threatened a cascading crisis that might engulf vulnerable economies in Latin America, and even wash back into the very heartlands of capitalist power. It made little sense to try to control that crisis by appeal to a rhetoric of market freedoms, structural adjustments, privatizations, and entrepreneurial initative and competition. The whole question of security and stability and the role of governments, individually and collectively, suddenly came back into play as corporate and transnational capitalist powers overtly recognized the need for regulatory and institutional supports to keep capital accumulation going.

Put all this together, and we have a climate of opinion somewhat more conducive to a thoroughgoing critique of the neo-liberal version of capitalism in particular, if not capitalism in general. And signs of that critique abound. Pierre Bourdieu (1993, 1998) takes a remarkable series of stands in support of the French workers' struggles which erupted in the 1990s, and publishes massive materials to indict the soulless qualities of contemporary free-market capitalism. Richard Rorty (1997) suddenly proclaims the importance of class and class struggle; and Henry Louis Gates argues in a public TV programme that class is now far more important than race in the social fragmentations that are fissuring the United States. Judith Butler (1998), a major theorist of feminism and advocate of queer theory, seeks some sort of *rapprochement* with the Marxist tradition. Even the New Yorker, hardly a radical rag, in its special issue on 'The next of everything' (October 1997), has a lengthy article by someone friendly to Wall Street explaining (with considerable insight and sophistication) why Karl Marx is the 'next great thinker' (Cassidy, 1997). If you want to understand how capitalism works, the argument runs, you can do no better than read Marx, because he understood it better than anyone before or since. (Marx was not, of course, rated as a political thinker or activist in the *New Yorker*'s eyes.) And then, to cap it all (at least for self-styled postmodern radicals), someone as eminent as Jacques Derrida (1994) insists that the spectre of Marx can never be erased. With all this fluttering going on in the wings, can that other spectre – the communist alternative – be far behind?

This sudden resurgence of interest in the critique of capitalism makes it a propitious moment in which to reconsider Marx's arguments in general, and *The Limits to Capital* in particular. *Limits* was written in an attempt to make Marx's political economic thought as a whole both more accessible and more relevant to the specific problems of the time. The time was the 1970s, when words like 'globalization', 'financial derivatives' and 'hedge funds' were not part of our vocabulary; when 'securitization' had barely got under way; and when figures like Michael Milken and Ivan Boesky were just beginning their spectacular careers. Nick Leeson, who single-handedly brought down Barings Bank in six months of wildly uncontrolled trading in financial futures, was a mere child. *Limits* was largely written before Thatcher and Reagan came to power, before neo-liberalism assumed the importance that it did (as an ideology as well as a set of political practices) and before the full assault against working-class power, the welfare state and state regulation came into play.

There were, however, all manner of portentous signs of change. The oil embargo subsequent to the Arab–Israeli war in 1973 masked some deeper shifts such as the simultaneous collapse of several financial institutions throughout the world (largely hooked to a speculative building boom) and the final folding of the Bretton Woods global financial system (the de-materialization of money in 1973 was a major shift in the rules of capitalist engagement). Financial difficulties seemed to cascade onwards into all manner of events, such as the spectacular technical bankruptcy of New York City in 1975, and financial deregulation was already being touted (particularly in the United States) as the answer. Meanwhile, high rates of inflation during the 1970s were eroding the value of savings as nominal rates of interest (base rates jumped to heights of 12 or more per cent in the USA) were still outpaced by inflation. De-industrialization in the advanced capitalist countries was proceeding apace as the relocation of manufacturing capacity to the lesser developed countries (together with the rise of the newly industrializing economies in Asia backed by the success of the so-called Japanese 'model' of capitalism) radically altered the geographical context of political economic power. Unemployment exploded, along with labour unrest throughout the advanced capitalist world, to levels that would have been unthinkable in the 1960s, and it soon became apparent that this was a structural rather than a transitional or temporary problem. The Keynesian (or social contract) compromise of the post-World War II era was gradually unravelling as the welfare state apparatus became less easily sustainable, and open to right-wing assault. And the power of the nation-state to control capital was already in question as the British Labour Government succumbed to International Monetary Fund discipline in the mid-1970s, and took the path towards austerity and 'structural adjustment' of its economy to meet the demands of international competition.

My immediate attempt to explore the relevance of Marx's thinking to issues of urbanization and regional development (see my Introduction below) was undoubtedly influenced by these more general contextual concerns. Topics such as how the credit system, and money and finance capital, operated to modify the 'laws of motion' of capitalism, and how geographical displacements and reconfigurations (what I called 'the spatial

fix') affected the paths of capitalist crisis formation and resolution, had
general as well as particular interest. But I also had to pick my way through
the minefield of Marxist scholarship and political argumentation concerning the 'correct' interpretation of Marx's arguments.

   This proved not to be so easy, because a certain climate of Marxist
scholasticism (which continues to this day) then held sway. Initial drafts of
Limits were rejected for publication largely on the grounds that various
publishers' readers felt I had not paid enough attention to – or 'correctly'
positioned myself with respect to – serious questions such as the transformation problem, the law of value, the reduction of skilled to simple labour,
Okishio's theorem, or whatever. I countered by expanding my comments
on such subjects. But the effect was not to convince anyone very much,
while making the text harder to read, and therefore less accessible (no
matter how much I struggled to simplify the arguments). These issues of
interpretation of Marx's concepts are not, of course, irrelevant. They need
to be debated. And I think *Limits* provides some pioneering and suggestive
interpretations as to how some of the controversies that have bedevilled
Marxian theory (e.g. the falling rate of profit argument, the idea of value,
the problems of devaluation and overaccumulation, etc.) might best be
understood, albeit in provisional rather than definitive ways. But the habit
of rejecting *any* argument that does not bear the exact imprimatur of a
particular ('correct') reading of, say, the value theory (or the transformation
problem, or whatever) is something to be deplored within the Marxist
tradition. It tends to inhibit rather than enhance politics, and to keep the
terms of debate confined within a fragmented Marxist left rather than
projected outwards to a potentially much wider audience.

   If contextual conditions played a role in the way *Limits* was written,
then this immediately raises the issue of how 'dated' it might be. Here I
make a strong claim. *Limits* was (in spite of the scholasticism) peculiarly
prescient for the 1970s, and it is now even more deeply relevant to
understanding how a 'globalizing' capitalism impelled by a powerful
financial system has worked and is working. *Limits* was – and continues to
be – the only text I know of that seeks to integrate the financial (temporal)
and geographical (call it global and spatial) aspects to accumulation within
the framework of Marx's overall argument. It attempts to do so in a
holistic rather than segmented way. It provides a systematic link between
the basic underlying theory (for which there are many excellent and
competing expositions) and the expression of those forces on the ground as
mediated through uneven geographical developments and financial
operations.

   I wish I could claim authorship of such insights. But that honour lies
with Marx himself, because my idea was to excavate Marx's ideas on these
topics from the cavernous depths of his writings rather than to innovate on

my own account. I still find, for example, Marx's arguments concerning 'fictitious capital' formation and the circulation of credit (see chapters 9 and 10) as brilliantly insightful and relevant as ever (particularly in the light of what has been happening to stock markets in the USA). The connection back through problems of differential turnover times and fixed capital circulation (including that on the land) to the basic theory of accumulation and its crisis tendencies is of profound importance. Marx's fragmentary arguments on the potentialities of and limitations to a 'spatial fix' to crisis tendencies through geographical restructuring are exemplary for the time, as befits someone who clearly saw as early as *The Communist Manifesto* how bourgeois power rests on a distinctive mode of geographical strategizing (see Harvey, 1998).

My main contribution lay, then, in doing the hard excavatory work with the persistence and care it required. But I did need to knit the materials together if I was to capture what Marx called 'the mutual interaction' that 'takes place between the different moments' within any 'organic whole'. Marx tentatively listed some of the different moments to be combined in the *Grundrisse* (a text which became available in English, it must be recalled, only in 1973, and was extremely influential on my thinking at the time):

> (1) the general, abstract determinants which obtain in more or less all forms of society. . . . (2) The categories which make up the inner structure of bourgeois society and on which the fundamental classes rest. Capital, wage labour, landed property. Their interrelation. Town and country. The three great social classes. Exchange between them. Circulation. Credit system (private). (3) Concentration of bourgeois society in the form of the state. Viewed in relation to itself. The 'unproductive' classes. Taxes. State debt. Public credit. The population. The colonies. Emigration. (4) The international relation of production. International division of labour. International exchange. Export and import. Rate of exchange. (5) The world market and crises. (*Grundrisse*, p. 108)

This loosely forms the framework upon which I hung the enquiries that led to *Limits*. The thread I used to link the moments into a unity was dialectics. Here I found myself following Marx's practice rather than appealing to abstract formulations. The latter lean heavily on Marx's undoubted indebtedness to Hegel, while Marx's practice (see Ollman, 1993; Harvey, 1996, chapter 2 for fuller accounts) entails a rather different and, in my view, far subtler process-based dialectics that can better capture the free flows of capital circulation in space and time. 'Every historical social form,' writes Marx in *Capital*, must be captured 'as in fluid movement' and this is what dialectics has to do. Hardly surprisingly, Marx's definition of capital is also as a process, as 'value in motion', rather than as a thing. This shifts the

note: there are 2 kinds of value: material wealth +

capital as capitalizing

idea of value away from an accounting tool to an understanding of how
capital must continuously seek to augment its powers through circulation
and motion (this is what 'the law of value' is all about). I increasingly see
Marx as a magisterial exponent of a process-based philosophy rather than
as a mere practitioner (albeit 'right side up with feet upon the ground') of
Hegel's *Logic*.

My appeal to dialectics (of whatever sort) did not sit well, of course,
with those who preferred and (and in some instances insisted upon) appeal
to analytical mathematics and mathematical modelling as the only rational
way in which to reformulate Marx's political–economic arguments. I was
not then, nor am I now, opposed to exploration of Marx's arguments by
such methods. I found, as the reader will see, the works of economists like
Morishima and Desai particularly helpful in unravelling many of the
difficulties that arise with Marx's general theory of accumulation, and in
more recent years I have gained much from the mathematical and statistical
explorations of Shaikh and Tonak (1994) and Webber and Rigby (1996).
But I insist that such explorations must be embedded in a somewhat larger
sense of dialectics. I therefore found myself at loggerheads not only with
economists (and to this day, *Limits* remains totally ignored in the history
of something called 'Marxist Economics', thus testifying to the curious way
in which bourgeois academic divisions of labour exact their own toll within
Marxian theorizing) but also with so-called 'analytical' Marxists such as
G.A. Cohen, Jon Elster, Erik Olin Wright and Robert Brenner, who regard
dialectics as mumbo-jumbo reasoning given over to mystification of otherwise rational argument. But if we are to understand the world broadly in
Marx's own terms, then I fail to see how those terms can be anything other
than dialectical.

I claim that *Limits* was prescient because it took up matters which were
generally ignored at the time, but have become even more self-evidently
important since. On the matter of finance capital and its contradictions, for
example, there was almost nothing of substance written from a Marxist
perspective when I began, subsequent to Hilferding's major work of 1910
(itself lacking translation into English until 1981). I had to reconstruct
Marx's views almost entirely from scratch, with a little help from some of
the French theorists. The geographical angle was better served in works on
imperialism, dependency, the development of underdevelopment, accumulation on a world scale, and the first wave of work on world systems
theory. But even here, the tendency was to segregate the geographical and
spatial arguments from the general theory of accumulation that Marx
proposed, and to cast the whole argument in a fixed rather than malleable
spatial frame. That tendency continues to this day. There are now several
strong accounts of financial systems and their internal contradictions
written from a broadly Marxist perspective, and lengthy analyses of the

new international divisions of labour, the geography of capital accumulation, the new industrial geography, and the like. But it is amazing how so many of these accounts drift loose from their moorings in the Marxian theory of accumulation, and – either deliberately or by default – disrupt what I would see as Marx's major contribution: the capacity to see capitalism as an integrated whole.

Tying disparate moments together dialectically did entail some intuitive jumps and, on occasion, speculative leaps. By the time I had spent nearly ten years immersed in Marx's texts, I felt confident enough about my command of the general flow of his argument to make such jumps and leaps. In some instances Marx clearly indicated where the links lay. Several times, for example, he insists that the problem of differential turnover times in general, and fixed capital circulation in particular, cannot be solved without appeal to a sophisticated credit and financial system. On that point I was on very solid ground. He was much vaguer about the geographical aspects to capital accumulation, usually alluding to town–country distinctions, urban concentrations, transport structures and regional/territorial divisions of labour, capital and labour mobilities in a rather haphazard way. It was therefore left to me to infer how the processes of crisis formation and devaluation would always be place- or region-specific in the first instance, and that a general crisis would crucially depend upon a geographical and spatial process of entrainment of the sort that occurred in the 1930s and the early 1970s, and became so threatening in 1998. Holding the line geographically (as the US economy did in 1998) or seeking geographical adjustments as a way out of the crisis (the famed process of 'globalization' that galloped away in the mid 1970s) had to be written into Marxian theory in a much more explicit way than Marx himself achieved.

But I here want to re-emphasize one very strong warning sign which I set out in the original Introduction, but which was frequently ignored in subsequent reviews and commentaries. Marx held that the method of presentation (considered quite distinct from the method of discovery) should proceed from the abstract to the concrete. This presumption, coupled with the linearity of the narrative form of exposition in *Limits*, makes it seem as if capital has some spectral existence all to itself before it comes to earth in tangible forms in space and time. It seems as if, for example, the crisis tendencies of capitalism can be set up *sequentially* from the general, to the temporal (financial), to the spatial (uneven geographical development and geopolitics). This is how the structure of *Limits* works as we move through the three 'cuts' at crisis formation. In particular, it seems as if the 'final cataclysm' in the sequence is global war, culminating in nuclear apocalypse.

It is, however, wrong to see these three cuts as *sequential*. They should be understood as *simultaneous* aspects to crisis formation and resolution within the organic unity of capitalism. I offer two supportive arguments for this position. To begin with, materialism of any sort demands that the triumvirate space–time–process be considered as a unity at the ontological level. Of course it is possible to hold space and time, in the fashion of Newton, as absolute and immovable external frameworks within which processes (such as capital accumulation) occur. But in Marx's case, nothing other than a relational theory of space and time will do (how else can we interpret principles like 'the annihilation of space through time'?). We have to see space and time as social metrics produced through capital accumulation. This argument is well-embedded even in volume 1 of *Capital* where we find value defined as 'socially necessary labour time', where money circulation 'burst through all the temporal, spatial and personal barriers imposed by the direct exchange of products', 'moments are the elements of profit', struggles over time control (e.g. the working day) become endemic, and the factory becomes the spatially bounded panopticon of capitalist control over labour. The social production of space and time are internal relations rather than external conditions of the dynamics of capital accumulation. This insight, of course, later permitted me to formulate ideas about 'time–space compression' in *The Condition of Postmodernity*, and 'the social production of space and time' in *Justice, Nature and the Geography of Difference*. But in *Limits*, the idea emerges through the text rather than being stated clearly at the outset.

The second supportive argument depends on looking more closely at the actual history of class positionalities. *The Communist Manifesto* makes it clear, for example, that the bourgeoisie came to power in part through a geographical strategy of using trade and mobility to undermine land-based feudal powers (see Harvey, 1998). In *Capital*, Marx argues that:

> In the course of our investigation, we shall find that both merchants' capital and interest-bearing capital are derivative forms, and at the same time it will become clear why historically, these two forms appear before the modern primary form of capital. (*Capital*, vol. 1, p. 165)

Why this might be so requires explanation. The answer lies mainly in the way money has always been crucially dependent upon historical and geographical connections. It is always internalizing effects of the spatio-temporal world which its circulation is constructing, and in which its valuations are occurring (see Harvey, 1985a, chapter 1; 1996, chapters 8 and 9). This implies that money – the central accounting measure for capital – is nothing without credit, trust, and linkages within a space economy. Contemporary work which suggests that credit and trust preceded the rise of the money form support this view. Bourgeois power is, furthermore, always about geopolitical positioning. Interestingly, immediately after describing how money bursts through temporal and spatial barriers, Marx refers to the possibility of crises in which 'all the antitheses and contradictions which are immanent in commodities' assert themselves (*Capital*, vol. 1, p. 114). Crises have no existence outside the matrix of spatio-temporalities that capitalism itself creates. Crises are as much about reconfiguring the spatio-temporal form of class relations (through all manner of stressful adjustments) as about the internal class contradictions of capitalism specified in some absolute and immutable space and time.

Breaking the rigidities of an existing spatio-temporal form through speed-up and globalization (to note two obvious forces at work in recent times) becomes, for example, a crucial aspect of what crises are about. It is not hard to identify this aspect to past crises. Who can dispute, for example, that the difficulties in the Far East in 1998 had much to do with the temporality of the debt and financing structure that had existed in that region for some time? The three 'cuts' at understanding crisis formation in *Limits* must, I emphasize, be read as distinguishable but simultaneously co-present moments within the internal contradictions of capitalism.

This argument assumes even greater importance for present understandings. The recent travails of capitalism have spawned a variety of interpretations, some from a Marxist perspective. The danger is that such attempts may become what Fine *et al.* (1999) call 'exercises in nostalgia', merely replicating the debates of the early 1970s (including their scholastic turns). The immediate target of this critical comment is Robert Brenner's essay on 'The economics of global turbulence', which occupied a whole issue of *New Left Review* in 1998. There is much in Brenner's argument to recommend it. I welcome, for example, the emphasis upon individual behaviours, which is consistent with my view (see below, p. 188) that 'individual capitalists – coerced by competition, trapped by the necessities of class struggle and responding to the hidden dictates of the law of value – make technological adjustments which drive the economy away from a "sound", "normal" development of the process of capitalist production'. The emphasis upon fixed capital formation and sunk costs is laudatory, as is the attempt to pull together extensive data on the subject. But – if I read Marx correctly (see chapter 8 below) – the mode of fixed capital formation and circulation cannot be understood without connecting it to the way in which (1) surpluses get formed and disbursed; (2) capital handles disparate turnover times through the credit and financial system; and (3) fixed capital in and on the land (including state investments in infrastructures) creates distinctive geographical patterns.

As an analytical Marxist, of course, Brenner has every reason not to engage with *Limits*. This is a pity, because his failure to say anything about the financial system – its deep implications in fixed capital formation and circulation, its instabilities and its gyrations – seriously limits the efficacy of his work. Marx's theses on fictitious capital circulation (set out in *Limits*, chapters 9 and 10) are ignored, and the 'second-cut' or 'temporal' dimension to crisis formation is evaded. Brenner thereby erases – as Fine *et al.* (1999) correctly complain – one of the most important facets of the way capitalism works. He similarly inadmissably reduces uneven geographical development to the comparative performance of the United States, Germany and Japan. This eliminates the production, destruction and reconfiguration of space (both within and between countries) as a key element in capitalism's restless dynamic. It casts capital accumulation in a Newtonian frame of absolute space (and time). The geographical splitting up of production processes under the control of multinational enterprises (an institutional form that Brenner largely neglects) and the complex value transfers that then ensue (cutting the connection between, say, manufacturing activity – in places like Bangladesh – and geographical concentrations of wealth and power in places like the United States) have reconfigured the spatio-temporal matrix (as well as the geographical scale) of capital accumulation. Brenner, in short, ignores the spatio-temporal aspects to capitalist development and crisis formation. It should be clear from any analysis of recent instabilities that these aspects of crisis formation must be central rather than marginal to our understandings.

The celebration of Brenner's account is odd, given the fact that several other far more sophisticated and far-reaching accounts of capitalist dynamics are readily available (see, for example, the extensive critique by Fine *et al.* 1999). I cite, however, just one work, that of Webber and Rigby (1996), because of the close theoretical and empirical attention they pay to historical and geographical transformations and spatio-temporal forms. Webber and Rigby go beyond *Limits* in a number of important ways (using analytical and statistical tools to do so). Their sophisticated and fine-grained empirical work on uneven geographical development demonstrates how capital accumulation moved sectorally and regionally according to disparate rhythms throughout the whole postwar period, thus calling into question any simple cross-national periodization (such as the break in capital accumulation patterns that supposedly occurred in the early 1970s). While the problems of fictitious capital formation remain rather too undeveloped for my taste, multinational and financial powers are not ignored, particularly in relation to the disposal and dispersal of capital surpluses from the late 1960s onwards. But – most important of all – Webber and Rigby show, with a great deal of theoretical and empirical sophistication, how late-twentieth-century capitalism has crucially depended upon a particular dynamics of uneven geographical development. Impelled by multinational capital aided, abetted and occasionally cut across by the powers of credit and finance, these shifts have kept capital accumulation in a perpetual state of dynamic uncertainty. Investment strategies (in most instances backed by state power) have, they argue, played a crucial role in generating geographical shifts relative to the more usual explanations of 'globalization' through lower labour costs, technological advantages, and the like. This leads to certain important counter-intuitive conclusions:

> First, low profit (high cost) regions may grow more rapidly than high profit (low cost) regions. Secondly, the net flow of capital may point from high profit to low profit regions. And, thirdly, rates of profit are not necessarily equal at equilibrium (unless central financial institutions direct all international capital flows and adhere to a particular rule to allocate investment). (Webber and Rigby, 1996, p. 236)

There exists, they go on to say, 'no necessary tendency for rates of profit to be equal in dynamic equilibrium'. Those analyses (both conventional and Marxist) which depend explicitly or tacitly upon the concept of equilibrium cannot capture what capitalist spatio-temporal dynamics are about. This is a remarkable and challenging finding which deserves some commentary. Marx, of course, has sometimes been depicted as an 'equilibrium theorist', and – as I show throughout *Limits* – he often invokes equilibrium (in wage rates, profit rates, intersectoral flows, or whatever) as a means to advance his arguments. As I see it, however, the role of equilibrium in his work is mostly to describe an impossible condition which capital seeks to realize but cannot, given its dominant social relations and productive forces. This broadly reflects Marx's dialectical view in which change is the general condition of any social system (see Ollman, 1993).

But there is a further implication. In effect, Webber and Rigby show that equilibrium becomes less and less meaningful the more the geographical aspects of capital accumulation are invoked. This echoes a remarkable technical finding by Koopmans (1957) which states that equilibrating prices cannot form in any spatial location/allocation model. Projected into the matrix of process–space–time relations, this means that the dynamic of capitalism is always bound to be highly unstable unless it is held down by some coercive force (such as US hegemony backed by powerful central institutions like the World Bank and the IMF). On this point, the linearity of the argument in *Limits* is again potentially misleading unless the three cuts at crisis formation are held together as simultaneous rather than sequential aspects of the dynamics of capital accumulation on the world stage. To put it another way: the argument in *Limits* progresses in such a way as to make the concept of equilibrium less and less feasible or relevant as the argument moves on to the terrain of spatial forms and uneven geographical developments. I owe this insight to Webber and Rigby's cogent analysis.

Limits is, of course, an unfinished text. As I remark in the Afterword, dialectics of the sort that Marx practised precludes closure. There is always something more to be discovered, something more to be said. While I managed to weave together certain facets of historical–geographical processes of capital accumulation into a tolerably coherent representation, much is left out or given short shrift. In the Afterword (which readers may wish to consult at the outset) I indicate two major problems: the struggles around reproduction of labour power (including even the full power and significance of class formation and class struggle itself) are not as central as they could be, while the processes of state and civil society formation are also given a tangential rather than the central positioning they deserve. To these I would now add the pressing need to incorporate a more thorough accounting of the 'metabolism' of capital accumulation in relation to environmental issues on local, regional and global scales. And then, of course, the familiar problems of cultural differentiations, local histories, identities, gender issues, and the like are not brought into the argument in ways that today are quite properly regarded as essential (though not necessarily in an essentialist way).

It is an all too familiar trope in these times, however, to criticize texts for what they leave out rather than to appreciate them for what they accomplish. *The Limits to Capital*, with all its shortcomings, pioneered a way to integrate our understandings of how capital accumulation operates not only in but through the active production of time and space. It thereby brings the Marxian theory of capital accumulation closer to understanding contemporary realities, and provides a base from which to help interpret all manner of other seemingly incomprehensible phenomena. My own subsequent work on urbanization and cultural change (see, for example, Harvey, 1985a, b; 1989) rested fundamentally upon the bedrock of argument set up in *Limits*. But, as I think that work demonstrates, resting on a certain secure basis in no way confines argument to that basis.

Limits is, I claim, a foundational as well as a prescient text which repays careful study. It helps to shed light on current events. It can add some theoretical heft to our renascent efforts on the left both to understand the world and to change it. It may even help to inform more subtle geopolitical practices on the part of oppositional forces committed to finding an alternative to capitalist hegemony and the disastrous social, political and environmental consequences of never-ending 'accumulation for accumulation's sake, production for production's sake'.

DH
May 1999

BIBLIOGRAPHICAL NOTE

The edition of *Capital* used throughout *The Limits to Capital* was the 1967 imprint from International Publishers. Unfortunately, subsequent printings of this edition changed the page numbers, making it hard to track the exact

locations of citations. I am powerless to do anything about this except to
warn readers of the problem and suggest that they consult the first printing of
the International Publishers edition if they wish to identify particular passages.

FURTHER REFERENCES

Bourdieu, P. (1993), *La Misère du Monde*, Paris.

Bourdieu, P. (1998), *Acts of Resistance: Against the Tyranny of the Market*,
New York.

Brenner, R. (1998), 'The economics of global turbulence', *New Left
Review*, 229.

Brooks, R. (1992), 'Maggie's man: We were wrong', *The Observer*, Sunday
21 June, 21.

Butler, J. (1998), 'Merely cultural', *New Left Review*, 227, 33–44.

Cassidy, J. (1997), 'The Return of Karl Marx', *The New Yorker*, 20 and
27 October, 248–59.

Derrida, J. (1994), *Specters of Marx*, New York and London.

Fine, B., Lapavitsas, C. and Milonakis, D. (1999), 'Addressing the world
economy: two steps back', *Capital and Class*, 67, 47–90.

Friedman, T. (1996), 'Revolt of the Wannabes', *New York Times*, 7
January, A19.

Gray, J. (1998), *False Dawn: The Illusions of Global Capitalism*, London.

Harvey, D. (1985a), *Consciousness and the Urban Experience*, Baltimore.

Harvey, D. (1985b), *The Urbanization of Capital*, Baltimore.

Harvey, D. (1989), *The Condition of Postmodernity*, Oxford.

Harvey, D. (1996), *Justice, Nature and the Geography of Difference*,
Oxford.

Harvey, D. (1998), 'The geography of class power', *Socialist Register*,
49–74.

Koopmans, T. (1957), *Three Essays on the State of Economic Science*,
New York.

Moody, K. (1997), *Workers in a Lean World*, London.

Ollman, B. (1993), *Dialectical Investigations*, London.

Rorty, R. (1997), 'Back to class politics', *Dissent*, Winter, 31–4.

Schwab, K. and Smadja, C. (1999), 'Globalization needs a human face',
International Herald Tribune, 28 January, 8.

Shaikh, A. and Tonak, E. (1994), *Measuring the Wealth of Nations*,
Cambridge.

Soros, G. (1998), *The Crisis of Global Capitalism: Open Society Endan-
gered*, New York.

Webber, M. and Rigby, D. (1996), *The Golden Age Illusion: Rethinking
Postwar Capitalism*, New York.

Introduction

Everyone who studies Marx, it is said, feels compelled to write a book about the experience. I offer this work in partial proof of such a proposition. But I do have an additional excuse. After the completion of *Social Justice and the City* (nearly a decade ago), I determined to improve upon the tentative, and what I later saw to be erroneous, formulations therein and to write a definitive statement on the urban process under capitalism from a Marxist perspective. The more deeply enmeshed I became in the project, the more I became aware that some of the more basic aspects of Marxian theory to which I sought to appeal lay quite undeveloped and in some cases almost empty of consideration. So I set out to write the theory of urbanization, to integrate it with detailed historical studies of the urban process drawn from Britain, France and the United States, and to casually fill in a few 'empty boxes' in Marxian theory *en route*. The project soon became totally unwieldy. In this book, long as it is, I deal only with the 'empty boxes' in the theory. Let me explain how that came to be.

It is both a virtue and difficulty in Marx that everything relates to everything else. It is impossible to work on one 'empty box' without simultaneously working on all other aspects of the theory. The bits and pieces I had to understand – such as the circulation of capital in built environments, the role of credit and the mechanisms (such as rent) that mediate the production of spatial configurations – could not be understood without careful attention to the relationships they bore to the rest of the theory. I saw, for example, that earlier errors on the interpretation of rent arose precisely out of a failure to integrate this single aspect of distribution into the general theory of production and distribution that Marx proposed. The trouble is, however, that there are many different interpretations of that general theory. Furthermore, as is to be expected, investigation of the topics of particular interest to me suggested new ways to think about value theory, crisis theory and so on. I had no option except to write a treatise on Marxian theory in general, paying particular attention to the circulation of capital in built environments, the credit system and the production of spatial configurations.

All of this took me very far from my original concern with urbanization under capitalism; with the details of Haussmann's administration in Paris and the subsequent glories and horrors of the Paris Commune; with the processes of urban transformation and class struggle in my adopted city of Baltimore. Yet the links are there. I think it is possible to pull all of this together, to transcend the seeming boundaries between theory, abstractly formulated, and history, concretely recorded; between the conceptual clarity of theory and the seemingly endless muddles of political practice. But time and space force me to write down the theory as an abstract conception, without reference to the history. In this sense the present work is, I fear, but a pale apology for a magnificent conception. And a violation of the ideals of historical materialism to boot.

In self-defence I have to say that no one else seems to have found a way to integrate theory and history, to preserve the integrity of both while transcending their separation. Marx went to great pains to keep the history–theory relation intact in the first volume of *Capital,* but covered probably about one-twentieth of what he intended as a result (he never finished *Capital,* and projected books on foreign trade, the world market and crises, the state, etc., were left totally untouched). And the history disappears almost entirely from the preparatory studies that make up volume 2 of *Capital.* For my part, I wanted to get through the materials Marx assembled in the three volumes of *Capital,* the three parts of *Theories of Surplus Value* and in the *Grundrisse* in order to deal with the particular topics that interested me. There was no way to do it except by stripping the theory of any direct historical content.

But I hope that the general theory set out here will be helpful to the study of history and the formulation of political practices. I have found it so. It has helped me to understand why capitalism engages in periodic splurges of insane land speculation; why Haussmann was brought down in 1868 by the same kinds of financial difficulties that beset New York in the 1970s; why phases of crisis are always manifest as a joint reorganization of both technologies and regional configurations to production; and so on. I can only hope that others will find the theory as helpful. And if not, then I suppose the burden rests on me to demonstrate the utility of the theory in future works that have a more explicit historical, geographical and political content. This should not be taken to mean, however, that I regard the theory as correct and sacrosanct. It surely deserves all kinds of modification in the light of critical review, better and more general theory construction and thorough testing against the historical record, as well as in the fires of political struggle. I publish these theoretical findings as a contribution to a collective process of discovery. I do so now because I cannot take the subject much further without a radical change in direction which will take several more years to bear fruit.

H's book is comprehensive T

Marx was overambitious, or at least not comprehensive as he intended

I could puff out this introduction with learned-sounding comments on matters such as epistemology and ontology, on the theory and practice of historical materialism, on the 'true' nature of dialectics. I prefer to let the methods of both enquiry and presentation speak for themselves through the text and to let the object of enquiry emerge in the course of study rather than to set it up *a priori* like some cardboard cut-out on a back-lit stage. But some general comments on what I have tried to do, and how, may be helpful to the reader.

The general objective has been to combine a mode of thinking that I conceive to be dialectical with as much simplicity of exposition as a manifestly complicated subject matter will allow. Such aims are not easily reconciled. At some points, the striving for simplicity takes me dangerously close to the perils of reductionism, while at others the struggle to keep faith with the intricate integrity of the subject matter brings me to the brink of obscurantism. I have not avoided either error to my own satisfaction. And I am only too well aware that what appears as reductionist to the expert long steeped in Marxian theory may appear unnecessarily obscure to the newcomer. My tactic in the face of this has been to strive for enough simplicity in the opening chapters to give newcomers, willing to struggle with admittedly difficult concepts, the greatest possible opportunity to grapple with the more substantive contributions of later chapters. I have tried to keep better faith with the intricacy of the subject matter in the chapters on fixed capital, finance and money, rent and the production of spatial configurations.

I do not, however, want the argument to be construed as a linear argument, in spite of the apparent linearity in the flow. The first chapters are not firm and fixed building blocks upon which all subsequent chapters are erected. Nor are the later chapters derived or deduced out an original set of propositions advanced at the outset. I begin, rather, with the simplest abstractions that Marx proposed and then seek to expand their meaning through consideration of them in different contexts. The view of the whole should evolve as more and more phenomena are integrated into the vast composite picture of what capitalism, as a mode of production, looks like. The difficulty here is to come up with a mode of presentation – a form of argumentation, if you will – that does not do a violation to the content of the thoughts expressed. Each chapter focuses on a particular aspect of the whole. The difficulty is to preserve the focus while keeping the relation to everything else broadly in view. Constant invocation of 'everything else' would needlessly clutter later chapters and render the initial chapters incomprehensible, because subjects not yet analysed would have to be invoked without explanation. Marx tried to deal with the problem in the opening chapters of *Capital* by fashioning a language of such density and utter abstraction that most ordinary mortals are left quite bewildered, at least on first reading. I have sought a middle ground. I use notions of opposition, antagonism and contradiction as connecting threads to bind the materials together. In so doing I employ a logical device which Marx uses to great effect. The details will be explored later, but the general tactic is worth elucidating in advance, if only to provide the reader with some idea of how the subsequent argument will unfold.

At each step in the formulation of the theory, we encounter antagonisms that build into intriguing configurations of *internal* and *external* contradiction. The resolution of each merely provokes the formation of new contradictions or their translation on to some fresh terrain. The argument can spin onwards and outwards in this way to encompass every aspect of the capitalist mode of production. For example, Marx opens *Capital* with the idea that the material commodity is simultaneously a use value and an exchange value, and that the two forms of value necessarily oppose each other. This opposition (which is internal to the commodity) achieves its external expression in the separation between commodities in general (use values) and money (the pure representation of exchange value). But money then internalizes contradictory functions within itself which can in turn be resolved only if money circulates in a certain way, as *capital*. And so the argument proceeds to encompass the class antagonism between capital and labour, the contradictory dynamics of technological change, and ultimately evolves into an elaborate and lengthy disquisition upon those seemingly irreconcilable contradictions that lead capitalism into the cataclysms of crises. The first seven chapters summarize and interpret Marx's argument, according to such a logic, up to the point of what I call 'the first cut' at crisis theory, as exemplified by Marx's theory of the falling rate of profit.

In the remaining chapters I use the same logical device to extend Marx's argument on to less familiar terrain. The analysis of fixed capital and consumption fund formation in chapter 8 shows that the surpluses of capital and labour produced under the conditions described in the 'first cut' at crisis theory can be absorbed by the creation of new forms of circulation oriented to future rather than present uses. But we then find that these new forms are at odds, in the long run, with a continuous dynamics of technological change, itself a necessary condition for the perpetuation of accumulation. The 'value' put upon fixed capital becomes an unstable magnitude as a result. The continued circulation of capital is threatened with severe disruption.

The credit system then comes to the rescue. In chapters 9 and 10 we discover that the credit system, as a kind of 'central nervous system' for the regulation of capital flow, has the potential to resolve all of the imbalances to which capitalism is prone, to resolve the contradictions earlier identified. But it can do so only at the price of internalizing the contradictions within itself. Massive concentration of financial power, accompanied by the machinations of finance capital, can as easily de-stabilize as stabilize capitalism. And a fundamental opposition arises in any case between the financial system – the creation of money as credit money – and its monetary base (the use of money as a measure of value). This sets the stage to examine the financial and monetary aspects of crisis formation, including financial panics and inflation. This forms the 'second cut' at crisis theory.

The chapter on rent nominally completes the theory of distribution but also allows us to consider the spatial as well as the temporal dynamics from a theoretical perspective. Further analysis of the geographical mobilities of capital and labour shows how the contradictions of capitalism are, in principle at least, susceptible to a 'spatial fix' – geographical expansion and uneven geographical development hold out the possibility for a contradiction-prone capitalism to right itself. This leads directly to the 'third cut' at crisis theory, which deals with crisis formation in its spatial aspects. Under this heading we can approach the problems of imperialism and inter-imperialist wars from a fresh perspective. We see once more that pursuit of a 'spatial fix' to capitalism's internal contradictions merely ends up projecting them, albeit in new forms, upon the world stage. This, I argue, allows us to construct a framework for theorizing about the historical geography of the capitalist mode of production.

I do not claim this is the end of matters – how could it be, given the mode of theorizing? I indicate some areas of unfinished business in the Afterword. Nor do I claim that everything I have to say is original or beyond dispute. Which brings me to another matter that deserves to be broached by way of introduction.

The Marxist intellectual tradition has undergone a remarkable resurgence during the past decade, a resurgence marked by lively disputations and vigorous polemics spiked with not a little vitriol. I have struggled, not always successfully, to keep up with a literature that has grown enormously even during the space of the five years or so of writing. To acknowledge the stimulus to every thought in the text would require footnotes beyond belief. So I simply want to acknowledge here the deep debt I owe to the collective efforts of many writers, thinkers and practitioners. The courage of those such as Paul Sweezy, Maurice Dobb, Paul Baran, Edward Thompson, Eric Hobsbawm, R. Rosdolsky and others, who kept the flame of Marxist thought alive during incredibly difficult years, was always an inspiration. Without the stimulus of the resurgence in Marxist thinking, which writers as diverse as Althusser, Poulantzas, Wallerstein, Amin, Mandel and others, engineered, I probably would have given up on this project long ago. Amongst these thinkers I count Manuel Castells and Vicente Navarro as personal friends who time and again offered help and encouragement.

I have also struggled to sort out the debates as best I could (although I must confess I gave up on some of them in deep frustration). But to confront the various positions taken on every point of controversy would extend the text endlessly while some works, such as Kozo Uno's came upon the scene too late for me to pay them the close attention they warranted. So I decided to deal directly with only the most fundamental debates, as these impinge upon key points in my own argument. And even then I tend to forgo polemics and simply mention in passing those who have been the most active participants in the debate. I hope the smoothness of the flow will make up for the lack of verbal pyrotechnics.

Finally, there are those people and institutions to whom I am directly indebted in one way or another. I am pleased to acknowledge receipt of a Guggenheim Memorial Fellowship to Paris, which allowed me time to study the French urbanization experience but, perhaps more importantly, allowed me to come to grips with the active intricacies of the French Marxist tradition. M. G. Wolman, chairman of the Department of Geography and Environmental Engineering in The Johns Hopkins University, demonstrated a deep commitment to the principle of freedom of enquiry and helped thereby to create conditions of work that were extremely favourable.

I had the good fortune, also, to meet up with a group of people in the early 1970s who participated in a remarkably invigorating exploration of Marxist thought. Dick Walker and Lee Jordan, Gene Mumy, Jörn and Altrud Barnbrock, Flor Torres and Chuck Schnell, Ric Pfeffer, Lata Chatterjee and Barbara Koeppel shared their insights and helped peel back the layers of mystification that surround us, through their collective efforts. And what is more, they did it with a sense of fun and joy that is truly rare in human companionship. And in recent years Beatriz Nofal and Neil Smith continued that tradition. They also went, page by page, over the manuscript. I owe them an enormous debt. Barbara, Claudia, John and Rosie provided very special support. Finally, John Davey, of Basil Blackwell, waited patiently and encouragingly for the final product and kindly allowed me to commandeer a sometimes sunny corner of his kitchen to pen these and many other lines.

CHAPTER 1

Commodities, Values and Class Relations

The method of analysis which I have employed, and which had not previously been applied to economic subjects, makes the reading of the first chapters rather arduous. . . . That is a disadvantage I am powerless to overcome, unless it be by forewarning and forearming those readers who zealously seek the truth. There is no royal road to science, and only those who do not dread the fatiguing climb of its steep paths have a chance of gaining its luminous summits. (*Capital*, vol. 1, p. 21)

Marx opens his analysis in *Capital* by examining the nature of commodities. At first blush this choice seems somewhat arbitrary. But if we review the writing preparatory to *Capital* – stretching over almost three decades – we see that the choice was not arbitrary at all. It was the result of extensive enquiry, a long voyage of discovery which led Marx to a fundamental conclusion: to unlock the secrets of the commodity is to unravel the intricate secrets of capitalism itself. We begin with what is in effect a conclusion.

Marx considers the commodity as a material embodiment of *use value*, *exchange value* and *value*. Once again, these concepts are presented to us in a seemingly arbitrary way so that it appears 'as if we had before us a mere *a priori* construction' (*Capital*, vol. 1, p. 19). These are the concepts that are absolutely fundamental to everything that follows. They are the pivot upon which the whole analysis of capitalism turns. We have to understand them if we are to understand what it is that Marx has to say.[1]

In this there is a certain difficulty. To understand the concepts fully requires that we understand the inner logic of capitalism itself. Since we cannot possibly have that understanding at the outset, we are forced to use the

---

[1] It is the hallmark of Marx's materialist method to begin the discussion by examining the characteristics of material objects with which everyone is familiar. 'I do not proceed on the basis of "concepts" hence also not from the "value concept". . . . What I proceed from is the simplest social form in which the product of labour in contemporary society manifests itself, and this is as "commodity" ' (*Notes on Adolph Wagner*, p. 214)

concepts without knowing precisely what they mean. Furthermore, Marx's relational way of proceeding means that he cannot treat any one concept as a fixed, known or even knowable building block on the basis of which to interpret the rich complexity of capitalism. We cannot interpret values, he seems to say, without understanding use values and exchange values, and we cannot interpret the latter categories without a full understanding of the first. Marx never treats any one concept in isolation as if it could be understood in itself. He always focuses on one or other of the triad of possible relations between them – between use value and exchange value, between use value and value, between exchange value and value. The relations between the concepts are what really count.

In the course of *Capital* we can observe Marx shifting from one relational pairing to another, using insights garnered from one standpoint to establish interpretations for another. It is rather as if, to borrow an image of Ollman's, Marx sees each relation as a separate 'window' from which we can look in upon the inner structure of capitalism. The view from any one window is flat and lacks perspective. When we move to another window we can see things that were formerly hidden from view. Armed with that knowledge, we can reinterpret and reconstitute our understanding of what we saw through the first window, giving it greater depth and perspective. By moving from window to window and carefully recording what we see, we come closer and closer to understanding capitalist society and all of its inherent contradictions.

This dialectical way of proceeding imposes a great deal upon the reader. We are forced to grope in the dark, armed with highly abstract and seemingly *a priori* concepts we have very little understanding of, working from perspectives we are not yet in a position to evaluate. Most readers therefore encounter great difficulty on reading the first few chapters of *Capital*. But after a painful and often frustrating period of groping, we begin to perceive where we are and what it is that we are looking at. Shadowy understandings emerge as Marx bit by bit illuminates for us different aspects of the intricate complexity of capitalism. The meaning of the concepts use value, exchange value and value become clearer in the course of the analysis. The more we understand how capitalism works, the more we understand what these concepts refer to.[2]

All of this contrasts vividly with the 'building-block' approach to

---

[2] Ollman (1973). Engels also specifically warns us against 'the false assumption that Marx wishes to define where he only investigates, and that in general we might expect fixed, cut-to-measure, once and for all applicable definitions in Marx's works. It is self-evident that where things and their interrelations are conceived not as fixed, but as changing, their mental images, the ideas, are likewise subject to change and transformation; and they are not encapsulated in rigid definitions, but are developed in their historical or logical process of formation.' (*Capital,* vol. 3, pp. 13–14)

knowledge so typical of bourgeois social science and deeply ingrained in widely accepted bourgeois modes of thought. According to this line of thought, it is both possible and desirable to build solid foundations to knowledge by isolating basic components within the social system and subjecting them to detailed investigation. Once the component is understood, we can build upon it as if it were a fixed and immutable foundation for subsequent enquiry. From time to time, of course, the cornerstones of knowledge appear wanting, and when the cracks in them become obvious to all, we witness one of those dramatic revolutions in thought – paradigm shifts, as they are sometimes called – so characteristic of bourgeois science.

Most of us raised in 'Western' traditions of thought feel at home with such a strategy of enquiry. We find Marx's departure from it, if we understand it at all, disconcerting if not downright perverse. And the temptation is always there to try and reduce the unfamiliar to the familiar by re-stating Marx's arguments in more readily comprehensible terms. This tendency lies at the root of many misinterpretations of Marx by Marxists and non-Marxists alike. It produces what I shall call a 'linear' interpretation of the theory laid out in *Capital*.[3]

This 'linear' interpretation runs along the following lines. Marx, it is said, sets up three potential building blocks for interpreting commodity production and exchange, by presenting us with the concepts of use value, exchange value and value. He supposedly abstracts from questions of use value on the first page of *Capital* and thereafter regards the study of them as irrelevant to his purpose although it still remains of historical interest. An investigation of exchange values merely serves to show that the secrets of capitalism cannot be revealed through a study of them alone. And so Marx constructs the labour theory of value as the solid foundation, the fixed building block which, when built upon, will tell us all we need to know about capitalism. The justification of the labour theory of value, according to this view, lies in Marx's discovery that 'all history is the history of class struggle', and that the labour theory of value must hold because it is the expression of the class relations of capitalism.

Such a 'linear' version of Marx's theory runs into a variety of difficulties, of which we will briefly consider one. In the third volume of *Capital*, Marx examines the 'transformation of values into prices'. The accuracy of his transformation procedure is vital to the 'linear' interpretation because Marx

---

[3] Such a 'linear' interpretation of Marx characterises both Robinson's (1967) and Samuelson's (1971) presentations on the subject (this appears to be one of the few points they do agree upon). More troublesome 'structuralist' versions can be found in Bronfenbrenner (1968) and Elster (1978), while even Sweezy (1968) – in a work that is otherwise deserving of the utmost admiration – seems to fall into this trap. He got into the difficulty, in my opinion, by not fully appreciating the relationship that Marx builds between the concepts of use value and value (see notes 5 and 9).

appears to be deriving exchange values out of the fixed building block of the value theory. Since everyone concedes that capitalists operate with exchange values and not with values, Marx's analysis of the 'laws of motion' of capitalism stands or falls, according to this interpretation, with the logical coherence of the transformation.

Unfortunately, Marx's transformation is incorrect. There seems to be no necessary relation between the values embodied in commodities and the ratios at which the latter exchange. Bourgeois detractors (and some sympathizers) have had a field day. They portray the first and third volumes of *Capital* as being irreconcilably in contradiction. Marx, they say, finally came to his senses in the third volume and realized that the value theory of the first was an irrelevant distraction as far as understanding the real processes of commodity production and exchange was concerned. All that was required to accomplish the latter was a theory of relative prices without any reference to values. And this argument, given the linear interpretation, is sufficiently powerful to lead Marxists into a certain self-doubt as to the relevance of Marxian value theory or into lines of defence of it which sound merely assertive as opposed to coherent and convincing.

But an examination of Marx's work shows that exchange values, far from being derived out of value theory at some late stage in the game, are fundamental to the enquiry at the outset. Without some understanding of them we could not say anything meaningful about value. Exchange value and value are relational categories, and neither of them can be treated as a fixed and immutable building block. Marx's study of the transformation problem is but one step in a continuing investigation of the intricate relations between them. And he is most definitely not seeking to derive exchange values out of values, as appears to be the case under the linear interpretation. This explains why Marx, who was fully aware of the logical defects of his argument (although not, perhaps, of all of the implications), could dismiss them as unimportant in relation to the actual topic he was there concerned with. This is, however, a matter to which we will return in chapter 2.

It follows that we should eschew anything that smacks of a 'linear' interpretation of Marxian theory. But if we follow Marx's method, then this means that we are bound to encounter the kinds of difficulties that face any reader of *Capital*. We have to begin by groping in the dark, armed with Marxian categories which are at best partially understood. There is, unfortunately, no way in which we can avoid this difficulty – 'there is no royal road to science'.

In this chapter I shall try to reconstruct Marx's argument concerning the relations between use values, exchange value and values under conditions of commodity production and exchange. At the same time I shall seek to explain what Marx is doing and why. In this way I hope to make the steep climb to the luminous summits of Marxian theory a little less fatiguing.

I USE VALUES, EXCHANGE VALUES AND VALUES

1 *Use values*

At the basis of Marx's conception of the world lies the notion of an appropriation of nature by human beings in order to satisfy their wants and needs. This appropriation is a material process embodied in the acts of production and consumption. Under conditions of commodity production, the acts of production and consumption are separated by exchange. But the appropriation of nature always remains fundamental. From this it follows that we can never ignore what Marx calls 'the material side' of commodities. To do so would be to remove the satisfaction of human wants and needs from any relation to nature.

The material side of commodities is captured in its relation to human wants and needs by the concept of its *use value*. This use value may be looked at 'from the two points of view of quality and quantity'. As an 'assemblage of many properties' which can 'be of use in various ways', the commodity possesses certain qualities that relate to different kinds of human wants and needs. Food satisfies our hunger, clothing our need for warmth and housing our need for shelter. And although Marx insists that 'as use values, commodities are, above all, of different qualities', he also insists that 'when treating of use-value we always assume to be dealing with definite quantities, such as dozens of watches, yards of linen, or tons or iron' (*Capital*, vol. 1, p. 36).

In relation to exchange value, which is seen primarily as a quantitative relation, Marx stresses the qualitative aspects of use values. But in a sophisticated and intricate system of commodity production, the quantitative aspects of use values become of great importance. Producers use a certain quantity of inputs – labour power, raw materials and instruments of production – to create a quantity of physical product which is used to satisfy the wants and needs of a certain number of people. The ratio of physical inputs to outputs in the production process provides a physical measure of efficiency. A description of aggregate inputs and outputs provides us with an overall picture of how the appropriation of nature relates to social wants and needs.

In a society characterized by division of labour and specialization of production, we can define the requirements for social reproduction in terms of the quantity of output in a particular industry (such as iron and steel) needed to satisfy the demands of all other industries (such as automobiles, construction, machine tools and so on). A state of reproduction is one in which the inputs and outputs balance. We can identify a surplus within such a system as a *surplus product*: that is, an amount of material use values over and above those needed to reproduce the system in a given state. This surplus product can be used in a variety of ways, such as building monuments or creating new means of production to help produce even more surplus product. The surplus product from different industries can be re-combined so that the total quantity of output expands over time, either by simple expansion of existing industries or by the formation of entirely new ones.

The quantitative characteristics of such a physical production system are of considerable interest, although there are, of course, some problems of specification. We need to know what use values are required to reproduce or expand labour power (never an easy subject), how to identify industries, how to account for fixed capital, joint products and so on. But the obvious need to balance quantities of inputs and outputs makes the direct study of the physical aspects of production both possible and potentially enlightening – they have therefore been the focus of attention ever since Quesnay first produced his *Tableau économique*. Marx picks up on the technique in volume 2 of *Capital,* and in more recent years Leontieff has fashioned an elaborate method to study the structure of physical flows within the economy. There are now input–output studies of national, regional and selected urban economies. The question is, then, what insights can we derive regarding the inner logic of capitalism from studying the physical characteristics of this production system in isolation?

Marx recognizes, of course, that all societies must physically reproduce themselves if they are to survive. From the standpoint of production, the physical aspect to social reproduction is captured by a description of the labour process. We could cast this description in universal terms: '(1) the personal activity of man, i.e. work itself, (2) the subject of this work, and (3) its instruments' (*Capital*, vol. 1, p. 178).[4]

Marx's studies of political economy led him to be deeply suspicious of universal categories of this sort. He saw categories themselves as a product of a particular society and sought concepts that could serve to distinguish capitalism from other modes of production and thereby serve as a basis for dissecting capitalism's internal logic. In this manner, Marx seeks to make his materialism genuinely historical.

On the first page of *Capital,* Marx seems to abstract from use values by arguing that an understanding of the exact nature of human wants and needs will 'make no difference' and contribute nothing to a study of political economy. We cannot discriminate between societies on the basis of their use values. 'To discover the various uses of things', therefore, is 'the work of history' rather than of political economy.

This has been interpreted by some to mean that Marx considered that the structural characteristics of capitalism could be investigated independently of

[4] Steedman (1977), building upon Sraffa (1960), reinterprets Marx in the light of the characteristics of physical production systems. Fine and Harris (1979) summarize the criticisms of this approach.

any consideration of use values. Nothing could be further from the truth. Indeed, had Marx truly taken that path he would have destroyed the materialist basis to his investigation. Having rejected use value as a universal category on the first page of *Capital,* he reintroduces it as a relational category on the second. The commodity is conceived of as an embodiment of both use value and exchange value. This sets the stage for considering use value in relation to both exchange value and value.[5]

In its relational form, the category 'use value' is extremely important to the subsequent analysis. 'Only an obscurantist who has not understood a word of *Capital*', Marx asserts, 'can conclude [that] use value plays no role in [the] work' (*Notes on Adolph Wagner*, p. 215). Marx explains his strategy in the *Grundrisse* (p. 881) quite explicitly. A use value is 'the object of the satisfaction of any system whatever of human needs. This is [the commodity's] material side, which the most disparate epochs of production may have in common, and whose examination therefore lies beyond political economy.' But, he then adds, 'use value falls within the realm of political economy as soon as it becomes modified by the modern relations of production, or as it, in turn, intervenes to modify them.'

This is an extremely important statement. It explains how and why Marx will weave the study of use value into his argument. Use values are shaped according to the modern relations of production and in turn intervene to modify those relations. Analyses of the labour process, the social and technical organization of production, the material characteristics of fixed capital, and the like – all considered from the standpoint of use values – are interwoven with the study of exchange values and values in most intricate fashion. In the case of fixed capital, for example, we find Marx asserting over and over again that use value here 'plays a role as an economic category' (*Grundrisse,* p. 646). A machine is a use value produced under capitalist relations of production. It embodies exchange value and value. And it has an extremely important role to play in modifying the labour process, the structures of production, the relations between inputs and outputs, and the like. The production and use of machines falls very much within the realm of political economy.

We are not yet in a position, of course, to understand how the concept of use value is modified by, at the same time as it modifies, capitalist relations of

[5] Rosdolsky (1977, pp. 73–98), has an excellent discussion on Marx's use of the concept 'use value' and the manner in which the concept is employed, chiefly in the *Grundrisse* but also in *Capital.* He also draws attention to the following rather surprising statement in Sweezy (1968, p. 26) to the effect that 'Marx excluded use-value (or as it would now be called, "utility") from the field of investigation of political economy on the ground that it does not directly embody a social relation,' Sweezy, as Rosdolsky points out, is here replicating a misinterpretation of Marx which stretches back at least to Hilferding's writings in the early 1900s.

production because we have yet to grasp the Marxian interpretations of exchange value and value. But it might be useful to consider how the Marxian understanding of use value evolves in the course of analysis by examining one important example at length.

Consider the conception of human wants and needs which Marx appears to relegate to a mere question of history on the first page of *Capital*. By the end of the very first section, after a brief examination of exchange values and values, Marx modifies his argument and insists that the producer of commodities 'must not only produce use values but use values for others, social use values'. Unless the commodity satisfies a social want or need, it can have neither exchange value nor value (*Capital*, vol. 1, p. 41). The category of use value, albeit now understood as social use value in relation to exchange value and value, is undeniably already performing an economic function.

This invites us to consider how social wants and needs are modified by capitalism. Throughout much of the first volume of *Capital*, Marx assumes that these social wants and needs are known. As far as the labourers are concerned, for example, they are seen as 'the product of historical development' dependent upon the 'degree of civilization of a country, more particularly on the habits and degree of comfort in which the class of free labourers has been formed' (*Capital*, vol. 1, p. 171). But then Marx shifts to consider how the accumulation of capital affects the conditions of life of the labourer. The 'standard of living' of labour is now seen as something that varies according to the dynamics of capitalist accumulation.

Towards the end of volume 2 of *Capital*, Marx takes a further step. The totality of the physical system of reproduction is disaggregated into three sectors producing means of production, wage goods (necessities) and luxuries. The flows between the sectors have to balance (in quantity, value and money terms) if simple reproduction is to occur or if an orderly expansion of production is to take place. The conception of wants and needs of the labourers now undergoes a further modification. The labourers rely upon capitalist commodity production to meet their needs at the same time as commodity producers rely upon the labourers to spend their money on the commodities the capitalists can produce. The production system (under capitalist control) both responds to and creates wants and needs on the part of the labourer.

This prepares the way for considering the production of new consumption as a necessary aspect to the accumulation of capital. And this production of consumption can be accomplished in a variety of ways – 'firstly quantitative expansion of existing consumption; secondly: creation of new needs by propagating existing ones in a wide circle; thirdly: production of new needs and discovery and creation of new use values' (*Grundrisse*, p. 408). The conception of use value thus shifts from something embedded in 'any system whatever of human needs' to a more specific understanding of how social wants and needs are shaped under the capitalist mode of production (see Lebowitz, 1977–8).

2 Exchange value, money and the price system

Nothing is more basic to the functioning of capitalist society than the elemental transaction in which we acquire a certain quantity of use value in return for a certain sum of money. The information generated by such transactions – that wheat sells at so much a bushel, that shoes cost so much a pair, that steel trades at so much a ton, etc. – provide signals that guide both production and consumption decisions. Producers decide how much of a commodity to produce given an average selling price and purchase certain quantities of commodities at some buying price in order to undertake commodity production. Households decide how much of a commodity to buy given its price in relation to their wants and needs and their disposable income. These transactions – so fundamental to daily life under capitalism – constitute the 'world of appearance' or the 'phenomenal form' of economic activity. The problem for political economy has ever been to explain why commodities exchange at the prices they do.

The exchange values expressed through the price system would be relatively easy to understand if we could unquestioningly accept two initial assumptions. First, one commodity functions as an unbiased *numéraire* – as money – so that the relative values of all other commodities can be unambiguously expressed as a price. Secondly, we live in a world of commodity production – all goods are produced for exchange in the market. In a capitalist society, these two assumptions appear almost 'natural' – they appear to pose no serious difficulties, if only because they reflect conditions with which we are very familiar. Armed with them, we can proceed to analysis of the price system directly. We see that commodities exchange according to relative prices and that the prices shift in response to supply and demand conditions. The price system evidently provides a highly sophisticated decentralized mechanism for co-ordinating the varied activities of innumerable and diverse economic agents. And it seems as if the laws of supply and demand will be sufficient to explain relative prices.

Marx accepts the importance of supply and demand in equilibrating the market, but he vehemently denies that supply and demand can tell us anything whatsoever about what the equilibrium prices of commodities will be.

If supply and demand balance one another, they cease to explain anything, do not affect market-values, and therefore leave us so much more in the dark about the reasons why market-value is expressed in just this sum of money and no other. It is evident that the real inner laws of capitalist production cannot be explained by the interaction of supply and demand. (*Capital,* vol. 3, p. 189)[6]

This is a very strong assertion, and we have to see Marx's justification for it. We will finally nail this down in chapter 3. But one of the linchpins of his argument lies in his analysis of money.

Marx opens his argument in *Capital* by treating exchange value as if it were a simple matter in order to arrive at his initial statement of the theory of value. But he then returns immediately to questions of exchange to show that it is indeed problematic and that a study of it, in relation to value, is very enlightening. His general tack is to show that the exchange value of a commodity cannot be understood without analysing the nature of the 'money' that permits exchange value to be expressed unequivocally as a price. In particular, he challenges the idea that any commodity can ever be an *unbiased numéraire,* and seeks to show that, on the contrary, money embodies a fundamental contradiction.

The basic task, he asserts, 'lies not in comprehending that money is a commodity, but in discovering how, why, and by what means a commodity becomes money' (*Capital,* vol. 1, p. 92). The money form is a social creation. 'Nature,' Marx argues, 'does not produce money, any more than it produces a rate of exchange or a banker' (*Grundrisse,* p. 239). And money is not established arbitrarily or out of mere convention. The money commodity is produced in the course of history by a specific social process – participation in acts of exchange – which has to be understood if we are ever to penetrate the inner logic of the price system.[7]

[6] We should note that Marx followed Ricardo on this. Ricardo considered supply and demand important as an equilibrating mechanism but, like Marx, did not consider it a powerful enough conception of the world to form the basis of value theory. 'You say demand and supply regulates value,' he wrote to Malthus, but 'this, I think, is saying nothing' (quoted in Meek, 1977, p. 158). Supply and demand lies at the heart of neoclassical and marginalist value theory, but Sraffa's (1960) critique of the latter has pushed at least a segment of contemporary economic theory back to the common basis provided, in at least this respect, by both Marx and Ricardo. Meek (1977, ch. 10) has a good discussion on this point.

[7] Studies on Marx's theory of money are few and far between. Rosdolsky (1977) has an excellent discussion of how Marx arrived at his final conception of money. De Brunhoff's *Marx on Money* (1976) is useful, but as her auto-critique at the end indicates, she misses out on a number of points which she seeks to include in her later works (1976b and 1978) which are generally excellent. Harris (1976; 1979) and Barrère (1977) also assemble some materials of interest. What is distressing, however, is the way in which general works on Marx often shunt the problem of money to one side as a special topic, instead of treating it as central to the whole analysis. The only exception is Mandel (1968), who commendably integrates money and credit into his text. By the same token there is a danger inherent in the rise of special studies of Marx's theory of money as something that can be treated in isolation from other aspects of Marx's theory. I hope to avoid this pitfall in chapters 9 and 10.

Marx treats the simple commodity form as the 'germ' of the money form. An analysis of direct barter shows that commodities can assume what he calls the 'equivalent' and 'relative' forms of value. When a community measures the value of goods being acquired against the single value of a good being disposed of, then the latter functions as its equivalent form of value. In an initial state, each community or bargaining agent will possess commodities that operate as the equivalent form of value. With the proliferation of exchange, one commodity (or set of commodities) will likely emerge as the 'universal equivalent' – a basic money commodity such as gold. The relative values of all other commodities can then be expressed in terms of this money commodity. 'Value' consequently acquires a clearly recognizable, unique and socially accepted measure. The shift from many different (subjective and often accidental) determinations of exchange value to one standard money measure is produced by a proliferation of exchange relations to the point where the production of goods for exchange becomes 'a normal social act'. But we can also see, on the other hand, that a general system of commodity exchange would be impossible without money to facilitate it. The growth of exchange and the emergence of a money commodity therefore necessarily go hand in hand.

The commodity that assumes 'the mantle of money' becomes distinct from all the others. And analysis of its special characteristics proves enlightening, since 'the riddle presented by money is but the riddle presented by commodities . . . in its most glaring form' (*Capital,* vol. 1, p. 93).

The money commodity, like any other commodity, has a value, exchange value and use value. Its value is determined by the socially necessary labour time taken up in its production and reflects the specific social and physical conditions of the labour process under which it is produced. The exchange values of all other commodities are measured against the yardstick formed by these specific conditions of production of the money commodity. From this standpoint, money functions as *a measure of value,* and its exchange value ought presumably to reflect that fact. The use value of money is that it facilitates the circulation of all other commodities. From this standpoint it functions as *a medium of circulation.* In the course of lubricating exchange, however, money acquires an exchange value formed as 'the reflex, thrown upon a single commodity, of the value relations between all the rest' (*Capital,* vol. 1, p. 90). Money becomes worth what it will buy. The result: the money commodity acquires a dual exchange value – that dictated by its own conditions of production (its 'inherent' exchange value), and that dictated by what it will buy (its 'reflex' value).

This duality arises, Marx explains, because exchange value, which we initially conceived of as being an internalized attribute of all commodities is now represented by a measuring rod which is external to and quite separate from the commodities themselves (*Grundrisse,* p. 145). The problem of how to represent and measure values is thereby solved. But the solution is arrived at only at the expense of internalizing the duality of use value and value within the exchange value of money itself. Money, in short, 'solves the contradictions of direct barter and exchange, only by positing them as general contradictions' (*Grundrisse*, p. 200). All of which has some very important ramifications.

We can see, for example, that the total quantity of money circulating in society at a given velocity has to be sufficient to facilitate a given quantity of commodity exchange at appropriate prices. We can designate the demand for money as $P \cdot Q$ (where P is a vector of prices and Q the respective quantities of commodities in circulation) and the supply of money as $M \cdot V$ (where M is the quantity of money available and V is its velocity of circulation). In equilibrium, $MV = PQ$ (*Capital*, vol. 1, p. 123). If the quantity of commodities in circulation suddenly increases, while both M and V remain constant, then the reflex value of the money commodity will rise to a level that may be far above its inherent value. An increase in the supply of money or in its velocity of circulation can rectify this. But the volume of commodity exchange is perpetually fluctuating, day by day, while the very conditions that led a particular commodity to be selected as the money commodity (scarcity, etc.) militate against instant adjustability in its supply. One possible way out of this difficulty is to create a reserve fund, a *hoard*, which can be used flexibly in the face of potentially wide fluctuations in the volume of commodity exchange. Another possibility is to use some kind of credit system and then use the money commodity to pay the balance of accounts at the end of a given period of time (a day, month or year). In this way the demand for money can be much reduced and the effects of day-to-day fluctuations in the volume of commodity exchange neutralized.

This immediately focuses our attention upon certain additional functions of money – as a *store of value* and as a *means of payment*. Both depend upon the capacity of money to operate as an independent form of social power which in turn derives from the fact that money is the social expression of value itself. 'The individual', Marx suggests, consequently 'carries his social power, as well as his bond with society, in his pocket' (*Grundrisse*, p. 157). This social power is 'alienable without restriction or conditions', and it can become, therefore, the 'private power of private persons' (*Capital*, vol. 1, pp. 110, 132). Greed for that social power leads to appropriation, stealing, hoarding, accumulation – all become possible. Marx goes to considerable lengths, particularly in the *Grundrisse* (see particularly pp. 145–72), to describe the disruptive effects of monetization, through social power relations, on traditional societies.

But in *Capital* he is concerned to make another point. If the use of money as a store of value or as means of payment provides the only way to keep the two forms of exchange value that money internalizes in line with each other, then this requires that the social power of money be used in a certain way. If hoarding is necessary to equilibrate the exchange process (*Capital,* vol. 1, p. 134), then this implies that the hoarded money is used according to certain rational principles – money must be withdrawn from circulation when commodity production is down, and thrown back into circulation when commodity production revives. When money is used as means of payment, all agents in the exchange process become both debtors and creditors, and this again implies certain coherent principles for contracting and settling debts. In both cases our attention is focused on a particular form of circulation. We understand why the circulation of money, as an end in itself, arises as a 'social necessity springing out of the process of circulation itself' (*Capital,* vol. 1, p. 136).

Marx defines the commodity form of circulation (commodity–money––commodity, or C–M–C, for short) as an exchange of use values (the use of shoes against bread, for example) which depends essentially upon the *qualities* of the goods being exchanged. Money functions here as a convenient intermediary. We now encounter a form of circulation, M–C–M, which begins and ends with exactly the same commodity. The only possible motivation for putting money into circulation on a repeated basis is to obtain more of it at the end than was possessed at the beginning. A *quantitative* relation replaces the exchange of *qualities*. Money is thrown into circulation to make more money – a profit. And money that circulates in this way is called *capital*.

We have arrived at the point where we can see that the conditions of general commodity exchange make the capitalist form of circulation socially necessary. The social implications of this are legion. A social space is created in which the operations of the capitalist become necessary in order to stabilize exchange relations. But

> it is only in so far as the appropriation of ever more and more wealth in the abstract becomes the sole motive of his operations, that he functions as a capitalist, that is, as capital personified and endowed with consciousness and a will. Use values must therefore never be looked upon as the real aim of the capitalist. . . . The restless never-ending process of profit-making alone is what he aims at. This boundless greed after riches, this passionate chase after exchange value, is common to the capitalist and the miser; but while the miser is merely a capitalist gone mad, the capitalist is a rational miser. The never-ending augmentation of exchange value, which the miser strives after, by seeking to save his money from circulation, is attained by the more acute capitalist, by constantly throwing it afresh into circulation. (*Capital*, vol. 1, pp. 152–3)

And so we arrive at the most fundamental question we can possibly ask of a capitalist society: where does profit come from? But only value theory can equip us with the wherewithal for an assault on that question.

3 *The value theory*

We now consider the value theory implicit in the processes of commodity production and exchange. Unlike use values and prices, there is no self-evident starting point for the analysis. We either start with *a priori* assumptions about the nature of value, or seek an objective theory of value through a material investigation of how society functions. Marx takes the latter course. Since the world of appearance is dominated, in our own society, by the prices of quantities of use values, these provide the data for establishing an initial version of the value theory. Once the latter is in place, the dialectical relationship between values, prices and use values can be examined as a means to dissect the inner logic of capitalism.

The opening argument in *Capital* is strikingly simple. Marx defines the commodity as an embodiment of use and exchange values, abstracts immediately from the former, and proceeds directly to analyse exchange values. Putting two different use values (which are themselves qualitatively different) equal to each other in exchange implies that both use values have something in common. The only attribute that all commodities have in common is that they are products of human labour. When 'commodities are looked at as crystals of this social substance, common to them all, they are – Values' (*Capital*, vol. 1, p. 38).

The argument is almost identical to that laid out in Ricardo's *Principles of Political Economy and Taxation*. Marx appears to follow Ricardo entirely in treating the problem of value, at this stage, as one of finding an appropriate standard of value.[8] The only modification is his introduction of a distinction between 'concrete useful labour' defined as 'human labour exercised with a definite aim, to produce use values' and 'human labour in the abstract', which 'creates and forms the value of commodities' (*Capital*, vol. 1, pp. 41–6). But Marx's argument now appears purely tautological – the standard of value is that aspect of human labour which creates value!

Marx breaks out of the tautology by an analysis of the difference between abstract and concrete labour. All labour is concrete in the sense that it involves the material transformation of nature. But market exchange tends to obliterate individual differences both in the conditions of production and on the part of those doing the labouring. If I paid according to actual labour time embodied, then the lazier the labourer, the more I should pay. But generally I pay the going market price. What happens in effect is that the commensurability of commodities achieved through exchange renders the labour embodied in them equally commensurable. If it takes one day to make a pair

[8] Itoh (1976) provides an excellent study of the way in which Marx uses Ricardo's arguments to fashion his own conception in *Capital*, and Pilling's (1972) article is also of considerable interest. See also Elson (1979).

of shoes on average, then the abstract labour embodied in a pair of shoes is one day no matter whether it takes the individual labourer two or fifty hours to make. Abstract labour is defined then as 'socially necessary labour time' (*Capital*, vol. 1, p. 39).

All that this does is to insert the qualification 'socially necessary' into Ricardo's theory of labour time as the standard of value. It hardly makes Marx's version strong enough to bear the weight of all the subsequent analysis, nor does it seem profound enough to justify treating it as *the* solid foundation of Marxian theory and therefore as a proposition to be defended at all costs. Until, that is, we ask what, exactly, is meant by 'socially necessary'?

The invocation of social necessity should alert us. It contains the seeds for Marx's critique of political economy as well as for his dissection of capitalism. What Marx will eventually show us, in a discourse pervaded by a profound concern with marking the boundaries between freedom and necessity under capitalism, is that human labour in the abstract is a distillation, finally accomplished under very specific relations of production, out of a seemingly infinite variety of concrete labour activities. We will discover that abstract labour can become the measure of value only to the degree that a specific kind of human labour – wage labour – becomes general.

This immediately differentiates Marx's theory of value from conventional labour theories of value (Ricardo's in particular). Marx turns an a-historical, universal statement into a theory of value that operates solely under capitalist relations of production. At the same time, the value theory reaches out beyond the problem of simply defining a standard of value for determining the relative prices of commodities. The value theory comes to reflect and embody the essential social relations that lie at the heart of the capitalist mode of production. Value is conceived of, in short, as a social relation. But Marx does not throw this conception at us arbitrarily, as an *a priori* construct. He seeks, rather, to show us, step by step, that this is the only conception of value that makes sense; that the law of value as he conceives of it indeed operates as a guiding force within capitalist history. And the proof of this must necessarily lie at the end of his analysis, not at the beginning.[9]

Marx begins on the explication of 'socially necessary' almost immediately. It is, we are told, 'the labour required to produce an article under the normal conditions of production and with the average degree of skill and intensity prevalent at the time'. This cannot be understood without returning to an analysis of use values. First, the productivity of labour is considered in purely physical terms: it is set 'by the average amount of skill of the workman, the state of science, and the degree of its practical application, the social organization of production, the extent and capabilities of the means of production,

[9] The contrast between this view and other interpretations of the value theory will be considered in the Appendix on p. 35 below.

and by physical conditions' (*Capital,* vol. 1, p. 40). Second, labour can create no value unless it creates social use values – use values for others. Marx does not elaborate on what is meant by a 'social use value' at this stage. He simply asserts that value has to be created in production and realized through exchange and consumption if it is to remain value. This brief return to the sphere of use values is a foretaste of much that is to come.

But at this point Marx chooses to focus more closely on value in relation to exchange value. His investigation of the material forms of value achieved through exchange reveals that the substance of value – human labour in the abstract – can regulate commodity production and exchange only if there is some way that value can be represented materially. The conclusion quickly follows: 'money as a measure of value, is the phenomenal form that must of necessity be assumed by that measure of value which is immanent in commodities, labour time (*Capital,* vol. 1, p. 94).

Notice, once more, the invocation of *necessity*. When we relate this back to the idea of 'socially necessary labour time' we arrive at an important proposition. The existence of money is a necessary condition for the separation and distillation of abstract out of concrete labour.

We can see why this is so by examining the consequences of a growth in exchange relations. This growth, we have already seen, is dependent upon, at the same time as it gives rise to, the money form. But it also has consequences for the distinction between concrete and abstract labour:

> It is only by being exchanged that the products of labour acquire, as values, one uniform social status, distinct from their varied forms of existence as objects of utility. This division of a product into a useful thing and a value becomes practically important, only when exchange has acquired such an extension that useful articles are produced for the purpose of being exchanged. . . . From this moment the labour of the individual producer acquires socially a two-fold character. On the one hand, it must, as a definite useful kind of labour, satisfy a definite social want, and thus hold its place as part and parcel of the collective labour of all, as a branch of a social division of labour that has sprung up spontaneously. On the other hand, it can satisfy the manifold wants of the individual producer himself, only in so far as the mutual exchange-ability of all kinds of useful private labour is an established social fact, and therefore the private useful labour of each producer ranks on an equality with that of all others. The equalization of the most different kinds of labour can be the result of an abstraction from their inequalities, or of reducing them to their common denominator, viz., expenditure of human labour-power or human labour in the abstract. (*Capital,* vol. 1, p. 73).

Marx's rapid movement from one 'window' to another in the first chapter of *Capital* has brought us to the point where we can clearly see the interconnections between the growth of exchange, the rise of the money form and the emergence of abstract labour as a measure of value. But we have also gained sufficient perspective on these interrelations to see that the way things appear to us in daily life can conceal as much as it can reveal about their social meaning. This idea Marx captures in the concept of 'the fetishism of commodities'.

The extension of exchange puts producers into relations of reciprocal dependency. But they relate to each other by way of the products they exchange rather than directly as social beings. Social relationships are expressed as relationships between things. On the other hand, the things themselves exchange according to their value, which is measured in terms of abstract labour. And abstract labour becomes the measure of value through a specific social process. The 'fetishism of commodities' describes a state in which 'the relations connecting the labour of one individual with that of the rest appear, not as direct social relations between individuals at work, but as what they really are, material relations between persons and social relations between things' (*Capital*, vol. 1, p. 73).

It is no accident that Marx lays out this general principle of 'the fetishism of commodities' immediately after considering the emergence of the money form of value.[10] He is concerned at this point in the analysis to use the general principle of 'fetishism' to explain the problematic character of the relation between value and its monetary expression:

> It was the common expression of all commodities in money that alone led to the establishment of their character as values. It is, however, just this ultimate money form of the world of commodities that actually conceals, instead of disclosing, the social character of private labour, and the social relations between the individual producers. (*Capital*, vol. 1, pp. 75–6)

The exchange of commodities for money is real enough, yet it conceals our social relationships with others behind a mere thing – the money form itself. The act of exchange tells us nothing about the conditions of labour of the producers, for example, and keeps us in a state of ignorance concerning our social relations as these are mediated by the market system. We respond solely to the prices of quantities of use values. But this also suggests that, when we exchange things, 'we imply the existence of value . . . without being aware of it.' The existence of money – the form of value – conceals the social meaning of value itself. 'Value does not stalk about with a label describing what it is' (*Capital*, vol. 1, p. 74).

Consider, now, the relationship between values and prices that this implies. If the price system permits the formation of values at the same time as it

---

[10] Rubin (1972) has some fascinating comments on the theme of fetishism in Marx's *Capital*.

conceals the social basis of values from view, then the magnitude of relative prices does not necessarily have to correspond to the magnitude of relative values. Marx considers the deviations between the two magnitudes as 'no defect' because they 'admirably adapt the price form' to a social situation characterized, seemingly, by lawless irregularities that compensate each other (*Capital*, vol. 1, p. 102). The ebb and flow of commodity production for exchange, arising out of the spontaneous decisions of myriad producers, can be accommodated by the price system precisely because prices are free to fluctuate in ways in which a strict measure of values could not. Values, after all, express an equilibrium point in exchange ratios after supply and demand have been equilibrated in the market. The flexibility of prices permits that equilibration process to take place and is therefore essential to the definition of values.

More troublesome, however, is the fact that 'the price form may also conceal a qualitative inconsistency' to the point where 'price ceases altogether to express value.' Objects that are not products of human labour – land, conscience, honour and so on, 'are capable of being offered for sale by their holders and thus acquiring through their price the form of commodities' (*Capital*, vol. 1, p. 102). Commodities that are products of human labour must be distinguished, then, from 'commodity forms', which have a price but no value. This topic is not seriously broached again until volume 3 of *Capital*. There we will discover the fetishism that attaches to the categories of rent (which puts a price on land and makes it seem as if money grows out of the soil) and interest (which puts a price on money itself). For the moment we, too, will leave such thorny questions aside.

Marx's characterization of the fetishism of commodities encourages us to consider the social meaning of value in greater depth. In one of his earliest statements on the subject, Marx viewed value as 'the civil mode of existence of property' (*Collected Works* (with Engels), vol. 1, p. 229). In *Capital* Marx is nowhere near as blunt, but this dimension to his argument is nevertheless of great importance.

Exchange of commodities presupposes the right of private proprietors to dispose freely of the products of their labour. This juridical relation is 'but the reflex of the real economic relations' of exchange (*Capital*, vol. 1, p. 84). If exchange ratios are to be established that accurately reflect social requirements, then producers must 'treat each other as private owners of alienable objects and by implication as independent individuals'. This means that 'juridical individuals' (persons, corporations, etc.) must be able to approach each other on an equal footing in exchange, as sole and exclusive owners of commodities with the freedom to buy from and sell to whomsoever they please. For such a condition to exist supposes not only a solid legal foundation to exchange but also the power to sustain private property rights and enforce contracts. This power, of course, resides in 'the state'. The state in some form or another is a necessary precondition to the establishment of values.

To the extent that private property rights and enforcement of contracts are guaranteed, so production can increasingly be carried on 'by private individuals or groups of individuals who carry on their work independently of each other' and who express their relation to society through the exchange of their products (*Capital,* vol. 1, pp. 72–3). The price system, which also requires state regulation if only to guarantee the quality of the money in circulation (see chapter 10 below), facilitates the co-ordination of the spontaneous activities of innumerable individuals so that production achieves 'the quantitative proportion . . . which society requires' (*Capital,* vol. 1, p. 75). We can, under these conditions, study the 'behaviour of men in the social process of production' as if it were 'purely atomic', so that 'their relations to each other in production assume a material character independent of their control and conscious individual action' (*Capital,* vol. 1, pp. 92–3).

This working model of a market society and all of its political and legal trappings was, of course, quite prevalent in the political economy of the time and stretches back, as Professor MacPherson has so ably shown, at least to Hobbes and Locke.[11] Marx clearly took the view that the operation of the law of value depended upon the existence of these basic societal conditions. Furthermore, he considers that notions of 'individuality', 'equality', 'private property' and 'freedom' take on very specific meanings in the context of market exchange – meanings that should not be confused with more general ideologies of freedom, individuality, equality and so on. To the degree that these highly specific meanings are universalized in bourgeois notions of constitutionality, we create confusions in thought as well as in practice.

Consider, for example, the notion of *equality,* which plays a key role in Marx's argument. Aristotle had long before argued that 'exchange cannot take place without equality' – a principle that Marx quotes approvingly. This does not mean that everyone is or should be considered equal in all respects. It simply means that we would not exchange one use value for another under conditons of free exchange unless we valued the two at least equally well. Or, put in money terms, a dollar equals another dollar in terms of its purchasing power no matter whose pocket it is in. The whole rationale for the operation of the price system rests on the principle that 'the circulation of commodities requires the exchange of equivalents' (*Capital,* vol. 1, p. 160). The definition of values therefore rests upon this restricted and quite specific idea of equality in the sense that diverse use values produced under diverse concrete condi-

[11] I do not mean to imply by this that I agree entirely with MacPherson (1962), whose *Political Theory of Possessive Individualism* ignores, among other things, the patriarchal organization of families at the same time as it skips over many of the real complexities – see Tribe (1978) and Macfarlane (1978). Marx himself picks up on these themes in some detail in the *Grundrisse* (pp. 157–65).

tions of human labour are all reduced in the course of market exchange to the same standard. They can be brought into a relation of equivalence. But once we have this idea of equality firmly in place, we can use it as a lever to push the whole discussion of the inner logic of capitalism on to a new and more fruitful plane of discourse. Let us see how Marx does this.

4 The theory of surplus value

We have now arrived at the point where we can lay out a conception of capital that integrates our understanding of the relationships between use values, exchange values and values. Capital, Marx insists, should be defined as a process rather than as a thing. The material manifestation of this process exists as a transformation from money into commodities back into money plus profit: $M-C-(M+\Delta M)$. But since we have defined money as the material representation of value, we can also say that capital is a process of expansion of value. And this Marx calls the production of *surplus value*.

Capital must, in the course of its circulation, assume the forms of money (exchange value) and commodities (use values) at different moments:

> In truth, however, value is here the active factor in a process, in which, while constantly assuming the form in turn of money and commodities, it at the same time changes in magnitude, differentiates itself by throwing off surplus-value from itself.

We ought not, however, divorce our understanding of this process of 'self-expansion of value' from its material expression. For this reason,

> Value . . . requires some independent form, by means of which its identity may at any time be established. And this form it possesses only in the shape of money. It is under the form of money that value begins and ends, and begins again, every act of its own spontaneous generation. . . . Value therefore now becomes value in process, money in process, and, as such, capital. (*Capital*, vol. 1, pp. 153–5)

This definition of capital has some wide-ranging implications. First of all, it implies that the functioning capital in society is not equal to the total stock of money, nor is it equal to the total stock of use values (which we can define as the total *social wealth*). The money that sits in my pocket as a means to purchase the commodities that I need to live on is not being used as capital. Nor are the use values of the house I live in or the spade I dig the garden with. There is, therefore, a great deal that goes on in society that is not directly related to the circulation of capital, and we should therefore resist the temptation to reduce everything to these simple Marxian categories. *Money capital* is, then, that part of the total stock of money, *productive* and *commodity capital* are those portions of the total social wealth, caught up in a very specific process of circulation. Capital, it follows, can be formed by converting money and use values and putting them into circulation in order to make money, to produce surplus value.

Secondly, this 'process' definition of capital means that we can define a 'capitalist' as any economic agent who puts money and use values into circulation in order to make more money. Individuals may or may not relish this role, personify it and internalize its rationale into their own psychology. Capitalists may be nice or evil people. But this need not concern us: we can simply treat 'the characters who appear on the economic stage' as 'personifications of the economic relations that exist between them' (*Capital,* vol. 1, p. 85). For the purposes at hand we can concentrate on *roles* rather than upon people themselves. This permits us to abstract from the diversity of human motivations and to operate at the level of social necessity as this is captured in a study of the roles of economic agents.

Last, but not least, Marx's definition of capital demonstrates a necessary rather than fortuitous relation between the capitalist form of circulation and the determination of values as socially necessary labour time. Since this is a very important proposition, we should recapitulate the basis for it.

We have seen that the extension of exchange and the rise of money are integral to each other. We also saw that the internalized contradiction within the money form (between its use value and value) could be resolved only if there were a reserve fund of money that could be thrown into or withdrawn from circulation as conditions of commodity exchange required. Money must begin to circulate in a certain way. Since $M-C-M$ yields no qualitative change in the nature of the commodity held at the beginning and end of the process, the only systemic motivation for this form of circulation is through a quantitative change, which means a circulation process of the form

$$M-C-(M+\Delta M).$$

What Marx shows us is that, even in the absence of diverse human motivations (the lust for gold, the greed for social power and the desire to dominate), the capitalist form of circulation would have had to come into existence in response to the contradictory pressures exerted on money through the expansion and extension of exchange. But exchange also establishes values as the regulators of exchange ratios. And so we can derive the connection: the rise of the capitalist form of circulation and of values as the regulators of exchange go hand in hand because both are the product of extension and expansion of exchange.

But in Marx's book, contradictions are rarely resolved, nearly always displaced. And so it is in this case. The capitalist form of circulation rests upon an *inequality* because capitalists possess more money (values) at the end of the process than they did at the beginning. But values are established by an exchange process which rests on the principle of *equivalence*. This poses a difficulty. How can capitalists realize an inequality, ΔM, through an exchange process which presupposes equivalence? Where, in short, does profit come from under conditions of fair exchange?

Try as we might, Marx argues, we cannot find an answer to that question in the realm of exchange. By violating the principle of equivalence (by cheating, forced exchanges, robbery and the like) we can only make one individual's profit another's loss. This can result in the concentration of money and means of production in a few hands, but it cannot form a stable basis for a society in which innumerable producers are supposed to seek and make a 'fair' profit without cannibalizing each other in the process.

We have, therefore, to seek the answer by way of a careful scrutiny of the realm of production. We have to switch our 'window' on the world from that formed by the relation between exchange value and value and consider the relation between value and use value. From the sixth chapter of volume 1 of *Capital* until well into volume 3, Marx will, with a few significant exceptions, generally assume that all commodities trade at their values, that there is no distinction between prices and values. The problem of profit then becomes identical to that of the expansion of values. And the solution to that problem has to be sought without in any way appealing to the idea of deviations between prices and values. From this new 'window' on the inner logic of capitalism, Marx sees his way clearly forward to the construction of the theory of surplus value. Let us see how this argument flows.

Production occurs in the context of definite social relations. The social relation that dominates under the capitalist mode of production is that between wage labour and capital. Capitalists control the means of production, the production process and the disposition of the final product. Labourers sell their labour power as a commodity in return for wages. We presuppose, in short, that production occurs in the context of a definite class relation between capital and labour.

Labour power as a commodity has a two-fold character: it has a use value and an exchange value. The exchange value is set, in accordance with the rules of commodity exchange, by the socially necessary labour time required to reproduce that labour power at a certain standard of living and with a certain capacity to engage in the work process. The labourer gives up the use value of the labour power in return for its exchange value.

Once capitalists acquire labour power they can put it to work in ways that are beneficial to themselves. Since capitalists purchase a certain length of time during which they maintain the rights to the use of labour power, they can organize the production process (its intensity, technology, etc.) to ensure that the workers produce greater value during that time span than they receive. The use value of labour power to the capitalist is not simply that it can be put to work to produce commodities, but that it has the special capacity to produce greater value than it itself has — it can, in short, produce *surplus value*.

Marx's analysis is founded on the idea that 'the value of labour power, and the value which that labour power creates in the labour process, are two entirely different magnitudes' (*Capital,* vol. 1, p. 193). The excess of the value that labourers embody in commodities relative to the value they require for their own reproduction measures the exploitation of labour in production. Notice, however, that the rule of equivalence in exchange is in no way offended even though surplus value is produced. There is, therefore, no exploitation in the sphere of exchange.

This solution to the origin of profit is as simple as it is elegant. It strikes home, as Engels put it, 'like a thunderbolt out of a clear sky' (*Capital,* vol. 2, p. 14).

Classical political economy could not see the solution because it confused labour as a measure of value and labour power as a commodity traded on the market. There is in Marx's theory, therefore, a vital distinction between labour and labour power. 'Labour,' Marx asserts, 'is the substance, and the immanent measure of value, *but has itself no value.*' To suppose otherwise would be to suppose that we could measure the value of value itself. Furthermore, 'if such a thing as the value of labour really existed, and [the capitalist] really paid this value, no capital would exist, his money would not be turned into capital' (*Capital,* vol. 1, pp. 537–41). What the labourer sells to the capitalist is not labour (the substance of value) but labour power – the capacity to realize in commodity form a certain quantity of socially necessary labour time.

The distinction between labour and labour power leads Marx to a quite pivotal conclusion – one that allows him to rectify and transform Ricardo's labour theory of value. In a society in which labour and labour power were indistinguishable (as they are in Ricardo's theory), the law of value could operate only in a very restricted degree. The law of value 'begins to develop freely only on the basis of capitalist production' (*Capital,* vol. 1, p. 536). And this presupposes social relations of wage labour. In other words, the contradiction between capital and wage labour is 'the ultimate development of the *value-relation* and of production resting on value' (*Grundrisse,* p. 704).

This means, quite simply, that value and the production of surplus value are part and parcel of each other. The full development of the one is predicated on the flowering of the other. Since the production of surplus value can occur only under certain specific relations of production, we have to understand how these first came into being. We have to understand the origin of wage labour.

And the one thing we can be certain of is that:

> Nature does not produce on the one side owners of money or commodities, and on the other men possessing nothing but their own labour power. This relation has no natural basis, neither is its social basis one that is common to all historical periods. It is clearly the result of a past

historical development, the product of many economic revolutions, of the extinction of a whole series of older forms of social production. (*Grundrisse,* p. 169)

Marx has now pulled together all of the logical threads of a complex argument. He began, as we did, with the simple conception of the commodity as an embodiment of use value and exchange value. Out of the proliferation of exchange he derived the necessity for money as an expression of value and showed a necessary relation between the capitalist form of circulation and the determination of exchange ratios according to socially necessary labour time. He has now shown us that the contradiction this generates between the equivalence presupposed by exchange and the inequality implied by profit can be resolved only by identifying a commodity that has the special characteristic of being able to produce greater value than it itself has. Labour power is such a commodity. When put to work to produce surplus value it can resolve the contradiction. But this implies the existence of wage labour. All that remains is to explain the origin of wage labour itself. It is to this task that we must now turn.

II CLASS RELATIONS AND THE CAPITALIST PRINCIPLE OF ACCUMULATION

Marx's investigations of the relations between use values, prices and values in the context of commodity production and exchange yields a fundamental conclusion. The social relation that lies at the root of the Marxian value theory is the class relation between capital and labour. The value theory is an expression of this class relation. This conclusion sets Marx apart from Ricardo and constitutes the essence of his critique of bourgeois political economy. But what, exactly, is meant by a class relation?

The class concept is inserted into the analysis of *Capital* with the utmost caution. There are no direct professions of faith of the sort that 'all history is the history of class struggle', nor do we find 'class' introduced as some *deus ex machina* which explains everything but does not have to be explained. The conception of class evolves in the course of investigating the processes of commodity production and exchange. Once an initial definition is in place, Marx can broaden the scope of his enquiry immeasurably, incorporate specific ideas on class relations and move freely between use values, prices, values and class relations in dissecting the inner logic of capitalism. This is what permits him to break out of the strait-jacket of traditional political economy.

The analysis of commodity production and exchange reveals the existence of two distinctive and opposed roles in capitalist society. Those who seek profit take on the role of capitalist, and those who give up surplus labour to nourish that profit take on the role of labourer. Throughout *Capital* Marx treats the capitalist as 'capital personified' and the labourer simply as the bearer of a commodity, labour-power (*Capital,* vol. 1, p. 85). They are treated, in short, as 'personifications of the economic relations that exist between them'. Marx elaborates on the social, moral, psychological and political implications of these distinctive roles and departs from a two-class representation of capitalist social structure only to the extent that such elaborations and departures are deemed necessary to the analysis.

This formal and quite severe treatment of the class concept is, however, juxtaposed in *Capital* with richer, more confused meanings which derive from the study of history. Contemporary commentators in the Marxist tradition are consequently fond of distinguishing between concepts of class as they relate to the *capitalist mode of production* and those relating to *capitalist social formations.*[12] The distinction is useful. The formal analysis of the capitalist mode of production seeks to unravel the stark logic of capitalism stripped bare of all complicating features. The concepts used presuppose no

[12] The term 'mode of production' is liberally scattered throughout Marx's work, the concept 'social formation' less so. The distinction between the two concepts became a hot topic of debate through the work of Althusser (1969), Althusser and Balibar (1970), Poulantzas (1975) and others working in what became known as the 'Althusserian' tradition of structuralist Marxism. The subsequent debate has gone from the unnecessarily obscure and difficult (Althusser and Balibar) to the ridiculous (Hindess and Hirst, 1975) and reached its nadir of self-destructiveness in the work of Hindess and Hirst (1976) and Cutler, Hindess, Hirst and Hussain (1978); see also the review of the latter by Harris (1978). A measure of sanity, together with some important insights, has been injected into the debate by writers such as Ollman (1971), Godelier (1972), Therborn (1976), Laclau (1977) and more recently Cohen (1978). E. P. Thompson (1978), justifiably incensed by the *a*-historical and unenlightened character of much of the debate, dismisses it all as arrant and arrogant theoretical nonsense, but in the process is rightly rebuked by Anderson (1980) for throwing out the nuggets of gold within what he admits to be a good deal of turgid dross.

Marx himself uses the term 'mode of production' in three rather different ways. He writes the 'mode of production of cotton', for example, and means the actual methods and techniques used in the production of a particular kind of use value. By the *capitalist* mode of production he often means the characteristic form of the labour process under the class relations of capitalism (including, of course, the production of surplus value), presuming production of commodities for exchange. This is the main way in which Marx uses the concept throughout *Capital* (see, for example, vol. 1, pp. 510–11). The concept is an abstract representation of a reasonably narrowly defined set of relationships (see chapter 4 below for a discussion of the manner in which productive forces (the capacity to transform nature) and the social (class) relations combine within the labour process to define the characteristic mode of production).

But Marx sometimes, particularly in his preparatory writings such as the *Grundrisse,* uses the concept holistically and for comparative purposes. The concept then refers to the whole gamut of production, exchange, distribution and consumption relations as well as to the institutional, juridical and administrative arrangements, political organization and state apparatus, ideology and characteristic forms of social (class) reproduction. In this vein we can compare the 'capitalist', 'feudal', 'Asiatic', etc., modes of production. This all-embracing but highly abstract concept is in some ways the most

more than is strictly necessary to that task. But a social formation – a particular society as it is constituted at a particular historical moment – is much more complex. When Marx writes about actual historical events he uses broader, more numerous and more flexible class categories. In the historical passages in *Capital* for example, we find the capitalist class treated as one element within the ruling classes in society, while the bourgeoisie means something different again. In the *Eighteenth Brumaire of Louis Bonaparte,* which is often held up as a model of Marx's historical analysis in action, we find the events in France of 1848–51 analysed in terms of lumpenproletariat, industrial proletariat, a petite bourgeoisie, a capitalist class factionalized into industrialists and financiers, a landed aristocracy and a peasant class. All of this is a far cry from the neat two-class analytics laid out in much of *Capital.*[13]

---

interesting, but it also creates the greatest difficulties. It is over this use of the term that most of the debate has raged.

I shall treat this third sense of 'mode of production' as a preliminary concept, the content of which has yet to be discovered through careful theoretical, historical and comparative study. The ambiguity that some have correctly detected in Marx's own use of the concept testifies to the tentative nature of his own formulations, and we would do well to follow him in this regard. The trouble with Althusser's approach is that it presumes that a complete theorization can be achieved through some kind of rigorous 'theoretical practice'. While he does generate some important insights, the full meaning of the idea will become apparent only after a long-drawn out process of enquiry which must surely include historical and comparative studies. But we have to start our enquiry somewhere, armed with concepts that have yet to be filled out. To this end, I shall primarily appeal to the second, more limited, conception of the mode of production in order to build, step by step, towards a more comprehensive understanding of the capitalist mode of production as a whole. This is, I would emphasize, only one of the ways in which we can approach the full meaning of the concept.

The idea of a 'social formation' serves primarily to remind us that the diversity of human practices within any society cannot be reduced simply to the economic practices dictated by its dominant mode of production. Althusser and Balibar suggest two ways in which we can think about a social formation. First, we must recognize the 'relative autonomy' of the economic, political, ideological and theoretical practices in society. Which is one way of saying there is abundant opportunity, within limits, for a good deal of cultural, institutional, political, moral and ideological variation under capitalism. Second, in actual historical situations we will certainly find several modes of production intertwined or 'articulated' with each other, even though one mode may be clearly dominant. Residual elements of past modes, the seeds of future modes and imported elements from some contemporaneously existing mode may all be found within a particular social formation. All such features, we should note, are explicable rather than accidental or purely idiosyncratic, but to understand them we have to adopt a far more complex frame of analysis than that dictated by the analysis of any one particular mode of production (conceived of in the narrow sense). The coupling of the terms 'mode of production' and 'social formation' is for this reason very useful.

[13] In the third volume of *Capital,* Marx begins to disaggregate the capitalist class into separate 'factions' or 'classes' of merchant capitalist, money capitalist, financier

The interplay between two seemingly disparate conceptual systems — the historical and the theoretical — is crucial to the explication of the class concept in all of its fullness. And by extension the interplay is crucial for understanding the nature of value itself. But the links are hard to forge, and Marx most certainly did not complete the task. Throughout much of *Capital*, for example, Marx 'clings to the fact' of wage labour 'theoretically' in exactly the same way that the contemporary capitalist accepts the fact 'practically' (*Capital*, vol. 1, p. 169). But behind this theoretical fact there lurks an important historical question: how and why did it ever come about that the owner of money finds a labourer freely selling the commodity labour power in the market place? The relation between capital and labour has no 'natural' basis — it arises as the result of a specific historical process. And so at the end of the first volume of *Capital* Marx describes the processes whereby capitalism came to replace feudalism.

The story Marx tells is controversial in its details but simple in its basic conception.[14] The rise of the capitalist class proceeds hand in hand with the formation of a proletariat. The latter is 'the product of centuries of struggle between the capitalist and the labourer' (*Capital*, vol. 1, p. 271) as those engaging in the capitalist mode of circulation struggled to find an appropriate mode of production as a systematic basis for generating profit. Both classes are caught in a symbiotic but inexorable opposition. Neither can exist without the other, yet the antithesis between them is profound. Their mutual development takes on a variety of intermediate forms and proceeds unevenly by sector and by region. But ultimately the relation between capital and labour becomes hegemonic and dominant within a social formation in the sense that the whole structure and direction of development dances mainly to their tune. And at this point we are justified in calling such a society a *capitalist* society. But the essential point has been made. Wage labour is not a universal category. The class relation between capital and labour, and the theory of value that is expresses, is an historical creation.

---

and landlords, on the basis of the distinctive role each plays in relation to the circulation of capital. He also considers, briefly, the implications of the separation between ownership and control and the 'wages of superintendence' paid to management. It seems that he thought the theory of class structure under the capitalist mode of production was to be one of the final products, to be pulled out at the end of the analysis, of his detailed investigations of how the law of value operated.

[14] Marx's version of 'primitive accumulation' in Britain has been gone over again and again by historians and cannot be considered separately from the whole argument over the transition from feudalism to capitalism. Dobb's (1963) study of the economic development of capitalism still has much to recommend it, and the general lines of debate within the Marxist camp are detailed in Hilton (1976). The debate that has swirled around Thompson's (1968) classic study, *The Making of the English Working Class*, also repays careful study.

1 *The class role of the capitalist and the imperative to accumulate*

The sphere of exchange, recall, is characterized by individuality, equality and freedom. It is 'not admissible to seek here for relations between whole social classes' because in the realm of exchange (which includes the buying and selling of labour power) 'sales and purchases are negotiated solely between particular individuals' (*Capital,* vol. 1, p. 586). So under what conditions can we seek for relations between whole social classes, and what are the implications of the fact that individuality appears to have precedence over class in the realm of exchange?

Marx demonstrates that, beneath the surface of exchange relations, 'entirely different processes go on in which this apparent individuality, equality and liberty disappear' because 'exchange value already in itself implies compulsion over the individual' (*Grundrisse,* p. 248). The compulsion arises from the need to provide a use value for others at a price that is regulated by the average conditions of production of a commodity. And the mechanism that lies behind this compulsion is competition.

It is important to understand the manner in which Marx appeals to the principle of competition.[15] He argues that competition can explain why things are sold at or close to their value, but it cannot reveal the nature of value itself; nor can it shed any light on the origin of profit. The equalization of the rate of profit is to be explained in terms of competition, but where profit comes from requires an entirely different framework for analysis. Marx does not find it necessary, therefore, to analyse competition in any detail in the first two volumes of *Capital,* with one very important exception.

The behaviour of the individual capitalist does not depend on 'the good or ill will of the individual' because 'free competition brings out the inherent laws of capitalist production, in the shape of external coercive laws having power over every individual capitalist' (*Capital,* vol. 1, p. 270). In so far as individuals adopt the role of capitalist, they are forced to internalize the profit-seeking motive as part of their subjective being. Avarice and greed, and the predilections of the miser, find scope for expression in such a context, but capitalism is not founded on such character traits – competition imposes them willy-nilly on the unfortunate participants.

There are other consequences for the capitalists. Consider, for example, what they can do with the surplus they appropriate. They have a choice of consuming or reinvesting. There arises a 'Faustian conflict between the passion for accumulation and the desire for enjoyment' (*Capital,* vol. 1, p. 594). In a world of technological innovation and change, the capitalist who

---

[15] The assumption of perfect competition plays a very different role in Marx's theory to that which it plays in conventional economics. Marx uses it to show how, even when capitalism is operating in a manner considered perfect by the bourgeois political economists, it still entails the exploitation of labour power as the source of profit.

= 741

reinvests can gain the competitive edge of the capitalist who enjoys the surplus as revenues. The passion for accumulation drives out the desire for enjoyment. The capitalist does not abstain from enjoyment by inclination:

> Only as personified capital is the capitalist respectable. As such, he shares with the miser the passion for wealth as wealth. But that which in the miser is a mere idiosyncrasy, is, in the capitalist, the effect of a social mechanism, of which he is but one of the wheels. Moreover, the development of capitalist production makes it constantly necessary to keep increasing the amount of the capital laid out in a given industrial undertaking, and competition makes the immanent laws of capitalist production to be felt by individual capitalists as external coercive laws. It compels him to keep constantly extending his capital in order to preserve it, but extend it he cannot except by means of progressive accumulation. (*Capital,* vol. 1, p. 592)

The rule that governs the behaviour of all capitalists is, then, 'accumulation for accumulation's sake, production for production's sake' (*Capital,* vol. 1, p. 595). And this rule, enforced by competition, operates independently of the individual will of the capitalist. It is the hallmark of individual behaviour, and thereby stamps itself as the distinguishing characteristic of all members in the class of capitalists. It also binds all capitalists together, for they all have a common need: to promote the conditions for progressive accumulation.

2 The implications for the labourer of accumulation by the capitalist

Competition among the capitalists pushes each of them towards use of a labour process that is at least as efficient as the social average. But those who accumulate more quickly tend to drive out of business those who accumulate at a slower rate. This implies a perpetual incentive for individual capitalists to increase the rate of accumulation through increasing exploitation in the labour process relative to the social average rate of exploitation. The implications of this for the labourer are legion.

The maximum limit of the working day, for example, is set by physical and social constraints, which are, however, 'of a very elastic nature and allow the greatest latitude' (*Capital,* vol. 1, p. 232). Through competition or inclination, capitalists may seek to gain *absolute* surplus value by extending the working day. Labourers, on the other hand, demand a 'normal' working day, and will obviously suffer if the capitalists' necessary passion for accumulation is allowed to pass unchecked. The battle is engaged:

> The capitalist maintains his rights as a purchaser when he tries to make the working day as long as possible. . . . On the other hand . . . the labourer maintains his right as seller when he wishes to reduce the working day to one of definite normal duration. There is here, therefore, an antinomy, right against right, both equally bearing the seal of the law of

exchanges. Between equal rights force decides. Hence is it that in the history of capitalist production, the determination of what is a working day, presents itself as the result of a struggle, a struggle between collective capital, i.e., the class of capitalists, and collective labour, i.e., the working class. (*Capital*, vol. 1, pp. 234–5)[16]

We have finally arrived at the point where it is not only admissible but *necessary* to seek the relationships between whole social classes. And we now can see more clearly why a world of equality, freedom and individuality in the arena of exchange conceals a world of class struggle, which affects both capital and labour alike, in the realm of production.

Individual labourers are free to sell their labour under whatever conditions of contract (for whatever length of working day) they please – in principle. But they also have to compete with each other in the labour market. All of which means that 'the isolated labourer, the labourer as a "free" vendor of labour power . . . succumbs without any power of resistance' before the capitalists' drive to accumulate. The only remedy is for labourers to 'put their heads together . . . as a class' to resist the depredations of capital (*Capital,* vol. 1, pp. 299–302). And the more the labourers offer collective forms of resistance, the more the capitalists are forced to constitute themselves as a class to ensure collectively that the conditions for progressive accumulation are preserved.

The study of class struggle over the length of the working day reveals a further point. In the absence of class organization on the part of labour, unbridled competition among the capitalists has the potential to destroy the work force, the very source of surplus value itself. From time to time, the capitalists must in their own interest constitute themselves as a class and put limits upon the extent of their own competition. Marx interprets the early English factory acts as an attempt 'made by a state that is ruled by capitalists and landlord' to 'curb the passion for a limitless draining of labour power' which had 'torn up by the roots the living force of the nation' (*Capital*, vol. 1, p. 239). There is, then, a distinction – often rather hazy – between regulation of this sort and regulation obtained through victories of the working class and its allies in the struggle to obtain a reasonable working day.

Capitalists can also accumulate by capturing *relative* surplus value. Marx identifies two forms. A fall in the value of labour power results when the productivity of labour in the sectors producing 'wage goods' – the commodities the labourer needs – rises. The absolute standard of living, measured in terms of the *quantities* of material goods and services that the labourer can command, remains unchanged: only the exchange ratios (the prices) and the

---

[16] The idea that, in a class-bound society such as capitalism, force is the only way to decide between two rights leads Marx to make strong criticisms of those, such as Proudhon, who sought to fashion a socially just society by appealing to certain bourgeois conceptions of justice. Tucker (1970) has an excellent chapter on this topic.

values change. The systematic cheapening of wage goods is, however, beyond the capacity of individual capitalists. A class strategy of some sort (subsidies on basic commodities, cheap food and housing policies, etc.) is required if this form of relative surplus value is to be translated into a systematic as opposed to sporadic and uncontrolled means for accelerating accumulation.

The second form of relative surplus value is within the grasp of individual capitalists. Individuals can leverage the gap between socially necessary labour time and their own private costs of production. Capitalists employing superior production techniques and with a higher than average productivity of labour can gain an excess profit by trading at a price set by the social average when their production costs per unit are well below the social average. This form of relative surplus value tends to be ephemeral, because competition forces other producers to catch up or go out of business. But by staying ahead of the field in productivity, individual capitalists can accelerate their own accumulation relative to the social average. This then explains why the capitalist 'whose sole concern is the production of surplus value, continually strives to depress the exchange value of commodities' by driving up the productivity of labour (*Capital,* vol. 1, p. 320).

Herein lies the mainspring for organizational and technological change under capitalism. We will return to this point later (see chapter 4 below). For the moment we are simply concerned to spell out the consequences for the labourer as individual capitalists seek relative surplus value through the extension of co-operation, division of labour and the employment of machinery.

Co-operation and division of labour within the labour process imply the concentration of work activity and labourers in one place and the setting up of means for co-ordination and control under the despotic authority of the capitalist. Competition forces progressive concentration of activity (until, presumably, all economies of scale are exhausted) and the progressive tightening of authority structures and control mechanisms within the work place. Hand in hand with this goes an hierarchical organization and forms of specialization which stratify the working class and create a social layer of administrators and overseers who rule – in the name of capital – over the day-to-day operations in the work place.

The employment of machinery and the advent of the factory system have even more profound results for the labourer. A reduction occurs in the individual skills required (a process now described, rather inelegantly, as 'de-skilling' or 'de-qualification') – the artisan becomes a factory operative. The separation of 'mental' from 'manual' labour is emphasized, while the former tends to be converted into a power 'of capital over labour'. Women and children can also be brought into the work force more easily, and the labour power of the whole family is made to substitute for the labour of the individual. The intensity of the labour process increases, and stricter and tighter work rhythms are imposed. And in all of this the capitalist has at hand a new and much more powerful device for regulating the activity and productivity of the labourer – the machine. The labourer has to conform to the dictates of the machine, and the machine is under the control of the capitalist or his representative.

The overall result is this. The competition for accumulation requires that the capitalists inflict a daily violence upon the working class in the work place. The intensity of that violence is not under individual capitalists' control, particularly if competition is unregulated. The restless search for relative surplus value raises the productivity of labour at the same time as it devalues and depreciates labour power, to say nothing of the loss of dignity, of sense of control over the work process, of the perpetual harassment by overseers and the necessity to conform to the dictates of the machine. As individuals, workers are scarcely in a position to resist, most particularly since a rising productivity has the habit of 'freeing' a certain number of them into the ranks of the unemployed. Workers can develop the power to resist only by class action of some kind – either spontaneous acts of violence (the machine-breakings, burnings and mob fury of earlier eras, which have by no means disappeared) or the creation of organizations (such as the unions) capable of waging a collective class struggle. The capitalists' compulsion to capture ever more relative surplus value does not pass unchallenged. The battle is joined once more, and the main lines of class struggle form around questions such as the application of machinery, the speed and intensity of the labour process, the employment of women and children, the conditions of labour and the rights of the worker in the work place. The fact that struggles over such issues are a part of daily life in capitalist society attests to the fact that the quest for relative surplus value is omnipresent and that the necessary violence that that quest implies is bound to provoke some kind of class response on the part of the workers.

3 Class, value and the contradiction of the capitalist law of accumulation

The explication of the class concept is, at this point, nowhere near complete. We have said nothing about the manner in which a 'class' constitutes itself socially, culturally and politically in a given historical situation; nor have we ventured to say anything whatsoever about the complex problems of class consciousness, ideology and the identifications of self which class actions inevitably presuppose. But the limited version of the class concept we have set out is sufficient to permit some reflections and conclusions.

Consider, first, the meaning we must now attach to 'socially necessary labour time' as the measure of value. The capitalist class must reproduce itself, and it can do so only through progressive accumulation. The working class must also reproduce itself in a condition appropriate for the production of surplus value. And, above all, the class relation between capital and labour must be reproduced. Since all of these features are socially necessary to the reproduction of the capitalist mode of production, they enter into the concept of value. Value thereby loses its simple technological and physical connotation and comes to be seen as a social relation. We have penetrated the fetishisms of commodity exchange and identified its social meaning. In this manner, the concept of class is embedded in the conception of value itself.

But we are now in a position to be much more explicit about the nature of the law of value. Consider how the matter stands historically. Wage labour is an historical product. So is the class relation between capital and labour. The capitalist law of value is an historical product specific to societies in which the capitalist mode of production dominates. The description of the passage from pre-capitalist to capitalist society is meant to reveal to us how such a transition might have taken place. First, the emergence of the money form and the growth of exchange steadily dissolve ties of personal dependency and replaces them with impersonal dependencies via the market system. The growth of the market system gives rise to a distinctively capitalist mode of circulation which rests on profit-seeking. This mode of circulation contains a contradiction, for on the one hand it presupposes freedom, equality and individuality while on the other hand profit itself presupposes an inequality. This fundamental contradiction gives rise to various unstable forms of capitalism in which profits are sought without commanding the production process. Bankers put money to work to command more money, merchants seek profit through exchange, land speculators trade in rents and properties, and so on. Unfair exchange, pillage, robbery and all manner of other coercive practices can sustain such systems for a while. But in the end it becomes necessary to master production itself in order to resolve the fundamental contradiction between the equality presupposed by exchange and the inequality required to gain profit. Feeble at first, various phases of industrialization, such as experiments with the plantation system, pave the way for the institutionalization of the industrial form of capitalism which rests upon wage labour and the production of surplus value. The advent of the capitalist mode of production resolves the contradictions of exchange. But it does so by displacing them. New contradictions of a quite different sort arise.

The class analysis of *Capital* is designed to reveal the structure of these new contradictions as they prevail at the heart of the capitalist mode of production. By extension, we come to see the value theory as embodying and internalizing powerful contradictions which form the mainspring of social change.

Recall, first of all, the manner in which the equality, individuality and freedom of exchange is transformed by competition into a world of compulsion and coercion so that each individual capitalist is forced willy-nilly into accumulation for accumulation's sake. The realm of equality, individuality and freedom is never entirely abrogated, however. Indeed, it cannot be, because exchange continues to play a fundamental role, and the laws of exchange remain intact. The production of surplus value resolves the contradiction within the capitalist mode of production in accordance with the laws of exchange. Only in production does the class character of social relations become clear. Within the capitalist class this produces a contradiction between the individuality presupposed by exchange and the class action necessary to organize production. This poses problems, because production and exchange are not separate from each other but organically linked within the totality of the capitalist mode of production.

We saw this contradiction in action in Marx's analysis of struggles over the length of the working day. Individual capitalists, we there discovered, each of them acting in his or her own self-interest and locked in competitive struggle with each other, can produce an aggregative result which goes against their class interest seen as a whole. By their individual action they can endanger the basis for accumulation. And since accumulation is the means whereby the capitalist class reproduces itself, they can endanger the basis for their own reproduction. They are then forced to constitute themselves as a class – usually through the agency of the state – and to put limits upon their own competition. But in so doing they are forced to intervene in the exchange process – in this instance in the labour market – and thereby to offend the rules of individuality and freedom in exchange.

The contradiction within the capitalist class between individual action and class requirements can never be resolved within the laws presupposed by the capitalist mode of production. And this contradiction lies at the root, as we shall later see, of many of the internal contradictions within the capitalist form of accumulation. It also serves to explain many of the social and political dilemmas that have beset the capitalist class throughout the history of capitalism. There is a continuous wavering line between the need to preserve freedom, equality and individuality and the need to take often repressive and coercive class action. The production of surplus value resolves the contradictions within the capitalist mode of circulation only by positing a new form of contradiction within the capitalist class – that between the individual capitalist and the interest of the capitalist class in reproducing the general preconditions for accumulation.

Consider, secondly, the relation between capital and labour that the production of surplus value presupposes. Like any other commodity, labour power exchanges in the market place according to the normal rules of exchange. But we have seen that neither the capitalist nor the labourer can truly afford to let the market for labour power operate unhampered, and that both sides are forced at certain moments to take class action. The working class must struggle to preserve and reproduce itself not only physically but also socially, morally and culturally. The capitalist class must necessarily inflict a violence upon the working class in order to sustain accumulation, at the same time as it must also check its own excesses and resist those demands on the part of the working class that threaten accumulation. The relation between capital and labour is both symbiotic and contradictory. The contradiction is the fount of class strugle. This also generates internal contradictions within the capitalist form of accumulation at the same time as it helps to explain much of the unfolding of capitalist history.

Only in the final chapters of the first volume of *Capital* do we finally appreciate the transformation that Marx has wrought on Ricardo's labour theory of value. We now see socially necessary labour time as the standard of value only in so far as a capitalist mode of circulation and a capitalist mode of production with its distinctive social relations have come into being. And this is the result of a specific historical process of transformation which created wage labour as a vital category in social life. *En route* to this fundamental conclusion, Marx has collected a mass of valuable insights into the structure of capitalism. We have seen the importance of certain juridical relations expressed through property rights and state enforcement of those rights. We have noted the importance of certain kinds of freedom, individuality and equality.

The value theory therefore internalizes and embodies the fundamental contradictions of the capitalist mode of production as these are expressed through class relations. Social necessity requires that both capital and labour be reproduced as well as the class relation between them. The capital–labour relation is itself a contradiction which forms the fount of class struggle, while the reproduction of both capital and labour incorporate a contradiction between individuality and collective class action. The concept of value cannot be understood independently of class struggle.

The concept of socially necessary labour time now stretches far beyond what Ricardo ever dreamed of when he enunciated his labour theory of value. We must be prepared to follow it wherever it takes us, for we have created a powerful vehicle indeed with which to analyse the inner logic of capitalism.

APPENDIX: THE THEORY OF VALUE

The proper interpretation of Marx's theory of value is a matter of great contention. Rival schools of thought have drifted so far apart in recent years that their common roots are by now almost indiscernible. The seriousness of the rift is illustrated by the growing clamour on the part of some to drop the concept of value altogether, since it is a 'major fetter' to an historical materialist investigation of capitalism (Steedman, 1977; Hodgson, 1980; Levine, 1978; Morishima, 1973; Elster, 1978). The demand may be justified when applied to that interpretation of value as a pure accounting concept, as a fixed and immutable measuring rod tied to labour inputs, which is then supposed to explain not only relative prices of commodities, but also distributive shares, exploitation and so on. Such a narrow conception is soon found wanting when matched against so grandiose ends. It is hard to account unambiguously for the relation between values and relative prices, and fixed capital and joint products pose seemingly insurmountable problems (see chapter 8). The critics of value theory have mounted a quite successful campaign against traditional interpretations, such as those put forward in Dobb (1940), Sweezy (1968) and Meek (1973).

The response of many has been to reassert what they say was the true meaning of the traditional position all along, that value is a unified expression of quantitative and qualitative aspects of capitalism and that neither makes sense without the other (Sweezy, 1979). Value is thereby invested with 'more than strictly economic significance' – it expresses 'not merely the material foundation of capitalist exploitation but also, and inseparably, its social form' (Clarke, 1980, p. 4). Although some, such as Desai (1979), evidently feel there is no problem in exploring quantitative and qualitative aspects jointly, the effect of more 'radical' interpretations of value has been to deny the rigours of quantitative mathematization employed by the 'model-builders' (mostly professional economists like Morishima, 1973; Roemer, 1980; etc.) and to push Marxian theory towards a more trenchant critique of political economy (which sometimes includes pouring scorn upon the model-builders) and a more vibrant exposition of historical materialism. The danger here is that 'value' will degenerate into a pure metaphysical conception. What will be gained in moral outrage will be lost in scientific cogency. Or else value theory, in encompassing 'the whole grand sweep of the materialist interpretation of history', will fall prey to Joan Robinson's (1977) objection that 'something that means everything means nothing'. Such accusations do not sit well with those who identify with Marx's claim to have built a truly scientific foundation for understanding the capitalist mode of production.

All of this has set the stage for a more careful reconstruction of what Marx himself said (in the tradition of scholars like Rubin, 1972; Rosdolsky, 1977; etc.). While the idea of value as an accounting tool or as an empirically observable magnitude plainly had to be abandoned, it could still be treated as a 'real phenomena with concrete effects' (Pilling, 1972; Fine and Harris, 1979, ch. 2). It could be construed as the 'essence' that lay behind the 'appearance', the 'social reality' behind the fetishism of everyday life. The validity of the concept could then be assessed in terms of the concrete effects that it helps us interpret and understand. The value concept is crucial since it helps us understand, in a way that no other theory of value can, the intricate dynamics of class relations (in both production and exchange), of technological change, of accumulation and all its associated features of periodic crises, unemployment, etc. But to accomplish this, traditional interpretations of value as whatever is achieved by labour in production have to give way to a more complex understanding of *social* labour as expressed and co-ordinated within a unity of production and exchange, mediated by distribution relations (Fine and Harris, 1979, ch. 2).

But even this conception, though obviously much closer to Marx's intent, does not quite capture the significance of the real revolution which Marx wrought in his method of approach. Elson (1979) has recently collected together a set of interesting essays (and added an extraordinarily penetrating piece of her own) that explore the revolutionary aspects to Marx's value theory in terms of the unity of rigorous science and politics. I have great sympathy with these arguments and view my own work as an exploratory essay along the lines that Elson and others have begun to define.

I base my own interpretation upon a reading of Marx's texts in which certain ideas stand out as dominant. Value is, in the first place, 'a definite social mode of existence of human activity' achieved under capitalist relations of production and exchange (*Theories of Surplus Value,* pt I, p. 46). Marx is not primarily concerned, therefore, with fashioning a theory of relative prices or even establishing fixed rules of distribution of the social product. He is more directly concerned with the question: how and why does labour under capitalism assume the form it does? (cf. Elson, 1979, p. 123). The *discipline* imposed by commodity exchange, money relations, the social division of labour, the class relations of production, the alienation of labour from the content and product of work and the imperative 'accumulation for accumulation's sake' helps us understand both the real achievements and the limitations of human labour under capitalism. This discipline contrasts with the activity of human labour as 'the living form-giving fire', as the 'transitoriness of things, their temporality', and as the free expression of human creativity. The paradox to be understood is how the freedom and transitoriness of living labour as a process is *objectified* in a *fixity* of both things and exchange ratios between things. Value theory deals with the concatenation of forces and constraints that discipline labour as if they are an externally imposed necessity. But it does so in the clear recognition that in the final analysis labour produces and reproduces the conditions of its own domination. The political project is to liberate labour as 'living form-giving fire' from the iron discipline of capitalism.

It follows that labour is not and never can be a fixed and invariable standard of value. Marx mocks those bourgeois economists who sought to establish it as such (*Theories of Surplus Value,* pt 1, p. 150; pt3, p. 134). Through analysis of the fetishism of commodities, Marx shows us why 'value cannot stalk around with a label describing what it is' and why bourgeois political economy cannot address the real question: 'why labour is represented by the value of its product and labour time by the magnitude of that value' (*Capital,* vol. 1, pp. 74–80). 'The proof and demonstration of the real value relation', Marx wrote to Kugelmann in a high state of dudgeon at the critics of *Capital,* lies in 'the analysis of the real relations' so that 'all that palaver about the necessity of proving the concept of value comes from complete ignorance both of the subject dealt with and of scientific method.' Value cannot be defined at the outset of the investigation but has to be discovered in the course of it. The goal is to find out exactly how value is put upon things, processes, and even human beings, under the social conditions prevailing within a dominantly capitalist mode of production. To proceed otherwise would mean 'to present the science *before* science'. The science consists, Marx concludes, 'in demonstrating *how* the law of value asserts itself' (*Selected Correspondence* (with Engels), pp. 208–9).

A full accounting of that 'how' calls for rigorous theorizing. Marx in part achieves the latter through ruthless application of dialectical modes of reasoning – the principles of which are very different from but just as tough and rigorous as any mathematical formalism. The task of historical materialism is also 'to appropriate the material in detail, to analyse its different forms of development, to trace out their inner connexion' with all of the integrity and uncompromising respect for the 'real relations' that characterize the materialist forms of science. 'Only after this work is done can the actual movement be adequately described' so that 'the life of the subject-matter is ideally reflected as in a mirror' (*Capital,* vol. 1, p. 19).

The method of exposition in *Capital* – the method I have tried to replicate in this book – is to unravel the contraints to the free application of human labour under capitalism step by step, to see contradictions of this or that form as containing the seeds of other contradictions that require further exploration. The reflection, like the subject matter it depicts, is perpetually in the course of transformation. The rigorous depiction of 'how' is not a charter for dogmatism, but an opening towards a truly revolutionary and creative science of human history. And that science is only a part of a much broader struggle to discipline discipline itself, 'to expropriate the expropriators' and so to achieve the conscious reconstruction of the value form through collective action.

CHAPTER 2

Production and Distribution

The relationships between value creation through production and the distribution of values in the forms of wages, profits, interest, rent, etc., have never been easy to pin down. Marx set out to resolve the contradictions and to correct the errors in classical political economy. In this he thought he had succeeded very well. Judging by the sound and fury of the controversy surrounding his interpretations, he either succeeded too well or deluded himself as to the success of his enterprise.

Although the nuances were considerable, Marx found himself faced with two basic lines of argument, both of which had their origins in Adam Smith's rather confusing presentation of value theory. On the one hand, Smith appears to hold that the value of commodities is set by labour and that this regulates wages, profit and rent. There is, then, more than a hint of a theory of surplus value in Smith because profit and rent can, under this interpretation, be regarded as deductions out of the value produced by labour. On the other hand, Smith also argued that in 'civilized society', wages, profit and rent were 'the three original sources of revenue as well as of all exchangeable value'. Value, in this case, appears to arise out of adding together the separate values of rent, wages and profit as these are embodied in a commodity.

Ricardo spotted the contradiction and firmly rejected the second interpretation in favour of a labour theory of value. But there then arose an awkward gap between the theory of value (set solely by labour time) and the theory of distribution (set by the relative scarcities of land, labour and capital). This was all very distressing, since Ricardo considered that the 'principal problem of political economy' was to determine the laws that regulate the distribution of the product among the three classes in society – the proprietors of land, the owners of stock and the labourers. He even confessed, 'in a moment of discouragement' (according to Sraffa), that he thought 'the great questions of rent, wages and profits' were quite separate from the doctrine of value and that they had to be explained 'by the proportion in which the whole produce is divided between landlords, capitalists and labourers.'[1] The implication that

[1] See Sraffa's introduction to Ricardo (1970 edn).

distribution was the result of a social process independent of that ruling production was rendered explicit by J. S. Mill, who drew a firm distinction between 'the laws of production of wealth which are real laws of nature . . . and the modes of its Distribution, which, subject to certain conditions, depend upon human will.' Mill's socialism consequently focused upon questions of distribution and treated the social relationships of production as separate and immutable.[2]

There are various echoes of this separation between production and distribution in present day neo-Ricardian representations. Sraffa demonstrates that the relative values and prices prevailing in a system of commodity production cannot be determined without fixing the wage rate. Since labour is not a reproducible commodity in the normal sense, the wage rate becomes a variable which has to be determined outside of the technical relations prevailing within the system of commodity production. And since the wage rate in Sraffa's system moves inversely to the profit rate, it is a short step to seeing class struggle as fundamental. Although the appeal to class struggle as the ultimate determinant of the relative shares of profit and wages sounds very Marxian, the conception that Sraffa advances is rather different from that set out by Marx, and a somewhat acrimonious debate has ensued of late between 'neo-Ricardians' and Marxists.[3]

The second line of argument to be considered takes up Smith's conception of rent, wages and profit as being simultaneously sources of value and sources of revenue. This ultimately led to the notion that the distributive shares of rent, wages and profit were mere reflections of the contribution of land, labour and capital to the production process. To Marx, the notion that capital was the source of value, that land was the source of rent or even that labour was the source of wages amounted to a most extraordinary fetishistic representation of the relations of capitalist production – 'it is their form of existence as it appears on the surface, divorced from the hidden connections and intermediate connecting links'. Rarely was Marx more scathing than when he was railing against the fetishisms of what he was wont to call 'vulgar political economy'. The notion that rents could somehow grow out of the soil was nothing but a 'fiction without fantasy, a religion of the vulgar', which presented reality in terms of 'an enchanted perverted, topsy-turvy world, in which Monsieur le Capital and Madame la Terre do their ghost-walking as social characters and at the same time directly as mere things' (*Theories of Surplus Value,* pt 3, pp. 453–540; *Capital,* vol. 3, ch. 48).

[2] Dobb (1973, p. 125). In general, Dobb provides an excellent overview.
[3] Sraffa (1960); Steedman (1977) is one of the chief exponents of the 'neo-Ricardian' position, and Rowthorn (1980) one of his chief opponents. Fine and Harris (1979) provide a good summary of the debate (while coming down against neo-Ricardianism), and Dobb (1975–6), shortly before his death, issued a somewhat impatient clarion call for better understanding on both sides.

The 'vulgarity' of this view derived not so much from the errors *per se* as from what Marx considered the deliberate cultivation of concepts for apologetic purpose (a motivation that he most certainly never attributed to Adam Smith). Separating land, labour and capital as independent and seemingly autonomous factors of production had a double advantage for the ruling classes since it permitted them to proclaim 'the physical necessity and eternal justification of their sources of revenue' at the same time as it suppressed any notion of exploitation since the act of production could in principle be portrayed as the harmonious assembly of separate and independent factors of production.

In this regard, the neoclassical framework is almost identical to the vulgar political economy about which Marx complained so bitterly. The essence of the neo-classical argument is that competition for productive factors – land, labour and capital – forces entrepreneurs to pay an amount equal to the value that the marginal (last employed) unit of each factor creates. Given a particular technological state and relative factor supplies (scarcities), then competition ensures that each factor 'gets what it creates', that 'exploitation of a factor cannot occur.' It is then a short step to infer that the distributive shares of rent, wages, interest, etc., are socially just fair shares. The political implication is that there is no point in, or call for, class struggle, and that government intervention should be confined largely to ensuring that perfect competition prevails. In the lexicons of many Marxist writers, this qualifies as 'vulgar political economy' with a vengeance.[4]

Marx lays out his general conception of the relationship between production and distribution in the 'Introduction' to the *Grundrisse* as well as in the third volume of *Capital* (ch. 51). He vigorously criticized those who hold to an economic conception 'that distribution dwells next to production as an autonomous sphere' and characterizes as 'absurd' those (like J. S. Mill) 'who develop production as an eternal truth, while they banish history to the realm of distribution.' He is equally critical of those who are content to treat everything 'twice over' as an agent of production and as a source of income. The general conclusion Marx reaches 'is not that production, distribution, exchange and consumption are identical, but that they all form members of a totality, differences within a unity' and that the 'reciprocal effects' between these different 'moments' have to be understood in the context of capitalist society considered as an 'organic whole'. This is all very abstract, and we must consider what he means more explicitly.

Marx emphasizes that the forms of distribution are reflections of the social relations of production. He suggests that 'the determinate way of sharing in

---

[4] Gerdes (1977), Benetti (1976) and Benetti, Berthomieu and Cartelier (1975) take strong anti-marginalist positions, while Meek (1977, ch. 9) takes a somewhat less antagonistic view.

production determines the forms of distribution', and that distribution relations are 'merely the expression of the specific historical production relations' (*Capital*, vol. 3, p. 882). From this standpoint, distribution appears as if it is determined by production considerations.

But Marx then plays upon alternative meanings of distribution. His purpose is to show how production and distribution relations interpenetrate and intertwine. He points out that both are the product of the same historical process which depended upon the separation of the labourer from the instruments of production as well as upon the expropriation of the direct producers from the land. Distribution, he goes on to argue, should not be thought of simply as the distribution of product or value among the social classes, but also as the distribution of the instruments of production, of land and the distribution of individuals (usually by birth) among the various class positions. These forms of distribution 'imbue the conditions of production themselves . . . with a specific social quality', and production cannot therefore be considered apart from the 'distribution included in it', for to do so would be to produce an 'empty abstraction' (*Grundrisse*, p. 96). It is in this sense that production and distribution are to be thought of as 'differentiations within a totality' which cannot be understood without considering the relationship that each bears to the other.

Once more, Marx breaks out of the straitjacket of conventional political economy in order to see production and distribution in the context of class relations. And the whole framework for thinking of distribution gets reformulated in the process. 'In the study of distribution relations,' he observes, 'the initial point of departure is the alleged fact that the annual product is apportioned among wages, profit and rent. But if so expressed it is a misstatement' (*Capital*, vol. 3, p. 878). If we build carefully upon the results already obtained through the investigation of use values, prices, values and class relations, we will see why this 'alleged fact' is indeed a 'misstatement' of the problem.

Recall, first, that Marx defines capital as a *process* (above, pp. 20–1). The expansion of value occurs through the production of surplus value by capitalists who employ a specific kind of labour – *wage* labour. This in turn presupposes the existence of a class relation between capital and labour. When we subject this relation to careful scrutiny we see immediately that the wage cannot be conceived of as a 'revenue' or as a 'distributive share' in the ordinary sense at all. The labourer does not claim a share of the product by virtue of his or her contribution to the value of the product. The essence of the transaction is something quite different. The labourer gives up rights to control over the process of production, to the product and to the value incorporated in the product in return for the value of labour power. And the latter has nothing directly to do with the contribution of labour to the value of the product.

The labourer receives, then, the value of labour power, and that is that. Everything else is appropriated as surplus value by the capitalist class as a whole. The manner in which this surplus value is then split into the different forms of profit on industrial capital, rent on land, interest on money capital, profit on merchants' capital and so on is set by quite different considerations. The class relation between capital and labour is of an entirely different sort compared with the social relations holding between different fractions of the capitalist class (industrialists, merchants, rentiers and money capitalists, landlords, etc.). When Marx insists that we focus on production in order to uncover the secrets of distribution, he does so because it is there that the fundamental relation between capital and labour becomes very clear.

Marx frequently congratulated himself on his ability to explain the origin of profit by way of a theory of surplus value that made no reference to the distributive categories of rent and interest. But it is one thing to show the *origin* of profit in surplus value – and by extension in the class relation between capital and labour – and quite another to determine the *magnitude* of that profit, and to come up with the rules that fix the division of the total social product into wages, profit on industrial capital, rent, interest and so on.

It should be said at the outset that Marx was less concerned with magnitudes than he was with understanding social relationships. But he did struggle gamely with certain quantitative aspects of distribution, as the innumerable numerical examples in *Capital* adequately attest to. Unfortunately, as his editor Engels remarked, 'firmly grounded as Marx was in algebra, he did not get the knack of handling figures. . .' (*Capital,* vol. 2, p. 284). His various mathematical errors have allowed many of his critics – particularly those positivists who take the view that nothing meaningful can be said of a social relationship unless it can be accurately quantified – to punch a variety of gaping holes in Marx's handling of the practical and quantitative aspects of distribution which, when taken together, can be used to discredit Marx's version of the *origin* of profit itself.

A long and involved controversy has consequently ensued surrounding Marx's theory of distribution. There is no question that this controversy broaches matters of considerable weight and moment. The difficulty, however, is to keep Marx's concern with social meaning and historical origins in the forefront of a controversy that, in its details, is inevitably dominated by quantitative and mathematical concerns. This task is rendered even more difficult by the sophistication of the mathematical technique required to evaluate the various mathematic 'proofs' set forth to show that Marxian value theory is, or is not, totally inconsistent in its treatment of production and distribution.

In this regard, the recent work of Morishima and Catephores (1978) is of interest. They point out that the labour theory of value has, until very recently, been exclusively formulated in terms of a system of simultaneous equations. Using such an approach, Morishima had previously shown that Marxian value theory performed unsatisfactorily when confronted with a variety of problems and had therefore concluded that it should be abandoned – a suggestion that was predictably received with bad grace by many Marxists. In their new work, Morishima and Catephores show that, if the theory of value is formulated in terms of linear inequalities, then most of the problems disappear. This leads them to withdraw their earlier proposal 'to remove the concept of value from Marxian economics'.[5]

The point of this is to show that, in spite of all of its rigour – a rigour Marx himself clearly admired and aspired to – the mathematization of Marxian theory is itself a contentious matter. We must, therefore, treat mathematical proofs for what they are: rigorous deductions on the basis of certain *assumptions* which may or may not capture the intricacy of social relationships with which Marx deals.

There are, however, two arenas of controversy which, according to Marx's critics, threaten the very foundations of Marxian theory in general. Interestingly enough, neither of them is concerned with the general process of distribution of the total social value among the various categories of wages, rent, interest and profit. The first of these deals with the reduction of heterogeneous to simple labour – the 'reduction problem', as it is usually referred to – and is concerned with the impact on the value theory of the manner in which the variable capital (or total wage bill) is split up among the various individuals within the working class. The second deals with the manner in which Marx transforms values into prices of production – the 'transformation problem', in short. This is concerned with the manner in which surplus value is distributed among capitalist producers. Both matters have been the focus of bitter debates which, far from being stilled in the course of time, have become ever more contentious.

In what follows, therefore, I shall try to deal with these substantive controversies in the course of elaborating upon Marx's arguments concerning the relations between production and distribution. In accordance with Marx's concerns, I shall try to concentrate upon social and historical meanings without denying the importance of rigorous mathematical argument wherever that is appropriate. It will, I think, become evident that the Marxian challenge to both past and present theories of production and distribution – all of which face chronic internal problems of their own – is a powerful one. Indeed, the elaborate attempts to discredit it seem to suggest that Marx was on to something of great import. Which is not to say, of course, that the Marxian theory is free of serious difficulty: in this regard, the barrage of criticism from bourgeois political economists, both past and present, has been helpful in defining what has to be done to make the Marxian theory of production and distribution a more coherent enterprise.

[5] See Morishima (1973) and Morishima and Catephores (1978, esp. p. 19).

1 THE SHARE OF VARIABLE CAPITAL IN THE TOTAL SOCIAL PRODUCT, THE VALUE OF LABOUR POWER AND WAGE RATE DETERMINATION

The value of the total social product in a given year can be expressed as $C + V + S$, where C is the value of constant capital (machines, raw materials, energy inputs, etc.), V is the value paid out for labour power, and S is the total surplus value produced. On an annual basis we can treat the constant capital as labour power expended to replace the value equivalent of the means of production used up. It does not, therefore, enter in as an important category in distribution theory. The latter is concerned, then, to explain the manner and proportion in which newly created value is divided between labourers (V) and capitalists (S). We must also consider how V is divided among individual labourers and S among individual capitalists or among the various factions of the bourgeoisie (as rent, interest, profit of enterprise, taxes, etc.).

In order fully to understand Marx's theory of distribution we have to explore the relationships between value, use value and exchange value as these define the value of labour power, the standard of living of labour and the wage rate. This exploration will help bring out Marx's critique of conventional political economy and capitalism alike. We begin with the relationship between the wage rate (an exchange value concept) and the value of labour power.

The total wage bill in an economy can be regarded as the product of the number of labourers employed (n) and the *average wage rate* (w). The total variable capital can likewise be represented as $v \cdot n$, where v is a magnitude called the *value of labour power*. We can see immediately that both the total wage bill and the share of V in total social product will vary, everything else remaining constant, according to the total numbers employed. While this is an important principle, we are at this juncture more interested in the relationship between the wage rate and the value of labour power. Why even distinguish between them?

Marx's primary purpose here is to expose the social meaning of the wage payment.[6] The wages system, he argues, masks the difference between abstract human labour as the substance of value and the value of labour power which, like any other commodity, is fixed by its costs of production. Those, like Smith and Ricardo, who failed to make that distinction typically fell into 'inextricable confusion and contradiction', while their more 'vulgar'

[6] Not much has been written on Marx's theories of wage determination. Both Mandel (1971) and Rosdolsky (1977) have useful accounts, but by far the most interesting recent contribution is that by Rowthorn (1980, ch. 7), which deals with the substantive issues at the same time as it lays out the historical evolution of Marx's thought in relation to the basis provided by Ricardo.

brethren could find here a 'secure basis' for concealing the true origin of profit in exploitation of the labourer. 'The wage form', Marx claims, 'extinguishes every trace of the division of the working day into necessary labour and surplus labour', because 'all labour appears as paid labour.' And this 'forms the basis of all the juridical notions of both labourer and capitalist, of all the mystifications of the capitalistic mode of production, of all its illusions as to liberty, of all the apologetic shifts of the vulgar economists' (*Capital,* vol. 1, pp. 539–40). Value is, we have argued, a concept that is meant to reflect the class relationship between capital and labour. The concept of the value of labour power primarily serves to keep the idea of exploitation in the forefront of the analysis.

But what, exactly, does Marx mean by the value of labour power? That value is set, he argues, by the value of the commodities necessary to maintain and reproduce labouring individuals in their 'normal state'. The particular commodity bundle required to do that will vary according to occupation (increased expenditure of energy requires more sustenance, for example) and according to 'climatic and other physical conditions'. It includes, also, the costs of raising children, and to the degree that special skills take time and effort to acquire and maintain, these too effect the cost of reproduction of labour power. But in 'contra-distinction to the case of other commodities', there enters into the determination of the value of labour power 'a historical and moral element' which depends upon 'the degree of civilization of a country, more particularly on the conditions under which, and consequently upon the habits and degree of comfort in which the class of free labourers has been formed' (*Capital,* vol. 1, p. 171; cf. *Wages, Price and Profit,* p. 72).

This statement requires some elaboration, particularly since the last sentence has been the subject of some contentious argument. Recall, first, that the labourers eke out their separate existences through a form of circulation of the type C–M–C. They trade the use value of the only commodity they possess in return for a money wage. They then convert this money into commodities sufficient to reproduce their own existence. The concept 'value of labour power' relates to the totality of that circulation process whereby the class of labourers gets reproduced.

We can, however, consider what is involved at each link in this general flow of social reproduction. The negotiation over the nominal money wage and conditions of contract (the length of the working day, the rate for the job, the speed and intensity of work, etc.) focuses on the first link. Marx's main point, of course, is that the haggling over the wage contract that takes place in the market does not have to violate the rule that all commodities should exchange at their value, because the use value of labour power to the capitalist is precisely its capacity to produce surplus value. Moreover, the infinite variety of forms the wage bargain can take (hourly wages, piece work, day rates, etc.) effectively conceals the class relation of exploitation in production by putting all emphasis upon the various modes of market exchange. Furthermore, the individual wage rate can conceal much about the social costs of reproduction. If, as frequently happens, the labour power of a whole family is substituted for that of the individual labourer, then the quantity of labour power supplied may increase dramatically, the individual wage rate may fall, while the costs of reproduction (measured as the bundle of commodities needed to guarantee the reproduction of the family) may still be fully met (*Capital,* vol. 1, p. 395).[7]

Clearly, the higgling and haggling over the wage contract in a supposedly 'free' market can produce an infinite variety of results with respects to individual wage rates, wage structures and conditions of contract. But Marx follows the classical political economists in observing that wages tend to hover around some kind of social average which they called the 'natural price'. The problem is then to explain how this natural price is arrived at. Classical political economy came up with a variety of answers to this question. Marx focuses on real, as opposed to nominal, wages. This directs our attention to the next step in the process, the conversion of wages into commodities.

As holders of money, labourers are free to buy as they please, and they have to be treated as consumers with autonomous tastes and preferences. We should not make light of this (*Grundrisse,* p. 283). Situations frequently arise in which labourers can and do exercise choice, and the manner in which they do so has important implications. And even if, as is usually the case, they are locked into buying only those commodities capitalists are prepared to sell, at prices capitalists dictate, the illusion of freedom of choice in the market plays a very important ideological role. It provides fertile soil for theories of consumer sovereignty as well as for that particular interpretation of poverty that puts the blame fairly and squarely upon the victim for failure to budget for survival properly. There are, in addition, abundant opportunities here for various secondary forms of exploitation (landlords, retail merchants, savings institutions), which may again divert attention from what Marx considered to be the central form of exploitation in production.

We must drive beyond these surface appearances, however, and try to discover the essential meaning of the value of labour power as a process of social reproduction of the labourer. Plainly, labourers need use values if they are to survive. To the degree that these use values are provided in commodity form, labourers need a wage sufficient to pay the market price. The value of labour power can at this point be interpreted in relation to the real wage – the intersection of that particular bundle of use values necessary for the labourer's

---

[7] This phenomenon has frequently been observed in the early stages of capitalist development in many countries, but it can also be identified in advanced capitalist countries – witness the strong movement of married women into the labour force in the United States since 1950.

survival and the exchange value of the commodities within that bundle.

Consider the matter first from the standpoint of use values. Not all use values are provided as commodities. Many are fashioned within the household. To the extent that labourers meet their own needs, they gain a certain autonomy from capital (see below, chapter 6). Let us assume, for the moment, that the labourers have to purchase all the basic use values they need as commodities. We then have to define that particular bundle of use values that meets the labourers' needs. This we cannot do without due consideration of the 'historical and moral elements' that enter into the standard of living of labour. Marx is not very helpful here. He simply abstracts from the whole question by asserting that 'in a given country, at a given period, the average quantity of means of subsistence necessary for the labourer is practically known' (*Capital*, vol. 1, p. 171). For purpose of analysis we can hold the standard of living of labour, defined in use value terms, constant. This device allows Marx to generate a very important theoretical insight. If the exchange value of that fixed bundle of use values falls (as it surely must do, given the increasing productivity of labour), then the value of labour power can fall without any detrimental effect upon the standard of living of labour. And this, of course, is a primary source of relative surplus value to the capitalist. S increases because V declines.

Armed with that finding, we can conjure up all kinds of possible combinations. The share of V in the total social product can fall (implying a rise in the overall rate of exploitation) at the same time as the standard of living of labour improves, or a declining rate of exploitation might be accompanied by a falling standard of living.

But Marx definitely did not mean to imply that the standard of living of labour remained constant. It evidently varied greatly according to historical, geographical and 'moral' circumstances, and he put great stress upon 'the important part which historical tradition and social habitude play in this respect' (*Wages, Price and Profit*, pp. 72–3). He also saw needs as relative rather than absolute:

> Rapid growth of productive capital calls forth just as rapid a growth of wealth, of luxury, of social needs and social pleasures. Therefore, although the pleasures of the labourer have increased, the social gratification which they afford has fallen in comparison with the increased pleasures of the capitalist.... Our wants and pleasures have their origin in society; we therefore measure them in relation to society; we do not measure them in relation to the objects which serve for their gratification. Since they are of a social nature, they are of a relative nature. (*Wage Labour and Capital*, p. 33)

Needs are, according to Marx, produced by a specific historical process.[8]

[8] Lebowitz (1977–8) summarizes Marx's views.

To the degree that the evolution of capitalism is predicated upon the production of 'a constantly expanding and constantly enriched system of needs' (*Grundrisse,* p. 409), so we must anticipate perpetual shifts in the datum formed by the 'normal' standard of living of labour. Like most of Marx's key concepts, that of the value of labour power yields up its secrets only at the end of the analysis, not at the beginning. But we are now in a position at least to appreciate the direction in which he was headed. The value of labour power can be understood only in relation to the concrete modalities of the reproduction of the working class under the specific historical conditions imposed by capitalism.

But this grandiose formulation comes close to qualifying as something that can mean everything and therefore nothing: until, that is, we bring it back down to earth by considering the historical processes whereby the standard of living, the value of labour power and the share of variable capital in the total social product are actually regulated. The classical political economists offered a variety of hypotheses on the subject, which Marx either rejects or re-shapes as part of his own distinctive theory of distribution. We will consider the four major hypotheses in turn.

1 *The subsistence wage*

Marx is sometimes depicted as a subsistence wage theorist.[9] Nothing could be further from the truth. He vigorously opposed LaSalle's doctrine of the supposed 'iron law' of wages and, as we have already seen, denied that wages were inexorably tied to the requirements of pure physiological reproduction of the labourer. Capital, as process, is much more flexible and adaptable than that.

The misconception may be based, in part, upon Marx's view that the *minimum* value of labour power is set by the commodities 'physically indispensable' to the renewal of the labourer's vital energies (*Capital,* vol. 1, p. 173). And he certainly saw tendencies at work within capitalism that would drive wages down to, and even below, this physiological minimum, so threatening even the physical reproduction of labour power. But there were also countervailing tendencies that would push the wage rate in the other

---

[9] Marx's condemnation of LaSalle's propositions may be found in the *Critique of the Gotha Programme.* Rosdolsky (1977, pp. 295–7) comments on Marxist version of subsistence wage theories, while Baumol (1976) criticizes those, like Maarek (1979), who find a trace of an 'iron law of wages' in Marx's work when there is none. Baumol, however, takes the very curious position that 'it is a matter of semantics whether we prefer to think of the value of wages departing from the value of labour power, which we *define* to be at a physiological subsistence, or we would rather interpret the value of labour power to be an extremely flexible quantity.' Far from being a 'matter of semantics', I think a flexible concept of value is fundamental to the whole Marxian argument.

direction. The misconception might also have its roots in Marx's habit, throughout much of the influential first volume of *Capital*, of assuming that labour usually trades at its value and that the standard of living is indeed constant in terms of the use values required for social reproduction. By means of such assumptions he can derive the theory of relative surplus value. In the process he often uses the language of 'subsistence', 'minimum costs of reproduction', 'basic needs', etc., without firmly relating such conceptions to the idea of the 'historical and moral elements' involved in the determination of the value of labour power.

There is, in all of this, danger of considerable confusion as to the true nature of Marx's argument. For, beyond the physiological minimum (which perpetually lurks in the background) there appear to be somewhat varying conceptions of what fixes the value of labour power and what constitutes 'subsistence'. As Rowthorn correctly complains,

> Marx defines the value of labour-power in three different ways, basing himself successively on: (1) the cost of production of labour-power under given historical conditions, (2) the traditional standard of life to which workers are accustomed, and (3) the standard of living which prevails in non-capitalist modes or forms of production. (Rowthorn, 1980, p. 210)

(The last is important because it fixes the 'minimum wage required to induce people to seek work or remain working in the capitalist sector.') These definitions are not conceptually equivalent. But Rowthorn goes on to make what seems to me to be the vital point. There is, he says, a 'common thread' running through all the various definitions: if the minimum (however defined) is not met, then there 'are very serious consequences: either the supply of good quality labour-power declines, as workers fail to maintain or reproduce themselves properly, or leave the capitalist sector altogether; or else there is conflict and disruption as workers fight for what they consider is their just reward' (Rowthorn, 1980, p. 210). The unifying thread turns out to be the threat posed to the further accumulation of capital. We will take up this idea in section I.4 below.

2 Supply and demand for labour power

The idea that the wage rate varies in response to supply and demand conditions is not at all hard to accept. But Marx firmly rejects the argument that supply and demand dictate the natural price of labour power, let alone its value or the standard of living of labour. Demand and supply are fundamental to the equilibration of the market, but in equilibrium they 'cease to explain anything' – even the natural price of labour power must be determined 'independently of the relation of demand and supply' (*Capital*, vol. 1, p. 538).

We must be careful to interpret Marx's point correctly. He never argued that the exchange process was irrelevant to the determination of values. Indeed, he is firmly of the opinion that values in general and the value of labour power in particular come into being only to the degree that market exchange flourishes. The forces that fix the value of labour power must, in the end, be expressed through this market process. What Marx is objecting to is the erroneous identification of demand and supply mechanisms as these are clearly visible in the market with the underlying forces that operate *through* the market. Marx here follows Ricardo by asking what determines supply and demand in labour markets in the first place. And when we pursue that question we find that the accumulation of capital has a certain power in relation to both. Let us see how this can be so.

Demographic variables play a very important role on the supply side. Ricardo cheerfully accepted Malthus's law of population as the means whereby the supply of labourers would adjust to accumulation via rising wage rates. Marx does not deny the existence of such a mechanism (*Capital*, vol. 1, pp. 581–643).[10] But, presumably out of repulsion for anything that even remotely smacked of Malthusianism, he makes very little of the idea (cf, below, chapter 6). He concentrates instead upon processes of primitive accumulation (forced proletarianization), mobilization of latent sectors of the industrial reserve army (women and children), migration (rural to urban or from pre-capitalist social formations such as Ireland) and the production of relative surplus populations by mechanisms unique to capitalism. Direct action on the part of capital or action taken on behalf of capital through the agency of the state (enclosures, etc.) become the main focus of his analysis of the forces regulating the supply of labour power. And although he does not do so, we can easily see that population and immigration policies implemented by the capitalist state would fit into this perspective of the overall management of the supply of labour power by capital.

On the demand side, capital is capable of adjusting its requirements – not without stress and difficulty, to be sure – through reorganization, restructuring and technological change. In addition, the mobility of money capital on the world stage provides capital with the capacity to adapt to differing demographic situations as well as to the various 'historical and moral' circumstances which, initially, at least, might affect the value of labour power differentially from region to region and from country to country. To the degree that the accumulation of capital entails the perpetual shifting of capital from one line of production to another, from one place to another, to say nothing of the perpetual drive to re-structure the social and technical organization of production, so the demand for labour power is expressive of the requirements of accumulation.

[10] Morishima and Catephores (1978, ch. 5) attempt to build in some explicit argument regarding population growth into Marx's theory.

Again, we come back to the idea that the overall requirements of the accumulation of capital have the capacity to assert a hegemonic controlling influence with respect to both the demand for and the supply of labour power. 'Capital works on both sides at the same time' (*Capital,* vol. 1, p. 640). This, I believe, is where Marx wants to position himself with respect to the underlying forces that fix the value of labour power. This is not to say, however, that all forces operating in the market have this quality to them. Scarcities can arise for reasons that are entirely outside of the influence of capital. But we find Marx asserting under such circumstances that wages may be 'above value', and that they may so remain for extended periods of time (*Capital,* vol. 1, p. 613). In phrasing things thus, Marx indicates, in effect, that he wishes to distinguish between those *contingent forces* that can push wage rates hither and thither and the *socially necessary* forces that attach to the accumulation of capital in general and which dictate the value of labour power. In this he is entirely consistent with his overall strategy: to see value as an expression of social necessity under the class relations of capitalism and to assert that values (including that of labour power) become the regulators of economic life only to the degree that the capitalist mode of production becomes hegemonic within a social formation.

3   *Class struggle over the wage rate*

The idea that the relative shares of V and S in the total social product (and by implication v, the value of labour power) is fixed by class struggle, by the power relation between capital and organized labour, sounds very Marxian. It has been put to use in recent times in the form of a 'profits-squeeze' hypothesis of capitalist crisis. The argument runs roughly as follows. A successful struggle on the part of labour (because labour is either scarce or better organized) raises real wages and diminishes profits. The 'profits-squeeze' that results slows accumulation and leads ultimately to stagnation, Capital's response is to create (either by conscious design or because there is no choice) a severe recession (such as that of 1973–4), which has the effect of disciplining labour, reducing real wages and re-establishing the conditions for the revivial of profits and, hence, of accumulation. A number of Marxists have vigorously attacked this schema, often dubbing it pure neo-Ricardianism.[11]

---

[11] Glyn and Sutcliffe (1972) and Boddy and Crotty (1975) provide the two simplest and direct statements on the 'profits-squeeze' as an empirical phenomenon, while Itoh (1978a) provides a more theoretical argument. The best of several critiques of the thesis are those of Yaffe (1973) and Weeks (1979), with the latter providing a very tough, and in my view quite correct, evaluation of the thesis as a theoretical proposition.

The issues raised here are of great importance. We have to consider in particular the degree to which the shifting power relation between capital and labour can substantially alter the relative shares of the two parties in the total product and the degree to which the daily struggles over nominal and real wages, as well as over the standard of living of labour (conceived of in use value terms), can substantially effect the value of labour power.

Marx readily concedes that the shifting magnitudes of wages and profit limit each other, and that the balance between them 'is only settled by the continuous struggle between capital and labour, the capitalist constantly tending to reduce wages to their physical minimum, and to extend the working day to its physical maximum, while the worker constantly presses in the opposite direction. The matter resolves itself into a question of the respective powers of the combatants' (*Wages, Price and Profit,* p. 74).

But Marx also argues that a rise in the real wage meant a fall in the profit rate only under the supposition of no changes in the productive powers of labour, no expansion in the amounts of capital and labour power employed and no expansion of production. Otherwise, depending upon the rate and conditions of accumulation, real wages and profit rates could rise or fall together or move inversely (*Theories of Surplus Value,* pt 2, p. 408). The real wage can rise, Marx argues, provided the rise 'does not interfere with the progress of accumulation' (*Capital,* vol. 1, p. 619). The question is, then, could the organized power of the working class keep the real wage from rising even when that would threaten accumulation?

Failing the transition to socialism, Marx denies such a possibility as a long-run proposition. His reason is not hard to adduce. Struggles over distribution, after all, take place in the market. The key relation for Marx lies in production – that is where surplus value has its origin. To interpret the share of labour in the total social product as the result of a pure power relation in the market place between capital and labour is an inadmissible abstraction. And so Marx reduces class struggle over distributional shares to the status of an equilibrating device, rather like supply and demand. Over the course of the industrial cycle, for example, the enhanced power of labour during the upswing should push wages above value if only to compensate for the fall of wages below value during the ensuing depression. Shifting power relations could generate wage fluctuations around the natural price that reflects the underlying value of labour power. And if, as the result of strong labour organization, wages remain above value for any extended period, then this is because it does not interfere with accumulation. Marx therefore explicitly warns the workers 'not to exaggerate to themselves the ultimate working of these every-day struggles' and 'not to be exclusively absorbed in these unavoidable guerilla fights incessantly springing up from the never-ceasing encroachments of capital or changes in the market'. Instead of the 'conservative motto, "*A fair day's wage for a fair day's work*!" they ought to inscribe on their banner the *revolutionary* watchword, "*Abolition of the Wages system!*" ' (*Wages, Price and Profit,* p. 78)

Class struggle plays an ambivalent role here. On the one hand it helps to preserve some sense of dignity and to repulse the crasser forms of violence that the capitalists are wont to visit upon those they employ. It also forms the basis for struggles over the definition of the bundle of use values that make up the standard living of labour (health care versus forced consumption of military protection, for example). By focusing on the realm of use values and human needs, such struggles can form the basis for a truly revolutionary movement, which has as its aim the abolition of a system founded on the ultimate irrationality of accumulation for accumulation's sake. But struggle within the confines of capitalism over the real wage merely serves, in Marx's view, to ensure that labour power trades at or close to its value. That value may be arrived at *through* a process of class struggle, but this is no way means that it simply reflects the relative powers of capital and labour in the market.

Interestingly enough, the 'profits-squeeze' hypothesis properly interpreted, supports rather than rebuts this conclusion. The changing balance of power between capital and labour can indeed alter the real wage in such a way as to restrict or augment the rate of profit. This kind of thing is exactly what we would expect to happen within the realm of exchange. It is, however, a description of a surface movement, and leaves the value of labour power itself untouched. If real wages move out of line with accumulation, then compensating forces are set in motion which pull them downwards and, if necessary, diminish the relative power of organized labour in the market place (either through the rise of unemployment or through political and other restrictions upon the power of organized labour).[12] As a description of these surface movements, the 'profits-squeeze' hypothesis is entirely plausible, even unobjectionable. But, as its critics maintain, it is an entirely inadequate conception of the overall laws of motion of capitalism, and certainly an inadmissible rendition of Marx's theory of crisis formation. Class struggle of this sort has little or nothing to do with the determination of the underlying value of labour power, although it does have a vital role to play, like demand and supply, in equilibrating the market.

[12] The point, of course, is that if the balance of power between capital and labour is such as to seriously threaten accumulation, then steps must be taken to rectify that power balance. The intent of the Wagner Act 1933 in the United States was, therefore, to improve the bargaining power of trade unions in the market in order to help resolve what was generally interpreted as a crisis of under-consumption. By way of contrast, we may note the present attempt in many advanced capitalist countries to curb union power at a time when wage demands (and the power to make those demands stick) are seen as the main cause of chronic inflation. Such shifts in the balance of power do not occur automatically, nor do they occur without often awesome struggles. But the balance does change over time, and there is every reason to believe that the shifts are themselves in part a response to problems of accumulation.

4 *The accumulation process and the value of labour power*

Marx rejects outright all formulations that immutably fix the value of labour power (such as the physiological subsistence wage) or the share of variable capital in total output (such as the so-called 'labour-fund' theory) on the grounds that 'capital is not a fixed magnitude, but is a part of social wealth, elastic and constantly fluctuating', and that labour power forms one of the 'elastic powers of capital' which must likewise be construed to be in perpetual flux (*Capital*, vol. 1, p. 609). He also argues that both class struggle over distributional shares and demand-supply play vital roles in equilibrating the market and can, on occasion, force real wages to depart from values, sometimes for extended periods. But, in the final analysis, they operate as market mediators only for the more fundamental forces which fix the value of labour power. So what are these 'more fundamental forces'?

Marx's general answer to that question is not hard to spot. An initial 'production-determining' distribution of means of production divides capital from labour, but thereafter distribution relations have to be regarded as 'merely the expression of the specific historical production relations'. Moreover, production and distribution 'form members of a totality, differences within a unity', which also includes exchange and consumption (see above, pp. 41–2). The value of labour power cannot be fixed in abstraction from the internal relations within this totality – a totality which, furthermore, is dominated by the imperative, accumulation for accumulation's sake. We remarked earlier (p. 2) that Marx builds his concepts relationally. We now encounter a specific instance of that strategy at work. As always, the problem is to make this highly abstract conception more accessible to concrete interpretation.

We are not yet in a position to unravel the whole argument. But the general conception is roughly this. There is an *equilibrium distribution* between variable capital and surplus value determined in relation to the rate of accumulation and the overall structure of production and consumption.[13] There is also an equilibrium growth path for total employment which, when divided into V, yields an equilibrium value of individual labour powers. If there is a general rise in the standard of living of labour (measured in use values commanded), and if these become a part of the 'historical and moral element' encompassed in the value of labour power, it is because the accumulation of capital requires the production of new needs, or because the laws of

[13] Those who would turn Marx into a general equilibrium theorist, replete with all the neoclassical tools, have a hard time of it at this point in the analysis. They invariably find that they cannot determine the equilibrium wage rate and that they are therefore forced to take either the standard of living or the equilibrium wage as a permanent structural and exogenously determined factor – see Maarek (1979), Roemer (1980) and Morishima and Catephores (1978, ch. 4).

accumulation are indifferent with respect to the specific forms of use value produced. The value of labour power has to be construed as a perpetually moving datum point regulated by the accumulation process. It can be defined, in short, as the *socially necessary remuneration of labour power*; socially necessary, that is, from the standpoint of the continued accumulation of capital. The invocation of social necessity is important. It permits us to distinguish between the equilibrium concept of the value of labour power and the innumerable accidental and contingent circumstances that can push wages above or below this equilibrium value.

This conclusion, it should be emphasized, applies solely to that very narrow conception of the standard of living that rests on the quantity of material use values the labourer can command through commodity exchange. It does not dictate which particular bundle of use values will be provided (health care or discos), nor does it deal with those aspects of life and culture within the working class that are outside the sphere of commodity exchange. In both of these respects, the working class can exercise a certain autonomy and, through its own struggles and its own choices, can make much of its own culture and much of its own history. That it is in a position to do so must be attributed precisely to the fact that it shapes its existence out of an exchange of *qualities* through a form of circulation defined by C–M–C.[14]

The significance of this exchange for capital is, of course, entirely different. The capitalist looks to gain surplus value from it. At first blush it appears that, the less for labour, the more for capital. But when we look at the accumulation process as a whole we see, first, that 'the maintenance and reproduction of the working class is, and must ever be, a necessary condition to the reproduction of capital' (*Capital,* vol. 1, p. 572). Capital must itself limit its own 'boundless thirst after riches' to the extent that it destroys the capacity to reproduce labour power of a given quality. But we also notice that capitalists pay out wages, which they receive back as payment for the commodities they produce. Distribution here functions as a mediating link between production and consumption, or, as Marx prefers it, between the creation of value in production and the realization of value in exchange. The capitalist must, after all, produce *social* use values – commodities that someone can afford and that someone wants or needs. Individual capitalists cannot reasonably expect to diminish the wages of their own employees while preserving an expanding market for the commodities they produce.

[14] This point has been taken up and elaborated into a strong critique of Marxist theories of class struggle by Burawoy (1978). He points out that, if workers are interested only in the use values they can command, then they may accede or even co-operate in their own exploitation in the work place providing that this redounds to their benefit in the form of material goods. The fact that capitalists are interested in values and workers in use values provides a basis for co-operation rather than confrontation in the work process. Burawoy has a point, but generally makes far too much of it.

All of this leads us beyond the narrow confines of distribution *per se*. But that is exactly where Marx wants to take us. He wants us to see that the value of labour power and the share of labour in newly created value cannot be understood outside of the general process of production and realization of surplus value. We will take up the study of this process in chapter 3.

II THE REDUCTION OF SKILLED TO SIMPLE LABOUR

The total variable capital is not split up equally among individual workers. The manner in which it is divided depends upon a wide variety of factors – degree of skill, extent of union power, customary structures of remuneration, age and seniority, individual productivity, relative scarcity in particular labour markets (sectoral or geographical) and so on. We are faced, in short, with *heterogeneous labour powers* that are *differentially rewarded*.

This poses a double problem for Marxian theory. First, the wage differentials themselves require explanation. Second, and this is the question we will mainly be concerned with here, the heterogeneity of labour power has been regarded by some bourgeois critics as the Achilles heel of Marx's theory of value. Let us see why.

Marx explained the exchange values of commodities by reference to the socially necessary labour time embodied in them (we will see how this conception must also be modified in the next section). To do this he had to construct a standard of value consisting of *simple abstract labour,* and that presumed that there was some satisfactory way to reduce the manifest heterogeneity of concrete human labour, with all of its diversity as to skill and the like, to units of simple abstract labour. Marx's own treatment of the problem is ambivalent and cryptic. He simply states that 'experience shows' that the reduction is 'constantly being made' by a 'social process that goes on behind the backs of the producers' (*Capital,* vol. 1, p. 44). In a footnote he makes clear that 'we are not speaking here of the wages or the value that the labourer gets for a given labour time, but of the value of the commodity in which the labour is materialized'. All of which is thoroughly consistent with the distinction between the value of labour power and social labour as the essence of value. The process whereby heterogeneous skills are reduced to simple labour must be independent of the processes of wage rate determination in the market place.

Marx does not bother to explain what he means by a 'social process that goes on behind the backs of the producers'. The appeal to 'experience' suggests that he thought it all self-evident. It may have been to him but it certainly has not been so to his critics. If, as Böhm-Bawerk (1949) insists, the only social process that can do the job is the exchange of the products of that labour power in the market, then 'we have the very compromising circumstance that the standard of reduction is determined by the actual exchange relations' when the exchange relations are supposed to be explicable in terms of the social labour they embody. There is, it seems, a 'fundamental and inescapable circularity' in Marx's value theory. Values, it is then said, cannot be determined independent of market prices, and the latter, not the former, are fundamental to understanding how capitalism works. Marx's more violent opponents, from Böhm-Bawerk to Samuelson (1957), have consequently derided Marxian value theory as an 'irrelevant abstraction', and argue that the modern price theory that they espouse is far superior to Marx's formulation. Even a relatively sympathetic critic, like Morishima (1973), concludes that the reduction involves either differential rates of exploitation (which seriously disturbs the theory of surplus value) or the conversion of different skills to a common measure through wage rates (which destroys the value theory altogether). In the face of such strong criticism, a solution to the reduction problem becomes imperative.

One line of response has been to reduce skilled to simple labour by assuming that labour power imparts value in proportion to its cost of production. This fails to establish the reduction independently of the exchange process, and cannot by itself avoid the circularity of which Böhm-Bawerk complains. Both Rowthorn (1980) and Roncaglia (1974), therefore, seek to identify a production process which accomplishes the reduction without reference to exchange. Rowthorn argues:

> Skilled labour is equivalent to so much unskilled labour performed in the current period *plus* so much labour embodied in the skills of the worker concerned. Some of the labour embodied in skills is itself skilled and can in turn be decomposed into unskilled labour *plus* labour embodied in skills produced in each earlier period. By extending this decomposition indefinitely backwards one can eliminate skilled labour entirely, replacing it by a stream of unskilled labours performed at different points in time. . . . The reduction . . . can be performed quite independently of the level of wages and the analysis avoids Böhm-Bawerk's charge of circularity. (Rowthorn, 1980, ch. 8)

This approach runs into a variety of difficulties. Simple labour becomes the unit of account, and it is presumed that the cost of production of that simple labour has no effect upon the system. Also, the skills that labourers acquire appear as a form of constant capital held by them. The reduction is accomplished, according to Tortajada (1977), at the expense of introducing a version of human capital theory. This obliterates class exploitation issues and buries real social processes in a mythology of self-advancement which most certainly runs counter to the general thrust of Marxian theory. These difficulties originate, Tortajada continues, 'in the very way in which the problem of reduction has been posed, as much by the critics of Marxist theory as by those who tried to reply'. In short, Marxists have sought to respond to the problem on a terrain defined by the bourgeois critics rather than in the terms that Marx defines. Abstract labour comes into being, recall, through a process that expresses the underlying unity of both production and exchange under a distinctively capitalist mode of production.

So let us go back to Marx's argument. Abstract labour, he says:

> develops more purely and adequately in proportion as labour loses all the characteristics of art; as its particular skill becomes something more and more . . . irrelevant, and as it becomes more and more a purely abstract activity, a purely mechanical activity, hence indifferent to its particular form. (*Grundrisse,* p. 297)

> Indifference towards any specific kind of labour presupposes a very developed totality of real kinds of labour, of which no single one is any longer predominant. As a rule, the most general abstractions arise only in the midst of the richest possible concrete development, where one thing appears as common to many, to all. Then it ceases to be thinkable in a particular form alone. . . . Indifference to specific labours corresponds to a form of society in which individuals can with ease transfer from one labour to another, and where the specific kind is a matter of chance for them, hence of indifference. . . . Such a state of affairs is most developed in the most modern form of existence of bourgeois society — in the United States. . . . This example of labour shows strikingly how even the most abstract categories . . . are nevertheless, in the specific character of this abstraction, themselves likewise a product of historic relations, and possess their full validity for and within these relations. (*Grundrisse,* pp. 104–5; cf. also *Results of the Immediate Process of Production,* p. 1033)

Abstract labour becomes the measure of value to the degree that labour power exists as a commodity capitalists can freely command in the market. The accumulation process requires a fluidity in the application of labour power to different tasks in the context of a rapidly proliferating division of labour. The capitalist can create such fluidity by organizing the division of labour within the firm and transforming the labour process so as to reduce technical and social barriers to the movement of labour from one kind of activity to another. Skills that are monopolizable are anathema to capital. To the degree that they become a barrier to accumulation they must be subdued or eliminated by transformation of the labour process. Monopolizable skills become irrelevant because capitalism makes them so (*Wages, Price and Profit,* p. 76).

The reduction from skilled to simple labour is more than a mental construct; it is a real and observable process, which operates with devastating effects upon the labourers. Marx therefore pays considerable attention to the destruction of artisan skills and their replacement by 'simple labour' — a process that, as Braverman documents in great detail, has gone on relentlessly throughout the history of capitalism (consider, for example, the transformation of the automobile industry from skilled craft production to mass assembly-line technology and the reduction from skilled to simple labour which this implied).[15]

This is not to say that capital has everywhere been successful in forcing such reductions, and Marx was the first to admit that the historical legacy of craft and artisan skills was often strongly resistant to the attacks mounted by capital. Nor is the history of this process of reduction free of contradictions. Routinization of tasks at one level often requires the creation of more sophisticated skills at another level. The job structure becomes more hierarchical, and those at the top of this hierarchy – the engineers, computer scientists, planners and designers, etc. – begin to accumulate certain monopolizable skills. This poses problems for class analysis and for understanding the labour process under capitalism – problems to which we will return in chapter 4.

We conclude, then, that the 'social process' to which Marx refers is none other than the rise of a distinctively capitalist mode of production under the hegemonic control of the capitalist in a society dominated by pure commodity exchange.[16] The reduction to simple abstract labour could not occur in any other kind of society – petty commodity producers, artisan, peasant, slave, etc. Values form as the regulators of social activity only to the degree that a certain kind of society, characterized by specific class relations of production and exchange, comes into being.

In the light of this conclusion it is instructive to go back to the kind of example to which Marx's critics appeal when they seek to discredit his argument. Böhm-Bawerk considers the example of exchange between a sculptor and a stone-breaker in order to show that labour as value is indistinguishable from the value of the different labour powers as determined through the exchange of their products. His example is not wrong. But it is the kind of particular and individualized form of labour that ceases, in Marx's view, even to be 'thinkable' in a well developed totality of exchanges. Furthermore, both labourers in Böhm-Bawerk's example are self-employed, while one – the sculptor – possesses special monopoly skills. The condition that Marx is interested in is one in which both labourers are employed by capitalists producing commodities – statues and roads – while neither has any monopolizable skill, even though the labour imparted may be of differing productivity. Böhm-Bawerk abstracts entirely from capitalist relations of production – hardly an adequate basis to fashion a valid critique of Marx. The circular reasoning Böhm-Bawerk thought he spotted is a product of

---

[15] Braverman (1974). There have been innumerable criticisms of Braverman's argument, which we will go into in chapter 4.

[16] Desai (1979, p. 20) writes: 'The labour value ratio is therefore simultaneously a formula and a historical process. This is why the category of abstract, undifferentiated labour is not an abstraction but a historical tendency.' See also Arthur's (1976) study on the concept of abstract labour.

tearing the reduction problem free from its roots in real historical processes, which re-shape the labour process and generalize commodity exchange. Put back into this broader context, the reduction problem disappears into insignificance. We are then left with two distinctive issues. First, we need to explain the wage differentials that do exist with the full understanding that these have nothing necessarily to do with the manner in which social labour becomes the essence value. Second, we have to consider the degree to which the reorganization of the labour process under capitalism has indeed eliminated monopolizable skills and thereby accomplished the reduction which is the basis for the theory of value. We will take up this second question in chapter 4, since it poses some serious theoretical challenges to the Marxian system.

III THE DISTRIBUTION OF SURPLUS VALUE AND THE TRANSFORMATION FROM VALUES INTO PRICES OF PRODUCTION

Marx felt that one of the 'best points' in his work was the 'treatment of surplus value independently of its particular forms as profit, interest, ground rent, etc.' (*Selected Correspondence* (with Engels), p. 192). The theory of surplus value explains the *origin* of profit in the exploitation of labour within the confines of the production process under the social relation of wage labour. The theory of distribution has to deal with the conversion of surplus value into profit. Marx attached great importance to such a step. 'Up to the present time,' he wrote, 'political economy . . . either forcibly abstracted itself from the distinctions between surplus value and profit, and their rates, so it could retain value determination as a basis, or else it abandoned this value determination and with it all vestiges of a scientific approach.' In the third volume of *Capital* (p. 168), Marx claims that 'the intrinsic connection' between surplus value and profit is 'here revealed for the first time'. This is a strong claim, which would bear some examination even if it had not been the focus of an immense and voluble controversy.

Marx's argument concerning the relation between surplus value and profit is broadly this. Surplus value originates in the production process by virtue of the class relation between capital and labour, but is distributed among individual capitalists according to the rules of competition.

In considering how surplus value is distributed among capitalist producers in different sectors, Marx shows that commodities can no longer exchange at their values – a condition that he assumed to hold in the first two volumes of *Capital*. They must exchange according to their 'prices of production'. We would do well at the outset to eliminate a potential source of confusion. These prices of production are still measured in values and are not to be confused with monetary prices realized in the market. Marx still holds to socially necessary labour time as a measuring rod. What he now shows is that commodities no longer exchange according to the socially necessary labour time embodied in them.

In order to follow Marx's argument, we must first lay out some basic definitions and notations. The time taken to produce a completed commodity is called the 'production period'. The time taken to realize the value embodied in the commodity through the exchange process is called the 'circulation time'. The 'turnover time' of capital is the time taken for the value of a given capital to be realized through production and exchange – it is, then, the sum of the production period and circulation time. The 'capital consumed' is the total value of raw materials and instruments of production used up in the course of one production period. Since fixed capital may be fully employed during the production period but not fully used up, the capital consumed during a production period will be equal to or less than the 'capital employed'. We may treat the 'constant capital', c, either as the capital consumed or the capital employed, depending upon what it is we are seeking to show. The 'variable capital', v, is the value of labour power consumed in a production period. The 'rate of surplus value' (or 'rate of exploitation') is given by the ratio of surplus value to variable capital, s/v. The 'value composition of capital' is defined as c/v. The 'rate of profit', p, is $s/(c + v)$ which, when reformulated, becomes:

$$p = \frac{s/v}{(c/v) + 1}.$$

Notice that all of these measures are expressed in *values*.

We now assume a competitive process which equalizes the rate of profit across all industries and sectors. What then becomes clear is that the exchange ratios are affected by differences in the value composition of capital. Consider the following example. An economy has two industries. The first employs 80 units of constant capital and 20 units of variable capital and creates 20 units of surplus value, while the measures for the second are $20c$, $80v$ and $80s$. The total capital advanced in both industries is exactly the same. We define these as the 'costs of production', $c + v$. The rate of exploitation, s/v, is the same in both industries. We also assume an identical production period. But we now notice that the rate of profit in the first industry (with high value composition) is 20 per cent while in the second industry (of low value composition) the rate of profit is 80 per cent. The rate of profit is not equalized.

Let us now suppose that the two industries are of equal weight and that the average rate of profit, p, is 50 per cent. The effect of equalizing the rate of profit is to change the exchange ratios of the two commodities. Each commodity now exchanges according to the ratios indicated by $c + v + p$, instead of $c + v + s$. The first of these measures is called the 'price of production'. It is, we emphasize once more, measured in values not money prices. Under competition we can expect commodities to exchange according to their prices of production rather than according to their values.

We can construct an identical argument with respect to capitals having different turnover times. Marx did not do so directly, but we should also acknowledge the importance of turnover time in forming exchange ratios. Since the capitalist is interested in profit over an average time period (an annual rate of return on capital, for example), capital that turns over many times in a year will earn a much higher rate of return compared with capital that turns over only once (assuming similar value compositions and identical rates of exploitation). Capital and labour will tend to be reallocated from sectors with lower turnover times to those with higher until the annual rates of return are equalized. Relative prices will be affected, and we have an additional reason why commodities will no longer exchange according to their values.

What Marx is doing here is implementing his general rule that production determines distribution but that the former cannot be considered independently of the distribution included in it. Marx's transformation procedure in fact plays upon a double sense of 'distribution'. It is the distribution of the capital among the different industries in accordance with the general rate of profit that leads to the formation of prices of production, which have the effect of distributing the surplus value differentially according to the value compositions and turnover times of the different capitals.

The general distributive effect can be quite simply stated. Each capitalist contributes to the total aggregate surplus value in society according to the labour power each employs, and draws upon the aggregate surplus value according to the total capital each advances. Somewhat facetiously, Marx called this 'capitalist communism' – 'from each capitalist according to his total workforce and to each capitalist according to his total investment' (*Selected Correspondence* (with Engels), p. 206). More specifically, this means that industries with low value composition ('labour-intensive' industries) or rapid turnover time produce greater surplus value than they get back in the way of profit, while the opposite is the case for industries with high value composition (so-called 'capital-intensive' sectors) or low turnover time. This is an important result. It provides the basis for some erroneous Marxist interpretations of imperialism – countries dominated by industries with low value composition will give up surplus value to countries dominated by high value composition.[17]

So why all the controversy? Marx's own strong claims, together with some provocative comments by Engels in his prefaces to the second and third

[17] Emmanuel (1972); the error arises because when proper solutions to the transformation problem are derived they do not necessarily show a transfer of value from sectors with low value composition to sectors with high composition.

volumes of *Capital,* served to focus attention upon what is indeed a key feature in Marxian theory: the relation between surplus value and profit. Unfortunately, the solution Marx proposes is either in error or incomplete. Bourgeois critics have pounced upon what they see as a fundamental error and used it to discredit the whole Marxian theory of production and distribution, insisting, all the while, that distribution must be restored to the rightful place from which Marx sought to dislodge it. Let us consider the nature of the supposed 'error'.[18]

Marx sets up a tableau for five industries of varying value composition in order to illustrate how prices of production will be formed when the profit rate is equalized through competition (*Capital,* vol. 3, ch. 9). He assumes, for purposes of exposition, that capitalists purchase commodities at their values and sell them according to their prices of production. He also assumes that the average profit rate is known and that this can be calculated in advance by giving an equal weighting to each of the five sectors and averaging surplus value production in relation to total capital advanced.

We can spot two problems immediately. If all commodities exchange according to their prices of production, then this applies as much to inputs as to outputs. Capitalists buy at prices of production and not, as Marx sets it out in his schemas, according to values. Marx is perfectly well aware of this, but considered that 'our present analysis does not necessitate a closer examination of this point' (*Capital,* vol. 3, pp. 164–5). Secondly, as capital is redistributed from sectors with low to high value composition, so the total output of surplus value changes and this alters the rate of profit. Clearly, the transformation procedure Marx devises is incomplete. It is, at best, an approximation. Marx did not emphasize that this was so, and Engels went on to confuse matters greatly by triumphantly proclaiming in his preface that Marx had established *the* solution to the problem, which would confound and silence his critics for ever more.

Böhm-Bawerk (1949) promptly pointed out the defects in Marx's procedure, treated them as fundamental errors, and derided the whole Marxian scheme of things to great effect. Far from silencing the critics, Marx's solution to the transformation problem provided them with abundant ammunition to use against him.

The transformation problem assumed its current guise with mathematical attempts to correct for Marx's error. von Bortkiewicz was the first to provide a mathematical solution in 1907. He used a simultaneous equation approach and showed that it was possible to solve the transformation problem under

---

[18] There is an immense literature on the transformation problem. Baumol (1974), Desai (1979), Laibman (1973–4), Gerstein (1976), Howard and King (1975), Morishima (1973), Samuelson (1971) and Shaikh (1978) all provide good accounts from a variety of perspectives. The early history of the debate is covered in an excellent work by Dostaler (1978a).

certain rigorously defined conditions. The problem then becomes one of identifying and justifying the conditions for the solution.

The formal mathematical problem arises because it is necessary, given the simultaneous equation approach, to hold something invariant between the value structure and the price of production structure if a solution is to be identified. Since Marx himself argued that the sum of the prices of production should equal the sum of the values, and that the total surplus value must equal the total aggregate profit, these two have most commonly been chosen as the invariants. The trouble is that these two conditions cannot hold simultaneously given this particular mathematical representation. Consequently, a whole host of different mathematical solutions have been proposed, each using a different invariance condition.[19]

This allows Samuelson (1971) to argue that, since there is no logical reason to choose one invariant over another, Marx's transformation from values into prices of production is not a mathematical transformation in any real sense at all, but simply a process of erasing one set of numbers and replacing them with another set. The price of production analysis in the third volume of *Capital* has no necessary logical relation to the value theory proposed in the first volume. The latter, then, can be viewed either as an essay in metaphysics or 'an irrelevant detour' *en route* to the more fundamental price theory of the third volume. Since price theory has been 'revolutionized' since Marx's time (principally through the marginalist 'revolution', which lies at the basis of contemporary neoclassical theory), Marx can, as far as his contribution to price theory is concerned, be relegated to the history books as a 'minor post-Ricardian'. Thus does Samuelson joust with the Marxian ghost.

One line of response to Samuelson has been to accept his mathematical contribution and then to argue that, although he may be 'a crackerjack mathematical economist', he is a 'terrible political economist'. Laibman (1973–4) thus chooses the rate of exploitation as the invariant on the grounds that class struggle and the social tension between capital and labour is the qualitative hallmark of the capitalist mode of production. True as the latter may be, this implies that the balance between wages and profits in a capitalist economy is set by class struggle and by nothing else – a proposition we denied earlier. This is far too high a price to pay to get past Samuelson's objections.

A second line of defence requires treating the transformation problem as an historical problem. Under this interpretation, commodities did indeed exchange at their values under conditions of simple commodity exchange among independent producers not subjected to the rule of capital. With the rise of capitalist relations of production, the value relations become obscured and ultimately buried under prices of production. This interpretation finds

[19] Sweezy (1968) gives an account of the Bortkiewicz solution and the various mathematical solutions are reviewed by Laibman (1973–4).

some justification in Marx's comment that 'the exchange of commodities at their values . . . requires a much lower stage than their exchange at their prices of production, which requires a definite level of capitalist development.' It is, therefore, 'quite appropriate to regard the values of commodities as not only theoretically but also historically *prius* to the prices of production' (*Capital*, vol. 3., p. 177). Engels opined that, 'had Marx had the opportunity to go over the third volume once more, he would doubtless have extended this passage considerably (*Capital,* vol. 3., p. 896). And so Engels set about elaborating on the idea for him, and in his '*Supplement*' to *Capital* (vol. 3) wrote out a lengthy historical version of the transformation problem. A number of more restrained versions of it have been since advanced by writers such as R. L. Meek (1977, ch. 7).

There are two problems to this historical approach, even though it sounds very Marxian to appeal to history to resolve a logical dilemma. We note, first of all, that this account runs entirely contrary to the argument we set out earlier, namely, that values cannot be fully established in the absence of capitalist relations of production. It contradicts the idea of an integral relation between the value theory and the capacity to produce surplus value. Furthermore, as Morishima and Catephores (1978) document in great detail, Marx's general approach indicates that what he was 'looking for in the labour theory of value was not the abstract description of a pre-capitalist period from which he could derive developed capitalism genetically, but rather the theoretical tools which would allow him to get to the bottom of capitalist economic relations.' The historical version of the transformation problem – even in its more moderate and sophisticated renditions – must, therefore, be rejected.[20]

Since we cannot appeal either to class struggle or to history to solve the problem, we have to revert to treating the transformation as a 'static, atemporal, analytical device' for dissecting the social relations of capitalism. We are obliged to find a reasonable mathematical technique for dealing with the problem. Rather late in the day, Shaikh (1978) has proposed to follow the technique that Marx used and designed iterative solutions which, at each round of the iteration, adjust input costs and the profit rate until equilibrium prices of production are identified. According to this view, Marx simply performed the first calculation in this sequence and didn't bother with the rest because it did not seem as important to arrive at the correct mathematical solution as to draw the important social conclusion. Morishima (1973), with his customary mathematical ingenuity, shows that, if the transformation procedure is treated as a markov process, many of the difficulties that arise when it is treated in terms of simultaneous equations disappear – the equality between the sum of the prices of production and the

[20] Morishima and Catephores (1978) provide detailed, and in my view quite correct, arguments for why they think Marx would have rejected such an historical approach.

sum of values can happily coexist with the equality of surplus value and total profit, as Marx insisted it should. What is truly surprising, in Morishima's view, is how close Marx came to solving the problem in spite of its inherent difficulty and his extremely limited mathematical technique.[21]

Several interesting insights into the transformation problem have, in fact, come from the non-Marxist camp. Both Baumol (1974) and Morishima (1973) have had much to say that is positive and germane to the problem. Baumol correctly argues, for example, that Marx's fundamental concern was to establish a theory of distribution and that the actual transformation from values into prices of production is a side issue.[22] Morishima likewise defends the view that Marx was striving for social insights rather than for mathematical exactitude, and that, from this standpoint, what Marx set out to do he did quite well.

So what is the social meaning for which Marx was searching? He lays out his conclusions forcefully, by comparing the effect of the transformation with that produced by the capitalist appropriation of relative surplus value:

> With the development of relative surplus value . . . the productive powers . . . of labour in the direct labour process seem transferred from labour to capital. Capital thus becomes a very mystic being, since all of labour's social productive forces appear to be due to capital, rather than labour as such, and seem to issue from the womb of capital itself. . . .
>
> All this obscures more and more the true nature of surplus value and thus the actual mechanism of capital. Still more is this achieved through the transformation of . . . values into prices of production. . . . A complicated social process intervenes here, the equalization process of capitals, which divorces the relative average prices [of production] of the commodities from their values, as well as the average profits in the various spheres of production . . . from the actual exploitation of labour by the particular capitals. Not only does it appear so but it is true in fact that the average prices [of production] of commodities differ from their value, thus from the labour realised in them, and the average profit of a particular capital differs from the surplus value which this capital has extracted from the labourers employed by it. . . . Normal average profits themselves seem immanent in capital and independent of exploitation. (*Capital*, vol. 3, pp. 827–9)

The fact that profit has its origin in the exploitation of labour power is no longer self-evident but becomes opaque to both capitalist and labourer alike. 'Disguised as profit, surplus value actually denies its origin, loses its character, and becomes unrecognizable.' This leads in turn to the 'utter incapacity of

[21] Morishima (1973), Shaikh (1978) and Desai (1979) are all helpful here.
[22] Baumol (1974) seems best to have captured what Marx was trying to do with the transformation, and repays careful reading. Dostaler (1978b) provides a similar account and tries to reconcile the issues within the framework of the sort of value theory we are here adopting.

the practical capitalist, blinded by competition as he is, and incapable of penetrating its phenomena, to recognize the inner essence and inner structure of this process behind its outer appearance' (*Capital,* vol. 3, pp. 167–8). And to the extent the theorists of capital reflected this confusion, they too failed to penetrate to the secrets that were concealed by the phenomena of competition. And it is these secrets Marx claims to have revealed fully and effectively for 'the first time'.

The fetishism that arises out of the transformation from values into prices of production plays a crucial role in Marx's argument. It performs an obvious ideological and apologetic function at the same time as it mystifies the origin of profit as surplus value. Such a mystification is dangerous for capital because the reproduction of the capitalist class depends entirely upon the continuous creation and re-creation of surplus value. But even if the capitalists could penetrate beneath the fetishism of their own conception, they would still be powerless to rectify a potentially serious state of affairs. Competition forces them willy-nilly to allocate social labour and to arrange their production processes so as to equalize the rate of profit. What Marx now shows us is that this has nothing necessarily to do with maximizing the aggregate output of surplus value in society. We find in this a material basis for that systematic misallocation of social labour, and that systematic bias in the organization of the labour process, that lead capitalism into periodic crises. Competition necessarily leads individual capitalists to behave in such a way that they threaten the very basis for their own social reproduction. They so behave because the logic of the market forces them to respond to prices of production rather than to the direct requirements for the production of surplus value. This is the crucial insight that arises out of a study of the transformation problem. It is a result we shall pursue to its bitter logical conclusion in subsequent chapters.

IV INTEREST, RENT AND PROFIT ON MERCHANTS' CAPITAL

Given the sound and fury of the debate over the reduction and transformation problems, it is somewhat surprising to find that the other components of Marx's theory of distribution have sparked so little controversy. This can be explained, in part, by the appallingly muddled state in which Marx left his theories of rent and interest and the failure of Marxists to come up with cogent and agreed-upon clarifications of the mess Marx left behind.

Since each of these aspects of distribution will be examined at length in later chapters, I shall at this stage limit myself to a few general comments on the direction in which Marx seemed headed and the reasons he provides for heading there.

The theory of surplus value, recall, stands on its own independently of any theory of distribution apart from that most fundamental of all distributional arrangements, which separates labour from capital. The surplus value is converted into profit through the social process of competition. Profit is in turn split into the components of profit on merchants' capital, interest on money capital, rent on land and profit of enterprise. The task of any theory of distribution is to explain the social necessity for, and the social processes that accomplish, this distribution of surplus value.

The sequential manner of presentation – moving from surplus value production to distribution – should not deceive us into thinking that distribution relations have no importance for understanding production. Since Marx argues that production cannot be considered apart from 'the distribution included in it', we have to consider the very real possibility that rent and interest play important roles as conditions of production.

Indeed, I shall later seek to show that fixed capital formation – and in particular the creation of the physical infrastructures in the built environment – cannot be understood independently of the social processes that regulate distribution. Distribution relationships therefore affect the conditions of production. Marx plainly does not deny this. But he does insist that, however significant these impacts might be, they could never explain the origin of surplus value itself.

Marx opened up a perspective on the underlying logic dictating distribution relations by examining the general process of circulation of capital. He depicts the process of expansion of value as passing through a sequence of metamorphoses – changes of state. The simplest way to look at it is as a process in which money is thrown into circulation to obtain more money. Money is laid out to purchase labour power and means of production, which are together shaped through production into commodities to be sold on the market:

$$M - C \begin{pmatrix} LP \\ MP \end{pmatrix} \dots P \dots C' - M' \text{ (etc.)}.$$

The money at the end of the process is greater than that at the beginning and the value of the commodity produced is greater than the value of the commodities used as inputs. The two phases $M–C$ and $C'–M'$ are transformations brought about through buying and selling, whereas P, the production process, involves a material transformation in the product and the embodiment of socially necessary labour.

The circulation process that begins with money and ends with money (plus profit) is the paradigm form of circulation of capital. But when we look at circulation as a never-ending process, we find that we can dissect it in a number of different ways. We could look at it as beginning and ending with the act of production or with capital in a commodity state. We can create three separate windows to look in on the overall characteristics of the circulation of capital (see figure 2.1.) From each window we see something different. Marx describes what we can see from each in the opening chapters of volume 2 of *Capital*.

We see that the conditions and concerns regulating the circulation of *money capital* are rather different from those that govern capital tied down as *productive capital* to a specific production process, and that both are different again from those regulating the circulation of *commodity capital*. In the end, of course, we are interested in the circulation of capital as a whole, but we cannot understand this, in Marx's view, without first examining the differentiations within it.

These differentiations, together with the problems that attach to transforming capital from one state to another, can give rise to specializations of function. Merchant capitalists, for example, take on specific responsibility

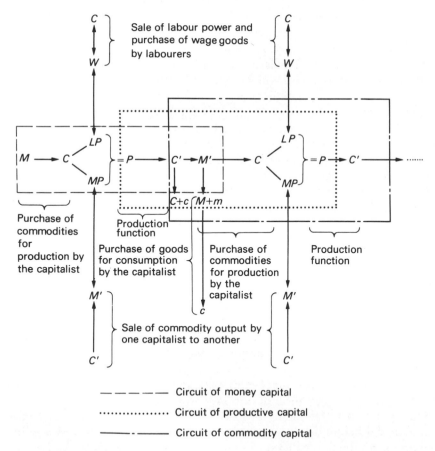

Figure 2.1   The circulation of capital (from Desai, 1979, p. 33)

for capital in commodity form and specialize in transforming commodities into money. The circulation of money likewise calls for the special skills of banker and financier who, once they assume command of the general use of money as capital, become *money capitalists* who receive interest. This leaves the productive capitalist in command only over the production of surplus value itself.

The disaggregation of the different circuits of capital permits us to establish certain necessary conditions regulating the relations between production of surplus value and its distribution. It does not, however, yield us the sufficient conditions that determine the distributional arrangements that must prevail under capitalism. We will consider these sufficient conditions in later chapters. For the moment we must remain content with a simple description of the distributional categories that Marx identifies.

1 *Merchants' capital*

When capital is held in commodity form it exists as *commodity capital*. But since capital remains capital only as value in motion, it follows that commodity capital must continuously be transformed into money capital if it is to retain its character as capital. The speed and efficiency of this transformation is of great importance to the capitalist. The circulation time (the time during which capital assumes the commodity form) affects the turnover time and thereby the rate of profit. The transformation incurs certain costs which are necessary deductions out of the surplus value produced – marketing a commodity realizes value but does not create it. Reducing circulation time and economizing on the necessary costs of circulation are important for capitalists engaged in production, because by both means the surplus value that remains within their hands increases. This provides an opportunity for merchants' capital. The merchant assumes all of the costs and responsibility for marketing in return for a slice of the surplus value produced. With the equalization of the rate of profit, the merchant should receive exactly the same rate of profit on the capital advanced as does the producer. The advantage of all of this to capitalist producers is, of course, a shortening of the turnover time, and economies in the costs of circulation (through economies of scale, specialization of function, etc.).

Put in value terms, this means that producers sell below value to the merchants, who then sell the commodity at its value. The difference is an appropriation of surplus value that covers the necessary expenses incurred and the profit on the capital the merchant advances. This puts merchants' capital into an odd relationship to the production of surplus value. On the one hand, the relationship is parasitic in the sense that the merchant creates no value but merely appropriates it. On the other hand, merchants' capital can expand the surplus value realized by the producer through accelerating the turnover of capital and reducing the necessary costs of circulation.

2 *Money capital and interest*

When capital takes on the money form and becomes *money capital,* it manifests itself as capital in its purest form – as exchange value divorced from any specific use value. The paradox, of course, is that it cannot retain its character as capital without being put into circulation in search of profit. The normal process of circulation under the capitalist mode of production entails the use of money capital to create surplus value through production of commodities. This implies that the *use value* of money capital is that it can command labour power and means of production, which can then be used to produce greater value than that money originally represented. The capacity to produce surplus value then appears to be a power of money capital itself. Money capital, as a consequence, becomes a commodity like any other. It possesses a use value and an exchange value. This exchange value is the rate of interest.

'Interest-bearing capital' Marx observes, 'is the consummate *automatic fetish* . . . money making money, and in this form it no longer bears any trace of its origin' (*Theories of Surplus Value*, pt 3, p. 455). '[To the] vulgar economist who desires to represent capital as an independent source of value, a source which creates value, this form is of course a godsend, a form in which the source of profit is no longer recognizable.'

The result is that interest on money capital becomes separate from what Marx calls 'profit of enterprise' – the return gained from engaging in the actual production of commodities. The separation arises because when individual capitalists hold money they have a choice between putting it into circulation as money capital earning interest, or putting it directly into circulation through the production of commodities. This choice is to some degree dependent upon the organization of production itself, because the purchase of large items – plant and machinery, for example – entails either hoarding or a system of capitalist saving and borrowing in order to smooth out what would otherwise be an extremely uneven investment process.

We will deal with the details of the credit system and interest on money capital in chapters 9 and 10. All we are concerned to show here is that the difference between capital in money or productive form ultimately leads to the separation between interest on money capital and profit of enterprise. This distinction amounts to a division of the surplus in two different forms, which may ultimately crystallize into a division between money capitalists and producer entrepreneurs. While both have a common interest in the expansion of surplus value, they do not necessarily see eye to eye when it comes to the division of the surplus value produced.

3 Rent on land

Since we will have much to say on the nature of rent in a later chapter, we need to consider it only in the most peremptory manner here. At first sight there appears to be no logical position for rent in the circulation of capital as we have portrayed it. The monopoly power that accrues to landowners through the private ownership of land is the basis of rent as a form of surplus value. The power this privilege confers would come to nought, however, were it not for the fact that land is an indispensable *condition* of production in general. In agriculture the land becomes even a *means* of production in the sense that it is cleared, improved and worked upon in a way that makes the land itself an integral part of the production process.

The circulation of capital encounters a barrier in the form of landed property. The landowner can exact a tribute – appropriate a portion of the surplus value – in return for the use of the land as a condition or means of production. The degree to which this barrier is manifest as the class power of landowners depends upon the historical circumstances. But all the time the power to appropriate a part of the surplus in the form of rent exists, it must of necessity reflect a pattern of social relationships that penetrate willy-nilly into the heart of the production process and condition its organization and form.

4 Distribution relations and class relations in historical perspective

With the exception of rent, which rests on the monopoly power of private property in land, the splitting of the surplus value into interest on money capital, profit on productive capital (profit of enterprise) and profit on merchants' capital is implicit in the three circuits of capital and the three fundamental forms capital can assume in the process of circulation. But we are not dealing here simply with the logical relationship between the circulation of capital and the distribution this entails.

Marx, for example, emphasizes that all of these forms of capital – merchants' capital, money capital and rent on land – had an historical existence which stretches back well before the advent of industrial capital in the modern sense. We therefore have to consider an historical process of transformation in which these separate and independently powerful forms of capital became integrated into a purely capitalist mode of production. These different forms of capital had to be rendered *subservient* to a circulation process dominated by the production of surplus value by wage labour. The form and manner of this historical process must therefore be a focus of attention.

These forms of appropriation of surplus value, all of which hide the origin of surplus value, have also to be considered in terms of the social relationships that they both presuppose and sustain. The result is that we have now to modify the notion of the class relations that prevail within the capitalist mode of production. Although there is a certain community of interest among both capitalist appropriators and capitalist producers of surplus value – a community of interest that underlies the overall conception of the bourgeoisie in capitalist society – there are also differentiations within the bourgeoisie which have either to be interpreted as 'fractions' or as autonomous classes. A 'class' of rentiers that lives entirely off interest on their money capital is not to be confused with the industrial capitalists who organize production of surplus value, the merchant capitalists who circulate commodities or the landlord class which lives off the rent of land. Whether or not we use the language of class or fractions or strata does not matter too much at this juncture. What is essential is to recognize the social relationships that must attach to the different forms of distribution, and to recognize both the unity and diversity that must prevail within the bourgeoisie as a result. For in the same manner that the distinction between wages and profits as a generic category cannot be considered except as a class relation between capitalists and labourers, so the distribution relations are social in nature, no matter how hard the vulgarizers might seek to conceal them in terms of the fetishistic notion that money and land magically *produce* interest and rent. Once more we have to recognize that, although these distribution relations enter into and condition production in important ways, it is the study of the production process itself that reveals the secrets of distribution. To pretend otherwise is to fall victim to the world of appearance, which is clouded with fetishisms, and to fail to penetrate 'the inner essence and inner structure . . . behind its outer appearance'.

CHAPTER 3

Production and Consumption, Demand and Supply and the Realization of Surplus Value

The notion that there must be some sort of balance or equilibrium between production and consumption, between demand and supply appears innocuous enough. The primary role of the market in a general system of commodity exchange appears to be to equilibrate demand and supply and thereby achieve the necessary relation between production and consumption. Yet the whole relation between demand and supply, between production and consumption, has been the focus of an immense and occasionally awesome battle in the history of political economy. The intensity of the debate is understandable, since the stakes are high. Not only do we here confront, head-on, the interpretation of business cycles and the short- or long-run stability of capitalism, but we enter into the heart of the controversy over the ultimate viability of the capitalist mode of production itself.

In Marx's time the central point of controversy was over the proposition that supply necessarily created its own demand. There was a variety of nuanced versions of Say's Law, as it is usually called.[1] The simplest states that the incomes paid to the suppliers of factors of production (land, labour and capital) in the form of wages, profits and rents must equal the total price of the goods produced with these factors. This means that 'the income generated during the production of a given output is equal to the value of that output', and that any increase in the 'supply of output means an increase in the income necessary to create a demand for that output' with the general consequence that 'supply creates its own demand'. A corollary of the law is that there can be no general overproduction or 'general glut' and that crises are the result either of 'exogenous shocks' (wars, revolutions, widespread harvest failures, etc.) or of temporary disproportionalities in production. There could be overproduction within an industry or geographical region, but this meant

[1] I have relied heavily here on an excellent study of Say's Law by Sowell (1972).

underproduction somewhere else. Transfers of capital and labour could equilibrate the system. What Say's Law precluded was a *general* glut.

Classical political economy was divided on the validity of Say's Law. Ricardo, James Mill, John Stuart Mill and most of the respected economists of the time accepted some version of it. The 'general glut theorists', like Malthus and Sismondi, could provide explanations for the periodic crises of capitalism but could not match the intellectual reputations of their opponents. The main cause of a general glut, in Malthus's view, was the want of effective demand for production. The intensity of the desire for consumption (and in this Malthus had a primitive version of the theory of consumer utility) formed the mainspring that drove accumulation. To Ricardo's view that human wants are limitless and that frugality and saving were the mainspring of accumulation, Malthus opposed the barriers owing to an insufficient desire for consumption and the problem that 'saving, pushed beyond a certain limit, will destroy profits.'

Marx characterized Say's Law as 'pitiful claptrap' and 'childish babble' and was deeply critical of Ricardo – whom he generally admired – for his 'miserable sophistry' in accepting a version of Say's Law. Ricardo, Marx pointed out, 'has recourse to Say's trite assumption, that the capitalist produces use value directly for consumption . . . [and] overlooks the fact that the commodity has to be converted into money (*Theories of Surplus Value*, pt 2, p. 468). The Ricardians clung to 'the concept of unity' between demand and supply and between production and consumption 'in the face of contradiction'. When it came to crises of general overproduction, therefore, they were reduced to insisting 'that if production were carried on according to the textbooks, crises would never occur' (*Theories of Surplus Value*, pt 2, p. 500).

Marx was equally vociferous in his condemnation of Malthus, whose analysis was 'childishly weak, trivial and meaningless' and whose main work on political economy was a 'comical exertion of impotence' (*Theories of Surplus Value,* pt 2, p. 53). The verbal thunderbolts Marx hurls at Malthus had more to do with the latter's apologia 'for the existing state of affairs in England, for landlordism, "State and Church", pensioners, tax-gatherers, stock-jobbers, beadles, parsons and menial servants' than with Malthus's position on the 'general glut' controversy. With respect to the latter, Marx credits Malthus with not seeking to conceal 'the contradictions of bourgeois production' even if he exposed them in order to 'prove that the poverty of the working class is necessary' and to demonstrate 'to the capitalists the necessity for a well-fed Church and State hierarchy in order to create an adequate demand for the commodities they produce' (p. 57). Marx had a good deal more sympathy with Sismondi who, he felt, had 'grasped rather crudely but none the less correctly' the 'fundamental contradiction' within a capitalist system 'compelled by its own immanent laws . . . to develop the productive forces as if production did not take place on a narrow restricted social

foundation.' Sismondi could consequently see that 'crises are not accidental
. . . but essential outbreaks – occurring on a large scale and at definite periods
– of the immanent contradictions', which form the 'deepest and most hidden
causes of crises' (pp. 56, 84). Unfortunately, Marx does not say much more
about Sismondi in *Theories of Surplus Value* on the ground that 'a critique of
his views belongs to a part of my work dealing with the real movement of
capital (competition and credit) which I can only tackle after I have finished
this book' (p. 53).

Since Marx did not complete his project, we can find no full and coherent
theory of crisis in his writings; nor do we know exactly what aspects of the
'general glut' theory he was prepared to accept. His critical comments on
Say's Law and his scattered remarks on the relations between production and
consumption have led some Marxists to interpret Marx as an 'under-con-
sumptionist' who saw the imbalance between supply and the effective
demand exercised by the mass of the proletariat as the main barrier to
accumulation and as the fount of periodic and recurrent crises. This is Paul
Sweezy's view, for example.[2] And did not Marx himself say that 'the ultimate
reason for all real crises always remains the poverty and restricted consumption of the masses as opposed to the drive of capitalist production to develop
the productive forces as though only the absolute consuming power of society
constituted their limit'? (*Capital,* vol. 3, p. 484).

Rosa Luxemburg (1951), on the other hand, has an entirely different
complaint. Marx's analysis of social reproduction in the second volume of
Capital appeared to show that capital accumulation could continue indefinitely and without limit. And that seemed to put Marx in accord with
Ricardo's version of Say's Law – that there is no amount of capital that
cannot be employed in a country since the only limit to aggregative demand is
that imposed by production itself.

Marx has been variously represented, by Marxists and non-Marxists alike,
as, among other things, as underconsumptionist, an equilibrium growth
theorist, and a theorist of the tendency towards long-run secular stagnation.[3]
His evident sympathy with Sismondi's view that the level of aggregate output
was not arbitrarily chosen, and that there is an equilibrium point for aggregate income distribution and output that would facilitate the reproduction
and expansion of both output and income over successive time periods, has
led some bourgeois economists to see Marx as the precursor of Keynes.
Keynes himself, while appealing to Malthus and ignoring Sismondi, certainly
placed Marx in that 'furtive underworld' of theorists who kept the question
of deficient effective demand alive. Keynes's attack upon Say's Law – which

[2] Sweezy (1968); for a critical history of underconsumption theories see the excellent study by Bleaney (1976).
[3] Osadchaya (1974) takes an interesting look at the different ways in which Marx's
arguments have been appropriated by the different schools of thought.

had been handed down from Ricardo and John Stuart Mill to the neoclassical economists – was no less vigorous than that which Marx had launched many years before. It also covered much of the same ground. And it is interesting to note that the Polish economist Kalecki, who independently derived many of the same results that Keynes laid out in his *General Theory of Employment, Interest and Money,* started off with firm roots in Marxian theory.

The relationships between Marxian and Keynesian theory are not easy to pin down, however. Apart from obvious differences in methodology, philosophy and political persuasion, Keynes himself was very much concerned with short-run phenomena and the stabilization policies government could pursue, whereas Marx was far more concerned with long-run dynamics and the inner logic of capitalism as the motor of historical change. But when Keynesian theory is projected into the long run, it begins to exhibit parallels to certain aspects of Marxian theory, while the Marxian theory of interest, fixed capital formation and business cycles – weakly articulated though these are – can be profitably compared to Keynesian theory. We are, besides, dealing with two theories that are evolving rapidly, and in which there is a good deal of mutual influence. It is just as easy to view Marx through Keynesian-coloured glasses as it is to see Keynesian theory as a 'special case' of the Marxian.[4]

Marx has also been treated as the precursor of modern growth theory. The lineage of descent here is interesting to follow. Feldman, a Soviet economist working in the 1920s, tried to elaborate upon the models of social reproduction contained in the second volume of *Capital* (the very ones that had so bothered Luxemburg). He came up with a 'model' of economic growth which anticipated in certain respects the conclusions reached many years later by Harrod and Domar. The Harrod-Domar growth model sought a middle path between the Ricardian emphasis upon production and the Keynesian emphasis on demand. Domar – who freely acknowledged his debt to Feldman – emphasized that his purpose was to solve the dilemmas left open by Marx and Keynes by tracing 'the effects of capital accumulation on current investment, profit rates, and the level of income and employment.' He also sought to show that 'there exists a rate of growth of income, however vaguely defined, which, if achieved, will not lead to diminishing profit rates, scarcity of investment opportunities, chronic unemployment and similar calamities . . . and as far as we can now judge, this rate of growth is not beyond our physical possibilities.' This possibility for balanced growth – a dynamic equilibrium – did not mean its automatic achievement in practice, and so Harrod and

[4] Keynes (1936) makes just a passing reference to Marx, but Kalecki (1971) and Robinson (1967; 1968) were much more directly influenced. On the relationship between Keynesian and Marxian thought see Dumenil (1977), Fine (1980), Mattick (1969) and Tsuru (1968).

Domar both used the notion of equilibrium – much as Marx did – as the basis for understanding the chronic instability of capitalism.[5]

I outline all of this to show that Marx's analysis of the relationship between production and consumption is susceptible of diverse interpretations and can therefore be seen as the precursor of many different, and often quite incompatible, contemporary bourgeois theories. Marx's formulations have generated equally diverse interpretations within the Marxian tradition with the works of Luxemburg, Bauer, Bukharin, Grossman and Sweezy charting what seem to be quite different courses, depending upon which aspect of Marx's own writings on production and consumption relations are accorded priority of place.[6]

So what, precisely, did Marx say on these matters? If there were a simple answer there would be no ground for controversy. As to why Marx did not make his position clear – this we can establish with reasonable certainty. The crises in the world market in which 'all contradictions of bourgeois production erupt collectively' would be fully understood only after a thorough study of competition, the credit system, the state, etc. Marx delayed consideration of Sismondi's views for example, because he wanted first to prepare the ground for theory – he did not wish to postulate a theory on an inadequate conceptual base. He therefore approaches the relations between production and consumption, between demand and supply, with the greatest circumspection. And when these questions are broached it is usually in a very specific context under quite restrictive assumptions. Marx left us with several partial analyses but no picture of the totality. This explains why his work has spawned such a wide variety of often conflicting theories. The synthesis that he was after was presumably to be presented in his work on the world market and crises – a work which was never to be prepared. We cannot, of course, determine with any accuracy what that work might have looked like. But we can go over some of the terrain that Marx prepared with his characteristic thoroughness and search for some clues as to where he was headed.

I   PRODUCTION AND CONSUMPTION, DEMAND AND SUPPLY AND THE CRITIQUE OF SAY'S LAW

Marx sets out, in highly abstract fashion, his thoughts on the relations between production and consumption in the celebrated 'Introduction' to the

[5] Osadchaya (1974) discusses this (the quote from Domar comes from there) but see also Blaug (1978), Erlich (1978), Kühne (1979) and Krelle (1971).

[6] The tremendous debate over whether or not capitalism was bound to collapse produced an incredible outpouring of literature at the beginning of this century. Sweezy summarizes much of the debate as does Kühne (1979); but see also Luxemburg (1951), Luxemburg and Bukharin (1972), Grossman (1977), Pannekoek (1977) and Rosdolsky (1977).

Grundrisse. He there argues that 'production, distribution, exchange and consumption . . . all form members of a totality, distinctions within a unity', and that the mutual interactions between these different moments are extremely complex in their structure. He is critical of what he calls 'the obvious, trite notion' that 'production creates the objects which correspond to the given needs; distribution divides them up according to social laws; exchange further parcels out the already divided shares in accord with individual needs; and finally, in consumption, the product steps outside this social movement and becomes a direct object and servant of individual need, and satisfies it in being consumed.' Such a conception is, for Marx, quite inadequate. So what does constitute an adequate representation?

In terms of the relation between production and consumption, Marx sees three fundamental forms that this can assume. First, consumption and production can constitute an *immediate identity,* because the act of production entails the consumption of raw materials, instruments of labour and labour power. Production and consumption are here one and the same act, and we can call this 'productive consumption'. Consumption likewise usually requires a simultaneous production process (this is particularly true of personal services) and this 'consumptive production' (such as the preparation of food at home) similarly rests upon an immediate identity between production and consumption. The distinction between productive consumption and consumptive production becomes important under capitalist relations of production because the former lies wholly within the sphere of the production of surplus value whereas the latter – in so far as it involves personal services to the bourgeoisie or productive activity within the workers' family (cooking, washing, etc.) – may remain outside of the sphere of direct production of surplus value.

Secondly, Marx sees production and consumption in a *mediating* relation to each other. Production creates the material for consumption, dictates also the manner or mode of consumption, at the same time as it provides the motive for consumption through the creation of new social wants and needs. On the other hand, consumption produces production in the two-fold sense that production is rendered entirely redundant without consumption, while consumption also provides the motive for production through the representation of idealized human desires as specific human wants and needs.

Thirdly, and most difficult of all to grasp, is the manner in which production and consumption relate so that 'each of them creates the other in completing itself, and creates itself as the other.' This is the Marxian sense of dialectics, of relational meanings, at work with a vengeance. Marx intends here to convey the sense of a process in which a process of production flows into – 'completes itself in' – a process of consumption, and vice versa. The unity of the two processes constitutes a social process of reproduction. 'The important thing to emphasise here is only that [production and consumption] appear as moments of one process in which production is the real point of departure and hence also the dominant moment.' But lest this be misunderstood as meaning that production determines consumption, Marx quickly adds that consumption 'as need' is itself an intrinsic moment of production when set within the context of a process of social reproduction – 'the individual produces an object and, by consuming it . . . is reproduced as a productive individual.' In a society characterized by division of labour and exchange and by the social relationship between labour and capital, the processes of reproduction must embrace the reproduction of labour power as well as the reproduction of the social relation between capital and labour. We will work out the implications of this shortly.

This 'dialectical' view of the relation between production and consumption constitutes, for Marx, the only adequate way of conceptualizing the problem. It emphasizes that *value* must be understood in terms of the underlying *unity of production and consumption,* though broken by the separation between them. From this standpoint we can unravel the secrets of supply and demand and lay the basis for a critique of Say's Law. Let us follow Marx down that path.

'Nothing can be more childish,' Marx thunders in *Capital* (vol. 1, p. 113), 'than the dogma that, because every sale is a purchase and every purchase a sale, therefore the circulation of commodities necessarily implies an equilibrium of sales and purchases. If this means that the number of actual sales is equal to the number of purchases, it is mere tautology. But its real purport is to prove that every seller brings his buyer to market with him. Nothing of the kind.' The first step Marx takes is to put the question of the relation between purchases and sales in the context of a generalized system of commodity exchange as opposed to simple barter situations. It was not admissible, in Marx's view, to establish 'the metaphysical equilibrium' of 'supply and demand' by reducing the process of circulation to direct barter (*Critique of Political Economy,* p. 97).

Commodity circulation entails continuous transformations from material use value to exchange value form. But each sequence, C–M–C, has to be seen as just one link in 'many such sequences' constituting an 'infinitely intricate network of such series of movements which constantly end and constantly begin afresh at an infinite number of different points'. Thus, each individual sale or purchase 'stands as an independent isolated transaction, whose complementary transaction . . . does not need to follow immediately but may be separated from it temporarily and spatially' (*Critique of Political Economy,* p. 93). This separation of sales and purchases in space and time creates the possibility – *and only the possibility* – for crises (*Capital,* vol. 1, p. 114; *Theories of Surplus Value,* pt 2, pp. 500–13). And it is money that makes this separation possible because a person who has just sold is under no immediate obligation to buy but can hold the money instead. Marx hints at a very simple conception of crisis in the course of fashioning a direct rebuttal to Say's Law:

> [Purchase and sale] fall apart and can become independent of each other. At a given moment, the supply of all commodities can be greater than the demand for all commodities, since the demand for the *general commodity,* money, . . . is greater than the demand for all particular commodities. . . . If the relation of demand and supply is taken in a wider and more concrete sense, then it comprises the relation of *production* and *consumption* as well. Here again, the unity of these two phases, which does exist and which forcibly asserts itself during the crisis, must be opposed to the *separation* and *antagonism* of these two phases. (*Theories of Surplus Value,* pt 2, pp. 504–5)

This announces an important theme in Marx's analysis. 'Crisis,' he argues, 'is nothing but the forcible assertion of the unity of phases of the production process which have become independent of each other', or, as he prefers to put in it *Capital* (vol. 3, p. 249): 'From time to time the conflict of antagonistic agencies finds vent in crises. The crises are always but momentary and forcible solutions of the existing contradictions. They are violent eruptions which for a time restore the disturbed equilibrium.'

Marx frequently makes use of the concept of equilibrium in his work. We ought to specify the interpretation to be put upon it; otherwise we are in danger of misinterpreting his analysis. In considering supply and demand, for example, Marx comments that 'whenever two forces operate equally in opposite directions, they balance one another, exert no outside influence, and any phenomena taking place in these circumstances must be explained by causes other than the effect of these two forces.' Therefore, 'if supply and demand balance one another they cease to explain anything', and it follows that 'the real inner laws of capitalist production cannot be explained by the interaction of supply and demand' (*Capital,* vol. 3, p. 190). The equilibrium between supply and demand is achieved only through a reaction against the constant upsetting of the equilibrium.

As proof of this last proposition Marx cites the perpetual adjustments being achieved through competition, which incontrovertibly shows 'that there is something to adjust and therefore that harmony is always only a result of the movement which neutralises the existing disharmony.' Also, 'the necessary balance and interdependence of the various spheres of production' cannot be achieved except 'through the constant neutralization of a constant disharmony' (*Theories of Surplus Value,* pt 2, p. 529).

All of this sounds and is fairly conventional. What differentiates Marx from bourgeois political economy (both before and since) is the emphasis he puts upon the *necessity* for departures from equilibrium and the crucial role of crises in restoring that equilibrium. The antagonisms embedded within the capitalist mode of production are such that the system is constantly being forced away from an equilibrium state. In the normal course of events, Marx insists, a balance can be achieved only by accident (*Capital,* vol. 2, p. 495). Marx thus reverses the Ricardian proposition that disequilibrium is accidental and seeks to identify the forces internal to capitalism that generate disequilibrium. But to do this Marx has to generate equilibrium concepts suited to such a task. And this is precisely why Marx found it necessary to drive beyond the surface appearance of demand and supply and even the superficial characterizations of production and consumption in order to articulate a value theory appropriate to his purpose. Only after the value theory has done its work can we return to the questions of supply and demand and production and consumption to explore them in detail. Meanwhile, the focus of attention shifts to that of the production and realization of surplus value as capital – for that, after all, is what the capitalist mode of production is really all about.

II THE PRODUCTION AND REALIZATION OF SURPLUS VALUE

The relation between production and consumption has so far been considered in terms of use values and prices. We will now examine it from the standpoint of values and embed an understanding of it in the context of surplus value production.

Recall, first, that capital is defined as a process – as value 'in motion' undergoing a continuous expansion through the production of surplus value. Consider, now, the structure of the circulation process as laid out in Figure 2.1 above. In its simplest form, and considered from the standpoint of the individual capitalist, capital circulates through three basic phases. In the first, the capitalist acts as *buyer* in commodity markets (including the market for labour power). In the second, the capitalist acts as an organizer of production, and in the third he appears upon the market as a *seller.* Value takes on a different material guise in each phase: it appears in the first as money, in the second as a labour process and in the third as a material commodity. The circulation of capital presupposes that continuous translations can occur from one phase to another without any loss of value. The translations are not automatic, and the different phases are separate in both time and space. As a consequence, 'there arise relations of circulation as well as of production which are so many mines to explode' the smooth functioning of bourgeois society:

> Capital describes its circuit normally only so long as its various phases
> pass uninterruptedly into one another. If capital stops short at its first
> phase M–C, money capital assumes the rigid form of a hoard; if it stops
> in the phase of production, the means of production lie without func-
> tioning on the one side, while labour power lies unemployed on the
> other; and if capital is stopped short in its last phase C'–M', piles of
> unsold commodities accumulate and clog the flow of circulation. (*Capi-
> tal*, vol. 2, p. 48)

Confusions arise, however, because Marx puts a double meaning on the word 'circulation'. As the 'circulation of capital' we think of capital moving through all of its phases, one of which is the sphere of *circulation* – the time when a finished commodity is on the market in the course of being exchanged. The circulation of capital can be conceived of in the following manner: surplus value originates in production and is realized through circulation. Although the fundamental moment in the process may be production, capital 'which does not pass the test of circulation' is no longer capital.

Marx defines the 'realization of capital' in terms of the successful movement of capital through each of its phases.[7] Money capital has to be realized through production; productive capital must be realized in commodity form; and commodities must be realized as money. This realization is not automatically achieved because the phases of circulation of capital are separated in time and space.

Capital that is not realized is variously termed 'devalued', 'devalorized', 'depreciated' or even 'destroyed'. Marx – or his translators – seem to use these terms interchangeably and inconsistently. I shall restrict my own uses of them in the following way. The 'destruction of capital' refers to the physical loss of use values. I shall restrict the use of the idea of 'depreciation of capital', largely in accordance with modern usage, to deal with the changing monetary valuation of assets (from which it follows that appreciation is just as important as depreciation). And I shall reserve the term 'devaluation' for situations in which the socially necessary labour time embodied in material form is lost without, necessarily, any destruction of the material form itself.

These are all very important concepts and will play a key role in the analysis that follows. Marx himself adopts some confusing phrases – such as the 'depreciation of values' and 'moral depreciation', and even extends such phrases to talk about the 'depreciation of labour power' as well as the 'depreciation of the labourer' as a person. The play on words is interesting because it focuses attention on the relationships. But it can also be confusing if the sense that what is being depicted is not clearly kept in view.

By restricting my own use of these terms so that destruction relates to use

---

[7] Some translators and theorists prefer the term 'valorization process' to cover the creation of surplus value through the labour process (see Ernest Mandel's introduction to the Penguin edition of *Capital*). While this has the virtue of making a clear distinction between processes of realization in production and processes of realization in the market (and emphasizes the crucial differences between them), it has the disadvantage of diverting attention from the necessary continuity in the flow of capital through the different spheres of production and exchange. Since I am interpreting value in terms of the unity of production and exchange, I prefer to use the term 'realization' to refer to the perpetual motion and self-expansion of capital and leave either the context or a suitable modifier to indicate whether I am talking about realization through the labour process (valorization), realization through exchange or the unity of both.

values, depreciation to exchange values and devaluation to values, I shall hope to clarify some of Marx's meanings. But this clarification will be purchased at great expense if we fail to recognize that use values, exchange values and values are expressive of an underlying unity which requires that the destruction, depreciation and devaluation of capital be seen as part and parcel of each other.

All crises are crises of realization and result in the devaluation of capital. An examination of the circulation of capital and its possible disaggregations suggests that this devaluation can take different tangible forms: (1) idle money capital; (2) unutilized productive capacity; (3) unemployed or under-employed labour power; and (4) a surplus of commodities (excessive inventories).

In the *Grundrisse* (pp. 402 *et seq.*) Marx makes much of this general idea. Again, to avoid misunderstanding, we must take steps to clarify his argument. A common mistake, for example, is to regard a 'realization' crisis as that particular form of crisis that arises from failure to find a purchaser for commodities. Realization and sale of commodities would then be treated as the same thing. But Marx argues that barriers to realization exist both within and between each of the phases of circulation. Let us consider the different form these barriers to the circulation of capital assume.

1 The time structure and costs of realization

In the *Grundrisse,* Marx sets up an argument that at first sight seems some-what peculiar. He suggests that, when capital takes on a particular form – as a production process, as a product waiting to be sold, as a commodity circulat-ing in the hands of merchant capitalists, as money waiting to be transferred or used – then that capital is 'virtually devalued' (p. 621). Capital lying 'at rest' in any of these states is variously termed 'negated', 'fallow', 'dormant' or 'fixated'. For example, 'as long as capital remains frozen in the form of finished product, it cannot be active as capital, it is *negated* capital' (p. 546). This 'virtual devaluation' is overcome or 'suspended' as soon as capital resumes its movement (p. 447). The advantage of seeing devaluation as a necessary 'moment of the realization process' (p. 403) is that it enables us to see immediately the possibility for a general devaluation of capital – a crisis – and gets us away from the identities assumed under Say's Law. Any failure to maintain a certain velocity of circulation of capital through the various phases of production and realization will generate a crisis. The time structure of production and realization thus becomes a crucial consideration. Crises will result if inventories build up, if money lies idle for longer than is strictly necessary, if more stocks are held for a longer period during production, etc. For example, a 'crisis occurs not only because the commodity is unsaleable, but because it is not saleable within a *particular period of time*' (*Theories of Surplus Value*, pt 2, p. 514).

But something more is also involved. The time taken up in each phase is, in a sense, a loss for capital, if only because 'time passes by unseized' (*Grundrisse*, p. 546):

> As long as [capital] remains in the production process it is not capable of circulating; and it is virtually devalued. As long as it remains in circulation it is not capable of producing. . . . As long as it cannot be brought to market it is fixated as product. As long as it has to remain on the market, it is fixated as commodity. As long as it cannot be exchanged for conditions of production, it is fixated as money. (*Grundrisse*, p. 621)

There is, therefore, considerable pressure to accelerate the velocity of circulation of capital, because to do so is to increase both the sum of values produced and the rate of profit. The barriers to realization are minimized when 'the transition of capital from one phase to the next' occurs 'at the speed of thought' (*Grundrisse*, p. 631). The turnover time of capital is, in itself, a fundamental measure which also indicates certain barriers to accumulation. Since an accelerating rate of turnover of capital reduces the time during which opportunities pass by unseized, a reduction in turnover time releases resources for further accumulation.

Certain costs also attach to the circulation of capital. Commodities have to be moved from their point of production to their final destination for consumption. Marx treats these physical movements as part of the material production process (see chapter 12) and therefore as productive of value. But other aspects of circulation are treated as unproductive of value since they are to be regarded as transaction costs which are paid for as deductions out of surplus value, no matter whether these costs are born by the producer or by some specialized agent (a merchant, retailer, banker, etc.). Costs of accounting, storage, marketing, information gathering, advertising, etc., are all viewed as necessary costs of circulation. The same applies to costs that attach to the circulation of money – banking facilities, payment mechanisms and so on. Marx calls these the '*faux frais*' (necessary costs) of circulation because they are unavoidable costs which must be incurred if capital is to circulate in the form of money and commodities. And we must include here certain basic state functions in so far as these are necessary to preserve and enhance the mechanisms of circulation. The necessary costs cut into accumulation because they must be paid for out of surplus value produced. Economies in these costs (including those that derive from the exploitation of labour power) have the effect of releasing capital for accumulation and are therefore an important means for increasing accumulation.

The imputed losses imposed by the time taken up, as well as the real costs that attach to circulation, comprise a whole set of barriers to the realization of capital. It follows that the drive to accumulate must also be manifest as a drive to reduce these costs of circulation – of transport, of transaction costs, marketing costs and so on. The removal or reduction of these barriers is as much a part of the historical mission of the bourgeoisie as is accumulation for accumulation's sake. And in what follows we will have frequent occasion to resurrect this idea, both in a theoretical and in its historical context.

2 The structural problems of realization

At each moment or phase in the circulation of capital we encounter particular kinds of problem, and it is worth examining each of these in turn as we consider the transition from money into means of production and labour power, and the translation of these 'factors of production' into a work activity that produces a commodity which must then find a buyer in the market.

(a) If capitalists cannot find upon the market the right quantities and qualities of raw materials, instruments of production or labour power at a price appropriate to their individual production requirements, then their money is not realizable as capital. The money forms a hoard. This barrier appears somewhat less awesome because money is the general form of value and can be converted into all other commodities without any difficulty. The capitalist has a wide range of options. These options are narrowed if the capitalist employs large quantities of fixed capital which have a relatively long life. In order to realize the value of the fixed capital, the capitalist is forced to sustain a specific kind of labour process with particular input requirements for a number of years. When viewed in aggregate, however, we cannot be so sanguine that all capitalists will find their total needs met for raw material inputs and labour power. Furthermore, with a portion of the surplus being reinvested, those capitalists producing means of production for other industries must expand their production in anticipation of future requirements which may or may not materialize. An aggregative expansion in the demand for labour power also poses a whole host of problems. Some of the structural problems that arise in the aggregative case will be examined later. The point here is to recognize that difficulties and uncertainties arise even in this first phase in which money has to be converted into raw material inputs and labour power.

(b) Within the confines of the production process, capitalists must enjoy that relation to labour power and must possess that technology which permits the value of the commodities purchased to be preserved and surplus value added. Marx notes, somewhat ironically, that the realization of capital in production depends upon the 'devaluation' of the labourer.[8] The point is

---

[8] Magaline (1975) builds a very interesting argument on this basis.

well taken. Capitalists must shape the labour process to conform to the social average at the very least and impose a rhythm and intensity of labour upon the worker adequate to the extraction of surplus value. They must counter the incessant guerilla warfare that accompanies class struggle in the work place and impose, if they can, a despotic control over the work process. Failure so to do means that surplus value is not produced and that the money capital which sat in the capitalist's pocket at the outset has not been realized as capital. And competition puts a further obligation upon the capitalist: to keep pace with the general process of technological change. Reorganization of the work process leads to 'revolutions in value': the socially necessary labour time is reduced and the value of the unit output falls. The capitalist who fails to keep pace experiences a devaluation of capital – capital is lost because the individual concrete specific conditions of labour do not correspond to the conditions for embodying abstract labour. There are, evidently, many barriers to be overcome if money capital is to be realized in production.

(c) As sellers, capitalists find themselves possessed of material commodities which must find users willing to part with an exchange value equivalent to the value embodied in each commodity. The conversion of specific material use values into the general form of exchange value – money – appears more difficult in principle than does the conversion of money into commodities. For this reason Marx does put particular emphasis upon it. We encounter here the barrier of consumption. This barrier has a dual aspect. First of all, the commodity must fulfil a social need; be a social use value. There are clear limits for specific kinds of use values – by the time everyone in capitalist society is proud possessor of a bicycle, for example, the market for bicycles is strictly limited to replacement requirements. When faced with market saturation of this sort, capital is forced towards the stimulation of new social wants and needs by a variety of strategems. The continuous evolution of social wants and needs is therefore seen as an important aspect of capitalist history – an aspect that expresses a basic contradiction. In the *Economic and Philosophic Manuscripts of 1844* (p. 148) Marx argues that capitalism 'produces sophistication of needs and of their means on the one hand, and bestial barbarization, a complete, unrefined, abstract simplicity of need, on the other.' And there is much in the *Grundrisse* and in *Capital* to validate that contention.

But from the standpoint of capitalists seeking to convert their commodities into money, the problem is not simply one of fulfilling social wants and needs, but of finding customers with sufficient money to buy the commodities they want. The *effective* demand for product – need backed by ability to pay – is the only relevant measure (*Theories of Surplus Value*, pt 2, p. 506). If an effective demand for commodities does not exist, then the labour embodied in the commodity is useless labour and the capital invested in its production is lost, devalued.

It is, therefore, at this point in the circulation of capital that capitalists are most vulnerable. As holders of money or masters of the production process, capitalists exercise direct control. But when the commodity has to be exchanged, the fate of capitalists depends upon the actions of others – workers, other capitalists, unproductive consumers and the like – all of whom hold money and must spend it in certain ways if the value embodied in commodities is to be realized.

When we view the aggregative processes of circulation of capital, however, we are struck immediately by the semblance of an important problem. If the capitalist mode of production is characterized by perpetual expansion of value through the production of surplus value, then where does the aggregative effective demand come from to realize that expanding value through exchange?

III THE PROBLEM OF EFFECTIVE DEMAND AND THE CONTRADICTION BETWEEN THE RELATIONS OF DISTRIBUTION AND THE CONDITIONS OF REALIZATION OF SURPLUS VALUE

The 'social demand', i.e., the factor which regulates the principle of demand, is essentially subject to the mutual relationship of the different classes and their respective economic position, notably therefore to, firstly, the ratio of total surplus value to wages, and, secondly, to the relation of the various parts into which surplus value is split up (profit, interest, ground-rent, taxes, etc.). And this thus again shows that nothing can be explained by the relation of supply to demand before ascertaining the basis on which this relation rests'. (*Capital,* vol. 3, pp. 181–2)

An investigation of effective social demand will lead Marx to the following conclusion:

The conditions of direct exploitation, and those of realising it, are not identical. They diverge not only in place and time, but also logically. The first are only limited by the productive power of society, the latter by the proportional relation of the various branches of production and the consumer power of society. But this last named is ... determined ... by the consumer power based on antagonistic conditions of distribution. (*Capital,* vol. 3, p. 244)

There is, then, an underlying contradiction between the distributional arrangements characteristic of capitalism and the creation of an effective demand sufficient to realize the value of commodities through exchange. Let us follow Marx *en route* to this conclusion.

Consider, first, the demand exercised by the working class. This can never be an 'adequate demand' in relation to sustained capital accumulation, because the 'labourers can never buy more than a part of the value of the social product equal to . . . the value of the advanced variable capital' (*Capital,* vol. 2, p. 348). But this does not mean that the demand of workers for wage goods is unimportant or that it does not warrant some careful scrutiny.

Considered from the standpoint of the class relation between capital and labour, the individual consumption of the labourer becomes 'a mere factor in the process of production', since it serves to reproduce the labour power required for the production of surplus value (*Capital,* vol. 1, p. 573). At the same time the workers find themselves in a 'company store' relation to capitalist commodity production. 'Capital pays wages e.g., weekly; the worker takes his wages to the grocer etc.; the latter directly or indirectly deposits them with the banker; and the following week the manufacturer takes them from the banker again, in order to distribute them among the same workers again.' (*Grundrisse,* p. 677)

The reproduction of the working class and the consumer power that goes with it is caught within the circulation of capital. The capitalists must collectively produce enough wage goods and lay out sufficient variable capital in the form of wages to ensure that the working class possesses the effective demand required for its own reproduction. Yet individual capitalists are under continuous competitive pressure to cut back wages and reduce the value of labour power, while those producing wage goods look to the labourers as a source of effective demand. And so Marx notes:

> Contradiction in the capitalist mode of production: the labourers as buyers of commodities are important for the market. But as sellers of their own commodity – labour power – capitalist society tends to keep them down to the minimum price.
>
> Further contradiction: . . . production potentials can never be utilized to such an extent that more value may not only be produced but also realised; but the sale of commodities, the realisation of commodity capital and thus of surplus value, is limited, not by the consumer requirements of society in general, but by the consumer requirements of a society in which the vast majority are always poor and must always remain poor. (*Capital,* vol. 2, p. 316)

This contradiction cannot be overcome by wage increases or alterations in the value of labour power. Changes of this sort either result in the conversion of luxuries into necessities – which illustrates how 'social wants are very elastic and changing' – when 'equilibrium is restored, the social capital, and therefore also the money capital, is divided in a different proportion between the production of necessities of life and that of luxury articles' (*Capital,* vol. 2, p. 341; vol. 3, p. 188).

Although the variable capital that forms the effective demand of the labourers has its origin with capital, the capitalists producing wage goods are potentially vulnerable to the consumer habits of the working class. On occasion, therefore, 'the capitalist, as well as his press, is often dissatisfied with the way in which the [labourer] spends [his] money', and every effort is then made (under the guise of bourgeois philanthropy and culture) to 'raise the condition of the labourer by an improvement in his mental and moral powers and to make a rational consumer of him' (*Capital,* vol. 2, pp. 515–16). 'Rational' is defined, of course, in relation to the accumulation of capital and has nothing necessarily to do with fundamental human wants and needs. So even the labourers, particularly in advanced capitalist societies, are subjected to the blandishments of the ad-men while government also steps in – usually in the name of social welfare – to collectivize consumption in ways that give it the possibility to manage consumption (through fiscal policies and government expenditures) in a manner consistent with accumulation. All of this does not negate, however, that other side of capitalist 'rationality' which perpetually pushes for lower real wages. Which takes us back to the fundamental contradiction which precludes the demand of the labourers acting as a solution to the effective demand problem.

Capitalists generate an effective demand for product as buyers of raw materials, partially finished products and various means of production (which includes machinery, buildings and various physical infrastructures required for production). The total value of constant capital purchased furnishes the total demand for the output of industries producing these commodities. As with variable capital, this effective demand for constant capital originates with the capitalist. The expansion of production requires increasing outlays on constant capital and on expansion of effective demand. To the degree that technological change forces substitutions between variable and constant capital inputs (production becomes more constant – capital-intensive), so we will witness a progressive shift towards the production and consumption of means of production.

We should note, however, that the total aggregative demand at any one point in time is equal to $C + V$, whereas the value of the total output is $C + V + S$. Under conditions of equilibrium, this still leaves us with the problem of where the demand for S, the surplus value produced but not yet realized through exchange, comes from.

We can seek an answer to this first of all by considering the consumption of luxuries on the part of the bourgeoisie. What must happen, if demand and supply are to balance, is that the capitalist class must throw money into circulation for the purchase of commodities exactly equivalent to the surplus value produced:

> Paradoxical as it may appear at first sight, it is the capitalist class itself that throws the money into circulation which serves for the realisation of the surplus value incorporated in the commodities. But, *nota bene,* it does not throw it into circulation as advanced money, hence not as

capital. It spends it as a means of purchase for its individual consumption. (*Capital,* vol. 2, p. 334)

This indicates to us immediately that one of the necessary conditions for sustained accumulation is that 'the consumption of the entire capitalist class and its retainers keeps pace with that of the working class' and that the capitalists must spend a portion of their surplus value as revenues for the purchase of consumption goods (*Capital,* vol. 2, p. 332). For this to happen requires either 'a sufficient prodigality of the capitalist class' (p. 410) or a disaggregation of the capitalist class into capitalists who save and 'consuming classes' who 'not only constitute a gigantic outlet for the products thrown on the market, but who do not throw any commodities on to the market' (*Theories of Surplus Value,* pt 3, pp. 50–2). These 'consuming classes' represent 'consumption for consumptions' sake' and exist as a kind of mirror image to the 'accumulation for accumulations' sake' that prevails among the productive capitalists.

Malthus, of course, saw the necessity for conspicuous consumption on the part of the bourgeoisie and parlayed it into a necessary and sufficient condition for the accumulation of capital. Marx accepts that bourgeois consumption must keep pace with accumulation if crises are to be avoided, but pours scorn upon Malthus's notion that such a class of unproductive consumers – of purchasers – can function as the *deus ex machina* for accumulation – furnishing both the stimulus for gain and the means to realize surplus value through consumption. Individual capitalists generally have the capacity, of course, to survive quite well and live off their wealth while waiting for surplus value to return to them. From this standpoint it does indeed seem as if capitalists throw money into circulation to acquire consumer goods that will, at the end of the production period, be paid for out of the production of surplus value. But there are clear limits to this as a general social process. We have to consider where, exactly, these financial resources come from in the first place if not out of surplus value? Which brings us to the brink of a tautology of the following sort: the financial resources to realize surplus value come out of the production of surplus value itself. We will ultimately have to penetrate that tautology and find out what lies behind it.

We can already see, however, that the prevailing conditions of distribution in capitalist society erect barriers to realization through exchange which are much more restrictive than those that exist in the sphere of production itself. 'It is,' says Marx, 'in the nature of capitalist production to produce without regard to the limits of the market' (*Theories of Surplus Value,* pt 2, pp. 522–5). 'Since market and production are two independent factors,' he continues, 'the expansion of one does not correspond with the expansion of the other.' Overproduction, a glut of commodities, 'is specifically conditioned by the general law of production of capital: to produce to the limit set by the productive forces ... without any consideration for the actual limits of the market or needs backed by ability to pay; and this is carried out through continuous expansion of reproduction and accumulation ... while on the other hand the mass of the producers (the working class) remain tied to the average level of needs, and must remain tied to it according to the nature of capitalist production.' (*Theories of Surplus Value*, pt 2, p. 535)

A potential way out of this difficulty is to expand commercial relations with non- or pre-capitalist societies and sectors. This was to be Luxemburg's solution to the problem of effective demand, and it led her to establish a firm connection between the accumulation of capital and the geographical expansion of capitalism through colonial and imperialist policies. Marx, for the most part, excludes questions of foreign trade from consideration in *Capital* and assumes 'that capitalist production is everywhere established and has possessed itself of every branch of industry' (*Capital*, vol. 1, p. 581). But in the *Grundrisse* (pp. 407–9) he does not so restrict himself. He there argues that a 'precondition of production based on capital is ... the production of a constantly widening sphere of circulation', so that 'the tendency to create the world market is directly given in the concept of capital itself.' This leads Marx to a general proposition which applies as much to the geographical spread as to the deepening of the influence of capitalism over social life:

> Capital drives beyond national barriers and prejudices as much as beyond nature worship, as well as [beyond] all traditional, confined, complacent, encrusted satisfactions of present needs, and reproductions of old ways of life. It is destructive towards all of this, and constantly revolutionizes it, tearing down all the barriers which hem in the development of the forces of production, the expansion of needs, the all-sided development of production, and the exploitation and exchange of natural and mental forces.

The ability of capitalism to generate such revolutionary transformations in the way of life and to become a world system was not appreciated by the general glut theorists. From this standpoint, Marx concludes, 'those economists who, like Ricardo, conceived of production as directly identical with the self-realization of capital – and hence were heedless of the barriers of consumption ... grasped the positive essence of capital more correctly and deeply than those who, like Sismondi, emphasized the barriers of consumption (*Grundrisse*, p. 410). What Ricardo failed to appreciate was that the incessant and inexorable breaking down of old barriers and the revolutionary transformation of needs on a world scale 'only transfers the contradictions to a wider sphere and gives them greater latitude' (*Capital*, vol. 2, p. 468).

Although Marx accepts the idea that accumulation inevitably results in the penetration and absorption of non-capitalist sectors – including those in distant places – by capitalism, he specifically denies that this can resolve the effective demand problem. He plainly thought that if a solution was to be found it must lie within the capitalist mode of production itself.[9]

And so Marx turns to consider another possible solution to the problem. 'The surplus value at one point requires the creation of surplus value at another point . . . if only, initially, the production of more gold and silver, more money, so that, if surplus value cannot directly become capital again, it may exist in the form of money as the possibility of new capital.' (*Grundrisse*, p. 407) Perhaps the extra effective demand required to realize the surplus value can come simply from an expansion of the quantity of money, either directly through the production of a money commodity, such as gold, or indirectly through the credit system.

At first sight, such a solution appears to make some sense. An analysis of money shows that insufficiency in the quantity of money can seriously check the circulation of commodities. Under conditions of insufficiency of money we often observe an acceleration in accumulation when the money supply is increased. From this we might be tempted to draw the unwarranted inference that an expansion in the money supply always leads to accumulation, and that it does so by furnishing the effective demand for product that would otherwise be lacking. While Marx accepts that the organization of the credit system is a necessary condition for the survival of accumulation (see chapter 9 below), he warns us against entertaining 'any fantastic illusions on the productive power of the credit system' (*Capital*, vol. 2, p. 346). But it is still tempting to see the source of the extra effective demand in the credit system itself. Furthermore, from the standpoint of the money circuit of capital, $M-C-(M + \Delta M)$, it seems as if more money is required at the end of each turnover in order to accommodate ΔM, the profit.

For all of these reasons, it is tempting to accept a version of the monetarist illusion in which the effective demand problem is solved by an expansion in the money supply. While Marx notes that the gold producers do indeed create more money than they advance in production (since they produce surplus value which is thrown directly into circulation as money), he rejects outright that this can provide a solution to the effective demand problem. Since money is a cost of circulation rather than productive activity, reliance upon the money producers to furnish the extra effective demand would have the effect of switching capital away from the production of surplus value into the absorption of surplus value as circulation costs. The historical tendency has been, Marx points out, to seek to economize on costs of circulation by way of the credit system which illustrates the futility of turning to the producers of money commodities as a source of effective demand. Dispelling the 'fantastic illusions' that surround the credit system is a more complex matter which we

[9] Marx appears to be following Hegel's *Philosophy of Right* here. See chapter 12 below.

will examine in detail in chapters 9 and 10, but we will find, in the end, that similar arguments apply.

Marx delivers the *coup de grâce* to the monetarist illusion, however, by considering the role of money in relation to the commodity and productive circuits of capital. The quantity of money required at a given velocity of circulation (plus whatever is required as a reserve stock) is related to the total value of commodities being circulated. From this standpoint, 'it changes absolutely nothing ... whether this mass of commodities contains any surplus value or not.' The money stock may need replacement or augmentation in order to accommodate the proliferation of exchange, but this has nothing directly to do with the realization of surplus value through exchange (*Capital*, vol. 2, p. 473).

This investigation of the monetary aspects to the realization of surplus value appears to lead to a dead end. But a proper analysis of it provides us with certain clues as to what the only possible resolution to the effective demand problem can be. The monetarist illusion arose in part, for example, by a confusion of the total quantity of money with the total quantity of money functioning as capital. Money capital can be augmented by converting an increasing quantity of a constant stock of money into capital. And so Marx arrives at his own solution. *It is the further conversion of money into capital that furnishes the effective demand required to realize surplus value in exchange.* Let us explore this simple, if somewhat startling, solution to the problem.

Money must exist before it can be converted into capital. Furthermore, an insufficiency of money relative to the quantity of commodities in circulation will indeed act as a check to accumulation. But the creation of money in no way guarantees its conversion into capital. This conversion involves the creation of what Marx calls 'fictitious capital' – money that is thrown into circulation as capital without any material basis in commodities or productive activity. This fictitious capital, formed by processes we will consider in detail in chapter 9, is always in a precarious position precisely because it has no material basis. But this then provides it with its distinctive power: in searching for a material basis it can be exchanged against the surplus value embodied in commodities. The realization problem, as it exists in the sphere of exchange, is resolved.

But this solution to the effective demand problem means the creation of new money capital, which must now be realized in production. And so we come full circle. We are back in the sphere of production, which is, of course, where Marx insists we should be all along. The solution to the problems of realization in exchange is converted into the problem of realizing surplus value through the exploitation of labour power in production. We see, once more, the social necessity for perpetual accumulation, but we now derive that necessity out of a study of the processes of realization within the continuous flow of production and consumption.

It was in the first volume of *Capital,* in a chapter entitled, significantly enough, the 'Conversion of Surplus-Value into Capital', that Marx first established the social necessity of 'accumulation for accumulation's sake, production for production's sake', given the social relations prevailing under capitalism. It is in the parallel chapter in the second volume of *Capital,* entitled the 'Circulation of Surplus Value', that Marx tentatively derives the same principle from a study of the relations between production and consumption. We see that a balance between production and consumption can be achieved under the capitalist mode of production – given its 'antagonistic' relations of distribution – only through perpetual accumulation.

Perpetual accumulation depends, however, on the existence of labour power capable of producing surplus value. The necessary geographical expansion of capitalism is therefore to be interpreted as capital in search for surplus value. The penetration of capitalist relations into all sectors of the economy, the mobilization of various 'latent' sources of labour power (women and children, for example), have a similar basis. And so we come to see capitalism for what it truly is: a perpetually revolutionary mode of production, constantly labouring under the social necessity to transform itself from the inside, while it just as constantly presses up against the capacities of the social and physical world to sustain it. This is, of course, a contradictory process. To begin with, capitalism encounters external barriers because the 'original sources of all wealth' – the soil and the labourer – do not have limitless capacities (*Capital,* vol. 1, p. 507). But also it encounters 'barriers within its own nature' (*Grundrisse,* p. 410) – and these are the 'internal contradictions of capitalism' that Marx will seek to expose.

What Marx has now done for us is to put a very specific interpretation upon the idea that 'production, distribution, exchange and consumption . . . all form members of a totality, distinctions within a unity' (*Grundrisse,* p. 99). He has re-fashioned the idea of *value* as a concept that must capture the relations within this totality. He has demonstrated, with respect to the relationship between production and consumption, how each 'creates the other in completing itself, and creates itself as the other', and shows us precisely what must happen when 'distribution steps between production and consumption' (*Grundrisse,* p. 94).

But Marx has also shown us that the merry-go-round of perpetual accumulation is not an automated or even a well-oiled machine. He has shown us the necessary relationship that must prevail between production and distribution, surplus value production and realization, consumption and new capital formation, and between production and consumption. He has also identified a whole host of necessary conditions – particularly with respect to the creation of money and credit instruments – which must hold if equilibrium is to be achieved.

But he has also shown us that there is nothing to guarantee that this equilibrium point will be found in practice. The best we can hope is that the balance will be achieved 'by accident'. The worst, and this is what Marx is beginning to show us, is that there are strong forces driving the system away from equilibrium, that accumulation for accumulation's sake is an unstable system in both the short and long run. Crises then appear as the only effective means to counter disequilibrium, to restore the balance between production and consumption. These crises entail, however, the devaluation, depreciation and destruction of capital. And that is never a comfortable process to live with – particularly since it also entails the devaluation, depreciation and destruction of the labourer.

CHAPTER 4

Technological Change, the Labour Process and the Value Composition of Capital

Technology discloses man's mode of dealing with Nature, the process of production by which he sustains his life, and thereby also lays bare the mode of formation of his social relations, and of the mental conceptions that flow from them. (*Capital,* vol. 1, p. 372)

Of all the misinterpretations of Marx's thought, perhaps the most bizarre is that which makes a technological determinist of him.[1] He did not regard technological change as the moving force of history. This misinterpretation of his argument has arisen, in part, by imposing contemporary meanings on Marx's words, and also out of a failure to understand his method of enquiry. Commonly accepted definitions would now have it, for example, that tech-

---

[1] Hook (1933) long ago sought to eliminate this interpretation, but it has undergone somewhat of a revival in recent years. By far the most powerful argument is that advanced by Cohen (1978), who accepts the appelation 'technological' but not that of 'determinist' in his interpretation of the primacy of the productive forces within Marx's version of historical materialism. Cohen's work, although extremely helpful in clarifying many points in Marx, demonstrates the consequences that arise when Marx is interpreted according to 'the standards of clarity and rigor which distinguish twentieth century analytical philosophy' (p. ix). Marx, according to Cohen, defines a productive force as "the property of objects" rather than a relation holding between objects (p. 28). The list of productive forces includes labour power (and all of its qualities) and means of production (including instruments of production, raw materials and spaces). Cohen analyses Marx's statements and finds that, while there are innumerable occasions on which Marx asserts that changes in the productive forces generate changes in social relations, there 'are not generalizations asserting the putative reverse movement . . . in the corpus of Marx's work' (p. 138). The 'dialectical' relationship between productive forces and social relations does not hold, and the primacy of the productive forces is thereby established. The only cause for doubt is the statement that it is the bourgeoisie that revolutionizes the productive forces that

nology implies the application of scientific knowledge to create the physical hardware for production, exchange, communication and consumption. Marx's meaning is both broader and narrower than that.

When Marx speaks of 'technology' he means the concrete form taken by an actual labour process in a given instance, the observable way in which particular use values are produced. This technology can be described directly in terms of the tools and machines used, the physical design of production processes, the technical division of labour, the actual deployment of labour powers (both quantities and qualities), the levels of co-operation, the chains of command and hierarchies of authority and the particular methods of co-ordination and control used.

The task is then to penetrate beneath this surface appearance and understand why particular labour processes take on the specific technological forms they do. To this end, Marx considers the labour process in terms of the *productive forces* and the *social relations of production* embodied within it.[2] By 'productive force' Marx means the sheer power to transform nature. By 'social relations' he means the social organization and the social implications of the what, how and why of production. These are abstract concepts, and we must mark their meaning well. Much that follows rests upon their proper interpretation. They will be used to unravel the contradictions within production in much the same way that the duality of use and exchange value provides the conceptual lever to expose the contradictions of commodity exchange. The parallel is apt. Productive force and social relations are initially to be regarded as two aspects of the same material labour process, in the same way that use and exchange value are two aspects of a single commodity. The exchange value in commodities has an external referent in the shape of

---

change the social relations. Cohen concedes that capitalist production relations 'are a prodigious stimulus to the development of the productive forces', but makes this compatible with the primacy of productive forces thesis by the assertion that 'the function of capitalist relations is to promote growth in productive power – they arise and persist when they are apt to do so'.

The characterization of Marx's initial definition of productive force is, in my view, correct. But like 'use value', this initial conception is in itself of little interest to Marx. Again, like use value, productive forces are integrated back into the argument only when they are understood as a social relation specifically embedded within the capitalist mode of production. Cohen, however, sticks to the initial definition and fails to mark the transformation in Marx's usage of the term. The whole flow of the argument in *Capital* is precisely geared to unravelling the dialectical interpenetration of productive forces and social relations as the locus of contradictions which push capitalism perpetually into new configurations. Analytical philosophy may be good at analysing sentences but is not so good, apparently, at capturing the total flow of an argument.

[2] Therborn (1976, pp. 356–86) reconstructs the genesis of these concepts throughout Marx's intellectual development in very thorough fashion.

money, and the social relations of production have an external referrent in the form of the class relations that prevail in society at large and that permeate exchange, distribution and consumption as well as production. And in the same way that use value becomes re-integrated into political economy as *social* use value, so the purely physical idea of productive force is re-integrated into political economy as the power to create surplus value for capital through material commodity production. Given the importance of these concepts, we must move to establish their meaning with care.

We begin by eliminating a common source of confusion. The identification of 'technology' with the 'forces of production' is erroneous and the mainspring of that misreading of Marx that turns him into a technological determinist. Technology is the material form of the labour process through which the underlying forces and relations of production are expressed. To equate technology with productive forces would be like equating money, the material form of value, with value itself, or equating concrete with abstract labour. But in the same way that an analysis of money can reveal much about the nature of value, so an analysis of actual technologies can 'disclose' the nature of the productive forces and the social relations embedded within the capitalist mode of production. This is the sense to be attributed to the quotation with which we began this chapter.

Analysis of existing technologies can be a useful (and necessary) preliminary exercise. But Marx conceives of his method rather differently (*Grundrisse*, pp. 100–7). He begins with the simplest possible abstractions, drawn from 'the actual relations of life', and then builds up richer and ever more complex conceptualizations so as to 'approach, step by step' the concrete forms which activities assume 'on the surface of society' (*Capital,* vol. 3, p. 25). This is, he claims, 'the only materialistic and therefore the only scientific' way to interpret the phenomena with which we find ourselves surrounded – commodity production, money and exchange, concrete technological forms, crises and so on (*Capital,* vol. 1, p. 372).

Marx's materialist method and his concern for the 'actual relations of life' lead him to concentrate attention upon the labour process as a fundamental point of departure for enquiry. 'Human action with a view to the production of use values, appropriation of natural substances to human requirements,' he writes, 'is the necessary condition for effecting exchange of matter between man and Nature; it is the everlasting Nature-imposed condition of human existence' (*Capital,* vol. 1, p. 184). And what can be more fundamental than that? The relation with nature is treated dialectically, of course. The separation between the 'human' and the 'natural' is viewed as a separation within a unity because the 'interdependence of the physical and mental life, of man with Nature has the meaning that Nature is interdependent with itself, for man is part of Nature' (*Economic and Philosophic Manuscripts,* p. 127). The language is very Hegelian, but Marx does not depart from this position in his later works.[3] The focus shifts, however, to a study of the separation within the unity:

> Labour is, in the first place, a process in which both man and Nature participate. . . . He opposes himself to Nature as one of her own forces, setting in motion arms and legs, head and hands, the natural forces of his body, in order to appropriate Nature's production in a form adapted to his own wants. (*Capital*, vol. 1, p. 177)

We here encounter the concept of 'productive force' in its simplest and most easily comprehensible form: it represents the *power* to transform and appropriate nature through human labour. That power can be augmented by the use of various instruments of labour which, together with the land itself, form the means of production and constitute the necessary basis for productive labour (*Capital*, vol. 1, pp. 180–1). The specific form the relation to nature takes is, however, a social product, 'a gift, not of Nature, but of a history embracing thousands of centuries' (*Capital*, vol. 2, p. 512). The actual technology of the labour process is shaped by historical and social processes and necessarily reflects the social relationships between human beings as they combine and co-operate in the fundamental tasks of production. The productive powers of labour cannot be gauged in abstraction from these social relationships.

Furthermore, the work process is both instrumental and purposive in relation to human wants and needs – 'what distinguishes the worst architect from the best of bees is this, that the architect raises his structure in imagination before he erects it in reality' (*Capital*, vol. 2, p. 178). Mental conceptions of the world can become a 'material force' in a double sense: they become 'objectified' in material objects and materialized in actual production processes. The activity of production therefore incorporates a certain knowledge of the world – knowledge that is also a social product. Each mode of production evolves a specific kind of science, a 'knowledge system' appropriate to its distinctive physical and social needs. Marx will make much of how capitalism seeks to unify 'the natural sciences with the process of production' and how the principle of 'analysing the process of production into its constituent phases, and of solving the problems thus proposed by the application of mechanics, of chemistry, and of the whole range of the natural sciences,

---

[3] Schmidt (1971) provides a comprehensive study of *The Concept of Nature in Marx*. He errs, as Smith (1980) shows, by defining nature as the realm of use values and forgetting that Marx's concern is with *social* use values or, in this instance, with the production of use values in the form of a 'produced nature' (the built environment, a physical landscape modified by human action). This produced nature assumes a commodity form and is therefore to be conceived of in terms of the relationship between use values, exchange values and values. Nature, under these circumstances, can no longer be seen as wholly external to human existence and human society. We will take up this matter further in chapters 8 and 11.

becomes the determining principle everywhere' (*Capital,* vol. 2, pp. 387, 461). He even comments upon how invention itself becomes a business and the production of new scientific understandings becomes necessarily integrated into the dynamics of capitalism (*Grundrisse,* pp. 704–5).[4]

The labour process is initially conceived of, then, as a *unity* of productive forces, social relations and mental conceptions of the world. The importance of the separation within the unity, in the first instance, is that it fashions the questions we ask of any technology, any labour process, we might encounter.

Consider, for example, a person digging a ditch. We can describe the use of nerve and muscle and perhaps measure the physical expenditure of energy on the part of the digger. We can likewise describe the qualities of nature (the ease with which the earth can be dug) and the instruments of labour (spade or earth-mover). And we can measure the productivity of labour in terms of feet of ditch dug per hour of work. But if we limit ourselves to this direct physical description, we miss much that is important. Indeed, Marx would consider the measure of productivity a meaningless abstraction. To interpret the activity properly we must first discover its purpose, the conscious design of which it is a part and the mental conception of the world that is embodied in the activity and its result. We must also know the social relationships involved. Is the work being done by a slave, a wage labourer, an artisan, a dedicated socialist, a religious fanatic participating in a religious ceremony, or a rich lord with a penchant for strenuous physical exercise? Identical physical actions could have an infinite variety of social meanings. We cannot interpret the activities without some understanding of their social purpose. Only in this way can we come up with a meaningful measure of productivity. Marx will, in this vein, make much of the idea that productivity in relation to human wants and needs is very different from productivity in relation to the creation of surplus value. And finally, only when we fully comprehend the social meaning and social purpose will we be able to understand why certain technologies are chosen rather than others; why certain mental conceptions of the world take precedence over others. It is the relation between the productive forces, social relations of production and mental conceptions of the world, all expressed within a single unique labour process, that counts in the end.

From this it follows that revolutions in the productive forces cannot be accomplished without a radical re-structuring of social relationships and of the knowledge system. Yet the impetus to such change lies, according to Marx, in the very nature of the labour process itself – 'by acting on the external world and changing it, [man] at the same time changes his own nature' (*Capital,* vol. 1, p. 177). The reciprocal (dialectical) relation between

[4] Noble (1977) explores in detail how engineering science, technological innovation and corporate capitalism related to each other in the United States after the Civil War. For all its defects, J. D. Bernal's (1969) work still remains a classic.

the subject and object of work therefore lies at the heart of the process of development. This process, when generalized to social and historical contexts, leads to the idea that 'in acquiring new productive forces, men change their mode of production; and in changing their mode of production . . . they change all their social relations' as well as their mental conceptions of the world (*Poverty of Philosophy*, p. 109).

We can dissect this process more exactly by considering the separations within the unity of the labour process. What happens, for example, if the social co-operation required to operate a certain kind of production system is not forthcoming, or if the social capacity and desire to transform nature is not matched by the means of production available? What happens when the result desired is not matched by the scientific understanding of the production process needed to produce that result? The potentiality exists for all kinds of oppositions and antagonisms between the productive forces, social relations and mental conceptions of the world. It is however, one thing to speak of potentiality and quite another to establish, as Marx seeks to do, the *necessity* of such contradictions within capitalism.

His general argument proceeds as follows. In order to produce and reproduce, human beings are compelled to enter into social relationships and to struggle to appropriate nature in a manner consistent with these social relationships and their knowledge of the world. In the course of that struggle they necessarily produce new relations with nature, new knowledges and new social relations. Powerful social checks may hold down societies in relatively stationary states – states that Marx refers to as 'pre-history'. But once the social checks are broken down (by whatever means), the equilibrium is upset and contradictory forces come into play. The contradictions between the productive forces, social relations and mental conceptions of the world become the central source of tension. The perpetual struggle to overcome the contradictions becomes the motor force of history.

This general interpretation of the forces governing the trajectory of human history is put to work to understand the dynamics of capitalism. The insatiable quest on the part of capitalists to appropriate surplus value impels perpetual revolutions in the productive forces. But these revolutions create conditions that are inconsistent with the further accumulation of capital and the reproduction of class relations. This means that the capitalist system is inherently unstable and crisis-prone. Though each crisis may be resolved through a radical re-structuring of productive forces and social relations, the underlying source of conflict is never eliminated. New contradictions arise which generate ever more general forms of crisis. The only ultimate resolution to the contradictions lies in the elimination of their source, in the creation of fundamentally new social relationships – those of socialism.

Put in these terms, this argument will, presumably, convince no one. Its utility lies in the questions it serves to pose. It directs our attention, first of all, to the social relations that spawn changes in the productive forces and in particular impels us to confront the class basis for such changes. Secondly, we are challenged to show that the pace, form and direction of revolutions in the capacity to transform nature can ever be consistent with stable, balanced growth. And if it is not, do we not have here a fundamental explanation for the evident periodic crises of capitalism? These are the grand questions we shall seek to answer in the next few chapters. But first we need to tie down our conceptual apparatus rather more carefully to the specific historical form taken by the capitalist mode of production.

I   THE PRODUCTIVITY OF LABOUR UNDER CAPITALISM

Initially, we might be tempted to treat the productivity of labour in purely physical terms and measure it by the amount of raw material that a labourer can transform, using certain instruments of production, into a given amount of finished or semi-finished product within some standardized time period. Marx is at war with such a conception.[5] It fails to distinguish between concrete labour and abstract labour and presumes that capitalists are interested in the production of use values rather than value in general and surplus value in particular. Marx proposes a distinctively capitalistic definition of labour productivity:

> That labour is alone productive, who produces surplus value for the capitalist, and thus works for the self-expansion of capital. . . . Hence the notion of a productive labourer implies not merely a relation between work and useful effect . . . but also a specific, social relation of production, a relation that has sprung up historically and stamps the labourer as the direct means of creating surplus value. (*Capital*, vol. 1, p. 509)

Marx goes on to add, cryptically, that 'to be a productive labourer is, therefore, not a piece of luck but a misfortune'. This value definition of productivity provides Marx with a powerful tool to beat the vulgar economists with. 'Only bourgeois narrow-mindedness, which regards the capitalist forms of production . . . as eternal . . . can confuse the problem of what is productive labour from the standpoint of capital with the question of what labour is productive in general . . . and consequently fancy itself very wise in giving the answer that all labour which produces anything at all . . . is by that very fact productive labour.' (*Theories of Surplus Value,* pt 1, p. 393)

Armed with this conception of *value* rather than *physical* productivity, Marx can also debunk the commonly held notion that capital is itself some-

[5] Blaug (1968, p. 231), accuses Marx of a 'horrible confusion between physical productivity and value productivity', but the confusion arises more out of Blaug's misinterpretation of Marx's relational manner of proceeding than it does out of Marx.

how productive. Increases in physical productivity, particularly those brought about through the application of machinery, appear to be an attribute, a product, even, of capital. Capital 'becomes a very mystic being since all of labour's social productive forces appear to be due to capital, rather than labour as such, and seem to issue from the womb of capital itself' (*Capital*, vol. 3, p. 827). But what does this appearance truly denote? It simply represents, Marx argues, the ability of the capitalist to appropriate the productive powers of social labour in such a way that the latter appear to be productive powers of capital (*Theories of Surplus Value*, pt 1, pp. 389–91). And this can happen only because of the specific class relations that prevail within production, relations that give the labourer access to the means of production under conditions broadly dictated by capital.

Marx's value definition of productivity also raises difficulties. It has spawned, for example, a long and somewhat tedious debate on the difference between 'productive' and 'unproductive' labour.[6] Since only that labour that produces surplus value is deemed 'productive' under Marx's definition, a variety of physically productive activities (chiefly in services and circulation) end up being characterized as 'unproductive', no matter how socially necessary they might be. The point of Marx's argument was to take what was a mere classification of labourers as discussed by the political economists (Adam Smith, in particular) and to convert it into terms that reflected capitalist relations of production. There is very little evidence that Marx wished to go any further than this. He certainly was not proposing a new and more elaborate classification of occupations into productive and unproductive groupings – to do so would have been to put the debate precisely back upon the terrain defined by the physiocrats and Adam Smith, the very terrain from which Marx sought to dislodge it. All that Marx was suggesting here was, in effect, that any definition of productive labour under capitalism had to be seen in relation to the actual process of production of surplus value. As we broaden our perspective on that process – from, for example, within the labour process outwards to embrace the total circulation process of capital – so the definition of productive labour will broaden also. 'In order to labour productively, it is no longer necessary for you to do manual work yourself; enough, if you are an organ of the collective labourer, and perform one of its subordinate functions' (*Capital*, vol. 1, p. 509).

---

[6] Those interested in following up the debate should consult Fine and Harris (1979, ch. 3), Gough (1972), Hunt (1979), O'Connor (1975) and the various issues of the *Bulletin of the Conference of Socialist Economists* (1973–5). There is also a considerable literature in French on the matter: see Berthoud (1974), Freyssenet (1971; 1977) and Nagels (1974). The debate assumes added significance to the degree that some writers, such as Poulantzas (1975), trace differentials in subjective states of consciousness within certain fractions of the working class to the different statuses of productive and unproductive worker.

The idea that it is the productivity of the collective, rather than the individual, labourer that counts has implications for our conception of productive force. The ways in which labourers relate to and mutually reinforce each other in the performance of their various tasks clearly has a bearing upon their collective productivity. Efficiency is not a purely technical matter but, as every industrial relations expert knows, at least in part a social question. The dilemma for the capitalist is to mobilize the positive powers of co-operation as a productive force of capital through mechanisms that, in the last instance, must be judged coercive. Strategies of job enrichment, co-operation and worker–management integration seem specifically designed to mask the basic relation of domination and subordination that necessarily prevails within the labour process. This brings us to consider, however, the decisive role of class struggle within the labour process itself.

II THE LABOUR PROCESS

One of the most compelling aspects to the first volume of *Capital* is the way in which Marx switches so fluently from the deepest and simplest possible abstractions (like value) to reflections on the history of struggles over the working day and mechanization, on through to the political implication of the necessity for a revolutionary overthrow of capitalism. While the work is executed with consummate artistry, its very achievements can in themselves be somewhat misleading. Put in the context of his overall project, even as articulated in the other two volumes of *Capital,* we could well argue that the tie between history and theory in volume 1 is prematurely knotted and that the political implications are far too hastily derived. Marx was not necessarily wrong in this. Neither historical interpretation nor political action can wait upon the perfection of theory, while the latter itself can emerge only out of perpetual testing against historical experience and political practice. But the first volume of *Capital* is such a seductive document that many Marxists treat it as the final word when it should be viewed as an extraordinary but preliminary stab at how theory, historical interpretation and strategies for political action mutually determine and relate to each other.

The controversial character of Marx's argument becomes immediately apparent in the contemporary debate over the nature of the labour process under capitalism. The debate is important because the labour process is fundamental to the workings of any mode of production. If Marx's manner of representing it is wrong, then almost everything else must also be called into question. The debate has taken on added urgency and direction since the publication of Braverman's *Labor and Monopoly Capital* in 1974. With the exception of Gramsci's (1971) fascinating essay on 'Fordism', this was the first major work in the Marxist tradition to grapple with changes in the labour process in the twentieth century. Subsequent work has called into question both Marx's original conception and Braverman's extension of it.

Marx organizes his thoughts on the matter around the distinction between 'formal' and 'real subjection of labour to capital' (*Capital*, vol. 1, p. 510). 'Formal subjection' is sufficient for the production of absolute surplus value and comes about as soon as labourers are compelled to sell their labour power in order to live. The labour process goes on as before, apart from the introduction of 'an economic relationship of supremacy and subordination', which arises because capitalists 'naturally' direct and supervise the activities of the labourer, and because of a tendency for the labour to become far more continuous and intensive 'since every effort is made to ensure that no more (or even less) socially necessary labour time is consumed in making the product' (*Results of the Immediate Process of Production*, p. 1025). Through competition in exchange, socially necessary labour time begins to be felt as the regulator of the labour process even though labourers retain substantial control over their traditional skills and over the methods employed. The reduction of skilled to simple labour does not occur. And the only compulsion involved arises out of the necessity for the labourer to sell labour power in order to live.

The 'real subjection of labour to capital' arises when capitalists begin to reorganize the labour process itself in order to acquire relative surplus value. With this, the entire mode of production 'is altered and a specifically *capitalist form of production* comes into being' together with 'the corresponding relations of production' (*Results*, p. 1024). In other words, the class relations that prevail within capitalism in general now penetrate *within* the labour process through the reorganization of the productive forces.

Capitalists mobilize the powers that arise out of co-operation and the detailed division of labour, and profit from the increased productivity of labour that results. Workers increasingly become 'special modes of existence of capital' and are increasingly subjected to the 'despotic' control of the capitalists and their representatives. An hierarchical and authoritarian structure of social relations emerges within the work place. The methods of work may remain the same, but the specialization of labourers on specific tasks may allow the latter to be so simplified that they can be performed by workers with little knowledge or skills. 'In order to make the collective labourer, and through him capital, rich in productive power, each labourer must be made poor in individual productive powers' (*Capital*, vol. I, p. 361). A general distinction between skilled and unskilled labour emerges, but the technical basis of production also requires the preservation of a hierarchy of labour powers and skills, together with wage differentials (the reduction of skilled to simple labour is not complete). In these instances also, the increasing productive power of labour arises out of a reorganization of existing work processes and does not necessarily entail any major investment on the part of the capitalists – although new premises and buildings may be needed, since co-operation often means the aggregation of various processes under the same roof (pp. 320, 355).

Capitalism overcomes the 'narrow technical basis' of manufacturing through the introduction of machinery and the organization of the factory system. The transition to a truly *capitalist* mode of production then becomes possible. Although this does involve active investment on the part of the capitalists, the advantage is that the machine can be used to increase the physical productivity of labour at the same time as it permits the capitalists to control the intensity and rhythm of the work process through regulating the speed of the machine. The worker then becomes a mere 'appendage' – a slave – of the machine. The separation of mental from manual labour, the destruction of craft and artisan skills and their replacement by mere machine-minding skills, the employment of women and children – all follow as a consequence. For Marx, the impoverishment of the labourer under capitalism had as much if not more to do with the degradation forced upon the worker in the labour process, than with low wages and high rates of exploitation. With the capitalist use of machinery, 'the instrument of labour becomes the means of enslaving, exploiting, and impoverishing the labourer; the social combination and organization of labour processes is turned into an organized mode of crushing out the workman's individual vitality, freedom, and independence' (*Results*, p. 506).

The violence the capitalist class must necessarily visit upon the labourer in order to extract surplus value is nowhere more readily apparent than in the degraded relation to nature that results in the labour process. This provokes its own response. Workers resort to individual acts of violence, sabotage – industrial pathology of all kinds – as well as collective forms of resistance to the use and abuse of machinery. The social struggles to which this violent resistance gives rise form a central theme in the social and political histories of those countries that have taken the capitalist road to industrialization. But Marx appears to insist that, in the long run, individual or collective forms of worker resistance *within* the work process must fall before the overwhelming forces that capital can muster. The isolated forms of resistance only delay the inevitable. Only a broadly based revolutionary movement can regain for labour what will otherwise almost certainly be lost.

Yet this whole process is not without its compensations and contradictions either. The routinization of tasks requires sophisticated managerial, conceptual and technical (engineering) skills. This entails a new kind of hierarchical ordering (which Marx pays scant attention to, though it is implied by the necessary persistence of co-operation and detailed division of labour within the factory system). Workers also come to be indifferent to the particular tasks they perform, ready to adapt to each and every new technology and able to switch freely from one line of production to another. These powers of adaptability – which often entail literacy, numeracy, the ability to follow instructions and to routinize tasks quickly – counter the tendency towards the degradation of labour in important ways. Skills of this sort, though very different from those of the traditional craftsman, imply the creation of a new kind of worker: 'the fully developed individual, fit for a variety of labours, ready to face any change of production, and to whom the different social functions he performs are but so many modes of giving free scope to his own natural and acquired powers' (*Capital*, vol. I, p. 488). By 'liberating' workers from their traditional skills, capital at the same time generates a new and peculiar kind of freedom for the worker.

We should note in this how the word 'skill' undergoes a subtle transformation of meaning. On the one hand, there is the traditional craft and artisan skill which confers a certain power upon whoever possesses it because it is, to some degree, monopolizable. Such skills are anathema to capital. They can act as a barrier to the accumulation of capital (wage rates are sensitive to their scarcity) and prevent the penetration of capitalist social relations of domination and subordination within production. These are the skills that have to be eliminated if capitalism is to survive. On the other hand, it is important for capital that new skills emerge: skills which allow for flexibility and adaptability and, above all, for *substitutability* – that are non-monopolizable. The 'de-skilling' of which Marx writes often entails a direct transformation from monopolizable to non-monopolizable skills. But the former kind of skill can never disappear totally. The skills of the engineers, the scientists, managers, designers and so on often become monopolizable. The only question is, then, whether the monopoly powers that attach to such skills are totally absorbed as a power of capital, through the formation of a distinctive faction of the bourgeoisie (the managers and scientists), or whether they can be captured as part of the collective powers of labour.

Braverman (1974), in a work that is both rich and compelling, updates Marx's account and seeks also to show how the labour process has been modified as capitalism has moved into its 'monopoly stage'. It is difficult to deal with a very subtle argument in a few paragraphs. However, Braverman attaches prime importance to *scientific management* and the *scientific–technical revolution* as two aspects of capital that 'grow out of monopoly capitalism and make it possible.' Both have deep implications for the social relations within production and the form the labour process takes. Scientific management (Taylorism) entails a systematic separation of the mental labour of conception from the manual labour of execution and so fragments and simplifies the latter that even a 'trained gorilla' could do it. The mobilization of science and technology gives capital the organized capacity to revolutionize the productive forces almost at will. It furthers the separation of manual from mental labour and, when combined with scientific management, ensures that control over the labour process passes from the hands of the worker into those of management – 'this transition presents itself in history as the progressive *alienation of the process of production* from the worker' (Braverman, 1974, pp. 57–8). This ensured 'that, as craft declined, the worker would sink to the level of general and undifferentiated labour power, adaptable to a wide range of tasks, while as science grew, it would be concentrated in the hands of management (Braverman, 1974, pp. 120–1). The 'de-skilling' of the mass of the workers proceeded apace, and as capital gained an ever more thoroughgoing and complete control over the labour process, labour 'comes ever closer to corresponding, in life, to the abstraction employed by Marx in an analysis of the capitalist mode of production' – the reduction of skilled to simple abstract labour is complete (Braverman, 1974, p. 182). The problem posed above (pp. 57–61) is resolved.

The only substantive problem that remains, for capital, is to habituate and reconcile workers – living human beings with real aspirations and concerns – to the degradation of work and the destruction of traditional skills. The apparent shift in managerial strategy from control of work to control of the worker through industrial relations programmes designed to increase job satisfaction, diminish feelings of alienation, etc., is interpreted by Braverman as an extension and deepening of the tactics of Taylorism to penetrate within the very psychological makeup of the workers themselves. But this, too, has to be put in its context. For what is most striking about Braverman's contribution is the way in which he relates the very specific manner in which industrial work processes are transformed under monopoly capitalism to the transformation of all aspects of life in the twentieth century (Braverman, 1974, p. 271).

He shows, for example, how realms other than production are affected by the same trends. Much of the labour of conception and control becomes routinized so that the very opportunities for new forms of skill capitalism creates are by and large denied. The labour engaged in the circulation of commodities, money, information, and the like – activities that have become increasingly important as monopoly capitalism has become more complex – has also been degraded and de-skilled, as has much of the work of administration. But Braverman does not stop at office work. He pursues his argument into the community and into the heart of family life, where he shows the deep implications for the sexual division of labour, family organization, and so on. He deals, as Burawoy puts it, with

> the penetration of the entire social structure by the commodification of social life and with it the degradation of work as manifested through the separation of conception and execution. Like a cancerous growth the spirit of commodification and degradation appears with a momentum of its own. . . . It cannot rest until it has subordinated the entire fabric of social life to itself. A concern with specific causes, bringing it about here

rather than there, now rather than later, are irrelevant to the broad sweep of history. (Burawoy, 1978, pp. 295–6)

Braverman's work, while drawing universal praise as a major contribution, has also provoked a storm of criticism and commentary. Since Braverman explicitly roots his arguments in Marx's, a general debate has arisen as to the adequacy with which either or both have handled the labour process under capitalism. The discussion has been highly nuanced and often idiosyncratic. Some seek more rigorous and more accurate representations within the broad framework that Marx and Braverman define; others object not to Marx but to Braverman's extension of Marx into the conditions of twentieth-century capitalism; while others have voiced strong criticisms of both. I cannot possibly do justice to this debate here. In what follows I will present a collage of criticisms as these have been directed at both Marx and Braverman.[7]

The latter have been indicted by their critics for a variety of offences. For all their compassion and concern, both Braverman and Marx treat the workers within the labour process as objects, dominated by and subordinate to the will of capital. They ignore the workers as living human beings, endowed with a consciousness and will, capable of articulating ideological, political and economic preferences on the shop floor, able (when it suits them) to adapt and compromise, but also prepared, when necessary, to wage perpetual war against capital in order to protect their rights within production. Class struggle within the labour process is thereby reduced to a transient affair of relatively minor importance, and 'worker resistance as a force causing accommodating changes in the capitalist mode of production' is totally neglected.[8] Marx and Braverman erroneously depict technological and organizational change as an inevitable response to the operation of the law of value, to the rules that govern the circulation and accumulation of capital, when struggles waged by workers on the shop floor have affected the course of capitalist history.[9] That history, when properly reconstructed by techniques faithful to historical materialism, tells a quite different story from that set out by either Marx or Braverman. The latter imposed theoretical constructs upon historical realities and so distorted history. Worse still, their

[7] In constructing a collage of criticism in this way, I am all too aware that I am not doing justice to the point of view of any one individual, while I am not being entirely fair to Braverman and Marx either. The numerous contributions to the debate have been summarized and reviewed by Elger (1979), who also provides an extensive bibliography. The collage also draws heavily upon Burawoy (1978; 1979), Edwards (1979), Friedman (1977a; 1977b), and Palmer (1975). The special issues of *Politics and Society* (vol. 8, nos 3–4, 1978) and *Monthly Review* (vol. 28, no. 3, 1976), and the symposium published in the *Cambridge Journal of Economics* (vol. 3, no. 3, 1979), which contains an important opening statement by Elbaum *et al.* and detailed articles by Lazonic, Zeitlin and others, have also been used extensively.

[8] Friedman (1977a; 1977b) is particularly strong on this point.

[9] Edwards (1979) adopts this as his basic theme in his book, *Contested Terrain*.

theories reflected capitalist ideology rather than capitalist practice. Marx, says Lazonick (1979, pp. 258–9), gives a 'misleading portrayal of the effects of the self-acting mule . . . because he derived his conclusion of the omnipotence of technology in the subjection of labour to capital from an uncritical acceptance of capitalist ideology' (particularly that espoused by Ure and Babbage). Palmer, Edwards and Burawoy likewise see Braverman as a victim of the ideology of Taylorism because the real history shows, they claim, that the working class defeated Taylorism on the shop floor and forced capitalists to seek out new and more acceptable (to labour) means of control.[10] Capitalists had to compromise, in part because of the sheer tenacity of working-class struggle on the shop floor, but also because the new processes of production, far from reducing the power of labour to fight back against capital, have, by their very intricacy and interdependency, increased the capacity for sabotage and disruption. Capitalists have therefore had to 'manufacture consent' and to elicit the willing co-operation of workers.[11] The net result has been to transform the 'contested terrain' within the work place into a 'terrain of compromise'.[12] Co-operation between capital and labour, over the form taken by the labour process (job enrichment schemes, 'responsible autonomy', etc.), over the definition of job and wage structure (hierarchically ordered so as to offer the worker job mobility within the enterprise and even a career), becomes the order of the day and gradually replaces confrontation and conflict on the shop floor.

Such criticisms are potentially devastating. Not only do they challenge the basic lines of historical and theoretical interpretation which Marx laid down, but they also challenge the very basis of Marx's revolutionary politics.[13] The criticisms have been seriously advanced and in some cases carefully

[10] Palmer (1975), Edwards (1979) and Burawoy (1978) all make this point.

[11] Burawoy's careful study of *Manufacturing Consent* (1979) is an excellent attempt to document this idea.

[12] The phrases are from Edwards (1979) and Elbaum *et al.* (1979).

[13] Edwards (1979) argues, for example, that the perpetuation and augmentation of hierarchical ordering of job and wage structures under the 'bureaucratic' control of the large corporation (a system that he sharply distinguishes from the 'technical' control through Taylorism) has fragmented rather than homogenized the working class. Individuals and groups of workers pursue their own interests through some mixture of confrontation and compromise, and the more privileged of them (who often turn out to be those with traditional craft skills) can win much of what they want (wages and pensions, job security, on-the-job responsibility, etc.). And under conditions of oligopoly, capital has the leeway to make such concessions. The working class in the United States has never been, nor will it likely become, truly revolutionary, and Marx's clarion call for a revolutionary transformation of the mode of production is bound to fall upon deaf ears. The only political strategy for the left is to protect the 'terrain of compromise' so laboriously built up through years of class struggle (particularly in the political arena) and to seek, by social democratic methods, to extend that terrain wherever possible, in the name of socialism. Pungent criticisms of this approach can be found in two reviews of Edward's work in *Monthly Review* (December 1979).

documented. They cannot, therefore, be cavalierly dismissed. The virtue of constructing defences against them is that it sharpens and in some respects corrects our interpretation of what it was that Marx was driving at.

The charge that Marx treats the worker as an 'object' is in one sense true. It was precisely Marx's point that the world cannot be understood solely through direct subjective experience of it, and that the working class's own vision of its potentialities and powers was seriously emasculated without the achievement of a truly materialist science. To make such an argument does not deny the validity of the workers' subjective experiences, nor does it say that the sheer inventiveness and variety of workers' responses are unworthy of comment or study. It is vital to understand how workers cope, the 'games' they invent to make the labour process bearable, the particular forms of camaraderie and competition through which they relate to each other, the tactics of co-operation, confrontation and subtle avoidance with which they deal with those in authority, and above all, perhaps, the aspirations and sense of morality with which they invest their daily lives. It is important, too, to understand how workers build a distinctive culture, create institutions and capture others for their own, and build organizations for self-defence.

But what Marx seeks is an understanding of what it is that workers are being forced to cope *with* and to defend *against*; to come to terms with the manifest forces that impinge upon them at every turn. Why is it that workers have to cope with new technologies, speed-ups, lay-offs, 'deskilling', authoritarianism in the work place, inflation in the market place? To understand all this requires that we construct a materialist theory of the capitalist mode of production, of the circulation and accumulation of capital through commodity production. And the theory shows that, from the standpoint of capital, workers are indeed objects, a mere 'factor' of production – the *variable form* of capital – for the creation of surplus value. The theory holds up to the workers, as in a mirror, the objective conditions of their own alienation, and exposes the forces that dominate their social existence and their history. The construction of this theory, by techniques that went beyond the simple replication of subjective experience, was, surely, Marx's most signal achievement.

But the undoubted revelatory power of Marxian theory does not by itself guarantee its absorption by the proletariat as a guide to action. Political and class consciousness is not forged, after all, by appeal to theory. It has its roots deep in the very fabric of daily life and in the experience of working in particular. Yet the theory shows that capitalism is characterized by fetishisms that obscure, for both capitalist and worker alike, the origin of surplus value in exploitation. The immediate subjective experience of the labour process does not necessarily lead, therefore, to the same conclusions that Marx expressed, for the very reasons that Marx himself divined. The subjective experience is none the less real for all that. So a gap may exist between what daily experience teaches and what theory preaches – a gap that the ideologists of capitalism are by no means loath to play upon and exacerbate. Marx, for his part, was more than a little inclined to deny the authenticity of experience (the unfortunate category, 'false consciousness', springs immediately to mind), in pushing so strongly for the revelatory power of theory. Furthermore, his deep and uncompromising hostility to those socialists who spun utopian webs out of subjectivism and fancy made it all the more difficult for him to create a space in his own thought in which the subjective lived experience of the working class could play out its proper role. He could not, as a consequence, solve the problem of political consciousness, and it is interesting to note that Braverman likewise thought it wise to avoid that question.[14]

Yet the question is fundamental and will not go away. It has dogged some of the best Marxist thinkers – for example, Lukacs, Gramsci and those of the Frankfurt school, such as Fromm, Marcuse, Horkheimer and Habermas – who sought an explanation of the non-revolutionary character of the working classes in the advanced capitalist countries through an integration of Marx and Freud. But it is fair to say that the duality of worker as 'object for capital' and as 'living creative subject' has never been adequately resolved in Marxist theory. Indeed, it has been the cause of an immense and continuing friction within the Marxist tradition. Those, like E. P. Thompson in his epic *Making of the English Working Class*, who dwell primarily on the labourer as creative subject, frequently find themselves castigated and ostracized as 'moralists' and 'utopians' by their more theoretically minded colleagues whose prime concern appears to be the preservation of the integrity and rigour of Marxist materialist science. Thompson condemns the latter for an 'arbitrary separation of a "mode of production" from everything that actually goes on in history' – a self-validating 'theoretical practice' which 'ends up by telling us nothing and apologising for everything'. More specifically, he pours scorn on 'authorities on "the labour process" who have never found relevant to their exalted theory Christopher Hill's work on "the uses of sabbatarianism", nor mine on "time and work discipline", nor Eric Hobsbawm's on "the tramping artisan", nor that of a generation of (American, French, British) "labour historians" (a group often dismissed with scorn) on time-and-motion study, Taylorism, and Fordism.' Not surprisingly, the critics of Marx and Braverman have drawn much strength from Thompson's work.[15]

[14] Braverman (1974, p. 27); Burawoy (1978) focuses most directly on this point in fashioning his critique of Braverman.
[15] Thompson (1978, pp. 347–54). The debate between Thompson and Anderson (1980) revolves around this duality, and read in the right spirit holds out some hope of reconciling the different viewpoints within new and much more powerful formulations.

So what happens to our theory when we allow back the worker as 'creative subject'? Thompson is quite explicit. 'Contrary to the view of some theoretical practitioners,' he writes, 'no worker known to historians ever had surplus-value taken out of his hide without finding some way of fighting back (there are plenty of ways of going slow); and, paradoxically, *by* his fighting back the tendencies were diverted and the "forms of development" were themselves developed in unexpected ways' (1978, pp. 345–6). Here we come to the root of the problem: the role of class struggle and worker resistance in modifying and guiding the evolution of the labour process itself. Can workers, as creative subjects who resist the depredations of capital, become thereby at least partial authors of their own history? Can they alter the forms of technological change, the systems of managerial control and authority, the organization, intensity and speed of work, the patterns of investment and re-investment and, hence, the direction, pace and content of the accumulation of capital itself? Immediate experience would suggest a positive response to such questions. The theory appears to indicate otherwise. Can we reconcile the two?

What Marxian theory teaches is that capitalism operates under the perpetual and relentless imperative to revolutionize the productive forces (understood in terms of the value productivity of labour power). This is, we have argued, an abstract proposition rendered concrete by reference to the specifics of technological change.[16] Both Marx and Braverman may here be judged guilty of a too facile transition from the abstraction to the very concrete strategies of deskilling. A closer inspection of what happens on the shop floor indicates that the intersection of worker resistance and managerial counter-pressure is a very intricate affair, which does not have entirely predictable results; the subtle mixes of coercion, co-optation and integration that make up the strategy of management are met with equally subtle responses of resistance and co-operation on the part of workers. And we also become aware, as Friedman points out, of the limitations of both repression and worker autonomy within the production process. When taken to their limits, neither strategy appears entirely viable, and social relations within the enterprise will therefore almost inevitably entail a fluctuating balance between the two.[17]

But what does all this signify? First, it most definitely says that we cannot understand the political consciousness of workers without careful consideration of how these processes operate. But this, in itself, says nothing in

[16] Various attempts exist to tighten up Marx's interpretation, and some of them are extremely useful; see, for example, Brighton Labour Process Group (1977) and Palloix (1976). Elger's (1979) review is also well worth consulting, both for the information it contains and for the position it espouses.

[17] Friedman (1977a; 1977b) and Burawoy (1978; 1979) both explore this process with some care.

particular about the pace, direction and content of the accumulation of capital. The concrete forms of technology, organization and authority can vary greatly from one place to another, from one firm to another, as long as such variations do not challenge the accumulation process. There are, evidently, more ways to make a profit than there are to skin a cat. And if the value productivity of labour can be better secured by some reasonable level of worker autonomy, then so be it. Capital is, presumably, indifferent to how the value productivity of labour is preserved and enhanced. And it is this indifference that is captured in the abstract concept of productive forces.

What Marx, for his part, primarily focuses upon is the extraordinary power of capital to adapt to the varying circumstances in which it finds itself — circumstances that include tremendous diversity 'in nature' as well as in 'human nature'. For example, the threat of capital mobility, plant closures, 'runaway shops' and consequent job loss is a powerful force with which to discipline labour. Such adaptations on the part of capital are not without their costs or internal contradictions, but in the long run what Marx predicts is that worker resistance must give way before these tremendous powers of adaptation. And the guiding force behind all this is the tendency to equalize the profit rate through competition. The noble rearguard action fought here, the specific resistance offered there, may be important for understanding the uneven development of world capitalism (why, for example, British industry lagged behind that of other nations), but they fade into insignificance, become irrelevant, when judged against the broad sweep of the history of capitalist accumulation.

It is precisely in relation to the adaptive powers of capital in general and to the processes of competition in particular that Marx's critics get into the most frightful tangles. On the one hand, Friedman and Elbaum et al. seem to want to deny the efficacy of competition as the guiding imperative to perpetual revolutions in the productive forces in order to replace it by class struggle within production.[18] It is rather as if, having got inside the labour process in a most instructive way, they then forget there is a whole world out there of competitive pricing, disinvestment and reinvestment, mobility of money capital, etc. What Marx depicts as the mutual disciplining effect of the law of value in exchange and within production is totally ignored. Burawoy, for his part, while making much of the ideological, political and economic significance of shop floor struggles, is forced to come back to competition in order to explain why such struggles have not themselves become the source of change in the labour process. And in so doing he comes up with a conclusion,

---

[18] Elbaum et al. (1979, pp. 228–9) argue that competition divides capitalists and thereby checks the ability of capitalists to use new technologies to undermine the power of their workers. We take up the manner in which competition and class struggle intersect in relation to technological change in section III below.

frequently implied in other works of this sort, that 'class struggle was not the gravedigger of capitalism but its saviour' (1979, pp. 178–9, 195).

Interestingly enough, this provides us with the clue for putting struggles on the shop floor into proper perspective. Like economistic struggles over the wage rate (see above, chapter 2), they are a part of the perpetual guerilla warfare between capital and labour. Workers place limits on the leverage of capital with respect to technological change, but managerial counter-pressure likewise prevents any real movement towards genuine worker autonomy or self-management. Within the ebb and flow of worker militancy and managerial counter-pressure, we can spot a trend towards 'the introduction of long-term uni-directional change in the labour process'. The cyclical dynamics of shop floor struggles are equilibrators for long-term changes within the overall trajectory of capitalist development (Burawoy, 1979, p. 178). From this standpoint, such struggles must indeed by viewed as frictional and transient, which is not to say that they are politically or ideologically unimportant. They can provide the basis for broader and grander political struggles, although the necessary fetishisms that surround them prevent any automatic translation of the experience of them into more general states of political consciousness.[19]

Struggles of this sort play a very important role for capital. They are, on the one hand, a perpetual threat to the system. But, on the other, they help stabilize affairs for one basic and very fundamental reason. Perpetually accelerating technological change can be extraordinarily destructive for capital – it is, as we shall see, a major source of instability (imagine a society in which technologies were changed every night!). Worker resistance can restrain the pace of technological change, and to the degree that this puts a floor under competition it can help stabilize the course of capitalist development. There is here a 'terrain of compromise' upon which capital may be reluctantly willing to operate. In much the same way that capitalists came to see the benefits to be had from regulating the working day once the social costs of not so doing had become readily apparent, so they may come to recognize the benefit of institutionalized forms of negotiation with labour over the pace and direction of technological change. The problem for capital is to avoid unnecessary disruptions within the work process and to achieve that pace and configuration of technological change consistent with sustained accumulation. Capital is not necessarily successful in this, and, as we shall see, there are forces at work that militate against any successful resolution to this problem. But capitalists are surely aware of the immense dangers that lurk in unrestricted technological change, and almost certainly come to regard negotiation with labour on the shop floor as part of a package of controls – others include monopolization and state regulation – that contain technological

[19] We are here simply echoing Marx and Lenin on the difference between economistic 'trade union' consciousness and 'revolutionary socialist' consciousness.

change within certain bounds acceptable to them. From this standpoint, the modest restraints placed upon them through worker militancy may be regarded as helpful. The problem, of course, is that workers' demands are not always known for their modesty, and at that point capital must react with all the force and power it can muster.[20]

This leaves us with one residual problem of some importance. Both Marx and Braverman indicate that the reduction from skilled to simple abstract labour comes about through the technical division of labour, mechanization, automation and scientific management. Furthermore, 'for Marx, the tendency of the evolution of the labour process was to create a homogeneous industrial proletariat which would discover its unity in its common subjection to capital through the destruction of "traditional" and "pre-industrial" skills.' Elbaum et al. claim that such views are too simple.

> Whatever the technical structure of production, capitalists may require hierarchical divisions of labour as modes of management. And in the determination of the structure of these hierarchies, formal and informal struggles by strategic groups of workers often play a crucial role. . . . not only did the . . . development of industrial capitalism fail to eliminate all such 'traditional' groups as craftsmen and even out-workers, but also the relations between different groups of workers (especially craftsmen and the less skilled) have played a crucial role in determining the structure of the division of labour which emerges from technical change. (Elbaum et al., 1979, pp. 228–9)

A variety of issues are involved here – questions of historical veracity in different accounts of the evolution of the labour process, questions of political strategy and ideology, of class consciousness, etc. But the most important issue at this point in our investigation of the capitalist mode of production concerns the reduction from skilled to simple labour. If the historical evolution of the labour process has not moved towards such a reduction, then what credence can we place upon a theory of value that presupposes that such a reduction has occurred? Certainly, the accounts labour historians now provide indicate that, if the reduction has occurred at all, it is by a process that has taken a most tortuous and convoluted path.[21] We find ourselves forced to reflect, once more, upon the relation between the theory of the capitalist mode of production as a whole and the historical evolution of capitalist social formations.

[20] The widespread existence of co-operation between management and labour that Burawoy (1979) finds ought, I believe, to be interpreted in the light of this. When two parties co-operate and one holds considerably more power (in the final analysis) than the other, then the voluntary nature of the co-operation might reasonably be called into question. I feel somewhat similarly sceptical when I read that suspects are 'co-operating' with the authorities in the investigation of some crime.

[21] The works of Montgomery (1979), Stone (1974) and Zeitlin (1979) provide some excellent examples.

We can begin by simplifying the problem. First, the separation of managerial and technically based hierarchies is in principle irrelevant because both have a role in mobilizing the productive powers of labour for the creation of surplus value. Secondly, Marx most certainly did not argue that the reduction of skilled to simple abstract labour entailed the homogenization of the work force to the point where no skills were left. The reduction meant the elimination of *monopolizable skills* and the creation of a flexible skill pattern which allowed of relatively easy substitutions. The skills then remaining could reasonably be accounted for as so many multiples of simple abstract labour. Finally, we must recall Marx's insistence that the reduction itself has nothing to do directly with the pattern of wage differentials based on costs of production or 'on distinctions that have long ago ceased to be real, and that survive only by virtue of a traditional convention' (*Capital,* vol. 1, p. 197). The wage system, by obscuring the origin of surplus value, characteristically contains all kinds of distortions and oddities – piece work, for example, could have substantial differential effects on the rewards of labourers and so give 'wider scope' to 'individuality, and with it the sense of liberty, independence and self-control of the labourers' as well as to 'their competition one with another' (*Capital,* vol. 1, p. 555). Marx was undoubtedly not finely attuned to the details of wage determination or its hierarchical ordering. But this was simply because he did not attribute great importance to this 'surface appearance' of things. The essential measure of the reduction of skilled to simple labour lies in the degree to which capitalism has created skills that are easily reproducible and easily substitutable. All of the evidence suggests that this has been the direction in which capitalism has been moving, with substantial islands of resistance here and innumerable pockets of resistance there. To the extent that the reduction of skilled to simple labour is still in the course of being accomplished, we have to conclude that capitalism is in the course of becoming more true to the law of value implied in its dominant mode of production.[22] From this standpoint, at least, there seems to be little ground for disputing Marx's or Braverman's basic line of argument.

III THE SOURCES OF TECHNOLOGICAL CHANGE UNDER CAPITALISM

That capitalist society has exhibited an extraordinary degree of technological and organizational dynamism throughout its history is self-evident. The difficulty is to explain this dynamism in a way that locates its origins within

[22] We ought to remark that perfection of competition is similarly vital to the achievement of pure value relations in the sphere of exchange, but nowhere has such perfection ever existed, even though, as we shall see in chapter 5, the historical tendency within capitalism has been towards a perfection of competition.

society rather than treating it as some external force with its own autonomous dynamic.[23] It is in this regard that we find Marx at his most powerful as
both analyst and critic. He will broadly ascribe the technological and organizational dynamism of capitalism to a desperate struggle, waged by capital, to
stabilize the inherently unstable conditions of class reproduction. He will
measure the limits to this process and explore its contradictions. He will
fashion a theory of crisis formation. And he will in part base his plea for the
transition to socialism upon the need to cure the gross irrationalities that arise
out of the burgeoning contradiction between growth in the productive forces
and the social relations upon which the capitalist mode of production is
based.

When we turn to consider the matrix of social relations that impel technological change, we find ourselves confronted with some confusing cross-
currents which run into each other in interesting ways. Competition among
capitalists and, to a lesser degree, within the working class plays an important
role, but we cannot judge the response to that competition in isolation from
the central cleavage between capital and labour which is the hallmark of
capitalist social relations. Consider, for example, the possible responses of
capitalists to heightened competition. They can (1) lower the wage rate, (2)
increase the intensity of use of an existing production system, (3) invest in a
new production system, (4) economize on constant capital inputs (run old
machinery longer, use energy and raw material inputs more efficiently, seek
cheaper raw materials in the market, etc.), (5) seek out more efficient 'factor
combinations' and substitutions, (6) change the social organization of production (job structures, chains of command) in the search for more efficient
management, (7) appeal to the workers to co-operate and work harder in
order to save their jobs, (8) come up with new strategies for marketing
(product differentiation, advertising, etc.), (9) change location (see chapter
12). Through one, or any combination, of these responses, individual
capitalists can hope to preserve or improve their competitive position. The
strategy that is chosen will depend upon circumstances and possibilities as
well as upon managerial predilections. The course of technological change
under such conditions appears hard to predict.

But Marx's central point is that competition impels capitalism towards
perpetual revolutions in the productive forces by whatever means of whatever sort. Capitalists compete with each other in the realm of exchange. Each
has the possibility to alter his own production process so that it becomes more
efficient than the social average. This is a source of relative surplus value to
them. Once the competitors have caught up, the original innovators have
every incentive to leap ahead once more in order to sustain the relative surplus
value they were previously capturing. There is plenty of opportunity here, of

[23] Magaline (1975) has an excellent review of both Marxian and non-Marxian
perspectives on these questions. For a good example of the latter see Heertje (1977).

course, for the enterprising, imaginative and individualistic entrepreneur – that inspiring and noble individual so important to the folklore of capitalism and so frequently depicted as the sole fount of its technological dynamism.[24]

The social consequence of competition is, of course, to force continuous leap-frogging in the adoption of new technologies and new organizational forms independent of the will of any particular entrepreneur – provided, of course, markets remain competitive. The only question posed is: what are the limits to such a process?

But capitalists are also highly interdependent upon one another, and the degree of interdependency increases with proliferation in the division of labour. Spillover and multiplier effects become significant:

> A radical change in the mode of production in one sphere of industry involves a similar change in other spheres. This happens at first in such branches of industry as are connected together by being separate phases of a process, and yet are isolated by the social division of labour, in such a way, that each of them produces an independent commodity. Thus spinning by machinery made weaving by machinery a necessity, and both together made the mechanical and chemical revolution that took place in bleaching, printing and dyeing, imperative. . . . But more especially, the revolution in the modes of production of industry and agriculture made necessary a revolution in the general conditions of the social process of production, i.e., in the means of communication and of transport [which] . . . became gradually adapted to the modes of production of mechanical industry, by the creation of a system of river steamers, railways, ocean steamers, and telegraphs. But the huge masses of iron that had now to be forged, to be welded, to be cut, to be bored, and to be shaped, demanded, on their part, cyclopean machines. . . . Modern Industry had therefore itself to take in hand the machine, its characteristic instrument of production, and to construct machines by machines. It was not till it did this, that it built up for itself a fitting technical foundation, and stood on its own feet. (*Capital,* vol. 1, pp. 383–4)

There seems to be no end to such a spiral of multiplier effects. To begin with any uneven development of the productive forces within different phases of a vertically integrated system of production will pose problems for the smooth flow of inputs and outputs from unworked raw material to finished product. And it is hard to imagine how technological structures can ever be exactly right to equilibrate such a process. The general spillover effects into other spheres will also likely be marked by uneven development and spiralling side-effects. Consider, for example, those technological changes that decrease the cost and time of circulation. As the division of labour proliferates and

[24] Schumpeter (1934; 1939) is probably the most unabashed advocate of this idea within intellectually respectable circles.

market interactions become more complex, so these costs tend to rise and the pressure to reduce them mounts. From the physical standpoint this means pressure to reduce the cost and time of movement of commodities and to economize on costs of wholesaling, retailing and merchandizing. Innovations that affect the speed with which money can circulate (the credit system), and with which information can be gathered and disseminated – the telegraph, telephone, radio, telex, etc. – also become imperative. Even the household is not immune: the technology of final consumption must keep pace with the requirement to absorb the increasing quantities of commodities produced.

At one point in time there will likely be considerable unevenness in the development of the productive forces as between individual firms, industries and even whole sectors and regions. But the technological states are not independent of each other. Each serves to define the other through multiple interaction effects. These are extremely difficult to trace. Indeed, so extensive are the interactions, so wide the ramifications, that technological change appears to assume an autonomous dynamic, entirely divorced from its origins in capitalist competition and class relations. Technological change can become 'fetishized' as a 'thing in itself', as an exogenous guiding force in the history of capitalism. The presumption of the necessity and inevitability of technological change becomes so strong that the striving for it – embodied in a prevailing ideology of technological progress – becomes an end in itself.

What this all points to is a never-ending and ever-accelerating spiral of technological change, sparked by competition and sustained by way of multiplier effects reverberating through increasingly integrated spheres of economic activity. The remarkable thing under such circumstances is not that capitalist society is technologically dynamic, but that its dynamism has been so muted and controlled. That this is the case must in part be attributed to barriers that arise out of the social relations of capitalism. Consider, then, the barriers capital itself erects against the tendency towards perpetually accelerating technological and organizational change.

Any technological and organizational change incurs direct and indirect costs. Among the former are outlays on new plant and equipment, the cost of retraining the work force and other direct costs of implementation. Among the latter are managerial inexperience with new techniques or new systems of authority, worker resistance and even sabotage of methods to which workers are not accustomed or which they find degrading, hours lost learning on the job, plus a wide variety of unforeseen externality effects that did not enter into the initial calculations. Any firm has to weigh the costs and benefits of change in relation to existing and expected states of competition. Since many of these costs and benefits are unknown and the state of competition ever unpredictable, the individual capacity and penchant for taking risks – again, made much of by bourgeois interpreters of capitalist history – enters in as a mediating element.

Chief among the potential costs, however, are those that attach to the premature retirement of fixed capital that has not yet been fully amortized. The value embodied in machinery and other forms of fixed capital can be recouped only over a certain time period. Revolutions in the productive forces can have disastrous impacts here and force producers to take large losses if new equipment (cheaper and more efficient) comes on to the market. This takes us into territory we will explore in detail in chapter 8. For the moment we simply note the irony that fixed capital, which is itself one of the chief means employed to increase the productivity of social labour, becomes, once it is installed, a barrier to further innovation. Thus does capital constitute barriers to its own dynamic within itself.

The potential disruptive effects of technological change can be traced throughout the whole system of production and realization of value. Major changes are hard to absorb and can deliver a severe shock to the stability of the system. When development becomes too uneven it can spawn crises of disproportionality between, for example, the capacity to produce means of production in relation to the capacity to produce consumer goods. Leaving aside the disciplining effects of crises, other forces are at work which serve to moderate the arbitrary and potentially catastrophic insertion of technological change into what is often a rather delicately balanced system of production and realization. Individual firms will naturally be reluctant to adopt innovations that increase their output beyond what the system can absorb. Aware of bottlenecks in transport and communications, or in market capacity, firms will temper their push towards competitive technological change and settle for average rather than excess profits. And, in so far as the end result of competition is always some degree of monopolization, monopolistic practices become part of a strategy to control the overall pace of technological change. The active participation of the state through patent laws, funding of basic research and so on can add to an impressive battery of potential controls which hold the tendency towards perpetual acceleration in technological progress in check. We will take up these matters in chapter 5.

The barriers to technological and organizational change are there. In serving to keep the pace of change in bounds reasonable to capital, they help to equilibrate what could otherwise be a dangerously unstable process. When taken to extremes, such barriers act as barriers to accumulation itself and must therefore be overcome if capitalism is to survive. The path of technological change has never been exactly smooth, but the forces that regulate it have to be quite delicately balanced if the smooth continuation of the accumulation of capital is to be assured.

Some of the mechanisms whereby such a delicate balance is maintained become more evident when we introduce the class relation between capital and labour into the picture. We have already seen that the value of labour power, assuming a constant standard of living in physical terms, is reduced by the rising productivity of labour in the wage goods sector, but that countervailing forces are also at work to ensure that labour gets an 'equilibrium share' of total value produced. If labour gets more than its share and wages move above value in a way that threatens accumulation, so pressure will mount to introduce technologies that save on labour power and induce unemployment. The production of a relative surplus population which brings wages down and checks the power of labour relative to capital becomes a crucial device for ensuring the perpetuation of accumulation in the face of changing conditions of labour supply. Technology can likewise be put to work to diminish the power of organized labour, either on the shop floor or at the bargaining table. Machinery, Marx argues, 'is the most powerful weapon for repressing strikes, those periodical revolts of the working class against the autocracy of capital'. The steam engine, for example, 'enabled the capitalist to tread under foot the growing claims of workmen, who threatened the newly-born factory system with a crisis'. Indeed, 'it would be possible to write a history of the inventions made since 1830, for the sole purpose of supplying capital with weapons against the revolts of the working class' (*Capital,* vol. 1, pp. 435–6). The dynamics of capitalist competition would again seem to point towards complete destruction of the economic and political power of labour.

But there are countervailing tendencies at work also – tendencies that put a floor under competition and therefore serve to regulate the pace of technological change. Whether or not fixed capital would be employed depends, for example, upon 'the difference between the value of the machine and the value of the labour power replaced by it.' Given international differences in the quantity of price of labour power, it was in no way surprising that machines invented in England would be 'employed only in North America' and that England, 'the land of machinery', should at the same time be characterized by a 'shameful squandering of human labour power for the most despicable purposes'. The reason could be put quite brutally: 'in England women are still occasionally used instead of horses for hauling canal boats, because the labour required to produce horses and machines is an accurately known quantity, while that required to maintain the women of the surplus population is below all calculation' (*Capital,* vol. 1, pp. 392–4). At times when the industrial reserve army becomes massive, capital will have abundant incentives to go back to labour-intensive techniques (hence the contemporary revival of the sweatshop even in advanced capitalist countries). The stimulus for more complex forms of technological and organizational change is certainly blunted at times of chronic labour surplus.

We have also argued that class struggle on the shop floor has an important role to play as an equilibriating device. Such struggles can serve to check the dangerous acceleration of technological change in myriad ways (new technologies require some degree of worker co-operation when they are introduced, for example). The perpetual guerilla warfare on the shop floor can therefore play both positive and negative roles in the stabilization of capitalism.

But the exact relations here are very complex. We can be sure that the imperative to accumulate lies perpetually in the background. The problem is that the actual forms of technological and organizational change are so various, and the forces that regulate them are so intertwined, that we cannot readily distinguish them. Although technological change plays a central role in Marxian theory, we do not have a complete understanding of it. That capitalist competition and interdependency as well as class struggle between capital and labour form the pivot on which the analysis turns there can be no doubt. But the interaction and multiplier effects are incompletely analysed, as are the consequences of the direct production of new scientific knowledges.

This indicates a serious lacuna in Marx's exposition. The gap is there, but we must interpret its meaning correctly. If, after all, the technology of a particular labour process is an expression and an embodiment of the central contradictions of capitalism, as Marx frequently avers, then a full understanding of the former depends upon a complete unravelling of the latter. An understanding of technology must therefore be regarded as an end-product of that line of enquiry that Marx did not complete.

Yet we cannot even begin upon the analysis of the laws of motion of capitalism without laying down some conceptualization of technology at the outset. This Marx does by way of the abstract concepts of productive force and social relations as these are embodied within the concrete materiality of the labour process. Marx can thereby abstract from the specific details of actual technological changes and simply argue that revolutions in the productive forces are a necessary product of the social relations of capitalism. But a deeper understanding of that, like the understanding of the law of value itself, must emerge in the course of the subsequent investigation. What Marx seeks to prove is that the revolutions in the productive forces are ultimately antagonistic to the very social relations that spawned them. Herein, in Marx's view, lay the central contradiction of capitalism: that between the evolution of the productive forces and the social relations.

Marx's proof of this general proposition is partial and incomplete. We must first see how far he progressed down this difficult road, and then, through critical evaluation, try to push his argument to its limits.

IV THE TECHNICAL, ORGANIC AND VALUE COMPOSITIONS OF CAPITAL

We now take up the difficult question of the impact of perpetual revolutions in the productive forces upon capital itself. In so doing, it will be convenient to assume that the concrete technologies employed (in Marx's broad sense of that term, which includes all organizational characteristics) faithfully express the underlying configuration of productive forces. We will likewise work with *values,* on the assumption that all commodities trade at their values (prices reflect values). Such assumptions permit a greater degree of generality to the discussion and allow us to talk more freely of the *potential* concrete effects of underlying forces in a way that is *potentially* generalizable to historical experience. The tentative character of such identifications and the hypothetical character of the resulting generalizations should be apparent from our previous remarks.

A particular technological state is associated, in the first instance, with a certain physical productivity of labour power. This physical productivity is measured in diverse, non-comparable units – the number of yards of cloth woven, the number of shoes made, the tons of iron and steel produced, etc., per labourer per hour. Marx calls such ratios 'the technical composition of capital'. When reduced to a common basis of values, these ratios are expressed in terms of proportion of constant to variable capital employed in a standardized production period. The ratio c/v is called 'the value composition of capital'. In some cases the ratio $c/(v + s)$ is preferred as the measure, since this more accurately captures the ratio between past 'dead' labour (means of production of all sorts owned by the capitalist) and the new value added by 'living labour'. Different industries and sectors may then be compared according to the different value compositions of their capitals. Constant capital-intensive industries exhibit high value compositions, while those industries that employ a lot of living labour lie at the other end of the scale of value composition.

We have already seen how and why capitalists must resort to technological change. This means that the technical compositions of capital are perpetually shifting. The next step is to show how changes in technical composition affect value composition. To do this Marx introduces the concept of the 'organic composition of capital'. This, he says, is 'the value composition, in so far as it is determined by its technical composition and mirrors changes in the latter' (*Capital,* vol. 1, p. 612). The immediate implication of this remark is that the value composition can also change for reasons that have nothing to do with the technical composition.

We have here three concepts crucial to the argument that follows. Unfortunately, there is a good deal of confusion in Marx's thought – and a quite massive confusion in the subsequent literature – as to the relations between the technical, organic and value compositions of capital. The distinction between the value and organic compositions, for example, appears very important. Yet at some points we find Marx using the terms interchangeably while at others he seems to stress that the terms should be kept separate. The inconsistency of usage can in part be explained by the fact that he came to these concepts relatively late and did not manage a proper refinement of them. The concept of organic composition, for example, appears only with the third printing of the first volume of *Capital,* presumably as a foretaste of ideas to come in the unfinished third volume. However this may be, there is a good deal of confusion here which must be sorted out.[25]

Consider, first, the idea that the value composition can alter for reasons other than changes in technical composition. In his critiques of Ricardo and Cherbuliez (*Theories of Surplus Value,* pt 2, pp. 275–89; pt 3, pp. 382–96), Marx suggests value composition can and does alter independently of the forces that regulate the organic composition. In the chapter on 'Absolute Rent' in *Capital,* (vol. 3, p. 766), he goes even further: 'capitals of equal organic composition may be of different value-composition, and capitals with identical percentages of value-composition may show varying degrees of organic composition and thus express different stages in the development of the social productivity of labour'. Since there is, presumably, only one value-ratio that can prevail within a production process, this rather extraordinary statement puts us in something of a quandary as to the exact interpretation to be put upon the organic composition *vis-à-vis* the value composition. After this, certainly, we cannot treat organic and value composition as identical terms (as is so frequently done in the literature).

Marx apparently intended to reserve the term 'organic composition' to indicate those shifts in technology *within* an enterprise that affect the value composition of capital. It is a label that identifies a particular *source* of shifts in value composition. The significance of such an identification lies in this: the technological mix within the enterprise is broadly under the control of individual capitalists, who can and do (as far as they are able) alter it in their restless pursuit of surplus value, either in response to competition or out of concern for the state of class struggle. The dynamics of such a process can be understood independently of the fluctuating costs of inputs into production.

But the value compositions will also be altered by a variety of considerations over which individual capitalists have no control. The external forces regulating value composition are diverse in their origin, but we can usefully separate them into two groups. First, we should consider 'accidental and conjunctural' forces that affect the value of inputs capitalists purchase on the market. These vary from climatic 'accidents' (no matter whether they are induced by human action), disruptions in trade, wars, the systematic exploration of the earth's surface for more 'productive' resources, etc., all of which affect the socially necessary labour time required to produce commodities.

[25] The position I take is broadly similar to that laid out in Fine and Harris (1979), but I am particularly indebted to Dumenil (1975; 1977) for stimulating ideas on the subject. There is a good deal of literature now emanating from the more mathematically minded, such as Roemer (1977; 1978), but by far the most instructive work is that by von Weizsäcker (1977). Robinson (1978), as might be expected, also provides a spirited contribution which cannot too easily be dismissed.

Second, we have to consider the multitude of interaction and multiplier effects that link the productivity of labour in one sector with the value of the inputs to another. These interaction effects, which have their origins within the work process, are nonetheless not under the control of the individual capitalist. Put another way, the value composition of capital within one production process is crucially dependent upon the state of technology adopted by entrepreneurs producing the inputs to that production process.

This contrast between the forces internal and external to the enterprise is very significant, and it is, I believe, the idea Marx was seeking to capture in distinguishing between value and organic compositions. Individual capitalists control their own production process and select their technology according to economic circumstances. But they operate in a market environment in which the values of inputs are fixed by forces over which no one individual has control, even though the individual technological choices of entrepreneurs have systemic multiplier effects. What Marx will eventually seek to prove is that seemingly rational individual choices on the part of individuals will threaten the basis for accumulation and therefore the very survival of the capitalist class. It was this contradiction that Marx sought to capture by way of the twin concepts of value and organic composition.

The first volume of *Capital* considers production from the standpoint of the individual entrepreneur seeking to maximize profits under competition. Only those technological innovations that capture relative surplus value within the firm are considered. Although the multiplier effects of technological innovations are mentioned, the impact these might have upon the value ratios of inputs are generally ignored except in the case of variable capital – the falling value of labour power as a result of rising productivity in industries producing wage goods is considered a prime source of relative surplus value to the capitalists. We here encounter the supposed 'labour-saving bias' in Marx's account of technological innovation. But with the focus of attention upon technological change within the firm, Marx can conclude that there is an inevitable tendency for the value composition to rise as a result of the increasing physical productivity of labour. This idea emerges strongly in the third volume of *Capital* (p. 212):

> The same quantity of labour-power set in motion by a variable capital of a given value, operate, work up and productively consume in the same time span an ever-increasing quantity of means of labour, machinery and fixed capital of all sorts, raw and auxiliary materials – and consequently a constant capital of an ever-increasing value. This continuous relative decrease of the variable capital *vis-à-vis* the constant . . . is identical with the progressively higher organic value composition of the social capital in its average. It is likewise just another expression for the progressive development of the social productivity of labour.

The supposed 'law' of the 'rising organic composition of capital' plays a vital role in Marx's argument, and we must therefore consider it carefully. What Marx is saying is that the ratio of 'dead' to 'living' labour tends to rise as a result of technological innovation within the firm. But he does not prove to us that this is necessarily the case. Indeed, as we probe deeper into his argument we find that all kinds of difficulties attach to the manner in which he formulates the problem. It turns out that he has not entirely freed himself from the misconceptions of traditional political economy. Let us see in what respects this is so.

Traditional political economy handled the structure of capitalist production in terms of a stock of fixed capital and flows of circulating capital. Profit was then interpreted as a flow of real gains to be had from the proper employment of a stock of assets (money or physical plant). Marx broke with this conception and substituted the distinction between constant and variable capital. He conceived of both as flows.[26] Capital, recall, is defined by Marx as a *process* in which value undergoes an expansion, and he therefore sought definitions that reflected the flow of this process. Labour power is used to preserve the value of means of production used up at the same time as it adds value – 'by the very act of adding new value, [the labourer] preserves former values' (*Capital,* vol. 1, p. 199). The value composition of capital represents the ratio between the value being preserved and the value being added. It is a ratio between two flows. The concept of organic composition, we have seen, focuses our attention on the manner in which technological change within the production process enables the same quantity of applied labour power to preserve and expand greater value than previously. Two difficulties then arise.

First of all, we can see directly that the value composition of capital as Marx measures it is highly sensitive to the degree of vertical integration in production processes. If a production process starts with raw cotton and ends with a shirt, the value of the initial input of constant capital is small compared with the variable capital applied. If that same production process is split into two independent firms, one of which produces cotton cloth and the other shirts, then the quantity of constant capital appears to increase because the labour embodied in the production of cloth now appears as the constant capital purchased by the shirt-makers.

We can illustrate this idea diagrammatically (see figure 4.1).[27] Consider a process that commences at time t_0 with an initial input of constant capital, c_0,

[26] Blaug (1968, p. 229) complains bitterly at the way Marx 'shuffled freely between stock and flow definitions without warning the reader', while von Weizsäcker (1977, p. 201) comments that 'what Marx was really after is the ratio of constant capital (a stock) to the product of variable capital and the speed of turnover of variable capital (a flow)'. The latter part of this definition is helpful, but I would argue that Marx is also interested in the labour process as a flow which actively preserves constant capital.

[27] The idea comes basically from Dumenil (1975).

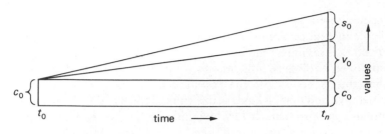

Figure 4.1

and which proceeds until time t_n by adding variable capital to the value of v_0 and adding surplus value, s_0. The value composition of capital in this case is c_0/v_0. Now consider this same production process broken into two segments at time t_k such that the total value at that moment becomes the constant capital input, c_2, into the second segment of the process (see figure 4.2). The average value composition in this case is $(c_1 + c_2)/(v_1 + v_2)$, which is obviously much greater than c_0/v_0.

A stocks-and-flows model of this process finds the quantity of constant capital stock sensitive to the degree of vertical integration. A pure-flow model degenerates quickly into the *reductio ad absurdum* that only that labour which is being embodied at this very moment is living labour, while all other labour has to be characterized as past 'dead' labour. The latter model can be saved only by considering how these flows are broken by market exchanges, which brings us back, once more, to the question of degree of vertical integration.

This difficulty is by no means as damaging to Marx's argument as it seems at first sight. After all, he includes organizational characteristics, in his characterization of technology, and the levels of centralization and concentration, in which the problem of vertical integration must also be included, are of vital concern to him. Indeed, we can use this apparent difficulty in creative ways. If vertical concentration has the effect of lowering the value

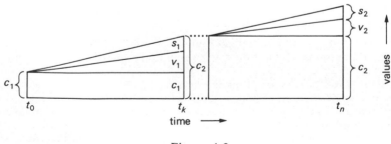

Figure 4.2

composition of capital – always assuming, of course, that the actual production technology remains constant – then it can provide a mechanism that counteracts the supposed 'law of rising organic composition'. Before we get too carried away with this idea, we had better consider certain important circumstances that modify it.

The second volume of *Capital* deals with the process of circulation of capital. The act of production is now treated as a moment in a circulation process. We here learn to appreciate fully what it means to conceive of capital as a process, as a *flow*. We are exposed to an analysis of circulation costs, turnover, production and circulation times, as well as to the peculiarities of circulation of fixed capital. Most important of all, from the standpoint of the problem we are presently considering, the turnover times of variable and constant capital as well as surplus value are examined in some detail.

Technological change is seen to be important and necessary in each of these respects. The diminution of circulation costs and the shortening of turnover times can serve to accelerate accumulation. The use of fixed capital poses a problem, since on the one hand it can serve to increase the value productivity of labour while on the other hand it requires a longer turnover time and so diminishes accumulation. The impact of these technological changes upon value composition – within firms as well as in society as a whole – is not explored in any coherent fashion. In a few scattered passages Marx seems to suggest that faster turnover times increase value compositions. But by and large the concept of value or organic composition is totally ignored in the second volume of *Capital*.

Plainly, the value composition of capital is very sensitive to the relative turnover rates of both variable and constant capital. If the time taken to regain the variable capital decreases, then the variable capital advanced decreases and the value composition rises, even though the quantity of labour power employed remains exactly the same. The turnover time of constant capital is even more problematic. We have to deal with various raw material and energy inputs, which may be turned over at different rates, as well as with fixed capital (machinery, buildings, etc.), which may be turned over very slowly relative to other items. It is not easy to come up with a measure of volume of constant capital being preserved under these conditions. Even leaving aside the thorny problems that attach to the circulation of fixed capital (see chapter 8), it should be evident that an acceleration in the turnover time of constant capital reduces the value composition of capital.

Independently of the degree of vertical integration, therefore, the relative turnover times of variable and constant capital within the firm have a direct impact upon the value compositions of the capitals used in production. Under the right circumstances, the falling value composition achieved through increasing vertical integration could be more than offset by the increasing turnover time of the constant relative to the variable capital used.

But the analysis presented in the second volume of *Capital* also indicates to us other circumstances that militate directly against increasing vertical integration in production. The general circulation of capital takes the form

$$M–C \begin{pmatrix} LP \\ MP \end{pmatrix} \dots P \dots C'–M' \text{ (etc.).}$$

How long should capital remain within production before testing its value in the sphere of exchange? Marx's answer to that question is: as short a time as possible, since capital is value only when it is in motion, i.e., in the act of being transformed from money into productive activity into commodities into money, and so on. There is a strong incentive, therefore, to accelerate the turnover of capital as much as possible. This militates against vertical integration of production, since the latter requires that capital remain for a longer period in production before entering the sphere of exchange. The splitting of a production process into many different phases and firms linked through market exchange appears to be highly desirable, since it diminishes the turnover time of capital. For this reason, even large corporations prefer to sub-contract a lot of production to small firms with shorter turnover times. But the effect of this, as we have seen, is to increase the value composition of capital independently of any changes that may be instituted with respect to production processes. We will examine the implications of this for the capitalist organization of production in the next chapter.

There is one other respect in which the framework built up in the second volume of *Capital* provides us with a means to analyse the forces that regulate the value composition of capital. In the last two chapters of that volume Marx constructs a disaggregated model of an economy and examines the conditions for equilibrium growth (see below, chapter 6). This disaggregated model provides an interesting format for exploring some of the interaction effects of technological change in different sectors of an economy. Consider an economy divided into two sectors producing necessities (which fix the value of labour power) and means of production (the elements of constant capital). If the rate of technological change is higher in the sector producing necessities, then the overall value composition of capital will tend to increase because of the relative saving on outlays of variable capital. Otherwise, the rising productivity of labour in the sector producing means of production becomes a lever for lowering the aggregate value composition of capital. Whether or not, therefore, the aggregate value composition of capital increases in response to technological innovation depends entirely upon the sectors in which these technological changes occur and the interaction effects these changes have throughout the economy as a whole.[28] We have here the

[28] Howard and King (1975, pp. 198–9) summarize the argument on this. See also Heertje (1972) for a technical presentation.

possibility to discriminate between constant-capital saving, variable-capital saving or neutral forms of technological change.

There are, it seems, a whole host of considerations that derive from the volume 2 analysis, which have implications for understanding the impact of technological and organizational change upon the value composition of capital. Few of these considerations are picked up in the third volume. Since the latter is supposed to deal with capitalist production as a whole, as a unity of production, exchange and realization, the omission is somewhat surprising. It has a simple enough explanation. The draft of the third volume that has come down to us was written relatively early, before the extensive investigations recorded in the second volume were undertaken.

We can only speculate as to what Marx might have written in the third volume of *Capital* if he had revised it subsequent to completing the unfinished business of the second. But we can avoid some unnecessary confusions if we keep the overall thrust of his project in mind. And we can even take some fairly modest and simple steps to clarify and advance his argument.

V   TECHNOLOGICAL CHANGE AND ACCUMULATION

We have shown why capitalism is necessarily technologically dynamic, why it exists under the imperative: 'innovate or perish!' Quite simply, the dominant class relations of capitalism enforce and ensure perpetual reorganizations of the labour process in the search for relative surplus value. To be sure, capitalists do not operate in a void, and they encounter a variety of checks – class struggle within the labour process, the limits of scientific and technological knowledge, problems of writing off values embodied in old machinery and equipment, the sheer cost of change, etc. The pace, form and direction of technological change is constrained in important ways. And we also know that the underlying imperative perpetually to revolutionize the productive forces (understood as an abstract proposition) can be realized through the achievement of a wide variety of actual technological states (understood as the particular configuration of hardware and social organization which preserves and promotes the productivity of labour). And, above all, we have seen how important it is to emphasize that it is the *value* productivity of labour which is, in the end, all that matters. Changes in physical productivity are but a means to that end. Technological change exists, therefore, as the prime lever for furthering the accumulation of capital through perpetual increases in the value productivity of labour power.

If we subject this whole process to careful scrutiny, we immediately become aware of its contradictory character. These contradictions, it must be stressed, are internal to capital itself and would be a main source of confusion and stress even in the absence of any barriers 'in nature' (the limitations of the resource base) or in the specific forms of class struggle that the real subjection of labour to capital is bound to spark. So let us, for a moment, imagine a world in which the bounty of 'nature' is limitless and in which labourers do the bidding of capital with a docility and slavishness more characteristic of an automaton than of a human being. The purpose of such an awful fiction is to help us understand how capitalism creates barriers within itself, thereby continually frustrating its own process of development.

Consider, first, what happens to the rate of exploitation, s/v, with the rising productivity of labour power. There is the irony, of course, that 'hand in hand with the increasing productivity of labour goes the cheapening of the labourer, therefore a higher rate of surplus value' (*Capital*, vol. 1, p. 604) – but then this is exactly what is meant by increasing the value productivity of labour power. Marx generally holds, however, that the kinds of technological changes that increase the rate of exploitation can do so only at a decreasing rate (*Grundrisse*, p. 340). This is a strong proposition, which requires a rigorous proof. Marx offers us only a mathematical limit, which says that the smaller the proportion of variable capital in the total value added, the more difficult it is to reduce that proportion further. But the necessary limits here are social, not mathematical. We can invoke the need to maintain the consuming power of the workers as a necessary source of effective demand for the realization of capital through exchange. We can, in short, invoke all of the arguments laid out in chapter 2, which suggest that there is an equilibrium share of variable capital in the total social product that cannot be departed from without destroying the equilibrium conditions for the production and realization of capital in general. We see here the necessary contradiction that arises when each capitalist strives to reduce the share of variable capital in value added within the enterprise while speculating on selling his output to workers employed by other capitalists. This dilemma arises independently of any struggles over the real wage rate, and we can readily see how such struggles, under the right set of circumstances, can help bail capitalists out of the difficulties they themselves create.

Consider, secondly, what happens to the aggregate rate of profit under conditions of general technological change. If we measure the rate of profit as $s/(c + v)$, which is the same as $s/v/(1 + c/v)$, then obviously the rate of profit will fall if the value composition of capital increases while the rate of surplus value remains constant. We will take up this idea in detail in chapter 6, but we can see immediately that a stable value composition of capital has a potentially important role to play in stabilizing the aggregate rate of profit. Yet the idea of organic composition tells us that technological change within the firm is primarily and necessarily oriented to increasing the value composition. To be sure, a variety of countervailing influences can be identified – the interaction effects *may* be such as to keep the overall value composition stable in the face of a rising organic composition. But we can also clearly see that individual capitalists, pressured by competition and in perpetual quest of relative surplus value, capture the ephemeral form of the latter from temporary technological advantage, but in the process tend to create an aggregate technological mix in society that is inconsistent with a stable rate of profit. Individual capitalists, in short, behave in such a way as to threaten the conditions that permit the reproduction of the capitalist class.

All of this puts the question of technological mix at the centre of the contradictions of capitalism. To accord it this central position is not, of course, to give it autonomous agency in the shaping of capitalist history. It merely says that the actual technology embodied in a labour process is a locus of contradictions spawned by antagonistic requirements. It is this fundamental antagonism Marx captures, albeit in a rather hazy and confused way, through the dual concepts of organic and value composition. The problem for capital in general is somehow to stabilize the value composition in the face of a perpetual tendency to increase the organic composition through technological change within the enterprise. What Marx will ultimately seek to show us is that there is only one way that this can be done: through crises. The latter can then be interpreted as the forced re-structuring of the labour process so as to bring the system as a whole back into something that roughly conforms to the conditions of balanced accumulation.

Marx does not lay out the argument in this form, nor does he explore all of its complexities and dimensions. We will push the argument further in subsequent chapters. There is, however, one dimension to it worthy of further comment here since it is implicit in the considerations we have already advanced in this chapter.

Marx often made much of the contrast between the anarchy and disorder characteristic of market relations and the despotism, authority and control which exists within the enterprise. This polarization is not, in practice, quite as fierce as Marx depicted it – class struggle within the labour process modifies the latter, and monopolistic, oligopolistic and 'price leadership' behaviour modifies the former. But even taking account of such modifications, the general principle to which Marx appealed seems reasonably valid. Notice that the concept of organic composition is tied to determinations within the enterprise and is therefore within the arena of capitalist control. The value composition, on the other hand, represents the general relationship between living and dead labour after all the interaction effects and other diverse forces within the market have been ironed out – it is therefore tied to determinations expressed through the anarchy and disorder of the market.

The boundary between the realm of control and the anarchy of the market is set by the size of enterprise. Where, exactly, this boundary is drawn is of great significance to the workings of the economy as a whole. We must therefore consider the forces, if any, that roughly determine the position of this boundary. The analysis of the flow definition of value composition here yields some interesting results. The greater the degree of vertical integration, we have shown, the lower the value composition of capital within the enterprise and the greater is the arena of direct capitalist control. To this is opposed the requirement to accelerate the turnover time of capital by fragmenting activity, sub-contracting and generating a proliferation in the division of labour. This serves to increase the value composition of capital at the same time as its extends the arena of chaotic and anarchistic exchange relationships at the expense of regulated and controlled production. Between these two forces we can begin to spot the requirement for some equilibrium organization of production that fixes the degree of vertical integration, size of firm, etc., and thereby fixes the boundary between the market and the (relatively) controlled environment within the enterprise. Since this equilibrium is the product of fundamentally opposed forces, it is inherently unstable. But there is a connection here with the prospects for accumulation. The value composition of capital cannot be determined independently of these organizational characteristics. If a stable value composition of capital is essential for stable profits, then it follows that there is some equilibrium form of organization consistent with balanced accumulation. This is a fundamental and very simple idea, which is helpful to understanding the changing organization of capitalist production. We take up this idea in more concrete fashion in the next chapter.

CHAPTER 5

The Changing Organization of Capitalist Production

In its surface appearance, at least, we live in a very different world from that which prevailed in Marx's time. This is nowhere more apparent than in the dramatic changes that have taken place in the capitalist forms of organization for production and marketing. 'Since the beginning of the Industrial Revolution,' Hymer writes, 'there has been a tendency for the representative firm to increase in size from the *workshop* to the *factory* to the *national corporation* to the *multidivisional corporation* and now to the *multinational corporation*' (Hymer, 1972, p. 113). While governments were never exactly *laissez-faire* with respect to economic activity throughout the nineteenth century (they always played key roles with respect to money and large-scale 'public' works, as well as ensuring the legal basis of contracts and private property), the by now all too familiar intervention of the state through fiscal and monetary policies was virtually unknown before the 1930s. The sheer scale and complexity of organization – in both government and business – have changed out of all recognition in the last two hundred years.

Any theory of the economic evolution of capitalism must take these massive organizational changes into account and explain their historical necessity. Marx himself frequently referred to what he called the 'laws of centralization of capital', and Engels elaborated at length on the idea. The need to resolve the 'antagonism' between the control exercised within the workshop and the 'anarchy of production in society generally,' Engels wrote, inevitably led to the centralization of capital as a means to extend the islands of systematic control within the sea of blind market forces. Joint stock companies were the first organizational step in this direction, but soon 'this form also becomes insufficient' and gives way to large-scale monopolies (trusts, cartels, etc.), which seek market domination and vertical integration in production and distribution. Finally, 'the official representative of capitalist society – the state – will ultimately have to undertake the direction of production.' These necessary transformations, Engels argued, do not 'do away with the capitalistic nature' of production but simply serve the better to accomplish the production of surplus value.

After Engels, Hilferding attempted a comprehensive analysis of 'finance capital', conceptualized as a unification of banking capital and productive capital through a variety of organizational arrangements. Lenin, drawing much upon Hilferding's argument while rejecting the latter's politics, dubbed imperialism 'the highest stage of monopoly capitalism' and shortly thereafter coined the expression 'state-monopoly capitalism' to describe the new forms of economic organization then evolving in the advanced capitalist countries. Since then, a whole host of writers have sought to characterize these organizational changes and to interpret them. This has not proved easy, and a lively debate on some of the fundamentals of Marxian theory has ensued.[1]

For the most part, the debate centres upon a supposed transition from 'competitive' through 'monopoly' or 'finance' forms of capitalism to a present stage of 'state-monopoly' capitalism. Some writers challenge the terminology of stages, while others accept the terminology as descriptively useful but interpret the meaning of the terms quite differently. In what follows I shall endeavour to analyse the *process* of transition without bothering particularly about the labels to be put upon it. In this way I hope to identify an interpretation of organizational transformation that is consistent with Marxian value theory, and thereby lay to rest a number of ghosts that haunt the Marxist literature.

It might be useful at the outset to remind ourselves that if Marx taught us anything it was, surely, that the world of appearances deceives and that it is the task of science to penetrate beneath the appearances and identify the forces at work beneath. If Marx's theory is as robust as he claims, then it should provide us with the necessary basis to interpret the dramatic and very evident forms of organizational change that have occurred under capitalism over the past century or so.

We begin by connecting the question of organizational change with the general argument on technological change as it was worked out in the last chapter. This connection is direct and obvious, if only because Marx specifically includes organizational characteristics in his definition of technology. The necessity to accomplish perpetual revolutions in the productive forces implies, then, that there must be perpetual revolutions in the organization of production. But if Marx's general approach to technological change holds, then we must interpret organizational change as a response to contradictory forces. We must also anticipate that the organization achieved at a particular moment will embody powerful contradictions which will likely be the source of instability and crises.

---

[1] Hilferding (1970 edn); Lenin (1970 edn). Much of the contemporary debate in the English-speaking world stems from Baran and Sweezy (1966), but in Europe the debate took a rather different turn – see Boccara (1974), Poulantzas (1975), Altvater (1973) and the recent summary statements by Fine and Harris (1979, chs 7 and 8), Holloway and Picciotto (1978) and Fairley (1980).

There is no intent in this to try to divorce the analysis of organizational change from the analysis of changing forms of the work process. Each has to be seen as integral to the other. Focusing on the organizational side of this relation provides us with some special insights, however. It will also permit us to consider the degree to which Marx's arguments, fashioned in a world organized along quite different lines to those with which we are now familiar, still apply.

The competitive striving for surplus value and the need to discipline labourers to the laws of accumulation form, as we have seen, the basis for the technological dynamism of capitalism. The appropriation by capital of the productive powers of labour requires organizational innovation. The analysis of co-operation, the detail division of labour and machinery, indicates the need for an hierarchical organization of the work process and the separation of mental from manual labour. The increasing scale of production also calls for the concentration of capital, primarily through accumulation.

But concentration could also be accelerated by a process of centralization of capital. Larger-scale capitalists could gobble up the smaller either through competition or by employing a variety of financial strategems (takeovers, mergers, etc.). All of this requires new institutional and organizational arrangements, often explicitly sanctioned or encouraged by the state. Centralization completes 'the work of accumulation by enabling industrial capitalists to extend the scale of their operations'. This forms the 'starting point' for 'the progressive transformation of isolated processes of production, carried on by customary methods, into processes of production socially combined and scientifically arranged.' Centralization can accomplish 'in a twinkling of an eye' what would take many years of concentration through accumulation to bring about. Marx concludes that there is a 'law of centralization of capital' which plays a vital role in regulating the changing organization of production under capitalism (*Capital*, vol. 1, pp. 626–8).

Much play has been given to this supposed 'law' in the subsequent literature, since it seems to explain only too well the observable and quite massive centralization of economic and political power within a few dominant corporations. But like all of Marx's 'law-like' statements, we should be chary of attributing absolute and unchecked powers to it. In the same manner that we can identify countervailing forces to the 'law of rising organic composition of capital', so we can conceive of a variety of forces that counteract the tendency towards centralization.

Marx himself paid most attention to the phenomenon of centralization. He argues that monopoly is the inevitable end result of competition and that the drive for control will lead to progressive vertical integration within the capitalist system of production. The ultimate limit to this would be reached only 'when the entire social capital was united in the hands of either a single capitalist or a single capitalist company' (*Capital,* vol. 1, pp. 626–8). But he argues elsewhere that the tendency towards centralization 'would soon bring about the collapse of capitalist production if it were not for counteracting tendencies, which have a continuous decentralizing effect' (*Capital,* vol. 3, p. 246; *Theories of Surplus Value,* pt 3, p. 311). Certain 'forces of repulsion' are always at work to ensure that 'portions of the original capital disengage themselves and function as new independent capitals' (*Capital,* vol. 1, p. 625).

What Marx seems to be proposing is that there is some 'equilibrium' organization of production – expressed in terms of size of firm, degree of vertical integration, level of financial centralization or whatever – that is consistent with capitalist accumulation and the operation of the law of value. Furthermore, he seems to be suggesting that this equilibrium point would be struck, in theory at least, by the working out of opposed tendencies towards centralization and decentralization. As usual, we should view the concept of equilibrium as a convenient means to identify the disequilibrium conditions to which capitalist society is prone. And, as usual also, we should look to identify the forces that disturb the equilibrium organization of production under capitalism and promote either excessive centralization or decentralization.

The problem, of course, is that Marx is not explicit as to the kind of centralization he is talking about (financial, productive, etc.), and that he does not explicitly state what are the 'forces of repulsion' that make for decentralization, although he does in various places discuss the incentive for capital to engage in extensive sub-contracting of its operations (*Capital,* vol. 1, p. 553) and the tendency within capitalism to open up new branches of production that are typically small-scale and labour-intensive (*Grundrisse,* p. 751).

We can, however, theorize about this process, given the findings of the previous chapter on the limits to vertical integration and the necessary boundary between production and exchange. Increased vertical integration decreases the value composition (which is advantageous for profit-making) but increases the turnover time (which diminishes the prospects for profits). The degree of vertical integration can, in the first instance, be interpreted as the product of these two opposed incentives.

General considerations that fix the boundary between the sphere of capitalist control within production and market exchange also now come into play. In the market, it is true, 'chance and caprice have full play.' But we must also remember that the law of value, backed by the 'authority' of competition and 'the coercion exerted by the pressure of . . . mutual interests', is established in part through market co-ordinations which determine 'how much of its disposable working-time society can expend on each particular class of commodities' (*Capital,* vol. 1, p. 355–6). The spheres of production and exchange mutually condition each other. Capitalism cannot do without market co-ordinations and still remain capitalism. Centralization extends the sphere of controlled production at the expense of exchange. If the sphere of operation of the latter is cut back to the point where market co-ordinations are seriously impaired, then the processes that allow values to be determined (see chapter 1) are rendered less effective and the operation of the law of value is emasculated. This, presumably, explains why excessive centralization without countervailing 'forces of repulsion' would soon 'bring about the collapse of capitalist production.' The spheres of production and exchange, as separations within a unity, are important to the perpetuation of capitalism. The boundary between them may be fluid, but it cannot, evidently, stray too far from some equilibrium point without seriously threatening the reproduction of capitalism itself.

Marx's comment that the law of value asserts itself like 'a law of nature' under capitalism was not a chance or flippant remark. The law of value, to be sure, is a social product, but the social relations of capitalism ensure that a capitalist society is not only wedded to the law's consequences but must also perpetually search to perfect the law's functioning. This implies that organizational change ought to be interpretable in terms of such a process. If this idea is accepted as a hypothesis, then the task before us is to explain how the manifest and far-reaching changes in organizational structure under capitalism have served to perfect the operation of the law of value. In this spirit, presumably, Engels argued that the observable organizational changes during the nineteenth century were promoted by the desire to enhance the production of surplus value.

But the transition from competitive to monopoly to state monopoly forms of organization certainly appears to represent a movement away from the 'authority' of competition and therefore a movement away from the regulatory power of the law of value. Some Marxists have drawn such a conclusion. Baran and Sweezy, for example, argue:

> We cannot be content with patching up and amending the competitive model which underlies [Marx's] economic theory. . . . In an attempt to understand capitalism in its monopoly stage, we cannot abstract from monopoly or introduce it as a mere modifying factor; we must put it at the very center of the analytical effort. (Baran and Sweezy, 1966, pp. 5–6)

The abandonment of the 'competitive model' in Marx certainly does entail abandoning the law of value – which, to their credit, Baran and Sweezy are fully prepared to do. The trouble is that we cannot withdraw this, the linchpin of Marx's analysis, without seriously questioning or compromising all of the other Marxian categories. After all, when categories are defined relationally, then it follows that one cannot be altered or magically whisked out of the analysis without disturbing all of the others.[2]

Boccara likewise accepts the idea of a transition from a competitive through a monopoly to a state-monopoly stage, but seeks to reconcile these transitions with Marxian theory by viewing them 'dialectically' rather than one-sidedly. The movement from one form to another is, in his view, an attempt to overcome the contradictions implicit in an earlier form by the creation of a new form of capitalism which is, in turn, doomed to express the fundamental underlying contradictions of capitalism, albeit in new and seemingly quite different guises. We should not

> confound the fact that capitalism always remains capitalism with the idea that the relations of production and the overall economic structure remain un-transformed. According to Marxist theory, the relations of production are the object of an incessant process of transformation. . . . This does not prevent the essentially capitalist nature of these relations being preserved and deepened; the fundamental relation of exploitation of the proletariat persists. (Boccara, 1974, p. 31)[3]

The kind of reconciliation that Boccara proposes must, if it is to be convincing, be both theoretically secure and historically appropriate. A Marxian theory of capitalist dynamics must be united with the results of historical materialist investigation – a unification that Marx insisted was vital to both. Since this is ever a difficult task, I shall proceed schematically. Theoretically, I will presume that the operation of the law of value depends upon the articulation of a set of competitive mechanisms which serve three fundamental purposes: to equalize the prices of commodities, to equalize the rate of profit between firms and among sectors and, finally, to channel the movement of capital and allocate labour power so that accumulation can be sustained. For the sake of simplicity I shall also abstract entirely from the actual mechanics of the process whereby new organizational structures are formed. The basic task is then to compare the supposedly different stages of capitalism with respect to degree of competition, price and profit equalization and the self-sustaining flow of capital into lines of activity productive of surplus value.

Consider, now, the supposedly 'competitive stage' of capitalism as it existed in, say, the 1840s in the 'advanced' capitalist world. Industrial activity at that time was organized almost entirely on the lines of the family business enterprise, using methods of accounting and business practices which were

---

[2] There is a certain irony here. While Baran and Sweezy prepare to abandon the law of value in exchange, Braverman (1974), deriving inspiration from their work, shows convincingly how the Marxian notion of value captures with devastating accuracy the conditions that prevail within production (see above, chapter 4, section II). How values can prevail within production but not in exchange is a mystery to me.

[3] For a strong criticism of Boccara's formulation see Theret and Wievorka (1978).

extremely traditional in the sense that the entrepreneur of the 1840s would have felt quite at home in the business milieu of fourteenth-century Italian merchants. Ownership and management were one and the same, the size of firm was such that the whole industrial structure could reasonably be characterized as highly decentralized. Of course, there were at that time plenty of examples of vertically integrated industries in which the social division of labour had yet to take hold, as well as older monopoly forms which had not yet been eliminated – the British East India Company lasted until 1845, for example. We might reasonably suppose that the latter would pass with time, as would the extensive sectors of activity still organized along pre-capitalist lines (artisan production, peasant agriculture, *petit bourgeois* commerce and workshop production, etc.). All of these forms would ultimately be reduced to the pure capitalist model. The only activities that were large-scale and centralized were public or quasi-public works — railroads, canals, port and harbour facilities, etc. – and government finance. Some of the major banking houses, such as Barings and Rothschilds, were in a position to make or break governments, and the taxing powers of the latter were increasingly integrated into the world of high finance via government debt. In these arenas there were abundant complaints concerning the immense concentrations of economic and financial power. But industrial and agricultural activity, by and large, was small-scale, fairly decentralized and generally independent of direct financial control by the 'high financiers' who, by and large, resisted direct long-term involvement with industrial and agricultural production. The main connection between productive activity and the world of finance lay in the provision of short-term commercial credit.

But it is one thing to point to the small scale of enterprise and fragmentation of economic activity, and quite another to presume that this entailed perfect competition, the equalization of prices and profits, let alone an adequate basis for sustained accumulation. Price variations from locality to locality were quite marked. While there are not many systematic studies on differentials in profit rates, what evidence we do have – all of which is in money-price terms – suggests that it varied greatly from firm to firm, from industry to industry and from place to place.[4] The mechanisms for equalizing prices and profits through competition were anything but perfect, and labour allocations were haphazard at best. And it is not hard to see why.

To begin with, transport costs were relatively high and the spatial integration of national economies, let alone the international economy, was in its very early stages. Quite small firms could operate as monopolists in the local markets they commanded. Transaction costs – the necessary expenses of circulation – were also relatively high in relation to volume and value, while the flow of information was slow, sporadic and incomplete with respect to

---

[4] Studies on what actually happened to profit rates are few and far between. Bouvier *et al.* (1965) have produced one of the best and most instructive works on the subject.

price movements, profit opportunities, techniques of production, and so on. Capital markets were in a very primitive state; they were often local rather than national, and the whole institutional framework for facilitating the flow of money (whether to permit commodity exchange or in its function as money capital) was scarcely adapated to bring about rapid adjustments in production. And to cap it all, the traditional family structure of ownership was as much a barrier as a virtue when it came to being able to respond to a new profit opportunities. Since ownership and control were identical and the joint stock company form had yet to penetrate far into industrial and agricultural activity, the potential for expansion of business, either through large-scale operation or be geographical spread, was strictly limited by the managerial capabilities of the family or a limited partnership.

A high degree of organizational decentralization went hand in hand, therefore, with localized monopoly power and all manner of frictions and barriers that inhibited true competition and prevented the equalization of prices and profits.[5] The virtue of the pioneering entrepreneurial capitalists, those legendary figures of nineteenth-century capitalism, lay precisely in their remarkable ability to sustain accumulation in the face of all of these barriers – including, we should note, their own mode of organization. And if the technological transfers and the capital movements were quite remarkable, given the general state of affairs, this did not and could not amount to perfection of competition by any standards. So why on earth do we typically dub this period of capitalist history as 'the classical competitive stage'?

The answer presumably lies in the manner in which the 'firm' has been idealized in bourgeois thought and the hegemonic role that this thought plays in fashioning our understandings of the world. The vision of entrepreneurs, pursuing their own individual self-interest but guided by the invisible hand of the market in such a way that they enhanced the general social welfare, is common to Adam Smith and contemporary neoclassical economics. The latter, in particular, idealizes firms in ways that never existed and fetishizes the small-scale enterprise, which lacks any degree of monopolistic market power, as the ideal agent for achieving competitive equilibrium. Hence has arisen an unjustified association between small scale of organization and competitiveness.

Marx was not deceived by such a vision. And we should not be either. In the supposedly 'competitive' stage of capitalism, when firms were indeed relatively small, the law of value operated imperfectly and the laws of motion were but partially felt. The problem in the 1840s, therefore, was to perfect competition, enhance the operation of the law of value and continue to

---

[5] Chandler (1962, p. 3) writes: 'companies bought their raw materials and their finished goods locally. When they manufactured for a market more than a few miles away from the factory, they bought and sold through commission agents who handled the business of several other firms.'

increase the productivity of labour so that accumulation could be sustained. The barriers to circulation and movement had to be overcome and local monopolies eliminated through spatial integration. Transaction costs had to be much reduced, mechanisms for the collection and dissemination of information improved and an institutional structure to facilitate money payments, capital flows, etc., had to be created. Solutions had to be found to all of these problems. The irony here is that the traditional small-scale organization of the firm – so idealized in bourgeois theory as the paragon of competitiveness – was one of the most serious barriers to finding solutions to these problems. The traditional organization of the firm had to be overcome in order to perfect the competitiveness of exchange and profit-making.

To some extent the barriers to competition were reduced by massive improvements in transport, communications and banking techniques. In each of these sectors, however, we can witness the rise of large-scale, quasi-monopolistic forms of organization with quite immense market power by nineteenth-century standards. The railroads, in particular, provided the teething ground for modern corporate forms of organization. The 'organizational revolution' that took place at the end of the nineteenth century, and which culminated in the emergence of trusts and cartels, can in part be seen as an attempt to deal with all of these barriers to competition by replacing the family business by modern business enterprise. This replacement occurred, according to Chandler, when 'administrative coordination permitted greater productivity, lower costs and higher profits than coordination by market mechanisms.' The advantages of the new form were many:

> By routinizing the transactions between units, the costs of these transactions were lowered. By linking the administration of producing units with buying and distributing units, costs for information on markets and sources of supply were reduced. Of much greater significance, the internalization of many units permitted the flow of goods from one unit to another to be administratively coordinated. More effective scheduling of flows achieved a more intensive use of facilities and personnel employed in the processes of production and distribution and so increased productivity and reduced costs. (Chandler, 1977, pp. 6–12)

Modern business enterprise of this sort, Chandler maintains, 'appeared for the first time in history when the volume of economic activities reached a level that made administrative coordination more efficient and more profitable than market coordination.' The quest for profit diminished the role of exchange and extended the sphere of production because, at a certain scale of output, the transaction and circulation costs were higher in the market than they were within the firm. By internalizing these costs, the firm could diminish barriers to the circulation of capital and improve upon the capacity to equalize the profit rate. The centralization of capital may, therefore, improve rather than diminish the capacity to equalize profits.

The modern business enterprise also entails, as Marx saw, a 'transformation of the actually functioning capitalist into a mere manager, administrator of other people's capital, and of the owner of capital into . . . a mere money-capitalist' (*Capital*, vol. 3, p. 436). The financial form which capitalism then assumed permitted 'an enormous expansion of the scale of production and of enterprises', far beyond that which individual capitalists could ever hope to achieve. And this meant 'the abolition of capital as private property within the framework of capitalist production itself' (*Capital*, vol. 3, p. 436).

This separation of ownership and management helped to overcome the managerial limitations of the old-style family firm and to open up the field of application of techniques of modern management and organization. But there were dangers attendant upon it. Adam Smith, doubtless with the speculative bubbles of the early eighteenth century in mind, regarded joint stock companies as licences for irresponsible entrepreneurs to speculate with other people's money. The reluctance to sanction joint stock forms of organization except for large-scale semi-public works – canals, railroads, docks, etc. – derived precisely from such objections. The whole history of speculative crashes from the mid-nineteenth century to the present time suggests that the objections are far from unfounded, and that the 'finance' form of capitalism faces a perpetual problem of keeping its own house in order (see below, chapters 9 and 10).

But the net effect of increasing scale, centralization of capital, vertical integration and diversification within the corporate form of enterprise has been to replace the 'invisible hand' of the market by the 'visible hand' of the managers. How, then, does this visible hand or managerial co-ordination within the sphere of production relate to the expression of value which, our theory tells us, must at least partially be arrived at through exchange?

Monopoly control and market power permit the large corporation to be a 'price-maker' rather than a 'price-taker' in the market. But although managers have a variety of pricing strategies available to them, none is exactly arbitrary and some, such as marginal cost pricing, are as well attuned to supply and demand conditions as any open market pricing ever was. While it is true the resulting prices are not the same as those arrived at through competitive pricing, the deviations are by no means substantial enough to warrant abandoning the idea that values are expressed through market prices. Supply and demand simply replaces open competition as the mechanism. The objection that managers make decisions based on considerations of relatively long-term stability and growth has more substance to it (although for many the long-term is not very long). The shift of time horizons and the capacity for planning obsolescence is particularly important when it comes to questions of the use of fixed capital (see chapter 8).

There can be little doubt also that the 'managerial class' has to some degree taken on a life of its own, become 'relatively autonomous' from the owners of capital and thereby become a 'source of permanence, power and continual growth'.[6] To the degree that managerial structures have become bureaucratized, they have become rigid, inflexible and incapable of major adaptation. To the extent that the modern corporation has captured science, technology and planning – and, via the patent laws, evolved a capacity to regulate innovation — it has successfully internalized the processes of technological change.[7] The corporation sets out to produce new kinds of work processes and new organizational structures, as well as new products and new product lines. To the extent that it dominates certain branches of production, it promotes these at the expense of all others, often to the detriment of overall economic structure. And to the extent that corporations are forced, by virtue of their size and importance, to negotiate with governments, they play politics overtly, covertly and unscrupulously in their own self-interest.

In all of these respects the modern corporate form of organizations appears to be the antithesis of competitiveness and, by implication, incapable of equalizing prices and profits in accordance with prices of production and the average rate of profit.

But let us look at the other side of this picture. The large financial conglomerate has achieved the capacity to switch capital and manpower from one line to another and from one part of the world to another 'in the twinkling of an eye'. It can and does evolve extremely sophisticated systems for gathering and using information on production techniques, market and profit opportunities. Transaction costs are minimized within the corporation, and production and distribution can be planned down to the last detail as if no internal barriers to realization existed. It can likewise respond to many of the difficulties attendant upon increasing reliance upon fixed capital by planning for obsolescence. In all of these respects, the modern corporation has increased the potentiality to achieve an equalization of the rate of profit *within* its confines.[8]

It is, however, one thing to speak of potentiality and quite another to point to the necessity of achievement. To discover the secrets of profit equalization and the contemporary forms of competition, we have to penetrate the maze of modern managerial structures in much the same way that Marx insisted we

[6] Chandler (1977) provides a lot of good history on this. The general problem of the 'managerial class' has been taken up by a number of writers such as Poulantzas (1975), Becker (1977) and Wright (1978).

[7] Noble (1977) provides an excellent account of how this came about.

[8] This is the principle conclusion to be drawn from the work of Palloix (1971, 1973); see also the readings edited by Radice (1975). In contrast with the disjunction that prevails between Barran and Sweezy on the one hand and Braverman on the other (above, n. 2), Palloix couples this vision of increasing penetration of the law of value through international exchange with increasing penetration of the law of value in production (see Palloix, 1976).

should penetrate 'into the hidden abode of production, on whose threshold there stares us in the face "No admittance except on business" [in order to] force the secret of profit making' (*Capital,* vol. 1, p. 176).

Chandler is one of the few historians who have been privileged to enter into this difficult territory. His discoveries are of interest. Most important from the standpoint of our present argument is that what appears on the outside as a steady and seemingly irreversible movement towards centralization has been accompanied on the inside by a progressive, controlled decentralization in the structure of management. Here, perhaps, we can find the secret of the counteracting movement towards decentralization which prevents the collapse of capitalist production through excessive centralization. The idea of an equilibrium organization, achieved by a balance between the forces of repulsion, making for decentralization, and the forces of centralization is not at all remote. But it is now expressed by an internalization of competition within a corporation that presents itself to the world as a centralized monopolistic monster.

The historical evidence is not inconsistent with such an argument. Decentralized, multidivisional structures within the large corporation began to emerge in the 1920s in response to specific kinds of problems which the centralized systems of the immediately preceeding period had had great difficulty in handling. As Chandler put it, 'by placing an increasingly intolerable strain on existing administrative structures, territorial expansion and to a much greater extent product diversification brought the multidivisional form.' The structural reorganization undertaken at General Motors in the midst of the crises of 1921–2 created a decentralized organization that: 'not only helped it to win the largest share of the automobile market in the United States, but also to expand and administer successfully its overseas manufacturing and marketing activities. Furthermore, because of its administrative structure, it was able to execute brilliantly a broad strategy of diversification in the making and selling of all types of engines, and products using engines, in the years after the automobile market fell off in the late 1920s.' Competition, even of the limited variety that operates under market oligopoly, soon forced the other automobile companies to follow suit. The decentralized, multidivisional corporate structure had become general throughout the world by the 1960s.[9]

The interesting point, of course, is that this decentralized structure is so organized that each division (whether it be a product line or a territory) can be held financially accountable. The managerial performance of each division can be measured in terms of a rate of return on capital from each division. The function of central management is to monitor performance and to allocate resources – labour power, managerial skills and finance – in relation to the

[9] Chandler (1962, pp. 44–6); Hannah (1976) provides an anologous study of the British experience. See also Scott (1979).

present or estimated future profitability of each division. With transaction costs held to a minimum, the modern managerial structure generates a form of competition within itself which often has the effect of equalizing the profit rate. The central conclusion to which this points is that the modern financial conglomerate is, in terms of its internal organization at least, far more efficient and effective at equalizing the profit rate than its supposedly perfectly competitive forebears were in the first half of the nineteenth century.

This multidivisional corporate structure and the internalization of competition did not come about by accident. The large trusts and cartels formed at the beginning of this century in a phase of massive centralization of capital were, within a short period, in deep financial difficulty, in spite of all of their supposedly immense market power. And they were in difficulty precisely because they did not know exactly where, in the midst of their complex operations, profits were coming from or unnecessary costs were being incurred. The collapse of capitalist production indeed appeared imminent, had not 'the forces of repulsion' been unleashed to create the multidivisional structure.

The 'forces of repulsion' were mobilized, however, by external constraints operating through the market – constraints that forced even the largest of corporations into some kind of conformity to the law of value. This brings us to the question of how competition is maintained between financial conglomerates and the degree to which this competition produces an equalization of prices and profits across all economic units no matter what their size or type.

The main test of oligopoly and monopoly lies in the degree of market power and the ability to dictate prices free of competitive pressures in the market place. Market prices are equalized at the dictates of the monopoly or according to strategies of 'price leadership' within an oligopoly. Profit rates may still be equalized, but the equalization is distorted by monopoly prices which supposedly deviate from the prices of production that would be realized under competition.

It is easy to make rather too much of this argument. Large corporations, operating within an oligopolistic market environment, are subject to a variety of competitive pressures. They compete through product differentiation, marketing sophistication and so on. The separation between ownership and management also has an important impact upon the form that competition now takes. To the extent that the corporation operates on borrowed funds and raises money through issuing stocks and bonds, it enters into a general competition for money capital. The performance of an enterprise is measured in terms of yield (surplus value distributed as profits to stock and bond holders) and prospects for long-term growth. An inefficient and low-paying enterprise cannot stay alive for long, no matter what its market power with respect to prices.

Competition, therefore, takes many forms besides those that attach to price competition in the market. Managerial practices and reorganizations have internalized competitive processes within the firm (even created internal labour markets), while competition for money capital has shifted the focus to capital markets as the means for disciplining even the most powerful of economic units. These forms of competition may be just as effective at equalizing prices and profits, given the superior efficiency achieved in other respects, as was the classic form of market co-ordination in which the 'invisible hand' supposedly guided entrepreneurs unerringly to behave in accordance with the law of value.

This is not to say, however, that competition functions perfectly under oligopoly. Indeed, there are many problems as epitomized by the interlocking relations between financial institutions and industrial corporations, the proliferation of holding companies and large financial conglomerates (which often pay little attention to details of day-to-day management), etc. Competitive processes – of whatever sort – are always liable to be emasculated by excessive centralization. And the very size, weight and power of the economic actors involved mean that it becomes less and less certain that capitalist forms of organization will approximate to that equilibrium state which would ensure the equalization of prices and profits and sustained accumulation.

The problem of maintaining competitive processes through organizational arrangements becomes even more acute when we consider state involvement in the spheres of production and exchange. We are speaking here of the varieties of direct intervention on the part of the state rather than of the state as protector of private property rights, contracts, etc., or the state as 'manager' of the processes of production and reproduction of labour power (through investments in health, education, welfare services, etc.). While the whole question of state interventionism is far too complex to be dealt with thoroughly here, we can identify straight away countervailing tendencies towards centralization and decentralization being expressed both within and through the state apparatus.

On the one hand, we see the state seeking to prevent excessive centralization either by regulating capitalist forms of organization (through a battery of laws designed to prevent monopolization) or by generating decentralized administrative arrangements within itself. The political and administrative structure of federalism and the organization of the banking industry in the United States provide excellent examples of highly decentralized arrangements maintained through the agency of the state itself.

On the other hand, government frequently acts to stimulate the centralization of capital. Mergers and takeovers may be encouraged and even subsidized as part of a government-sponsored policy of industrial reorganization. Large-scale undertakings that are beyond the scope of private capital may be financed, built and even managed by government – no new large-scale iron and steel plants have been built in Europe in recent years without extensive government participation, for example. Public utilities, transport and communications are fields in which the government either participates directly or regulates, in part because of the scale of investment required and in part because we are here dealing with 'natural monopolies' which arise because it is physically impossible to have a large number of competitors operating in the same area (15 different railroads between two points just does not make sense). And governments may seek, under certain circumstances, to consolidate failing enterprise in some key sector of the economy and to subsidize it in order to lower the cost of constant capital inputs to private firms. This leads, of course, to a distortion of market prices in relation to prices of production, and this can lead to a re-structuring of profit rates according to the lines dictated by government.

The fiscal and monetary policies that governments pursue likewise have profound impacts. Designed to maintain 'economic stability and growth', these policies, whether constructed along Keynesian lines or not, cannot avoid having implications for capitalist forms of organization. To begin with, the channelling of the flow of capital through the government apparatus itself yields highly centralized fiscal and monetary powers to the government. Military expenditures and large-scale public works can, under certain conditions, absorb large portions of the total social product. In addition, laws governing taxation, depreciation arrangements, etc., which may themselves be constructed as part of the battery of tools for guaranteeing economic stability and growth, often have profound consequences for corporate organization.

These are all very complex matters, which deserve careful study. The purpose in broaching them here is to consider in general theoretical terms the degree to which these kinds of organizational arrangements can possibly be consistent with the operation of the law of value as Marx defined it. On the surface at least, the activities of government seem to have little or nothing to do with the maintenance of that competitive exchange process through which Marxian theory sees the law of value operating. 'State monopoly capitalism', as it is sometimes called, appears even more fundamentally antagonistic to the operation of the law of value than does monopoly or finance capitalism.[10]

[10] The theory of the state has been the subject of intensive discussion among Marxists in recent years. The debate has been many-sided and impossible to summarize in a short space. Fine and Harris (1979), Holloway and Picciotto (1978) and Wright (1978) provide interesting perspectives and summaries. The way in which I introduce the state into the argument here suggests a certain sympathy with the approach advocated by Holloway and Picciotto. They argue for a materialist theory of the state constructed out of a careful examination of the necessary relationship between state forms on the one hand and forms of production and social relations as these are expressed through the contradictory processes of accumulation on the other. Stripped of its potentially arid logical formalism, this approach has, I believe, a lot to offer in helping us understand many aspects of the state under capitalism. Whether or

We can reduce the complexity of this question by focusing on the mechanisms whereby the state may be disciplined by capital. This does not, unfortunately, resolve all difficulties, but it indicates one path we can follow to extricate ourselves from what appears to be a serious theoretical impasse.

We could conceive of the state as being controlled politically in the interest of the capitalist class. The idea that the state is 'the executive committee of the bourgeoisie' is not unfamiliar in Marxist circles. While there is often an element of truth in such a conception, we do not necessarily have to invoke it here since there are other forces at work which can equally well serve to discipline the state to the requirements of capital – assuming, of course, that the basic legal and institutional arrangements of capitalism are preserved. These forces are primarily financial. In the first place, taxes – which form the life-blood of state activity – are themselves a slice out of surplus value or out of variable capital. The state cannot take out more than some 'equilibrium share' of surplus value or variable capital without fundamentally disrupting the distributional arrangements that underlie the circulation of capital. We should note here, of course, that, since production and consumption can never be equilibrated under the antagonistic relations of distribution, it becomes a distinctive aim of Keynesian policies to undertake the impossible – hence, the more Keynesian policies succeed in equilibrating production and consumption in the long run, the more they threaten the social relations of distribution which are central to capitalism. When public policy is forced to revert to protect those social relations of distribution, the ability to equilibrate production and consumption is immediately diminished.

Secondly, to the degree that the state engages in direct production on a long-term basis, it usually has to borrow from capital markets. It cannot borrow what is not there, and it is forced to compete, albeit on a somewhat privileged basis, for its share of money capital. It must also provide a rate of return on the capital it borrows – a return that must come either directly out of the exploitation of labour power in the sector under its control or indirectly by taxation of surplus value produced elsewhere.

What all of this means is that at some point or other the state has to be financially accountable in relation to the fundamental processes of capital circulation and surplus value production. The mechanisms whereby this accountability is pressed home are often intricate and subtle. But there are enough examples of the gross exercise of disciplinary powers to make this argument more than merely plausible. A dominant capitalist power, such as the United States, or an international agency, such as the International

---

not it can lead us all the way to the complete theory of the state is another matter, which at this juncture I am not prepared to speculate upon. I will come back to this in the concluding comments to this work.

Monetary Fund, will likely put strong pressure on weaker governments to conform to certain standards of behaviour. Government participation in certain sectors that are judged to be the domain of private enterprise may be curtailed and the excessive centralization of economic power within the government checked. Stringent requirements may be put upon the operations of state enterprises (with respect to their efficiency and profitability, for example) as governments seek financial support. Britain, Italy and Portugal number among the several countries that have been financially disciplined by the International Monetary Fund in recent years. The government of New York City was similarly disciplined by forces mobilized within the financial system of the United States in the period 1973–8.

The conclusion we can reasonably draw is that states that stray too far from organizational forms and from policies that are consistent with the circulation of capital, the preservation of the distributional arrangements of capitalism and the sustained production of surplus value soon find themselves in financial difficulty. Fiscal crisis, in short, turns out to be the means whereby the discipline of capital can ultimately be imposed on any state apparatus that remains within the orbit of capitalist relations of production.

The whole history of organizational change under capitalism can, it seems, be interpreted as a progression dictated by a striving towards perfection in the operation of the law of value. Capitalism has, by this account, become more rather than less responsive to the law of value. The surface appearance of a movement away from competitiveness to monopoly and state-monopoly forms – while descriptively accurate in certain respects – turns out on inspection to be historically and theoretically misleading if taken too literally. Capitalism has never been perfectly competitive or even remotely in accordance with that ideal. In striving to become more competitive, capitalism has evolved structures that diverge from a predominant imagery of what a truly competitive organization should look like. But in its practices it has evolved new modes of competition that permit the law of value to operate in diverse but ever more effective ways. Daily life for the mass of people held captive within the social relations of capitalism has grown ever more competitive. Competition on the international stage sharpens; the disciplining of governments by financial mechanisms becomes part of our daily diet of news. Divisional managers feel the sharp edge of competition daily in their communications with central management. From all of these standpoints we see the laws of motion of capitalism still in the course of perfection, the law of value finally coming into its own as the absolute dictator over our lives.

But to say that the law of value is being perfected is not to suggest that we are moving into an era of capitalist harmony. Far from it. The law of value embodies contradictions and the organizational arrangements that are fashioned in accordance with its workings cannot, under such circumstances, themselves be free of contradictions. The result is a tendency towards chronic organizational instability within the capitalist mode of production.[11]

The drive to control all aspects of production and exchange tends to create an over-centralization of capitals – in both the private sector and the state – that is indeed a threat to the perpetuation of capitalist production itself. To the degree that the compensating forces making for decentralization are difficult to set in motion, so the system stagnates, becomes bogged down, held captive by the weight and complexity of its own organizational structure. Conversely, excessive decentralization and the chance and caprice of the market can create such a climate of uncertainty, so many gaps between production and realization, that it, too, has to be compensated for by moves towards centralization. The equilibrium point between these two opposed tendencies is inherently unstable. It is, at best, achieved only by accident, and there are no mechanisms to prevent the antagonistic relations of capitalism forcing organizational structures into disequilibrium. At this point we can perceive that crises have a constructive role to play not only in forcing through new technologies in the narrow sense but also in forging new organizational structures which are more in accordance with the law of value in that they provide the basis for renewed accumulation through the production of surplus value. This, however, is a matter to which we will return in chapter 7.

Beneath all of this, there exists an even deeper irony. The law of value is a social product. And the social relation that lies at the bottom of it is none other than that between capital and labour. Yet the law of value itself entails a whole series of organizational transformations which cannot be accomplished without simultaneously transforming class relations. The rise of a 'managerial class', separate and distinct from the owners of capital, of government structures of intervention and regulation, of increasingly hierarchical orderings in the division of labour; the emergence of corporate and governmental bureaucracies – all of these obscure the simple capital – labour relation that underlies the law of value itself.[12]

That these extensive social changes are the product of the law of value should not be viewed with surprise. It simply confirms the basic Marxian proposition with which we started out. We seek to create a technological–organizational structure appropriate to a particular set of social relation-

---

[11] Hilferding (1970 edn) saw very clearly that the impact of oligopoly, cartels, etc., distorted prices of production even more than otherwise would be the case, and that monopolization therefore tended to exacerbate rather than cure the underlying problems of instability.

[12] We noted in chapter 4, section I, that the transformation of the labour process has tended towards an ever greater capacity to obscure the origin of profit in surplus value, and here we see the mirror image of that idea as expressed in capitalist forms of organization. All of which indicates that the theme of necessary fetishism that Marx enunciates in that extraordinary passage in the first volume of *Capital* is more relevant than ever to our understanding of the world.

ships, only to find that the latter must change to accommodate the former – in seeking to change the world, we change ourselves. Or, put in more classical Marxian form, the resolution of one set of contradictions within the social and technological apparatus of capitalism inevitably engenders others. The contradictions are replicated in new and frequently more confusing forms. And it is, of course, the working out of such a process that is writ so large in the history of capitalist forms of organization and the transformations they have undergone.

CHAPTER 6

The Dynamics of Accumulation

Capitalism is highly dynamic and inevitably expansionary. Powered by the engine of accumulation for accumulation's sake and fuelled by the exploitation of labour power, it constitutes a permanently revolutionary force which perpetually reshapes the world we live in. How can we represent and analyse the complex dynamics – the inner laws of motion – of the capitalist mode of production?

Marx addresses this question by fashioning a variety of 'abstract representations' of the processes of production and circulation of capital. He then treats these representations as 'theoretical objects', systematically investigates their properties, and so builds various 'models' of the dynamics of accumulation. Each 'model' forms a particular 'window' or vantage point from which to view an extraordinarily complex process.

There are three major 'models' of the dynamics of accumulation set out in *Capital*. Each reflects the manner in which the 'theoretical object' is constituted in each of the three volumes of *Capital*. In the first volume Marx seeks to uncover the origin of profit in a production process carried out under the aegis of the social relationship between capital and labour. The theory of surplus value is constructed and elaborated upon, and great emphasis is placed upon the processes of technological and organizational change. But questions or difficulties that might attach to the circulation of capital are excluded from the analysis entirely under the simple assumption that capitalists experience no difficulty in disposing of the commodities they produce – commodities generally trade at their values. This leaves Marx free to constitute his first model of accumulation, which explores the social and technological conditions that fix the rate of exploitation. The model, though firmly anchored within the theoretical domain of *production*, therefore deals with the *distribution* of the values produced as between capitalists and labourers. The model is argued out in tough, rigorous and uncompromising terms.

The second volume of *Capital* focuses upon the circulation of capital through all of its phases

$$M–C\begin{pmatrix} LP \\ MP \end{pmatrix} \ldots P \ldots C'–M' \text{ (etc.).}$$

Production and purchase of labour power are viewed as relatively un-problematic 'moments' in this process. The focus is upon problems that arise as capital moves from one state to another and in the exchange relations that must prevail if capital is to be realized. Technological change is very little emphasized, and the grand lines of class struggle, so evident in the first model, disappear almost entirely from the picture. This permits Marx to construct a quite different 'model' of accumulation through the expanded reproduction of the circulation of capital. The model is grounded in the theoretical domain of *circulation of capital and exchange,* and deals with the conditions of realization of capital through consumption (see above, chapter 3). But it is argued imaginatively and tentatively rather than rigorously.

The intent in the third volume of *Capital* is to synthesize the findings of the first two volumes and to build a model that integrates production–distribution relationship with production–realization requirements. A synthetic model of capitalist dynamics – of 'capitalist production as a whole' – is built around the theme of 'the falling rate of profit and its countervailing tendencies.' This model, deceptively simple in form, is used as a vehicle to expose the various forces making for disequilibrium under capitalism and thereby to provide a basis for understanding crisis formation and resolution. Unfortunately, the model makes very little reference to the findings of the second volume, and therefore lacks firm grounding in a theoretical domain which ought to encompass production and circulation jointly. The model has to be treated, then, as a preliminary and quite incomplete stab at understanding a difficult and complex problem. Just how incomplete this third model is we shall shortly see.

The intent of this chapter is to outline the characteristics of each of these 'models' of accumulation and to assess their shortcomings as well as the insights they generate. Like Marx, I shall try to lay out the argument in such a way that the fundamental underlying contradictions between *production* and *exchange,* between the equilibrium requirements for the production of surplus value and the circulation of capital, become readily apparent. These contradictions do indeed provide a valid basis for understanding the formation and resolution of crises under capitalism. The actual mechanics of that process, so vital to the inner logic of capitalism, will then be taken up in chapter 7.

I THE PRODUCTION OF SURPLUS VALUE AND THE GENERAL LAW OF CAPITALIST ACCUMULATION

If, as Marx avers, 'the historical mission of the bourgeoisie' is 'accumulation for accumulation's sake, production for production's sake' (*Capital*, vol. 1,

p. 595), then a portion of the surplus value must be converted into new capital to produce more surplus value. Towards the end of the first volume of *Capital,* Marx spells out the 'influence of the growth of capital on the lot of the labouring classes' and in the process builds a model of the dynamics of accumulation. Certain assumptions are tacitly incorporated in order to facilitate the argument. There are just two classes in society, capitalists and labourers. The former are forced by competition to reinvest at least a part of the surplus value they appropriate in order to ensure their own reproduction as a class. The labourers, denied any access to means of production, are entirely dependent upon employment by the capitalists for their livelihood (the working class can produce nothing for itself). Capitalists encounter no barriers to the disposal of commodities at their value. Costs of circulation as well as all transaction costs are ignored. The economy is considered as a single aggregate, so that input–output relationships between different sectors can be ignored.

In such a highly simplified economy there are only two forms of revenue: wages and aggregate profits, or, as conceptualized in value terms, variable capital and surplus value. Since s/v represents the rate of exploitation, we can explore certain facets of 'the lot of the labourer' by examining changes in the rate of exploitation under the social relations of capitalist production and exchange. To do this requires that we examine the relative shares of variable capital (the total wage bill) and surplus value (prior to distribution) in the total social product. Although Marx conducts the analysis in value terms, there is tacit appeal to market prices because wages are considered free to vary from the underlying value of labour power. The wage rate, the actual rate of exploitation, is fixed by the supply of and demand for labour power. What Marx now has to explain is how the day-to-day realities of supply and demand are themselves structured so as to ensure a rate of exploitation consistent with the requirements of accumulation.

Marx builds two versions of his accumulation model. The first excludes technological and organizational changes and presumes that the physical and value productivities of labour power remain constant. Accumulation under these conditions entails an increasing outlay on variable capital. It therefore 'reproduces the capital relation on a progressive scale, more capitalists or larger capitalists at this pole, more wage-workers at that.' Put another way, 'accumulation of capital is, therefore, increase of the proletariat' (*Capital,* vol. 1, p. 613).

Where does this increase in the supply of labour power come from? We can envisage either an increase in the total population or increasing participation of an existing population in the work force. This quantitative increase is not necessarily accompanied by any increase in the rate of exploitation – the mass of labour power exploited simply increases to keep pace with accumulation. Indeed, the lot of the labourer may improve. Wages may rise and may continue to do so, provided this does not interfere with the progress of accumulation. If, however, wages rise above the value of labour power in such a fashion that accumulation is diminished, then the rate of accumulation will adjust:

if wages 2 hi, fewer machines, less total product

> A smaller part of the revenue is capitalized, accumulation lags, and the movement of rise in wages receives a check. The rise of wages therefore is confined within limits that not only leave intact the foundations of the capitalistic system, but also secure its reproduction on a progressive scale. (*Capital*, vol. 1, p. 620)

The pace of accumulation appears to move inversely with the wage rate. But Marx insists that, in spite of appearances, accumulation remains the independent and the wage rate the dependent variable. It is accumulation for accumulation's sake, after all, that forced the wage rate up in the first place by pushing the demand for labour power over and beyond its available supply.

The first version of this model permits us to explain short-term oscillations in wage rates in relation to fluctuations in the pace of accumulation. The rate of actual exploitation, represented by wages, fluctuates around the underlying equilibrium value of labour power. But there is nothing in the model's specification to guarantee that major departures from equilibrium do not occur in the long run. In the face of strong barriers to any increase in the supply of labour power, wage rates could rise so far above the value of labour power that scarcely anything was left over for accumulation. Under these conditions the reproduction of capitalism would be threatened.

And so Marx builds his second version of the accumulation model. He now drops the assumption that the physical and value productivities of labour remain constant. Technological and organizational changes can be used as means to sustain accumulation in the face of labour scarcity. By reducing the demand for variable capital in relation to the total capital advanced, these changes lower the wage rate and thereby permit an increase in the actual rate of exploitation. This result is achieved, Marx notes, by increasing the value composition of capital. An increase in the 'productivity of social labour', therefore, 'becomes the most powerful lever of accumulation' (*Capital*, vol. 1, p. 621).

Marx specifies the exact mechanisms that allow a rising rate of exploitation to be achieved no matter what the pace of accumulation. Technological and organizational changes so reduce the demand for labour in relation to the available supply that a 'relative surplus population' or 'industrial reserve army' is produced. A portion of the workforce is, in short, thrown out of work and replaced by machines.

> But if a surplus labouring population is a necessary product of accumulation . . . this surplus population becomes, conversely, the lever of capitalistic accumulation, nay, a condition of existence of the capitalist

mode of production. It forms a disposable industrial reserve army, that belongs to capital quite as absolutely as if the latter had bred it at its own cost. Independently of the actual increase of population, it creates, for the changing needs of self-expansion of capital, a mass of human material always ready for exploitation. (*Capital,* vol. 1, p. 632)

This technologically induced unemployment not only provides a reserve pool of labour power to facilitate the conversion of surplus value into new variable capital, but it also exerts a downward pressure on wage rates:

The industrial reserve army, during the periods of stagnation and average prosperity, weighs down the active labour-army; during the periods of over-production and paroxysm, it holds its pretensions in check. Relative surplus population is therefore the pivot upon which the law of demand and supply of labour works. It confines the field of action of this law within the limits absolutely convenient to the activity of exploitation and to the domination of capital. (*Capital,* vol. 1, p. 639)

We finally discover here the secret of those mechanisms that hold the share of wages in total product to that proportion 'absolutely convenient' to the accumulation of capital (see above, chapter 2). Technological change, broadly under the control of the capitalists, can be used to ensure that the rate of exploitation is held close to an equilibrium condition defined by the requirements of accumulation. There is nothing to ensure that this equilibrium will be achieved exactly. Cyclical oscillations in the relative shares of wages and profits will reflect the 'constant formation, the greater or less absorption, and the re-formation of the industrial reserve army or surplus population (*Capital,* vol. 1, pp. 632–3).

Wage rates may also be kept systematically depressed below the value of labour power under certain conditions. Technological change, we saw in chapter 4, has its origins in competition as well as in the need to deal with labour scarcity or heightened class struggle. Growth in the industrial reserve army blunts the stimulus for technological change only when wage rates fall so low that fixed capital costs more than the labour it is designed to supplant. Conversely, wage rates cease to fall only when the stimulus to technological change is blunted. There is nothing whatsoever to guarantee that the lower bound set to wage rates by considerations of this sort will correspond to the equilibrium wage required for balanced accumulation. The stage is thus set for the derivation of Marx's celebrated theorem regarding the inevitable and progressive impoverishment of the proletariat.

The theorem follows quite naturally from the assumptions built into this model of accumulation. Marx shows that accumulation and technological change under capitalism means an increase in the absolute number of unemployed – a trend that could be reversed, under the assumptions of the model, only briefly in periods of extraordinary expansion. Unemployment and underemployment are produced by capital. The working class is consequently faced with an endemic crisis with respect to job security, wage rates, conditions of work, etc.

The forces making for an 'increase in the proletariat' are so powerful that they can, unless checked, reduce the labourers to 'mere animal conditions of existence'. The only check that exists within the assumption of Marx's model is that associated with the diminishing incentive to innovate as wage rates fall to ever lower levels. Since this check is relatively weak, the general law of accumulation does indeed imply increasing proletarianization of the population and increasing impoverishment. This is frequently regarded as one of Marx's erroneous 'predictions' as to the future of the working class under capitalism. Although Marx was in no way loath to exploit this proposition politically, it is not in fact a prediction at all but a proposition entirely contingent upon the assumptions of the first model of accumulation. That there are other countervailing influences at work will become apparent when we examine the second model of accumulation through expanded reproduction.

There are three fundamental conclusions to be drawn from Marx's first model of accumulation. First, the accumulation of capital is structurally tied to the production of unemployment and thereby generates an endemic crisis of fluctuating intensity for much of the working class. Secondly, the forces that regulate wage rates tend to keep them below that level required to sustain balanced growth. This second conclusion is vital to the argument laid out in the second and third models of accumulation. Thirdly, capitalist control over the supply of labour power (through the production of an industrial reserve army) undermines the power of labour within the labour process and tips the balance of class struggle in production to capital's advantage (see chapter 4).

The whole theoretical structure Marx builds in order to derive the general law of capitalist accumulation rests upon certain strong and quite restrictive assumptions. While some of these will be dropped in the course of subsequent analysis, others remain unquestioned. It is to these latter assumptions that we now turn.

Consider, for example, the definition of the value of labour power. Technological change, which reduces the value of necessities, can reduce the value of labour power and hence outlays on variable capital without in any way diminishing the number of labourers employed or their physical standard of living. This is, as we have seen, a source of relative surplus value to the capitalist. But it also means that the share of wages in total social product can be diminishing while the real standard of living of labour, measured in use value terms, remains constant or even rises (see above, chapter 2). Marx does not include this possibility in his model and presumes, in effect, that the value of the commodities required to reproduce the labourer at a certain standard of living (measured in use value terms) remains constant over time. The impoverishment of the workers is judged relative to this standard. Under these assumptions, any fall in the share of variable capital in total social product can automatically be represented as absolute impoverishment of the proletariat.

The presumption that the worker's family has no capacity to produce for itself and that the value of labour power is entirely defined by exchange of commodities in the market also creates problems of both theoretical and historical interest. To the extent that workers can support themselves, the value of labour power is diminished and the rate of accumulation increased. It is in the self-interest of capitalists from this standpoint to force the costs of reproduction of labour power back into the framework of family life (and therefore generally on to the shoulders of women) as much as possible.[1] This then implies that workers must have at least limited access to their own means of production. But if workers can in part take care of their own reproduction needs, then they have less need to participate as wage labourers and will certainly be more resilient when it comes to strikes and other forms of labour struggle. From this standpoint, it is in the interest of the capitalist class to increase the workers' dependency upon commodity exchange. But this means allowing a rising standard of living of labour and an increase in the value of labour power.

Individual capitalists, left to their own devices, will doubtless do all they can to keep wages down. The 'constant tendency of capital', therefore, 'is to force the cost of labour back to . . . zero.' The more successful they are in this enterprise, the less control they will be able to exert over the labour force: 'if labourers could live on air they could not be bought at any price (*Capital*, vol. 1, p. 600). There is, therefore, a potential conflict between the need to economize on outlays on variable capital in order to increase the rate of exploitation, and the need to control the labour force by strong economic ties of dependency. Only when the workers are totally dependent upon the capitalist for the maintenance of a reasonable standard of living can the capitalist fully claim the power to dominate labour in the work place.

This contradiction has played an important role in the history of capitalism, and has had much to do, presumably, with changes in the physical standards of living, changes in the labour process in the household, changes in the role of women in the family, the structure of family life, states of class consciousness, forms of class struggle and so on. Marx excludes such considerations from his model of accumulation. We can scarcely blame him for that, since these are all difficult and complex questions. A critical scrutiny of the

---

[1] It is in this context that we have to consider the whole question of the role of housework in setting the value of labour power. See the debate in *New Left Review* subsequent to the publication of Seccombe's (1974) article; Conference of Socialist Economists (1976); Himmelweit and Mohun (1977) and Malos (1980).

assumptions in his model does allow us, however, to generate some interesting speculations into the contradictory forces governing capitalist history.

Do the evident changes in the material standard of living of labour in the advanced capitalist countries reflect an extension of capital's control over labour through the greater material dependency a rising standard of living brings? Has this drive for control also meant a secular tendency to reduce the degree to which workers and their families have to bear their own costs of reproduction? These are the sorts of questions that can be asked.[2]

But most important of all, this leads us to consider Marx's rather surprising failure to undertake any systematic study of the processes governing the production and reproduction of labour power itself. Labour power is, after all, the one commodity that is fundamental to the whole system of capitalist production. It is also the one commodity that is not produced directly under capitalist relations of production. It is produced by a social process in which the working-class family has had, and still has, a fundamental role to play in the context of social institutions and cultural traditions which may be influenced by the bourgeoisie and hedged around by all manner of State interventions but which, in the final analysis, are always within the domain of working-class life. Since the quantity and quality of labour supply is an important feature to the general law of capitalist accumulation, we might expect Marx to make some reference to it, if only to stave off more detailed consideration of it until later. But very little play is given to the problem, and it is most certainly not taken up later. This omission is, perhaps, one of the most serious of all the gaps in Marx's own theory, and one that is proving extremely difficult to plug if only because the relations between accumulation and the social processes of reproduction of labour power are hidden in such a maze of complexity that they seem to defy analysis.[3]

We could defend Marx against such criticism by pointing out that the purpose of the general law of accumulation was to establish that capital produced an industrial reserve army no matter what the supply of labour

[2] To the degree that a rising material standard of living of labour increases the dependency of labourers and their families on capital, so it may be associated with an increasing degree of co-operation and negotiation of the sort that Burawoy (1979) reports. Capitalists are presumably aware of the benefit to them of increasing dependency and certainly, through the agency of the state, have often gone out of their way to encourage increasing indebtedness, etc.

[3] This is a topic that warrants extensive historical and theoretical analysis. Thompson (1963), Foster (1975), Scott and Tilly (1975), Meillassoux (1981) and many others have taken up the task, while the feminist literature has called many traditional Marxist ideas into question and reshaped both the content and direction of the discussion in important ways – see, for example, Eisenstein (1979), Humphries (1977), Hartmann (1979) and Leacock's 'Introduction' to Engels, *The Origin of the Family, Private Property and the State* (1942; 1972 edn). See also Zaretsky (1976), Donzelot (1979) and Merignas (1978).

power, and that we could explain poverty and unemployment without reference to the processes of social reproduction that were frequently invoked
though poorly understood by the classical political economists. Marx's
attacks upon Malthusian population theory – a theory Ricardo cheerfully
and uncritically accepted – were explicit and violent. What Marx complained
about so bitterly was the Malthusian view which attributed poverty and the
misery of the mass of the population to a supposedly 'natural' law of population. Marx argued that there is no such thing as a 'universal law of population', but that 'every special historic mode of production has its own special
laws of population, historically valid within its limits alone' (*Capital,* vol. 1,
p. 62). What the general law of accumulation does, very successfully, is to
demonstrate that the production of a relative surplus population by capital is
'at the bottom of the pretended "natural law of population" ' that Malthus
formulated and Ricardo accepted.

Problems arise, however, as soon as we seek to push the general law of
accumulation into more realistic territory. Marx hints that in order to do that
a theory of accumulation and population growth would have to be constructed as an integrated whole. Accumulation, he states, entails 'as a fundamental condition, maximum growth of population – of living labour
capacities' (*Grundrisse,* p. 608). Furthermore, 'if accumulation is to be a
steady continuous process, then this absolute growth in population –
although it may be decreasing in relation to the capital employed – is a
necessary condition. An increasing population appears as the basis of
accumulation as a continuous process' (*Theories of Surplus Value,* pt 2, p. 47;
cf. *Grundrisse,* pp. 764, 771). Growth of population, as Sweezy points out,
appears to be an important hidden assumption in Marx's general law of
capitalist accumulation. Generally speaking, it seems that the processes Marx
invokes could not operate effectively under conditions of absolute population
decline, and that the more rapid the rate of expansion in labour supply
through population growth, the less marked would cyclical fluctuations
become.[4]

But we are provided with few insights as to the mechanisms that link
population growth with accumulation. When it comes to features promoting
a high rate of population growth (earlier age of marriage, rising birth rates,
etc.), Marx does not read very differently from Malthus. The only addition,
and that one of great importance, is that the labouring family, denied access
to the means of production, would strive in times of prosperity as much in
times of depression to accumulate the only form of 'property' it possessed:
labour power itself (*Capital,* vol. 1, p. 643). But the laws of population
growth under capitalism – if such laws there be – remain to be specified. And
Marx seems to be trapped in the same general swamp of ignorance with

[4] See Sweezy (1968, pp. 222–6) and Morishima and Catephores (1978).

respect to the processes of reproduction of labour power as were his contemporaries.

The work force can also be expanded by increasing the proportion of the total population participating as wage labourers. This 'latent' industrial reserve army, as Marx calls it, can exist in a variety of forms: women and children in the family not yet employed as wage labourers, independent peasant proprietors and craftsmen, artisans of all kinds and a whole host of others who can make their living without selling their labour power as a commodity. Marx holds that the expansion of the capitalist mode of production tends to be destructive of all of these social forms – many of which are relics of a pre-capitalist economic system – and to increase the proportion of the population that has to sell its labour power in order to live. In Marx's own time that proportion was relatively small even in advanced capitalist countries like Britain. The social relations of capitalism have penetrated slowly into all spheres of life to make wage labour the general condition of existence only in fairly recent times. In this regard, also, we find ourselves moving progressively towards a perfection of those conditions that permit the law of value to operate unrestrainedly. The creation of the modern proletariat was, however, no easy matter, and from the first moments of primitive accumulation up until the present, it has involved violent expropriation, legal manoeuvres of all kinds and not a little chicanery. The mobilization of a latent industrial reserve army is not therefore to be regarded as a simple or easily accomplished task.[5]

The expansion of the labour supply by these means reaches its limits when the whole of the able-bodied population participates in the labour force. While this limit is close to being reached in some of the advanced industrial economies, there are massive reserves of labour power in other parts of the world. The history of capitalism is replete with examples of pre-capitalist economies that have been destroyed and their populations proletarianized either by market forces or physical violence. This happened to the Irish in the mid-nineteenth century (it was one of Marx's favourite examples), but we can see the same processes at work today as Mexicans and Puerto Ricans are brought into the work force in the United States; as Algerians become part of the French proletariat; as Yugoslavs, Greeks and Turks become part of the Swedish labour force and so on. All of which brings us to the edge of another problem that touches the general law of capitalist accumulation – the relative mobilities of capital and labour on the world stage (see chapter 12).

The mobilization of an industrial reserve army – particularly the 'latent' portion – depends upon both social and geographical mobility of both labour and capital. With respect to labour, for example, 'the more quickly labour

---

[5] Lenin's study on *The Development of Capitalism in Russia* (1956 edn) is still worth reading.

power can be transferred from one sphere to another and from one production locality to another', the more quickly can the rate of profit be equalized
and the passion for accumulation satisfied (*Capital,* vol. 3, p. 196; vol. 1, p.
632). A highly mobile labour force becomes a necessity for capitalism. But
here, too, we can spot a contradiction. The industrial reserve army can play
its role in depressing wage rates only if it remains in place, as a permanent
threat to those already employed. Labour cannot be so mobile that it escapes
entirely from the clutches of capital. In this regard the superior mobility of
capital on the world stage, pre-empting possibilities for escape the world over
and drawing more and more of the world's population into commodity
exchange relations if not into capitalist relations of production, becomes vital
to the sustenance of accumulation for accumulation's sake.

The sociological, demographic and geographical aspects of labour supply
are important for any general theory of accumulation. But they can reasonably be put upon one side considering Marx's main purpose in building this
first model of accumulation. What Marx demonstrates, convincingly, rigorously and brilliantly, is that if misery, poverty and unemployment are found
under capitalism, then they have to be interpreted as the product of this mode
of production and not attributed to 'nature'. A more general theory of
accumulation requires, however, dropping some of the more restrictive
assumptions, and this Marx proceeds to do in his second and third models.

II   ACCUMULATION THROUGH EXPANDED REPRODUCTION

At the end of the second volume of *Capital* Marx takes accumulation out of
the realm of production and models its characteristics in the realm of
exchange. The models of 'expanded reproduction' explore the conditions
that would permit accumulation to proceed in balanced fashion through
exchanges of commodities between different sectors or 'departments' of an
economy. The 'reproduction schemas' that Marx constructs have continued
to fascinate both Marxist and non-Marxist writers ever since and have
exercised a profound, though often subterranean, influence upon all aspects
of economic thought. The schemas have, as a consequence, been dissected
and analysed in detail, and investigators have played with variants of them
and used them to shed light on both Marxian and bourgeois theory. Since
there are many accounts of the schemas published elsewhere, I shall simply
summarize their main features and offer an interpretation and evaluation of
them.[6]

Marx appeals to use value criteria to disaggregate an economy into 'depart-

[6] Full accounts can be found in Desai (1979); Howard and King (1975); Morishima
(1973); and Sweezy (1968).

ments'. Department 1 produces fixed and circulating constant capital – use values destined for productive consumption. Department 2 produces use values for individual consumption – necessities for workers and luxuries for the bourgeoisie. A two-sector model of accumulation is built to show how definite proportionalities and relative growth rates have to be maintained in the production of means of production (Department 1) and consumption goods (Department 2) if balanced long-run accumulation is to be achieved. At various points in the text, however, Marx suggests that further disaggregations should be made – distinguishing between fixed and circulating capital in Department 1 and between necessities and luxuries in Department 2, for example.

The physical quantities of inputs and outputs in the two departments have to be in exactly the right proportions if accumulation is to take place smoothly. Department 1 must produce exactly that quantity of means of production to satisfy the needs of all producers for machinery, raw materials, etc. Department 2 has to produce exactly that quantity of consumer goods to sustain the labour force at its customary standard of living and to satisfy the wants and needs of the bourgeoisie. The material shape and quantity of commodities has an important potential role to play in these models of accumulation (*Capital,* vol. 2, p. 94).

The physical exchanges between departments are achieved through the market, and from this it follows that money exchanges between the departments must also be in balance. In order to study this process free of too many complications, Marx assumes that all commodities exchange at their values. This means that the effect of capitalist competition is ignored, as is the fact that commodities exchange at prices of production rather than of values. Marx also abstracts entirely from fluctuations in monetary market prices, actual money flows, the credit system and so on. The schemas purport to deal only with use values and values. But in practice the analysis is conducted almost entirely in value terms, with very little reference to physical material magnitudes.

Marx's analysis of the value flows is part verbal and part numerical. The ideas can be expressed much more simply in algebraic terms. The total output of Department 1, W_1, can be expressed as $C_1 + V_1 + S_1$, and for Department 2, $C_2 + V_2 + S_2 = W_2$. If there is to be accumulation, then a part of the surplus value in each department has to be ploughed back to purchase additional means of production and labour power. We can then break down the value components in the total output for each department in the following fashion:

Department 1
(means of production) $C_1 + V_1 + S_{01} + \Delta C_1 + \Delta V_1 = W_1$

Department 2
(consumption goods) $C_2 + V_2 + S_{02} + \Delta C_2 + \Delta V_2 = W_2$

Here S_0 stands for the amount of surplus value that remains for consumption after reinvestment in additional means of production, ΔC, and additional variable capital, ΔV.

In order for this system to be in equilibrium, the total output of means of production in Department 1 (W_1) has to be exactly equal to the demand for means of production in both Departments 1 and 2 ($C_1 + \Delta C_1 + C_2 + \Delta C_2$). Presuming that workers and capitalists spend all of their revenues on consumer goods, then $W_2 = V_1 + \Delta V_1 + S_{01} + V_2 + \Delta V_2 + S_{01}$. It is then easy to show that the exchange ratio required *between* departments in order to sustain balanced growth is:

$$C_2 + \Delta C_2 = V_1 + \Delta V_1 + S_{01}.$$

Put in words, this simply means that the total demand for means of production in Department 2 must be exactly equal to the total demand for consumer goods emanating from Department 1. If this proportionality is not maintained, then balanced accumulation cannot be sustained and a crisis of disproportionality (over- or underproduction of either means of production or consumer goods) ensues.

Marx's numerical example has some interesting properties and so it is worth reconstructing. The outputs of the two departments are:

Department 1 $4000C + 1000V + 1000S = 6000 = W_1$
Department 2 $1500C + 750V + 750S = 3000 = W_2$

Notice that the rate of exploitation, s/v, is the same in both departments but that both the value compositions of capital, c/v, and the rates of profit, $s/(c + v)$, differ between the departments. There is no equalization in the rate of profit – this follows from Marx's simplification that commodities trade at their values rather than according to their prices of production.

The reinvestment proportions which will keep this system in balance are:

Department 1 $4000C + 40\Delta C + 1000V + 10\Delta V + 500S_{01} - 6000 = W_1$
Department 2 $1500C + 100\Delta C + 750V + 50\Delta V + 600S_{02} = 3000 = W_2$

The way Marx sets this up presumes that only capitalists save, and that they reinvest in their own department only – a somewhat strange assumption, given the usual characterization of capital as highly mobile between sectors. Notice also that the reinvestment occurs in such a way that the value compositions of capital remain undisturbed. No technological change is built into the model. This, too, is a strange assumption, which runs entirely contrary to the emphasis given to technological change in the first model of accumulation. The reinvestment rate also differs between the two departments – capitalists in Department 1 convert one-half of their surplus value into additional means of production and variable capital, whereas capitalists in Department 2 convert only one-fifth of the surplus value they produce.

Something odd happens to this reinvestment function when we take Marx's numbers and continue accumulation over a number of years. In order to keep the system in balance, capitalists in Department 2 have to raise their rate of reinvestment in the second year and every year thereafter from 20 to 30 per cent.

While these peculiarities may be attributed in part to Marx's choice of numbers, they do serve to focus attention upon the relative rates of reinvestment in the two departments as critical to preserving the stability of the system. Designating these rates as a_1 and a_2 respectively, and the value compositions of capital in the two departments likewise as k_1 and k_2, it can be shown that a condition for equilibrium exchange under expanded reproduction is:

$$\frac{a_2}{a_1} = \frac{1 + k_2}{1 + k_1}$$

which says that the relative rates of reinvestment must reflect differences in value compositions in the two departments (Howard and King, 1975, p. 191). It follows also that the relative rates of expansion in employment in the two departments vary according to reinvestment rates and value compositions.

The two-sector accumulation model Marx builds appears to show that, under the right conditions, including correct reinvestment strategies on the part of capitalists, accumulation can continue relatively trouble-free for ever. A model depicting the reproduction of capitalism in perpetuity has certain attractions for bourgeois economists, but it poses serious dilemmas for Marxists. If capitalism can continue to accumulate in perpetuity, then on what grounds do Marxists predict the inevitable demise of capitalism or even the inevitability of crisis formation? Luxemburg, for example, was so exercised by these questions that her whole treatise on *The Accumulation of Capital* is given over to a vigorous denunciation of Marx's errors and omissions in his formulation of the reproduction schemas. To better understand this debate we must consider the assumptions embodied in the schemas and Marx's intent in building them.

Marx's purpose is not hard to divine. He wished to improve upon Quesnay's remarkable *Tableau économique,* in which 'the innumerable individual acts of circulation are at once brought together in their characteristic social mass movement — the circulation between great functionally determined economic classes of society' (*Capital,* vol. 2, p. 359). He wishes, in short, to study the 'process of circulation' of the 'aggregate social capital' in terms of the *class relations* of capitalism.

But he also wants to disentangle the contradictions embodied in such a process. So he fashions a device that allows him to identify the proportionate growth rates in the different departments, in production quantities, in value exchanges and in employment which, if they are not fulfilled, will result in crises. The reason for taking so much trouble to define equilibrium is, as always, to be better able to understand why departures from that condition are inevitable under the social relations of capitalism.

The balanced harmonious growth the reproduction schemas depict have also to be judged against the restrictive assumptions embodied in them. We should notice, first of all, that the manner of Marx's exposition runs counter to the concept of capital as a continuous process and therefore diverges from the general line of attack taken throughout the second volume of *Capital*. The reproduction schemas measure capital as the value of a stock of inputs available at the beginning of a production period (the initial constant and variable capital) augmented by the surplus value redistributed to purchase additional constant and variable capital by the end of a production period. The necessary balances are defined by a 'beginning- and end-of-the-year' accounting procedure which ignores everything that goes on in between. The accounting also presumes that all capital exists in the form of commodities that are totally used up during the production period – no capital exists as money, as inventories or as fixed capital carried over from one production period to the next. By modelling accumulation in highly simplified stock terms, Marx gains greatly in analytical tractability. But the price he pays is a departure from the very basic but much more difficult flow conception which he sought to hammer out in preceeding chapters, particularly those dealing with the circulation of variable capital and surplus value.

Secondly, the emphasis on the value exchanges to the exclusion of all else is inconsistent with Marx's stated purpose, and violates his rule of never treating any one of the triumvirate of value, use value and exchange value in isolation. Balanced growth would in fact require that physical use value and money exchanges also balance. While Marx might be forgiven for dropping one of these dimensions of analysis, he cannot be excused for dropping two, particularly since his stated intent was to consider use value as well as value aspects in his model. Had he followed through on this intent he would have come up with some helpful insights.

In order to know, for example, whether a balanced exchange of values coincides with balanced exchange of use values, we would first need information on the technological coefficients that relate physical inputs to outputs and fix the relative values of the commodities being exchanged. This leads us directly to the very important concept of a *viable technology* – defined as that production technology which can equilibrate physical and value exchanges between departments simultaneously. The socially necessary labour time embodied in means of production has to be in exactly the right ratio to that embodied in consumption goods if balance is to be achieved simultaneously on both use value and value dimensions. This plainly puts severe restraints upon the technology that can be adopted.

Marx seems to be aware of some of the difficulties, because he holds technology constant in his models of expanded reproduction. This treatment contrasts markedly with the emphasis placed upon technological change in the first volume model of accumulation. The contrast is so vivid that it immediately suggests a very important hypothesis: that there is a serious potential conflict between the 'viable technology' defined from the standpoint of balanced exchange and the technological change required to sustain accumulation through production. This clash of requirements, properly identified and understood, provides us with a tool to dissect crises under capitalism. Had Marx firmly laid out such an argument, then the problems besetting the synthetic model of accumulation in the third volume of *Capital* would have been much more easily resolved. This 'clash of technological requirements' is, therefore, a theme to which we will return in detail in the next section and the subsequent chapter.

There are various other restrictive assumptions built into Marx's model of expanded reproduction that call for critical examination. There are presumed to be only two classes in society – capitalists and labourers – and other aspects of distribution are ignored. Money functions purely as a means of payment; there is no hoarding; the surplus value produced in one department cannot be invested in another; there is no equalization in the rate of profit; there is an infinite supply of labour power; etc. With modern mathematical techniques it is possible to explore what happens when some of these assumptions are dropped, and in some cases valuable insights have been achieved.

Morishima's work along these lines is particularly interesting because it helps to illuminate some of the basic themes with which Marx was pre-occupied. Morishima considers what will happen when the surplus value created in one department can be reinvested in another. He concludes that the balanced growth Marx's numerical examples depict would then become unstable with 'explosive oscillations . . . around the balanced growth path, if department II, producing wage and luxury goods, is higher in the value composition of capital (or more capital-intensive) than department I.' We have 'explosion without fluctuations', or 'monotonic divergence from a balanced growth path', when the value composition of capital is higher in Department 1 than in Department 2. It takes very little, therefore, to generate strong cyclical fluctuations or chronic instability out of the reproduction schemas – and this, presumably, was what Marx was wishing to analyse. The case that Morishima models is of particular interest, however, since it suggests that equalization of the rate of profit under competition will disrupt the balance required for equilibrium growth. This in itself is a neat illustration of the fundamental Marxian theme that balanced growth is impossible under the social relations of capitalism (Morishima, 1973, pp. 125–7).

Morishima's model also embodies assumptions that have been duly criticized. Desai thus points out that, by varying their rates of reinvestment instead of reinvesting at a constant rate as Morishima assumes, capitalists may be able to dampen the tendency towards long-run instability and explosive cyclical oscillations. But in so doing the capitalists may generate cyclical movements in the unemployment rate, which points up another difficulty: there is no guarantee whatsoever that the 'viable technology' and the 'appropriate rate of reinvestment' will increase the demand for labour in a manner consistent with its supply. Which brings us back to the contradiction between the conditions set out for sustained accumultion in the first and second models of accumulation (Desai, 1979, chs 16 and 17).

We have also, it turns out, done less than justice to the intricacy of Marx's own thought. The long, tortuous, laboured but nevertheless deeply imaginative chapter Engels reconstructed out of Marx's notes on simple reproduction contains a mass of materials that are hard to integrate into the simplified model of expanded reproduction. And we ought not to ignore, either, the interesting chapters on the circulation of variable capital and surplus value which precede it. Marx was overly aware of the difficulties that lurked in the line of analysis he was taking. While it may appear somewhat invidious to pick and chose issues out of this mass of materials as being of particular importance, there are three problems that stand out.

First, we should note that the reproduction of labour power becomes integrated into the circulation of capital. The worker becomes, in effect, an 'appendage of capital', in the sphere of exchange as well as in the sphere of production. While Marx does not pay great attention to specifics, he sees that 'balanced accumulation' requires that the labourers use the variable capital they receive to purchase commodities from the producers in Department 2. The effective demand of the working class – which depends on the wage rate – becomes a factor that can contribute or detract from balanced growth. The processes described in the first volume of *Capital* explain why wages cannot rise much above some equilibrium proportion of national output, and furthermore suggest a prevailing tendency to depress wages much below that equilibrium. In the second volume of *Capital* we see why wages cannot fall much below this equilibrium level without precipitating a crisis in the circulation of capital within and between the department: rapid shifts in the share of labour in the total product will disrupt balanced accumulation through exchange.

The social consequences of transforming the working class into a mere appendage of capital – as 'variable capital' – in the realm of exchange are legion. Once the consumption of workers becomes integrated into the circulation of capital, their independence and autonomy in the sphere of exchange relations becomes a potential threat which capitalists must take steps to diminish. The capitalists producing wage goods are obliged to produce the specific use values that workers want and need. As possessors of money, after all, the workers are 'free' to exercise choices as consumers. Yet we can also see that 'rational consumption' – rational, that is, from the standpoint of capital accumulation – is a necessity for the smooth translation of variable capital paid out as wages into commodities produced in Department 2. The mechanisms whereby capital reaches out into the living place to ensure 'rational consumption' on the part of the workers and the reproduction of the requisite quantities and qualities of labour power are complex. Marx himself mocks the manner in which 'the capitalist and his press . . . philosophises, babbles of culture and dabbles in philanthropical talk' when '[the capitalist] is dissatisfied with the way in which labour-power spends its money' (*Capital,* vol. 2, p. 515). To this we should add the various instruments of persuasion and domination, including those mobilized through the agency of the state (usually, of course, in the name of public welfare), by means of which working-class culture and consumption habits are brought roughly into line with the requirements of 'rational consumption for accumulation'. The more we venture along this road, however, the more we are forced to enter into that domain of the reproduction of labour power which Marx generally ignores.[7] But the translation of the living labourer into mere variable capital allows us to perceive, however dimly, the lines of a different form of class struggle over the quality of life for labour.

Secondly, Marx makes a brief sally into the question of fixed capital formation and use. This posed far too many difficulties to be integrated into the model of expanded reproduction, but in the long chapter on simple reproduction Marx has a fair amount to say about the problems of finding an equilibrium rate of investment for fixed capital items that last over several production periods. He there points out that Department 1, which produces fixed capital as well as circulating constant capital, has to face up to some peculiar problems of timing in reinvestment, money flows and the like. He suggests that investment in fixed capital will likely engender strong cyclical movements, which have the potentiality to burgeon into crises, even under the most stringent simplifying assumptions. The circulation of capital between the two departments is therefore at least bound to oscillate around equilibrium as soon as fixed capital is introduced into the picture. This is a major item of unfinished business in Marx's theory – so major that we will consider it separately in chapter 8.

Thirdly, while money is treated as a means of payment in the model of expanded reproduction, there are innumerable statements in the text that indicate that the production and circulation of money are not as simple as they seem. Marx eliminates the problems posed by money capital and the credit system on the grounds that they obscure the actual processes of

---

[7] We should in no way gloss over the difficulty of transforming working-class life and culture into patterns amenable to exploitation through the accumulation of capital. It gives rise to forms of conflict and struggle in the living place that are a very important aspect to capitalist life – see Castells (1977) and Harvey (1978).

circulation of values (*Capital*, vol. 2, p. 421). But he also recognizes that the circulation of money and the creation of credit have real effects, while the production of a money commodity cannot simply be subsumed as a branch within Department 1 because it has some very peculiar characteristics (it is, for example, the one branch of production that throws more money into circulation than it absorbs in the purchase of constant and variable capital). Marx tries to deal with all of this by assuming that 'a certain supply of money, to be used either for the advancement of capital or for the expenditure of revenue . . . [exists] beside the productive capital in the hands of the capitalists' (*Capital*, vol. 2, p. 420). Where this money comes from, who is responsible for its supply and how that supply 'promotes' exchanges and 'facilitates the advancement of capital' are bothersome questions, to which we will return in chapters 9 and 10. All of this does not necessarily interfere with the model of expanded reproduction, since this model assumes that capital exists only as commodities. But if we seek more realistic models, in which capital also takes the form of money and of productive apparatus carried over from one production period to the next, then the whole issue of money and credit becomes fundamental to the analysis.

These three topics in no way exhaust the issues that Marx raises, but does not resolve, in the analysis of accumulation through exchange. I have selected them for mention in part to illustrate the richness of Marx's imaginative treatment of the processes of reproduction of capital and in part to make points of great import for the general argument I am seeking to establish. With respect to the circulation of variable capital, for example, we can now see countervailing forces to those making for increasing impoverishment of the proletariat. By putting the first and second models of accumulation in relation to each other, we can identify the forces that make for an equilibrium wage rate, or share of wages in total output. Any radical departure from that equilibrium share of wages in total values will likely generate a crisis in the circulation of capital – a crisis that can strike either in the sphere of exchange or in the sphere of production, depending upon whether wages more above or below their equilibrium value. The social processes of wage determination – inter-capitalist competition, class struggle, etc. – are such as to ensure that this equilibrium is achieved only by accident. Production and consumption cannot be kept in balance under antagonistic relations of distribution (see section III below).

So where does this leave us in terms of an overall evaluation of the schemas of expanded reproduction? Marx was most certainly not trying to build a framework with which to model the actualities of the capitalist growth process or the realities of input–output structures. Judged against those kinds of projects, the reproduction schemas would be of mere historical interest – innovative and imaginative for their time, but lacking the power of con-temporary models. Judged in relation to Marx's own project, the schemas have a quite different interpretation. They are designed to yield us *theoretical* insights into the inner logic of capitalist accumulation, insights generated by intensive modelling of a 'theoretical object' defined with respect to the domain of circulation of capital through exchange. Let us consider the nature of these insights and the manner in which they may legitimately be used.

In the first volume of *Capital* (p. 578), Marx writes:

> Capitalist production, therefore, under its aspect of a continuous connected process, of a process of reproduction, produces not only commodities, not only surplus value, but it also produces and reproduces the capitalist relation: on the one side the capitalist, on the other the wage labourer.

We also saw, in the first model of accumulation, how 'reproduction on a progressive scale, i.e., accumulation, reproduces the capital-relation on a progressive scale, more capitalists or larger capitalists at this pole, more wage-workers at that' (*Capital,* vol. 1, p. 613).

The reproduction schemas allow us to examine the reproduction of the class relationship between capital and labour from the standpoint of exchange relations. Capital circulates, as it were, through the body of the labourer as variable capital and thereby turns the labourer into a mere appendage of the circulation of capital itself. The capitalist is likewise imprisoned within the rules of circulation of capital, because it is only through the observance of these rules that the reproduction and expansion of constant capital and the production of further surplus value is ensured. We are, in short, looking at the rules that govern the reproduction on a progressive scale of whole social classes.

Viewed solely from the standpoint of exchange, this process of social reproduction does indeed appear to be relatively unproblematic. There are, to be sure, innumerable peculiarities and complications which ought to be taken into account in any full accounting of balanced accumulation. The difficulties posed by the circulation of fixed capital, the problem of accounting for inventories, stocks of money capital, the operations of the credit system, etc., all loom large. But many of these problems either disappear on analysis or at best impart cyclical oscillations to an otherwise smoothly functioning secular reproduction process.

An elaborate exploration of these additional features makes no more than a dent in models that depict the reproduction of the class relations of capitalism in perpetuity and in relatively trouble-free states. Taken directly for what they are, divorced entirely from Marx's overall project, the models deserve the vigorous denunciations to which Luxemburg subjects them. And Luxemburg is in fact quite correct in her principle objection: that Marx nowhere explains in his reproduction schemas where the effective demand is to come from that will serve to realize the value of commodities in exchange. But in this Marx is only being true to himself. It was, after all, his principle point in the first volume of *Capital* that we could never discover the secrets of where profit came from by analysing the realm of exchange. And in the chapter on the circulation of surplus value in the second volume of *Capital,* Marx makes exactly the same point about effective demand. Dig as deep as we can, we can never find how capital is realized in exchange without going back into the realm of production – that 'hidden abode . . . on whose threshold there stares us in the face "No admittance except on business." ' It is, then, in the realm of production that 'we shall see, not only how capital produces, but how capital is produced' (*Capital,* vol. 1, p. 176). It is also in that realm of production that capital is realized (see above, chapter 3). That is, after all, what is meant by 'accumulation for accumulation's sake' as the *primus agens* within the capitalist mode of production.

What all of this does, of course, is force us to consider the stark contrast between the rules regulating accumulation in the realm of production and those that regulate balanced accumulation in the realm of exchange. Read in the context of Marx's overall project, the reproduction schemas yield most of the theoretical insights we need. Balanced accumulation through exchange is indeed possible in perpetuity, provided that technological change is confined within strict limits, provided that there is an infinite supply of labour power which always trades at its value, and provided that there is no competition between capitalists and no equalization in the rate of profit. Once we relax these assumptions, the crucial variables in the first model of accumulation, then chronic disruptions will arise in the exchange process. The 'viable technology' that must prevail in exchange is perpetually disturbed by the revolutions in the productive forces.

Put simply, the conditions that permit equilibrium to be achieved in the realm of production contradict the conditions that permit equilibrium to be achieved in the realm of exchange. Capitalism cannot possibly be in such a state that it can satisfy these conflicting requirements simultaneously. The stage is set for building a third model of accumulation – one that exposes the internal contradictions of capitalism and demonstrates how these contradictions are the fount of all forms of capitalist crisis.

III THE FALLING RATE OF PROFIT AND ITS COUNTERVAILING INFLUENCES

The reproduction schemas in the second volume of *Capital* demonstrate that the capitalist process of production as a whole represents a synthesis of production and circulation. In the third volume Marx seeks to drive beyond 'general reflection relative to this synthesis', to 'locate and describe the concrete forms which grow out of the *movements of capital as a whole*' and thereby 'approach step by step the form which they assume on the surface of society' (*Capital,* vol. 3, p. 25).

If Marx is to complete his project, he must build a third model of accumulation which synthesizes the insights of the first two. The model must depict and mirror the internal contradictions of capitalism and describe their manifestations in the world of appearance. For Marx this meant explaining the origin, functions and social consequences of crises.

Unfortunately, Marx does not complete his project effectively. He leaves us instead with a preliminary sketch of what the third model of accumulation might look like. He hinges his ideas on 'the most important law of modern political economy' – that of a tendency towards a falling rate of profit. This is, he claims, 'a law which, despite its simplicity, has never before been grasped and, even less, consciously articulated' (*Grundrisse*, p, 748). The idea that profit rates would tend to decline was not new, however. Smith, Ricardo and John Stuart Mill all depicted capitalism gradually running out of steam until it lapsed into a 'stationary state' with a zero rate of accumulation. Ever eager to turn *Capital* into a critique of political economy as well as into an exposition of the 'true laws of motion' of capitalism, Marx attempts to build a model that will explain the supposed tendency towards a falling rate of profit at the same time as it identifies the origins of crises under capitalism.

Classical political economy (with the exception of Smith) explained the tendency towards a falling rate of profit by way of factors external to the workings of capitalism. The fault, Ricardo suggested, lay in nature, because agricultural productivity was subject to diminishing returns. Appeals to 'nature' of this sort were anathema to Marx; when faced with the problem of falling profits, he says scathingly of Ricardo, 'he flees from economics to seek refuge in organic chemistry' (*Grundrisse*, p. 754). Marx seeks the cause of the phenomena within the inner logic of capitalism. The argument he constructs is both brilliant and simple.

Let us define the rate of profit, he says, as:

$$p = \frac{s}{c+v} = \frac{s/v}{1+c/v}$$

From the second of these expressions we can see that the rate of profit varies inversely with the value composition and positively with a rising rate of exploitation. If the rate of exploitation increases more slowly than the value composition, then we will have a falling rate of profit.

Marx in general holds that the rate of exploitation can increase only at a decreasing rate (see above, pp. 55; 155–6). The increasing difficulty in squeezing higher rates of exploitation out of an already severely pauperized work force, the state of class struggle and the need to maintain a modicum of working-class consumption exercise a restraining influence. Furthermore, it can be shown that the rate of profit becomes less and less sensitive to changes in the rate of exploitation, the greater the value composition becomes (see Sweezy, 1968).

The burden of proof for the falling rate of profit 'law' therefore lies in showing that the value composition of capital tends to rise without restraint. Marx simply invokes here the supposed 'law of the rising organic composition of capital' as sufficient to this task. He then concludes that it is the 'progressive development of the social productivity of labour' which, under the social relations of capitalism, provokes a perpetual tendency towards a falling rate of profit (*Capital*, vol. 3, p. 212). By means of this simple strategem, Marx makes the law of falling profits compatible with the 'laws of motion of capitalism'.

But given the 'enormous development of the productive forces of social labour' under capitalism, 'the difficulty which has hitherto troubled the economist, namely to explain the falling rate of profit, gives place to its opposite, namely to explain why this fall is not greater and more rapid' (*Capital*, vol. 3, p. 232). The 'law' turns out to be a 'tendency' because it is modified by an array of counteracting influences.

Marx lists six such counteracting influences in *Capital*, but two of these (foreign trade and in increase in stock capital) fail to conform to his usual assumptions (a closed economy and a concept of surplus value that precludes the facts of distribution). This leaves us with (1) a rising rate of exploitation albeit at a decreasing rate; (2) falling costs of constant capital (which checks the rise in value composition); (3) depression of wages below the value of labour power; and (4) an increase in the industrial reserve army (which preserves certain sectors from the ravages of technological progress by lessening the incentive to replace labour power by machines). In the *Grundrisse* (pp. 750–1), Marx lists a variety of other factors that can stabilize the rate of profit 'other than by crises'. He writes of 'the constant devaluation of a part of the existing capital' (by which I presume he means planned obsolescence), the 'transformation of a great part of capital into fixed capital which does not serve as agency of direct production' (investment in public works, for example) and 'unproductive waste' (military expenditures are now often used as an example in the contemporary literature). He also goes on to say that the fall in the rate of profit can be 'delayed by creation of new branches of production in which more direct labour in relation to capital is needed, or where the productive power of labour is not yet developed' (labour-intensive sectors are opened up or preserved). And, finally, monopolization is treated as an antidote to the falling rate of profit.

This is, to put it mildly, a somewhat motley array of factors to be taken into account. They all deserve far more scrutiny than Marx gives them. And we are nowhere provided with a firm analysis of them. Some, such as wages moving below values, appear to be temporary palliatives at best, while others, such as savings in constant capital and the opening up of labour-intensive lines of production, appear to have the potential to keep the profit rate stable in the long run. We should also note that some factors, such as investment in

[handwritten margin note:] unused productive capacity

[handwritten note at bottom:] (3) so when does mrx say that there is unused capacity resulting from paying workers less than the going rate

public works and in unproductive expenditures, can probably best be construed as responses to falling profits, while others, such as the preservation or opening up of labour-intensive lines of production and savings in constant capital, occur 'naturally' with the technological changes spawned under capitalist relations of production.

However all this may be, Marx leaves us with the definite impression that none of this motley array of counteracting influences, when taken separately or all together, can successfully counter the long-run tendency towards a falling rate of profit. At best they delay the inevitable. He can then press home his argument to its final conclusion:

> The growing incompatibility between the productive development of society and its hitherto existing relations of production expresses itself in bitter contradictions, crises, spasms. The violent destruction of capital, not by relations external to it, but rather as a condition of its self-preservation, is the most striking form in which advice is given it to be gone and to give room to a higher state of social production. (*Grundrisse*, pp. 749–50)

Marx has, apparently, killed two birds with one stone. He has set the political economists straight as to why the rate of profit must fall at the same time as he has sketched a model that reflects the contradictions of capitalism and its concrete manifestations in 'the world of appearance'. Unfortunately his argument is incomplete and by no means rigorously specified. And although Engels imposes a very clear shape to the argument by his editing, the text is plagued by all manner of ambiguities.

Marx's explanation and use of the law have therefore been the focus of an immense and continuing controversy within the Marxist tradition at the same time as they have been subject to a good deal of disparagement in bourgeois quarters (which, given what the law depicts, is hardly surprising). The law has been investigated from a variety of standpoints (theoretical, historical, empirical), examined carefully for its political implications and interpreted in quite different ways. I shall not attempt to review the controversy or its manner of unfolding, since those who wish to can regale themselves at length with innumerable articles on the subject.[8] But some evaluation of this, Marx's third model of accumulation, is plainly called for.

The evaluation can proceed at two levels. On the first, we can consider the rigour, logical coherence and historical meaning of the 'law' of falling profits as a proposition in its own right. At a second, more general, level we can consider how far the law (or some version of it) effectively synthesizes the findings of the first two models of accumulation to provide thereby a firm interpretation of the laws of motion of capitalism as a whole.

[8] The surveys by Fine and Harris (1979) and Wright (1978) are useful. A good sampling of opinion would by Cogoy (1973); Desai (1979); Hodgson (1974); Morishima (1973); Steedman (1977); Sweezy (1968); and Yaffe (1973).

In what follows I shall argue that Marx, in his anxiety to straighten out the political economists, is lured into an erroneous specification of what should have been a synthetic model of the contradictions of capitalism. More specifically, by taking over the problem of the inevitability of a falling rate of profit from the political economists of the time and treating it as a question, Marx diverts from the logic of his own argument to such a degree that what should have been a tangential proposition appears fundamental while the fundamental proposition gets interred in a mass of tangential argument. As a result, Marx does not successfully synthesize the first two models of accumulation. Nor does he properly represent the 'concrete forms' which the internal contradictions of capitalism assume 'on the surface' of society. Yet, in spite of all these defects, he does manage to unmask what might well be *the* fundamental source of capitalist crises: the contradiction between the evolution of the forces of production on the one hand and the social relations upon which capitalist production are based on the other. Let us flesh out this general argument.

The exact status of the so-called 'law' ought first, however, to be clarified. It would be one thing, for example, to claim theoretically that, *if* there is a tendency towards a falling rate of profit, then it must be explained in a manner consistent with the overall laws of motion of capitalism, and quite another to maintain, as Marx most definitely does on several occasions, that the law captures *the* inner logic of capitalist dynamics at the same time as it explains real and observable historical trends in the actual rate of profit (*Grundrisse,* p. 748; *Capital,* vol. 3, ch. 13). There is, in fact, a good deal of confusion as to the exact epistemological status of the law – a confusion signalled by the way Marx variously refers to it as a 'law', a 'tendency' or even as a hybrid 'law of a tendency'. For the sake of convenience I shall continue to refer to the falling rate of profit argument as a law without presuming that such a label confers any particular epistemological status upon it.

The theoretical import of the law is fairly clear: the capacity to produce surplus value relative to the total value circulating as capital is diminished over time by the very technological revolutions that individual capitalists institute in their pursuit of surplus value. Marx spells out the law, however, in values rather than in market prices, so that both long- and short-term monetary considerations (such as endemic inflation or financial panics) cannot be included in the analysis. This means that the law cannot be used to describe the 'surface appearance' of capitalist dynamics. Furthermore, profit is construed as surplus value prior to its distribution as rent, interest, profit on industrial and merchants' capital, taxes and so on. This means that the rate of profit on, say, industrial capital can rise or fall as a result of changes in distribution rather than as a reflection of movements in the profit rate as Marx defines it (*Grundrisse,* p. 751).

We have to be particularly wary, therefore, of treating the law as a direct historical or empirical proposition. We cannot, for example, assemble data on corporate profits in the United States since 1945 and prove or disprove the law by appeal to that particular historical record. Even braver and more sophisticated attempts – such as that by Gillman (1957) – to chart changes in the value composition of capital and the rate of profit over a long time period are suspect because the necessary relationships between values and market prices are hard to establish while shifting distributional arrangements also muddy the waters considerably (accounting for taxes is particularly trouble-some). An historical record dominated by price movements and distribu-tional shares cannot easily be matched up against the law of falling profits.[9]

The most that the law can bear as an historical proposition is the not-insubstantial weight of explanation for long-run secular stagnation and violent periodic crises. Marx tends to emphasize the crises, but there is much confusion in the text as to whether or not capitalism could overcome an inherent tendency towards long-run decline by way of the perhaps increas-ingly violent shake-outs and rationalizations achieved in the course of crises. Different schools of thought exist on this point.[10]

Unfortunately, Marx's falling rate of profit argument is not particularly well-honed or rigorously defined even as a purely theoretical proposition. Consider, for example, the definition of profit which Marx uses:

$$p = \frac{s/v}{1 + c/v}.$$

It is not exactly clear, from Marx's text, what c, the constant capital, refers to. There are three possibilities; (1) the constant capital *used up* (preserved) in the course of a year; (2) the constant capital *employed* throughout a year (which would include fixed capital not used up); or (3) the capital *advanced* for the purchase of constant capital (in which case the turnover times of the various elements of constant capital become crucial to the calculation). Marx himself wavers between the first two definitions and occasionally invokes the third. Engels, cognizant that Marx had done less than justice to the findings of the second volume of *Capital*, inserted a whole chapter on the 'effect of turnover on the rate of profit' and frequently adds sentences and paragraphs to draw attention to what he saw as a serious omission in Marx's formulation of the problem.

In general, Marx's argument in the third volume of *Capital* reflects his thinking in the first volume but makes scant reference to the powerful formulations of the second (which is not surprising, since the text of the third volume that has come down to us was apparently written before the extensive investigations of the second were undertaken). The exclusion of fixed capital and turnover time from the analysis leaves us in practice with a definition of c

[9] See also the discussion by Desai (1979, pp. 193–8).
[10] Kühne (1979) and Sweezy (1968) summarize some of the debates.

as the constant capital used up in the course of a year and a definition of profit that in no way synthesizes the analytic structures of the first two models of accumulation. In short, Marx's measure of the rate of profit might be reasonable if we are prepared to assume that all capital is produced and used up in all sectors during a standard production period. Such a limited definition might be acceptable for some purposes, but it is hardly adequate to capture the inner logic of capitalism as a whole, let alone 'the concrete forms' assumed 'on the surface of society' by the laws of motion of capitalism.

Furthermore, all the theoretical objections we raised in chapter 4, concerning the relationships between technical, organic and value compositions of capital, now come fully into play as objections to Marx's specification of the law of falling profits. Let us inject these objections into the argument one by one.

Marx is fully aware, of course, that technological changes that reduce the value of fixed and circulating constant capital can, under the right conditions, raise the rate of profit or at least counteract its supposed tendency to fall. But he does not explain directly why such changes cannot stabilize the overall value composition of capital and, hence, the rate of profit in the long run. His critics have therefore pointed to a supposed bias in Marx's theory towards 'labour-saving' as opposed to what are called 'capital-saving' or 'neutral' innovations – a bias some regard as justifiable in Marx's own day but as no longer so given the predominant forms of technological progress since the latter half of the nineteenth century.[11] This is a somewhat unfortunate characterization of the problem – one which, we should note, stems from bourgeois theory – since Marx is concerned only with movements in the value ratio of constant and variable capital. In this regard, he has at hand, in the reproduction schemas of the second volume of *Capital,* a ready tool to explore the impacts of differential rates of technological change in the two departments producing constant and variable capital goods respectively.

Thus, Morishima (1973, pp. 160–3) and Heertje (1977) show that a special distribution of technological change – one that focuses in particular on certain sectors within Department 1, which produces means of production – can lead to a stable or even declining value composition of capital in the economy as a whole. The circumstance that allows of such a result is exactly that which Marx felt indicated the moment capital came truly into its own – when it evolved a capacity to produce machines with the aid of machines (*Capital,* vol. 1, p. 384). An economy dedicated to the production of machines by ever more sophisticated machines sounds somewhat insane, of course, but the technical possibility that it could stabilize the value composition of capital does indeed exist. We are then justified in asking whether or not the social processes that regulate technological change under capitalism are such as to guarantee such a result.

[11] See Blaug (1968) and Heertje (1977).

Since individual capitalists institute technological changes in response to competitive pressures and the state of class struggle, we can immediately conclude that the particular mix of technological changes required to keep the value composition of capital stable will at best be achieved by accident. Indeed, individual capitalists in command of their own production process can best proceed by seeking to increase the productivity of the labour they employ relative to the social average. The thrust of technological innovation within the firm is always towards savings in socially necessary labour time. And under conditions of labour scarcity or heightened class struggle there is every incentive for individual capitalists to economize on the labour power they employ. The parallel incentive for individual capitalists to seek economies in employment of constant capital is, by contrast, much weaker. The actual processes regulating technological change under capitalism are indeed systematically biased towards variable-capital as opposed to constant-capital saving. The anarchic character of inter-capitalist competition prevents any rational application of technological change – 'rational', that is, from the standpoint of sustaining accumulation through a stabilization of the value composition of capital. Crises therefore become the means to rationalize technological structures in relation to the requirements of accumulation. Put in these terms, Marx's falling rate of profit argument appears far less vulnerable to the barbs of his critics. This is not, then, where the real difficulties with Marx's formulation of the problem lie.

A different line of criticism might be constructed on the basis of ideas set out in chapter 4, section IV. We there showed that the measure of value composition *decreases* (everything else remaining constant) with increasing vertical integration. It then follows that the measure of the rate of profit captured by individual firms should *increase* with increasing vertical integration – again, assuming everything else remains constant. In one sense the effect is illusory, because Marx's argument on the falling rate of profit is directed at the economy viewed as a single aggregate. He is concerned with the rate at which capitalists, viewed in aggregate, use the values they command to create surplus value. And vertical integration, unless accompanied by technological change, different patterns of exploitation, etc., presumably has no impact upon that aggregate rate in and of itself. The manner in which capitalists share in the aggregate surplus value produced is affected. A simple increase in vertical integration appears to be one way of raising or protecting profit levels within the firm when actual surplus value produced is lower than average. There are evident opportunities for misallocation of labour power under these conditions.

Increasing vertical integration usually means increasing centralization of capital and change of technology away from the variable and towards constant capital. What may be gained through vertical integration may be lost through changing technology in the work process. On the other hand, smaller firm size has the advantage of faster turnover and a technological mix that usually depends more upon variable capital (though this is not always the case). The disaggregation of production, accompanied by shifts in techno-logical mix, may indeed provide a means to raise the aggregate profit rate. The trouble is that the advantages of vertical integration exert a pull in exactly the opposite direction. In this sense, the rate of profit may indeed be judged as sensitive to the exact mix of organizational and technological characteristics. We find ourselves considering, once more, the idea of an optimal degree of centralization–decentralization in production in relation to sustained accumulation (see above, pp. 139–50).

It is against such a background that we can evaluate some of the ways in which Marx thought the profit rate might be stabilized. In some cases these entail the mobilization of the 'forces of repulsion' which typically counter excessive centralization. First of all, new labour-intensive sectors could be opened up to supply new social wants and needs so as to compensate for increasing reliance upon constant capital in older, more centralized, sectors. We could here introduce the idea of 'product-innovation cycles', since it has frequently been observed that new products, initially produced on a small scale with labour-intensive technologies, are ultimately transformed into mass-production, constant-capital-intensive industries. We can then easily show that for product innovation to compensate fully for the falling rate of profit would require a perpetually accelerating rate of product discovery. This is inconceivable in the long run.

Increasing division of labour and specialization of firms within existing lines of production, on the other hand, provides a more powerful mechanism for stabilizing the value composition of capital. Historically, there has been a trend towards what is called increasing 'roundaboutness' in production – an increasing segmentation of previously integrated production processes into separate, specialized phases, co-ordinated through the market or more directly through sub-contracting. The advantage lies in a superior efficiency derived from specialization of function and the decreased turnover time of capital (a phenomenon we will shortly examine in greater detail). Since smaller firms, partly by virtue of their size, tend to be more labour-intensive, and since specialization of function permits a dramatic change in the charac-ter of labour power required as well as in labour relations, the result may be to stabilize the aggregate rate of profit in spite of the supposed disadvantages of disaggregation.[12]

The fall in the profit rate might also be checked by mechanisms that hold back the pace of technological change. There is a whole host of ways – takeovers, patent laws and the like – whereby large powerful organizations blunt competition and the impulsion to innovate. Large relative surplus

[12] Burawoy (1979) provides some interesting observations on the difference in labour relations between large and small companies and what this might mean for labour productivity.

populations can spur moves back towards labour intensive techniques, such as sweatshops (Koeppel, 1978), particularly if machines become more expensive than the labour power they replace. Some critics push this argument even further. There is nothing irreversible about technology, they say, and switching and re-switching from labour- to constant-capital intensive techniques can easily stabilize the profit rate (Howard and King, 1975, pp. 207–10). Van Parijs (1980), for his part, uses a proof of Okishio's (1961) to show that capitalists, under competition, will choose techniques which necessarily reduce the unit values of all commodities (including labour power), and increase the transitional rate of profit to themselves as well as the social rate of profit, no matter what happens to the value composition, provided only that the physical standard of living of labour remains constant. This powerful version of the theory of relative surplus value breaks down only under monopolization, increasing living standards of labour, or because of barriers posed by fixed capital circulation.

Innovation through competition does not necessarily produce the particular outcome Marx predicts. It can still function, however, as the fundamental underlying force making for disequilibrium and crises. If real wages are held constant, as Okishio assumes, the share of variable capital in total output declines sparking imbalances between production, distribution and realization, unless there is a compensating acceleration in demand for means of production and luxuries. An economy which stuck to such a trajectory would soon find itself in that 'lunatic' condition of producing ever more machines by machines or relying upon an ever-increasing disparity in wealth of the two great social classes. Also, switching of techniques, although a real possibility, is the kind of adjustment that will more likely be forced through in the course of crises than something achieved in the normal course of events.

Furthermore, switching and re-switching of technologies incurs costs. Marx definitely held that massive technological reorganizations could only ever be 'enforced through catastrophes and crises' (*Capital,* vol. 2, p. 170). This was particularly the case because of the 'peculiarities' that attached to the circulation and use of fixed capital. This, however, brings us to the point where we have to take up Marx's elaborate studies on the working period, production and circulation times, fixed capital circulation, etc., and integrate them into the model of falling profits. To do this we have to go back to basics and re-define profit in a way that genuinely reflects a synthesis of the thinking of both volume 1 and volume 2 of *Capital.*

Capital, we may recall, is conceived of as a process of circulation and expansion of value. From the second volume of *Capital* we see that capital takes on very different material expressions in the course of its circulation. This suggests a rather different formula for profit than the one which Marx uses.[13]

[13] Dumenil (1975) provokes thought along these lines.

$$P' = \frac{\text{surplus value}}{\begin{array}{c}\text{money} \\ \text{capital}\end{array} + \begin{array}{c}\text{inventories of} \\ \text{raw materials,} \\ \text{fixed capital} \\ \text{and labour} \\ \text{power}\end{array} + \begin{array}{c}\text{inventories of} \\ \text{partially fini-} \\ \text{shed and fini-} \\ \text{shed products}\end{array} + \begin{array}{c}\text{inventories of} \\ \text{commodites on} \\ \text{the market as} \\ \text{yet unsold}\end{array}}$$

The denominator is here meant to capture in value terms the total quantity of capital in the different phases of the circulation of capital. As it stands, this formulation takes no account of differential turnover times and presumes that all products are produced and consumed within one standard period of turnover. It also treats of surplus value as a flow in relation to the total stocks of capital in the various states.

Now consider what a flow version of this formula might look like. We cannot even begin to specify it without a knowledge of the structures and time requirements of production and circulation in different sectors of the economy. The models of expanded reproduction are helpful in elucidating the structures. We can see, for example, that capital which takes on the form of variable capital has a dual existence: on the one hand its money form lies somewhere in between the capitalists who have paid out wages and the commodity producers who have yet to receive back that money in return for the wage goods they supply, while in its commodity form its exists as labour power at work under the command of the capitalists. We can, in this fashion, examine the conditions of circulation of constant and variable capital and surplus value (*Capital,* vol. 2, chs 15–17).

But the time requirements vary greatly and are extremely hard to incorporate in any conception of profit (the different components of constant capital are used up in production at quite different rates, for example). Some way has to be found to reduce the infinite diversity of circulation times to some common denominator. Put another way, we have to identify both theoretically and practically some 'normal process of circulation of capital' or, as I shall prefer to call it, 'socially necessary turnover time'. I shall define the latter, by analogy with the concept of socially necessary labour time, as the 'average time taken to turn over a given quantity of capital within a particular sector, under the normal conditions of production and circulation prevalent at the time'.

Firms with shorter than necessary turnover times will receive excess profits or relative surplus value. There will likely be, therefore, a competitive struggle to accelerate turnover times. We can also see that a faster turnover time yields a higher rate of profit on an annual basis when all else is held constant. Turnover times can be reduced by a variety of means, one of which involves splitting a production process into independent phases under the command of independent firms. This, as we have seen, provides an incentive for creating increased 'roundaboutness' in production systems. The falling profits associated with increasing disaggregation may therefore be overwhelmed by the rising profits associated with faster turnover times. There is, presumably, an equilibrium point between these two opposed tendencies consistent with a stable rate of profit.

A closer inspection of the concept of socially necessary turnover time however, suggests, that we are using it to cover a multitude of complexities which ought not to be so cavalierly interred. Different elements of variable and constant capital turn over at different rates even within firms, and there will likely be widely divergent average turnover rates in different sectors. It may take decades to turn over the capital locked into a hydroelectric project and a few days to retrieve the capital laid out on setting up a sweatshop in the garment industry. How can such widely divergent turnover times be reduced to some common yardstick so as to be able to compare profit rates?

It is as crucial to find an answer to this problem as it was to explain how abstract labour becomes a yardstick against which diverse forms of concrete labour can be evaluated. Without a common measure of turnover time, there can be no equalization of profit rates because there would be no standard against which to determine whether the profit rate was higher or lower than average, or even rising or falling.

The solution that Marx is perpetually hinting at in the second volume of *Capital,* but which he fails to press home to its final conclusion, is that the credit system provides the mechanism to reduce different turnover times to a common basis, and that this 'common basis' is the rate of interest. In the same manner that the market exchange of commodities serves to reduce diverse concrete labours to the common denominator of abstract labour, so do the market processes surrounding money itself (in particular, that part of the money market called the capital market) reduce diverse concrete production processes with their specific and often highly idiosyncratic time requirements to a standard socially necessary turnover time.

This conclusion is, however, deeply disruptive of Marx's own argument. He insists that both the *origin* and the *rate* of profit can be discussed independently of the facts of distribution. While the *origin* of profit in the exploitation of labour power can indeed be so discussed, we now conclude that the *rate* of profit cannot be discussed independently to the distributive processes that form the rate of interest, except under certain highly restrictive assumptions (which we will shortly specify).

Marx's notorious reluctance to allow the facts of distribution into his analysis stemmed from his fierce struggle with a bourgeois political economy which treated distribution as fundamental while neatly side-stepping the need to consider the social relations of production. But Marx errs in the other direction. His refusal to take up the role of the credit system and the rate of interest in the second volume of *Capital* prevents the full flowering of a potentially rich analysis of the process of circulation of capital. His failure to integrate even the limited though deeply suggestive findings on turnover time into his falling rate of profit argument prevents the latter being used as a viable synthetic model of the contradictions of capitalism.

So where does this leave us with respect to the law of falling profits? Is there no way in which we can minimize the damage and rescue at least a part of Marx's argument?

At first blush, it seems that the best we can do is to lay out very clearly the assumptions that would allow Marx's argument to hold. Assume:

(1) a two-class society comprised solely of capitalists and labourers;
(2) an economy with an extremely simple structure in which all commodities are produced and consumed within the same standard time period: this means that all turnover times are considered equal, no inventories or hoards of commodities or money exist and that no fixed capital is carried over from one production period to the next;
(3) money functions purely as a means of exchange which reflects and measures values precisely;
(4) capitalist relations of production and exchange dominate every facet of life.

Then, given Marx's characterization of 'capitalist relations of production and exchange', we can deduce that the profit rate (again, assuming Marx's formula for profit is appropriate) must necessarily fall. The problem of falling profits, which had dogged the political economists of the time, is effectively solved. I do not, however, regard this as the most important insight to be garnered from a more rigorous specification of Marx's law.

The fundamental proposition emerges from a consideration of the *processes* that tend to generate the falling profits in the first place. What Marx in effect shows us is that individual capitalists – coerced by competition, trapped by the necessities of class struggle and responding to the hidden dictates of the law of value – make technological adjustments which drive the economy as a whole away from 'a "sound", "normal" development of the process of capitalist production' (*Capital*, vol. 3, p. 255). Put another way, individual capitalists, acting in their own self-interest under the social relations of capitalist production and exchange, generate a technological mix that threatens further accumulation, destroys the potentiality for balanced growth and puts the reproduction of the capitalist class as a whole in jeopardy. Individual capitalists, in short, necessarily act in such a way as to de-stabilize capitalism.

Unfortunately, Marx obscures this fundamental proposition by concentrating upon its supposed expression as a law of falling profits, with all of the historical, empirical and theoretical connotations that such a law implies.

We can rescue Marx from both his apologists and detractors by going back to the fundamental principle of a contradiction between the forces of production and the social relations of production under capitalism and tracing the expression of this contradiction in terms of the technological and organizational characteristics that capitalism must necessarily adhere to if it is to achieve balanced equilibrium growth.

In the first volume of *Capital* we see individual capitalists in command of their own production processes using technological change *within* the firm as a 'lever' for accumulation – a lever to be used against other capitalists in the struggle for relative surplus value and against the labourer in the struggle to prevent the working class from appropriating much or any of the surplus value produced. The result: perpetual revolutions in the productive forces and an ever-increasing productivity of social labour. This is the idea that Marx sought to capture in his concept of a rising organic composition of capital.

When we pushed the analysis of the reproduction schemas in the second volume of *Capital* somewhat further than Marx had time for, we came up with the concept of a *viable technology* which would permit the successful reproduction of class relations at the same time as it permitted 'balanced accumulation' among and within sectors in physical, monetary and value terms. What Marx is driving at in his third model is that, if accumulation is to be sustained, then the aggregate value composition of capital must remain reasonably stable. By stepping back into the framework of the reproduction schemas we can specify more clearly what that means. The viable technology now encompasses a specific distribution of technological change across sectors so as to keep the value composition of capital stable. What this tells us is that the dynamics of technological and organizational change are critical for the stability of capitalism and that the paths of change compatible with balanced growth are, if they exist at all, highly restricted.

The basic question Marx poses is this: how on earth can the processes of technological and organizational change, as regulated by individual capitalists acting under the class relations of capitalism, ever achieve the viable technology to permit balanced accumulation and the reproduction of class relations in perpetuity? While Marx does not prove the point beyond any possible shadow of doubt, he makes a pretty good case that the necessary technological and organizational mix could only ever be struck temporarily by accident and that the behaviour of individual capitalists tends perpetually to de-stabilize the economic system. This is, I believe, the correct interpretation to be put upon what Marx depicts as the fundamental contradiction between the productive forces and the social relations under capitalism. It is also, I would submit, the fundamental proposition that lies buried within the falling rate of profit argument.

CHAPTER 7

Overaccumulation, Devaluation and the 'First-cut' Theory of Crisis

The tendency of the profit rate to fall 'breeds overproduction, speculation, crises and surplus capital alongside surplus population.' Furthermore, it reveals 'that capitalist production meets in the development of the productive forces a barrier which has nothing to do with the production of wealth as such; and this peculiar barrier testifies to the limitations and merely historical transitory character of the capitalist mode of production . . .' (*Capital,* vol. 3, p. 242).'

Periodic crises, long-run secular decline, stagnation and even, perhaps, some ultimate economic catastrophe seem to be implied in Marx's comments. The exact interpretation to be put upon them is of great political importance. The 'big-bang' theorists assume a quite different political posture from those who see capitalism ending with a whimper. The political differences that split the international socialist movement in the period 1890–1926 – between Luxemburg and Lenin, between those who kept to a 'revolutionary' line and those who, like Bernstein, Kautsky and Hilferding, were to seek a social democratic path to socialism – were frequently expressed in terms of different interpretations of the long-run dynamics of capitalism. Today, the political posture of the French Communist Party is reflected in Boccara's theory of the transition to state-monopoly capitalism, and attacks upon that theory by writers like Magaline reflect the rather different political stance of other forces on the left. Strategies of class alliance, of 'historical compromise', of 'Eurocommunism' are likewise debated against the background of some theory of the long-run evolutionary path of capitalism. The search for a 'correct' interpretation of Marx's theory is not, therefore, an empty academic exercise, but a politically sensitive task that has to be undertaken with all the rigour we can command.

Marx himself is infuriatingly ambivalent. His writings have consequently been subject to widely divergent interpretations.[1] The ambivalence remains even when he appears to rule out certain possibilities. He firmly states, for example, that 'over-production does not call forth a constant fall in profit but *periodic* over-production occurs constantly . . . followed by periods of under-production', and that 'when Adam Smith explains the fall in the rate of profit from an over-abundance of capital . . . he is speaking of a permanent effect and this is wrong. . . . The transitory over-abundance of capital, over-production and crises are something different. Permanent crises do not exist (*Theories of Surplus Value*, pt. 2, pp. 468; 497). Yet long-run secular decline is still possible – perhaps even culminating in the ultimate catastrophe that some Marxists predict – through the broadening scope and deepening intensity of these periodic crises. And at certain points Marx seems to indicate that capitalism indeed faces such a fate (*Grundrisse*, p. 750).

All that we can say with absolute certainty is that Marx meant his exposition of the law of falling profits as a 'first-cut' statement of his theory of crisis formation under capitalism. I say 'first-cut' because, as we saw in the last chapter, his failure to integrate all of the insights from the first two volumes of *Capital* prevents a full statement of the internal contradictions of capitalism in the third. But we also find that in writing on crisis formation Marx is forced to move ahead on his own analysis in disconcerting ways – to invoke aspects of theory that lay quite undeveloped. And so we are left with a lot of unfinished business. An inspection of those brief sections where Marx does explicitly consider the shape and form of crises yields a check-list of matters invoked that have yet to be considered:

(1) the peculiar mode of production, circulation and realization of fixed capital and the difficulties that arise from differential turnover times;
(2) the process of organizational and structural change which affects the degree of centralization—decentralization of capital;
(3) the role of the credit system, interest-bearing and money capital (all of which require that the monetary aspects of circulation of capital be analysed);
(4) the interventions of the state in the circulation of capital;
(5) the physical aspects of circulation of commodities (the movement of commodities in space) together with foreign trade, the formation of the 'world market' and the whole geographical structure of capitalism;
(6) the complex configurations of class relations both within and between social formations (for example, factional distinctions within the capitalist class and distinctions within the proletariat based on different national values of labour power).

[1] Shaikh (1978) and Wright (1978) provide surveys of different interpretations of Marx's crisis theory.

This list does not exhaust the many features that ought to be included in any final version of crisis theory. Dislocations in the sphere of social reproduction – the reproduction of labour power, of bourgeois ideology, in the political and military apparatuses designed to ensure control, etc. – all require consideration. But Marx clearly regards the contradictions inherent in commodity production and exchange as basic to understanding crisis formation under capitalism. In this sense, the 'first-cut' theory of crisis is more than just a first approximation. It reveals, rather, the underlying rationale for the evident instability of capitalism as a mode of economic and social organization.

The structure of class relations implied in this 'first-cut' theory of crisis formation is not hard to schematize. From the first volume of *Capital* we see that accumulation 'reproduces the capital relation on a progressive scale, more capitalists at this pole, more wage workers at that'. We also see that unemployment, an industrial reserve army, is necessary to accumulation, and this translates into an endemic crisis for a fluctuating proportion of the working class. From the second volume of *Capital* we see the conditions that allow individual acts of circulation to be brought together into a process of 'circulation between great functionally determined economic classes of society' so as to permit the reproduction of both the capitalist and working classes. The contradictions are brought out in the third volume of *Capital*. They are expressed as a disruptive collapse of the processes of social reproduction of the two great social classes in society and take the form of 'an excess of capital simultaneously with a growing surplus population'. And we can see that 'a plethora of capital arises from the same causes as those that call forth relative over-population', which entails the peculiarly irrational condition of 'unemployed capital at one pole, and unemployed worker population at the other' (*Capital*, vol. 3, pp. 245, 251).

The crisis clearly strikes at both capital and labour alike as well as at the very basis of the reproduction of class relations. A technical understanding of the *modus operandi* of Marx's 'first-cut' theory of crisis formation has to be spelled out, therefore, against this backdrop of crisis in the reproduction of class relations.

I   OVERACCUMULATION AND DEVALUATION OF CAPITAL

Marx's falling rate of profit argument does convincingly demonstrate that the capitalists' necessary passion for surplus-value-producing technological change, when coupled with the social imperative 'accumulation for accumulation's sake', produces a surplus of capital relative to opportunities to employ that capital. Such a state of over-production of capital is called the 'overaccumulation of capital'.

If the amount of capital in circulation is to remain in balance with the limited capacity to realize that capital through production and exchange – a condition implied by the stabilization of the rate of profit – then a portion of the total capital must be eliminated. If equilibrium is to be re-established, then the tendency towards overaccumulation must be counterbalanced by processes that eliminate the surplus capital from circulation. These processes can be examined under the heading 'the devaluation of capital'.

At first sight, the concept of 'devaluation' appears somewhat odd if not nonsensical. Capital, after all, was initially defined as 'value in motion', so we are here talking, in effect, of the 'devaluation of value', which sounds like a contradiction in terms.[2] The thrust of Marx's argument is to concede the contradiction but to insist that it lies in the capitalist mode of production rather than in the terms *per se*. The latter are merely designed to reflect the contradictions inherent in capitalist production and exchange. All of which prompts some fundamental reflections upon the nature of the value concept itself.

In chapter 1 we noted that Marx departed from Ricardo's conception of value as embodied labour time only to the extent of inserting the qualifying phrase, 'socially necessary', into the definition. I then argued that it is the invocation of 'social necessity' that provides Marx with the leverage to fashion a critique of political economy and an account of the contradictory laws of motion of capitalism. The concept of value as embodied labour time is not to be construed, therefore, as a fixed and immutable building block on which an analysis of the contradictions of capitalism can be founded, but as a concept that undergoes perpetual modification in its meaning the more we grasp what the socially necessary characteristics of capitalism are. And if, as Marx shows us in the third volume of *Capital*, capitalism is necessarily riddled with contradictions, then the concept of value must necessarily reflect that fact. Put another way, 'value' is not a fixed metric for describing an unstable world, but an unstable, uncertain and ambivalent measure that reflects the inherent contradictions of capitalism.

Marx alerts us to this possibility in the very opening section of *Capital* (vol. 1, p. 41), when he notes that embodied labour that does not fulfil a social

[2] Those who interpret Marxian value theory as a pure accounting system can make no sense of the idea of 'devaluation', and it is noticeable that the concept never crops up in the presentations of Morishima (1973), Dobb (1973) or even of Desai (1979). Bourgeois interpreters have a very hard time of it. Thus von Bortkiewicz (1952) attributes to Marx 'the perverse desire to project logical contradictions onto the objects themselves, in the manner of Hegel'. It should be noted that Marx was indeed deeply influenced by Hegel's *Logic*, and that we should therefore not be surprised to find that the concept of value contains its own negation in the form 'not-value'. What is interesting about Marx's presentation is the manner in which he overcomes the 'idealist mode of presentation' characteristic of Hegel and gives the whole idea a materialist base. Quite simply, we can say that if value is interpreted as human labour in its social aspect under capitalism, then 'not-value' can be interpreted as human labour that has lost its social meaning owing to processes that are also unique to capitalism.

want or need, that is not a use value, is wasted labour and therefore not value. The problem that that notion poses is held in abeyance thereafter under the assumption that all commodities trade at their values or at their prices of production (which are still measured in values). But an analysis of the internal contradictions of capitalism shows a perpetual tendency to produce 'non-values', to waste labour power either by not employing it or by using it to embody labour in commodities that cannot fulfil social wants and needs as these are structured under the social relations of capitalism. Value, recall, is not a universal attribute of all human labour everywhere. It attaches specifically to capitalist production and exchange, and now has to be seen to include its opposite, the non-production of values and the production of non-values. This is what devaluation entails.

Interestingly enough, we have already put in place the conceptual apparatus to allow such modification. In chapter 3 we showed how and why Marx considered devaluation as a 'necessary moment' in the circulation of value. Capital, in the course of its circulation, undergoes a series of 'metamorphoses' from money into material commodities into production processes into commodities, etc. Since capital is value *in motion,* value can remain value only by keeping in motion. This allows Marx to provide a purely technical definition of devaluation as value that is 'at rest' in any particular state for more than a moment. An inventory of commodities not yet being used or not yet sold, a reserve of money, etc., can all be lumped together under the heading of 'devalued capital' because the value is not in motion. This necessary devaluation, inherent in the circulation of capital itself, is automatically suspended once value resumes its motion by undergoing the 'metamorphosis' of moving from one state to another. No permanent ill effects derive from devaluation provided that capital can complete its circulation through all phases within a particular period of time. From this technical standpoint we can see that the concept of 'socially necessary turnover time' is implied in the very notion of value itself, and that value can have no meaning independent of the 'necessary devaluations' entailed in the circulation of capital through the different states.

The purpose of Marx's argument, which in effect makes devaluation part of value itself, is to get away from the identities assumed under Say's Law, to show that supply does not necessarily create its own demand and that the potentiality for crises always lurks in the need perpetually to overcome the separation between the various 'moments' or 'phases' in the circulation of capital in time and space.[3] For most of *Capital,* Marx is content to invoke the

[3] If we conceive of 'value' as human labour in its social aspect expressed through the continuous circulation of capital through production and exchange, then Marx's critique of Say's Law, which emphasizes the 'separation within the unity' of production and consumption, means that value itself must internalize that separation as 'not-value'. In this way the possibility of crises and disruptions is internalized within the notion of value itself.

possibility and only the possibility of crises. But when Marx presents his 'first-cut' theory of crisis the concept of devaluation comes very much to the fore to help understand the permanent ill-effects of the contradictory laws of motion of capitalism. Devaluation is the underside to overaccumulation.

We are now in a position to draw upon insights generated by what must have seemed rather abstract and hair-splitting arguments advanced in chapter 3. The overaccumulation of capital in general can immediately be translated into particular manifestations of excess capital 'held up' in all of the states it assumes in the course of circulation. We can therefore have:

(1) an overproduction of commodities – a glut of material commodities on the market expressed as an excess of inventories over and beyond that normally required to accomplish the smooth circulation of capital;

(2) surplus inventories of constant capital inputs and partially finished commodities over and beyond those required for the normal circulation of capital;

(3) idle capital within the production process – particularly fixed capital which is not being used to its full capacity;

(4) surplus money capital and idle cash balances over and beyond the normal monetary reserves required;

(5) surpluses of labour power – underemployment in production, an expansion of the industrial reserve army over and beyond that normally required for accumulation, a rising rate of exploitation which creates at least a temporary devaluation of labour power;

(6) falling rates of return on capital advanced expressed as falling real rates of interest, rates of profit on industrial and merchants' capital, declining rents, etc.

This list summarizes the 'forms of appearance' of overaccumulation and ties them all to the fundamental underlying contradiction between the evolution of the productive forces and the barrier posed by the social relations of capitalism. It permits Marx to expose the theoretical error in the Ricardian view that there could be an excess of capital but no generally overproduction of commodities (*Capital*, vol. 3, p. 256). It was, Marx held, quite absurd to admit the 'existence and necessity of a particular phenomenon which is called A, but deny it as soon as it is called B' (*Theories of Surplus Value*, pt 2, pp. 496–9).

The analysis also helps us to deal with the perpetually rumbling and rather wrong-headed controversy in Marxist circles as to whether crises should be construed as arising out of 'underconsumption' (the inability of the masses to pay for the immense quantities of commodities which capitalists produce) or out of a tendency towards a falling rate of profit.[4] In the world of appearance,

[4] The confusions are discussed in detail by Bleaney (1976), Shaikh (1978) and Wright (1978).

note: describe how all these aspects of crisis play out in clothing etc.

falling rates of profit and a glut of commodities are both surface representations of the same underlying problem. Conceived of theoretically, the tendency towards perpetual revolutions in the productive forces as expressed in a rising value composition of capital becomes the basis for understanding crisis formation only when it is put into opposition to the 'antagonistic' relations of distribution and production upon which capitalism is founded. It is the opposition between the productive forces and the social relations that is fundamental, and we cannot therefore assign priority to one or the other side.

Furthermore, the analysis suggests that the tendency towards overaccumulation will surely be expressed in capitalist history by periods and phases in which we will witness gluts on the market, massive rises in inventories, idle productive capacity, idle money capital, unemployment and falling money rates of profit (after distribution). We can gain a certain confidence in Marx's 'first-cut' theory of crises to the degree that capitalist history is quite regularly and periodically scarred with events such as these. The interpretation has to be cautious, because Marx leaves a great deal out and the analysis of actual crisis formation has yet to be undertaken. The most that we can conclude at this point is that the signs are very hopeful.

If overaccumulation takes on such surface forms of appearance, then we can expect its nemesis – devaluation – to strike in the same tangible ways. Capital held in money form can be devalued by inflation; labour power can be devalued through unemployment and falling real wages to the labourer; commodities held in finished or partially finished form may have to be sold off at a loss; the value embodied in fixed capital may be lost as it lies idle. The mechanics are different in each case, and the impacts will vary depending upon which kind of devaluation we are talking about. And we are not yet in a position to render all aspects of such a process explicit – we have yet to put in place, for example, frameworks for considering inflation and fixed capital formation and use. But we can provide some more detailed analyses of the processes of devaluation given the conceptual apparatus we have at hand. This will be the subject of the rest of this chapter.

II   THE 'CONSTANT DEVALUATION' OF CAPITAL WHICH RESULTS FROM THE RISING PRODUCTIVITY OF LABOUR

There are, Marx claims, features to the inner logic of capitalism which delay the falling rate of profit 'other than by crises; such as, e.g., the constant devaluation of a part of the existing capital' (*Grundrisse,* p. 750).

What Marx has in mind here is in essence quite simple. Since the value of a commodity is set, in the first instance, by the socially necessary labour time taken to produce it, then that value falls with the rising productivity of labour power. The same principle holds even when we appeal to prices of production (the rate of change differs between sectors and in some cases can move up rather than down). The rising productivity of labour under capitalism is therefore accompanied in general by falling unit values of commodities (*Capital,* vol. 3, p. 226), provided all else remains constant. The value of the same commodity may alter from one moment to the next. In the sphere of exchange this fact is expressed as a difference between original purchase price and subsequent replacement cost in real terms.

This gap gives rise to the potentiality for *appreciations* and *depreciations* in the exchange value of commodities (*Capital,* vol. 3, p. 311). Under certain circumstances, depreciation can be understood as a form of devaluation. When the productivity of labour is rising rapidly, for example, the unit values of commodities fall fast so that the value embodied in inventories of constant capital, partially finished or finished products and of commodities on the market is perpetually being revalued in relation to the newly achieved social productivity of labour power. Under normal conditions, depreciation can have only a marginal impact upon commodities that are produced and used up within a very short time period. But production processes that require a long working period, large reserve inventories of constant capital or large quantities of fixed capital are much more sensitive. Commodities that necessarily remain long upon the market, or can be consumed only slowly, are likewise affected – housing, public facilities, transport networks, etc.

The incessant 'revolutions in value' promoted by the perpetual hunt for relative surplus value always threaten the value of any past, dead labour that has not yet been realized through production or final consumption. While this difficulty is felt to some degree everywhere, it is of much greater social significance in some spheres than in others. The individual capitalist probably notices it most directly when the introduction of cheaper and more efficient fixed capital effectively reduces the value of the machinery that he or she is employing. There is strong pressure to avoid such ill effects by using up the fixed capital as fast as possible, which means intensifying the work-process, going to a shift system, etc., (*Capital,* vol. 3, pp. 113–14). Society as a whole probably notices the problem most emphatically when there are revolutions in the value of the basic money commodity (gold), or when there is inflation in the imputed value of paper currencies – the latter being the social form assumed by devaluation in modern times *par excellence.* These are both matters that we will take up in later chapters, since we have not yet developed the technical basis for discussing them.

We can give some consideration here, however, to the relationship of overaccumulation–devaluation to the centralization of capital. Marx is at pains to emphasize that a falling *rate* of profit is accompanied by an increasing *mass* of profit, by which he means that crises tend to result not from absolute declines in the production of surplus value but because the mass of the surplus value produced cannot keep pace with the expansion of the amount of capital looking to capture it. If the reduction of the total quantity

avoid drval w/shifwork

stop dual thru centralization

of capital is all that is needed to bring the system back into equilibrium, then the centralization of capital – which involves the 'progressive expropriation of the more or less direct producers' (*Capital,* vol. 3, p. 219) – can be seen as one of the means available to accomplish such a task. The takeover of smaller capitalists by larger ones deprives the former of their capital through a kind of expropriation which in effect devalues their capital to the advantage of the large-scale capitalists. The latter can absorb the physical and financial assets of the small-scale capitalists at a reduced value. The same mass of profit is then shared among a smaller number of capitalists who have managed to reduce the total quantity of capital in circulation without in any way impairing their own activities. They have, in effect, visited the costs of devaluation upon the smaller capitalists who have been expropriated. To the degree that centralization is always going on under capitalism, it forms one of the means to achieve a constant devaluation of a part of the existing capital. We would also expect, on this basis, periodic crises to be accompanied by strong phases of centralization.[5]

When Marx suggests that an increase in 'stock capital' can help stem the falling rate of profit, he is referring to a rather different form of devaluation to that accomplished through centralization. If a part of the capital in society circulates in such a way that it claims only a portion of the surplus value it helps to produce, then surplus value is released which can be distributed among the remaining capitalists so as to stabilize the rate of profit. Marx quotes the example of railways, which can be produced and operated at cost plus interest paid out in the form of dividends (*Capital,* vol. 3, p. 240). The example is instructive. It suggests that a portion of the fixed capital socially required can be loaned out at interest to the users, that capital can be lent out in physical as well as in money form. The spread of the joint stock company form of organization and the advent of 'finance capitalism' (which can evolve such practices as bank-financed equipment leasing, etc.) can then be interpreted as an organizational and structural adjustment which compensates for overaccumulation, since a portion of the total social capital now circulates to capture interest instead of claiming the full share of surplus value it produces. Capital that so circulates is *relatively* devalued because it receives less than the average rate of profit. The tendency towards overaccumulation can therefore be offset by the organizational adjustments that increase the quantity of relatively devalued capital in circulation. The difficulty with this idea is, of course, that Marx is forced to invoke facts of distribution at a point in his argument where he has not yet laid the basis for considering the rate of interest or the impacts of finance forms of capitalism upon trends in the rate

[5] Hannah (1976, Appendix 1) has some interesting data on centralization of capital through mergers in Britain during the twentieth century, and Aglietta (1979, p. 000) assembles similar materials for the USA.

of profit. But this, as we have already noted, is a general area of weakness in Marxian theory which requires rectification.

This argument can be taken one step further. Boccara (1974), for example, points out that there can be *absolute* devaluation of capital if capital continues to circulate at a zero rate of profit. This can happen when the state intervenes to organize certain sectors (for example, public utilities and transportation) so as to contribute to the aggregate production of surplus value while claiming back no portion whatsoever of the surplus value produced. The state can thereby subsidize the private sector and artificially increase the rate of profit that individual capitalists receive. This, Boccara argues, is a major function of the state in the 'state-monopoly' stage of capitalism.

Indeed, Boccara sees the twin principles of overaccumulation and devaluation as the key to understanding the structural transformations that capitalism has experienced in the course of its history. He suggests that the only viable long-run response to overaccumulation is to accomplish 'structural devaluations', which permit the tendency towards a falling rate of profit to be countered by keeping more and more capital in circulation in both relatively and absolutely devalued states. The successive transitions from competitive to monopoly finance and then, finally, to state-monopoly capitalism are to be interpreted as social reorganizations of capitalism which permit of such a permanent structural solution to the internal contradictions of capitalism.

Boccara's argument is a special rendition of Marx's theory. It is not implausible, not without supporting evidence, and in certain respects it is very appealing. Critics claim, however, it is a gross simplification and seriously misleading.[6] It focuses primarily on the way in which capitalists share in surplus value rather than upon the crisis-prone processes of aggregate surplus value production. It takes a partial aspect of Marx's overaccumulation–devaluation thesis and erects it into a monolithic framework for interpreting capitalist history. Worst of all, it takes the processes of constant devaluation of capital and treats them as a general resolution to the chronic tendency towards overaccumulation, thereby seriously distorting Marx's version of how capitalist crises unfold. The criticisms are, in these respects, all broadly justified. But the constant devaluation of capital is, nevertheless, a real enough process with tangible material effects upon accumulation. Boccara's analysis is helpful in this regard. It is not a proper basis for the interpretation of capitalist history or of the formation and resolution of crises under capitalism.

Finally, we have to consider the devaluation of labour power. The theory of relative surplus value shows that there 'is immanent in capital an inclination

[6] Théret and Wievorka (1978) spell out the criticisms in detail. For the most part, I accept their arguments. See also Fairley (1980).

and constant tendency to heighten the productiveness of labour, in order to cheapen commodities, and by such cheapening to cheapen the labourer himself' (*Capital,* vol. 1, p. 319). Furthermore, Marx, in noting that 'this development of productive power is accompanied by a partial depreciation of functioning capital', also points out that 'so far as this depreciation makes itself acutely felt in competition, the burden falls on the labourer, in the increased exploitation of whom the capitalist looks for his indemnification' (*Capital,* vol. 1, p. 605).[7] And Marx is not beyond playing upon the idea of 'devaluation' in a moral sense in order to parallel the processes that lead to a declining value of labour power by processes that generate 'an accumulation of wealth at one pole . . . at the same time as [there is] accumulation of misery, agony of toil, slavery, ignorance, brutality, mental degradation at the opposite pole' (*Capital,* vol. 1, p. 645).[8] While these thunderous polemics are constructed around the one-sided model of accumulation presented in the first volume of *Capital,* the structural necessity for an industrial reserve army, for technologically induced unemployment, cannot be considered as anything other than a requirement to keep 'devalued' labour power on hand to fuel the fires of future accumulation.

III DEVALUATION THROUGH CRISES

The gentle imagery of 'depreciation' gives way to the more dramatic and violent imagery of 'destruction' when it comes to describing the devaluations that occur in the course of crises. At the moment of crisis, all of the contradictions inherent in the capitalist mode of production are expressed in the form of violent paroxysms which impose 'momentary and forcible solutions' and 'for a time restore the disturbed equilibrium' (*Capital,* vol. 3, p. 249). Overaccumulation is countered by the 'withdrawal and even partial destruction of capital' (*Capital,* vol. 1, p. 253). The destruction can affect use values or exchange values or both together:

> In so far as the reproduction process is checked and the labour process is restricted or in some instances completely stopped, *real* (productive) capital is destroyed. Machinery which is not used is not capital. Labour which is not exploited is equivalent to lost production. Raw material which lies unused is no capital. Buildings (also newly built machinery) which are either unused or remain unfinished, commodities which rot in warehouses – all this is destruction of capital. . . . The existing means of production are not really used as means of production, are not put into operation. Thus their use value and their exchange value go to the devil.

[7] Although Marx uses the term 'depreciation' here, he clearly means 'devaluation' in the sense that we are using the latter term.

[8] Magaline (1975) provides by far the most perceptive discussion of the implications of the devaluation of labour power for Marxian theory.

e.g. Great Depression

Secondly, however, the destruction of capital through crises means the depreciation of values. . . . A large part of the nominal capital of the society, i.e. of the *exchange value* of the existing capital, is once for all destroyed, although this very destruction, since it does not affect the use-value, may very much expedite the new reproduction. (*Theories of Surplus Value*, pt 2, pp. 495–6)

The destruction of exchange value simultaneously with the preservation of use values is particularly important in sectors that rely heavily upon fixed capital. In conditions of crisis the use value of fixed capital can often be acquired for almost nothing, which means that the exchange value that capitalists have to advance to acquire the fixed constant capital from their fallen competitors falls dramatically, as does the value composition of capital. Marx also notes that such a circumstance is of particular importance as it affects the introduction of innovations – 'the trail-blazers generally go bankrupt, and only those who later buy the buildings, machinery, etc., at a cheaper price, make money out of it' (*Capital*, vol. 3, p. 104).

Marx is even more explicit about the destruction of values in *Capital*, and if we look closely at his comments we can see most of the forms of over-accumulation–devaluation that we have already listed put in relation to each other:

The main damage, and that of the most acute nature, would occur in respect . . . to the *values* of capitals. That portion of the value of a capital which exists only . . . in the form of promissory notes on production in various forms, is immediately depreciated by the reduction of the receipts on which it is calculated. A part of the gold and silver lies unused, i.e., does not function as capital. Part of the commodities on the market can complete their process of circulation and reproduction only through an immense contraction of their prices, hence through a depreciation of the capital which they represent. The elements of fixed capital are depreciated to a greater or lesser degree in just the same way. . . . The process of reproduction . . . is halted and thrown into confusion by a general drop in prices. This confusion and stagnation paralyses the function of money as a medium of payment. . . . The chain of payment obligations due at specific dates is broken in a hundred places. The confusion is augmented by the attendant collapse of the credit system, which [leads to] sudden and forcible depreciations, to the actual stagnations and disruptions of the process of reproduction, and thus a falling off in reproduction. (*Capital*, vol. 3, pp. 254–5)

The consequence is that the reproduction of class relations is put in jeopardy. Lines of social conflict emerge which, in their broad outlines at least, reflect the underlying contradictions under which capitalism operates. For example, the latent antagonism between individual capitalists, acting in their own self-interest, and the class interests of capital (see above, p. 188) come to the fore:

constant devaluation and crisis Dval equal recession and depression

So long as things go well, competition effects an operating fraternity of the capitalist class . . . so that each shares in the common loot in proportion to the size of his respective investment. But as soon as it no longer is a question of sharing profits, but of sharing losses, everyone tries to reduce his own share to a minimum and to shove it off upon another. The class as such must inevitably lose. How much the individual capitalist must bear of the loss . . . is decided by strength and cunning, and competition then becomes a fight among hostile brothers. The antagonism between each individual capitalist's interests and those of the capitalist class as a whole, then comes to the surface. . . . (*Capital*, vol. 3, p. 253)

The fight as to who is to bear the brunt of the burden of the devaluation, depreciation and destruction of capital will likely be bitter and intense. The breaking of the fraternal bonds within the capitalist class has its reverberations with respect to distributive shares as landlords, financiers, industrial and merchant capitalists and state interests all vie to preserve their respective shares of surplus value. But what happens here is not simply a reflection of factional power. The existence of surplus capital in money form – which, recall, is 'the most adequate form of capital' – means that, without fail, 'the moneyed interest enriches itself at the cost of the industrial interest in the course of the crisis' (*Theories of Surplus Value*, pt 2, p. 496). The very structure and manner in which crises come into being dictate certain distinctive distributive effects.

And so it is in the relationship between capital and labour. By throwing workers out of work capitalists in effect discard variable capital and thereby transform the endemic problem of crisis for the industrial reserve army into a condition of chronic maladjustment and social breakdown. The labourers lucky enough to preserve their jobs are almost certainly likely to suffer a diminution in the wages they receive, which means at least a temporary depreciation in the value of labour power which can, under the right circumstances, be translated into a permanent reduction in that value. Competition among the workers will be exacerbated, as will the general antagonism between labour and capital.

However the losses are distributed, and whatever the power struggle that ensues, the general requirement for returning the system to some kind of equilibrium point is the destruction of the value of a certain portion of the capital in circulation so as to equilibrate the total circulating capital with the potential capacity to produce and realize surplus value under capitalist relations of production. Once the necessary devaluation has been accomplished, overaccumulation is eliminated and accumulation can renew its course, often upon a new social and technological basis. And so the cycle will run its course anew (*Capital*, vol. 3, p. 255). But the fundamental paradox remains:

this seems sustainable...
but it is not b/c crises get bigger

The highest development of productive power together with the greatest expansion of existing wealth will coincide with depreciation [devaluation] of capital, degradation of the labourer, and a most straitened exhaustion of his vital powers. These contradictions lead to explosions, cataclysms, crises, in which by momentous suspension of labour and annihilation of a great portion of the capital the latter is violently reduced to the point where it can go on. . . . Yet these regularly recurring catastrophes lead to their repetition on a higher scale, and finally to its violent overthrow'. (*Grundrisse*, p. 750)

This 'first-cut' theory of crisis formation under capitalism is a mixture of acute insight, muddled exposition and intuitive judgement, all spiced with a dash of that millenial vision to which Marx was prone. But the account, though incomplete, is of compelling power, at least in terms of the social consequences of the devaluation of capital that it depicts. We can begin to see how, why and according to what rules capitalists fall out with each other at times of crises, how each faction seeks political power as a means to shove off the damage on to others. And we can begin to see the very human tragedy of the working class consequent upon the devaluation of variable capital.

The inner logic that governs the laws of motion of capitalism is cold, ruthless and inexorable, responsive only to the law of value. Yet value is a social relation, a product of a particular historical process. Human beings were organizers, creators and participants in that history. We have, Marx asserts, built a vast social enterprise which dominates us, delimits our freedoms and ultimately visits upon us the worst forms of degradation. The irrationality of such a system becomes most evident at times of crisis:

The violent destruction of capital not by relations external to it, but rather as a condition of its self-preservation, is the most striking form in which advice is given it to be gone and to [make way] for a higher state of social production. (*Grundrisse*, p. 749)

CHAPTER 8

Fixed Capital

Marx's analysis of the contradictory 'laws of motion' of capitalism rests heavily upon understanding the swift-flowing currents and deep perturbations associated with technological change. Although Marx's conception of technology is very broad, he accords a certain priority to the instruments of labour – machinery in particular – as major weapons in the fight to preserve the accumulation of capital. Such instruments of labour can be used in the competitive struggle for relative surplus value, to increase the physical and value productivity of labour power and to reduce the demand for labour (thereby pushing wage rates down via the formation of an industrial reserve army). They can also be used to bring the power of past 'dead' labour to bear over living labour in the work process, with all manner of consequences for the labourer (see above, chapter 4, section IV). These are awesome weapons that the capitalists can command once the latter have assumed control over the means of production.

But instruments of labour, capable of yielding up such useful effects, have first to be produced:

> Nature builds no machines, no locomotives, railways, electric telegraphs, self-acting mules, etc. These are the products of human industry: natural material transformed into organs of the human will over nature. . . . They are *organs of the human brain, created by the human hand*; the power of knowledge, objectified. (*Grundrisse*, p. 706)

These forces of production, together with the skill and knowledge they embody, must be appropriated by capitalists, shaped to the latter's requirements and mobilized as a 'lever' for accumulation:

> The development of the [instruments] of labour into machinery is not . . . accidental . . . but is rather the historical reshaping of traditional, inherited [instruments] of labour into a form adequate to capital. The accumulation of knowledge and of skill . . . is thus absorbed into capital,

as opposed to labour, and hence appears as an attribute of capital, and more specifically of *fixed capital.* (*Grundrisse*, p. 694)

The capitalists take control of the instruments of labour in the first instance through a specific historical process – primitive accumulation. This implies, however, that at first 'capital subordinates labour on the basis of the technical conditions in which it historically finds it' (*Capital*, vol. 1, p. 310). But as the drive for relative surplus value becomes ever more powerful, so capitalism must devise means for producing instruments of labour 'adequate to its purpose'. And it can produce them in the only way it knows how: through commodity production. When the various instruments of labour are produced as commodities, exchanged as commodities, productively consumed within a work process given over to surplus value production and, at the end of their useful life, replaced by new commodities, they become, in Marx's lexicon, *fixed capital.*

The models of accumulation we considered in chapter 6 presumed that all production and consumption occurred within some standard time period. They deal with the effects of technological change while presuming that fixed capital, which carries over from one time period to the next, does not exist! We must now rectify this omission and consider how fixed capital formation, use and circulation (implicit in the idea of technological change) relate to accumulation.

Marx's definition of fixed capital is quite distinctive – very different indeed from that of classical or neo-classical economists. First, since capital is defined as 'value in motion', it follows that fixed capital must also be so regarded. Fixed capital is not a thing but a process of circulation of capital through the use of material objects, such as machines. From this it then also follows that the circulation of fixed capital cannot be considered independently of the specific useful effects that machines and other instruments of labour have within the production process. Fixed capital cannot be defined independently of the use to which material objects are put. Only instruments of labour actually used to facilitate the production of surplus value are classified as fixed capital.

A number of implications follow from this definition. For example, not all instruments of labour are fixed capital – the tools of the artisan are not used to produce surplus value and are therefore not defined as fixed capital. Items used in final, rather than productive, consumption, such as knives and forks and houses, are not fixed capital but form part of what Marx calls 'the consumption fund' (*Capital*, vol. 2, p. 210). Fixed capital is, then, only that part of the total social wealth, the total stock of material assets, that is used to produce surplus value. Since the same objects can be used in different ways, objects are defined as fixed capital 'not because of a specific mode of their being, but rather because of their use'. The total quantity of fixed capital can therefore be augmented or diminished simply by changing the uses of existing things (*Grundrisse*, pp. 681–7). This idea is sufficiently important to warrant an example. Out of the total stock of cattle in a country, only those being used as beasts of burden in capitalist agriculture would be considered fixed capital. The fixed capital could be augmented simply by using more of the cattle as beasts of burden. The example also suggests something else: to the extent that cattle can be used as both beasts of burden and milk- or meat-producers simultaneously, they have two uses, only one of which can be characterized as fixed capital. Marx quotes a similar example of the street, which can be used simultaneously 'as a means of production proper as well as for taking walks' (*Grundrisse*, pp. 681–7).

The flexibility of Marx's definition of fixed capital in relation to use is of great importance. But it also poses an interpretative danger. We dare not assume, Marx warns us, 'that this use value – machinery as such – is capital, or that its existence as machinery is identical with its existence as capital' (*Grundrisse*, p. 699). To assume such an identity would be to equate use value with value and to fall prey to that fetishism that transforms 'the social, economic character impressed on things in the process of social production into a natural character stemming from the material nature of those things' (*Capital*, vol. 2, p. 225). The end-point of such an erroneous conception is the idea that machines can become the active factor in the labour process, capable by themselves of producing value. When considering fixed capital we have, then, always to bear in mind the relationship between the use value, exchange value and value of an object in the context of accumulation through the production of surplus value.

Fixed capital can be distinguished from circulating capital in the first place by the manner in which its value is imparted to the final product. Unlike the constant capital, which functions as raw materials, the material elements that make up the instrument of labour are not physically reconstituted in the final product. The use value of the machine remains behind after the production process is completed. In so far as the machine wears out, fixed capital is entirely consumed within the production process and never returns to the sphere of circulation. Nevertheless, the value equivalent of the fixed capital circulates 'piecemeal, in proportion as it passes from it to the final product' (*Capital*, vol. 2, p. 158).

The second distinguishing characteristic of fixed capital is its peculiar 'mode of realization, mode of turnover, mode of reproduction' (*Grundrisse*, p. 732). It can be distinguished from other 'auxiliary' elements of constant capital that are not reconstituted in the final product (energy inputs, for example) by its use over several turnover periods. This ties the definition of fixed capital to the turnover process of other elements of constant capital, and we have already noted that turnover time is by no means homogeneous. The distinction between fixed and circulating capital is, therefore, in the first instance a mere quantitative distinction which 'hardens' into a qualitative difference as more durable and longer-lasting instruments of labour are used (*Grundrisse*, p. 692). Fixed and circulating capital then become 'two different modes of existence of capital', exhibiting quite distinctive circulation characteristics. Since instruments of labour are transformed into fixed capital through a specific historical process, it also follows that 'capital itself produces its double way of circulating as fixed and circulating capital' (*Grundrisse*, pp. 702, 727, 737). The relationship between fixed and circulating capital, as we shall see in section II below, then become a key consideration in charting the laws of motion of capitalism.

The categories 'fixed' and 'circulating' capital organize our thinking in ways that are fundamentally different to those implied by the categories 'constant' and 'variable' capital, which we have hitherto used. Both sets of categories have this in common: they are defined *within* production. Capital in commodity or money form is 'in a form in which it can be neither fixed nor circulating'. Since all capital must take on the form of money or commodity at some point in its existence, it follows that the relationship between fixed and circulating capital as well as that between constant and variable capital is 'mediated' through commodity and money exchanges and modified by the existence of capital in these other forms (*Capital*, vol. 2, pp. 207–9). But within the production sphere we can now identify two quite different ways of conceptualizing the organizational form of capital. The dual definitions, set out in table 8.1, are at first sight confusing. So what, exactly, is their purpose?

The categories of constant and variable capital reflect the class relation between capital and labour within 'the hidden abode of production'. They

TABLE 8.1

Material forms	Categories within production	
	Production of surplus value	Motion of capital
Plant and equipment physical infrastructures of production	Constant capital	Fixed capital
Raw materials auxiliary materials materials on hand		Circulating capital
Labour power	Variable capital	

thereby help us to understand the production of surplus value, the origin of profit and the nature of exploitation; they allow us to see 'not only how capital produces, but how capital is produced' (*Capital*, vol. 1, p. 176). But the movement or motion of capital through production also encounters certain barriers which can check and on occasion disrupt the overall circulation of capital. The fixed-circulating dichotomy is designed to help us understand these problems. It in no way helps us understand the origin of profit, however, because if 'all constituent parts of capital . . . are distinguished merely by their mode of circulation', and if capital laid out for wages is no longer distinguishable from other raw materials, 'then the basis for an understanding of . . . capitalist exploitation, is buried at one stroke' (*Capital*, vol. 2, pp. 216–19). Small wonder, then, that bourgeois economists made much of the distinction between fixed and circulating capital while ignoring the distinction between constant and variable capital.

It is, as we have noted before, characteristic of Marx to construct different 'windows' on the world in order to understand the complexity of economic systems from different viewpoints. We have hitherto examined capitalism from the standpoint of constant and variable capital and thereby understood much about the basic process of accumulation. But the investigation of circulation requires different categories. The task before us is to construct an understanding of the processes of circulation of capital through production by way of the concepts of fixed and circulating capital.

I   THE CIRCULATION OF FIXED CAPITAL

'The circulation of the portion of capital we are now studying', writes Marx, 'is peculiar' (*Capital*, vol. 2, p. 158). To get behind the peculiarities we will take the simplest case first. Consider, then, a machine produced as a commodity, used in a production process under the control of capital and replaced at the end of its useful life by another machine.

As a commodity, the machine is potential fixed capital only. It becomes fixed capital as soon as it is bought and incorporated into a production process by a capitalist. Through the act of exchange, the producer realizes the exchange value of the machine while the purchaser is now obligated to try and preserve that exchange value through productive consumption. Let us assume for the moment that the exchange value of the machine at the time of purchase is equivalent to its value.

Like other constant capital inputs, the value of the machine has to be passed on, realized, through the commodities produced. But, as a use value, the machine never leaves the production process. It retains its bodily material form as a use value which is productively consumed during several production periods. Yet the value of the machine must continue to circulate somehow if that value is to be realized. The peculiarity of this form of circulation lies in this: fixed capital continues to circulate as value while remaining materially locked within the confines of the production process as a use value (*Grundrisse,* p. 681; *Capital,* vol. 2, pp. 157–8).

This poses an immediate and obvious difficulty. We must establish what it is that regulates the relations between the productive consumption of the material use value and the circulation of value via the commodities produced. And we find that the transfer of value, and even value itself, is regulated by a social process of great complexity.

To begin with, the productive consumption of the machine depends to some degree upon its purely physical characteristics – durability and physical efficiency being of prime importance. The more durable the machine, therefore, the more slowly it transfers value to the final product. But Marx also insists that idle or under-utilized machines lose their value without transferring it: they suffer devaluation. Therefore, the rate of transfer of value to the final product depends upon those conditions within the work process – the length of working day, the intensity of labour and so on – that affect the rate at which machines are on average utilized.

Finally, and here we encounter a major difficulty, the use value of the machine to the capitalist depends upon the surplus value (or profit) that the machine helps to generate. In a competitive market situation in which all commodities trade at their values (or prices of production), the capitalist who owns more efficient or more durable machines relative to the social average will realize relative surplus value. The machine will be more or less useful depending upon the state of competition, the value of commodities in the market and the average efficiency of machines within a given industry. The capitalist could, hypothetically at least, exchange the machine at any point in its useful life, or even rent its use value on an annual basis. Even making allowance for the value already transferred through productive consumption, this exchange value would likely vary from moment to moment according to social circumstances – the pace of technological change within an industry clearly being a factor of great importance. The implication is that the value of the machine adjusts in the course of its lifetime, and that it is an unstable rather than a stable magnitude.

The final act in the drama of fixed capital circulation comes when the machine is worn out and requires replacement. If the fixed capital is to be reproduced, then a store of value must be built up sufficient to replace the machine at the end of its useful life. We here encounter another peculiarity: the initial exchange value to be recovered is not necessarily the same as the replacement exchange value required to ensure the reproduction of production capital.

There seem to be, therefore, three ways in which the 'value' of fixed capital can be determined: by initial purchase price, by the surplus value it helps to produce through productive consumption, or by replacement cost. So what is the 'true' value of the machine? And if we do not know the true value, then how on earth are we even to discuss the circulation of fixed capital as value? These are not easy questions to answer. I shall argue that the value of the machine at any one moment is a simultaneous determination of all three circumstances. This implies that the value of machinery is in a perpetual state of flux – a conclusion that is incompatible with a conception of value as 'embodied labour time' but which is surely consistent with Marx's conception of value as a social relation.

Marx avoids these difficulties by focusing narrowly on what happens within the realm of production when the value of fixed capital – as measured by its initial purchase price – is recouped through productive consumption. He proposes the following rule for the circulation of fixed capital: 'its circulation as value corresponds to its consumption in the production process as use value' (*Grundrisse,* p. 681). We must, therefore, pay careful attention to the physical use-value properties of machinery as the basis – and only the *basis* – for understanding the circulation process of fixed capital. Marx's lengthy investigations of the material properties of machines have to be understood in such a context. Ultimately we have also to consider the manner in which use values are themselves socially determined and integrated with the value theory. We begin, however, with the purely material properties of machines.

Machinery improves the physical efficiency of repeated labour processes. This efficiency can remain constant, improve, decline or exhibit a variety of ups and downs during the lifetime of the machine. While here, as elsewhere, it is the average that is important, Marx's rule implies value should circulate in a way which reflects the changing average efficiency of machines over their lifetimes. Marx also considered the durability of the machine was 'a material basis of the mode of circulation that renders it fixed capital' (*Capital,* vol. 2, p. 221). The durability of machines can vary, but here again, it is the average that decides (p. 157). The rate at which fixed capital circulates depends, in part, upon the average rate at which machines wear out through use.

This 'average' lifetime depends, in turn, upon 'normal wear and tear' and 'normal maintenance and repair'. These are hard concepts to pin down with any precision, although their general import is plain enough. Without proper maintenance, the lifetime of the machine will be shortened. But maintenance requires further inputs of labour power and materials over and above those involved in the machine's original production. The same is true for 'normal' repairs. Marx treats these expenditures as part of the value of the machine, with the difference that they are spread over the machine's lifetime rather than incurred all at once. For this reason Marx treats these expenditures as part of the circulating rather than fixed capital (*Capital,* vol. 2, pp. 173–4). The initial purchase of the machine obligates the capitalist to allocate a portion of the circulating capital to the maintenance and repair of the fixed capital: 'the transfer of value through wear and tear of fixed capital is calculated on its average life, but this average life itself is based on the assumption that the additional capital required for maintenance purposes is continually advanced' (*Capital*, vol. 2, p. 175).

The distinction between repairs and replacement is unfortunately rather hazy. Machines often 'consist of heterogeneous components, which wear out in unequal periods of time and must be so replaced' (*Capital*, vol. 2, p. 171). The machine as a whole can be *repaired* by *replacing* defective parts, but when all of the constituent parts of a machine have been replaced, has not the machine as a whole been replaced? Circumstances of this sort make it very difficult to calculate the lifetime of the machine. Marx spends a considerable amount of energy toying with such issues, without, however, resolving them to his own satisfaction (*Capital*, vol. 2, pp. 169–82).[1] He ends up setting all of these physical complications aside in order to define a highly simplifed model of the 'depreciation' of machinery in which the circulation of fixed capital exhibits the following characteristics:

> By the wear and tear of the instruments of labour, a part of their value passes on to the product, while the other remains fixed in the instrument of labour and thus in the process of production. The value fixed in this way decreases steadily, until the instrument of labour is worn out, its value having been distributed during a shorter or longer period over a mass of products originating from a series of constantly repeated labour processes. . . . The longer an instrument lasts, the slower it wears out, the longer will its constant capital-value remain fixed in this use-form. But whatever may be its durability, the proportion in which it yields value is always inverse to the entire time it functions. If of two machines of equal value one wears out in five years and the other in ten, then the first yields twice as much value in the same time as the second. (*Capital*, vol. 2, p. 158)

What Marx is proposing here is what is now known as 'straight-line depreciation' of machinery. To avoid confusion, I shall use the term 'value transfer' to refer to the rate at which the value embodied in machinery is realized through productive consumption. Marx was well aware that a model of 'straight-line value transfer' was an over-simplification. It is also deeply inconsistent with the overall tenor of Marx's argument in *Capital* since it gives an autonomous and seemingly determinant role to the physical and material mode of being of fixed capital. Marx seems to fall into the trap of the very fetishism he so frequently railed against. The admission of use value as an economic category is all very well, but Marx is not thereby relieved of the

[1] The problem of differentiating between repair and replacement is particularly acute in the case of the built environment, as we shall later see (below, pp. 232–5).

obligation of specifying how that use value is 'modified by the modern relations of production'. If we take the model of straight-line value transfer as sacrosanct, we quickly run into a variety of difficulties.

For example, straight-line value transfer calculated with respect to an original purchase price (assumed to be equivalent to value) will equal replacement investment only under special and quite unrealistic conditions – no technological innovation, no variations in the cost of machinery, etc. When such conditions do not hold, a discrepancy arises between the value recouped and the value needed for replacement. The continued circulation of fixed capital is threatened at its point of replacement.

Straight-line value transfer also presumes that the lifetime of the machine is known. So how is this lifetime determined? Marx provides two answers. Initially, he appeals to a purely *physical* concept – a machine is built with a certain physical capacity and durability and wears out within a certain time period. But he also recognizes that the *economic* lifetime may be different. The capitalist discards a machine not because it is worn out physically, but because a higher profit can be had by replacing it. The use value of the machine to the capitalist is that it allows the latter to produce greater surplus value, and this use value, as Marx clearly recognizes, changes with social circumstances. The economic lifetime of a machine cannot, therefore, be known in advance, since it depends upon changes in the design and cost of machinery, the general rate and form of technological change, the conditions affecting the rate of exploitation of labour power (the ebb and flow of the industrial reserve army, for example), profit rate differentials under different technologies within a given line of production, and so on. The lifetime of machines, being a social determination, is at best variable and at worst quite unpredictable – blown hither and thither by the winds of competition, the restless search for profit and an accumulation process that spawns such a dramatic pace of technological change. What began by seeming a solid material foundation for the analysis of value transfer is transformed by social processes into a quagmire of uncertainty.

The rate at which fixed capital transfers its value to the final product, originally conceived of as an issue that pertained only to production, cannot, evidently, be analysed independently of the effects of the chill winds of market competition. Interestingly enough, we have already encountered a parallel problem in determining the meaning of organic and value compositions of capital. And it is quite proper that we come up against this same issue here, since fixed capital has such an important role to play in determining organic and value compositions. We now encounter the rule that the use value of fixed capital within the confines.of production and the firm depends upon the ability of the firm to realize profits in a competitive market environment. How, then, can we come up with a method for handling the transfer of value of fixed capital under such circumstances? To do so obviously requires that we build some kind of bridge between the separate but related processes of production and circulation.

The difficulties can most easily be resolved by treating fixed capital circulation as a case of joint production. At the beginning of each production period, the capitalist advances a total quantity of value to purchase labour power, raw materials and instruments of labour. At the end of the period the capitalist has a commodity for sale on the market and a residual quantity of fixed capital value embodied in a machine which can be used again, replaced or even sold to somebody else. The residual value of the fixed capital is treated as one of the outputs of the production process. This way of handling the problem has been used to great effect by writers such as von Neumann, Sraffa, Steedman and Morishima. The last author shows how this artifice can be used to determine the economic lifetime of machines, to provide an 'economic criterion for entrepreneurs' decisions not to use [a machine] of a particular age any longer' and a method for bringing value transfer in line with replacement cost.[2] Interestingly enough, Marx himself pioneered the technique – as both Sraffa and Morishima are at pains to point out – with respect to the analysis of capital employed in the production of goods taking different time periods. And there are hints that Marx saw an analysis of joint products as a way out of the dilemmas posed by his straight-line model of value transfer. (*Capital,* vol. 2, p. 153; *Theories of Surplus Value,* pt 3, p. 391). He simply failed to press home the possibility (for whatever reasons) and thereby to break open what has turned out to be one of the most complex of all issues for economic theory to handle.

This theoretical artifice of joint products is more than a convenient fiction, however, because second-hand markets for machines do exist, while renting and leasing of equipment on a periodic basis is not an uncommon feature. In addition, to the degree that titles to production capacity can be traded in the form of stocks and shares, we can identify another sort of market which reflects, in part, the current productivity of fixed capital stock in relation to surplus value production. There is, then, a material and social basis for revaluing fixed capital stock from one moment to the next.

Those who have pursued the matter in rigorous fashion in recent years have concluded, however, that the treatment of fixed capital circulation as a particular case of joint production poses serious dilemmas for Marxian value

[2] Morishima (1973, p. 178). In Sraffa's (1960) hands, this method produces the interesting insight that the choice of technology, and, hence, the use value of machines, depends upon the profit rate, and that switching and re-switching of technologies can occur with variations in the profit rate. We have already seen that one of the basic criticisms of Marx's falling rate of profit argument is the failure to admit of the possibility of such switching (above, p. 185), and we will now endeavour to show more concretely why there is a conflict between the circulation process of fixed capital and the capacity to switch technologies at will.

theory. Morishima, for example, states that 'the recognition of joint production and alternative manufacturing processes . . . encourages us to sacrifice
Marx's own formulation of the labour theory of value' (Morishima, 1973,
p. 180), while Steedman is even more emphatic:

> In the presence of fixed capital, the choice of the optimal life of a
> machine is determined only in the course of maximizing the rate of
> profit, so that the value magnitudes, which depend on the effective life
> of the machine, are determined only *after* the profit rate is determined.
> The physical conditions of production and the real wage rate are the
> proximate determinants of the profit rate. The task is to show what
> determines these physical production conditions and real wages, not to
> engage in pointless value calculations. (Steedman, 1977, p. 183)

Levine likewise argues that if Marx had applied the rule of 'socially
necessary labour time' to fixed capital value transfer, he would have discovered 'essential difficulties in the calculation of the labour-value of commodities' produced with the aid of fixed capital:

> The value contributed by the fixed capital to the product is determined
> neither by its original value nor by its current value, but by the change in
> value during the relevant period. It is this inherently dynamic compo-
> nent of the determination of the value of the commodity product which
> is lost in its reduction to a quantity of labour time. The quantity of value
> 'transferred' to the product within a given period varies with the rate at
> which the value of the fixed capital employed changes over that period.
> Since the determination of commodity value is governed by a rate of
> change of value, it is inherently irreducible to any fixed quantity of labor
> time. The determination of exchange value in a sum of past and current
> labour time is excluded (Levine, 1978, p. 302)

Levine goes on to add, by way of a footnote, that 'in order to retain the labour
theory of value as a theory of the determination of exchange value . . . it would
be necessary, in effect, to exclude fixed capital' (Levine, 1978, p. 302).

All of these accounts accurately reflect the difficulty of arriving at some
appropriate way to calculate the rate at which the value of fixed capital is
transferred to the product.[3] And they all indicate that the value of fixed
capital will necessarily alter over time according to social circumstances.
Furthermore, they all prove conclusively that the circulation of fixed capital
can not be reconciled with a theory of value that rests solely on past and
present embodied labour time. Marx himself drew exactly that conclusion.
Once fixed capital separates from circulating, we encounter circumstances

---

[3] The debate over 'positive profits with negative surplus value' under conditions of
joint production is instructive in this regard. See Steedman (1977, ch. 11), Morishima
and Catephores (1978, pp. 29–38) and the rejection of the argument as spurious by
Fine and Harris (1979, pp. 39–48).

that 'wholly contradict Ricardo's doctrine of value, likewise his theory of profit, which is in fact a theory of surplus value' (*Capital*, vol. 2, p. 223).

Ricardo's doctrine of value as embodied labour time must indeed be rejected. But Marx's theory of value as socially necessary labour time is very different.[4] While Marx frequently equates socially necessary labour with embodied labour for the sake of convenience, the latter does not embrace all aspects of value as a social relation. Value, recall, 'exists only in articles of utility', so that if 'an article loses its utility, it also loses its value' (*Capital*, vol. 1, p. 202). This is a simple extension of the Marxian rule that commodities 'must show that they are use values before they can be realised as values' and that 'if the thing is useless, so is the labour contained in it; the labour does not count as labour, and therefore creates no value' (*Capital*, vol. 1, pp. 41, 85). The changing utility of the machine during its lifetime does not, therefore, leave its value unaffected. And chief among the factors affecting the value of machinery are the frequent 'revolutions in value' associated with technological change. 'It is precisely capitalist production to which continuous change of value relations is peculiar, if only because of the ever changing productivity of labour that characterizes this mode of production' (*Capital*, vol. 2, p. 72). Technological change plays as much of a de-stabilizing role with respect to fixed capital circulation as it does in the simple models of overaccumulation and devaluation which we examined in the previous chapter.

Value, we have already argued, is not a fixed metric to be used to describe a changing world, but is treated by Marx as a social relation which embodies contradiction and uncertainty at its very centre. There is, then, no contradiction whatsoever between Marx's conception of value and the circulation of fixed capital. The contradiction is internalized within the very notion of value itself.

II THE RELATIONS BETWEEN FIXED AND CIRCULATING CAPITAL

Marx held that 'fixed capital is as much a presupposition for the production of circulating capital as circulating capital is for the production of fixed capital' (*Grundrisse*, p. 734). Both the machines that are used as fixed capital and the inputs of circulating constant capital are produced in the first place through the use of fixed and circulating capital (*Capital*, vol. 2, p. 209). Furthermore, because fixed capital loses its value when not in use, a continu-

---

[4] Fine and Harris (1979, p. 45) point out that 'neither Steedman nor Morishima employ Marx's concept of value. The most fundamental divergence from Marx's concept in both cases is that each writer sees value simply as an accounting concept whereas Marx treats it as a real phenomena which has concrete effects.' The same criticism can be made of Roemer's (1979) abortive attempt to integrate fixed capital formation and use into Marx's argument on the falling rate of profit.

ous flow of circulating capital – both labour power and raw materials – is a necessary condition for the realization of its value.

Since each is necessary to the other, a certain relationship must exist between the flows of circulating and fixed capital. If balanced accumulation is to be achieved, for example, the total capital in society must be divided into fixed and circulating proportions according to some 'rational' rule – rational, that is, from the standpoint of accumulation. The classical political economists frequently attributed crises to a disproportionality between fixed and circulating capital, and Marx does not disagree. But he treats the disproportion as a symptom rather than a cause, and seeks the mechanisms that produce it.

Consider, then, the simple case of a machine with a known lifetime which transfers value to the final product according to the 'straight-line' rule. Values in the form of commodities are withdrawn from circulation at the moment of purchase. No further commodities are taken out of circulation (except for repairs and maintenance) until the machine is replaced. Each year, however, commodities are returned to circulation through productive consumption of the machine until the commodity equivalent of the value embodied in the machine is totally returned to circulation in the last year of its life. The circulation of money takes a very different course. It is thrown into circulation 'all at one time [but] withdrawn from circulation only piecemeal according to the sale of the commodities produced' (*Capital,* vol. 2, pp. 161–7). In the absence of a credit system, the capitalist has to build up a hoard of money until there is enough to buy a new machine (p. 182).

The peculiarity in this exchange lies in its time features. Money and commodities circulate according to quite different temporal patterns. Immediately after the purchase of the machine there is an excess of money in circulation in relation to commodities. Towards the end of the machine's lifetime the opposite condition arises. In the long run such imbalances will counteract each other (under the assumptions we have specified), so that there are no aggregative ill-effects while the credit system can function to smooth out money payments over the lifetime of the machine. But fixed capital circulation nevertheless exercises short-run disruptive influences even on the processes of simple reproduction. The money and commodity exchanges between Departments 1 and 2 (see above, chapter 6) would correspond only under the unlikely condition that an equal proportion of the total fixed capital in society be 'retired' and replaced each year. This would require a fixed rate of value transfer and a particular age structure to the stock of fixed capital. Imbalances would arise also in the absence of a credit system because capitalists would have to hoard money to cover replacement costs while the circulating capital needed to build the machine would have to be advanced prior to replacement. And so, Marx concludes, 'a disproportion of the production of fixed and circulating capital . . . can and must arise even when the fixed capital is merely preserved' (*Capital,* vol. 2, p. 469).

This technical insight – which Marx, in his customary manner, establishes by way of tortuous arithmetic examples – brings us to the brink of the much broader questions that arise when technological change requires that the proportion of fixed capital be expanded in relation to the circulating capital. This happens because the production of machinery entails the 'production of means of value creation' rather than the direct creation of use values for individual consumption (*Grundrisse,* p. 710). Put another way:

> The part of production which is oriented to the production of fixed capital does not produce direct objects of individual gratification. . . . *Hence, only when a certain degree of productivity has already been reached . . . can an increasingly large part be applied to the production of means of production.* This requires that society be able to wait; that a large part of the wealth already created can be withdrawn from immediate consumption and from production for immediate consumption, in order to employ this part for the labour which is *not immediately productive.* (*Grundrisse,* p. 707)

Marx then goes on to specify the conditions that will allow fixed capital to be formed:

> This requires a certain level of productivity and of relative overabundance, and, more specifically, a level directly related to the transformation of circulating capital into fixed capital. . . . *Surplus population* (from this standpoint), as well as *surplus production,* is a condition for this. (*Grundrisse,* p. 707)

Furthermore, this 'relative surplus population and surplus production' must be all the greater if the fixed capital is of large scale, long life and only indirectly related to production – 'thus more to build railways, canals, aqueducts, telegraphs, etc. than to build the machinery' (*Grundrisse,* p. 707). So how are such surpluses of product and labour power to be procured or produced in the first place? There are two possible answers to that question.

First of all, the surpluses can be procured through direct appropriation and primitive accumulation. The formation of a landless proletariat out of a peasant population, for example, can create the necessary surplus labour power. Thus the Irish became the railroad navvies and construction workers of the world, particularly after the potato famine, itself a product of the penetration of capitalist social relations into Irish society, finally forced them off the land. Capitalists can also, by appropriation or conversion, acquire the use value of fixed capital without that use value being first produced by other capitalists in commodity form. This can happen because fixed capital can be created simply by changing the uses of existing things. Means of production and instruments of labour can be appropriated from artisans and labourers;

consumption goods can be acquired and put to productive use. Under the 'putting out' system, for example, the cottages of the weavers, which had hitherto been part of the consumption fund, began to function as fixed capital (*Theories of Surplus Value,* pt 2, p. 23). A similar effect occurs when transport systems built primarily for consumption begin to be used more and more for production-related activities.

The advantage here is that fixed capital can be formed without in any way interfering with circulating capital. How much fixed capital can be formed in this way depends, however, on the pre-existing conditions – capital, after all, 'did not begin the world from the beginning but rather encountered production and products already present, before it subjugated them beneath its process' (*Grundrisse,* p. 675). Eighteenth-century Britain, for example, possessed a vast reservoir of material assets (perhaps two or three times the assets that Nigeria currently possesses), and these use values could easily be converted into fixed capital at little or no cost. The early industrialists acquired much of their fixed capital by putting old structures (mills, barns, houses, transport systems, etc.) to new productive uses. Rates of fixed capital formation never rose much above 5 or 6 per cent of national output, compared with the 12 per cent or more usually considered essential to get the accumulation of capital going.[5] The aberrant case of Britain, which is so vital because it was to lead the way in sustained capital accumulation, is explicable given the fluidity of Marx's definitions. Appropriation, conversion and primitive accumulation provided the fixed capital without diverting anything from circulating capital. These features continue to be of some importance throughout the history of capitalism – African immigrants, for example, play a vital role in French construction activity, as do southern Europeans throughout much of Western Europe. But if technological change is to play its proper role, then capitalism has to develop the capacity to produce surpluses of product and labour power within its confines.

This brings us to the second major mechanism for generating the necessary preconditions for fixed capital formation. Overaccumulation, which we have seen necessarily arises under capitalism on a periodic basis, involves the creation of 'unemployed capital at one pole and an unemployed worker population at the other' (see above, chapter 7). The surpluses of labour power, of commodities, of productive capacity and of money capital are potentially convertible into fixed capital. This is a fundamental and very

[5] According to Rostow's (1960) *Stages of Economic Growth* (with its interesting sub-title of a 'non-communist manifesto'), Britain achieved its 'take-off' into economic growth between 1783 and 1802 by doubling is rate of investment from 5 to 10 per cent. Deane and Cole (1962, pp. 261–4) find little evidence for such a surge in capital formation, and the subsequent debate – much of which is reprinted in Crouzet (1972) – gives strong support to that conclusion. Mathias (1973) is also well worth consulting on this point.

important theoretical insight. It says, in effect, that the contradictions of accumulation produce the necessary preconditions for fixed capital formation on a periodic basis. We will try to unravel some of the implications of this striking theoretical insight in what follows.

We begin with considering how the ebb and flow of the industrial reserve army relates to fixed capital formation in the absence of any 'primitive accumulation' or the mobilization of 'latent' sectors within a population. Under such conditions, a relative surplus population is primarily the product of technological change which creates unemployment. But technological change usually requires fixed capital formation. And the latter requires the prior formation of an industrial reserve army. The rhythm of supply and demand for labour power and the capacity to absorb excess labour power through fixed capital formation appear to be regulated by contradictory circumstances. The very processes that produce an industrial reserve army also absorb it. The contradiction is typically expressed through phases of fixed capital formation and surplus labour power absorption followed by widespread unemployment and stagnation in fixed capital formation. We cannot, however, understand such a process fully without considering how surplus products are also generated and absorbed.

The surpluses of commodities, productive capacities and labour power associated with overaccumulation cannot instantaneously be switched from, say, consumer goods industries (clothing, shoes, etc.) to the production of fixed capital items (machinery, railroads). It often takes a crisis to force such a switch from circulating to fixed capital – indeed, Marx argued that 'a crisis always forms the starting point for new investments', which lay 'a new material basis for the next turnover cycle' (*Capital*, vol. 2, p. 186). If such switches could occur instantaneously and costlessly, then the problems of overaccumulation and devaluation of circulating capital could be entirely resolved by fixed capital formation. The limit to such switching would lie only in the capacity to realize the value of the fixed capital investments. Since the employment of fixed capital means an increase in the productivity of labour, the switch from circulating to fixed capital can only exacerbate the problem of overaccumulation in the long run. A part of the fixed capital will be condemned to forced idleness through overaccumulation, and the fixed capital itself will undergo a devaluation. A short-run solution to problems of overaccumulation exacerbates the difficulties in the long run and puts part of the general burden of periodical devaluations upon fixed capital. The only difference would be that the timing and rhythm of crisis formation and resolution would now be deeply affected by the turnover process of fixed capital itself.

The devaluation of fixed capital might be staved off indefinitely by switching more and more capital into fixed capital formation. This possibility was discussed by Tugan-Baranovsky in the context of Marx's schemas of expanded reproduction.[6] He showed that accumulation could continue in perpetuity provided that investment in fixed capital grew in the right proportions. This would imply an economy in which machines would be built to produce machines that built machines – something that looks quite absurd from the standpoint of human needs but which capitalism is theoretically capable of developing, since capitalists are interested only in surplus value and care not a jot for which use values they produce. The limits to such a lunatic economy would be reached only when the flow of circulating capital became insufficient to support the continued use of the fixed capital, or when the pace of technological change implied by fixed capital formation became so fast that devaluations through shortened economic lifetimes of machines became a serious problem. While Tugan-Baranovsky's solution cannot be sustained in the long run, he helps to explain why capitalism has frequent bouts of excessive investment in high-technology production without regard to the surpluses of labour power that already exist or the human needs of populations. In the short run, therefore, capital can respond to overaccumulation by switching to fixed capital formation – and the longer the life and the larger the scale of the fixed capital, the better (for example, large-scale public works, dams, railroads, etc.). But sometime in the long run, problems of overaccumulation are bound to re-emerge, perhaps to be registered on an even grander scale in the devaluation of fixed capital itself.

The contradictions inherent in the fixed capital form of circulation can be approached from another angle. Marx argues that 'the greater the scale on which fixed capital develops . . . the more does the continuity of the production process . . . become an externally compelling condition for the mode of production founded on capital' (Grundrisse, p. 703). When capitalists purchase fixed capital they are obliged to use it until its value (however calculated) is fully retrieved. Fixed capital 'engages the production of subsequent years', 'anticipates further labour as a counter-value' and therefore exercises a coercive power over future uses (Grundrisse, p. 731). Marx focuses on the tyranny that fixed capital, in the form of the machine under the control of the capitalist, exercises over the conditions of work of the labourer (hence the long and very powerful chapter on machinery in the first volume of Capital). But the point can be generalized. The more capital circulates in fixed form, the more the system of production and consumption is locked into specific activities geared to the realization of fixed capital.

The contradiction involved in this should be readily apparent. On the one hand, fixed capital provides a powerful lever for accumulation while further investment in fixed capital provides at least temporary relief from problems of overaccumulation. On the other hand, production and consumption are

---

[6] Kalecki (1971, ch. 13) gives an interesting account of Tugan-Baranovsky's schema.

increasingly imprisoned within fixed ways of doing things and increasingly committed to specific lines of production. Capitalism loses its flexibility, and the ability to innovate is checked (*Capital,* vol. 2, p. 185).

This throws us back immediately into that complex world, which Marx was cognizant of but about which he did little to enlighten us, in which the economic lifetime of fixed capital no longer corresponds to its physical lifetime. Straight-line value transfer can no longer hold as an adequate description of fixed capital circulation. The most serious problem to arise here concerns the impact of new, cheaper and more efficient machinery on the use value and, hence, on the imputed value of the old. Resorting to the language of prices, Marx notes how the 'constant changes in the construction of the machines, and their ever-increasing cheapness, depreciate day by day the older makes, and allow of their being sold in great numbers, at absurd prices, to large capitalists, who alone can thus employ them at a profit' (*Capital,* vol. 1, p. 474; vol. 3, pp. 114–15). Perpetual revolutions in technology can mean the devaluation of fixed capital on an extensive scale.

The exchanges between Departments 1 and 2 can also be subject to disruption. But if the pace of technological change is steady, and if capitalists can feel reasonably secure in their expectations with respect to future technologies, then it is possible to plan the obsolescence of their fixed capital and manage the circulation of fixed capital according to some rational plan.[7] In this way the disruptive effects of technological change can be minimized and the impact on the exchange relations between the two departments can be reduced to fairly minor oscillations. But planned obsolescence is possible only if the rate of technological change is contained. Monopolization, government sponsorship of research and development and legal constraints upon the application of innovations (patent and licensing laws in particular) play important roles, then, in regulating the pace of technological change and making planned obsolescence an available means to counter the evident tension between technological change and its inevitable corollary, fixed capital devaluation. Indeed, a case can be made that the incoherent and destructive effects of uncontrolled technological change call forth a capitalist response in the form of various arrangements – such as monopolies and patent laws – to control the pace of that technological change.[8]

In the absence of successful controls, planned obsolescence becomes impossible. What begin as minor oscillations and imbalances between departments and in the proportions of fixed to circulating capital quickly build into explosive oscillations or monotonic divergence from a balanced growth path (see above, p. 171). The circulation of fixed capital becomes

[7] The parallel with Boccara's views on relative devaluation – see chapter 7 above – is worth noting.

[8] Noble's (1977) account of the controlled use of the patent laws in the United States since the begining of this century fits very well with this theoretical account.

entangled in the mesh of contradictory forces associated with technological change, disequilibrium, crisis formation, overaccumulation and devaluation. It was just such a result that Marx had in mind in his studies of the circulation of fixed capital.

He argues explicitly, for example, that the competitive search for relative surplus value forces the replacement of 'old instruments of labour before the expiration of their natural life', and that if this occurs on 'a rather large social scale' it is 'mainly enforced through catastrophes and crises' (*Capital,* vol. 2, p. 170). He also notes that the 'continual improvements which lower the use value, and therefore the value, of existing machinery, factory buildings, etc.' have a 'particularly dire effect during the first period of newly introduced machinery . . . when it continually becomes antiquated before it has time to reproduce its own value.' Rapid reductions in replacement cost have similar effects. And so we find that 'large enterprises frequently do not flourish until they pass into other hands, i.e., after their first proprietors have been bankrupted, and their successors, who buy them out cheaply, therefore begin from the outset with a smaller outlay of capital' (*Capital,* vol. 3, pp. 113–14).

In the course of partial or general crises, the elements of fixed capital are devalued to a greater or lesser degree. This then forms 'one of the means immanent in capitalist production to check the fall of the rate of profit and hasten accumulation of capital value through formation of new capital' (*Capital,* vol. 3, pp. 249, 254). The aggregate value composition of capital is, in short, stabilized in the face of strong technological change by the forced devaluation of a part of the fixed constant capital. The concepts of over-accumulation and devaluation have, then, a particular role to play in relation to fixed capital circulation. Marx concludes:

> The cycle of interconnected turnovers embracing a number of years, in which capital is held fast by its fixed constituent part, furnishes a material basis for the periodic crises. During this cycle business undergoes successive periods of depression, medium activity, precipitancy, crisis. True, periods in which capital is invested differ greatly and far from coincide in time. But a crisis always forms the starting point for new investments. Therefore, from the point of view of society as a whole [it lays] a new material basis for the next turnover cycle. (*Capital,* vol. 2, p. 186)

Crises, then, take on a rather different aspect and a new dimension when we introduce fixed capital circulation into the picture. The fundamental contradiction between the evolution of the productive forces and the social relations of capitalism still remains at the very heart of things. The pace of technological change – itself primarily associated with the drive for relative surplus value (see chapter 4) – continues to be both the main lever for accumulation and the major force making for disequilibrium. But we now see

that the very manner in which many of the forces of production are constituted – through commodity and surplus value production – engenders a
form of circulation of value that is in contradiction with further technological
change. Technological change either slows down (thereby depriving capital
of its main lever of accumulation) or presses on apace with the inevitable
devaluation of fixed capital as its result. The whole material manifestation
and temporal rhythm of crisis formation is, however, fundamentally altered.
In such a situation, Marx's 'first-cut' theory of crisis (see chapter 7) plainly
will not do. How that theory should be adjusted to take account of fixed
capital formation and use remains to be seen.

III SOME SPECIAL FORMS OF FIXED CAPITAL CIRCULATION

By clinging to the example of machinery, we have been able to simplify the
conception of fixed capital. But fixed capital also includes such diverse items
as ships and docks, railroads and locomotives, dams and bridges, water
supply and sewage systems, power stations, factory buildings, warehouses
and the like. A pickaxe and a railroad may both be classified as fixed capital,
but their similarity thereafter quickly ceases. So we ought to disaggregate the
concept of fixed capital and consider some of the special 'peculiarities' that
then arise.

We have also hitherto excluded any detailed consideration of how the
interventions of the credit system affect matters even though the question has
lurked in the background of the analysis. Credit certainly appears, at first
blush, as an appropriate means to overcome the contradictions between fixed
and circulating capital. But, true to his colours, Marx will insist that to the
degree that credit successfully performs such a function it internalizes contradictions within its own sphere. The contradictions get displaced rather
than removed. Marx hints at such a displacement when he characterizes 'the
different kind of return on fixed and circulating capital' as the difference
between annuity, interest and the different forms of rent, on the one hand,
and selling and profit on the other (*Grundrisse*, p. 722). We will elaborate on
this theme in the sections that follow.

Since the sphere of money, credit and interest is extraordinarily complex,
we must delay consideration of it until the next chapter. The best we can hope
to do here is to show how and why the credit system must necessarily exist as
a means to deal with some of the chronic problems that arise in the context of
fixed capital formation and use. And this we can best do by considering
situations in which the problems of fixed capital circulation assume an
exaggerated and very special form.

1 *Fixed capital of large scale and great durability*

The turnover time of fixed capital is a function of its 'relative durability', and the 'durability of its material is therefore a condition of its function as an instrument of labour, and consequently the material basis of the mode of circulation which renders it fixed capital' (*Capital*, vol. 2, pp. 220–1). In so far as durability depends upon physical properties, the material qualities of use values have an important effect upon turnover time. But Marx also insists that 'the greater durability of fixed capital must not be conceived of as a purely physical quality' (*Capital*, vol. 2, p. 221). Durable materials are incorporated into fixed capital items because advantages arise from so doing – for example, 'the more often [a machine] must be replaced, the costlier it is' (*Grundrisse,* p. 711). On the other hand, the longer the fixed capital lasts, the more likely it is to be exposed to devaluation through technological change.

The durability of fixed capital therefore varies according to economic circumstances and material and technological possibilities. We have already noted that 'different constituents of the fixed capital of a business have different periods of turnover, depending upon their different durabilities', and the same proposition applies to the fixed capital in society as a whole. We need to consider, then, the special problems that arise when, for whatever reason, fixed capital of great durability is created under capitalist relations of production.

The amount of value that has to be thrown into monetary circulation and withdrawn from commodity circulation at the outset also varies a great deal depending upon the nature of the fixed capital formed. Docks and harbours require much more than simple agricultural implements. And it also happens that some fixed capital items can be produced incrementally – expanded bit by bit, like a railroad line – while others have to be totally finished before they can enter into use – a dam, for example. In all of these cases, the physical and material mode of being of the fixed capital affects the degree of difficulty encountered in forming it. There are, as it were, barriers to the entry of capital into certain kinds of activities because of the scale of initial effort involved. These barriers are in part a reflection of the material and physical properties of the use value required, but here, also, economic circumstances play their part. The scale of fixed capital investment depends in part upon the drive to achieve economies of scale in production, economies in employment of constant capital, and is not independent of the degree of concentration and centralization of capital.

Be all of this as it may, the production and circulation of fixed capital of large scale and great durability poses some very specific problems which have to dealt with. Consider, then, the difficulties that arise in relation to the investment and use of such items as a modern integrated iron and steel production facility, a petrochemical complex, a nuclear power station or a large dam.

To begin with, the *working period* required to produce such items will itself be quite long, and puts a very considerable burden upon producers. Marx argued that in 'the less developed stages of capitalist production, undertakings requiring a long working period, and hence a large investment of capital for a long time, such as the building of roads, canals, etc. . . [are] . . . not carried out on a capitalist basis at all but rather at communal or state expense' (*Capital,* vol. 2, p. 233). In the advanced capitalist era, however, the concentration and centralization of capital and the organization of a sophisticated credit system allows such projects to be carried out on a capitalistic basis.

Similar problems arise because of the massive outlay of money by the users of this fixed capital and because of the long time it takes – say, 30 years or more – to get that money back through production. Individual capitalists may therefore seek, of necessity, 'to shift the burden' of such projects 'on to the shoulders of the state' (*Grundrisse,* p. 531). Certainly, fixed capital of this scale and durability could not be either produced or used without resort to the credit system. The latter relieves individual capitalists of the obligation to hoard massive amounts of money capital preparatory to the purchase of the fixed capital and converts the payment for that fixed capital into an annual payment. What in effect happens – presuming no personal savings on the part of other classes in society – is that capitalist producers investing in the present borrow from other capitalists who are saving with an eye to future investment or replacement. In this manner capital is kept fully employed in spite of the long turnover of large-scale fixed capital items.

Credit makes it theoretically possible to balance the money exchanges between the various departments producing wage goods, constant circulating or constant fixed capital, although the commodity exchanges are in no way directly modified. But for harmony to exist in the money exchanges aggregate savings must be in equilibrium with investment needs. We are immediately led to enquire how such an equilibrium might be established under the social relations of capitalism. And this can be dealt with only in the full context of an analysis of the credit system. If this equilibrium condition does not hold – and we will later see why it cannot 'except by accident' (see chapter 9) – then credit may end up exacerbating rather than resolving the problem.

The exchanges of material commodities between departments are still subject to disruption on their own account and these disruptions become magnified by the introduction of large-scale and long-lived fixed capital. After all, 'the smaller the direct fruits borne by fixed capital', the greater must be the 'relative surplus population and surplus production; thus more to build railways, canals, aqueducts, telegraphs, etc. than to build machinery' (*Grundrisse,* p. 707). This means that either massive appropriation (slave labour, primitive accumulation, etc.) or very strong overaccumulation is required if such projects are to be completed. And to the extent that they anticipate the 'future fruits of labour' for a very long period in the future, they also imprison capital in ways that are not always desirable.

If, in the course of capitalist development, there were an even progression on all fronts from small to large scale and from short- to long-term investment in fixed capital, then it would be easier to incorporate the theory of fixed capital formation and circulation into the general theory of accumulation. While there are objective reasons why 'the magnitude and the durability of the applied fixed capital develop with the development of the capitalist mode of production' (*Capital,* vol. 2, p. 185), it is also true that 'the development of the productivity in different lines of industry proceeds at substantially differerent rates and frequently even in opposite directions', owing not only to natural and social conditions but also to the 'anarchy of competition and the peculiarity of the bourgeois mode of production' (*Capital,* vol. 2, p. 260). There are, for example, a variety of forms of fixed capital – physical infrastructures such as docks and harbours, transport systems and so on – which are relatively large-scale and which need to be produced early on in the history of capitalist development. And to the degree that tensions arise between the degree of centralization–decentralization of capital, between the spheres of market exchange and production, so we should expect that these factors also will interact with decisions on the use of fixed capital of a certain scale and durability. Differences in the scale and durability of fixed capital are destined, it seems, to be an essential feature to the uneven development of capitalism.

2 Fixed capital of an 'independent' kind

Circumstances arise in which fixed capital 'appears not as a mere instrument of production within the production process, but rather as an independent form of capital, e.g. in the form of railways, canals, roads, aqueducts, improvements of the land, etc.' (*Grundrisse,* pp. 686–7). Fixed capital of an 'independent' kind can be distinguished from fixed capital enclosed within the immediate production process by the very specific functions it performs in relation to production – it acts, as Marx puts it, as 'the general preconditions of production' (p. 739).

For the individual capitalist the difference can be expressed as that between the machinery and the buildings that house the machinery. But in society as a whole we can observe many situations in which capitalists make use of the independent kinds of fixed capital in common and, as individuals, on a partial, intermittent or temporary basis (*Grundrisse,* p. 725). The peculiar relation that this kind of fixed capital has to production is associated with a specific kind of circulation process – 'the realization of the value and surplus value contained in it appears in the form of an annuity, where interest represents surplus value and the annuity the successive return of the value advanced' (*Grundrisse,* p. 723). The capitalist, in effect, purchases the use value of this kind of fixed capital on an annual or fee-for-service basis – the building that houses production is rented for the year, a fork-lift truck is rented for a week, a container is rented to take the commodity to its final destination.

This implies that the independent form of fixed capital is owned by someone other than the capitalist producer. And herein lies the rational basis for the form of circulation that then arises. In effect, owners of capital lend it out to users in fixed rather than money form:

> Commodities loaned out as capital are loaned either as fixed or circulating capital, depending on their properties. Money may be loaned out in either form. It may be loaned as fixed capital, for instance, if it is paid back in the form of an annuity, whereby a portion of capital flows back together with interest. Certain commodities, such as houses, ships, machines, etc., can be loaned out only as fixed capital by the nature of their use values. Yet all loaned capital, whatever its form, and no matter how the nature of the use value may modify its return, is always only a specific form of money capital. (*Capital,* vol. 3, p. 344)

It follows, therefore, that we cannot go very far in discussing this form of circulation of fixed capital without a thorough examination of money capital and interest. And it was for this reason that Marx excluded further examination of the problem in the passages dealing with fixed capital and dealt exclusively with fixed capital enclosed within the production process. He does come up with some provocative comments which deserve some explication. He notes, for example, that large-scale undertakings relying heavily upon fixed capital – such as railways – 'are still possible if they yield bare interest, and this is one of the causes stemming the fall of the general rate of profit, since such undertakings, in which the ratio of constant capital to the variable is so enormous, do not necessarily enter into the equalization of the general rate of profit' (*Capital,* vol, 3, p. 437). It is possible to stave off crises, therefore, by transforming 'a great part of capital into fixed capital which does not serve as agency of direct production' (*Grundrisse,* p. 750).

It is rather odd that Marxists have not taken up this idea and explored its implications – both theoretical and historical.[9] Marx is making two claims. First, if fixed capital is lent out rather than sold, then it functions as a material

---

[9] Boccara's (1974) account of devaluation picks up on this point but then emasculates its true import by attaching it to a theory of structural devaluation under state monopoly capitalism – see above, chapter 7. Magaline (1975), in the course of correctly rejecting Boccara's general theoretical position, omits to concede the partial truth of the latter's argument concerning the circulation of fixed capital at a lower rate of remuneration than the social average.

equivalent of money capital. As such, it can circulate provided the value embodied in it is recovered over its lifetime and provided that it earns *interest*. Since interest is only a part of surplus value, fixed capital of an independent kind circulates without claiming all of the surplus value that it helps to produce. This releases surplus value which can be competitively divided among the remaining capitalists as they struggle to equalize the rate of profit. Plainly, a growth in the independent relative to the enclosed forms of capital releases surplus value and can so counteract, in the short run at least, the falling rate of profit as Marx defined it. It was for this reason, presumably, that Marx considered it important to analyse 'the proportion in which the total capital of a country is divided into these two forms' (*Grundrisse,* p. 686). And this, in turn, has implications for our interpretation of both the changing scale and organization of capitalism over the past two hundred years (see chapter 5).

We can, secondly, examine this whole question from the standpoint of the individual capitalist. If we accept one of Marx's definitions of the rate of profit as the ratio of surplus value produced to total capital employed, then an increase in the use of fixed capital within the production process increases the capital employed in relation to the actual capital consumed in a production period. The use of independent forms of fixed capital does not have the same effect because the total capital employed now includes only the payment that the capitalist makes to use the fixed capital for that one time period. Substituting the independent for the enclosed forms of fixed capital reduces the total capital employed by individual capitalists even though the total capital consumed may be increasing. The rate of profit for the individual capitalist can be raised by such a strategem. A shift towards fixed capital of an independent kind helps to stem the tendency towards a falling rate of profit. In the context it is important to recognize that to some degree the relationship between the independent and enclosed forms of fixed capital is fluid – an industrialist can either rent buildings and machinery or purchase the items outright. And when times get difficult we might anticipate a growth in equipment leasing of the sort we have witnessed in the past few years in advanced capitalist countries.

But all of this assumes that forms of organization are created capable of supplying fixed capital of an independent kind, and that its circulation is not beset by any peculiar difficulties or inhibited by any serious barriers. An actively functioning credit system is essential, and forms of organization – such as joint stock companies – have to be created. These are necessary conditions. In addition, the fixed capital that circulates independently incurs a certain risk in so doing. In one sense the problems of realization of the value embodied (and the calculation of value-transfer, etc.) are more serious here than in the case of fixed capital enclosed within production – the use of the fixed capital depends entirely upon general economic conditions and is much more vulnerable to sudden devaluations because of declines in use. On the other hand, since we are here dealing with fixed capital which is often used in common and which acts as the general preconditions for production, the competitive search for surplus value within the firm will not prompt devaluations through technological change to anywhere near the same degree — unless, that is, the suppliers of independent fixed capital are in competition with each other. Plainly, we cannot press this matter much further without very specific consideration of how the supply and demand for the independent kinds of fixed capital is organized.

Marx's views on this particular form of capital are far from being well developed. And the summary of his argument that we have provided raises as many questions as it answers. But, like Marx, we must necessarily defer deeper evaluation until we have at least some understanding of the credit system in place. Here we can only broach ideas that appear to be of great import, but which we are not yet equipped to explore in all their fullness.

IV THE CONSUMPTION FUND

Certain commodities perform in the realm of consumption a somewhat analogous role to that played by fixed capital in the production process. The commodities are not consumed directly but serve as *instruments of consumption*. They include items as diverse as cutlery and kitchen utensils, refrigerators, television sets and washing machines, houses, and the various means of collective consumption such as parks and walkways. All such items can conveniently be grouped together under the heading of the *consumption fund*.

The distinction between fixed capital and the consumption fund is based on the use of commodities and not upon their material mode of being. Items can be transferred from one category to another through a change in use (see above, p. 205). The fixed capital embodied in warehouses and workshops can be converted, for example, into consumption fund items such as apartments and art galleries, and vice versa. Some items function simultaneously as means of both production and consumption (highways and automobiles, for example). Joint uses are always possible.

Instruments of consumption do not have to be produced as commodities. Workers can produce their own housing in their own time and through their own efforts, and barter the products of their own labour among each other. Systems of this sort, common in the early years of capitalist industrialization, persist in the so-called 'informal' sector of Third World economies and in the 'underground' economies of the advanced capitalist countries.[10] The value of

[10] Portes (1980) surveys the literature on the informal sector and capital accumulation (primarily with references to Latin America).

labour power is sensitive to the form that provision of the consumption fund takes, because it is fixed according to the commodities purchased in the market. But since our primary concern at this point is with the circulation process of capital, we will assume that the consumption fund is produced solely through capitalist commodity production.

A commodity is circulating capital for its producer no matter how it is used. It disappears from circulation when it is sold to the final consumer and the value equivalent of the commodity is returned to the capitalist in money form. If the commodities have a long life and remain in use, they then form a part of the total social wealth of society. But they no longer function as capital in motion. In this regard, there is a crucial difference between the continued use of fixed capital (which keeps value circulating as capital) and the continued use of consumption fund items.

If this was all there were to the matter, then we could cheerfully leave the question of the consumption fund to one side. But consider the matter from the point of view of buyers. The latter have to pay the full value equivalent of the commodity at one point in time in order to gain a stream of future benefits. They can hoard money or borrow either the item itself (in which case they pay rent) or the money to purchase it (in which case they pay interest). Rent and interest payments are a standard accompaniment to the use of many consumption fund items. It is important to understand why.

Some consumption fund items, such as housing, require such a large initial outlay that they are beyond the means of direct purchase for all but the very wealthy. If housing is to be produced as a commodity, then renting or borrowing of money becomes essential. Without the interventions of the landlord, the credit system and the state, capital would be denied access to an extensive and very basic form of production.[11] Hoarding of money to purchase expensive consumer goods also disrupts the circulation of capital since it ties up money (which could otherwise be converted into capital) and acts as a barrier to the smooth transformation of the circulation of revenues into the realization of capital through exchange. When the credit system comes to the rescue, it permits some consumers to save (in return for interest) and others to borrow and pay back both the interest and the principal over an extended period of time. The interchanges between the various departments can thereby be protected against excessive hoarding of revenues.

The immediate effect, however, is to integrate the use of much of the consumption fund into the circulation of interest-bearing capital. Money is lent out against the future revenues of those who use the consumption fund item. The item acts as security for the loan, which means that it must retain its commodity character as a potentially marketable material use value. If the

---

[11] The housing sector has been the focus of much research done from a Marxian perspective in recent years. See the survey by Bassett and Short (1980).

borrower defaults on the payments, then the lender must be able to re-possess the commodity and offer it for sale upon the market. The formation of a second hand market in many consumption fund items (houses, automobiles, etc.) is a necessary corollary to debt financing of their purchase.

Capital can and does circulate within and through the consumption fund. To the degree that money capital penetrates, so the instruments of consumption take on the form of stored commodity capital. The rules of circulation of capital within the consumption fund become an important aspect to the circulation of capital in general. Marx himself puts off any detailed consideration of this on the grounds that it 'is connected with further determinations (renting rather than buying, interest, etc.)' which have yet to be explored (*Grundrisse*, p. 711). The point is well taken. But a number of initial points concerning the consumption fund can usefully be set down here.

(1) The physical and economic lifetimes of items within the consumption fund are fixed by forces different to those that prevail in the case of fixed capital. The competition for relative surplus value that perpetually revolutionizes and periodically devalues fixed capital is noticeably absent within the consumption sphere. The competition that does exist is tied to changing whims, fashions and the desire to exhibit signs of status. To the degree that 'rational consumption' for accumulation depends upon sustaining a certain turnover of consumption fund uses, the forces of fashion and status have to be mobilized by capital. However this may be, the economic obsolescence of consumption fund items does not occur in response to the same pressures that shape the use of fixed capital. Revolutions in the productive forces create economic obsolescence only indirectly – cheaper and more efficient consumer goods make it uneconomical to maintain the old; revolutions in transport relations and industrial relocation make housing in certain regions redundant; and so on. The physical material lifetime of objects has a more important role to play in the case of the consumption fund. Built-in physical obsolescence is therefore just as important to sustaining markets as economic obsolescence.

(2) The exchange value of second-hand items within the consumption fund is broadly dictated by the value of new equivalent items. The marketability of such items depends upon their alienability and their capacity (at whatever stage of their physical lifetime) to yield a flow of future revenues in return for their use. The price of the asset is then fixed by the revenue it can generate capitalized at the going rate of interest (see chapters 9 and 11).

(3) The purchase of consumption fund items via mortgages and other forms of consumer credit is sensitive to the availability of money. The cyclical impulses that derive from the tendency towards overaccumulation are therefore as active in consumption fund formation as they are with respect to investment in fixed capital. However, the capacity to absorb idle money capital within the consumption fund is limited by the circulation of future

revenues. Over-indebtedness with respect to the consumption fund can be just as serious a problem as over-investment in fixed capital. The claim on future revenues derived from future labour can far exceed the value-creating capacities of that future labour. The marketable assets within the consumption fund consequently stand to be devalued in the course of a crisis, while over-indebtedness can be a source of disequilibrium. On the other hand, the credit system has the capacity to stimulate production (through fixed capital formation) *and* realization in exchange (through consumption fund formation). We will consider the deeper ramifications of that in future chapters.

(4) The distinction between 'necessities' and 'luxuries' within the consumption fund is worth noting. The manner, often conspicuous, in which the bourgeoisie consumes its revenues has far different ramifications from the creation of a consumption fund for the reproduction of labour power. Reduction in the cost of necessities, recall, is a source of surplus value. Cheap housing and low rent or interest payments benefit capital because 'economy in these conditions is a method of raising the rate of profit' (*Capital,* vol. 3, p. 86). The formation of housing for workers often sparks cross-currents of conflict between landlords, builders, money capitalists, wage labourers and capitalists in general.[12] State intervention often results.

V THE BUILT ENVIRONMENT FOR PRODUCTION, EXCHANGE AND CONSUMPTION

A part of the instruments of labour, which includes the general conditions of labour, is either localized as soon as it enters the process of production . . . or is produced from the outset in its immovable, localized form, such as improvements of the soil, factory buildings, blast furnaces, canals, railways, etc. . . . The fact that some instruments of labour are localized, attached to the soil by their roots, assigns to this portion of fixed capital a peculiar role in the economy of nations. They cannot be sent abroad, cannot circulate as commodities in the world market. Title to this fixed capital may change, it may be bought and sold, and to this extent may circulate ideally. These titles of ownership may even circulate in foreign markets, for instance in the form of stocks. But a change of the persons owning this class of fixed capital does not alter the relation of the immovable, materially fixed part of the national wealth to its movable part. (*Capital,* vol. 2, pp. 162–3)

Marx insists that we should not confuse *fixed* with *immovable* capital (ships and locomotives are fixed capital even though they move, while some elements of circulating capital, such as water power, have to be used *in situ*). But we do have to consider the 'peculiar role' that immovable fixed capital

---

[12] I examine this in greater detail in Harvey (1977).

performs under capitalism in general and in the economy of nations in particular. A portion of the consumption fund (housing, parks, etc.) is also immovable in space.

This leads us to the conception of a *built environment* which functions as a vast, humanly created resource system, comprising use values embedded in the physical landscape, which can be utilized for production, exchange and consumption. From the standpoint of production, these use values can be considered as both general preconditions for and direct forces of production. We have to deal, then, with 'improvements sunk in the soil, aqueducts, buildings; and machinery itself in great part, since it must be physically fixed, to act; railways; in short, every form in which the product of industry is welded fast to the surface of the earth' (*Grundrisse*, pp. 739–40). The built environment for consumption and exchange is no less heterogeneous.

The built environment comprises a whole host of diverse elements: factories, dams, offices, shops, warehouses, roads, railways, docks, power stations, water supply and sewage disposal systems, schools, hospitals, parks, cinemas, restaurants – the list is endless. Many elements – churches, houses, drainage systems, etc. – are legacies from activities carried on under non-capitalist relations of production. At any one moment the built environment appears as a palimpsest of landscapes fashioned according to the dictates of different modes of production at different stages of their historical development. Under the social relations of capitalism, however, all elements assume a commodity form.

Considered purely as commodities, the elements of the built environment exhibit certain peculiar characteristics. Immobility in space means that a commodity cannot be moved without the value embodied in it being destroyed. Elements of the built environment have spatial position or location as a fundamental rather than an incidental attribute. They therefore have to be built or assembled *in situ* on the land so that land and the appropriation of land rent (see chapter 11) become significant. Furthermore, the usefulness of particular elements depends upon their location relative to others – shops, housing, schools and factories must all be reasonably proximate to each other. The whole question of the spatial ordering of the built environment has then to be considered; the decision where to put one element cannot be divorced from the 'where' of others.

The built environment has to be regarded, then, as a geographically ordered, complex, composite commodity. The production, ordering, maintenance, renewal and transformation of such a commodity poses serious dilemmas. The production of individual elements – houses, factories, shops, schools, roads, etc. – has to be co-ordinated, both in time and space, in such a way as to allow the composite commodity to assume an appropriate configuration. Land markets (see chapter 11) serve to allocate land to uses, but finance capital and the state (primarily through the agency of land use

regulation and planning) also act as co-ordinators. Problems also arise because the different elements have different physical lifetimes and wear out at
different rates. Economic depreciation, particularly of elements that function
as productive forces for capital, also plays its part. But since the usefulness of
individual elements depends, to large degree, upon the usefulness of surrounding elements, complex patterns of depreciation and appreciation (with
ramifications for value relations) are set in motion by individual acts of
renewal, replacement or transformation. The 'spillover' effects of individual
investment decisions are localized in space. Similarly, disinvestment in one
part of the built environment is likely to depreciate surrounding property
values.

To say that there is commodity production for the built environment
implies that markets can form for the production and sale of individual
elements which consequently have a use value, an exchange value and a value.
Here we encounter some further problems. Exclusivity of use and private
appropriation of use values can be established for some elements (houses,
factories, etc.), whereas collective uses are possible for other elements (roads,
sidewalks, etc.). The built environment as a whole is part public good and
part private, and markets for the individual elements reflect the complex
interactions between the different kinds of markets. Also, because the various
elements within the built environment function as localized use values, the
possibility exists of attaching a price tag to them even after their value has
been fully returned to capital. A rent can be extracted for their use and
capitalized, at the going rate of interest, into a market price on land and its
appurtenances. Two kinds of exchange value then exist side by side: the
capitalized rental on old elements and the price of production on the new. The
two prices are derived quite differently but are reconciled into a single price
structure by the market system. If I can buy an old house for less than it takes
to produce a new one with nearly identical characteristics, then why should I
bother to construct a new one?

The formation of land and property markets has an extremely important
impact upon the circulation of capital through the built environment in
general. A rate of return on money capital can be had by investing in old
property as well as in the production of new. Idle money capital can just as
easily be lent out as property as it can in money form. Since a part of the use
value of a property depends upon its relative location, money capitalists can
even invest in the land and in the future rent it can command. Since rent is
regarded as a portion of surplus value appropriated by landowners, money
capital is now being invested in appropriation rather than in production. As a
theoretical proposition this appears quite irrational. The material relevance
is, however, that all aspects of production and use of the built environment
are brought within the orbit of the circulation of capital. If things were not so,
then capital could not establish itself (replete with all its contradictions) in the

physical landscape in a manner generally supportive of accumulation – the built environment that capital requires for production, exchange and consumption could not be influenced in the interests of capital.[13]

Marx himself was all too aware of the broader implications of all this. The conception of capital circulating through the built environment implies, he wrote, that the mere 'technological conditions for the occurrence of the process (the site where the production process proceeds)' can in itself be considered a 'form of fixed capital'. The appropriation of 'natural agencies . . . such as water, land (this notably) mines, etc.' is in principle no different from the appropriation of other material uses values and their transformation into fixed capital by putting them into use as such (*Grundrisse,* pp. 691, 715). The improvement of land – be it for agriculture or industry – means that the land itself 'must ultimately function as fixed capital . . . in some local process of production' (*Capital,* vol. 2, p. 210).

How, then, can we possibly discuss the circulation of capital in the built environment without giving due consideration to landed property? And once we permit the entrance of landed property, can the theory of rent be far behind? (*Grundrisse,* p. 715). We cannot gain full command of what is going on without a full understanding of the theories of rent and interest. We can now see why Marx argues that the different kind of return on fixed and circulating capital is the difference between annuity, interest and various forms of rent on the one hand and the direct selling for profit on the other. The tasks before us in the next three chapters are hereby clearly defined. Rent and interest as forms of distribution have to be fully integrated into the theory of the capitalist mode of production.

VI FIXED CAPITAL, THE CONSUMPTION FUND AND THE ACCUMULATION OF CAPITAL

Capitalists cannot for long look to capture the benefits of technological change without forming fixed capital. They thereby create a distinctive and rather peculiar mode of circulation of capital which in due course 'hardens' into a 'separate mode of existence of capital'. A consumption fund is likewise necessary to the reproduction of labour power and special forms of circulation of capital arise to embrace its production in commodity form.

The aggregate effects upon the accumulation process are dramatic. Specific temporal relationships are introduced into models of accumulation, which are initially specified (see chapter 6) without reference to any particular time scale. The creation of a built environment obligates us to consider place and spatial arrangements as specific attributes of the capitalist mode of production. The accumulation process has now to be seen as operating within a

[13] See Harvey (1978) for a more detailed analysis of this theme.

time–space framework defined according to the distinctive logic of capitalism. Since we will take up the problem of place and space in chapters 11 and 12, I shall confine attention here to a few reflections upon the temporal aspect of affairs.

For convenience, I shall refer to the totality of processes whereby capital circulates through fixed capital and consumption fund formation and use as the *secondary circuit of capital*. Within this secondary circuit we must accord a certain priority of place to fixed capital formation and use in relation to surplus value production, since this defines the relative time scale within which different elements of constant capital circulate. It is interesting, however, to observe how the rhythm of consumption fund formation and use is gradually drawn into a pattern of broad conformity to that experienced by fixed capital. We will shortly show why this is so.

The circulation process of fixed capital does not establish an absolute time scale against which accumulation can be measured. Marx's investigation of the material properties of machinery comes close on occasion to pinning the circulation of fixed capital to the rates of decay of material substance given 'normal wear and tear'. But normal wear and tear cannot be defined without some prior notion of intensity of use, and the concept of economic, as opposed to physical, lifetime quickly upsets any easy construction of a temporal metric. The latter turns out to be a reflection of the general intensity of surplus value production within the labour process. Necessary and surplus labour *time* are, after all, a central feature in Marx's initial conceptual apparatus. The striving for relative surplus value is thus perpetually reshaping the temporality of social labour and social life.

Beyond this, Marx demonstrates that the separation of fixed from circulating capital imparts a cyclical rhythm – potentially explosive – to the interchanges between Departments 1 and 2. Given the ebb and flow in the volume of the industrial reserve army and the leads and lags involved in fixed capital formation (particularly large-scale works, which take up a long working period), strong cyclical fluctuations in the pace of accumulation appear inevitable. These impart in turn cyclical impulses to consumption fund formation which may, under certain circumstances, magnify the departures from equilibrium through a multiplier effect.

We also notice that the overaccumulation of capital entails the production of surpluses of labour power, commodities and money capital – conditions that are exactly right for stimulating flows of circulating capital into the secondary circuit of capital as a whole. Provided the switch into the secondary circuit of capital can be engineered – a process that may well involve a 'switching crisis' of some sort – the secondary circuit appears as a godsend for the absorption of surplus, overaccumulated capital. The capacity for absorption of excess capital is limited in two distinctive ways. The realization of fixed capital depends upon enhanced productive consumption which, in the long run, generates ever more capital to be absorbed. The realization of capital in the consumption fund depends upon the expansion of future revenues to cover indebtedness on present purchases. In both cases, then, the prospect of devaluation looms if the proper conditions are not fulfilled. But at this point the interaction between fixed capital and consumption fund formation and use becomes of paramount importance. Circumstances can arise in which the expanded fixed capital in production can be realized through the expansion of capital circulating within the consumption fund. That this is a chimerical solution to the problem of overaccumulation should be evident (see chapter 10). But to the degree that the two processes can bolster and feed off of each other, so they stave off the inevitable denouement.

The implication is that crisis formation takes on a particular temporal rhythm defined, in the first instance, by the relative circulation times at various components of fixed capital in relation to surplus value production. The diversity of potential circulating times is considerable, however. The system appears headed towards total incoherence – unless, that is, we can track down a single unifying force which puts its stamp upon the temporal processes as a whole. The central idea that emerges from the study of fixed capital formation is that the rate of interest performs just such a function. It relates present to future, defines a time horizon for capital in general. If we can discover what it is that regulates the rate of interest, we will uncover the secret of socially necessary turnover time – and that is the task of the next two chapters.

But there is in this a certain irony. The circulation of capital through the material form of fixed capital and the consumption fund is regulated by appeal to capital in its pure money form. Herein lie the seeds of a fundamental contradiction. On the one hand, fixed capital appears as the crowing glory of past capitalist development, the 'power of knowledge, objectified', an indicator of the degree to which 'social knowledge has become a direct force of production' (*Grundrisse,* p. 706). Fixed capital raises the productive powers of labour to new heights at the same time as it ensures the domination of past 'dead' labour (embodied capital) over living labour in the work process. From the standpoint of the production of surplus value, fixed capital appears as 'the most adequate form of capital'.

On the other hand, fixed capital is 'value imprisoned within a specific use value', associated with specific forms of commodity production under specific technological conditions. It must command future labour as a counter-value if its value is to be realized. For this reason fixed capital confines the trajectory of future capitalist development, inhibits further technological change and coerces capital precisely because it is 'condemned to an existence within the confines of a specific use value'. Capital in general is 'indifferent to every specific form of use value and seeks to 'adopt or shed any of them as equivalent incarnations'. From this standpoint circulating (money) capital appears 'the most adequate form of capital' because it is more instantaneously malleable to capital's requirements (*Grundrisse*, p. 694).

Fixed capital, which appears from the standpoint of production as the pinnacle of capital's success, becomes, from the standpoint of the circulation of capital, a mere barrier to further accumulation. Thus does capital 'encounter barriers in its own nature'. And there are only two ways to resolve such contradictions. They are either dealt with forcibly in the course of a crisis, or displaced on to some higher and more general plane where they provide the ingredients for crisis formation of a different and often more profound sort. Bearing this in mind, we now turn to the whole problem of money, credit and finance in relation to the accumulation of capital.

CHAPTER 9

Money, Credit and Finance

Marx did not complete his analysis of monetary and financial phenomena. He sets out a very general and highly abstract theory of money in the first volume of *Capital* (there summarizing the lengthier but more tentative analyses in the *Grundrisse* and in the *Contribution to a Critique of Political Economy*). His notes on the functioning of the credit system were left in great confusion. Engels had great difficulty in putting them into any kind of order for publication in the third volume of *Capital*. There was, Engels complained in his Preface to that work, 'no finished draft, not even a scheme whose outlines might have been filled out – often just a disorderly mass of notes, comments and extracts.' Engels was faithful to Marx and ended up replicating most of the disorder. Here was a major piece of 'unfinished business' in Marx's theory.

Just how important Marx thought this piece of unfinished business to be is difficult to tell. He thought the analysis of money of sufficient importance to place it before his investigation of the circulation of capital. But he also insists that the *origin* of profit (in surplus value) could be understood without appealing to any of the categories of distribution. The analysis of credit, finance and the circulation of interest-bearing capital is therefore left until after the analysis of general movements in even the *rate* of profit. It is doubtful if such a tardy introduction of the role of credit can be justified. Even *en route* to his derivation of the tendency towards a falling rate of profit, Marx frequently indicates that this or that problem could not be resolved without consideration of the role of credit. When we pull together these remarks, the credit system appears more and more as a complex centrepiece within the Marxian jigsaw of internal relations. But it is a centrepiece that depicts relations within the capitalist class – between individual capitalists and class requirements as well as between factions of capital. The credit system is a product of capital's own endeavours to deal with the internal contradictions of capitalism. What Marx will show us is how capital's solution ends up heightening rather than diminishing the contradictions.

Unfortunately, Marxists have paid little attention to this aspect of theory. This neglect is all the more surprising given the significance that many, taking their cue primarily from Lenin, have attached to the 'finance form of capitalism' as a specific stage in the history of capitalist development. Hilferding's work (which Lenin drew upon directly) was published in 1910 and remained, until very recently, the only major attempt to deal with the subject of the credit system head on.[1] Rosdolsky and de Brunhoff put Marx's analysis of money back into the center of things during the 1960s. But the pickings in the Marxist literature on the credit system are still remarkably slim.[2]

In what follows I will try to plug the theoretical gaps. The aim is to integrate the analysis of money and credit with the general theory of accumulation. This puts us in a better position to understand how and why the 'laws of motion' of capitalism are necessarily expressed through, and to some extent guided by, the circulation of interest-bearing money capital channelled through the credit system. A 'second-cut' theory of crises which integrates monetary and financial phenomena with the general theory of capitalist commodity production should not then be too far from our grasp.

It is difficult, however, to devise a method of exposition that portrays essentials without glossing over complexities. I have therefore split the materials into two chapters. In this chapter I deal with various aspects of money, credit and finance from a rather technical viewpoint. We begin with a fuller rendition of the role of money – a topic broached briefly in chapter 1. This reflects Marx's view that money has to be understood independently of the circulation of capital. The transformation of money into capital can then be seen as new configurations of basic money uses. Money thereby acquires the potential to circulate as interest-bearing money capital. So we then consider the functions of this form of circulation in order to show that it is a socially necessary aspect to the capitalist mode of production. The chapter closes with a brief description of the main instrumentalities and institutions that facilitate the circulation of interest-bearing capital in concrete ways.

The pieces are first put in place without too much concern for overall dynamics, the full flowering of contradictions or the supposed 'inner trans-

---

[1] See Lenin (1970 edn): Hilferding (1970 edn).

[2] Rosdolsky (1977) pays a lot of attention to the problem of money, while de Brunhoff's 1971; 1976; 1978; 1979) works are fundamental. Mandel (1968, chs 7 and 8) provides one of the few texts where money and credit are built into the analysis, and he has also sought to keep financial questions in the forefront of his later works. Other contributions of note are by Harris (1978; 1979) and Barrère (1977), with the latter trying to integrate a theory of money and credit with the general theory of state monopoly capitalism. Cutler, Hindess, Hirst and Hussain (1978, vol. 2, pt 1) have some very interesting things to say about money and financial institutions in general but totally misrepresent Marx's own position on these matters. Amin's (1974) contribution is also noteworthy.

formation of capitalism' which the rise of the credit system promotes. These broader and more exciting questions are taken up in chapter 10.

If there is a general theme that unites the two chapters, it is that money exists as the incarnation of general social power, independent of and external to particular production processes or specific commodities.[3] Money capital can function as the common capital of the capitalist class, but it can also be appropriated and amassed by private individuals. The contradiction between individual action and the requirements for the reproduction of the capitalist class (see chapter 7) is thereby rendered more acute. But Marx also insists that money expresses a contingent social power, ultimately dependent upon the creation of real value through the embodiment of social labour in material commodities. It is the relationship between money as the *general expression of value* and commodities as the *real embodiment of value* that forms the pivot upon which much of the analysis turns.

I MONEY AND COMMODITIES

A commodity, we may recall, is a material thing which embodies both a use value and an exchange value. This duality is the source from which all of the contradictions within the money form flow. Consider how this duality of use and exchange value is expressed in exchange. The *relative form* of value arises because the exchange value of a commodity cannot be measured in terms of itself but must always be expressed in terms of another (the idea that 20 yds of linen = 20 yds of linen tells us nothing, whereas 20 yds of linen = 1 coat tells us a lot). The exchange of two commodities also presupposes a relation of equivalence between them and indicates the existence of an *equivalent form of value* which Marx pins to socially necessary labour time or *value* itself. This equivalent form of value has to find a material 'earthly' representative if the exchange of use values is to become general. The proliferation of exchange guarantees that one commodity will become the *universal equivalent*, the socially recognized incarnation of human labour in the abstract. This

---

[3] The idea of money as social power, appropriated by capitalists and transformed into money capital, lies at the centre of the Marxian conception and differentiates it from bourgeois views, all of which tend, in the final analysis, to boil down to some version of the quantity theory of money (see Harris, 1979; de Brunhoff, 1979). Bourgeois texts in the neoclassical tradition (such as that by Niehans, 1978) modify the traditional neoclassical assumption as to the supposed neutrality of money within an economic system in favour of a more sophisticated analysis of transaction costs, supply and demand for cash balances, etc. The quantity and forms of money are thereby allowed to have real effects on accumulation, demand, growth, employment, output and so on. But the conception of money as a source of social power and the differentiation between money and money capital are totally absent.

commodity is called the *money commodity*. The relative values of all other commodities can then be represented by *prices,* the ratios according to which they exchange against this money commodity. But we can immediately spot a contradiction – labour in the abstract is being represented by a particular commodity produced under specific conditions of concrete human labour. This contradiction will always be with us in what follows, although, as we shall see, it usually takes on more mystified forms.

The money commodity, like any other commodity, has a value, a use value and an exchange value. Its value is fixed by the socially necessary labour time embodied in it (albeit through concrete labour). As the universal equivalent, money functions as *a measure of values* and provides a *standard of price* against which the value of all other commodities can be assessed. But the realization of those prices depends upon an exchange process and therefore involves exchange values. The intervention of exchange converts a necessary relation between value ratios into 'a more or less accidental exchange-ratio between a single commodity and another, the money-commodity'. Market prices deviate from values as a result. 'This is no defect,' Marx insists, because 'the lawless irregularities' of commodity production and exchange, the perpetual oscillations between demand and supply, could not possibly be equilibrated except by allowing prices to fluctuate around values (*Capital,* vol. 1, p. 102).

The use value of the money commodity is that it facilitates the circulation of commodities. It therefore functions as a *medium of circulation*. The value of the money commodity is in this case fixed as a reflection of the exchanges that it helps to bring about – 'we have only to read a price list backwards, to find the magnitude of the value of money expressed in all sorts of commodities' (*Capital,* vol. 1, p. 95). From this standpoint, money takes on the relative form of value. The antagonism between the relative and equivalent forms of value is preserved within the money form itself because the money commodity now embodies two measures of value: the socially necessary labour time it embodies, and the socially necessary labour time for which it can, on average, be exchanged. In a perfect world, of course, the two representations of value should coincide. But the 'lawless irregularities' of commodity production and exchange ever preclude the achievement of such perfection. The divergence between the two representations will frequently return to haunt us in the analysis that follows.

Consider, now, the function of money as a medium of circulation. Assume, for the moment, that gold is the only money commodity. The quantity of gold required to circulate a certain quantity of commodities at their prices is fixed by the mass of gold in circulation multiplied by its velocity of circulation. The formula $MV = PQ$ is identical to that employed by the quantity theorists such as Ricardo. Marx uses it also, but rejects the idea that the quantity of money determines the level of prices – a basic tenet of the quantity theorists (*Capital,* vol. 1, pp. 123–4).[4] Prices are, in the end, fixed by values (or the 'prices of production' – see above, chapter 2). But the velocity of circulation of both money and commodities fluctuates daily, and the prices and quantities of commodities also alter according to circumstances. The need for gold therefore fluctuates, and prices can deviate strongly from values unless some way can be found to augment and diminish the quantity of gold in circulation on relatively short notice. Marx argues that a reserve stock of gold – a hoard – is necessary to accommodate such fluctuations (*Capital,* vol. 1, p. 134). The total quantity of gold required is then equal to the gold needed to circulate commodities at their values plus whatever is needed for a reserve.

The gold must first be produced as a commodity, of course. Additional gold may be required to replace that lost through wear and tear or to facilitate expanded commodity production. But the capacity to supply gold is governed by concrete conditions of production, and since any money commodity must be rare and of specific qualities, we find that the supply of gold (or any other money commodity) is not instantaneously adjustable. Also, when gold functions purely as a medium of circulation its production costs have to be regarded as part of the necessary costs, or *faux frais,* of circulation. This is so because the gold that functions as money (as opposed to the gold that has non-monetary uses) must stay perpetually in circulation and never become a part of individual or productive consumption. As suppliers of the 'lubricant' of exchange, the gold producers take away resources from productive uses.

The weighing and calibration of gold is both risky and a nuisance. Gold, in common with other metallic moneys, is inflexible, costly and inconvenient when used as a pure money commodity, even though, and in some respects precisely because, it possesses the requisite qualities to function as money. The inconvenience of weighing can be replaced by simple counting as soon as the money commodity becomes coin:

> Coins are pieces of gold whose shape and imprint signify that they contain weights of gold as indicated by the names of the money of account, such as pounds sterling, shilling, etc. Both the establishing of the mint-price and the technical work of minting devolve upon the State. Coined money assumes *a local and political character,* it uses different national languages and wears different national uniforms. . . . Coined money circulates therefore in the *internal* sphere of circulation of commodities, which is circumscribed by the boundaries of a given community and separated from the *universal* circulation of the world of commodities. (*Critique of Political Economy*, p. 107)

With coins, however, the possibility arises of a separation between their real and nominal values. Debasement of the coinage can become a problem

---

[4] De Brunhoff (1971; 1979) and Harris (1979) review the quantity theory of money from a Marxist perspective.

while the production of coins has to be carefully controlled. Legislation becomes imperative, and the state usually takes on the responsibility of minting (although government-regulated 'free minting' – the production of coins by private persons – is also possible). The state necessarily takes on a role as an economic agent.[5] Coins can, in turn, be replaced by tokens or paper symbols. Convertible paper moneys link the face-value on the note with a given quantity of the basic money commodity. Such paper moneys have the advantage that their quantity can more readily be adjusted to any increase in the need for money owing, for example, to the expanding volume of commodity exchange, while they are also much less costly to produce and thereby help to cut down on the costs of circulation. Such economies are only possible, however, if the total quantity of paper money is allowed to exceed the quantity of the money commodity into which that paper money can be converted. Under normal conditions this difference poses no problems, but in times of crisis convertibility frequently has to be suspended. This points up a peculiar disadvantage of all paper moneys. Once notes are put into circulation they cannot be taken out again (at least, not in the same way that gold coins can be melted down and used for other purposes), so that it becomes impossible to adjust the supply of paper money downwards to accommodate a shrinking volume of commodity circulation. Inflation becomes a very real possibility.

Pure paper money – 'inconvertible paper money issued by the State and having compulsory circulation' (*Critique of Political Economy*, p. 127) – completely severs the connection between money and the process of production of any money commodity. The money supply is thereby liberated from any physical production constraints and the advantages of flexibility of supply and economy of circulation can better be achieved. But the power of the state then becomes much more relevant, because political and legal backing must replace the backing provided by the money commodity if users of pure paper moneys are to have confidence in their stability and worth.

From the standpoint of a pure medium of circulation, money can equally well take any number of forms. The capacity to lubricate exchange is all that matters. The choice of the form money takes then depends upon the relative efficiency of each in overcoming transaction costs. Indeed, transaction costs can be entirely eliminated and replaced by accounting costs to the degree that transactions can be recorded in a ledger and balanced out between economic agents at the end of the day, month, year, or whatever. From this standpoint money can be eliminated except as 'money of account'.

But money is more than a simple medium of circulation. Leaving aside its function as a measure of value – a function that both capitalist society and

---

[5] De Brunhoff (1978) picks up on the relation between money and the state in detail. Vilar (1976) provides an interesting history of the various forms of money.

bourgeois economists periodically but unsuccessfully seek to discard as irrelevant[6] – money still possesses some peculiar 'transcendental' properties. Money represents, after all, exchange value *par excellence,* and thereby stands opposed to all other commodities and their use values. Money assumes an independent and external power in relation to exchange because, as the universal equivalent, it is the very incarnation of social power. This social power, furthermore, can be appropriated and used by private persons. The significance of this has now to be worked out.

Money permits the separation of sales and purchases in space and time. The constraints of barter can be overcome because an economic agent can sell a commodity for money at one place and time and use the money to purchase a commodity of equivalent value at another place and a subsequent time. Exchange is thereby liberated from the tyranny of Say's Law (see above, pp. 79–83). But for this to happen requires that the social power of money remain constant with respect to both time and space. Money has to be able to function as a trusted store of value; but the more money is used to store value rather than circulate values, the greater the monetary costs of circulation become.

The use of money as 'money of account' comes to the rescue. And so credit moneys 'take root spontaneously' within the processes of commodity exchange (*Capital,* vol. 1, p. 127). Credit moneys have their origin in privately contracted bills of exchange and notes of credit which acquire the social form of money as soon as they begin to circulate as means of payment. Such moneys have the double advantage that they can adjust instantaneously to alterations in the volume of commodity production (producers simply increase or decrease the bills of exchange they circulate among each other) while they also economize greatly on transaction and circulation costs. The quantity of the money commodity required is reduced to that needed for active circulation plus whatever is needed to balance accounts and a reserve fund to meet contingencies.

Credit moneys are, in other respects, somewhat peculiar. No matter how

[6] Niehans (1978, p. 140) comments on the widespread tendency to denounce commodity money as a 'barbaric relic' from 'less enlightened stages of human society' in the following vein; 'Commodity money is the only type of money that, at the present time, can be said to have passed the test of history in market economies. Except for short interludes of war, revolution, and financial crisis, Western economies have been on commodity money systems from the dawn of their history almost up to the present time. More precisely, it is only since 1973 that the absence of any link to the commodity world is claimed to be a normal feature of the monetary system. It will take several more decades before we can tell whether the Western world has finally embarked, as so often proclaimed, on a new era of non-commodity money or whether the present period will turn out to be just another interlude.' The Marxian perspective would indicate that we are indeed in 'just another interlude', presumably characterized by financial crises, war and perhaps even revolution.

far afield a privately contracted bill of exchange may circulate, it must always return to its place of origin for redemption. The other forms of money do not circulate in this way. A gold piece can pass from hand to hand and always remain in circulation without ever returning to its point of origin. Such forms of money are social from the very beginning though put to private use. Credit money, by way of contrast, is privately created money which can serve a social purpose when put into circulation. When the original debt is paid off, however, the credit money disappears from circulation. Credit money is perpetually being created and destroyed through the activities of private individuals. This is a vitally important conception. On the one hand, it accounts for the ability of private individuals and institutions (such as banks) to adjust the quantity of money instantaneously to the volume of commodity transactions – credit money (unlike gold) can be expanded and contracted at will. On the other hand, those who issue the credit must be subject to some discipline, and the *quality* of the credit money must be guaranteed if credit moneys are to circulate securely.

In the first instance, credit money is tied to a particular set of commodity transactions engaged in by particular individuals. If the commodity trans- actions are not completed at the price envisaged, or if individuals fail, then the 'destruction' of credit money takes a rather more ominous turn. The credit money is 'devalued' or 'depreciated' directly because the debt cannot be paid. The credit money cannot be converted into other forms of money (except, perhaps, at a deep discount by someone willing to take the risk of buying up what might be a worthless bill of exchange). The 'normal' destruction of credit moneys is here expressed as an abnormality, characteristic of commer- cial and monetary crises. The 'devaluation' of credit money is, however, a private matter which may have social consequences. The 'devaluation' of state-issued paper moneys (through changes in convertibility or simply run- ning the printing presses overtime) is pre-eminently a social affair (with distinctive private and redistributive consequences). We take up the theme of the 'devaluation' and 'destruction' of money in chapter 10. For the moment we simply note the formal possibility of such processes through the use of credit money of whatever sort.

Monetary institutions are required to relate diverse credit moneys to each other as well as to 'real' money such as gold or state-backed money of legal tender. These institutions have their origin with money-dealers who, in return for a share of the diminished transaction costs that they achieve, manage the purely technical aspects of the circulation of money. When money is used as a means of payment, the money dealers may record the transactions and assemble together to found the prototypes of the clearing banks (*Capital*, vol. 1, p. 137). They may then use their own money and provide a centralized discounting function for the innumerable bills of exchange that originate and circulate among individual commodity producers. And at some point, the money dealers may find it more convenient, efficient and profitable to substi-tute their own bills of exchange for those of innumerable individual producers. The money dealers then become bankers. The issue of bank notes merely formalizes the matter because these notes are nothing more than drafts drawn upon the bank. With the emergence of banks the first tier of an hierarchical arrangement within the monetary system is put in place: bank money replaces the bills of exchange issued by individual producers as the medium of circulation.

The bank takes on two basic tasks. First, it provides a central clearing house for bills of exchange and thereby economizes greatly on transaction and circulation costs. Secondly, when banks issue their own notes or allow checks to be drawn upon them, they substitute their own guarantee for that of innumerable individual capitalists. When the system of exchange is relatively simple, the personal knowledge and trust of individual capitalists may guarantee the quality of debts incurred, but in a complex market system this cannot form an adequate foundation for the credit system. The bank seeks to institutionalize what was before a matter of personal trust and credibility among individual capitalists. The majority of the bills that originate with individual capitalists will be freely convertible into bank money. But if the bank is to maintain the quality of its own money it must retain the right to refuse bills it regards as risky or worthless. The bank monitors the credibility of individual capitalists and acts as an intermediary for the latter.

But banks are also private institutions in competition with each other. They must also, as facilitators of commodity exchange, enter into relationships with each other. Means have to be found to balance accounts between them. Each bank could preserve a stock of gold for this purpose. Under normal conditions, the gold reserve need be but a small proportion of the total value of commodities in circulation – sufficient simply to balance accounts between banks. When the value of the commodities on the market is in doubt, however, the need for an adequate reserve of the money commodity becomes more pressing – otherwise, the bank may fail. On the other hand, shipping gold around and storing it is cumbersome, risky and inefficient. Some other way has to be found to make diverse bank moneys freely convertible into each other.

A central bank of some sort can solve this problem. It provides the means for banks to balance accounts with each other without shipping gold around. To do this, the central bank must possess high quality money which can guarantee the safety of the transactions between banks. The money of indi-vidual banks is freely convertible into central bank money only when the central bank is satisfied as to the quality or soundness of the individual bank money. The central bank forms the next tier in the hierarchy of monetary institutions. From these commanding heights the central bank seeks to guarantee the creditworthiness and quality of private bank moneys.

A variety of institutional arrangements can meet the need for a central bank. A single very powerful bank or a consortium of banks can take on the role. Before the collapse of 1907, for example, J. P. Morgan, together with some of the other New York banks, carried out such a function in the United States. But there is a double difficulty with such a solution. In so far as banks are in competition with each other, 'bad money drives out good' and this undermines the quality of money the banks are supposed to protect. The ability of a private group to play the role of guarantor depends upon its power over the other banks in the system. Guaranteeing the quality of national money is a luxury only the most powerful can afford. It is no accident that the financial panic of 1907 in the United States took an uncontrollable turn, in part because the power of J. P. Morgan was by then being seriously challenged by the rise of mid- and far-western competitors. The other difficulty is that the immense power of any bank that can perform such a function is always liable to arbitrary and capricious use by its private directors.[7]

Most central banks are therefore set apart from other banks by the granting of certain monopoly privileges. Absolved from the necessity to compete, the central bank can dedicate itself to its sole task: to defend the quality of national money. In order to perform this function, the central bank becomes the guardian of the country's gold reserves. This gives it the power to drive out 'bad' bank money by refusing convertibility into central bank money, which is the only kind of money which is freely convertible into gold.

As guardian of the national stock of gold, the central bank can guarantee the quality of money only within the territory of the nation state. The central bank then takes on the task of balancing payments between nations. All the time that central bank money is convertible into gold, the latter functions as the universal equivalent in world exchange. But once countries abandon convertibility within their own borders, then it becomes progressively more difficult to keep the gold standard intact on an international scale (particularly when capital becomes multinational). If the only way to balance the accounts between nations is by means of the different national currencies, then these have to be freely convertible into each other at some determinate rate of exchange. The problem then arises of guaranteeing the quality of national moneys on the world market. Certain extremely powerful countries – such as Britain in the nineteenth century and the United States between 1945 and 1971 – can play the role of 'world banker'. When most of the world's gold reserves were locked up in Fort Knox and the United States had a dominant position in terms of balance of payments and world trade, the dollar standard fixed under the Bretton Woods Agreement of 1944 could

---

[7] Kolko (1977) provides a very appealing interpretation of the collapse of private guarantees of the quality of money in the United States and the subsequent formation of the state-backed Federal Reserve System in the period 1907–13.

prevail and the dollar became, in effect, the universal equivalent. But the deteriorating balance of payments and the increasingly fierce competition of West Germany and Japan did to the United States internationally what the competition of the mid- and far-western banks did to J. P. Morgan. The subsequent devaluation of the dollar in 1971 signalled the collapse of the Bretton Woods Agreement, and the search for a new international monetary order began. A series of stop-gap expedients have been devised and attempts to establish some kind of supra-national superior quality paper money – such as the special drawing rights of the International Monetary Fund ('paper gold') – have been made. But as de Brunhoff points out (1976, pp. 48–53), these attempts are founded on the fallacious proposition that a form of credit money can function as the ultimate measure of value. No way has yet been found to guarantee the quality of national moneys except by tying them to the production of some specific commodity.

This history also alerts us to the dilemmas of monetary policies as these are designed and carried out through the operations of the central banks. Countries (such as Britain and the United States) that permit their moneys to be used as reserve currencies for settling international accounts are perpetually plagued by a policy dilemma: whether to defend the interests of national capital or to defend the interests of capital on a global scale. When a particular economy dominates world commodity production and trade the dilemmas are relatively muted, but they become more acute as the international environment becomes more competitive. But world capitalism simply could not function without a stable reserve currency of some sort – and this is the difficulty that has faced the international monetary system since the early 1970s.

Although we have grossly over-simplified the structure and certainly abstracted from the complexities of historical circumstance, the nested hierarchical character of monetary institutions can be quite clearly established as a necessary corollary to the existence of credit moneys. The necessity for such an hierarchical ordering can be traced back to the underlying contradiction between money as a measure of value and money as a medium of circulation. For while credit moneys appear superbly adapted to function as almost frictionless media of circulation, their capacity to represent 'real' commodity values is perpetually suspect. The notion of some absolute measure of value may appear redundant at any one particular level in the hierarchy, but the problem of ensuring the quality of money remains – and what is this quality if not a guarantee that a nominal amount of credit money does indeed represent real commodity values?

Higher-order institutions guarantee the quality of money at a lower order in the hierarchy – as the banks do for the individual capitalists, as the central bank does for the private banks, as a *de facto* 'world banker' does for national central banks. But what is it that ensures the quality of money at the apex of this hierarchy? Gold? 'Paper gold'? 'Black gold' (petroleum)? Dollars? At this level the notion of money as a necessary measure of value refuses to die. 'It is,' Marx observes, 'only in the markets of the world that money acquires to the full extent the character of the commodity whose bodily form is also the immediate social incarnation of human labour in the abstract' (*Capital,* vol. 1, p. 142). The hierarchical ordering of monetary institutions overcomes the contradictions between the equivalent and relative forms of value, between money as a measure of value and a medium of circulation, at the local and national levels only to leave the antagonism unresolved in the international arena.

One further point has to be made about this hierarchical structure of monetary institutions. At first sight it seems as if those who sit at the apex of this hierarchy – the central bankers in particular – are in firm control of the circulation of money and therefore in a powerful position to influence commodity production and exchange. Marx explicitly rejects such a view. 'The power of the central bank,' he argues, 'begins only where the private discounters stop, hence at a moment when its power is already extraordinarily limited' (*Grundrisse,* p. 124). The monopoly status of a central bank within a country does not give it effective powers of control no matter how awesome the powers of the monetary authority. In like manner, private bankers exercise control only after individual discounters can go no further using their private bills of exchange.

The most that any monetary authority can do under such circumstances is to engage in 'financial repression' by refusing to discount the credit money that exists at lower orders in the hierarchy.[8] The International Monetary Fund can set about disciplining nation-states, central banks can discipline banks and banks can discipline commodity producers. The powers exercised are those of negation rather than creation, however. Marx, therefore, readily concedes that an inadequate supply of money, inappropriate financial structure or, in the present context, tight monetary policies can operate as barriers to the expansion of commodity production and, under certain circumstances, exacerbate crises – as happened in 1847–8 after the 'mistaken' Bank Act of 1844 in Britain (*Capital,* vol. 3, p. 516). But there is, in his view, no monetary power on earth that can by itself magically generate an expansion in commodity production. The real impetus to the system lies in accumulation through commodity production and exchange. Marx is violently opposed, therefore, to that version of the monetarist doctrine that supposes that the supply of money has creative effects.[9]

[8] The term 'financial repression' is used by McKinnon (1973, ch. 7), and I use it here not because I agree with McKinnon's technical definition but because it graphically describes the phenomena under investigation.

[9] De Brunhoff (1971) and Harris (1979) provide good accounts of the Marxist critique of monetarism.

This analysis of money under conditions of simple commodity production indicates that the central contradiction between money as a measure of value and money as a medium of exchange is never resolved: it is merely transposed to higher and higher levels within a hierarchy of monetary institutions. The various derivative functions of money – as store of value and means of payment, for example – give rise to further confusions. But we can best interpret the different forms money takes – the money commodity, coins, convertible and inconvertible paper currencies, various credit moneys, etc. – as an outcome of the drive to perfect money as a frictionless, costless and instantaneously adjustable 'lubricant' of exchange while preserving the 'quality' of the money as a measure of value. The uncertain and 'lawless' character of commodity production and exchange leads different economic agents to demand different kinds of money for definite purposes at particular conjunctures. In times of crisis, for example, economic agents typically look for secure forms of money (such as gold), but when commodity production is booming and exchange relations proliferating the demand for credit moneys is bound to rise.

Armed with these general insights, we can now go on to consider how money is specifically put to use under the capitalist mode of production. In what follows we will find that the basic contradiction between money as a measure of value and money as a medium of circulation will become even more marked under capitalism, but that the functions and forms of money will be put to quite remarkable and often extremely subtle uses.

II   THE TRANSFORMATION OF MONEY INTO CAPITAL

Marx constructs his theory of money out of an investigation of commodity production and exchange without any reference whatsoever to the circulation of capital. He takes this tack because a money economy is common to a variety of different modes of production and not unique to capitalism (*Capital,* vol. 2, p. 116). We would be seriously in error, he argues, if we sought to derive an understanding of money out of a study of the circulation of capital. But, by the same token, we would be equally remiss if we sought to understand the complex worlds of monetary circulation and financial operations under capitalism simply on the basis of some general theory of money (*Capital,* vol. 2, p. 30). We must avoid the confusion of *money* with *capital* at all costs and recognize that there is a 'palpable difference between the circulation of money as capital and its circulation as mere money' (*Capital,* vol. 1, p. 149). We must now consider this 'palpable difference' more carefully.

Under conditions of simple commodity production and exchange organized on non-capitalist lines, we find that 'money circulates commodities' and that 'commodities circulate money' – 'the circulation of commodities and the circulation of money thus determine one another' (*Grundrisse,* p. 186). Money basically circulates in reverse order to the circulation of commodities. Complications arise when money is used as a means of payment (the money flows and the commodity exchanges diverge in space and time as well as in quantity) and when money moves, for whatever reason, into or out of a hoard. Nor is it easy to integrate the money producers into such a monetary system without disturbing its otherwise simple logic.

Matters appear very differently, however, when we consider the capitalist form of circulation, of which the simplest expression is

$$M - C \begin{pmatrix} LP \\ MP \end{pmatrix} \ldots P \ldots C' - M'.$$

Yet Marx insists that when money functions as capital it still 'can perform only money functions' as medium of circulation (it facilitates the exchanges

$$M - C \begin{pmatrix} LP \\ MP \end{pmatrix} \text{ and } C' - M')$$

and measure of value (how else can the increase M–M' be validated?). Money functions, then, assume 'the significance of capital functions only by virtue of their interconnections with the other stages of [the circulation of capital]' (*Capital,* vol. 2, pp. 77, 81).

The 'palpable difference' between the circulation of money as capital and the 'mere circulation' of money through commodity exchange lies, in the first instance, in the new ways that capitals uses money. The 'transformation of money into capital' (*Capital,* vol. 1, pt 2) also depends upon social and historical conditions. Money can circulate as capital only when labour power, with the capacity to produce more value than it itself has, is available as a commodity:

> The owner of money and the owner of labour power enter only into the relation of buyer and seller. . . . [But] the buyer appears also from the outset in the capacity of an owner of means of production . . . the class relation between capitalist and wage labourer therefore exists. . . . It is not money which by its nature creates this relation; it is, rather, the existence of this relation which permits of the transformation of a mere money-function into a capital-function'. (*Capital,* vol. 2, pp. 29–30)

Wage labour consequently forms a bridge between what otherwise might be quite disparate spheres of production and exchange. On the one hand, the buying and selling of labour power is nothing more than a simple commodity transaction rendered special by the fact that it is a market reflection of a social relation in production. On the other hand a simple relation between buyer and seller 'becomes a relation inherent in production' (*Capital,* vol. 2, p. 117). The social relations of production have an expression both *within* and *without* the actual process of production. It is across the bridge provided by wage labour that capital can flow continuously (the disruptions of crises apart, of course) through the spheres of production and exchange. Money could not be converted into capital if wage labour did not exist.

Even then, the transformation of money into capital is not a painless affair. I cannot take the $10 or £10 in my pocket and convert it instantaneously into capital. In each line of production I must advance a certain amount of money capital in order to purchase the buildings, machinery, raw materials and labour power needed to get production of surplus value under way. I must hoard up enough money in order to go into business (the amount varies from one line of production to another – contrast railroads with sweatshops in the garment industry). But hoarding withdraws money from circulation, and this, if it occurs on any large scale, can disrupt the circulation of money and commodities. The credit system becomes a necessity. I can then indeed convert the $10 in my pocket into capital by depositing it in a bank where it can immediately be lent out as capital in return for interest.

The circulation of capital imposes additional obligations and burdens upon the monetary system, which can be met only through the organization of the credit system as the basis for financial operations. We will consider the functions of the credit system in detail in section IV below, but we can usefully sketch in here some of the demands that capital puts upon it. For example, the prservation and expansion of value requires continuity and smooth co-ordination when the material basis of production is characterized by discon-tinuity and discordance. Interchanges between departments and industries with different working periods, circulation and turnover times have some-how to be smoothed out and co-ordinations between the money, commodity and productive circuits of capital have also to be achieved. The profit rate can be equalized only if money capital can move quickly from one sphere of production to another while accumulation and reinvestment require periodic outlays of large sums, which would otherwise have to be hoarded.

For these and other reasons, the credit system emerges as the distinctive child of the capitalist mode of production and interest-bearing capital comes to play a very special role in relation to the circulation of capital. Yet this elaborate world of credit and finance is necessarily erected upon the monetary basis defined by conditions of simple commodity production and exchange. And this is so because money can only ever perform money functions even when it is thrown into circulation as capital or proffered as loan capital. To the degree that this monetary basis is riddled with contradictions, so the world of finance is erected upon shaky foundations. To the degree that capitalist finance breaks free from the shackles of the monetary system, so it both internalizes contradictions within itself and moves into an antagonistic posture with respect to its own monetary basis. Marx makes much of this antagonism, and in chapter 10 we will seek to understand how it imposes a peculiar monetary and financial twist to crisis formation under capitalism.

We can usefully sketch in the basic lines of this antagonism if only to indicate where the analysis is headed. The argument goes roughly along the following lines.

By virtue of their control over the means of production, capitalists can also appropriate the social power inherent in money and put it to work as *money capital,* and so produce surplus value through production. The logic of the overall circulation of capital forces them to create new financial instruments and a sophisticated credit system which pushes money and interest-bearing capital into a prominent role in relation to accumulation. But the coercive power of competition forces capitalists, as individual economic agents, to abuse that system and so undermine the social power of money itself: the currency may be debased, chronic inflation occurs, monetary crises are created, etc. It turns out that their use of money as a medium of circulation through the agency of the credit system undermines the utility of money as a measure and store of value. Steps must then be taken to preserve the quality of money. Tight and stringent monetary controls become necessary. Such controls either arise in the course of a crisis as capitalists rush to hold the basic money commodity (gold, for example) as the only legitimate representation of value, or else they are imposed as part of a conscious policy by a powerful monetary authority operating as an arm of the state. Under the latter circumstances, the politics of monetary policy as followed by the state becomes crucial to understanding the dynamics of capital accumulation.[10] Whatever the circumstances, however, the tendency towards excess in the realms of finance is ultimately checked by a return to the eternal verities of the monetary base.

In what follows, we will seek to unravel the relations between monetary and financial phenomena step by step. We begin with *interest* and *interest-bearing capital* as fundamental categories operating within the credit system. We will then proceed to a simple description of the functions and instrumentalities of the credit system in relation to the circulation of capital. We will proceed in both cases as if the conflict with the monetary basis has no significant role to play. This will then put us in a position to attack the broader and more complex issues concerning the monetary and financial aspects to crisis formation in the subsequent chapter.

[10] See de Brunhoff (1976) for a discussion on the relations between the state, finance and accumulation.

III   INTEREST

Interest-bearing capital, or, as we may call it in its antiquated form, usurer's capital, belongs together with its twin brother, merchant's capital, to the antediluvian forms of capital which long precede the capitalist mode of production and are to be found in the most diverse economic formations of society. (*Capital,* vol. 3, p. 593)

We can quickly establish the conditions that allow money-lending and usury to flourish. Through the proliferation of exchange relations, money 'establishes itself as a power external to and independent of the producers'. It thereby acquires a social power which can be appropriated and used by private persons. Usury arises out of the private use of this social power in the form of money-lending. It undermined 'ancient and feudal wealth and ancient and feudal property' and the forms of political organization characteristics of such societies. It helped break the power of feudal land-owners and separate small peasants, artisans and 'small burgher' producers from ownership of their own means of production. But although usury has a 'revolutionary effect', its impacts are destructive and negative rather than positive and creative. 'It does not alter the mode of production, but attaches itself firmly to [the mode of production] like a parasite and makes [the latter] wretched' (*Capital*, vol. 3, ch. 36). Prohibitions and legal sanctions against usury arise for these reasons.

To the degree that usurers appropriate the entire surplus value produced, they hold back the circulation of capital. That barrier has to be broken:

In the course of its evolution, industrial capital must therefore subjugate [usurer's and merchant's capital] and transform them into derived or special functions of itself. . . . Where capitalist production . . . has become the dominant mode of production, interest-bearing capital is dominated by industrial capital, and commercial capital becomes merely a form of industrial capital, derived from the circulation process. But both of them must first be destroyed as independent forms and subordinated to industrial capital. Violence [the state] is used against interest-bearing capital by compulsory reduction of interest-rates, so that it is no longer able to dictate terms to industrial capital. . . . The real way in which industrial capital subjugates interest-bearing capital is the creation of a procedure specific to itself – the credit system. . . . The credit system is its own creation. (*Theories of Surplus Value*, pt 3, pp. 468–9)

Interest, like the other major distributional categories of rent and merchant's capital, is viewed as an ancient form of appropriation, tamed by capitalism to its own specific requirements. 'Usury' and 'interest on money capital' have, therefore, entirely different social meanings in Marx's lexicon.

The difference cannot be attributed to the form of money itself because money can perform only money functions:

> What distinguishes interest-bearing capital – insofar as it is an essential element of the capitalist mode of production – from usurer's capital is by no means the nature or character of this capital itself. It is merely the altered conditions under which it operates. (*Capital,* vol. 3, p. 600)

The conditions that Marx has in mind are exactly those that permit the transformation of money into capital. Money must, in short, be able to command the labour of others – wage labour must already exist, brought into being through historically specific processes of primitive accumulation (in which usurious practices undoubtedly played their part). The social power of money can then be used by its owners to purchase both labour power and means of production – the first step down the rocky road of the production and realization of surplus value. The antagonism between capital and wage labour now takes on a wholly new dimension. On the one hand the concentration of the social power of money in the hands of the few is a necessary prerequisite to the initiation of the capitalist form of circulation. This presupposes that an appropriate 'production-determining distribution' of money wealth has already been achieved. On the other hand, the progressive concentration and centralization of money power in the hands of the capitalists is the result of the production of surplus value. Concentration of money power is a distributive condition which is both necessary to and perpetually reproduced under capitalism (*Capital,* vol. 3, p. 355).

All of this puts money in a very special position in relation to the circulation of capital and the production of surplus value. The money exists as a form of capitalist property *outside of* and *independent of* any actual production process. A distinction then arises between capitalists as *owners of money* and as *employers of capital* who use that money to set up the production of surplus value. The activity of lending and borrowing establishes a class relationship between these two different kinds of capitalists. Marx expounds upon this relationship in the following manner. The owners of money look to augment their capital by lending at interest which implies a form of circulation of the sort $M–(M + i)$. Suppose the money is lent to a capitalist engaging in production who has no money resources of his or her own. We then have:

$$\text{Owner of money} \quad M \searrow \qquad \qquad \qquad \qquad \nearrow (M + i)$$
$$\text{Productive capitalist} \qquad M - C\left(\begin{matrix} LP \\ MP \end{matrix}\right) \ldots P \ldots C' - (M + \Delta m)$$

But the owners of money and the employers of capital typically confront each other as independent juridical individuals. Lenders plainly will not lend their money unless they can get some kind of reward. Producers will not borrow money unless they, too, can gain something. And so, Marx argues, the surplus value is split between *owners of capital* who receive *interest* and the *employers of capital* who receive *profit of enterprise*. Since Marx is here, as elsewhere, concerned with roles rather than the particular ways in which those roles are personified, and since the employers of capital always have the option of lending out whatever money they have at interest rather than reinvesting, Marx concludes that 'the employer of capital, even when working with his own capital, splits into two personalities – the owner of capital and the employer of capital' (*Capital,* vol. 3, pp. 374–8). The basic conception which then emerges is this: interest is the 'mere fruit' of owning money capital as property *outside of* any actual process of production, whereas profit of enterprise is the 'exclusive fruit' of capital put to work *within* the process of production. The circulation of money as capital is to be interpreted as follows:

$$M - C \left(\genfrac{}{}{0pt}{}{LP}{MP} \right) \ldots P \ldots C' - (M + \Delta m) \quad \genfrac{}{}{0pt}{}{\nearrow \ i \ (\text{interest})}{\searrow p \ (\text{profit of enterprise})}$$

Interest-bearing capital can then be defined as any money or money equivalent lent out by owners of capital in return for the going rate of interest.

A number of observations and caveats can usefully be introduced into the argument at this point. To begin with, the owners of money can lend it to economic agents other than producers of surplus value – to merchants, landowners, governments, various factions of the bourgeoisie and even labourers. And the money can be lent for a variety of purposes that have nothing directly to do with production of surplus value. Since owners of money are concerned primarily to augment their money by interest, they are presumably indifferent as to whom and for what purposes the money is lent provided the return is secure. This creates some difficulties, which Marx is aware of but brushes aside for plausible enough reasons. If, in the final analysis, all interest payments have to be furnished, directly or indirectly, out of surplus value, then the crucial relationship to be examined is that between interest-bearing capital and surplus value production. Unfortunately, circumscribing the analysis in this way creates as many problems as it solves when we seek to bare the forces that determine the rate of interest. We shall return to this matter later.

The virtue of Marx's approach is that it focuses our attention upon the relation between two forms of capital and an immanent class relation between owners of money – money capitalists – and employers of capital – industrial capitalists. 'Interest is a relationship between two capitalists, not between capitalist and labourer' (*Capital,* vol. 3, p. 382). Marx rejects the bourgeois view that profit of enterprise is really a return to the managerial skills of the entrepreneur as *worker*. He does not deny that co-ordination and management are productive activities, but insists that wage determination here is ultimately brought into line with wages in general by 'the development of a numerous class of industrial and commercial managers' and the 'general development which reduces the cost of production of specially trained labour-power' (*Capital,* vol. 3, p. 89). While this is a rather simplistic view of wage determination for the so-called 'managerial classes', there is no reason to deny that profit of enterprise is a return over and above that paid out as wages of superintendence, however much bourgeois theory and practice may seek to disguise that profit as a form of wages. We will later encounter circumstances – joint stock company forms of organization in particular – where the disguise becomes even more effective (see below, pp. 276–8).

But if interest is a 'relationship between two capitalists', then we have to understand the nature and implications of that relationship. The existence of money as capital outside of production and the activity of lending and borrowing implies that money acquires 'an additional use-value, that of serving as capital'. This use value resides in its 'faculty of begetting and increasing value', the capacity to 'produce the average profit under the average conditions'. Money as capital becomes, in short, a commodity, albeit of a very special sort with its 'own peculiar mode of alienation' (*Capital,* vol. 3, pp. 338–52). The crux of the relation between money capitalists and industrial capitalists lies in the 'peculiarities' that arise when capital itself takes on a commodity character.

Consider, then, the relation between a money capitalist who lends to an industrial capitalist. The money capitalist parts with the use value of the money without receiving any equivalent in return, which in itself makes for a very peculiar kind of commodity transaction. What the money capitalist expects is the return of the original money capital plus interest *at the end of a specified time period*. First of all, a specific time dimension is thereby imposed upon the circulation of capital in general, which opens up all kinds of paths to deal with differential turnover times, circulation times, production periods and so on. We will return to these features shortly. Secondly, it makes it appear as if money 'grows' automatically over time and makes even time itself appear as money. Marx concentrates heavily upon exposing the fetishism of that conception by showing very concretely that, if money capital increases by interest over a given time period, this is because productive capitalists have managed to produce sufficient surplus value within that period to cover the interest payment (*Capital,* vol. 3 p. 348). The money capitalists, in so far as they can dictate rates of interest and times of repayment, directly control the intensity of surplus value production. We will return to the potential coercive powers of money capitalists over industrial capitalists later (see pp. 301–5 below).

The use value of money as a commodity is unambiguous enough, but what of its value and exchange value? We here encounter another peculiarity. Money is the representative of value and cannot possibly be more valuable than the value it represents. Yet the use value of the money is that it can be used to produce greater value in the form of surplus value. We then arrive at what Marx considers to be a totally irrational expression: the value of value is that it produces greater value! Since 'price represents the expression of value in money', it likewise follows that 'interest, signifying the price of capital, is from the outset quite an irrational expression' (*Capital,* vol. 3, p. 354). Money as a commodity has a use value but no 'value' or 'natural price'. This also follows because the transformation of money into capital does not involve a material production process and does not involve the embodiment of labour.

The argument is somewhat of a tongue-twister, but it leads directly to Marx's rejection of theories of a 'natural' rate of interest, a doctrine that was widespread in the political economy of the time. He similarly rejects, largely by implication, any 'marginal productivity theory' of the 'price' of money capital on the grounds that such theories fetishize capital as an 'independent factor of production' endowed with mystical powers of self-expansion (*Theories of Surplus Value,* pt 3, pp. 453–540).

So how is the rate of interest determined?[11] In the absence of any other explanation, Marx turns to demand and supply. In all other cases he rejects explanations of this sort on the grounds that, when supply and demand are equilibrated in the market, they serve to explain nothing. The interest rate is an apparent exception to this rule. It is set by the market forces of supply and demand for money as capital under conditions of competition. Furthermore, if there is 'no law of division except that enforced by competition', then the interest rate 'becomes something arbitrary and lawless' – 'the determination is accidental, purely empirical, and only pedantry or fantasy would seek to represent this accident as a necessity' (*Capital,* vol. 3, pp. 356, 354).

We can read these comments in two ways. Either Marx is saying that the determination of the rate of interest is *totally* arbitrary and lawless, and not susceptible to further scientific investigation except as an empirical regularity; or we can interpret him as saying that the interest rate is not regulated directly by the law of value. I lean to the second interpretation on two grounds. First of all, it would be very uncharacteristic of Marx, and wholly inconsistent with his wrestlings with the forces that determine the rate of interest, to take the first position. Secondly, we find Marx on a number of occasions making statements that suggest 'separate laws' determine interest and profit of enterprise (*Capital,* vol. 3, p. 375). He also indicates that, although the lower limit to the rate of interest can in principle be 'any low',

[11] Harris (1976) has a useful introduction to the forces that fix the rate of interest in Marx's analysis of the phenomenon.

there will 'always be counteracting influences to raise it again' (p. 358). Whenever Marx invokes counteracting influences we usually find some notion of equilibrium not far behind. That equilibrium is determined 'by the supply and demand of money capital *as distiguished* from the other forms of capital'. Marx then firmly indicates the direction in which he was headed: 'It could further be asked: How are demand and supply of money capital determined?' (p. 419).

There is, we can conclude, no 'natural rate of interest' regulated, as the bourgeois economists of the time frequently supposed, by the value of money as a commodity. The value and price of money are entirely 'irrational' expressions. The interest rate is regulated through a market process in which supply and demand have a key role to play. What we now have to establish is how supply and demand for money as capital are structured under the capitalist mode of production. Unfortunately, Marx does not provide us with any coherent analysis of this process. We shall have to fill in some gaps. But, clearly, we cannot understand the demand for money as capital without first understanding the various uses to which money capital can be put and the functions it is called on to perform under capitalism. By the same token, we cannot understand the supply of money as capital without having a general understanding of the institutional frameworks and mediations of financial operations in assembling and consolidating money as lendable capital. We need, in short, to dissect the functions and instrumentalities of the credit system as the distinctive product of the capitalist mode of production, as the system that permits capital to tame usury and convert it into forms of interest-bearing capital appropriate to its own inherently contradictory purposes.

In the next two sections we will take up an analysis of the credit system in detail. We shall do so, in the first instance, as if that system is contradiction-free and functioning perfectly in relation to the circulation of capital. This will prepare the ground for considering the contradictions in the subsequent chapter.

IV   THE CIRCULATION OF INTEREST-BEARING CAPITAL AND THE FUNCTIONS OF THE CREDIT SYSTEM

The circulation of money as interest-bearing capital presages the formation of a class of money capitalists who control the social power of money and who are sustained out of interest payments. The actual existence of such a class cannot be attributed simply to the desire of individuals to have done with the bother of engaging in production, although capitalists, given the opportunity, often tend to do just that. The extent and power of any class of money capitalists and the circulation of money as interest-bearing capital is in fact contained within fairly strict limits. 'If an untowardly large section of capitalists were to convert their capital into money-capital, the result would be a frightful depreciation of money-capital and a frightful fall in the rate of interest; many would . . . hence be compelled to reconvert into industrial capitalists' (*Capital*, vol. 3, pp. 377–8).

Indeed, since money capitalists absorb rather than generate surplus value, we may well wonder why capitalism tolerates such seeming parasites. There are two reasons. First, the circulation of capital confers a very special role upon money as the general equivalent of value, and this role inevitably provides a potential source of sustenance for a class of pure money capitalists. Secondly, the circulation of interest-bearing capital performs certain vital functions and the accumulation of capital therefore *requires* that money capitalists achieve and actively assert themselves as a power external to and independent of actual production processes. We will, in what follows, explain how and why this is so.

The general picture that will ultimately emerge is that balanced accumulation depends upon the achievement of a specific balance of power and allocation of functions between money capitalists operating *without* and industrial capitalists operating *within* the actual process of production. The task before us is to determine where this balance point lies and to explain how the internal contradictions of capitalism inevitably violate it only to restore it through crises.

As a first step towards this goal, we take up the functions of interest-bearing capital in relation to accumulation. This will help us fix the *need* for interest-bearing capital and the money capitalist as an independent power in relation to industrial capital. But in taking up such matters we must always remember that money can only ever perform money functions. The circulation of interest-bearing capital is ever bound by such a rule. This implies that the credit system is built up as an elaboration of money functions and forms that exist under simple commodity production and exchange. These functions and forms are 'extended, generalized and worked out' under capitalism in ways that were neither possible nor desirable under pre-capitalist modes of production (*Capital*, vol. 3, p.400). This 'working out' takes place in such a way, however, as to 'wrap the real movement in mystery' to the point where basics disappear almost entirely from view (*Capital*, vol. 2, p. 148). Our task is then a double one: to depict the relation between the credit system and accumulation while strictly observing the relation between the credit system and its monetary basis.

The functions of the credit system and the circulation of interest-bearing capital are considered under six main headings without regard to the way in which these functions fuse together or express contradictions.

1 *The mobilization of money as capital*

Money that does not circulate as capital can be regarded as *latent* or *potential* money capital. Under conditions of simple commodity production and exchange, much of the money in society is actively employed as a medium of circulation or is used as a store of value by economic agents who need to maintain a reserve fund for whatever purpose:

> The numerous points at which money is withdrawn from circulation and accumulates in numerous individual hoards or potential money-capitals appear as so many obstacles to circulation, because they immobilise the money and deprive it of its capacity to circulate for a certain length of time. . . . One can understand the pleasure experienced when all these potential capitals . . . become disposable, 'loanable capital', money-capital which indeed is no longer passive and music of the future, but active capital growing rank. (*Capital*, vol. 2, p. 493)

Money can be mobilized as capital via the credit system in two distinct ways. First of all, banks can convert a flow of monetary transactions into loan capital. They do so by substituting their own credit money (bank drafts or checks) for cash, internalizing the function of money as medium of circulation within their operations and relying upon compensating deposits and withdrawals to furnish a permanent money balance which can be converted into loan capital. The shift from cash to cheque payments (of wages and salaries, for example) can therefore be seen as part of a general strategy to generate loan capital out of ordinary monetary transactions.

Secondly, financial institutions concentrate the 'money savings and temporarily idle money capital of all classes' and convert this money into capital. 'Small amounts, each in itself incapable of acting in the capacity of money capital', can thereby 'merge together into large masses and thus form a money-power' (*Capital*, vol. 3, p. 403). The concentration and centralization of capital can proceed apace. Individual capitalists who are saving can lend at interest to capitalists who are reinvesting, and this cuts down on levels of hoarding because capitalists can amass credits while keeping their monetary reserves active as interest-bearing capital. The same principle applies to all economic agents in society who require a reserve fund for whatever reason. The savings of *all* classes can be mobilized as money capital. The consequence, however, is that capitalists, rentiers, landlords, governments, workers, managers, etc., lose their social identity and become *savers*. The reserve funds of all classes get indiscriminately lumped together into an 'undifferentiated homogeneous [mass] of independent value – money' (*Capital*, vol. 3, p. 368). This poses some conceptual problems at the same time as it provides more than a hint of potential confusions and contradictions.

Consider, for example, the position of workers. They typically save to purchase consumer durables, to meet the needs of old age, to pay out for extraordinary expenses (illness, pregnancy, burials, etc.), and they may also save when times are good and wages are above value to counter the 'rainy day' when times are bad and wages fall below value. The concept of the value of labour power ought to embrace a certain level of workers' savings. But when these savings are mobilized as capital, workers can also receive interest. This appears to make money capitalists of workers and contravenes the laws of value as we have so far specified them because workers are entitled to a part of the surplus value they produce (but see p. 274 below). Furthermore, workers then have a strong stake in the preservation of the very system that exploits them because the destruction of that system entails the destruction of their savings. On the other hand, to the degree that workers' savings become a significant source of money capital, worker organizations acquire considerable economic power – hence the fight for control over union pension funds, insurance funds, etc. A whole new dimension is introduced into class struggle.

Whatever the social significance of this may be, the supply of money capital is clearly affected by the distributional arrangements that prevail under capitalism and the various 'stores of value' different economic agents have to maintain to function effectively. The real relationships within the credit system become very difficult to discern while the behaviour of economic agents as *savers* is subject to quite different pressures compared with their behaviours as wage-earners, landlords, industrialists or whatever.

2   Reductions in the cost and time of circulation

'One of the principal costs of circulation,' Marx argues, 'is money itself' (*Capital,* vol. 3, p. 435). The credit system helps to promote the efficiency of monetary circulation and to economize on transaction costs. It thereby helps to reduce the necessary but unproductive costs of circulation incurred even under simple commodity production. Herein, in Marx's view, lies the 'natural basis' of the credit system in simple commodity production and exchange.

In like manner, the credit system can help remove all manner of barriers to the free flow of capital through the respective spheres of production and circulation. Commodities requiring extra long production periods, for example, can be paid for by instalments. This permits producers to turn over the same capital several times during a single production period. The dovetailing of money flows between industries requiring radically different production periods is also made possible by the use of credit. Differential circulation times and the growth of long-distance trade likewise form one of 'the material bases' of the credit system, while the growth of credit permits commodities to penetrate to more distant markets (*Capital,* vol. 2, pp. 251–2; vol. 3, pp. 480–2). Consumers who wish to acquire the use value of an object (such as a house) for a long period of time may also seek to do so by making periodic payments 'on credit'. In all of these respects, the credit system permits continuity in money circulation while embracing discontinuity in production, circulation and consumption of commodities. By way of the credit system, all turnover times are reduced to 'socially necessary turnover time'.

From the standpoint of capital, turnover time is lost time, and Marx frequently emphasizes that the need to accelerate the turnover of capital is a 'fundamental determinant of credit and capital's credit contrivances' (*Grundrisse*, p. 659; *Capital*, vol. 2, p. 282). The reduction of turnover time actually releases money capital, which can then be used for further accumulation. We can discern a multiplier effect within the credit system – the use of money capital to accelerate turnover releases more money capital.[12]

The need to maintain continuity of money flows and to reduce turnover times in the face of myriad commodity movements, proliferating division of labour and wildly divergent production and circulation times is a powerful stimulus towards the creation of a credit system. Without credit, the whole accumulation process would stagnate and founder.

> Credit is, therefore, indispensable here; credit whose volume grows with the growing volume of value in production and whose time duration grows with the increasing distance of the markets. A mutual interaction takes place here. The development of the production process extends the credit, and credit leads to an extension of industrial and commercial operations. (*Capital*, vol. 3, p. 481)

But by the same token, credit permits a far vaster wedge to be inserted into the identities presupposed by Say's Law than was ever possible given other forms of money. Purchases and sales can become increasingly separate from each other in both time and space. Under such conditions, the potentiality for crises becomes that much greater. Credit not only permits traditional money functions to be extended, generalized and worked out: it does exactly the same for the crisis tendencies within capitalism.

3 Fixed capital circulation and consumption fund formation

> Fixed capital . . . engages the production of subsequent years . . . [and] . . . anticipates further labour as a counter-value. The anticipation of future fruits of labour is . . . not an invention of the credit system. It has *its roots in the specific mode of realization, mode of turnover, mode of reproduction of fixed capital.* (*Grundrisse*, pp. 731–2)

What captures the attention in this statement is the implied relation be-

---

[12] De Brunhoff (1971) reviews the distinction in bourgeois theory between the money and credit multipliers from a Marxist perspective and demonstrates that the distinction has little relevance.

tween the formation and circulation of fixed capital, the rise of a credit system and the anticipation of future fruits of labour. The circulation of fixed capital imposes tremendous burdens upon capital. Sufficient money has to be hoarded up to cover the initial purchase price and to bridge the time until the return of values through production. The credit system becomes vital in facilitating the circulation of fixed capital. Even presuming no personal savings on the part of other classes in society, capitalists investing in the present can borrow at interest from capitalists who are saving with an eye to future expansion or replacement. As the circulation of fixed capital 'hardens' into an independent form of circulation, and as its scale, quantity and durability increase with accumulation, so must capitalism evolve an ever more sophisticated credit system to handle the problems that fixed capital circulation poses.

Investments of an 'independent kind', particularly in the built environment, would be impossible to achieve without access to credit. Long term investments can be converted into annual payments, or capital can be centralized on a scale capable of funding such vast undertakings as railroads, dams, docks and harbours, power stations and the like. Credit likewise facilitates the individual consumption of commodities that have a long life – motor cars and housing are good examples – while government can provide public goods through debt financing. Capital can also be lent out in commodity form. Equipment, buildings, etc., can be purchased by the money capitalist and lent out at interest to users. The net result is that interest-bearing capital can circulate in relation to fixed capital in a variety of ways. The only thing that all forms have in common is that the interest payment is linked to future labour as a counter-value.

For this reason credit becomes an essential mediating link between the flows of circulating and fixed capital. Over and beyond the direct problems of co-ordinating two flows that march according to very different drummers, we must also consider how the credit system functions to re-direct the surpluses of capital and population into fixed capital formation.

We noted, in chapter 8, the potential difficulty that arises when over-accumulated circulating capital has to be switched into fixed capital circulation. The idle money capital of, say, shoemakers can be syphoned off via the credit system and put to work with unemployed labourers to build, say, a railroad. But this leaves the surplus productive capacity and surplus commodities held by the shoemakers untouched. By creating money values equivalent to the surpluses of shoes and the idle productive capacity and putting that money into circulation as capital in railroad construction, capital can indeed be switched from one sphere to another. But this switch occurs without being backed by any real exchange of commodities. The credit system operates with a form of 'fictitious capital' – a flow of money capital not backed by any commodity transaction. The anticipation is, of course, that the expanded employment in railroad construction will increase the demand for shoes so as to mop up surplus inventories and to set idle productive capacity back to work. In this case, the fictitious capital advanced is subsequently realized in real value form.

The category of 'fictitious capital' is in fact implied whenever credit is extended in advance, in anticipation of future labour as a counter-value. It permits a smooth switch of over-accumulating circulating capital into fixed capital formation – a process that can disguise the appearance of crises entirely in the short run. But the creation of fictitious values ahead of actual commodity production and realization is ever a risky business. The credit system becomes the cutting edge of accumulation with all the attendant dangers such exposure brings. The gap between fictitious values within the credit system and money tied to *real* values widens. The stage is set for crises within the credit system. With such profound speculative dangers, why does capitalism tolerate fictitious capital in the first place? We must now answer that question in general terms.

4 *Fictitious capital*

We can, in the first instance, define the circulation of interest-bearing capital as an intersection between the money circuit of capital on the one hand and the circuits of commodity and productive capital on the other:

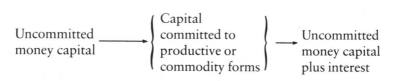

When capital exists as money it possesses all the virtues of general exchangeability, flexibility of use, mobility and the like. Interest-bearing capital can best fulfil its co-ordinating functions if it preserves its flexibility in relation to specific uses, if it remains perpetually *outside of* production and *uncommitted* to specific products. But in the course of its circulation, lenders must sacrifice the flexibility of their money for a specific period of time in return for an interest payment. During that time, money becomes tied down to specific use values (commodities, productive apparatus, etc.). Problems immediately arise. Lenders may not be able or willing to give up control over their money for the length of time that borrowers need to finance their operations. The difficulty of co-ordinating the seemingly infinite variety of needs on the part of both lenders (savers) and borrowers is symptomatic, however, of a deeper dilemma. To the degree that interest-bearing capital becomes committed to specific use values, it loses its co-ordinating powers because it loses its flexibility. Barriers arise within the very circulation process of interest-bearing capital itself. These barriers are removed by the creation of what Marx calls 'fictitious capital'.

The potentiality for 'fictitious capital' lies within the money form itself and is particularly associated with the emergence of credit money. Consider the case of a producer who receives credit against the collateral of an unsold commodity. The money equivalent of the commodity is acquired before an actual sale. This money can then be used to purchase fresh means of production and labour power. The lender, however, holds a piece of paper, the value of which is backed by an unsold commodity. This piece of paper may be characterized as *fictitious value*. Commercial credit of any sort creates these fictitious values. If the pieces of paper (primarily bills of exchange) begin to circulate as *credit money*, then it is fictitious value that is circulating. A gap is thereby opened up between credit moneys (which always have a fictitious, imaginary component) and 'real' moneys tied directly to a money commodity. (*Capital*, vol. 3, pp. 573–4). If this credit money is loaned out as capital, then it becomes *fictitious capital*.

In this case, the creation of fictitious capital can be viewed as more or less accidental. Accident is converted into necessity, however, when we connect the circulation processes of interest-bearing and fixed capital. The money capital has now to be advanced against future labour rather than against the collateral of already existing commodities. It has to be advanced, furthermore, for the full lifetime of the fixed capital and committed during that time to a specific use value. The only collateral is the value of the fixed capital, and this, as we saw in chapter 8, is subject to complex and unstable determinations. What in effect happens is that the claim upon future labour which fixed capital defines is converted via the credit system into a claim exercised by money capital over a share of future surplus value production. Money capital is invested in future appropriation. From the very outset, therefore, the money capital advanced has to be regarded as fictitious capital because it is not backed by any firm collateral. Furthermore, future surplus value production is uncertain and varies according to the state of competition, the pace of technological change, the rate of exploitation and the overall dynamics of accumulation and overaccumulation. Yet, even in the face of such uncertainty, the money capital must be advanced for at least the lifetime of the fixed capital. Serious barriers are posed to the circulation of interest-bearing capital.

A variety of solutions can be devised to deal with these barriers. Financial intermediaries can step into the breach and pool savings and risks so as to be able to borrow short-term and lend long-term. They can do this in anticipation of both future savings and future surplus value production (which ultimately must amount to the same thing, because savings are generated out of revenues that flow from production). The other solution is for producers to re-finance their debt on an annual basis or to market titles to shares of future surplus value production directly. The buying and selling of stocks and shares permits money owners to preserve flexibility and liquidity while share prices can adjust to the variations in surplus value production.

Such solutions, which institutionalize fictitious capital within the credit system, generate some confusions. 'The stocks of railways, mines, navigation companies, and the like, represent actual capital, namely the capital invested and functioning in such enterprises, or the amount of capital advanced by the stockholders for the purpose of being used as capital in such enterprises.' (*Capital,* vol. 3, p. 466) But the title of ownership does not 'place this capital at one's disposal', and the capital itself cannot be withdrawn because the title is only a claim upon a portion of future revenues. The title is a 'paper duplicate' of the real capital – the paper duplicate can circulate while the real capital can not. 'To the extent that the accumulation of this paper expresses the accumulation of railways, mines, steamships, etc., to that extent does it express the extension of the actual reproduction process.' But as paper duplicates the titles are purely 'illusory, fictitious forms of capital'. The prices of these titles may then fluctuate according to their own laws 'quite independently of the movement of the value of the real capital (*Capital,* vol. 3, pp. 466–77).

But in one respect these fluctuating prices can reflect something real with respect to the condition of productive capital. We noted in chapter 8 how the value of fixed capital was itself an unstable determination because the initial purchase price, the replacement cost and the rate of production of surplus value all provided different measures of value. From this arose the conception of the value of fixed capital as a perpetually shifting magnitude, affected by the state of competition, technological dynamism and the pace of accumulation itself. To some degree, the variation in stock prices can be viewed as a reflection of the shifting values of the stock of fixed capital itself.

Unfortunately, the shifting prices of titles are also shaped by many other forces. Profit, furthermore, is not the only form of revenue in capitalist society. There are, for example, rents and taxes. Marx holds that 'the form of interest-bearing capital is responsible for the fact that every definite and regular money revenue appears as interest on some capital, whether it arises from some capital or not' (*Capital,* vol. 3, p. 464). These revenues can be capitalized at the going rate of interest and titles to them can also be traded on the market. Government debt (the ultimate in fictitious capital as far as Marx was concerned) and land (see chapter 11) have no inherent value, yet they can assume a price:

> Government bonds are capital only for the buyer, for whom they represent the purchase price, the capital he invested in them. In themselves they are not capital but merely debt claims. If mortgages, they are mere titles on future ground rent. . . . All of these are not real

capital. They do not form constituent parts of capital, nor are they values in themselves. (*Capital,* vol. 3, p. 475)

In all such cases, money capital is invested in appropriation. The money capitalist is indifferent (presumably) to the ultimate source of revenue and invests in government debt, mortgages, stocks and shares, commodity futures or whatever, according to rate of return, the security of investment, its liquidity and so on. 'All connection with the actual expansion process of capital is thus completely lost, and the conception of capital as something with automatic self-expansion properties is thereby strengethened.' The result, Marx holds, is that interest-bearing 'is the fountainhead of all manner of insane forms' in which 'even in accumulation of debts' can 'appear as an accumulation of capital.' Everything, he says, 'is doubled and trebled and transformed into a mere phantom of the imagination'. The credit system registers the 'height of distortion' to the degree that the accumulation of claims far outruns real production (*Capital,* vol. 3, pp. 464–72).

Marx's primary purpose in all of this is to disabuse us of the idea that a marketable claim upon some future revenue is a real form of capital. He wishes to alert us to the insanity of a society in which investment in appropriation (rents, government debts, etc.) appears just as important as investment in production. Marx insists that in the end only the latter matters – 'if no real accumulation, i.e. expansion of production and augmentation of the means of production, had taken place, what good would there be from the accumulation of debtor's money claims on . . . production?' (*Capital,* vol. 3, p. 424.) If all money capital invests in appropriation and none in actual production, then capitalism is not long for this world. And when the 'height of distortion' is achieved in the credit system, the quality of money as a measure of value is threatened: so much so that in the course of a crisis, as Marx tirelessly points out, the system is forced to seek a more solid monetary basis than the one provided by credit moneys and fictitious capital. With so much insanity built into the credit system, why permit such a state of affairs to continue?

When we explore, step by step, the accumulation process and its contradictions, we find that fictitious capital is contained in the very concept of capital itself. Fixed capital formation and circulation is necessary for accumulation. The barrier fixed capital creates to future accumulation (see chapter 8) can be overcome only by way of the credit system in general and by the creation of fictitious forms of capital in particular. By permitting fictitious capital to flourish, the credit system can support the transformation of circulating into fixed capital and meet the increasing pressures that arise as more and more of the total social capital in society begins to circulate in fixed form. Fictitious capital is as necessary to accumulation as fixed capital itself. And we will later encounter circumstances that will make this conclusion even more emphatic. Given Marx's general line of argument concerning the manner in which the internal contradictions of capitalism are generalized and worked out, it should be no surprise that the circulation of interest-bearing capital is simultaneously the saviour of accumulation and 'the fountainhead of all manner of insane forms'. Thus can we understand the double-edged role of fictitious capital.

5 The equalization of the profit rate

There are innumerable barriers to the equalization of the profit rate. But the free flow of interest-bearing capital (enhanced by the existence of fictitious forms of capital) does much to eliminate them. The general rate of profit is, of course, 'never anything more than a tendency, a movement to equalize specific rates of profit' which are in perpetual flux among firms, industries and enterprises. The 'equilibration of constant divergences' through competition presumes that capital can flow from spheres with below-average profits to spheres with above-average profits (*Capital*, vol. 3, p. 366). Credit has an obvious role to play here. It is, for example, 'the means whereby accumulated capital is not just used in that sphere in which it is created, but wherever it has the best chance of being turned to good account' (*Theories of Surplus Value*, pt 2, p. 482). But credit is more than just a helpful means to accomplish a vital end:

> In the money-market only lenders and borrowers face one another. The commodity has the same form – money. . . . [Individual capitalists] are all thrown together as borrowers of money, and capital confronts them all in a form, in which it is as yet indifferent to the prospective manner of its investment. . . . [Capital appears] as *essentially the common capital of a class* – something industrial capital does only in the movement and competition of capital between the various individual spheres. On the other hand, money capital . . . possesses the form in which, indifferent to its specific employment, it is divided as a common element among the various spheres, among the capitalist class, as the requirements of production in each individual sphere dictate. (*Capital*, vol. 3, p. 368)

The credit system appears, in short, as a kind of central nervous system for co-ordinating the divergent activities of individual capitalists. Interest-bearing capital, representing the common capital of a class, flows in response to profit rate differentials. Furthermore, the rate of interest can function as a 'barometer and thermometer' for capitalism in a way that the profit rate cannot. This is so because the rate of interest is achieved as a 'simultaneous mass effect' of the supply and demand for money capital, a result that is known (it is quoted daily on the market) and that varies uniformly (although Marx does acknowledge interest rate differentials between different markets and different countries). Thus, when the long-term rate of interest moves substantially higher than the profit of enterprise received in a given line of production, industrialists have every incentive not to reinvest but to put whatever surpluses they may have on the money market. The information the interest rate provides and the functions interest-bearing capital can perform permit, therefore, far more rapid adjustments in capital flows, and they thereby perfect a set of mechanisms for equalizing the rate of profit (*Capital*, vol. 3, pp. 366–9). And this can happen because 'interest-bearing capital is capital as *property*' external to production, 'as distinct from capital as *function*' within production (p. 379). Unfortunately, the common capital of *the class* of all capitalists is converted, under the social relations of capitalism, into the common capital of *a class* of money capitalists whose specific interests do not always coincide with those of capital in general. We will take up *that* contradiction in the next chapter.

6 The centralization of capital

The credit system 'in its first stages furtively creeps in as the humble assistant of accumulation, drawing into the hands of individual or associated capitalists, by invisible threads, the money resources which lie scattered, over the surface of society, in larger or smaller amounts; but it soon becomes a new and terrible weapon in the battle of competition and is finally transformed into an enormous social mechanism for the centralisation of capitals' (*Capital*, vol. 1, p. 626). In this regard we find 'modern credit institutions are as much an effect as a cause of the concentration [centralization] of capital' (*Grundrisse*, p. 122). Let us consider how this might be.

The centralization of capital via the credit system unleashes the full power and potential of technological and organizational change as a prime lever for accumulation (see chapter 4). Economies of scale are more easily achieved, the barriers posed by the organizational capacities of the family firm can be overcome, and large-scale projects (particularly those embedded in the built environment) can be undertaken. And with the aid of fictitious capital, all of this can be done without unduly interrupting – except during crises, of course – the free flow of money capital. But the credit system also furnishes means to counter the de-stabilizing effects of technological and organizational change. For example, Marx lists an increase in stock capital as one of the influences counteracting the tendency towards a falling rate of profit. Undertakings of particularly high value composition comprised largely of fixed capital can be organized via the credit system so as not to 'enter into the equilization of the general rate of profit' since they can then be produced if they yield 'bare interest' only (*Capital*, vol. 3, pp. 240, 437). Overaccumulated circulating capital can be 'switched' into a form of fixed capital circulation which helps to increase the rate of profit.[13] The value composition of capital can likewise

[13] This is the import of Boccara's (1974) theory of relative devaluation discussed in chapter 7 above.

be reduced by increasing vertical integration and the rate of profit raised by accelerating turnover time. And if all else should fail, violent processes of primitive accumulation can continue in the very heart of capitalism as the 'roving cavaliers of credit' wreak havoc by making money out of devaluing other people's capital – 'the little fish are swallowed by the sharks and the lambs by the stock-exchange wolves' (*Capital*, vol. 3, p. 440). In all of these respects the credit system becomes a vital tool in the struggle to contain the destructive forces contained within the inner logic of capitalism.

And while it is true that Marx puts the greatest emphasis upon the centralization of capital via the credit system, it is also the case that the forces of decentralization – the opening up of new lines of production, the proliferation in the division of labour and the internal decentralization within contemporary forms of capitalist organization – can be marshalled via the credit system. The centralization of money capital can be accompanied by a decentralization in the organization of productive activity. A distinction thus arises between *financial* and *industrial* forms of organization at the same time as specific kinds of relations spring up to bind them together (see chapter 10). The proliferation of credit devices and financial strategems therefore appears vital to the preservation of capitalism and from this standpoint is indeed as much an effect as a cause of accumulation.

V THE CREDIT SYSTEM: INSTRUMENTALITIES AND INSTITUTIONS

Although we can certainly find many a sleight of hand in the slippery world of finance, the credit system does not operate by magic. Means have to be found to perform tasks, and means call forth institutions, and institutions need people to organize and run them. The bankers, financiers, stock brokers, *et al.* who populate the world of finance perform highly specialized functions within the division of labour. To some degree or other they constitute themselves as a special class within the bourgeoisie. And to the degree that the credit system does indeed function as a kind of central nervous system regulating the movement of capital, so this class occupies what seem to be the commanding heights of the economy from whence it confronts the industrial or merchant capitalists as the representatives of the total social capital.

The money capitalists, as we shall call them, are nevertheless caught in a welter of contradictions – the credit system internalizes the contradictions of capitalism and does not abolish them. For example, bankers are capitalists in competition with each other and must ply their trade with all the tricks at their command – tricks which, from time to time, pull them into the abyss of financial ruin. On the other hand, they are supposed to act as 'responsible' representatives of the total social capital and to use their powers wisely and well 'in the public interest'. They are supposed to keep everyone's money as 'safe as the Bank of England'.

Much of the complexity that has arisen in the world of finance reflects continuing and elaborate attempts to harmonize two irreconcilable roles. While this may be the simple truth of the matter, we are none the less obligated to examine the instrumentalities and institutions that have arisen under capitalism since these do have important material effects and theoretical implications. Marx himself focuses primarily on banks, gives a preliminary analysis of joint stock companies and makes mention, although usually in passing, of the wide range of specialized financial institutions, such as penny savings banks for workers, insurance companies and so on. He could not possibly have anticipated the extensive growth of consumer credit, pension funds and other accoutrements of the modern credit system. So it seems that there is much to do in up-dating Marx's analysis.

We are not, however, seeking categories with which to describe the seemingly infinite variety of institutional arrangements that have arisen in different countries throughout the history of capitalism. An exhaustive analysis, as Marx pointed out, is not necessary, since we seek here only a firm theoretical basis for understanding how the instrumentalities and institutions embedded in the credit system affect the laws of motion of capitalism. We consider this topic under four main headings.

1 The general principles of financial mediation: the circulation of capital and the circulation of revenues

At the basis of all financial operations, there always lies an elementary transaction between economic units possessed of surpluses of values and economic units that wish to make use of those surpluses for some purpose. The economic units may be individuals (from whatever class), corporations, governments, trade unions, institutions like church and crown, professional and business organizations, pension funds, charities, banks and so on, while the range of possible purposes is immense (to circulate as industrial or merchant's capital; to purchase a house, erect a monument, launch a political campaign, buy a country estate for a favoured mistress, build a church, etc.).

Financial institutions congregate around the need to find efficient ways to collect, concentrate and if necessary to convert these surpluses into money form preparatory to throwing the money into circulation as interest-bearing capital. In the midst of what appears to be immense confusion, we ought, at the outset, to make a firm distinction between the circulation of what Marx called the *money-form of revenue* and the *money-form of capital* (*Capital*, vol. 3, p. 443).

We have already dealt at length with the latter form of circulation – surplus value is converted into money and used to produce more surplus value. The circulation of the money-form of revenue is a very different process. Suppose, for example, workers set up institutions such as the early building societies in Britain or the savings and loan associations in the United States – which permit the savings of some workers to be used, in return for interest payments, to help other workers buy their houses. All that is happening here is that the revenues of workers (variable capital) are being redistributed within the working class from families with surpluses to families who need to go into deficit to acquire the housing they need. The problem is to interpret the interest payment that is plainly not a portion of the surplus value. The answer is simple enough. The monetization of relationships within the working class subjugates them to the *formal* as opposed to the *real* domination of interest-bearing capital as the centralized co-ordinator of the supply of workers' savings and the demand by workers for housing.

The circulation of revenues is extensive. It encompasses the hiring of menial servants by the bourgeoisie, payments for a whole host of services on the part of all classes. By way of the credit system, many of these transactions are converted into a relation of debtor and creditor with loans being made to consumers against future revenues. The transactions can become as fictitious in this sphere as in the sphere of circulation of capital. Marx did not regard the circulation of revenues as a primary target for investigation, since all such revenues have their origin in the circulation and accumulation of capital. He therefore focuses on the basic circulation process of capital to the exclusion of all else. Our understanding of the supply and demand for loanable funds, however, can become all too easily obscured because the credit system tends to merge the circulation of revenues and the circulation of capital indiscriminately.

Theoretically, we might distinguish several 'mini-circuits' within the credit system. Circuits can connect units in surplus with those in need within the working class, within the bourgeoisie, among governments and across and between these different kinds of economic units. In none of these cases can we interpret the interest payment as a direct slice out of the surplus value the loaned money helps to produce. The interest rate simply serves to regulate the borrowings and lendings out of revenues within the consumption sphere. The only connection to the circulation of capital – and an important one at that – lies in a diminution of personal hoarding and an increased demand for consumer goods which such credit arrangements can help to generate. These mini-circuits are very different from those that connect capitalist with capitalist or that link savings out of revenues with investment in the direct production of surplus value.

Let us suppose, for the moment, that the various mini-circuits are isolated from each other. The interest rate in each circuit would be set within that sphere and would presumably vary according to supply and demand conditions. But money is always money, no matter whose pocket it is in. Money would begin to flow from circuits where the interest rate is low to those where it is high. There would be *a tendency towards an equalization of the interest rate.*

Marx assumes a uniform and homogeneous rate of interest which presupposes the existence of a highly integrated credit system. The fragmentations could then be interpreted as a result of specialization in function. On the supply side, the mobilization of savings poses different problems according to the kind of economic unit. Penny savings banks, building societies and savings and loan associations, a national savings network, benefit societies, pension and insurance funds, etc., may be appropriate for workers, but such institutions are not well adapted to handle the savings of the Rockefellers or oil-rich Arab sheiks. The savings of large corporations and governments likewise require specialized handling. On the demand side, small business loans, agricultural credit, the financing of consumer purchases (motor cars, housing, etc.), the funding of government debt, the financing of large-scale projects (railways, public transport systems, public utilities) and meeting the needs of large multinational corporations are very different kinds of business calling for specialized expertise.

The financial structure that results is fragmented to some degree (although national systems vary a great deal in this regard, from being highly decentralized in the United States to highly centralized in France).[15] The fragmentations do indeed imply that there is not one financial market but many. And we can certainly discern interest rate differentials between markets and between nations, while different lending rates exist in relation to the financing of different kinds of activities. What is impressive about modern credit systems, however, is the manner in which a high level of integration exists within an often extremely fragmented structure. The flow of funds into and out of savings and loan associations in the United States, for example, is highly sensitive to the interest rates offered elsewhere. The supply of mortgage money to the housing market is thereby affected by the demand for money in other sectors of the economy. Interest rate differentials between countries (when adjusted for differential rates of inflation in local currencies) also quickly spark flows of 'hot' money capital to wherever the real rate of interest is highest. There are evidently strong forces at work which tend to equalize the long-term rate of interest. The consequence, however, is that the

[14] While Hilferding's (1970 edn) account is dated, the description of financial structures that he provides is still of consummate interest.

[15] Conventional accounts of French financial structure can be found in Coutière (1976) and Morin (1974), and comparative materials for Britain in Revell (1973) and for the United States in the Report of the Commission on Money and Credit (1961) updated by the Hunt Commission Report (1971). Goldsmith (1969) attempts some general comparisons around the theme of financial structure and development.

circulation of money as revenues and as capital become almost indistinguishable within the financial system.

2 Joint stock companies and markets for fictitious capital

We argued in chapter 5 that capital had to be liberated from the constraints imposed by the family firm if it was to expand and survive. The corporate form of organization unleashed the full powers of technological and organization change, stimulated the production of new knowledges and allowed the achievement of economies of scale in production, organization and marketing. It simultaneously separated ownership from management and led to a form of financing that liberated money capital as an independent power, as pure capitalist property external to production and commodity circulation.

Corporations organized according to the joint stock principle raise money by selling stocks, shares and bonds to money capitalists. The money raised is put to work as capital to produce surplus value (assuming, that is, the venture is intended as something more than 'pure swindle'). Investors hold titles of ownership and receive interest (fixed or varying as the case may be). The titles are simply marketable claims to a share in future surplus value production. Investors can retrieve their money at any time by selling off their stocks, shares and bonds to other investors. This buying and selling leads to the creation of a special kind of market – the *stock market*. This market is a market for fictitious capital. It is a market for the circulation of property rights as such.

But property rights come in many forms. Titles of any sort can in principle be traded. Governments can sell rights to a portion of future tax revenues. Property rights to commodities can be traded without the commodities actually changing hands or, as in commodity futures markets, prior to actual commodity production. Rights to land, buildings, natural resources (oil drilling, mineral exploration rights, etc.) can also be traded. There are, it seems, as many different markets for fictitious capital as there are forms of property ownership under capitalism.

The complexity of these markets is quite staggering, and a variety of specialized institutions and mechanisms arise to deal with the very specific problems that arise with respect to different kinds of property right (the mortgage market functions very differently, for example, from the commodity futures market). But all of these markets have one thing in common. Property titles are 'paper duplicates', which in themselves have no value even though they circulate at a price. This poses two questions: first, what is it that fixes the prices, and second, is the title a duplicate of any real value whatsoever?

The price of property titles is generally fixed by the present and anticipated future revenues to which ownership entitles the holder, capitalized at the going rate of interest. To the degree that the latter is fixed by the supply of and demand for money capital, prices plainly can shift in a manner entirely autonomous of alterations in anticipated revenues. The price is further modified by other considerations, such as ease of marketability, security, term of holding, taxation requirements and so on. We need not concern ourselves here with such details, since the main focus has to be upon the relation between these prices in general and the real values they must eventually represent. This relation provides us with an important clue in seeking to explain how and why the fictitious values (prices) achieved through the credit system can get so far removed from the values expressed in 'the monetary basis'.

In the case of joint stock companies, real capital (in the form of railroads, productive plant, etc.) does indeed exist, and the title of ownership that yields a dividend (interest) is backed to some degree or other by a real capacity to produce surplus value. The problem is to discern the firmness of the backing, and this can be known to investors only if full disclosure of company finances is required. Otherwise, corporations can find ways to make it seem as if they are in a far stronger (or weaker) position than they really are and to manipulate the prices of their stock accordingly. For example, borrowed money can be used to supplement dividend payments and so encourage further investment in an enterprise that seems profitable even though it is not (this process is known as 'stock watering', and was very common early in the twentieth century).[16]

Commodity markets usually operate with real value lurking somewhere in the background, and, leaving aside obvious cases of swindling, investors simply speculate over conditions of realization of values in different places and times. Such speculative activity is helpful in the sense that, if not subject to too much manipulation, it can lead to an equalization of prices. Commodity futures markets can perform a similar function by providing a guide to commodity owners as to whether they should store or release commodities at any given moment in time. But this requires an anticipation of future value production in commodity form. Mortgage markets (land and building prices) pose even more complex problems, which can be sorted out only after a thorough investigation of rent as an economic category (see chapter 11).

Government debt is likewise difficult to sort out. Marx considered it a purely illusory form of fictitious capital. The money represented by the national debt has been spent long ago (on fighting wars, meeting state expenses, etc.), so investors trade titles to the debt, which is backed simply by

[16] Some spectacular examples of speculators who made millions devaluing other people's investments by such activity can be found in the history of mass transit finance in the 1890s and early 1900s – see Hendrick (1907) and Roberts (1961) against the background described by Cheape (1980).

the powers of the government to tax surplus value production. This characterization is certainly appropriate for much of the national debt. But there are also forms of public expenditure that do not fit this model. If a municipal enterprise, financed by borrowings from the capital market, sells a commodity (electricity, gas, water, transportation) at a price that creates revenues sufficient to pay interest on the debt and to leave enough over for futher expansion of the business, then it is in principle no different from a joint stock company. The only difference lies in its form of ownership and its price-setting powers. If the activity is partially or wholly subsidized out of tax revenues, then the matter begins to appear very differently. But there are many productive activities that can be undertaken by the state with respect to physical and social infrastructures (health and education, for example). By improving the productive forces in society, the state can contribute, directly or indirectly, to surplus value production. The money invested in state debt does not automatically cease to circulate as capital simply because it enters into the framework of public finance. Interest-bearing capital can continue to circulate if the increase in surplus value production achieved through productive state investments generates the increasing tax revenues that form, in turn, the basis for the interest payments to those who invested in state debt in the first place. This is, of course, the theory 'productive expenditures' which has provided the rationale for all kinds of state activities.[17] But the fact that such an outcome is *possible* in no way guarantees that real values are indeed created by such state interventions.

In all of these cases, however, the relationship between the prices of titles and the real values such titles represent is necessarily obscured. The revenues themselves are not directly tied to surplus value production but are mediated by rules of distribution and a whole host of institutional arrangements which helpt to co-ordinate the flow of interest-bearing capital but which obscure the relation to real values. The supply of and demand for money capital also intervenes since prices are revenues capitalized at the rate of interest. Yet markets for fictitious capital are vital to the survival of capitalism, because it is only through them that the continuity of flow of interest-bearing capital can be assured. This flow, as we argued in the preceeding section, performs some vital co-ordinating functions. Markets for fictitious capital provide ways to co-ordinate the co-ordinating force in capitalist society.

---

[17] Baron Haussman pioneered this idea of 'productive expenditures' by the state in his dramatic reconstruction programme for Paris during the Second Empire (see Pinkney, 1958). The idea is now standard fare in most bourgeois theories of public finance. Marxist theories of the state are peculiarly reticent in handling this potentiality, although Barker (1978) proposes an interesting framework that deserves to be elaborated upon.

3 The banking system

The distinction between banks and other financial intermediaries is important.[18] Savings banks, pension and insurance funds, savings and loan associations and building societies, credit unions, post office savings accounts, etc., mobilize savings that are savings out of an existing quantity of values. Under these conditions, it is impossible to save ahead of the production of values. The same restriction does not apply to banks, which both give credit and create money values by virtue of the credit they give. The banks create fictitious money values when they substitute their own drafts for the bills of exchange which capitalists (and others) circulate among themselves. These fictitious money values can then be lent out as capital. This means that the banks can convert a flow of money being used as a means of payment into 'free' money capital. They can create money capital ahead of the production of values. The only limit to this capacity lies in the need to maintain a certain reserve of money to meet any sudden surge in demand for money on the part of their customers. A run on the bank occurs when depositors lose faith in the credit money of the bank and seek 'real money' (the money commodity or state-backed legal tender) in its stead.

The capacity of banks to create money capital out of fictitious values directly is important. There is, as we have seen, a perpetual problem under capitalism of finding the necessary slack resources to allow the reallocation of capital from relatively unproductive to more productive uses – always defined, of course, in terms of production of surplus value. In the early stages of capitalism, primitive accumulation and appropriation forced the reallocations directly or indirectly (through usury). In later stages, the mobilization of savings came to play an important role. But as primitive accumulation declined in relative importance, and as an increasing proportion of the total savings in society is wholly mobilized through the credit system, so the creation of money capital out of the flow of money within the banking system becomes the single most important source of the slack resoures needed to force reallocations in capital flows. The only other source lies in overaccumulation, but even here idle productive capacity and excess commodities must first be monetized via the banking system if reallocations are to occur. Furthermore, the capacity of the banking system to generate a supply of money capital ahead of real value production increases with the increasing volume of market transactions and the increasing proportion of such transactions accomplished through the banking system.

Marx focused on the role of the banks rather than on other kinds of

---

[18] This distinction is usefully discussed, albeit in bourgeois terms, by Gurley and Shaw (1960).

financial intermediary precisely because they combined both monetary and financial functions. As de Brunhoff (1978, p. 57) correctly concludes, 'the banking system is the strategic sector of the credit system' because the banks are 'the only institutions which combine both the management of means of payment and money capital.' These two managerial roles complement each other neatly in so far as the progress of accumulation requires the creation of fictitious values in money form ahead of any real production. But we have already noted (above, pp. 247–9) that the capacity of banks to create credit moneys without constraint poses an eternal threat to the quality of money as a measure of value. This threat is doubled and re-doubled as the creation of fictitious values becomes a necessity rather than just a standing temptation.

The potentiality for over-speculation under such circumstances is enormous. Fictitious values (credit moneys) are thrown into circulation as capital and converted into fictitious forms of capital. As a result, 'the greater portion of banker's capital is purely fictitious and consists of claims (bills of exchange), government securities (which represent spent capital) and stocks (drafts on future revenue)' (Capital, vol. 3, p. 469). Marx spends pages gleefully recounting examples of how the 'height of distortion' occurs within the banking sector of the credit system. The severity of the threat to the quality of money is obvious.

The response, as we saw in section I above, is to create a hierarchy of institutions with the express purpose of protecting the quality of money. Within any one country, a central bank typically sits at the apex of this hierarchy (we leave aside the international aspects of the problem for the moment). If the central bank is to succeed in its task, it must prevent fictitious values from moving too far out of line with real commodity values. It cannot impose a strict identity – even supposing it had the power to do so – because that would deny the production of free money capital to force new forms of accumulation. Nor can it let the creation of credit moneys run wild. Herein lies what even bourgeois economists concede to be the 'art' rather than the 'science' of central banking (see Niehans, 1978, ch. 12).

The result, however, is that 'the central bank is the pivot of the credit system' and 'the metal reserve, in turn, is the pivot of the bank' (Capital, vol. 3, p. 572). Stripped of its direct tie to a money commodity implied by the phrase 'metal reserve', this means that the central bank necessarily regulates the flow of credit in seeking to preserve the quality of money. A tension exists, then, between the need to sustain accumulation through credit creation and the need to preserve the quality of money. If the former is inhibited, we end up with an overaccumulation of commodities and specific devaluation. If the quality of money is allowed to go to the dogs, we have generalized devaluation through chronic inflation. Thus are the dilemmas of modern times neatly presented.

The monetary and financial systems are united within the banking system, and, within the nation state, the central bank becomes the supreme regulatory power. What in effect happens is this; the credit system provides a means to discipline individual capitalists and even whole factions of capital to class requirements. But someone has to regulate the regulators. The central bank strives to fulfil that function. But to the degree that these regulatory powers lie within the hands of a specific faction of capital, they are almost bound to be perverted and undermined. This brings us directly to the whole question of state involvement in monetary and financial affairs.

4 State institutions

Modern credit systems typically exhibit a high degree of integration between private and state activities, while a whole branch of the state apparatus is now given over to the direct or indirect management of the credit system. The reasons for such a high degree of state involvement are not hard to pin down.

Accumulation requires a free, untrammelled and continuous flow of interest-bearing money capital. This flow has to be sustained in the face of over-speculation, distortion and all the other 'insane forms' that the credit system inevitably spawns. Regulation of some sort is plainly required if the circulation of interest-bearing capital is to proceed free of severe and chronic disruption. The ability of the money capitalists – the bankers and financiers – to regulate themselves (no matter how perspicacious they may be as regards their obligations to the capitalist class as a whole) is strictly limited by their competitive stance *vis-à-vis* each other and their factional allegiance within the internal structure of capitalist class relations. Regulation of a limited sort can be achieved under oligopoly (the 'big five' banks in Britain did a fairly good job of regulating themselves until recently, for example), but firm regulatory powers necessarily rest on monopoly, and the latter must necessarily be brought under state regulation. The central banks are, therefore, not only the pivot of the modern credit system, but a central control point within the state apparatus.

The need for state regulation does not begin and end with the central bank, however. To the degree that the money capitalists fail to regulate their own excesses, so the state has to step in to eliminate the worst forms of abuse on the stock exchange ('stock-watering' and other kinds of swindling), while barriers to the supply of money capital can be removed by state guarantees for deposits and savings. The state may also find it necessary to stimulate certain kinds of credit flow for economic or social reasons (housing finance is usually set aside as a special kind of credit market for this reason). The state may even set up special purpose credit institutions (for agricultural credit, development projects in depressed areas, small business loans, student loans, etc.). The credit system is, then, a major field of action for state policy.

In many respects, these state interventions can be viewed as optional or contingent because they depend upon the success or failure of money capitalists in regulating themselves or upon the general state of class struggle as expressed through and within the state apparatus. It would likewise be foolish to deny that monetary and fiscal policy has a strong and overwhelming political content. But it is also necessary to understand that the state can never escape its general obligation to regulate, and that institutionalized state intervention is an inevitable response to the internalization and exacerbation of the contradictory forces of capitalism within the credit system itself.

Put in social terms, this implies that the powers of the state have to be invoked to regulate the operations of the money capitalists; and this leads immediately to the question, who controls the state? Put in more general theoretical terms, we find that the powerful contradictions mobilized within the credit system can be contained only by appeal to the higher-order institutionalized arrangements characteristic of the state apparatus; and that leads us to consider how the fundamental class antagonisms between capital and labour as well as between various factions of both are internalized within the state. These are, of course, huge and important questions. They are, unfortunately, beyond the scope of the present work.[19]

[19] Unfortunately, much of the recent Marxist theorizing on the state is rather badly informed when it comes to understanding the relation between the state and the money and credit systems. This latter relation is, in my view, quite fundamental to interpreting much of what the state does as well as the differentiated structure of state institutions under capitalism. The outstanding quality of de Brunhoff's work derives precisely from her sensitivity to this relation.

CHAPTER 10

Finance Capital and its Contradictions

The concept of finance capital has a peculiar history in Marxist thought. Marx himself did not use the term, but bequeathed a mass of not very coherent writings on the process of circulation of different kinds of money capital. The implied definition of finance capital is of a particular kind of circulation process of capital which centres on the credit system. Later writers have tended to abandon this process viewpoint and treat the concept in terms of a particular configuration of factional alliances within the bourgeosie – a power bloc which wields immense influence over the processes of accumulation in general. Yet, apart from Hilferding's basic work on the subject and the influential replication of some of his ideas in Lenin's seminal essay on imperialism, the concept has remained quite unanalysed. It has passed into the folklore of Marxian theory with hardly a flutter of debate.

From this privileged domain, the concept is periodically resurrected by Marxists whenever it is deemed polemically or scientifically appropriate. The use of the concept by this or that writer frequently draws critical commentary, of course, and occasionally bitter debates erupt over questions such as: do bankers control corporations or do corporations control banks?[1] The debates typically centre, however, on the manner in which a power bloc called 'finance capital' is constituted and the relative importance of this power bloc *vis-à-vis* other power blocs. The rationale for constituting such a power bloc in the first place, the social necessity of its existence, is not generally questioned.

The aim of this chapter is to contrast the process view of finance capital with the power bloc view, and to show how an exploration of the former, with particular emphasis upon its internal contradictions, helps identify the countervailing forces that simultaneously create and undermine the formation of coherent power blocs within the bourgeoisie. At the same time I shall also argue that the proper understanding of the processes has a certain

[1] See the debate between Fitch and Openheimer (1970) and Sweezy (1971) and its various echoes in Herman (1973; 1979) and Kotz (1978).

priority in Marxian theory because it yields us much deeper insights into the dynamics of accumulation and crisis formation than can any amount of delving into the mechanical intricacies of power bloc formation. The chapter therefore concludes with a 'second-cut' theory of crises which strives to integrate an understanding of the contradictions inherent in finance capital as a process with the understanding of the problems of disequilibrium in production laid out in chapters 6 and 7.

I   THE CREDIT SYSTEM ACCORDING TO MARX

In chapter 9 we considered in detail the various technical functions and benefits the credit system confers upon the circulation of capital. Taken as an integrated whole, the credit system may be viewed as a kind of central nervous system through which the overall circulation of capital is co-ordinated. It permits the reallocation of money capital to and from activities, firms, sectors, regions and countries. It promotes the dovetailing of diverse activities, a burgeoning division of labour and a reduction in turnover times. It facilitates the equalization of the rate of profit and arbitrates between the forces making for centralization and decentralization of capital. It helps co-ordinate the relations between flows of fixed and circulating capital. The interest rate discounts present uses against future requirements while forms of fictitious capital link current money capital flows with the anticipation of future fruits of labour.

Interest-bearing capital can perform all these roles because money represents general social power. When concentrated in the hands of the capitalists – a concentration that reflects the appropriation of surplus value – money therefore comes to express the power of capitalist property *outside of* and *external to* any specific process of commodity production. Money capital, when mobilized through the credit system, can operate as *the common capital of the capitalist class* (*Capital,* vol. 3, p. 368).

Properly organized and managed, the money capital amassed through the credit system has the potential to fine-tune the engine of accumulation through sophisticated co-ordination of investment decisions across an economy. Indifferent to any specific employment, this money capital can be used to impose the will of the capitalist class as a collectivity upon individual capitalists. To the degree that individual capitalists, acting in their own self-interest and seeking to maximize their profits in a competitive environment, adopt technologies and make decisions that are inconsistent with balanced accumulation, so does the credit system offer up the hope of controlling such errant behaviour. The deep contradiction between individual behaviours and class requirements, which, we argued in chapter 7, exercises such a powerful de-stabilizing influence over the path of accumulation, appears controllable, perhaps even reconcilable. Stability can be imposed upon an otherwise anarchistic and unco-ordinated capitalism through the proper organization and management of the credit system. Or so it seems.

The immense potential power that resides within the credit system deserves further illustration. Consider, first, the relation between production and consumption (see chapters 3 and 6). A proper allocation of credit can ensure a quantitative balance between them. The gap between purchases and sales – the basis for Marx's rejection of Say's Law – can be bridged, and production can be harmonized with consumption to ensure balanced accumulation. Any increase in the flow of credit to housing construction, for example, is of little avail today without a parallel increase in the flow of mortgage finance to facilitate housing purchases. Credit can be used to accelerate production and consumption simultaneously. Flows of fixed and circulating capital can also be co-ordinated over time via seemingly simple adjustments within the credit system. All links in the realization process of capital bar one can be brought under the control of the credit system. The single exception is of the greatest importance. While inputs can be acquired and outputs disposed of with the aid of credit, there is no substitute for the actual transformation of nature through the concrete production of use values. The latter can be subjected to overall class control only to the degree that financier and industrialist become one (an idea that both Lenin and Hilferding later take up).

Consider, secondly, those 'antagonistic' relations of distribution that act as a barrier to the production and realization of surplus value as a continuous process. Cannot the distributional shares of wages, rents, interest, taxes and profit of enterprise be modified by way of the credit system? Wages can certainly be whittled away by credit-fuelled inflation, and workers' savings can likewise be mobilized as capital through the credit system, perhaps to be devalued at time of crisis (*Capital*, vol. 3, p. 508). And then there are the various 'secondary forms of exploitation' – mortgages and consumer credit, for example – whereby workers real incomes can be modified (p. 609). Furthermore, the buying and selling of titles to future revenues of any sort integrates other aspects of distribution (the appropriation of rents, taxes and profit of enterprise) into the general system of circulation of money capital. The credit system also facilitates the centralization of capital, and allows capital to break free from the fetters of the family firm and to operate as corporate capital; the distributional arrangements within the capitalist class can thereby be altered and the degree of centralization–decentralization (see chapter 5) managed. If there is a perfect set of distributional arrangements for ensuring balanced accumulation, then banking and credit provide potential means for converging upon such an equilibrium point.

On the surface, at least, the credit system contains the *potential* to straddle antagonisms between production and consumption, between production and realization, between present uses and future labour, between production and distribution. It also provides means to arbitrate between the individual and class interests of capitalists and so to contain the forces making for crises. Armed with such a potentially powerful weapon, the capitalist class has every incentive to perfect it. And there is indeed abundant evidence that each successive crisis of capitalism has pushed the credit system into new configurations in the course of its resolution (the radical transformation of financial structure in the United States in the 1930s provides a splendid example). All of which confirms the basic message conveyed in chapter 9: that capitalism could not for long survive in the absence of a credit system, which daily grows more sophisticated in the co-ordinations it permits.

So how is it that crises still occur? Marx's answer is that credit 'suspends the barriers to the realization of capital only by raising them to their most general form' (*Grundrisse*, p. 623). What he means is that the use of credit tends to make matters worse in the long run because it can deal only with problems that arise in exchange and never with those in production. And there are, besides, a whole host of circumstances in which credit can generate erroneous price signals to producers and so aggravate the tendencies towards disproportionality and over-accumulation. Let us examine some of these circumstances.

First, the equalization of the rate of profit the credit system facilitates perfects competition and accelerates rather than diminishes the striving to gain relative surplus value through technological change. It also ensures that commodities trade at prices of production rather than according to values. Since the accelerating pace of technological change and the erroneous production signals given by prices of production lie behind the tendency for over-accumulation in the first place, it follows that in this respect credit exacerbates rather than diminishes the tendency towards disequilibrium.

Secondly, the credit system confers a certain independent power upon the financiers and sets them apart as representatives of 'capital in general'. A 'class' of bankers and other middlemen inserts itself between savers (many of whom belong to a 'class' of moneyed capitalists) and the 'industrial class of capitalists' (*Grundrisse*, p. 852). The managers of joint stock companies also congeal into a separate class of managers of other people's money (*Capital*, vol. 3, pp. 386–90). The growth of the credit system spawns new factions or 'classes' (Marx often uses that term to describe them) within the bourgeoisie. The different classes of moneyed capitalist, financiers and managers are supposedly responsible for the deployment of interest-bearing capital as the common capital of the capitalist class as a whole. They should, presumably, allocate money capital to facilitate accumulation in general. Yet, as individuals, they are bound by competition to act in their own immediate self- or factional interest.

Advantageously positioned as they are, the bankers and other 'gentlemen of high finance' can set about exploiting the credit system 'as if it were their own private capital' and thereby can appropriate 'a good deal of the real accumulation' at the expense of industrial capital (*Capital,* vol. 3, p. 478). The 'enormous centralization' possible via the credit system gives to 'this class of parasites the fabulous power, not only to periodically despoil industrial capitalists, but also to interfere in actual production in a most dangerous manner' (p. 545). The concentration of the external social power of money in the hands of a financial oligarchy is not, apparently, an unmixed blessing.

Because the power vested in the common capital of the class is open to individual appropriation and exploitation, the credit system becomes the locus of intense factional struggles and personal power plays within the bourgeoisie. The outcome of such power struggles is plainly important. Yet Marx pays singularly little attention to this aspect of affairs. It is almost as if he regards it as a self-evident conflict on the surface of bourgeois society, a conflict that conceals a much deeper set of underlying relations between the circulation of interest-bearing money as capital and the processes of production of surplus value. In this chapter I hope to show that the theory of finance capital as a process, as opposed to a particular set of institutional arrangements or a catalogue of who is dominating whom within the bourgeoisie, reveals a great deal about the contradictory dynamics of accumulation that would otherwise remain hidden.

The third barrier that prevents the credit system from functioning as a fine-tuner of accumulation arises because money capital is not particularly discriminating as to where it comes from or where it flows to. The savings of all social classes, for example, are lumped together so that everyone assumes the role of *saver* no matter what his or her social position. Workers' savings blend with those of moneyed capitalists in ways that often render them indistinguishable. The money power assembled via the credit system has an extraordinarily broad social base. Any shift in the propensity to save on the part of any class in society can alter the balance of power between financiers and other classes, particularly industrial capitalists.

Money capital is equally indiscriminate as to its uses since it typically flows to appropriate revenues of no matter what sort. While this permits the circulation of interest-bearing capital to integrate and perhaps even discipline government, consumer and producer debt, speculation in stocks and shares, commodity futures and land rent, there is nothing to prevent speculative investment in the appropriation of revenues from getting entirely out of hand. Worse still, an accumulation of claims can appear as an accumulation of money capital and the claims can continue to circulate even though they may have no basis in actual production. Speculation in titles to totally unproductive land, for example, can fuel a fictitious accumulation process if these titles can be used as collateral for other sales and purchases. A spectacular example occurred in the United States in the 1830s, when land titles held by individuals and banks effectively acted as money – the paper boom came to a jarring halt when President Jackson insisted that all payments towards purchase of federal lands be made in specie. Circumstances frequently arise, then, in which, 'all capital seems to double itself, and sometimes treble itself, by the various modes in which the same capital, or perhaps even the same claim on a debt, appears in different forms in different hands' (*Capital,* vol. 3, p. 470).

What started out by appearing as a sane device for expressing the collective interests of the capitalist class, as a means for overcoming the 'immanent fetters and barriers to production' and so raising the 'material foundations' of capitalism to new levels of perfection, 'becomes the main lever for over-production and over-speculation.' The 'insane forms' of fictitious capital come to the fore and allow the 'height of distortion' to take place within the credit system. What began by appearing as a neat solution to capitalism's contradictions becomes, instead, the locus of a problem to be overcome.

The credit system permits, Marx concludes, 'an enormous expansion of the scale of production and or enterprises', the replacement of the individual capitalist by 'social' and 'associated' forms of capital (joint stock companies, corporations, etc.), the separation of management from ownership, the creation of monopolies that call forth state interference, and the rise of a 'new financial aristocracy'. It thereby 'accelerates the material development of the productive forces' and establishes the world market. But it also accelerates crisis formation and brings the 'elements of disintegration' of capitalism to the fore. Marx calls this the 'abolition of the capitalist mode of production within the capitalist mode of production itself, and hence a self-dissolving contradiction (*Capital,* vol. 3, pp. 438–41).

Marx did not elaborate much on these ideas but history has, and so have a number of subsequent Marxist commentators. So we must consider how Marx's ideas have been interpreted, fleshed out and adapted to fit the realities of twentieth-century financial operations. In so doing, however, we should bear in mind that Marx nowhere fully explains exactly what he means by the high-sounding, very abstract and somewhat elusive phrase, 'a self-dissolving contradiction'. The aim, then, is to come up with an interpretation of that phrase and see how well it reflects the dilemmas of the use of credit under capitalism.

II   FINANCE CAPITAL ACCORDING TO LENIN AND HILFERDING

'The twentieth century,' Lenin wrote, 'marks the turning point from the old capitalism to the new, from the domination of capital in general to the domination of finance capital.' The banks, he argued, could concentrate the social power of money in their hands, operate as 'a single collective capitalist', and so 'subordinate to their will' not only all commercial and industrial operations but even whole governments. To the degree that industrialists seek monopoly power – largely through the centralization of capitals – industrial and banking capital tend to coalesce. 'Finance capital' is defined, then, as 'the bank capital of a few very big monopolist banks, merged with the capital of the monopolist associations of industrialists.'[2]

A controlling 'financial oligarchy' arises on the basis of finance capital. It systematically transforms the capitalist mode of production and projects the internal contradictions of capitalism upon the world stage in a new way. 'It is beyond doubt,' Lenin writes, that 'capitalism's transition to the stage of monopoly capitalism, to finance capital, *is connected* with the intensification of the struggle for the partitioning of the world.' Imperialism, he continues, 'is capitalism at that stage of development at which the dominance of monopolies and finance capital is established; in which the export of capital has acquired pronounced importance; in which the division of the world among the international trusts has begun, in which the division of all territories of the globe among the biggest capitalist powers has been completed.' The inherent contradictions of capitalism are now expressed in terms of an ever more dramatic uneven development of capitalism and a radical re-structuring of class relations. A dominant financial oligarchy backed by 'financially powerful states' buys labour peace in the 'core' countries by encouraging the formation of a 'labour aristocracy', while the rest of the world is driven deeper and deeper into states of dependency, subservience and rebellion. Competition within the financial oligarchy and between the financially powerful states is heightened rather than diminished. The end result: inter-imperialist rivalries and wars. Thus does Lenin, beginning with the concept of finance capital, arrive at a stunning analysis of twentieth-century imperialism.

Yet the theoretical content of Lenin's argument is by no means clear. He nowhere elaborates on the concept of finance capital, and the exact manner in which it transforms the internal contradictions of capitalism into inter-imperialist rivalries remains obscure. He drew many of his ideas, somewhat eclectically, from the rather disparate frameworks of thought proposed by Hobson, Bukharin and Hilferding.[3] Only the latter gives a very firm theoretical grounding to the concept of finance capital within a Marxian framework. While Lenin was strongly critical of Hilferding's political line, he appears to

[2] Lenin (1970 edn, vol. 1, p. 703); the subsequent quotes are all from *Imperialism, the Highest Stage of Capitalism.*

[3] Hobson (1965 edn), Hilferding (1970 edn) and Bukharin (1972a). Bukharin's work was published after that of Lenin's but was presumably influential since Lenin wrote a preface to it at least a year before he published his own work on the subject. Lenin's extensive background reading, as manifest in his notebooks, is documented by Churchward (1959), and the contribution of Hobson has been critically examined by Arrighi (1978).

accept with but one reservation the basic conception of finance capital that Hilferding advances. The single reservation concerns Hilferding's 'mistaken' views on money.[4] Lenin leaves us in the dark as to the nature of that mistake. We will shortly see how crucial an error it was. But first we must consider Hilferding's contribution.

Hilferding faithfully replicates Marx in the overall format of his argument. He begins by examining the various forms of money before proceeding to show – as we did in the previous chapter – how and why credit is essential to the perpetuation of capital accumulation. Initially, the banks merely mediate money flows, but the progress of accumulation puts increasing quantities of money capital in the hands of the banks which then have no choice but to 'fix an ever-growing part of their capitals in industry' and to integrate their activities with those of industrial capital. Since industrialists derive competitive advantages (particularly with respect to scale of operation) from access to bank capital, they must increasingly look to external sources of loan capital. Finance capital, says Hilferding (with Lenin's approval),

> significes the unification of capital. The previously separate spheres of industrial, commercial and bank capital are now placed jointly under the direction of high finance, in which captains of industry and the banks are united in intimate personal union. This association has as its basis the abolition of free competition of individual capitalists by the big monopolistic associations. This naturally has as a consequence a change in the relationship of the capitalist class to state power. (Hilferding, 1970 edn, p. 409)

Hilferding dwells at length, again with Lenin's approval, upon the institutional manifestations of this unity – the creation of monopolies, trusts, cartels, stock exchange operations and so on. He points out that speculation in property titles – fictitious forms of capital – necessarily plays a crucial role. The rise of a financial oligarchy changes the dimensions of class struggle in important ways. Hilferding assumes that the state becomes an agent of finance capital and that finance capital operates as national capital on the world stage. He then develops a particular interpretation of imperialism and its contradictions. The chain of argument is as follows.

The rise of finance capital (itself a necessary step to perpetuate capitalism) calls forth state interference just as Marx envisaged. State policies, forged in response to the requirements of finance capital, make the export of capital rather than commodities a primary concern. Relations between states (competition, protection, domination and dependency) transform the internal contradictions of capitalism into conflict-ridden uneven development on the world stage. The contradictions are now expressed in terms of an imbalance

---

[4] Lenin (1970 edn, vol. 1, p. 678). Lenin's views on the shortcomings of Hilferding's work are set out in Churchward (1959, p. 79).

of forces between monopolistic and non-monopolistic sectors, between the financial oligarchy and 'the rest' as well as between nation states. They originate in the basic processes of capitalist development.

Here Hilferding (1970 edn, ch. 17) appeals to a particular version of Marx's crisis theory. Variations in the value composition of capital, he argues, distort price signals and generate imbalances between departments (producing means of production and wage goods), between production and consumption, between fixed and circulating capital, etc. Cartels and monopolies can control the pace of technological change as well as prices, but this simply exacerbates price distortions between monopolistic and non-monopolistic sectors – 'the dislocations in the regulation of prices, which eventually lead to disproportionalities and to contradictions between the conditions of surplus value production and realization, are not modified by the cartels but only made more acute' (Hilferding, 1970 edn, p. 401). Cartels, in short, cannot abolish crises. The credit system, even though under the total domination of a financial oligarchy, likewise fails because the interest rate must, in the final analysis, be explained by the dynamics of production of surplus value rather than the other way round. Any attempt to fashion credit moneys to stabilize this inherently unstable system will ultimately result in a financial crisis. Hilferding then invokes, without further explanation, Marx's view that in the course of a crisis the system necessarily returns to its 'monetary basis', casting off the numerous fictitious capitals acquired during the phase of prosperity (1970 edn, p. 372). Protectionism, imperialism and relations between states as well as between monopolistic and non-monopolistic sectors are treated as particular expressions, modified by the oligarchic character of finance capital, of these basic tendencies towards crisis formation.

Lenin differs from Hilferding in two respects. First, while he seems to accept the identification of finance with national capital in the case of the main imperialist powers, he often switches to a supra-national conception of finance capital – a position similar to that of Hobson – when it comes to analysing the general condition of world capitalism. Lenin's formulation is, in this respect, more ambiguous than Hilferding's.[5] Secondly, he refers to Hilferding's mistake with respect to the theory of money. Lenin does not enlighten us as to the nature or implications of this mistake. De Brunhoff has recently confronted it directly. It is very important and warrants discussion.

Hilferding, de Brunhoff argues (1971, pp. 81–93), follows Marx in format only. His view of finance capital as a *unity* of banking and industrial capital leads him to construct a 'financial theory of monetary phenomena', where

[5] Churchward (1959, p. 78) indicates that Lenin even questioned Hilferding's basic concept of finance capital, writing in his notebooks, 'Isn't finance capital = bank capital sufficient?' The difference between Hobson and Hilferding is stressed by Arrighi (1978).

Marx built a 'monetary theory of finance'. The difference is important. Marx built his theory of money out of an analysis of commodity production and exchange without reference to the circulation of capital. In so doing, he first identified the contradiction between money as a measure of value and money as a medium of circulation in order to lay the basis for understanding how that contradiction is heightened when money circulates as capital. This contradiction disappears almost entirely from Hilferding's work. Monetary phenomena are reduced to 'pure organs of capitalist financing', completely under the control of finance capital. Hilferding depicts finance capital as both hegemonic and controlling, whereas Marx portrays it as necessarily caught in its own web of internal contradictions. The central contradiction for Marx lay between what he called the *financial system* (credit) and its *monetary basis*. Hilferding quotes Marx's view that a return to the monetary basis is essential during crises, but he fails to explain why or how. This is the topic we now take up.

III   THE CONTRADICTION BETWEEN THE FINANCIAL SYSTEM AND ITS MONETARY BASIS

Marx frequently asserts that, in the course of a crisis, capitalism is forced to abandon the fictions of finance and to return to the world of hard cash, to the eternal verities of the monetary basis. He jokingly characterizes the monetary system as 'essentially a Catholic institution, the credit system essentially Protestant' because the latter is powered by *faith* in 'money value as the immanent spirit of commodities, faith in the mode of production and its predestined order, faith in the individual agents of production as mere personifications of self-expanding capital.' But, he goes on to point out, 'the credit system does not emancipate itself from the basis of the monetary system any more than Protestantism has emancipated itself from the foundations of Catholicism' (*Capital,* vol. 3, p. 592). Though credit frequently 'crowds out money and usurps its place', the central bank always remains 'the pivot of the credit system' and 'the metal reserve, in turn, is the pivot of the bank' (pp. 572–3). Put another way, 'money – in the form of precious metal – remains the foundation from which the credit system, by its very nature, can *never* detach itself' (p. 606).

It is vital to understand what Marx meant by all of this. At first sight his ideas appear somewhat dated because he explicitly appeals to the precious metals as the 'pivot' of the monetary system – a peculiarly nineteenth-century notion. But if we enquire into the logic of Marx's argument we can identify a very important principle which applies to capitalism in general.

The inevitability of the contradiction between the financial system, and its monetary basis can be traced back directly to the dual functions of money as a measure of value and as a medium of circulation. When money functions as a measure of value it must truly represent the values it helps to circulate. Money here 'is in reality nothing but a particular expression of the social character of labour and its products' – an *external,* socially accepted measure of the value embodied in commodities. The reason for pinning that measure to a specific metal – such as gold – is to ensure that the measuring rod, when it takes on material form, is as precise and unambiguous as possible. The contradiction in so doing, of course, is that the product of a concrete, specific labour process – gold, for example is treated as the material representation of abstract labour. When money functions as a medium of circulation, on the other hand, it must divorce itself from the 'true' representation of value, permit market prices to deviate from values and prove itself the flexible lubricant of an exchange process that is unpredictable and perpetually changing. Paper moneys and credit moneys can operate unrestrainedly and creatively in this respect.

Under simple commodity production and exchange, these two aspects of money exist in an uneasy and antagonistic relation to each other. Indeed, the circulation of capital, as we noted in chapter 1, arises in part to bridge the gap between the 'inherent' value of gold and the 'reflected' value of money as measured against the value of the commodities which that money circulates.

A study of the processes of circulation of capital indicates, however, that capitalism must evolve a sophisticated credit system and create fictitious forms of capital if it is to survive. The 'fictitious' aspects of money – credit and paper 'moneys' – are pushed to extremes, and their links to the actualities of social labour become ever more tenuous. If social labour is firmly represented by the money commodity (gold), then we can argue that the separation between money in this latter sense and finance is exacerbated by the circulation of capital. This is what Marx meant by the concept of a contradiction between the financial system and its monetary basis. Let us explore the nature of this contradiction a little more explicitly.

Consider, for example, what happens when credit money and 'fictitious forms of value' usurp the place of the money commodity. If the pace of credit creation keeps pace with the socially necessary labour performed in society, then the effects of credit are beneficial rather than harmful with respect to the circulation of capital. But there is little to prevent credit creation from getting entirely out of hand, while, on the other hand, the problem of over-accumulation lurks perpetually in the background. If the fictitious values turn out not to be backed by the products of social labour, or if, for whatever reason, faith in the credit system is shaken, then capital must find some way to re-establish its footing in the world of socially necessary labour. There are two ways it can do this. It can either attach all of its operations firmly to the money commodity (gold) as *the* ultimate measure of value, or it can seek out some other way to establish a direct link with material processes of actual commodity production. Both solutions have defects.

In the first case, all values must be converted into the money commodity as a test of the value they represent. This was the general situation with which Marx was familiar – 'as soon as credit is shaken . . . all the real wealth is to be actually transformed into money, into gold and silver – a mad demand, which, however, grows necessarily out of the system itself.' The sudden surge of demand for liquidity and convertibility into gold far exceeds the available gold and silver, which 'amounts to but a few millions in the vaults of the Bank' (*Capital,* vol. 3, p. 574). The result:

> It is a basic principle of capitalist production that money, as an independent form of value, stands in opposition to commodities. . . . In times of squeeze, when credit contracts or ceases entirely, money suddenly stands out as the only means of payment and true existence of value in absolute opposition to all other commodities. . . . Therefore, the value of commodities is sacrificed for the purpose of safeguarding the fantastic and independent existence of this value in money. . . . For a few millions in money, many millions in commodities must therefore be sacrificed. This is inevitable under capitalist production and constitutes one of its beauties. (*Capital,* vol. 3, p. 516)

All of this assumes, however, that paper moneys are freely convertible into the precious metals. Marx did not consider the case of inconvertible paper moneys backed by the power of the state. Under such circumstances – which have become the rule in the twentieth century – things look very different. We have to determine whether we are dealing with fundamental differences or simply with a change in the form of appearance of the conflict between financial and monetary systems. We can approach an answer to that question step by step.

Under conditions of inconvertibility into gold, the burden of disciplining the credit system and fictitious capital falls upon the central bank. By raising the rate of interest, the central bank can 'put on the screw, as the saying goes', increase the cost of converting credit moneys into central bank money, and so cool off speculative fevers and keep the creation of fictitious capital in check (*Capital,* vol. 3, p. 543). By judicious management and manipulation of the interest rate and reserve requirements, a powerful monetary authority can hope to avoid the devaluation of commodities at the same time as it preserves the quality of its own money as a 'true' reflection of the value of social labour. This implies that the supply of central bank money should match the growth in value productivity in the economy as a whole. This kind of policy stance on the part of a central monetary authority has become the rule since the 1930s, when the blind defence of money as a measure of value entailed such a massive devaluation of commodities that the very survival of capitalism was at stake.

Marx would argue that such a policy stance is founded upon an illusion. In the first place, the central bank cannot totally isolate itself from world trade and sever its links with some sort of international money system: its autonomy is limited by its foreign exchange position. The national money may end up being devalued in relation to other national moneys if the central bank actively flouts the rules of the international money system. And at the international level within the hierarchy of moneys, the 'notion of money as a measure of value refuses to die' (see above, p. 250). The relation between national and international moneys constrains the power of any central bank. If there is no clear definition of world money – as has been the case since 1973 – the international monetary system itself falls into crisis.

Marx's second objection is that, even in the absence of any international monetary restraints, the power of the central bank, being strictly circumscribed, is totally insufficient to guard against crisis formation. There is, we have argued (chapter 7), a chronic tendency to produce surpluses of capital – states of overaccumulation. We now have to consider the additional circumstance that fictitious capitals must *necessarily* be created ahead of real accumulation, which means that 'the accumulation of money-capital must always reflect a greater accumulation of capital than actually exists' (*Capital,* vol. 3, p. 505). This is in no way problematic all the time the real expansion of commodity values keeps pace with the prior creation of fictitious capital. But as soon as overaccumulation becomes evident, the realization of the fictitious values as well as values in commodity form is threatened. The demand for money at such a point is strictly a demand for liquidity. A return to the monetary basis at such a moment will surely destroy fictitious capitals and devalue commodities. The only feasible defence by a central bank against such a condition is to print state-backed money to buy up the surpluses and so realize the values of the fictitious capitals. Marx explicitly rules out such a solution (*Capital,* vol. 3, p. 490) because he assumes a money system backed by gold – the limited gold reserves prevent the central bank from stepping in and buying 'up all the depreciated commodities at their old nominal values'.

But if the national money is not convertible into gold, then a central bank could indeed print money in order to defend against overaccumulation and devaluation. In so doing, however, it devalues its own money. The tendency towards overaccumulation is converted, in short, into a tendency towards rampant inflation. Marx did not consider such a possibility or examine its implications. But his failure to do so in no way undermines the general structure of his argument. Defending the nominal value of commodities that embody socially *un*necessary labour time is as irrational as defending money as a pure measure of value through blind adherence to a gold standard. Rampant inflation is just as hard to live with as the devaluation of commodities.

What Marx's theory tells us, however, is that the contradiction between the financial system and its monetary base ultimately boils down to a contradiction between 'capital in its money form and capital in its commodity form' (*Capital,* vol. 3, p. 460). Under conditions of overaccumulation, the capitalist class appears to have a choice between devaluing money or commodities, between inflation or depression. In the event that monetary policy is dedicated to avoiding both, it will merely end up incurring both (as the current state of capitalism illustrates).

The power of finance capital is evidently very limited. Marx argued explicitly, for example, that 'no kind of bank legislation can eliminate a crisis', though 'mistaken bank legislation . . . can intensify [it]' (*Capital,* vol. 3, p. 490). This conclusion applies to the whole range of possible monetary policies. 'As long as the *social* character of labour appears as the *money-existence* of commodities, and thus as a *thing* external to actual production, money crises – independent of or as an intensification of actual crises – are inevitable' (p. 517).

The contradictions between the financial system and its monetary basis heighten and become ever more awesome as capitalism progresses. These are the contradictions Hilferding misses entirely because of his mistaken interpretation of Marx's theory of money. The mistake is costly. And while Lenin recognizes the mistake, he does not rectify it but prefers instead to use Hilferding's definition of finance capital as a vehicle to show how the internal contradictions of capitalism are projected on to the world stage.

Yet, buried within those tortured chapters on banking and finance in the third volume of *Capital* lies a powerful interpretation of the internal contradictions within the finance form of capitalism itself. When connected with the basic theory of money laid out in the first volume of *Capital,* we can begin to comprehend how accumulation for accumulation's sake and the circulation of capital split asunder the functions of money as medium of circulation and as measure of value and erect on this basis a deeply antagonistic relation between the world of money as a measure of the value of social labour and the intricate and complex world of financial operations based on credit. Marx did not fully analyse all possible dimensions to this antagonism – the potentiality for devaluation through inflation or the manner in which the antagonism can be expressed as inter-imperialist rivalries and international competition, for example. But his deep insights still have to be appreciated for what they are, and Marxian theory extended on this basis.

IV THE INTEREST RATE AND ACCUMULATION

The rate of interest on high-quality (central bank) money plays a vital role in regulating the relations between the financial system and its monetary base. This resurrects the question: what fixes the rate of interest in general? The answer arrived at in chapter 9 was the forces that determine the supply and demand for interest-bearing money capital. The forces must now be identified.

On the demand side, a distinction must first be made between the demand for money as a *means of payment* and as a *means of purchase*. Both relate to the circulation of capital as a whole but occupy quite different moments of that process. The demand for money to launch new production is very different in its signification from the demand for money to realize values already produced. The latter is particularly prevalent at times of overaccumulation, whereas the former is typical of a state of heightened competition for relative surplus value. The two demands are not independent of each other, of course, and some kind of time-lagged relationship exists between them. A demand for investment credit now will likely lead to a demand for marketing credit later.

Capitalists are not the only economic agents who demand money either as means of purchase or as means of payment. All manner of demands emanate from the circulation of revenues. Workers and bourgeoisie alike seek consumer credit and mortgage finance (means of purchase), and also seek to monetize certain assets they hold prior to any actual exchange (means of payment). The aggregate demand for interest-bearing money comes from both the circulation of capital and the circulation of revenues. But the two forms of circulation are not independent of each other. An expansion of consumer credit can perform the same function (mediated through the market) as giving credit to capitalists for inventories of unsold goods on hand. Credit is needed to lubricate the circulation of capital and revenues and to balance the relation between them. Capital generates revenues, which must ultimately circulate back to capital if the system is to be reproduced smoothly. The underlying unity between realization through production and realization in exchange must be preserved.

The demand for money as capital is not, therefore, the sole determinant of the rate of interest, but is part of a very much more complex package of demands made upon the credit system and its monetary base. The disaggregations are important. They indicate the diverse points of origin of demand as well as the diversity of uses to which money can be put. They highlight the difficulty of gauging the 'correct' (from the standpoint of accumulation) allocation of interest-bearing money to the various activities of production, circulation, exchange, landlordism, administration, consumption, etc. They indicate the possibility – but only the possibility – of failures emanating from gaps in the total circulation process of capital. They demonstrate more concretely how the 'height of distortion' and all manner of 'insane forms' can erupt within the credit system to destroy the delicate balance that must always prevail between production and realization through exchange. Above all, they sensitize us to the fact that a demand for credit can signify quite different states within the dynamic of accumulation, ranging all the way from overaccumulation to untoward blockages in the circulation of revenues.

The supply of interest-bearing money is subject to equally complex determinations. This supply, Marx argues, is partly the product of accumulation, partly the result of 'circumstances which accompany [accumulation] but are quite different from it', and partly the result of seemingly quite independent events (*Capital,* vol. 3, p. 507):

(1) Part of the surplus value produced through accumulation can be held as money surpluses by industrialists, merchants, financiers, landlords and the state, while workers can also save out of variable capital. Rather than leave these surpluses idle, economic agents may strive to throw them into circulation as interest-bearing capital.

(2) Overaccumulation produces surpluses of idle money (and therefore a low rate of interest) because of dearth of opportunity to employ money as capital in general.

(3) The capacity of the banking system to mobilize money through the variety of techniques already described in chapter 9 can spark an accumulation of loan capital 'quite independently of the actual accumulation' (*Capital,* vol. 3, p. 495).

(4) Debts and fictitious capital can begin to circulate as loan capital to the degree that everyone has faith in the health of the economy – psychological states of expectation are, in the short run at least, important to that process which converts privately contracted debts into the social form of money.

(5) Distributional arrangements and the relative power of the factions involved can also have a dramatic effect upon the quantity of money accumulated in a form ready for use as interest-bearing money. Landlords may squeeze a peasantry; the state may appropriate from all classes through taxation; a strong financial oligarchy may use its power to assemble vast money resources under its command; and so on.

(6) An unusual fluctuation in the money supply (expansion or contraction of gold flow or printing of state moneys) can, in the short run, augment or diminish the total quantity of money available for conversion into interest-bearing money until the effects are absorbed by price adjustments.

The jumbled heterogeneity of forces that affect supply and demand for interest-bearing money guarantees considerable instability in the rate of interest. Short-term fluctuations need not concern us – such as the price of any commodity, the interest rate oscillates daily as supply and demand equilibrate each other in the market. The long-run underlying rate of interest is what matters. And there are two possible mechanisms that might give some semblance of order and coherence to the otherwise jumbled forces affecting supply and demand.

Consider, first, the possibility that the rate of interest is dominated by 'the struggle between moneyed and industrial capitalists' over the division of surplus value and the 'price' of capital before it 'enters into the production process' (*Theories of Surplus Value,* pt 2, p. 509). Signs of such a struggle abound in capitalist society. Marx by no means denies its importance: the point is to establish exactly what it signifies. Is the underlying rate of interest basically a reflection of the power relation between industrialists and financiers? To suppose so would be to relegate all other facets of interest rate determination (around the circulation of revenues, for example) to a peripheral and purely secondary role. Marx was, in general, not averse to putting the direct relations of production in the forefront of affairs. I shall argue, however, that the constant guerilla warfare between industrialists and financiers plays a similar kind of role to the struggle between capital and labour over the wage rate (see chapter 2): in the final analysis it is but a part of a whole complex of social processes that must serve to keep the interest rate close to an equilibrium position defined in relation to sustained accumulation. An imbalance in the power relation between industry and finance will force departure from equilibrium and so threaten accumulation. From this it follows that the survival of capitalism depends upon the achievement of some kind of proper balance of power between industrial and financial interests. This is an important conclusion, because it suggests that the power of finance capital (however that power bloc is institutionalized and defined) is necessarily a constrained power, and can never be unlimited or totally hegemonic.

This still leaves us in the dark as to what fixes the underlying rate of interest. The only option is to conceive of an equilibrium rate of interest in relation to accumulation. Such an equilibrium can be defined in terms of the relation between the circulation of interest-bearing money on the one hand and the activities of production and consumption (realization) on the other. It operates at the point where the circulation of revenues and capital necessarily intersect. Precisely because the credit system is a centralized co-ordinator, the interest rate has to move in a way that helps to sustain both the production and realization of surplus value on a sustained basis.

So why bother with such an elaborate enumeration of the forces that affect the demand and supply of interest-bearing money? The answer is simple enough. The material activities that structure demand and supply, and which, hence, fix the actual rate of interest, are so diverse that the equilibrium rate of interest will be achieved only by accident. The potential for disequilibrium is ever present. And if we inspect the forces that regulate supply and demand for interest-bearing money we can see how the inner logic of capitalism is disruptive of equilibrium in the interest rate and so leads the economy away from stable balanced growth, down the path of crisis formation. This is, I believe, the point that Marx wanted to bring us to. In order to illustrate that idea, I shall try to reconstruct his representation of the accumulation cycle and show how interest rate movements play a crucial role in translating the contradictory dynamics of accumulation into specific forms of monetary and financial crises.

V THE ACCUMULATION CYCLE

It is often said that Marx had no theory of the business cycle.[6] This is only partially true. He traced cyclical impulses in the relation between accumulation, industrial reserve army formation and the wage rate; he laid the groundwork for analysing explosive oscillations in output and exchanges between the various departments of production; he built a synthetic model of the general temporal rhythm of overaccumulation and devaluation (see chapter 6 and 7). His studies of fixed capital circulation (chapter 8) also reveal cycles of innovation, expansion, renewal and devaluation. The problem is to blend these partial insights into a unified representation of temporal dynamics. Otherwise it seems as if capitalism is beset by potentially divergent cyclical impulses which course through the economy in confusing ways.

Interest rate fluctuations lie at the heart of cyclical movements and impose some semblance of order upon the latter. Marx denies that they are a *primum agens*. They are a central mediating link through which the inner contradictions of capitalism are expressed. His investigation of the forces that fix the rate of interest establishes that point exactly. But we have also seen how the interest rate can be affected by all manner of arbitrary and capricious features. For this reason Marx tries to abstract from the day-to-day dynamics of the industrial cycle and its monetary and financial accompaniments (*Capital*, vol. 3, p. 358). He moves instead to construct a highly simplified representation of the cyclical course of accumulation in general. The intent is to capture the interactions between accumulation, technological change, fixed capital formation, employment and unemployment together with wage rates, consumer demand, the formation of fictitious capital, the surge of credit moneys and the ultimate return to the monetary basis during crises of over-accumulation–devaluation. Marx's representation can be reconstructed from a careful reading of volume 3 of *Capital* (chs 26–35). The accumulation process passes through various phases of stagnation, recovery, credit-based expansion, speculative fever and crash.

[6] See Smith (1937 edn), Wilson (1938) and Sherman (1967).

1 *Stagnation*

The phase of stagnation in the wake of a crash is characterized by a severe curtailment of production and low rates of profit. Prices are forced downwards as producers dispose of surplus inventories at less than their prices of production. Unemployment is widespread and wages typically adjust downwards. Effective demand is weak because of diminished disposable incomes (wages as well as the revenues of the bourgeoisie). The demand for money as a medium of circulation is at a low ebb (the volume of commodity exchanges is down). Faith in the credit system has been severely shaken, while the demand for loan capital is much reduced because of pessimistic expectations as to future revenues. Money is used primarily to measure values and strip away extraneous fictitious capital from the economy. The actual turnover time of commodities is drastically shortened since credit is not available to extend it. Yet the rate of interest is low; the plethora of loanable money capital produced out of overaccumulation is now in evidence. This surplus of money capital is relative to the opportunities to employ that money safely and securely.

The phase of stagnation is typically one of 'gentle' technological adjustment (in the broad Marxian sense, which includes organizational and institutional change) as opposed to the violent shake-out that accompanies crises. The adjustments gradually bring production technologies and price of production ratios into line with those consistent with balanced accumulation. The stage is then set for subsequent expansion.

2 *Recovery*

A variety of opportunities arises during the phase of stagnation. Falling wages and interest rates leave a larger share of surplus value to profit of enterprise, which may partially compensate for lower prices. Devalued capital (commodities, fixed capital, buildings, etc.) can be picked up for a song, so reducing outlays on constant capital and lowering the value composition of capital. Producers who have weathered the storm are usually blessed with a strong liquidity position – they can pay their bills with hard cash. Low interest rates and surpluses of labour power make conditions optimal for financing long-term fixed capital formation.

Modest expansion begins once most of the surplus inventories have been disposed of. This permits prices to rise, and, with wages remaining low, the larger share of surplus value going to profit of enterprise now takes hold. The profit rate revives and sparks the return of business confidence. A cautious expansion of production may begin based on the strong liquidity position of businesses that have survived – they use their own funds to finance expansion.

The low rate of interest may, with the return of some faith in the system, lead to the financing of certain long-term fixed capital investments (perhaps through the agency of the state). A concentration on this kind of investment expands employment in Department 1 and, because of the long production period involved, creates an effective demand without initially 'furnishing any element of supply' (*Capital*, vol. 3, p. 315). This effective demand is felt in the consumer goods sector (Department 2). The tendency towards explosive oscillations between the two sectors is gently set in motion.

The economic power of industrial capitalists tends to be strong relative to the bankers and financiers because the former have sufficient cash reserves to finance their own expansion and to extend commercial credit to each other so as to assure the continuity of production in the face of disparate turnover times, etc. Loan capital from the banks is not required for this purpose. The absorption of that loan capital through any large-scale fixed capital formation is more than matched by a gradual expansion in the supply of free money capital through increased savings on the part of all classes, increased flows of money to be converted into loan capital by the banks, etc. The interest rate therefore remains low.

The quantity of fictitious capital increases but new promotions are usually associated, at this stage, with direct investment in means of production, and the commercial credit extended is closely tied to actual commodities in circulation. This is the kind of fictitious capital creation that is both necessary and unproblematic because it is usually followed by a subsequent expansion in accumulation. It poses no threat, therefore, to the preservation of a sound monetary basis.

Competition is relatively relaxed during this phase. The auto-financing by business generates gradual and uneven concentration, and wide variations in actual rates of profit may coexist because the circuit of productive capital is what counts. The power of the credit system to force an equalization of the rate of profit is not strongly in evidence at this time.

The circulation of revenues picks up, as does the demand for money as a medium of circulation. Effective demand for final consumption goods strengthens, and the consumer goods sector begins to take on a leading role in the dynamic of accumulation.

3 Credit-based expansion

Faith in the economic system has by now recovered. The expansion of employment, rising wages and increased revenues for the bourgeoisie, presage a growing effective demand for final consumption goods. The increased circulation of revenues creates optimistic expectations with respect to future revenues of all types (land rents, taxes, mortgages, etc., as well as profit of enterprise).

But the piecemeal expansion of the preceding phase now reveals a whole host of imbalances in productive capacity and consequent bottlenecks in the inputs and outputs of the productive apparatus as a whole. All trace of surplus productive capacity now disappears. New investments appear necessary to create new supply, particularly of the elements of constant capital – raw materials, partially manufactured inputs and machinery. Attention switches back to investment in Department 1 as prices of constant capital rise in response to shortages in their supply.

At the same time, the capacity of industrial capitalists to finance their own investments and to extend credit to each other is exhausted as they reach the limits of their cash reserves. They are forced to turn to the banks and financiers who strengthen their power *vis-á-vis* industrial capital as a consequence. The credit system comes into its own as the general co-ordinator of commodity production and exchange. The demand for money capital and for medium of circulation expands. This demand calls forth its own supply since faith in the system is now sufficiently strong to allow even debt claims to circulate as a form of money capital. The quantity of fictitious capital moves steadily ahead of the actual accumulation, and the gap between the monetary basis as a real measure of values and the various forms of paper moneys in circulation begins to widen.

But the growing power of the credit system in relation to industry also tends to force an equalization in the rate of profit (the connection between profit of enterprise and the interest rate is now very strong). Competition for loanable funds becomes more acute, and the interest rate begins to rise. Industrialists are pushed into a competitive struggle for relative surplus value at a time when labour shortages emerge. Wages tend to move above the value of labour power. Strong technological adjustments are called for. We witness a 'great expansion of fixed capital in all forms and the opening up of new enterprises on a vast and far-reaching scale'. This requires yet more loan capital and puts industry ever more firmly at the service of money capital. But profit of enterprise is only one form of future revenue to attract loan capital: industrialists must compete for funds against land speculators, stock-jobbers, dealers in government debt, etc. 'Those roving cavaliers of credit who work on a money-credit basis begin to appear for the first time in considerable numbers' (*Capital*, vol. 3, p. 488).

4 *Speculative fever*

Credit-based expansion generates price rises if only because the total quantity of circulating medium now far outstrips the product of social labour. In addition, unemployment almost disappears and wage rates begin to soar – the condition of labour, Marx observes, is always at its best on the eve of a crisis. The effective demand for wage goods remains strong but high wages are now beginning to cut into accumulation at the same time as rising interest rates also cut into profit of enterprise. Caught in a 'profit squeeze', industrialists look desperately for ways to innovate their way out of their difficulties. In this they are aided and abetted by a credit system that is by now fuelling both production and realization. But this it can do only at the price of creating vast quantities of fictitious capital, of making room for 'the most colossal form of gambling and swindling'.

Beneath this speculative fever deep disturbances from equilibrium are evident. Disproportionalities between departments, between production and distribution and between the quantity of credit money in circulation and real output of values are growing. The value composition of capital is rising rapidly. The labour power is not there to permit the continued expansion of accumulation through production of surplus value, while the actual rate of exploitation is falling. Only the accumulation of fictitious capital can paper over the cracks. It is only a matter of time before the speculative bubble bursts.

5 The crash

The onset of a crisis is usually triggered by a spectacular failure which shakes confidence in fictitious forms of capital. The ensuing panic immediately focuses attention upon the quality of various credit moneys. The return to the 'Catholicism' of the monetary basis sets in with a vengeance. A chronic shortage of money of the right sort – closely tied to the money commodity – emerges at the very moment when producers and merchants are scrambling to meet their obligations. The rate of interest climbs to 'a point of extreme usury' (*Capital,* vol. 3, p. 360). The extended chain of payments is broken and the circulation of capital lies momentarily broken into a thousand disconnected pieces. At first sight the crisis appears to be 'merely a credit and money crisis', because it is only a question of 'the convertibility of bills of exchange into money' (p. 490). The demand for liquidity rises rapidly:

> On the eve of the crisis, the bourgeois, with the self-sufficiency that springs from intoxicating prosperity, declares money to be a vain imagination. Commodities alone are money. But now the cry is everywhere: money alone is a commodity! As pants the hart after fresh water, so pants his soul after money, the only wealth. (*Capital,* vol. 1, p. 138)

The disruption in the circulation of commodity capital makes money as a measure of value the only secure form of wealth. The search to establish the real basis of values destroys capital in commodity form:

> As soon as a stoppage takes place, as a result of delayed returns, glutted markets, or fallen prices, a superabundance of industrial capital becomes available but in a form in which it cannot perform its functions.

Huge quantities of commodity capital but unsaleable. Huge quantities of fixed capital, but largely idle due to stagnant reproduction. . . . Factories are closed, raw materials accumulate, finished products flood the market as commodities. (*Capital,* vol. 3, p. 483)

Masses of labourers are thrown out of work, the wage rate drops precipitously, and the circulation of revenues suffers a chronic disruption in reaction to the breakdowns in the circulation of capital. Effective demand for consumer goods founders and prices collapse. 'For a few millions in money, many millions in commodities must therefore be sacrificed.'

The devaluation of capital, and of the labourer, proceed apace. Capitalists seek to stay alive by cannibalizing upon each other. The labourer is likewise sacrificed on the altar of the underlying irrationality of capitalism. Crisis, as the irrational rationalizer of the economic system, cuts a grim swathe across the economic landscape of capitalist society.

VI THE POLITICS OF MONEY MANAGEMENT

The 'stripped-down' account of the accumulation cycle reveals a tightly interwoven texture of interactions between employment and accumulation, between technological change, the rate of reinvestment and the state of competition, between production and realization in the different departments, between the circulation of capital and the circulation of revenues, between the supply of and demand for interest-bearing money, between the relative power of industrial capitalists and financiers, between capital and labour, between money as a medium of circulation and a measure of social labour, and, finally, between money and commodities as expressions of capital.[7] The intent is to show how the various contradictions of capitalism interlock and build upon each other in dynamic sequence to produce the initial surge of accumulation and its final denouement: savage devaluation of both capital and labour.

The actual historical course of accumulation is, however, a much more complicated affair. It is affected, in the first instance, by a whole gamut of seemingly extraneous circumstances – wars, revolutions, harvest failures, droughts, etc. Secondly, there are innumerable nuances within the structure of internal contradictions themselves. The degree of organization of the working class can substantially modify wage rate adjustments and the pace

[7] Kalecki's (1971) early writings on the business cycle during the 1930s drew heavily upon Marx while arriving at results that were close to Keynes. The whole question of modelling the dynamics of Marxian aggregates was posed anew in the 1960s and has been a continuing focus of interest for the mathematically inclined ever since. See Sherman (1967), Weisskopf (1978) and the highly mathematical presentations of Morishima (1973).

and direction of technological change over the course of the cycle. The unification of industrial and banking capital modifies the power relation between them, while excessive centralization or decentralization of capital can also impart special twists to the accumulation process. Complications of this sort make every cycle unique. Marx evidently seeks to abstract from such conjunctural features, and in this we shall follow him.

There is, however, one matter that does deserve special consideration. This is the role of monetary and fiscal policy in relation to the cycle. It is difficult to take up this issue without a full analysis of the capitalist state.[8] But a skeletal investigation of the problem here will help us understand why certain aspects of the state apparatus, such as the central bank, are necessarily outside of democratic control. It will also help us understand, albeit in a very general way, the circumstances that permit the devaluation of capital to be transformed into the destruction of money through inflation.

The simplest way to regulate the quality of money in society is to tie it to some universally accepted money commodity such as gold. The disadvantage is that the value of social labour is tied to the condition of concrete labour in gold production. If the latter changes, then so does the general expression of social labour as a price. Marx was not unduly bothered by this problem. He considered that the occasional surges in the supply of gold (after the 'gold rush' of 1849, for example) would administer a temporary shock and then be absorbed by price adjustments (*Capital,* vol. 1, p. 98).

The state becomes involved in regulation of money as soon as coins, tokens, paper and credit moneys are introduced as means to circulate commodities. The state finds itself drawn willy-nilly into the politics of money management and may even take up an activist stance of some sort.[9] By the eighteenth century, for example, the main nations engaged in capitalist commerce were consciously pursuing strategies of devaluation and revaluation of their respective currencies in their perpetual jockeyings for commercial and political advantage. Mercantilist doctrines reflected such practices. The rise of a full-fledged credit system and the creation of fictitious forms of capital with legal backing posed the capitalist state with even more far-reaching problems.

Eventually, as we saw in chapter 9, the task of securing high-quality money devolves upon a central bank of some sort. Because the central bank has the power to set the conditions under which other moneys are convertible into its own money, it can, within certain limits, regulate the market rate of interest (*Capital,* vol. 3, p. 542). It cannot behave arbitrarily. It is constrained by its foreign exchange position, gold reserves and other links with some kind of

[8] De Brunhoff (1978) is one of the best presentations with respect to integrating questions of money and finance with the functioning of the capitalist state.

[9] Some background is given in De Brunhoff (1978, 1979), while Vilar (1976) constructs a fascinating history.

supra-national money on the world stage. We must also invoke Marx's rule that 'the power of the central bankers begins where that of the private discounters stops'. This means that the central bank can respond only to money market pressures emanating from within the heart of the system of production and realization of surplus value. How it responds is nevertheless important, because decisions made by the central bank (or foisted upon it by legislation) have a very important role in dampening or exacerbating cyclical oscillations. Stringent money policies at times of overaccumulation can intensify devaluation. The crisis often appears, in the first instance, as a money crisis, fored upon society by an unyielding and obdurate central bank.

When the central bank ties its money tightly to a gold standard, it has very little room for manoeuvre. A limited gold reserve forces it to raise interest rates to a point of extreme usury at a time when all capitalists seek refuge in high-quality money. When convertibility into gold is permanently (as opposed to temporarily) suspended, the quantity of central bank money and the rate of interest on that money can become policy instruments. The 'art' of central banking is to use these policy instruments to try to stabilize the inherently unstable course of accumulation. At the same time the severance of central bank money from gold gives rise to the formal possibility of sustained inflation. We now take up that possibility in greater detail.

VII   INFLATION AS A FORM OF DEVALUATION

Phases and instances of inflation abound in the history of capitalism. Any general interpretation of such phenomena has to be embedded in a complete theory of price determination. And it is clear that prices may rise or fall for a whole host of different reasons.[10] If we abstract from the various random shocks to which any economic system is heir – the bad harvests, the wars and rumours of war, etc. – as well as from the perpetual market price oscillations that accompany the equilibration of demand and supply in the market, we can identify a variety of forces that affect movements in the underlying prices of production of the various commodities.

The competitive struggle to acquire relative surplus value should increase the physical and value productivity of labour and so cheapen commodities (*Capital*, vol. 1, pp. 319–20). The expansion of production upon more fertile lands, the opening up of new sources of raw materials, the searching out of cheaper and more malleable labour power and the reduction in circulation costs (particularly transportation) add up to a whole battery of forces that tend to force prices downwards. Against these must be ranged the rising costs associated with natural resource depletion, congestion and other bottlenecks

[10] Marx is surprisingly respectful of Tooke's pioneering study of price movements – a subject that has continued to be the focus of bourgeois economic history since.

in the production apparatus, class struggle on the part of labour, increasing monopolization and the like. Price movements are, in the final analysis, dictated by the balance of incredibly divergent and particular forces.

The circumstance we are here considering has, however, a simpler logic.[11] Marx's representation of the accumulation cycle shows that prices are depressed in the phase of stagnation, rise gradually, and then accelerate rapidly during the boom. The return to the monetary basis during the crash forces a price collapse. If a more flexible monetary basis is constructed which, instead of being tied to the money commodity, permits the printing of inconvertible state-backed money during the crisis, then price falls at that time can presumably be kept in check.

Such a policy appears, on the surface, to be eminently sensible compared with its opposite – allowing commodity values to go to the wall in order to preserve the integrity of high-quality money. But it violates Marx's rule that the realization of values cannot be achieved through a mere increase in the supply of money (see chapter 3). It also means that money must abandon its role as a measure of the value of social labour. Furthermore, the idea that the severe crisis tendencies of capitalism, as we outlined them in chapter 7, can somehow be tamed by such a policy appears somewhat far-fetched. The most that can happen is that the form taken by the crisis will change. Let us see how.

Recall, first, what the theory of overaccumulation tells us. Too much capital is produced in relation to opportunities to use that capital because individual capitalists, driven by competition and striving to maximize their profits through the exploitation of labour power, adopt technologies that drive the economy away from a balanced accumulation path. The disequilibrium is made worse because prices of production, formed through the equalization in the profit rate, give erroneous price signals in relation to the potential for social surplus value production. In addition, the underlying disequilibrium tends to be obscured by the necessary creation of fictitious capitals ahead of real accumulation.

Fictitious capitals and the interest-bearing capital invested in them stand to be destroyed in the course of a crisis, while devaluation can strike at capital in any of the states within the circulation process

$$M - C \begin{pmatrix} LP \\ MP \end{pmatrix} \ldots P \ldots C' - M' \text{ etc.}$$

Consider, now, how an expansion of central bank money relates to all of this.

[11] Explicit Marxist theories of inflation are surprisingly thin on the ground. Harvey (1977) and Rowthorn (1980) are basic reading, while Jacobi *et al.* (1975) review some of the problems that attach to various Marxist approaches to the subject. Sherman (1976), Sweezy and Magdoff (1972), de Brunhoff (1979), Fine (1979a), Mattick (1980) and Mandel (1978) attempt analyses from rather different angles.

From the standpoint of the individual capitalist, the first sign of over-accumulation occurs with the increasing difficulty of converting commodities or property titles (fictitious capitals) into money at a price that allows the average rate of profit to be realized. The transition C–M is always difficult because it involves the movement from a specific concrete use value (or property title) into the most general form of social power that exists – money. This transition appears to be hindered by a lack of effective demand or, what amounts to the same thing, by a shortage of disposable money. Individual capitalists and other financial agents (private banks) can bypass this difficulty by extending credit. Capitalists receive the money equivalent of unsold commodities (including the average rate of profit thereon). The quantity of lower-order credit moneys expands rapidly. Pressure is then put upon the central bank to expand the supply of high-quality money. If the central bank obliges, then it seems as if overall liquidity can be maintained at the same time as all barriers to the realization of values through exchange are removed.

The matter is not, unfortunately, that simple. The central bank money issued can be used in a variety of ways. It could feed the circulation of fictitious capitals and so heighten speculative fevers. It could be converted into an effective demand for commodities (as opposed to property titles). Keynes insisted that the latter was more important to economic stability than the former and sought by specific fiscal policies (as opposed to pure monetary policies) to channel effective demand in ways that would contribute to stability rather than exacerbate the tendency towards disequilibrium. A simplified version of this idea goes like this. In times of depression, the state can create an effective demand for commodities by running a budget deficit which can be covered by borrowings from the capital market. While the increased effective demand solves the realization problem in the sphere of exchange, the increase in demand for loanable funds will, in the absence of any corresponding increase in supply, force interest rates upwards, perhaps to the point of 'extreme usury'. This has a disastrous impact upon industrial and commercial operations (though obviously not on banking capital) and can force the very devaluation that state policies were initially designed to avoid. There is, then, a strong pressure to increase the supply of high-quality money in order to bring interest rates down. The central bank, by engaging in such an action, can help avoid the devaluation of commodities.[12]

Unfortunately, such a strategy also contributes simultaneously to the realization of fictitious capital. If, for example, there has been considerable

[12] As Harris (1979) points out, both monetarists and Keynesians accept the same underlying theory of money, which is essentially a quantity theory. Keynesian policies always contain a strong monetarist perspective because the central bank has to play its proper part if the policies are to have any chance of short-run success. What divides monetarists and Keynesians is the degree of discretion allowed to the state in fixing fiscal and monetary targets.

speculative activity in land titles, then expanding effective demand for housing keeps that speculation very much alive at the same time as it increases the demand for commodities such as bricks, timber, etc. Support of this sort for fictitious capital implies, in effect, that the state substitutes its own fictitious capital (an increase in the stock of state-backed money) for the mass of privately held fictitious capital floating around in the credit system. Whether or not this is a good or bad thing depends entirely upon whether the fictitious values so created can be realized in subsequent phases of the circulation of capital.

With the successful, though problematic, negotiation of the link C–M, the burden now shifts on to money, which will itself suffer devaluation if it is not thrown back into circulation within its 'normal' time span. There are three possible uses for that money.

(1) Money reinvested in production must cross the divide

$$M - C\binom{LP}{MP}.$$

An increase in M increases the demand for labour power and means of production and mops up any surpluses in the supply of both. This puts upward pressure on prices, which, in the context of a crisis, means that costs of production do not decline anywhere near as much as they otherwise would. The 'technological shake-out' is nowhere near as vigorous as it normally would be, and there may even be pressure upon producers to continue a pattern of technological adjustment more characteristic of the phase of expansion than of retraction. Wages, for example, may not decline enough to stimulate the return to labour-intensive activities. The value composition of capital is unlikely to return to its equilibrium position under such conditions.

(2) Money can be invested in appropriation, in the purchase of titles to future revenues (land, stocks and shares, government debt, etc.). Fictitious values created by the state simply end up augmenting the quantity of privately held fictitious capital in the economy. The problem of the realization of such fictitious capitals through production is then posed anew.

(3) The bourgeoisie diverts a portion of the extra money into its own consumption. This increases the demand for luxury goods which, in turn, bids up the demand for labour power and means of production.

The extra money that the state throws into circulation has, therefore, at some point to be realized through production. This confirms Marx's fundamental finding in his investigation of the circulation of surplus value (*Capital*, vol. 2, ch. 17; cf. above, pp. 95–6): realization in the sphere of exchange is, in the end, contingent upon further realization in the realm of production.

Now it was Marx's basic argument that overaccumulation arises because the technological mix (including degree of centralization, vertical integration, etc.) in production is arrived at by processes that ensure that it is inconsistent with further balanced accumulation. Nothing is changed with respect to those processes by the creation of extra money in the sphere of exchange. The printing of money cannot cure the problem. Indeed, the distortion of price signals makes the disequilibrium worse. The full force of the shake-out, which would bring the system back into an equilibrium position as measured by the value composition of capital, is held back. Further technological innovations that de-stabilize the system are encouraged. The trend towards overaccumulation will likely be increased rather than curbed.

If individual capitalists and other private agents continue to extend credit to each other in the face of burgeoning overaccumulation and spiralling quantities of fictitious capital, and if they continue to be backed up by the printing of money by the central bank, then the insane aspects of the credit system can run amok. State-backed money breaks free from any pretence of acting as a firm measure of socially necessary labour. If money exercises little discipline over capitalists, there is nothing, except competition, to prevent their raising their prices arbitrarily. They realize profits in exchange in spite of the fall-off in real surplus value production. Such a situation is plainly untenable. Generalized inflation results and the underlying tendencies towards disequilibrium become worse – unless, that is, countervailing forces (such as the foreign exchange position of the central bank or conscious recognition on the part of the central bank that monetary discipline must be restored) come into play.

The result, however, is that the devaluation of commodities can be converted into the devaluation of money through inflation. We must reiterate that this is not the only form of inflation that can exist, and any actual historical interlude of strong inflation may be the outcome of a variety of different forces. Inflation of the sort we are here considering has a very specific interpretation.

The transformation of devaluation into inflation simultaneously entails the centralization and socialization of the devaluation process that accompanies overaccumulation. Devaluation, we should note, begins as a private affair (individual firms go bankrupt; particular commodities remain unsold) and ends up having social ramifications (unemployment, diminished circulation of revenues, etc.). Inflation is a social affair at the very outset, but has private and particular consequences. The transformation of devaluation into inflation, therefore, has certain technical, economic and political implications that deserve to be explored.

First, the socialization of devaluation reduces the impact of particular events upon the basic rhythm of the accumulation cycle. Potentially damaging bankruptcies of individual corporations can be avoided or absorbed (through government 'bail-outs', for example) and their costs spread over society as a whole. The possibility that events of this sort will bring the whole system crashing down is much reduced. Secondly, the 'constant devaluation' that attaches to technological change (see chapter 7) can be converted into a constant 'mild' inflation which, some Keynesians argue, helps to preserve balanced growth – shifting price structures provide signals for planned obsolescence and new investment. Thirdly, minor oscillations in the accumulation process can be controlled and sometimes even manipulated for short-run political ends (a case of the latter is the so-called 'political business cycle', in which monetary policy is used to create an artificial boom in the economy just prior to elections).[13] The costs of mild bouts of devaluation, which sometimes hit overly hard during the brief spasm of crisis, can, however, be attenuated and spread out as a mild surge of inflation over several years.

The socialization of devaluation through inflation also spreads the impacts of overaccumulation instantaneously over all social classes. But the effects are by no means equally felt. The distributive consequences vary according to circumstances. Marx pointed out, for example, that the depreciation of gold and silver in the sixteenth and seventeenth centuries 'depreciated the labouring class' as well as the landed proprietors relative to the capitalists and thereby helped concentrate money power in the hands of the latter (*Grundrisse*, p. 805). The incomes of 'the unproductive classes and those who live on fixed incomes' tend to remain 'stationary during the inflation of prices which goes hand in hand with over-production and over-speculation', and this 'diminishes relatively' their purchasing power at such times (*Capital*, vol. 3, p. 491). Those on fixed incomes stand to gain during the price deflation that occurs with the return to the monetary basis but are hurt when devaluation is transformed into permanent inflation.

Inflation also tends to redistribute money power from savers to debtors because the latter pay off their debts in depreciated currency. Whether or not this happens depends, however, upon the rate of interest, which becomes negative in real terms when the inflation rate is higher than the nominal interest rate. A negative real rate of interest betokens the general devaluation of money savings. If the nominal rate of interest varies according to money resources, then the savings of the big bourgeosie may be preserved from the ravages of inflation while those of the working classes may be devalued (cf. *Capital*, vol. 3, p. 508).

Most important of all, the transformation to permanent inflation allows capitalists to realize a long-cherished aim. 'The capitalist class', Marx observes, 'would never resist the trades' unions, if it could always and under all circumstances do what it is doing now by way of exception . . . to wit, avail

[13] Kalecki (1971) was probably the first to spot the likelihood for political manipulation of the business cycle. Boddy and Crotty (1975) take up the idea in the context of a 'profit squeeze' theory that we rejected above, pp. 52–4.

itself of every rise in wages in order to raise prices of commodities much higher yet and thus pocket greater profits' (*Capital,* vol. 2, p. 340). This possibility becomes real only when the strict discipline of the money commodity gives way to the looser and more flexible practices of state creation of inconvertible paper money. If the state takes care of the effective demand problem and expands the money supply to keep pace, then individual capitalists can stabilize their profit rates, in the face of falling surplus value production, simply by adjusting the prices of the commodities they produce. The only short-run limitation in the market is price competition. To the degree that monopoly, oligopoly and 'price leadership' behaviours develop, so price competition weakens. For this reason inflation is frequently attributed to corporate practices under 'monopoly capitalism'. Such practices have important secondary impacts, but inflation of the sort we are here considering has much deeper roots in the general transformation of devaluation of commodities into the devaluation of money.

Class struggle changes dramatically with inflation. Wage cuts are hard to impose directly and typically provoke a very targeted, concrete working-class response. With generalized inflation, employers can concede increases in nominal money wages and so reduce the intensity of direct worker opposition. What happens to real wages depends entirely upon the inflation rate, which individual capitalists can claim is not their personal responsibility. The devaluation of labour power is then achieved through inflation. To the degree that such a strategy is successful, it permits the problems of overaccumulation to be countered through a rising rate of exploitation achieved through a diminution in real wages. The mechanisms of wage adjustment that Marx describes in the 'general law of capitalist accumulation' (see chapter 6) are fundamentally altered. It may even become possible to manage wage adjustments through inflation without the help of a massive industrial reserve army. The significance of the so-called 'Phillips Curve' – which depicted a trade-off between inflation and unemployment – was that it appears to offer policymakers a ready-made target for fiscal and monetary policy.[14]

The struggle over the nominal wage is, as a result, gradually converted into a struggle over the real wage. Workers then find themselves fighting on two fronts. They seek strict cost-of-living clauses in wage contracts in order to prevent the costs of devaluation being visited upon them via inflation. From this derives a wage-push theory of inflation which blames greedy unions for rising prices. This theory is correct, in the theoretical context we are here

---

[14] The Phillips Curve refers to the empirical observation that there existed, for a number of years at least, an inverse relationship between the rate of wage increases and the level of unemployment. This was then parlayed into the general theoretical proposition that there is a trade-off between level of unemployment and inflation. Circumstances of the 1970s, when unemployment and inflation increased together, called the whole argument into question (see Fine, 1979a).

considering, only in the sense that workers prevent overaccumulation from being cured through a massive devaluation of labour power via inflation. But workers also have to confront the fiscal and monetary policies that allow devaluation to be transformed into inflation in the first place. The focus of class struggle can shift from the direct confrontation between capital and labour on to a confrontation between workers and the state. The latter thereby becomes a protective shield for capitalist class interests. It may even appear, with some not so subtle help from bourgeois propoganda, as if inflation has its origins in inefficient and ineffective government, in erroneous fiscal and monetary policies. This attribution is correct as regards the immediate cause. What it ignores is the underlying structure of class relations which generates crises of overaccumulation–devaluation in the first place.

The conversion of devaluation into inflation appears to have both positive and negative effects from the standpoint of capital. On the one hand, it can ease the pressure of direct forms of conflict over wages and even reduce the size of the industrial reserve army needed to equilibrate the wage rate. It also socializes the costs of devaluation across all classes behind the shield of fiscal and monetary policy carried out by the state. On the other hand, it prompts the formation of class alliances directed towards assuming state power. Inflation defuses conflict by broadening it and refocusing it on the state.

But inflation cannot cure the trend towards overaccumulation. If anything, it exacerbates the problem by attenuating and delaying the impacts. State policies allow an enormous head of inflationary pressure to build up to the point where it becomes potentially very explosive. The dead weight of unproductive fictitious capital is increasingly felt, the foreign exchange position of the central bank progressively weakens (bringing about devaluation of national currency in relation to world money), and price structures become so unstable that they lose their coherence as a co-ordinating power. Above all, the rationalization of production, which is the only solution to overaccumulation, cannot be properly set in motion. The problems of overaccumulation, in short, cannot be spirited away by the socialization of devaluation through inflation.

In this light, it is interesting to look at the range of proposed cures for inflation, all of which appeal to some kind of basic change in state involvement.

First, the state can reconstitute a strict monetary base for the economy. Though this need not be tied to a money commodity, it does imply very restrictive monetary policies (which force interest rates up), cuts in government stimulation of effective demand, and permission for the raw market forces that devalue commodities and labour power to take hold. A conventional depression, administered by the state, does its work of re-structuring the productive apparatus, eliminating excessive fictitious capitals, disciplining labour, and so on.

Secondly, the state can impose wage and price controls or seek to cool off inflation through some kind of incomes policy, a 'social contract' with labour (which usually amounts to some kind of negotiated devaluation of labour power) and an investment strategy for industry. Interventions of this sort must be accompanied by monetary and fiscal restraint if they are to have a chance of working. Monetarists argue that policies of this sort merely distort price signals and thereby destroy any proper basis for the resumption of accumulation. Marxian theory accords with that judgement, except under the unlikely circumstance that the price structure mandated and the investment strategies devised stabilize the value composition of capital. This would entail a phased and organized devaluation of capital and labour power through the agency of state policies.

Thirdly, the state, in conjunction with capital, can seek to accelerate the development of the productive forces and hope thereby to bring prices down to compensate for the inflationary surge. Failure to increase productivity, it is sometimes argued, lies at the root of inflation. The theory we are here adopting indicates that it is the uncontrolled and unbalanced development of the productive forces in the context of the class relations of capitalism that provokes overaccumulation in the first place. To the degree that inflation is a transformation of devaluation, it cannot be cured by an indiscriminate programme of raising productivity. The state can seek to change the technological mix (forced mergers, special tax incentives to certain sectors, state sponsorship of research and development). But if it is to cure the problems of overaccumulation it cannot avoid visiting the costs of devaluation upon certain segments of both capital and labour. And cures of this sort, to the degree that they entail direct or indirect state management of the productive apparatus, though they may not be socialistic, hardly bode well for the future of capitalism, either.

While it is true that the devaluation of commodities (including labour power) can be avoided by inflation in the short-run, it is equally true that problems of inflation cannot be cured without devaluing commodities. The Marxian theory tells us that, in response to overaccumulation, capital can devalue money or commodities (or some mix of both). But only the devaluation of commodities, including labour power, can force the re-structuring that will allow balanced accumulation to resume.

There is, perhaps, no better testimony to the fundamental underlying irrationality of capitalism than that the economic choices that exist within the confines of its dominant class relations are of so restricted and dismal a variety. The bigger, broader choice is between preserving those class relations or eliminating them together with the contradictions to which they give rise.

VIII   FINANCE CAPITAL AND ITS CONTRADICTIONS

There are two conceptions of finance capital at work in this chapter. The first is that of a *process* of circulation of interest-bearing capital; the second, of an institutionalized power bloc within the bourgeoisie. Neither conception is, in itself, entirely adequate. We must now strive to bring them together.

In its surface appearance, the organized power of finance is impressive, seemingly impenetrable and awe-inspiring. The financial system is shrouded in mystery born out of sheer complexity. It encompasses the intricate world of central banking, remote international institutions (the World Bank, the International Monetary Fund), a whole complex of interlocking financial markets (stock exchanges, commodity futures markets, mortgage markets, etc.), agents (brokers, bankers, discounters, etc.) and institutions (pension and insurance funds, merchant banks, credit unions, savings banks, etc.). And above all it includes an array of incredibly powerful private banks (the Bank of America, France's Credit Agricole, Britain's Barclays). Bankers and their cohorts shuttle back and forth between Basle, Zurich, London, New York and Tokyo. Decisions that clearly affect the fates of millions are made at international meetings, suggesting that the bankers of the world are indeed in control not only of the lives of individuals (capitalists and workers alike) but also of even the largest corporations and the most powerful of governments. This image achieves even greater credibility when we see that even that aspect of the state given over to the protection of monetary operations – the central bank – always eludes democratic control.

The average citizen can be forgiven for lapsing into a state of total awe when confronted with the sheer magnitude of money power that resides within such institutions and the sophistication of the elite that runs them. The mystery of the financial system, and the potency of the forces operating through its agency, generate a mystique. This mystique is the easy breeding ground for conspiracy theories – conspiracies to divide and rule the world, 'think-tanks' (like the celebrated Tri-Lateral Commission) to come up with strategies for global domination, plans to be executed by a powerful cabal of banks, corporate giants and their political representatives.

It is the task of science to demystify all of this, to reveal the compelling logic that courses through the veins of the financial system, to expose the inner vulnerability beneath what appears on the surface to be totally hegemonic controlling power. The task requires a subtle blend of theory and historical materialist investigation for its proper fulfilment.

Straight empirical studies typically run into impasses, founder upon seemingly insoluble conundrums. If, for example, a conspiratorially minded elite is so powerful, has at its fingertips such multiple and delicate instruments with which to fine-tune accumulation, then how can the periodic headlong slides into crises be explained? Or, to take another tack, how can financiers simultaneously appear as the sober guardians of an orderly process of accumulation, carried on in the interests of the bourgeoisie as a whole and operating with the common capital of the class, at the same time as they patently engage in venal and excessive appropriation, insane speculation and all manner of other parasitic practices which serve only to plunge society into paroxysms of chaos and disorder?

The conception of finance capital as a contradiction-laden *flow* of interest-bearing capital – a conception, we should note, that is entirely consistent with Marx's general view of capital as a *process* rather than a thing – helps penetrate the impasses and unravel the conundrums. It helps us understand the instability of the configurations that arise when 'finance capital' is considered as a power bloc within the bourgeoisie, or, what amounts to the same thing, the difficulty researchers experience when they seek a consistent definition of 'finance capital' in the first place. It also sheds further light on a topic first broached in chapter 5: the dynamics of the organizational transformation of capitalism. We now probe further into these questions.

1 Finance capital as the 'class' of financiers and money capitalists

Those who control the flow of money as an *external* power in relation to production occupy a strategic position in capitalist society. If that strategic position is to be converted into a real power base, then the centralization of money capital in a few hands is a first requirement. This centralization can occur in two ways. First, a few extraordinarily wealthy individuals or families can accumulate the mass of the money power in society in their hands. Secondly, a few powerful institutions can control the dispersed money power of innumerable individually powerless individuals. When a few wealthy families, such as the Mellons and Rockefellers, own much of the money wealth and participate strongly in the control of the remainder, then a unity of ownership and control prevails within the strategic centre of the circulation of interest-bearing capital. This provides a first working definition of finance capital.[15]

Excessive centralization of power within this strategic centre is, however, inconsistent with the proper exercise of its co-ordinating functions. Competition within the financial sector has to be maintained if the interest rate is to adjust in ways responsive to accumulation, if money capital is to flow freely and avoid the typical bias imposed by monopolistic practices. The form of competition within the financial sector varies, however. Sometimes it is manifest as intense rivalry between financial empires; sometimes it arises out

---

[15] Lenin wondered if this definition would be sufficient at one point (see Church-ward, 1959). This working definition underlies the perspective of Fitch and Openheimer (1970).

of social mechanisms that maintain a broad dispersal of money power within the bourgeoisie; in still other cases it is guaranteed by legal requirements which restrict certain institutions to certain kinds of activity (housing finance, for example), delimit the geographical area of operation (restrictions on inter-state branch banking in the United States, for example) or even dictate basic conditions of management of the portfolio of assets a particular kind of financial institution can hold (pension and insurance funds usually operate under such restraints). There is often a certain ambiguity as to where money power actually resides in such a fragmented system. The current concentration of much money wealth in the form of pension funds, for example, has given rise to a not very interesting debate over 'pension-fund socialism' (the idea that the mass of the people owns a large proportion of the fictitious capital in society through pension savings) and a real and very intense battle for control over the money power that pension funds represent. The accumulation of much of the money wealth in a few hands, likewise, does not necessarily mean that those few actively control the use of that money. They may seek to avoid risk by dispersing their wealth through a wide variety of institutions that operate independently of them.

The total fragmentation and decentralization of the financial system is, on the other hand, also detrimental. The quality of paper money is best guaranteed by a central bank with monopoly powers. Failure to centralize money power also acts as a barrier to the conversion of money into capital as well as to subsequent accumulation in so far as the latter depends upon the centralization of capital. The rapid reorganization of capitalism into its corporate and conglomerate form – steps that we saw in chapter 5 were necessary to the perpetuation of capitalism – could not have been brought about without a simultaneous shift in the capacity to centralize money power.

The tension between centralization and decentralization is as evident, therefore, within the financial power bloc as it is elsewhere (see chapter 5). It is evidenced in a variety of ways. For example, it helps explain why the United States exhibits a highly decentralized, seemingly chaotic financial system (kept in place by a weird assortment of piecemeal legislation enacted by a bourgeoisie that has spasmodically sought to counter the threat of excessive centralization) at the same time as it is characterized by immense concentrations of money wealth among a few families operating through a few large-scale financial institutions.[16] It helps explain also why banks simultaneously compete with each other in some arenas while in others they form alliances, consortia and, from time to time, conspiratorial cabals in order to assemble a sufficient concentration of money power to deal with the large-scale and long-term aspects of the financing of accumulation. The perpetually shifting realignments of both institutional structures and financial practices create a

---

[16] Domhoff (1978) and Zeitlin (1974) provide detailed information on this point.

good deal of confusion. Seen as material expression of the underlying tension within the circulation of interest-bearing capital itself, the confusions and contradictions make more sense. They are simply surface appearances of the underlying requirement to balance centralization and decentralization within the financial system.

2 Finance capital as the unity of banking and industrial capital

The conception of finance capital advanced by Hilferding and generally accepted by Lenin is of the unity of banking and industrial capital. The unity is selective in the sense that it is only the large banks and the grand industrial enterprises that form the basis for delimiting finance capital as a distinctive power bloc. For this reason the concept of finance capital, in Lenin's hands in particular, merges imperceptibly and indiscriminately at a certain point with that of monopoly capitalism in general.

The unity of banking and industrial capital, if it exists at all, is certainly a stressful one. It is obvious, of course, that large corporations cannot conduct their affairs without extensive use of banking services and that banks are desperately anxious to command the vast flows of money large corporations generate. In this sense large-scale banking and corporate capital are necessary to each other, exist in a symbiotic relation to each other. If this is all that is meant by the unity of banking and industrial capital, then there is no problem. But both Hilferding and Lenin mean something more: they assert that the unity is a working unity, which dominates the accumulation process and carves up the world into regions of subordination to the collective power of a few large banks and corporations.

The analysis of finance capital as a flow reveals the underlying unity and antagonism between financial and surplus value-producing operations. The accumulation cycle – assuming no active state interventions – suggests a shifting balance of power between industrial capital and banking capital over the course of the cycle. The shifting balance reflects the relative weight of commodity versus money expressions of value within the accumulation process. In the early phases of the upswing industrial capital is in the driver's seat because commodities are what count. During the later phases of the boom industrial and financial interests unite to promote a credit-based expansion of commodity values. In the crisis, money is everything and the banks appear to hold the fates of industrial capitalists entirely in their hands because excess commodities cannot be converted into money. But banks themselves may also go under as the demand for high-quality money (gold or central bank money) far exceeds the supply. In the depths of the crisis, power resides with those who hold money of last resort.

The accumulation cycle is much modified by contingent events and external interventions – particularly those of government. But shifting patterns of unity and antagonism between capital in commodity and money form are not eliminated. They are simply transformed into new configurations. They continue to form the basis for the shifting power relation between industrial and banking capital. In other words, the organizational and institutional arrangements, together with the practices of economic agents, have to be seen as a product of an accumulation process that can proceed in no other way except through perpetual opposition between money and commodities within the unity of capital as 'value in motion'. The conception of finance capital as a unity of industrial and banking capital is unobjectionable in principle, provided that the unity is seen as a unity that internalizes tension, antagonism and contradiction.

This leaves open the question as to the specific ways in which the contradictions are internalized within particular organizational structures. Consider, for example, a large-scale conglomerate corporation. Many financial operations are internalized within the firm and apparently united with production into an integrated whole. This appearance of unity is deceptive. In the same way that large corporations are forced to internalize mechanisms of competition if they are to survive (see chapter 5), so they are also forced to maintain the separation of finance from production. This opens up the prospect for conflict *within* the corporation – conflict that relates directly back to the antagonism between capital in money or commodity form. The unification of control does, however, provide the firm with alternative strategies for survival in times of crisis or for expansion in times of boom. Financial manouevres – take-overs, mergers, asset-stripping, etc. – are just as important as commitment to production operations. The struggle for survival between corporations therefore takes on a wholly new dimension. But the underlying problem is not thereby altered. If all corporations seek to survive by purely financial manouevres without enhancing or restructuring production, then capitalism is not long for this world. The form of appearance of struggle changes, as does the institutional and organizational framework, but the underlying essentials do not.

The somewhat acrimonious debate over whether banks control corporations or corporations control banks must be viewed in a somewhat similar light.[17] What actually constitutes control is by no means clear. Formal definitions (a certain percentage of the stock, for example) rarely capture perpetually shifting practices. And to the degree that the accumulation process invariably produces phases that are long on commodities and short on money and vice versa, so we have to anticipate perpetual shifts in the power relation between industrial and banking capital. From this standpoint, putting corporate chiefs on the boards of major banks and appointing bank presidents as directors of corporations appears a futile attempt to establish an organizational unity in the face of a contradiction-laden process.

[17] See the interchange between Fitch and Openheimer (1970) and Sweezy (1971).

But we would be wrong to leave matters there. The shifting patterns of control of corporations by banks or banks by corporations have also to be seen as part of a perpetual process of probing for an organizational form that will enhance the capacity of capitalism to survive in the face of its own internal contradictions. In exactly the same way that perpetual oscillations in market prices are fundamental to the establishment of equilibrium values, so perpetual oscillations in the balance of control between bankers and corporations are essential to the achievement of that equilibrium relation between finance and production of surplus value that is most appropriate at a particular moment of the accumulation process. The 'class' that occupies the strategic centre that joins finance and production may be clearly defined in a given situation; but it will surely remain an unstable configuration given the contradictory pressures and requirements that operate upon it.[18]

The unitary conception of finance capital Hilferding advances has to be judged, therefore, as too one-sided and simplistic because he does not address the specific manner in which the unification of banking and industrial capital internalizes an insurmountable contradiction. The best that he can do is to assert in very general, non-specific terms that finance capital can not overcome the contradictions of capitalism but merely serves to heighten them. What he fails to explain is exactly how and why this is necessarily so.

3 Finance capital and the state

At the level of the central bank, finance capital, however defined, integrates directly with a part of the state apparatus. But the state typically affects and relates to the circulation of interest-bearing capital across a far broader spectrum of activities than that. It fixes the legal and institutional framework and often designs the highly differentiated channels through which interest-bearing capital circulates into the different activities such as consumer debt, housing finance, industrial development and the like. It often regulates flows down the different channels by fixing interest-rate differentials or direct allocations of credit. The degree of centralization or decentralization of money wealth and control is likewise highly sensitive to state fiscal and redistributive taxation policies as well as to monetary strategies that affect inflation. The state itself absorbs a portion of the flow of interest-bearing capital in the form of state debt, and in the process creates fictitious capital of certain qualities (which may be further differentiated according to the governmental unit or agency doing the borrowing – US government debt is qualitatively different, for example, from New York City debt). And at the

---

[18] I am therefore strongly sympathetic to the definition of finance capital given by Thompson (1977, p. 247) as 'an articulated combination of commercial capital, industrial capital and banking capital' within which banking capital is *dominant* but not *determinant*.

centre of this intricate system lies the central bank with all of its powers in relation to the quality of national money.

A part of the state apparatus is entirely caught up in the circulation process of interest-bearing capital. There is an aspect, and only *an* aspect, of the state which cannot be considered even *relatively* autonomous of capital because it is necessarily constructed in the image of the motion of capital itself. The administrators of this aspect of the state apparatus manage the circulation of interest-bearing capital and function as 'the executive committee of the bourgeoisie' no matter what their political allegiance. A necessary unity is thereby established between a part of the state apparatus and the money capitalists, industrialists and financiers who similarly participate in the circulation of interest-bearing capital. From the outside it appears as if a section of the state colludes directly with industrial and financial interests. A new definition of finance capital comes to the fore: one in which all three interests are unified.[19]

This unity contains a contradiction as well as the potentiality for transformation. Marx argues that the credit system 'requires state interference' at the same time as it socializes capital and centralizes control over social labour. Socialized capital, brought under state regulation and control, is the inevitable product of the growth of capitalism. The credit system therefore constitutes 'the form of transition to a new mode of production' (*Capital*, vol. 3, pp. 438–41).

Our attention is immediately focused on the antagonism within the unity of the overall circulation of interest-bearing capital. The central bank, after all, has the unenviable task of disciplining errant industrialists and bankers and penalizing them for their inevitable excesses in the race to accumulate and capture the benefits of accumulation. Open conflict frequently erupts, particularly at times of crisis, between the state apparatus, necessarily exercising disciplining powers, and all other factions of capital. This conflict exists even in states where political power clearly lies in the hands of the bourgeoisie. The capacity for the regulation and control of capital, albeit in the interests of the capitalist class as a whole, necessarily resides within the state apparatus. It then seems as if a working-class movement can dominate capital if it can gain control of the strategic centre within the state apparatus. But then the reverse side of the medal immediately becomes evident. In so far as a part of the state apparatus is a pure reflection of capital itself, even a socialist government (as many have found to their cost) can do no more than

[19] Hilferding in practice tends to include the state in his theory of finance capital since the unity of banking and industrial capital is achieved within the nation state. Such a formulation poses problems because international finance is sometimes nationally based and sometimes supra-national in its form of organization. The connection between finance and the state is evidently very complex in nature – see de Brunhoff (1978) and Holloway and Picciotto (1978).

strive for a more effective management of the contradiction-laden flow of interest-bearing capital. To be sure, adjustments here and there in both institutional structures and in the direction and quantity of flows can bring benefits to workers. But the limits to such redistributions are strictly circumscribed by the necessary unity that also prevails within the circulation of interest-bearing capital. Only the total abolition of this form of circulation will suffice if the state is to escape from a position of collusion with capital. Failing that, class struggle is internalized within the state because of the dual obligation to service the flow of interest-bearing capital while striving to meet the needs of workers.

No matter what the circumstances, the state can never be viewed as an unproblematic partner of industrial and banking capital within a dominant power bloc. The underlying contradictions that plague the circulation of interest-bearing capital are frequently externalized as an opposition between the state (particularly the central bank) and industrial and banking capital. The role of the state is always, therefore, enigmatic and ambivalent. Even a purely capitalist state, run by and for the bourgeoisie, cannot circumvent the contradictions.

All of this becomes even more problematic when projected on to the international stage. The central bank, as guardian of the quality of national money, enters into relations with other central banks to constitute the core of the international monetary system, even when that system is based firmly on a money commodity such as gold. The gold reserves and the international exchange position of the nation state then materially affect the capacity of the central bank to respond to internal difficulties of capital accumulation within its borders. But the state also assumes certain powers to regulate the flows of capital – in commodity, money and even variable form through protective tarrifs, foreign exchange controls and immigration policies. And relations between states certainly cannot be discussed independently of economic, political, cultural and military competition between them.

What intrigued Hilferding and Lenin, of course, was the connection between finance capital, the state and inter-imperialist rivalries. Hilferding focuses on the unity between industrial and banking capital within the framework of state power – the internal contradictions disappear. The unified power blocs centred on nation states struggle with each other for world domination. Lenin takes Hilferding's line in the analysis of the 'core' imperialist powers. But he also draws upon Hobson, who saw financial operations as an independent means to control the governments of the world. Finance capital, Lenin wrote, is such a 'decisive' force 'in all economic and in all international relations, that it is capable of subjecting, and actually does subject, to itself even states enjoying the fullest political independence'. This can occur only if the flow of interest-bearing capital achieves a supra-national aspect, over and above the mere power relations between states. Governments contract debts outside their borders and are thereby subjected to a certain fiscal and monetary discipline, no matter whether it be exercised by powerful international bankers (like the Rothschild's and the Baring's in the nineteenth century or consortia of private banks and supra-national agencies like the International Monetary Fund today). The behaviour of national economies can likewise be subjected to the discipline of international flows, particularly of money capital. Finance capital, Lenin averred, is that stage in which capital 'spreads its net over all countries of the world', through the export of money capital rather than goods.

The enigmatic quality of the relation between finance capital and the state here becomes all too readily apparent. While the state apparatus forms the core of the strategic control centre for the circulation of interest-bearing capital, the latter is simultaneously free to circulate in such a way as to discipline the separate nation states to its purpose. The state is both controlled and controlling in its relation to the circulation of capital.[20] Which force dominates depends upon circumstance. But there, as elsewhere, the disequilibria have to be conceived of as perpetual oscillations around a moving point of equilibrium between countervailing forces. The equilibrium is that configuration in the relation between state powers and finance capital which can keep the capitalist system on its precariously evolutionary path. Failure to preserve that equilibrium, in the face of incredibly powerful forces that perpetually disturb it, can only push the capitalist system into a global crisis that necessarily invokes the might of competing economic, political and military capitalist states. War appears as a means to resolve the internal contradictions of capitalism (see below, pp. 438–45).

Some vital questions to be posed here are, unfortunately, beyond the immediate scope of the analysis: the central point I want to make, however, is that the relation between finance capital (however conceived) and the state is founded upon a contradiction within a unity. Any analysis of the state and of power relations between states must understand the nature and origin of the contradictions and place that understanding at the very centre of its concern.

IX   THE 'SECOND-CUT' THEORY OF CRISES: THE RELATION
BETWEEN PRODUCTION, MONEY AND FINANCE

The 'first-cut' theory of crises (chapter 7) revealed their origin within production. Given the contradictory unity that necessarily prevails between production and exchange, crises inevitably find expression in exchange. Capital can here appear either as commodities or money. Since money is the independent form by means of which the identity of value 'may at any time be established'

[20] Bukharin's (1972a) study on *Imperialism and the World Economy* makes much of this point and repays careful study.

(*Capital,* vol. 1, p. 154), it follows that crises must have a monetary expression. The analyses of credit and the circulation of interest-bearing capital, of the formation of fictitious capitals and all the other financial and monetary complications which have been the subject of the last two chapters add a new dimension entirely to the theory of crisis formation and expression under capitalism. We are now in a position to take a 'second-cut' at the theory of crisis – one that strives to integrate the financial and monetary aspect of affairs with the earlier analysis of the forces making for disequilibrium in production.

We confine attention for the moment to capitalism within one country or, what amounts to the same thing, within a world capitalist economy characterized by a single undifferentiated monetary system. The most singular fact with which we then have to deal is the manner in which the credit system brings capital together as the common capital of the class, with the potentiality to counteract those errant behaviours of individual capitalists that are a primary source of disequilibrium in production. To this we can then add all of those vital powers that permit the co-ordination of production with realization *and* consumption *and* distribution. Sufficient power apparently resides within the credit system to counteract the tendency towards disequilibrium in production. This power cannot be applied directly but must be transmitted via price and other signals in the sphere of exchange.

The existence of such powers does not guarantee that they will be so used. Indeed, in the early years of capitalism private appropriation of the benefits to be had from the use of the common capital of the class was so predominant that the credit system was the locus of speculative crises which erupted relatively independently of disequilibrium in production. Such speculative crises have substantial effects; they can put a strain upon surplus value production and disrupt the course of accumulation. It then appears as if the sole origin of crises lies in financial manipulations. Marx rejects this interpretation with good reason. Nevertheless, the 'second-cut' theory of crises must always allow for relatively autonomous speculative booms in fixed capital and consumption fund formation, in land sales, in commodity prices and commodity futures (including those of money commodities like gold and silver) and in paper assets of all kinds. Such speculative fevers are not necessarily to be interpreted as direct manifestations of disequilibrium in production: they can and do occur on their own account. But Marx demonstrates that they are surface froth upon much deeper currents making for disequilibrium. He also shows us that overaccumulation creates conditions ripe for such speculative fevers so that a concatenation of the latter almost invariably signals the existence of the former. The difficulty here is to disentangle the pure surface froth of perpetual speculation from the deeper rhythms of crisis formation in production.

The analysis of the accumulation cycle paves the way for a more integrated view of the relation between financial phenomena and the dynamics of production. It shows how the inner contradictions within production are manifest in exchange as an opposition between money and commodity forms of value which then becomes, via the agency of the credit system, an outright antagonism between the financial system and its monetary base. The latter antagonism then forms the rock upon which accumulation ultimately founders. The analysis appears to depict an accumulation cycle operating in the absence of extraneous speculative activity. Such is not the case. The formation of fictitious capital is essential to the whole dynamic, and how much or which of that is extraneous can be determined only after the crisis has done its work of rationalization. The surface of speculation, it turns out, is just as essential to the dynamics of accumulation as price movements are to the formation of values.

This focuses attention upon the single most important defect in the idea of an accumulation cycle – a defect that led Marx to bury the notion in such a tentative and fragmentary set of formulations that I may justly be accused of foisting upon him an idea he did not really hold. I refer to the ahistorical manner in which the cycle is specified. Each cycle looks like any other (see section V above) and therefore appears to return the capitalist system to its *status quo ante* after the crisis has run its course. This hardly fits with Marx's concern for the laws of motion that govern the historical evolution of capitalism unless, that is, we are prepared to see the latter accomplished over the course of successive accumulation cycles. And in such a case our interpretation of how the accumulation cycle works must be adjusted accordingly.

From the standpoint of the long-run evolution of capitalism, the accumulation cycle then operates as the means whereby much deeper processes of social transformation are achieved. These processes must at least temporarily relieve the underlying tension between the productive forces and social relations if capitalism is to survive. If the basic class relation remains unaltered, however, then the contradictions are merely displaced and re-created on a different plane. The accumulation cycle provides the 'open space' within which productive forces and social relations can adjust to each other. The speculative activity associated with the upswing allows individualized and private experimentation with new products, new technologies (including organizational forms), new physical and social infrastructures, even whole new cultures, class configurations, and forms of class organization and struggle. This atomistic ferment of experimentation creates much that is superfluous and ephemeral but simultaneously lays the material basis for later phases of accumulation. It is this aspect to speculation that Marx ignores. The crash rationalizes and re-structures production so as to eliminate extraneous elements – both old and new alike. It also disciplines all other aspects of social life to capitalist *class* requirements and hence typically sparks some kind of organized or unorganized response, not only on the part of labour (which goes without saying) but also from various affected factions within the bourgeoisie. This is the time for *class-imposed*, rather than individually achieved, innovation backed if necessary by repression. Roosevelt's New Deal fits exactly into such an interpretation. The net effect must be to bring productive forces and social relations back to some equilibrium position from whence the accumulation process can be renewed.

Marx depicts an analogous process in his schematic representation of how one mode of production transforms into another:

> No social order is ever destroyed before all the productive forces for which it is sufficient have been developed, and new superior relations of production never replace older ones before the material conditions for their existence have matured within the framework of the old society. Mankind thus sets itself only such tasks as it is able to solve, since closer examination will always show that the problem itself arises only when the material conditions for its solution are already present or at least in the course of formation. (*Critique of Political Economy*, p. 21)

The capacity to transform itself from the inside makes capitalism a somewhat peculiar beast – chameleon-like, it perpetually changes its colour; snake-like, it periodically sheds its skin. The study of the circulation of interest-bearing capital sheds light on the concrete material means whereby such internal transformations are wrought. We see that the circulation of capital in general must necessarily assume, at a certain point, a new guise: that of the circulation of interest-bearing capital. This is the chrysalis out of which finance capital emerges as an organized controlling force, replete with internal contradictions and characterized by chronic instability. The emergence is not an abstract affair but involves the creation of new instrumentalities and institutions, new class factions, configurations and alliances, and new channels for the circulation of capital itself. All of this is part and parcel of the necessary evolution of capitalism.

But if the power of the credit system is to be mobilized as a force to counteract disequilibrium in production, then it, too, must be transformed into an unambiguous instrument of class power, not in the sense that it falls into the hands of this or that faction of capitalists, but in the sense that it must be wielded in such a way as to ensure the reproduction of capital through accumulation. The state then takes on the burden of ensuring the reproduction of capital through fiscal and monetary policies executed by the central bank and various other branches of the state apparatus. The advantage of invoking other aspects of the state apparatus, rather then depending solely on the central bank to defend the quality of national money, is that it gives the capacity to respond to disequilibrium in production by structuring a wide range of market signals and powers within the credit system as a countervailing force. We saw in section VI how this can transform the immediate expression of crisis from the devaluation of commodities into the devaluation of money. The 'second-cut' theory of crisis must actively embrace this possibility.

But while the target of state policy may be unambiguous, the means for achieving it are of a quite different quality. Inflation does not achieve the restructing required in production and biases the outcome of the accumulation cycle in important ways which are unlikely to compensate for disequilibrium in production in the long run. The target of state policy has then to be to organize re-structuring, to organize what it is hoped will be a *controlled* crisis. Such a strategy encounters two barriers. First, class struggle (not only between capital and labour but also between the various factions of industrial, commercial, banking, etc., capital) becomes internalized within the state apparatus with all manner of unpredictable effects. Secondly, experience suggests that the degree of control is inversely proportional to the success of the enterprise. Bureaucratized innovation and re-structuring is a less vigorous and less viable process for evolving new forms of capitalism than the 'free market' version (outlined in section V above). Its only virtue, of course, is that it permits the worst aspects of the crash to be controlled.

Considerable debate exists in Marxist circles as to whether crises are to be regarded as temporary cyclical affairs, culminating, perhaps, in the ultimate denouement of capitalist catastrophe, or long-run secular declines, characterized by gradual degeneration and weakness in the face of burgeoning internal contradictions. The 'second-cut' theory of crises differentiates between periodic crashes, which are always the catalyst for the internal transformation of capitalism (and perhaps, ultimately, for the transition to socialism), and long-run problems that arise with the irreversible transformation of configurations in the circulation of capital, class formation, productive forces, institutions and so on. The latter, as Marx observed, are strongly affected by the increasing socialization of capital itself, first via the agency of the credit system and ultimately through socially necessary interventions on the part of the state. The character of periodic crashes is thereby also transformed. Instead of being the aggregate social effect of an essentially atomistic, individualized process, they become a social affair from the very outset. The state, via its policies, becomes responsible for creating what it hopes will be a 'controlled recession' that will have the long-run effect of putting accumulation back on track.

The options for the internal transformation of capitalism become increasingly limited, more and more confined to innovations within the state apparatus itself. And once the limit of the state's capacity to manage the economy creatively is reached, the increasingly authoritarian use of state power – over both capital and labour (though usually with far more devastating effects upon the latter) – appears the only answer. Crises embrace the legal, institutional and political framework of capitalist society and their resolution increasingly depends upon the deployment of naked military and repressive power. The whole problematic of the transformation of capitalism – either by evolutionary or revolutionary means – is thereby altered. The problems and prospects for the transition to socialism shift dramatically.

These shifts take on even starker meaning when we drop the assumption of a closed system and consider international aspects to crisis formation. The disciplinary power of 'world money' – however that is constituted – and the complex relations between different monetary systems become the background to the mobility of capital and labour on the world stage. Crises unravel as rival states, possessed of different money systems, compete with each other over who is to bear the brunt of devaluation. The struggle to export inflation, unemployment, idle productive capacity, excess commodities, etc., becomes the pivot of national policy. The costs of crises are spread differentially according to the financial, economic, political and military power of rival states. War, as Lenin insists, becomes one of the potential solutions to capitalist crisis (a splendid and immediate means of devaluation through destruction). Imperialism and neo-colonialism, as well as financial domination, become a central issue in the global economy of capitalism. We take these matters up in chapter 13.

CHAPTER 11

The Theory of Rent

Rent, it is fair to say, troubled Marx deeply. He sought 'a scientific analysis of ground-rent', of the 'independent and specific economic form of landed property on the basis of the capitalist mode of production' in its 'pure form free of all distorting and obfuscating irrelevancies' (*Capital,* vol. 3, p. 624). Yet his writings on the subject, all of which were published posthumously, are for the most part tentative thoughts set down in the process of discovery. As such they often appear contradictory. The formulations in the earlier *Theories of Surplus Value* differ substantially from the few well-honed passages in *Capital,* while his analysis in the latter work, though extensive and often penetrating, is dogged by certain difficulties which do not yield easily to the usual magic of his touch. The result is a good deal of confusion and an immense and continuing controversy among those few hardy souls who have tried to pick their way through the minefield of his writings on the subject.[1]

Rent, in the final analysis, is simply a payment made to landlords for the right to use land and its appurtenances (the resources embedded within it, the buildings placed upon it and so on). The land, conceived of in this very broad sense, evidently has both use value and exchange value. Can it also, then, have a value? If so, how can the existence of that value be reconciled with theories of value that rest on embodied labour time (such as Ricardo's) or, in Marx's case, on socially necessary labour time?

Improvements embodied in the land are, to be sure, the result of human

[1] Lenin's (1956 edn) *The Development of Capitalism in Russia* and Kautsky's (1970 edn) *La Question agraire* (see also Banaji's (1976) English summary) are the two post-Marx classics. More recent studies of interest are Rey (1973), Postel-Vinay (1974) and Tribe (1977; 1978), all of whom take a very critical line against what they consider to be Marx's more serious errors. Ball (1977) and Fine (1979) bring matters back much closer to Marx's original intent. Edel (1976) usefully reviews the recent attempts to find urban applications for Marx's concepts but does not deal with the French contributions on that subject – see Lipietz (1974), Topalov (1974) and Dichervois and Theret (1979). A good history of bourgeois theories of rent can be found in Keiper *et al.* (1961).

labour. Houses, shops, factories, roads and the like can be produced as commodities and therefore treated as values in course of circulation through the built environment (see chapter 8). A component of rent can then be treated as a special case of interest on the fixed capital or consumption fund. The part of rent that poses the problem is the pure payment to raw land, independent of the improvements thereon. This component Marx refers to as *ground-rent*. We will, unless otherwise specified, treat ground-rent as rent in what follows and assume that the interest on improvements is otherwise accounted for.

Marx insists, of course, that rental payments are not made to land and that rents do not grow out of the soil. Payments of this sort are made to landlords and would be impossible without general commodity exchange, full monetization of the economy and all of the legal and juridical trappings of private property in land. But he is equally aware that this legal basis decides nothing and that the full explanation of rent has to render compatible a payment made ostensibly to land with a theory of value that focuses on labour.

Marx could see quite clearly where Ricardo had gone wrong in seeking answers to this question. But he could not quite figure out how to get over the same difficulty. He had a strong prejudice against admitting the facts of distribution into the heart of his theorizing and was strongly inclined to treat rent as a pure relation of distribution and not of production. But distribution relations can, as the case of interest amply demonstrates, occupy strategic co-ordinating roles within the capitalist mode of production. The circulation of interest-bearing capital does not produce value directly but it helps to co-ordinate the production of surplus value (replete, of course, with all of its contradictions). Could it be, then, that the circulation of capital in search of rent performs an analogous co-ordinating role? I shall later seek to show that a positive answer to this question lies deeply buried within Marx's writings, that the 'proper' circulation of capital through the use of land and therefore the whole process of fashioning an 'appropriate' spatial organization of activities (replete with contradictions) is keyed to the functioning of land markets, which in turn rest upon the capacity to appropriate rent. Like interest-bearing capital, rental appropriation has both positive and negative roles to play in relation to accumulation. Its co-ordinating functions are bought at the cost of permitting insane forms of land speculation. But such an argument is barely discernible within Marx's texts, and he appears extraordinarily reluctant to admit of any positive role for the landlord under capitalism.

His dilemmas here can in part be traced back to his perpetual jousting with classical political economy. The Ricardians depicted landlords as parasites, as useless and superfluous holdovers from the feudal era. Malthus gave them a more positive role, as consumers and therefore as a source of effective demand. Where was Marx to put himself in all of this? He obviously did not want to put himself in Malthus's camp. How could he distance himself from Ricardo without appearing to support Malthus? He therefore overtly sides with Ricardo. But this then presents him with a dilemma. He cannot, on the one hand, treat the landlord as a purely passive, parasitic agent, appropriating surplus value without doing anything in return, and on the other hand provide a theoretical basis for the continued appropriation of rent under capitalism and for the social reproduction of a distinctive class of landed proprietors. When he considers landed property in this last aspect, it is difficult to avoid the conclusion that rent entails something more than a simple relation of distribution and that some kind of relation of production exists either within it or behind it.

He knew full well, of course, that landed property had played a vital role in that initial 'production-determining distribution' which separated labour from means of production in the land. But the suspicion also lurks that 'landed property differs from other kinds of property in that it appears superfluous and harmful at a certain stage of development, even from the point of view of the capitalist mode of production' (*Capital*, vol. 3, p. 622). Behind the ambiguous verb 'appears' lies the more assertive idea that indeed this could be so. And this view gathers some strength as he builds his case. If the dominant class relation is that between capital and labour, then 'the circumstances under which the capitalist has in turn to share a part of the . . . surplus value which he has captured with a third, non-working person, are only of secondary importance' (*Theories of Surplus Value*, pt 2, p. 152). And if that is not explicit enough, he later speaks of the 'reduction *ad absurdum* of property in land' and the total separation of the landowner from control over the land as one of 'the great achievements of the capitalist mode of production' (*Capital*, vol. 3, p. 618).

We might well wonder, of course, what compels capital to share its pickings with so diminished a social group. But, more disturbing, we then read on the very same page that ground-rent is that 'form in which property in land . . . produces value' and, even more surprisingly, that 'here, then, we have all three classes — wage labourers, industrial capitalists, and landowners constituting together, and in their mutual opposition, the framework of modern society.' And this last thought is expounded upon in the chapter on 'Classes', which Engels places at the very end of *Capital*. It seems passing strange to be told, at the end of a work that has built an interpretation of the dynamics of capitalism on the basis of the class relation between capital and labour, that in fact three classes constitute the 'framework of modern society'.

In what sense, then, can property in land 'produce value' when land itself is by definition not a source of value? And what is the exact class position of landowners within a capitalist mode of production stripped of all 'distorting and obfuscating irrelevancies'? Does rent pit landed property against capitalists, workers or both? The appropriation of rent, in short, entails the exploitation of who, by whom?[2]

The answers to such questions are all the harder to spot because of a world of appearance that makes it seem as if various factors of production – land, labour and capital – are endowed with magical powers that make them the source of value. Marx, as might be expected, is at his pungent best in dealing with such fetishistic notions (*Theories of Surplus Value*, pt 3, pp. 453–540; *Capital*, vol. 3, ch. 48). Yet he also concedes that it is 'natural' for producers 'to feel completely at home in the estranged and irrational forms of capital-interest, land-rent, labour-wages, since these are precisely the forms of illusion in which they move about and find their daily occupation'. Individual producers can afford to care only about the profit they make over and above what they pay out on wages, interest, rent and constant capital (*Capital*, vol. 3, pp. 830–5). The rent they pay is real enough, and their response to what indeed may be a fetishistic category has real enough effects which have to be taken into account. Armed with the theory of value, it is easy to strip away the necessary fetishisms that invest daily experience, but matters do not end there. And the theoretical challenge is to define a coherent theory of ground rent within the framework of value theory itself. This is the immediate task at hand.

I shall take on the problem in stages. I shall begin with the use value of land. This might be thought a somewhat incongruous starting point, but it poses no dangers if it is well understood that material qualities are here being examined in their social aspect. I shall then examine the role of landed property in the history of capitalism in order to try and identify the truly capitalist form of landownership. The first two sections lay the basis and necessary background to dissect the forms of rent, the contradictory role of landed property under the capitalist mode of production and the consequent distributional struggles that arise between capitalist and landlord. The final section considers landed property as a form of 'fictitious capital' operating in land markets, and attempts, on this basis, a full justification for the existence of ground rent by virtue of the co-ordinating functions that it performs in allocating land to uses and shaping geographical organization in ways reflective of competition and amenable to accumulation. These positive roles of landownership also have negative consequences. But the social basis for landowners as a faction of capital in general is thereby defined.

I THE USE VALUE OF LAND

The land, together with the labourer, constitute the 'original sources of all wealth' (*Capital*, vol. 1, p. 507). In its virgin state, the land is the 'universal

[2] Rey (1973, p. 24) poses the problem in this way.

subject of human labour', the 'original condition' of all production, and the repository of a seemingly infinite variety of potential use values 'spontaneously provided by Nature' (*Capital*, vol. 1, p. 178; *Theories of Surplus Value*, pt 2, pp. 43–4). Such a universal conception is only helpful, however, to the degree that it indicates conditions that capital must either cope with or modify. The use value of land and its appurtenances has to be considered in relation to the capitalist mode of production.

Private persons can, under the laws of private property, acquire monopoly powers 'over definite portions of the globe, as exclusive spheres of their private will to the exclusion of all others' (*Capital*, vol. 3, p. 615). Since the land is monopolizable and alienable, it can be rented or sold as a commodity. Certain circumstances arise in which clear private property rights are hard to establish – air, moving water and the fish that swim therein, for example. We will not consider such problems here.

The land itself is also a non-reproducible asset. By contrast, some (but not all) the use values embodied in it are not only reproducible but can be created through commodity production (factories, embankments, houses, shops, etc.). The quantity of land in a state fit for certain types of human activity can be altered through the creation of use values in the built environment. But the total quantity of land on the earth's surface cannot be significantly augmented or diminished through human agency (although reclamation from the sea can be important locally).

When we push beyond these very general points, an array of fine distinctions confronts us between, for example, wholly 'natural' use values and those created by human action, or land use actively for production and extraction versus land used simply as space (*Capital*, vol. 3, p. 774). Marx argues that landed property 'demands its tribute' in all of these senses. But we have to start somewhere, so we begin with the last of these distinctions.

1 *The land as the basis for reproduction and extraction*

The use values land contains can be extracted (as with minerals), mobilized in production as 'forces of nature' (wind and water power, for example) or used as the basis for continuous reproduction (as in agriculture and forestry). In the first two cases we can designate the use values as *conditions* or *elements* of production. Agriculture is somewhat special. The land here not only supplies a stock of nutrients to be converted by plant growth and animal husbandry into food and sundry raw materials, but it also functions as an *instrument* or *means of production*. The production process is partially embodied *within* the soil itself.[3]

[3] Marx's terminology is not always consistent. He variously refers to the land as a *condition of production*, a *precondition for production*, an *element of production*, an *element within which production takes place*, an *instrument* or *means of production*

This material condition is not the basis for rental appropriation. Much of Marx's analysis of agricultural rent is given over to attacking such an erroneous conception and explaining how it could arise. The distinction between *produced* and *unproduced* means of production suggests a valid basis for a distinction between profit on capital (regarded as produced means of production) and rent on land (considered as unproduced means of production). This is, Marx argues, one of the most pervasive of all illusions within bourgeois political economy (*Capital,* vol. 3, p. 825). It implies that 'rents grow out of the soil' and that land has value even though it is not the product of human labour – propositions that are as inconsistent with Ricardo's value theory as they are with that of Marx. But we see how such an illusion can arise. We attribute social meaning directly to purely use value distinctions. Marx argues, by way of contrast, that the hallmark of landed property under capitalism is the total separation of the 'land as an instrument of production from landed property and the landowner' (p. 618). Only capital commands the means of production, no matter whether these means are embodied in the soil or in the factory. This presumes, of course, that intermediate forms of landownership (such as peasant proprietorship) have given way to a purely capitalist mode of production on the land (see section II below).

The use values in and on the land are 'free gifts of Nature', and vary greatly as to their quantity and quality. The physical productivity of labour power therefore varies according to natural circumstances, which are monopolizable and non-reproducible. Relative surplus value (excess profits) can accrue to capitalists with access to use values of superior quality – easily mined mineral resources, powerful 'forces of nature' or land of superior natural fertility. The relative surplus value is a *permanent fixture,* however, as compared with the normal case where it is achieved only fleetingly through ephemeral technological advantage (*Theories of Surplus Value,* pt 2, p. 95). This distinction is important in understanding the basis for rent.

The illustration Marx provides is instructive. One capitalist uses a waterfall (not a product of human labour), while another uses coal (a product

---

(*Theories of Surplus Value,* pt 2, pp. 43, 48, 54, 245; *Capital,* vol. 3, p. 774). What he had in mind by these distinctions is best illustrated in the following passage: 'Actual agricultural rent . . . is that which is paid for permission to invest capital . . . in *the element land.* Here land is the *element of production.*' As such, it may be regarded as a form of constant capital (either fixed or circulating). 'The powers of nature which are paid for', in the case of rent for buildings, waterfalls, etc., 'enter into production as a *condition,* be it as productive power or as *sine qua non* [by which Marx evidently means as space pure and simple], but they are not the *element* in which this particular branch of production is carried on. Again, in rents for mines, coal-mines, etc., the earth is the reservoir, from whose bowels use values are to be torn. In this case payment is made for the land, not because it is the *element* in which production is to take place, as in agriculture, not because it enters *into* production as one of the conditions of production, as in the case of the waterfall or the building site, but because it is a reservoir containing the *use values.*' (*Theories of Surplus Value,* pt 2, p. 245) of human labour) to power machinery. Any capitalist can go on the market and purchase coal and machinery. But the waterfall 'is a monopolizable force of Nature which . . . is only at the command of those who have at their disposal particular portions of the earth and its appurtenances.' Furthermore, manufacturers who own waterfalls are in a position to 'exclude those who do not from using this natural force, because land, and particularly land endowed with water power is scarce' (*Capital*, vol. 3, p. 645). Such manufacturers stand to receive excess profits in perpetuity by virtue of the natural advantages they enjoy. Landowners can appropriate these excess profits and convert them into ground-rents without in any way diminishing the average profit.

The level of excess profit (and, by implication, the rent) is fixed by the difference between the individual productivity and the average productivity and price of production prevailing within the industry. The natural force, it must be stressed, 'is not the source of surplus profit, but its natural basis', and the excess profits would exist even without their conversion into ground rent. The circulation of capital, rather than landed property, is the active factor in this process. If, however, the average price of production falls below that achievable even with the aid of Nature's 'free gifts', then the latter will be rendered useless (in the way that steam engines eliminated the water wheel). The 'permanence' of excess profits must therefore be judged relative to the general processes of technological change.

This brings us to the general question of the modification of 'natural forces' by human action. The soil is capable of modification in ways that are very important for agricultural productivity. This form of technological change within the soil as means of production has some very peculiar characteristics. It can usually be accomplished only slowly – a fact that in Marx's view accounts at least in part for the relatively slow pace of technological change in agriculture compared with industry (*Theories of Surplus Value*, pt 2, pp. 93–6). Nevertheless, capital 'may be fixed in the land, incorporated in it either in a transitory manner, as through improvements of a chemical nature, fertilisation, etc., or more permanently, as in drainage canals, irrigation works, levelling, farm buildings, etc.' (*Capital*, vol. 3, p. 619). This capital is called *land capital*, a particular form of fixed capital which circulates and is presumably used up in the normal way (see chapter 8). This fixed capital ought to earn at least interest.

Consider, now, the implications of such investments for the fertility of the soil. Fertility, we should begin by noting, 'always implies an economic relation, a relation to the existing chemical and mechanical level of development in agriculture, and, therefore, changes with this level of development'. Fertility can be improved 'by an artificially created improvement in soil composition or by a mere change in agricultural methods' (*Capital*, vol. 3, p. 651). Consider the first of these two possibilities. Two peculiarities immediately stand out. Successive investments have the capacity to build upon one another and generate permanent improvements. Successive investments in machinery, by way of contrast, do not have such an effect. Indeed, technological revolutions in industry often entail the devaluation of old equipment. Soil improvements are not subject to devaluation in the same way. The soil, 'if properly treated, improves all the time' (p. 781). The circumstances that destroy the productive capacities of the land are not, therefore, comparable with those which reign in industry (p. 813).

The second peculiarity arises because permanent improvement on one plot of land usually means creating 'such properties as are naturally possessed by some other piece of land elsewhere' (*Capital,* vol. 3, p. 746). Capital creates in one place conditions of production that are free gifts of nature elsewhere. The boundary between interest on capital and rent on land appears somewhat blurred until the investment is amortized, when any permanent improvement becomes a free good and therefore in principle no different from free gifts of nature. 'The productivity of the land thus engendered by capital, later coincides with its "natural" productivity, hence swells the rent.' On these grounds, Marx disputes Ricardo's view that rent is a payment for the 'original and indestructible powers of the soil', because these powers are as much the product of history as they are of nature.

2 *Space, place and location*

Rent is that theoretical concept through which political economy (of whatever stripe) traditionally confronts the problem of spatial organization. Rent, we will later show, provides a basis for various forms of social control over the spatial organization and development of capitalism. This can be so because land serves not only as a means of production but also as a 'foundation, as a place and space providing a basis of operations' – space is required as an element of *all* production and human activity' (*Capital,* vol. 3, pp. 774, 781).

Marx did not tackle the use value of space systematically, but there are various scattered references to it throughout his work. His treatment of it in *Capital,* for example, is founded in pure common sense, untrammelled by appeal to any particular theory of space. But certain theoretical principles are implied: exactly which is a question that has bemused and divided those concerned with the problem ever since.[4] The difficulties are more apparent

---

[4] Of all major Marxist writers, Henri Lefebvre (e.g., 1974) has been by far the most persistent in his striving to incorporate a spatial dimension into Marxian thought. Lipietz (1977) attempts a more conventional 'spatialization' of the theory of accumulation, while a special issue of the *Review of Radical Political Economics* (vol. 10, no. 3, 1978) on uneven regional development broaches similar themes. Considerable controversy has arisen, particularly among geographers, over the problem of 'spatial

than real. Their solution lies readily to hand if we go back to the basic
concepts of use value, exchange value and value.

A use value, recall, is 'not a thing of air' but is limited by the 'physical
properties of commodities'. Spatial properties of location, situation, shape,
size, dimension, etc., are to be viewed, in the first instance, as material
attributes of all use values without exception. And we could, if we wished,
equalize all objects 'under the aspect of space', distinguish them 'as different
points in space' and examine the spatial relations between them (*Theories of
Surplus Value,* pt 3, p. 143). But the material properties of use values 'claim
our attention only in so far as they affect the utility . . . of commodities'. The
social aspect of use values is what counts in the end. But we cannot understand this social aspect to use values under capitalism independently of
exchange and the formation of values.

We note, then, that commodities 'have to be brought to market' for
exchange (although trading of titles can take place at one location), and that
this eventually involves a physical movement in space. The latter is essential
to the formation of prices. To the degree that exchange becomes general and
is perfected, so the circulation of commodities 'bursts through all restrictions
as to time, place and individuals'. Prices form which reflect production
conditions at diverse locations under varied conditions of concrete labour.
The exchange process is, in short, perpetually abstracting from the specifics of
location through price formation. This paves the way for conceptualizing
values in place-free terms. The abstract labour embodied at particular locations under specific concrete conditions is a social average taken across all
locations and conditions.

The accumulation of capital involves the expansion of value over time. At
first blush it would seem that space can be safely laid aside in such an analysis.
But stripped of its material reference point in both use values and money,
accumulation could be represented only ideally rather than materially. The
pivot upon which the analysis always turns, we saw in chapter 1, is the
relation between use value, exchange value and value. The trick, then, is to set
our understanding of material spatial properties of use values into motion
together with concepts of exchange value and value. The meaning of the
spatial properties of use values in their social aspect can then be unravelled.
We will, in what follows, take certain tentative steps down that path.

The ownership of private property in land confers exclusive power on
private persons over certain portions of the globe. This entails an *absolute*

---

fetishism' – making social relations between people appear as relations between places
or spaces. While all Marxists would agree in principle that class relations are of
paramount importance, the problem still arises as to how and when it is useful to
consider antagonisms between spatial categories, such as town and country, city and
suburb, developed versus 'Third World' and so on, as important attributes of
capitalism (see Peet, 1981; Smith, 1981; Soja, 1980).

conception of space, one of the most important properties of which is a principle of individuation established through exclusivity of occupation of a certain portion of space – no two people can occupy exactly the same location in this space and be considered two separate people.[5] The exclusivity of control over absolute space is not confined to private persons but extends to states, administrative divisions and any other kind of juridical individual. Private property in land, in practice usually recorded through cadastral survey and mapping, clearly establishes the portion of the earth's surface over which private individuals have exclusive monopoly powers.

When commodity producers take their products to market they move them across a space that can best be defined as *relative*.[6] Under this conception of space the principle of individuation breaks down because many individuals can occupy the same position relative to some other point – more than one producer can be exactly ten miles from market, for example – while the metric that prevails within the space can also be altered according to circumstance; distances measured in cost or time are not the same as each other, and both are very different from physical distances (see chapter 12).

Producers in more favoured locations ('more favoured' in this case is measured in terms of lower transport costs) can gain excess profits. These excess profits, like differences in natural fertility, are to be regarded in the first instance as permanently fixed as compared with the usual transitory form of relative surplus value associated with ephemeral technological advantage. It then follows that those who own land in favoured locations can convert the excess profits into ground-rent without affecting the average rate of profit.

But since space is used by everyone – not just producers – we have to consider the implications of 'more favoured' locations from the standpoint of all forms of human activity, including those of consumption. When we leave the realm of strict commodity production, a wide range of social and fortuitous circumstances can come into play. The consumption preferences of the bourgeoisie are, after all, not entirely predictable, shaped as they are by

---

[5] Absolute space in physics refers to a 'container view' of a space that is immutable, everlasting and unchanging. In practice this boils down to postulating a set of fixed co-ordinates through which matter moves. I argued elsewhere (Harvey, 1973, p. 13) that space is 'neither absolute, relative or relational in itself, but it can become one or all simultaneously depending on the circumstances. The problem of the proper conceptualization of space is resolved through human practice with respect to it.' I still hold to this view. In the case being considered here, we view private property or other territorial divisions as the fixed units through which capital circulates. The conceptualization of absolute space makes sense because that is how private property in land is expressed.

[6] The relative view of space has dominated Newtonian absolute space for a hundred years or so in physics, but geographers and other social scientists have picked up on the idea relatively recently (Harvey, 1969, ch. 13). Marx, as usual, was remarkably ahead of his time in clearly acknowledging the relativity of space with respect to exchange processes.

changing tastes, the whims of fashion, notions of prestige and so on. The
seeming incoherence can be reduced somewhat, however, if the implications
for the commodity labour power are quickly spelled out. The cost of reproduction, and therefore the value of labour power, is, given Marx's general
rule on transport costs, sensitive to the cost of getting to and from work. If all
workers receive a flat wage rate, then those who live in 'favoured locations'
have a relative advantage over those who live further away. If the wage is set
at a level needed to ensure the reproduction of the worker who lives furthest
away (as can sometimes happen under conditions of labour scarcity), then all
other workers receive a wage somewhat above value. It then follows that
those who hold land can convert the excess wage into ground-rent without in
any way disturbing the value of labour power. It is important to distinguish
cases of this sort from rack-renting and other secondary forms of exploitation
visited by landowners upon the labourers occupying their lands. In the latter
case, of course, the ground-rent is supplemented by a deduction out of the
value of labour power in exactly the same way that powerful landed interests
can, under certain circumstances, gain excess rents at the expense of
capitalist's profit.

The case of labour power illustrates that we can, in principle at least,
investigate each of the multitude of different activities within capitalism, seek
to discover the rational basis of each and the locational principles that guide
them, and so establish the basis for rental payments in different lines of
activity. Some – like wholesaling, retailing and money and financial functions
– are more amenable to treatment on this basis than others – for example the
location of administrative, religious, 'ideological' and scientific functions. In
the final analysis, however, the use value of a particular location can not be
understood independently of the variegated needs of a whole host of activities
with which Marx was only peripherally concerned, and which he therefore
excluded from his analysis (*Theories of Surplus Value*, pt 2, p. 270).[7]

The appropriation of rent on the basis of location becomes a much more
complicated affair as soon as we allow that relative advantages, though a
permanent feature of any landscape, are perpetually altering with respect to
particular land parcels. They alter 'historically, according to economic
development, . . . the installation of means of communication, the building of
towns, etc., and the growth of population' (*Theories of Surplus Value*, p.
312). The changing capacity of the transport industry is particularly
important since 'the relative differences may be shifted about . . . in a way that
does not correspond to the geographical distances' (*Capital*, vol. 2, pp.
249–50). The net effect in some cases may be to even out differences arising
from location, but in others exactly the opposite result can be achieved
(*Capital*, vol. 3, p. 650). The details of how and why this must necessarily

---

[7] What a genuinely Marxist approach to location theory would look like has yet to
be worked out. Some aspects of this problem will be taken up in chapter 12.

occur under capitalism will be taken up in chapter 12. For the moment, all we need to know is that locational advantages for specific land parcels can be altered by human agency. Which means that the action of capital itself (particularly through investment in transport and communications) can create spatial relationships. The spatial attributes of use values can then be brought back into the realm of analysis as socially created qualities and, therefore, as a fit and proper subject for full investigation in relation to the operation of the law of value.

3 Location, fertility and prices of production

The effects of location and differentials in 'natural productivity' intermingle in numerous and confusing ways, which sometimes reinforce and sometimes counteract each other. Fertile but poorly situated land may be abandoned in favour of less fertile but more favourably located land:

> The contradictory influences of location and fertility, and the variable-ness of the location factor, which is continually counterbalanced and perpetually passes through progressive changes tending towards equali-sation, alternately carry equally good, better or worse land areas into new competition with the older ones under cultivation. (*Capital,* vol. 3, p. 769)

But conversely, a mass of fertile soil can have a 'neighbourhood' or 'spillover' effect on poorer soil situated nearby: 'if inferior soil is surrounded by superior soil, then the latter gives it the advantage of location in comparison with more fertile soil which is not yet, or is about to become, part of the cultivated area' (*Capital,* vol. 3, p. 669).

Different activities also exhibit a different degree of sensitivity to location as opposed to the other qualitative attributes of particular sites. Agriculture is sensitive, generally speaking, to both fertility and location jointly, whereas factories, houses, shops, etc., are primarily sensitive to location. But the qualities of terrain – drainage, slope, aspect, healthiness, etc. – are not irrelevant to the siting of the latter, while certain kinds of industrialized agriculture depend scarcely at all upon the natural productivity of the land they occupy. 'The more agriculture develops,' Marx comments, 'the more all its elements enter into it as commodities' from outside and, by implication, the more it is liberated from specific qualities of the soil (*Theories of Surplus Value,* pt 2, p. 54).

Different activities compete with each other for the use of space. Marx explicitly abstracts from this process (*Theories of Surplus Value,* pt 2, p. 270), although he somewhat unwisely ventures the opinion (more or less as an aside) that the rent on all non-agricultural land 'is regulated by agricultural rent proper' (*Capital,* vol. 3, p. 773). He should have regarded the rents as simultaneously determined by many competing activities. Behind this conception lies the idea that landowners are indifferent as to whether the rent they receive is a deduction out of wages of labour, out of excess or even average profit of capital, or out of any other form of revenue. And Marx himself is certainly well aware that 'poverty is more lucrative for house-rent than the mines of Potosi ever were for Spain', and complains bitterly at how the 'monstrous power' of landed property is 'used against labourers . . . as a means of practically expelling them from the earth as a dwelling place' (*Capital,* vol. 3, p. 773).

More serious difficulties arise when we consider the manner in which the investment of capital modifies both spatial relations and the qualities of land at particular sites. Capital has, in this, a certain amount of choice. Money can be put to improving transportation and so opening up more fertile lands for exploitation, or it can be put to improving the inferior lands already in cultivation. The former strategy, because it deals with the relativity of space, will likely benefit many landowners, whereas the latter is more exclusively confined to individual owners. Leaving aside the obvious social problems that arise from such a difference, the complex interaction effects of investments on two aspects of use value that sometimes reinforce and sometimes contradict each other remains to be worked out. And if Marx had bothered to do so in any detail he would have picked up on certain aspects of rent that are now missing from his analysis.

As it is, Marx bypasses all such difficulties by eliminating the question of location and concentrating solely on differentials in fertility as these affect agriculture only. This simplification permits him to derive a very important principle. The price of production of agricultural commodities is usually fixed by the cost of production on the worst soil plus the average rate of profit. This is a radical departure from price determination in industry, where it is the social average that prevails. The departure can be justified on two grounds. First, 'naturally based' differentials in productivity cannot be eliminated by technological change in the same way as in industry (excess profits are a permanent fixture for those blessed with more fertile soils). Secondly, an expansion in agricultural production entails drawing more inferior lands into cultivation and intensifying production on superior soils only when that is more profitable. Whichever the case, the worst soil must always realize the average rate of profit if it is to stay in cultivation. This is the principle that Marx is most anxious to establish. It forms the basis for much of his theory of rent.

He recognizes, of course, that circumstances are by no means this simple. He presumes an equilibrium in demand and supply of agricultural commodities, for example. And he assumes also that the interaction effects between fertility and location, and the differential patterns of capital investment in both, as well as the competition among different lines and branches of production for the land, have, in the final analysis, no effect upon the theoretical coherence of the principle. In section III below we will return to consider the validity of such assumptions. But first we must consider the social position of landowners, with their exclusive rights to certain portions of the globe, under the social relations of capitalism.

II LANDED PROPERTY

'In each historical epoch,' Marx writes, 'property has developed differently and under a set of entirely different social relations' (*Poverty of Philosophy*, p. 154). The rise of capitalism entailed the 'dissolution of the old economic relations of landed property' and their conversion to a form compatible with sustained accumulation. From this standpoint capital can be regarded as 'the creator of modern landed property, of ground rent'. The latter has to be understood as a 'theoretical expression of the capitalist mode of production' (*Grundrisse*, pp. 276–7; *Capital*, vol. 3, p. 782). The hallmark of landed property under capitalism, Marx argues, is such a thorough dissolution of 'the connection between landownership and the land' that the landlord, in return for a straight monetary payment, confers all rights to the land as both instrument and condition of production upon capital. The landlord thereby assumes a passive role in relation to the domination of labour (which control of the land allows) and to the subsequent progress of accumulation (*Capital*, vol. 3, pp. 617–18, 636). It follows that, although 'the income of the landlord may be called rent, even under other forms of society', the meaning of that payment 'differs essentially from rent as it appears in [the capitalist] mode of production' (p. 883). The appropriation of rent can then simply be defined as 'that economic form in which landed property is realised under capitalism' (p. 634).

The actual history of the transformation of feudal rent into capitalist ground-rent, of the subjection of feudal property to the capitalist mode of production, is strewn with complexities generated to a large degree out of the cross-currents of class struggle and social conflict.[8] Difficulties also arise because 'capitalist production starts its career on the presupposition of landed property, which is not its own creation, but which was already there before it' (*Theories of Surplus Value*, pt 2, p. 243). The original conditions of landownership varied greatly, and some, such as those in England, appeared easier to transform than others.[9] Since the separation of labour from the land

[8] Rey (1973) and Tribe (1978) provide accounts of the origins of landed property, while the general problem of the transition from feudalism to capitalism is taken up in Dobb (1963) and Hilton (1976).

[9] Rey (1973, p. 73) argues that feudal property, subject to the influence of money and commodity production, was forced to create conditions for capitalist production (such as the expulsion of peasants from the land) because it was forced to increase its rents.

as a means of production was (and still is) an essential precondition for the formation of wage labour, the form of pre-capitalist landownership played just as important a role in primitive accumulation as capital played in the creation of the modern form of landed property. Private property in land, like merchant's capital and usury, is as much a prerequisite as a product of the capitalist mode of production:

> The history of landed property, which would demonstrate the gradual transformation of the feudal landlord into the landowner, of the hereditary, semi-tributary and often unfree tenant for life into the modern farmer, and of the resident serfs, bondsmen and villeins who belonged to the property into agricultural day labourers, would indeed be the history of the formation of modern capital. (*Grundrisse,* p. 252)

Marx's general version of this history can be divided into two phases. In the first, feudal labour rents are transformed into rent in kind and finally into money rents. This transformation presupposes 'a considerable development of commerce, of urban industry, of commodity production in general, and thereby of money circulation' (*Capital,* vol. 3, p. 797). The law of value begins to regulate prices through market exchange. The monetization of feudal rents opens up the possibility for leasing out land in return for money payments and, finally, to the buying and selling of land as a commodity. Urban-based capital can penetrate the countryside and transform social relationships there. To the gentler processes of monetization can be added the more grasping practices of the usurer (who does much to loosen the grip of traditional landholders on their lands) and, finally, violent expropriation (with or without the sanction of the state):

> The spoliation of the church's property, the fraudulent alienation of the State domains, the robbery of the common lands, the usurpation of feudal and clan property, and its transformation into modern private property under circumstances of reckless terrorism, were just so many idyllic methods of primitive accumulation. (*Capital,* vol. 1, p. 732)

But the privatization of land ownership and the formal subjection of the producer to a system of commodity production and exchange does not necessarily achieve that form of landed property which is a *pure* reflection of capitalist relations of production. All kinds of intermediate forms can arise that are perhaps better interpreted, in the manner of Rey, as 'complex articulations' of different modes of production, one upon the other. This does not imply acceptance of Rey's basic conclusion that rent under capitalism can be understood only as a relation of distribution, which reflects a relation of production of another mode of production (e.g. feudalism) with which capitalism is articulated (Rey, 1973, p. 60). Situations arise in the transition to capitalism, however, in which Rey's conception is highly appropriate.

Landowners frequently exploit the labouring producers directly, for example. This is as true for slave economies (the American South prior to the Civil War) as it is for systems of peasant production that have survived into the present era. In the latter case, the landlord has every incentive to extract the maximum rent, not only because this maximizes the landlord's revenues, but also because it forces the peasant to work harder and harder and to produce more and more commodities for the market at ever lower prices (given the increase in supply). The massive exploitation of a rural peasantry by a landlord class is, from this standpoint, entirely consistent with industrial capitalism when it provides cheap food for the urban workers and a cheap supply of raw materials for industry. A powerful alliance can be created between the landed interest and an industrial bourgeoisie on this basis.

But such a form of rural exploitation, like absolute surplus value in general, has its limits. The intermediate forms of production tend to inhibit 'the development of the social productive forces of labour, social forms of labour, social concentration of capital . . . and the progressive application of science' (*Capital,* vol. 3, p. 807). For this reason the intermediate forms ultimately give way to a production system which achieves the real subjection of labour to capital (rather than to the landlord) and which liberates the land from the barriers that inhibit the development of the productive forces. And the only way this can occur is through the complete removal of the landowner from any direct power over the use of the land, over the labour power employed thereon, and over the capital advanced, in return for a money payment.

Marx evidently did not feel too secure in his rendition of how the *capitalist* form of landed property came to be. He was later to claim that he had merely sought to 'trace the path by which, in Western Europe, the capitalist economic system emerged from the womb of the feudal economic system'. He attacked those who transformed 'my historical sketch of the genesis of capitalism into an historico-philosophical theory of the general path of development prescribed by fate to all nations, whatever the historical circumstances in which they find themselves', and freely admitted that 'events strikingly analogous but taking place in different historical surroundings led to totally different results' (Marx and Engels, *Selected Correspondence,* pp. 312–13).

He was, for example, somewhat exercised by the problem of the form landed property took in those countries, such as the United States, where there was no feudalism to replace. His argument here is that, where capital does not find landed property as a precondition, 'it creates it itself', for the very simple reasons that 'the separation of the labourer from the soil and from ownership of land is a fundamental condition for capitalist production and the production of capital' (*Theories of Surplus Value,* pt 1, p. 51; pt 2, p. 310). His chapter on the theory of colonization in the first volume of *Capital* makes the same point. But there are occasional hints that the form that landed property was taking in the United States was somewhat special (*Capital,* vol. 3, pp. 669–72; Marx and Engels, *Selected Correspondence,* pp. 226–8). It is a pity he did not examine this form in greater depth because the United States, as we shall see, is the one country in which land, from the very beginning, was treated in a manner that came closest to that dictated by purely capitalistic considerations (though even here the correspondence was far from exact).

Instead, Marx spent immense energy in his later years tracing the history of landed property in Russia. He was fascinated by the possibility that the Russian village commune might provide the basis for a direct passage to 'the highest communist form of landed property' without going through 'the same process of disintegration as that which has determined the historical development of the West'. Whether this could happen depended, in his view, upon the prior elimination of those 'deleterious influences' – chiefly those of money and merchant capital – that normally assailed such communal forms of property from every quarter. Under conditions of general socialist revolution, the traditional forms of communal property could indeed be the 'mainspring of Russia's social regeneration' (Preface to the Russian edition of the Communist Manifesto; *Selected Correspondence,* p. 340).

But even within the West, Marx had to concede that there was a great deal of historical variation which differentiated the experience of one nation from another and even one region from another. This could be attributed in part to residual features 'dragged over into modern times from the natural economy of the Middle Ages', but also to the uneven penetration of capitalist relations under historical circumstances showing 'infinite variations and gradations in appearance', which demand careful empirical study (*Capital,* vol. 3, pp. 787–93). The actual history of landed property under capitalism has been a confused and confusing affair. It is difficult to spot within that history the logic of a necessary transformation of landed property into its capitalistic form.

These confusions are still with us. They are the focus of great controversies in societies where pre-capitalist elements are strongly entrenched, where landed property exercises a powerful independent influence, and where the alliance between a rural oligarchy and an industrial bourgeoisie still reigns. In these societies, Rey's thesis still holds good, indicating that relationships on the land have been extraordinarily slow to adapt to the dictates of purely capitalist relations of production in many areas of the world.[10]

But the confusions are equally in evidence in advanced capitalist countries. In Britain, as Massey and Catelano (1978) have recently shown, landed property no longer exists (if it ever did) as a unified and relatively homogeneous class interest, but comprises motley and heterogeneous groups ranging all the way from ancient institutions (the Church, the Crown, large aristocratic

[10] Besides Rey (1973), Amin (1976), Laclau (1977) and Taylor (1979) fashion typical arguments from different points of view.

estates), through financial institutions (banks, insurance and pension funds) to a wide range of individual and corporate owners (including workers who own their own homes) and government agencies. This heterogeneity is hard to reconcile with the idea that landlords constitute 'one of the three great classes in capitalist society'. But if we probe hard within this diversity we can begin to spot a central guiding feature in the behaviour of all economic agents, regardless of exactly who they are and what their immediate interests dictate: this is the increasing tendency to treat the land as a pure financial asset. Herein lies the clue to both the form and the mechanics of the transition to the purely capitalistic form of private property in land.

If land is freely traded, then it becomes a commodity of a rather special sort. Because the earth is not the product of labour it cannot have a value. The purchase of land 'merely secures for the buyer a claim to receive annual rent' (*Capital*, vol. 3, p. 808). Any stream of revenue (such as an annual rent) can be considered as the interest on some imaginary, fictitious capital. For the buyer, the rent figures in his accounts as the interest on the money laid out on land purchase, and is in principle no different from similar investments in government debt, stocks and shares of enterprises, consumer debt and so on. The money laid out is interest-bearing capital in every case. The land becomes a form of fictitious capital, and the land market functions simply as a particular branch − albeit with some special characteristics − of the circulation of interest-bearing capital. Under such conditions the land is treated as a pure financial asset which is bought and sold according to the rent it yields. Like all such forms of fictitious capital, what is traded is a claim upon future revenues, which means a claim upon future profits from the use of the land or, more directly, a claim upon future labour.

When trade in land is reduced to a special branch of the circulation of interest-bearing capital, then, I shall argue, landownership has achieved its true capitalistic form. Marx does not reach this conclusion directly, although there are various hints scattered in the text to suggest that land-trading could indeed be treated as a form of fictitious capital (*Capital*, vol. 3, pp. 805−13). Once such a condition becomes general, then all landholders get caught up in a general system of circulation of interest-bearing capital and ignore its imperatives at their peril. Owner-producers, for example, are faced with a clear choice between purchasing the land or renting it from another. How that choice is exercised, under pure conditions of capitalist landownership, should make no difference. In the same way that capitalists can collect interest and profit on their capital when they use their own funds in production, so they can collect rent and profit on their capital if they own the land they use. But the roles are quite separate. A producer, as landowner, can just as easily sell off the land and lease it back from another, or mortgage it to a bank. The rent must be paid either directly to another or indirectly in the form of an income forgone because the producer fails to mobilize the fictitious capital that the land represents and put that money into motion to realize surplus value through production. But this also presupposes a capitalistic form of production upon the land itself (peasant proprietorship has been eliminated, etc.). Furthermore it is clear that the capitalistic form of private property would be unthinkable in the absence of a sophisticated and all-embracing credit system. Marx makes very little of this idea. We will return to it in section VI below.

It is all very well, and undoubtedly useful, to specify the characteristics of landed property as these ought to exist in pure capitalist state. But we ought also to specify the historical process whereby landed property is reduced to such a condition. The ability to alienate and to trade land in no way guarantees that it will be traded as a pure financial asset, and for much of the history of capitalism land has not been freely traded according to such a simple principle. The growth of commodity exchange, the spread of monetary relationships and the growth of the credit system all form contextual conditions favourable to the increasing treatment of land as a financial asset. The attractiveness of land as an investment (its security as well as the prestige that traditionally attaches to ownership of it) has always made it vulnerable to surplus capital. The more surplus capital there is (in both the short term, through overaccumulation, and the long term), the more likely will land be absorbed into the framework of capital circulation in general. The growth of mortgage markets, the taxation of land as a financial asset by the state (which forces monetization) and the whole complex history of primitive accumulation and the monetization of landed property relations (which Marx gives a partial account of in the *Grundrisse*) also play their respective roles. But in the final analysis, it is probably the need to revolutionize the productive forces on the land, to open up the land to the free flow of capital, that forces the reduction of landownership to the holding of a pure financial asset. This implies that traditional forms of rural exploitation (the absolute surplus value extracted from the peasantry) can no longer meet the needs of capital in general (the supply of food and raw materials). The alliance between rural landowners and industrialists becomes an antagonism of the sort that characterized the first half of the nineteenth century in Britain.

The treatment of land as a pure financial asset, and the reduction of landholders to a faction of money capitalists who have simply chosen, for whatever reason, to hold a claim on rent rather than on some other form of future revenue, is not free of its contradictory aspects.[11] The normal condition of ownership of a means of production entails, in the case of land, ownership of a claim upon revenue which attaches to a use value with peculiar qualities (see section I above). Monopoly power over the use of land – implied by the very condition of landownership – can never be entirely stripped of its

---

[11] Some of the more extraordinary episodes of out-of-control land speculation are recounted in Studenski and Kroos (1952).

monopolistic aspects, because land is variegated in terms of its qualities of fertility, location, etc. Such monopoly power creates all kinds of opportunities for the appropriation of rent which do not arise in the case of other kinds of financial asset except under special circumstances. Monopoly control can arise in any sector, of course, but it is a chronic and unavoidable aspect which inevitably infects the circulation of interest-bearing capital through land purchase. The 'insane forms' of speculation and the 'height of distortion' achieved within the credit system (see chapter 10) stand, therefore, to be greatly magnified in the case of speculation in future rents. The integration of landownership within the circulation of interest-bearing capital may open up the land to the free flow of capital, but it also opens it up to the full play of the contradictions of capitalism. That it does so in a context characterized by appropriation and monopoly control guarantees that the problem of land speculation will acquire deep significance within the overall unstable dynamic of capitalism. We will revert again and again to this theme in what follows.

III THE FORMS OF RENT

Marx considered that rent, under capitalism, could take four different forms: *monopoly, absolute,* and two types of *differential* rent. These categories are adapted from classical political economy. Fairly early on in his investigations, Marx declared:

> The only thing I have got to prove *theoretically* is the *possibility* of absolute rent, without violating the law of value. This is the point around which the theoretical controversy has turned from the days of the Physiocrats up till now. Ricardo denies this possibility. I maintain that it exists. (*Selected Correspondence* (with Engels), p. 134)

The odd thing is, however, that differential rent takes up hundreds of pages in *Capital* and *Theories of Surplus Value* while absolute rent is dealt with most summarily. I shall argue that Marx's initial concern for absolute rent was dictated more by his fascination with the contradictions of bourgeois political economy than by deep theoretical considerations, and that his real contribution lies in pushing the theory of differential rent into entirely new terrain.

1 *Monopoly rent*

All rent is based on the monopoly power of private owners of certain portions of the globe. But we can also assume, without contradiction, that users freely compete for plots of land of different quality in different locations and that landowners likewise compete with each other for the rent they can command.

Circumstances sometimes arise, however, in which such competitive conditions do not prevail. Monopoly rents can then be realized. Two different situations appear relevant (*Capital,* vol. 3, p. 775). First, property owners who control land of such special quality or location in relation to a certain kind of activity may be able to extract monopoly rents from those desiring to use that land. In the realm of production, the most obvious example is the vineyard producing wine of extraordinary quality which can easily be sold at a monopoly price. In this circumstance, 'the monopoly price creates the rent'. Marx did not, evidently, think this kind of monopoly rent would be very widespread in agriculture, but suggests that in densely populated areas house and land rents may be explicable only in these terms (*Theories of Surplus Value,* pt 2, pp. 30, 38). Prestige and status locations create all kinds of possibilities to realize monopoly rents from other factions of the bourgeoisie, for example. Secondly, landowners may refuse to release the unused land under their control unless paid such a high rent that the market prices of commodities produced on that land are forced above value. In this instance, which depends upon the scarcity of land and upon the collective class power and position of the landed interest, the rent charged creates the monopoly price. This form of monopoly rent can be important in all sectors and affect the cost of food grains as well as the cost of working-class housing.

In both cases, of course, the monopoly rent depends upon the ability to realize a monopoly price for the product (wine, grain or housing). And in both cases, also, the monopoly rent is a deduction out of the surplus value produced in society as a whole, a redistribution, through exchange, of aggregate surplus value (*Capital,* vol. 3, p. 833). The first case can be eliminated from consideration because, like trade in antiques and works of art, it is of peripheral concern to any study of general commodity production. The second case poses some more general problems, which can best be taken up in relation to absolute rent.

2 *Absolute rent*

The conditions for the existence of absolute rent are not hard to derive given the tools already to hand. We begin by noting the general difficulty of instituting technological change in sectors using land as a means of production (see above, p. 336). Agriculture is the most obvious example. There is, then, a strong likelihood that the value composition of capital in agriculture will be lower than the social average. If a complete equalization of the rate of profit across all sectors is assumed, then the prices of production in agriculture will be well below values (see chapter 2, section III). In other words, a capital of a certain size in agriculture produces greater surplus value than it receives in the way of profit, because sectors contribute to the total social surplus value according to the labour power they employ but receive surplus value according to the total capital they advance. But this supposition rests 'upon the constantly changing proportional distribution of the total social capital among the various spheres of production, upon the perpetual inflow and outflow of capitals', and assumes that no barriers exist to the equalization of the rate of profit. Absolute rent can arise when landed property erects a systematic barrier to this free flow of capital:

> If capital meets an alien force which it can but partially, or not at all, overcome, and which limits its investment in certain spheres, admitting it only under conditions which wholly or partially exclude that general equalisation of surplus-value to an average profit, then it is evident that the excess of the value of commodities in such spheres of production over their price of production would give rise to a surplus profit, which could be converted into rent and as such made independent with respect to profit. Such an alien force and barrier are presented by landed property, when confronting capital in its endeavour to invest in land; such a force is the landlord *vis-á-vis* the capitalist. (*Capital,* vol. 3, pp. 761–2)

It follows that agricultural products can trade above their prices of production, and so yield absolute rent, while selling below or even up to their values. An absolute rent can exist without in any way infringing the law of value. The apparent dilemma that led Ricardo to deny the possibility of absolute rent is neatly overcome. Part of the excess surplus value produced in agriculture by virtue of its labour intensity (lower value composition) is 'filched' (as Marx puts it) by the landlord, so that it does not enter into the equalization of the rate of profit. To be sure, the commodity sells at a monopoly price. But this represents a failure to redistribute surplus value from agriculture to sectors with higher than average value compositions, rather than an active redistribution of surplus value into agriculture, as would be the case under monopoly rent. The level of absolute rent depends upon supply and demand conditions as well as upon the area of new land taken into cultivation. The increase in the price of the product is not the cause of rent, 'but that rent is the cause of the increase in the price of the product', even though the commodity still trades at less than or equal to its value (*Capital,* vol. 3, pp. 762–3).

A number of comments on this conception of absolute rent are in order. First of all, its validity has frequently been attached to the successful resolution of the so-called 'transformation problem' (chapter 2, section III). Marx's 'errors' with respect to the latter, it is sometimes argued, totally destroy his conception of absolute rent. Certainly, the level of absolute rent would depend upon the excess profit available *after* all interaction and feedback effects had been taken into account. Far from disturbing Marx's conception of absolute rent, I believe his approach to the latter sheds light upon the proper interpretation to be put upon the tranformation process.[12] What Marx was after was to identify the rules of distribution of surplus value as these are achieved through social processes (market exchange in particular) and to show that these rules were entirely distinct from, and therefore in potential conflict with, the processes of production of surplus value. Without such a separation and opposition between production and distribution, the whole Marxian interpretation of crises would fall apart. We now encounter a specific version of this opposition. The social necessity for private landowner-ship under capitalism entails distributional arrangements – the capacity to appropriate rent – which are in potential conflict with sustained accumula-tion. What Marx will ultimately seek to show us is that a 'rational' organiza-tion of agriculture is impossible to achieve. The use of the land is necessarily irrational, not merely from the point of view of meeting human wants and needs (for that goes almost without saying), but also from the standpoint of sustained accumulation through expanded reproduction. This is a fundamen-tal contradiction, to which we will return in due course.

The second point is that absolute rent depends upon the power of landlords to create a barrier to the equalization of the rate of profit *and* the persistence of a low value composition of capital within agriculture. If the value composi-tion becomes equal to or higher than the social average, then absolute rent disappears (*Capital*, vol. 3, p. 765; *Theories of Surplus Value*, pt 2, pp. 244, 393). To what extent, then, does the barrier posed by landed property to the free flow of investment discourage agricultural improvement and thereby ensure the basis for the perpetuation of absolute rent? Marx barely hints at such a possibility on one occasion (*Theories of Surplus Value*, pt 2, p. 112), and this seems not to be his main point. Certainly, anachronistic social structures on the land – peasant proprietorship, for example – are associated with a retardation of the productive forces in agriculture, but Marx does not tie absolute rent to the persistence of such structures. He considers it, rather, in relation to large-scale landownership open to capitalistic agriculture. The low value composition of capital in agriculture is attributable more to tech-nological and scientific lag in that sector than to anything else. Once agriculture catches up, which at some point it must, then absolute rent disappears, leaving the landowners to take monopoly rents if they can.[13]

But if landlords are sufficiently powerful to extract absolute rent, then why do they not take monopoly rent also by forcing the price of commodities

[12] Rey (1973, p. 40) invokes Marx's correspondence of 1862 as evidence that the study of rent led Marx to the conception of price of production (as distinguished from values), rather than the other way round.

[13] Rey's (1973) characterization of Marx's theory of absolute rent as a 'fiasco' is partially correct in the sense that there is a lot of elaborate theorization about what ends up being of minor importance. But the tendency to damn all of Marx's rental theory on the basis of such a 'fiasco' is seriously misplaced.

above value to an arbitrary monopoly price? They can, and frequently do, artificially withdraw land from production and so raise the rents on the remainder (*Theories of Surplus Value,* pt 2, pp. 332–3; *Capital,* vol. 3, p. 757). The answer is that landlords may indeed do so under certain conditions. But the implications are fundamentally different. With absolute rent, landlords do not interfere with surplus value production directly. They simply intervene with respect to the distribution of the surplus value produced. Monopoly rent actively curtails surplus value production (though not, of course, when levied on consumption) and forces a redistribution of surplus value from other sectors not into agriculture but into the hands of the landlords. The effects on accumulation are likely to be quite different.

Both kinds of rent depend, however, upon the ability of the capitalist producers to realize monopoly prices. Competition between producers therefore limits the ability of landlords to appropriate either absolute or monopoly rent (the spatial aspects to this competition are dealt with in chapter 12). The capacity of landed property, by virtue of its ownership of land, to erect a barrier to investment does not automatically presume that the users of that land are in a position to charge a monopoly price for the commodities they produce, or that capitalist producers will be willing to pay the exorbitant rents charged. For this reason, Marx argues that 'under normal conditions' even the absolute rent charged in agriculture would be small, no matter what the difference was between price of production and value (*Capital,* vol. 3, p. 771). We can, on this basis, better interpret Marx's rather summary treatment of a problem that initially loomed so important to him. Absolute rent is not the important category. The real theoretical problems, he discovered, lay not so much with Ricardo's failure to admit of absolute rent, but in Ricardo's erroneous interpretation of differential rent. This is the topic to which we must now turn.

3 *Differential rent*

In his early works, Marx evidently viewed Ricardo's formulation of differential rent as reasonably unproblematic. But in *Capital* he begins to discover problems and wrinkles in the Ricardian formulation and generates the outlines of a quite different theory – one that is scarecely hinted at in *Theories of Surplus Value* and is by no means completely worked out in *Capital*. Recent works by Ball and Fine, however, have begun to unravel what it was that Marx was driving at in chapters full of seemingly convoluted argument and elaborate arithmetic calculations.[14]

The conditions necessary to derive differential rent of the first type (DR-1) have already been described. The market value of products in which land is used as a basic means of production is fixed by the price of production on the

[14] In what follows I will lean heavily upon Ball (1977) and more particularly on Fine (1979).

worst land – that land which has the highest price of production because of its particular combination of fertility and location. Producers on better land therefore receive excess profits. If we assume equal applications of capital to land of differing qualities, then the excess profits can be considered a *permanent* feature. They can be converted into DR-1 without affecting market values. In other words, DR-1 is fixed by the difference between individual prices of production and the market value determined by conditions of production on the worst land. This conception is, in principle, no different from that which Ricardo advanced.

True, Marx modifies Ricardo to the extent that he shows that, when the dual effects of location and fertility are taken into account, agriculture can just as easily expand on to more fertile as on to less fertile soils (depending upon where they are located), and that the general Ricardian assumption of diminishing returns in agriculture was not therefore justified. But, interestingly enough, Marx himself eliminates location from consideration and concentrates solely on fertility in fashioning his argument (*Capital*, vol. 3, p. 651). The exclusion is not entirely innocent. Locational advantages are as important to certain branches of industry as they are to agriculture, and this undermines the uniqueness of the agricultural case. It also happens that the 'permanence' of locational advantage is perpetually in the course of alteration through investment in transportation and the shifting geographical distribution of economic activity and population. Locational advantages therefore alter for reasons that may have nothing to do with agriculture *per se* and that are, in any case, generally outside the control of individual producers. Changes occur as the result of social processes of great complexity and generality, although we should note the important role played by speculation in land rents (of all sorts). But Marx eliminates speculation (*Capital*, vol. 3, p. 776) as well as location and competition of different uses from the picture. We will take these matters up in section VI, below.

DR-1 is easy to interpret given such simplifying assumptions. It reflects the material conditions that make fertility differentials permanent features to production. Landed property, which appropriates the DR-1, assumes a neutral position with respect to the determination of market value and can therefore be exonerated from all blame for lagging accumulation or any other social ills.

This interpretation undergoes substantial modification when we introduce the second form of differential rent (DR-2) into the picture. It is fairly easy to set up a version of DR-2 in isolation from DR-1. It simply expresses the effects of differential applications of capital to lands of equal fertility. But Marx insists that DR-1 must always be viewed as the *basis* for DR-2, while the whole thrust of his enquiries is to discover exactly how the two forms of rent 'serve simultaneously as limits for one another' (*Capital*, vol. 3, p. 737). The relationships between the two forms of rent are, in the end, what count. And these relationships are not so easy to untangle. It is here that Marx departs most radically from Ricardo and makes his original contribution to the theory of rent in general.

We begin, however, with the simplest case. If land is of equal fertility everywhere (and location has no effect), then DR-1 would not exist. If all producers invest exactly the same amount of capital on their land – call this the 'normal' capital invested – then there would be no DR-2 either. But if some producers invest more than the 'normal' capital, and gain returns to scale on the capital they invest, then their individual price of production will be lower than the market value fixed by the application of the 'normal' capital. All or some of this difference may then be appropriated as DR-2.

We are here dealing with the flow of capital organized by producers using land as a means of production. We assume that agriculture is completely organized on a capitalist basis, and that 'no soil yields any produce without an investment of capital, (*Capital*, vol. 3, p. 704). The problem is then to understand the logic that guides the flow of capital into agriculture given the peculiar conditions that attach to land as a means of production and the phenomenon of private landownership. This is, evidently, the most important of all the tasks we face in constructing the theory of ground-rent in its distinctively capitalist form. Here capital, conceived of as a flow of value, is confronted with the peculiar circumstance that it must flow actively through the soil itself (which is owned by another) in order to be realized as surplus value.

We can immediately enter certain observations. The flow of capital will be partly dependent upon the pace of accumulation and concentration of capital within agriculture, but it will also be highly sensitive to the existence of a credit system and to the general conditions that prevail within capital markets – 'in periods of stringency it will not suffice for uncultivated soil to yield the tenant an average profit', whereas 'in other periods, when there is a plethora of capital, it will pour into agriculture even without a rise in market price' (*Capital*, vol. 3, p. 770; cf. pp. 676, 690). For the sake of simplicity we will hold these external conditions constant, although the connection between the tendency towards overaccumulation (chapter 7) and the creation of fixed capital improvements in agriculture (chapter 8) should be noted as of great potential importance. We should also mark the possibility for some peculiar forms of circulation that arise when, as sometimes happens, landlords are also the financiers. In such cases, the money rents landlords appropriate may be circulated directly back into agriculture as credit. The landlord then receives both rent and interest while the producer is confined to profit of enterprise, which, under particularly repressive conditions, may end up being more like a managerial wage.

More important for our present purpose, however, is to consider the implications of shifts in the 'normal' flow of capital. This, Marx argues, can alter 'gradually' as the result of successive investments – 'as soon as the new method of cultivation has become general enough to be the normal one, the price of production falls' (*Capital,* vol. 3, p. 706). The basis for DR-2 is therefore likely to be eroded with the passage of time. Since DR-2 is the product of shifting flows of capital on to the land, it must also be regarded, in the first instance at least, as a *transient,* as opposed to *permanent,* effect. How is it, then, that landlords are in a position to appropriate DR-2? The most obvious, but least interesting, case arises when investments create permanent improvements (because successive investments, as we have seen, can often build upon rather than devalue each other). 'Such improvements, although products of capital, have the same effect as natural differences in the quality of the land' (p. 707). But what happens is that investment destroys the 'equal fertility' assumption and so creates a basis for the appropriation of DR-1. Fertility is, after all, a social product. DR-2 is converted directly into DR-1.

The more interesting cases arise because DR-2 'at any given moment occurs only within a sphere which is itself the variegated basis of differential rent 1' (*Capital,* vol. 3, p. 677). And we here find that DR-2 can be appropriated only on the *basis* of DR-1. It is the latter that converts the otherwise transient qualities of the former into permanent enough effects to allow a rental appropriation to occur. Let us see how this can be.

Since fertility always implies 'an economic relation', it changes with the 'level of development' (*Capital,* vol. 3, p. 651; above, p. 336). The worst soil cannot be identified, therefore, independently of the application of the 'normal' capital (and the technology and methods that go along with it). But the 'normal' capital must also vary according to the nature of the soil (what is 'normal' for heavy clay soils would not do for light loams, assuming the same commodity is produced). The concept of 'normal' capital becomes as variegated as the variegated fertilities to which that capital is applied. The 'normal' case is, therefore, the unequal application of capital to soils of unequal fertility. Marx then considers what happens when an extra investment of capital is made. He considers nine cases, cross-tabulated according to whether the market price is constant, rising or falling and whether the productivity of the second investment in relation to the first increases, declines or remains constant. Depending upon the particular combination, Marx is able to demonstrate situations in which the 'worst soil' goes out of cultivation, remains the regulator, or is replaced by an even more inferior soil. DR-1, which was originally conceived to be the reflection of permanent differentials, now becomes variable according to the condition of supply and demand (as reflected in market price movements) and the productivity of the capital flowing into agriculture. Furthermore, we can now see that even investments of decreasing productivity would lead to a rise in market price only when such investments were made on the worst land (p. 680). Since increasing investments will normally be on the better lands, it is entirely possible that increasing concentration of production on the better lands will, even under conditions where the investments entail diminishing returns, lead to a fall in market prices and a diminution of DR-1, because production on the worst soils ceases altogether (the regulator of market prices shifts to better soils).

There are two immediate implications of all this. First, as Fine (1979, p. 254) puts it, 'there is no presumption that the interaction of DR-1 and DR-2 is simply additive'. We see more clearly how the two forms of rent indeed do 'serve simultaneously as limits for one another'. But by the same token, it also becomes impossible for either landowner or capitalist to separate the two forms of rent, to distinguish what is due to the flow of capital and what is due to the 'permanent' effects of natural differences in fertility. The true basis for the appropriation of rent is rendered opaque. In the end, the landowner appropriates differential rent without knowing its origin. But exactly how the landowner appropriates it does indeed have implications for market prices and the accumulation of capital. And it is here that the second, even more interesting, implication of Marx's argument becomes apparent.

Consider the case of decreasing productivity of additional capital applied to the worst soil. 'Whether the price of production is equalised at the average price or whether the individual price of production of the second investment becomes regulating' depends entirely upon whether the 'landowner has sufficient time until demand is satisfied to fix as rent the surplus profit derived' at the price dictated by the second investment (*Capital*, vol. 3, p. 744). The intervention of landed property here affects market value, and the neutral posture of the landowner with respect to accumulation is undermined.

Consider, by way of contrast, the case of additional capital of decreasing, even negative, productivity moving on to superior soils when the market value remains constant at a level fixed by production conditions on the worst soil. In the absence of rental appropriation, 'additional capital with under-productiveness, or even increasing under-productiveness, might be invested until the individual average price per quarter from the best soils became equal to the general price of production', thus eliminating excess profit and differential rent on the superior soil. 'Under the law of landed property', however, 'the case in which the additional capital produces only at the general price of production would have constituted the limit. Beyond this point, the additional investment of capital in the same land would have had to cease. . . . The equalisation of the individual average price, in the case of under-productiveness, is thereby prevented.' (*Capital*, vol. 3, p. 735) In this case, then, it seems that the intervention of landed property and the appropriation of rent have a beneficial effect in relation to accumulation. They prevent the flow of capital down channels that would otherwise be unproductive of surplus value (though not of profit).

Finally, we contrast the impact of property relations in 'countries with maturer civilisations', where a 'reserve price' of some sort exists on uncultivated lands, with countries in which capital can flow with only the hindrance of clearing costs on to new land. That the latter will lead to extensive forms of investment and the former to intensive forms is obvious (*Capital*, vol. 3, p. 672). However, 'the concentration of capital – upon a smaller area of land increases the amount of rent per acre, whereas under the same conditions, its dispersion over a larger area . . . does not'. Consequently, 'given two countries in which the prices of production are identical, the differences in soil type are identical and the same amount of capital is invested – but in the one country more in the form of successive outlays upon a limited area of land, whereas in the other more in the form of coordinated outlays upon a larger area – then the rent per acre, and thereby the price of land, would be higher in the first country and lower in the second, although the total rent would be the same for both countries' (*Capital*, vol. 3, p. 692). property can have positive, negative or neutral effects upon market prices, the accumulation of capital, the degree of dispersal of production and so on. A subsidiary conclusion is that differential rent can, under certain conditions, arise even on the worst soil (*Capital*, vol. 3, ch. 44).[15] Marx had arrived at such general conclusions, without any evidence to back them up, much earlier. 'Rent,' he wrote, 'may not determine the price of the product directly, but it determines the method of production, whether a large amount of capital is concentrated on a small area of land, or a small amount of capital is spread over a large area of land, and whether this or that type of product is produced.' (*Theories of Surplus Value*, pt 3, p. 515) The appropriation of rent can be variously viewed as socially necessary, totally deleterious or a matter of indifference in relation to the accumulation of capital. This conclusion helps us to understand the contradictory role of landed property and rental appropriation under capitalism.

IV THE CONTRADICTORY ROLE OF GROUND RENT AND LANDED PROPERTY WITHIN THE CAPITALIST MODE OF PRODUCTION

The monopoly of landed property, besides being an 'historical premise', is also a 'continuing basis' for the capitalist mode of production (*Capital*, vol. 3, p. 617). The implication is that the appropriation of rent and the existence of private property in land are socially necessary conditions for the perpetuation of capitalism. The basis of such a social necessity has to be firmly established. We can then explain why the revolutionary force of capitalism, which is so frequently destructive of other social barriers that lie in its path, has left landed property intact (albeit in a transformed state) and permitted the appropriation of rent (a part of the surplus value that would otherwise accrue

---

[15] Fine (1979, pp. 266–8) examines how rent can arise on the worst land.

to capital) by 'a class that neither works itself, nor directly exploits labour, nor can find morally edifying rationalisations' for its continued existence (p. 829). What, in short, is the real social basis for the reproduction of landed property under capitalism?

Marx's answer is clear enough:

> Landed property has nothing to do with the actual process of production. Its role is confined to transferring a portion of the produced surplus value from the pockets of capital to its own. However, the landlord plays a role in the capitalist process of production not merely through the presure he exerts upon capital, nor merely because large landed property is a prerequisite and condition of capitalist production since it is a prerequisite and condition of the expropriation of the labourer from the means of production, but particularly because he appears as the personification of one of the most essential conditions of production. (*Capital*, vol. 3, p. 821)

Let us consider these three roles more carefully.

1 *The separation of the labourer from the land as means of production*

'If the land were . . . at everyone's free disposal, then a principal element for the formation of capital would be missing. . . . The "producing" of someone else's unpaid labour would thus become impossible and this would put an end to capitalist production altogether.' (*Theories of Surplus Value*, pt 2, pp. 43–4) Given the fundamental character of land as an original condition of production, those who work it must somehow be drawn or forced into commodity exchange. The extraction of rent from peasants by landlords plays a vital role in forcing the peasants to part with at least a portion of their product rather than consuming it themselves. But if the full domination of capital over labour is to be achieved, then a wage labour force, a *landless* proletariat, must first be brought into being. Primitive accumulation off the land produces wage labourers. A definite form of landed property fulfils this historical role and continues to fulfil it in so far as the widening and deepening of capitalism on the world stage requires it. When capital encounters situations in which private property in land does not exist, then it must take active steps to create it to ensure the production of wage labour. And the need to deny labour access to the land as means of production in no way diminishes with the advance of capitalism. Indeed, it remains a permanent necessity if the reproduction of the class relation between capital and labour is to be assured.

The barrier that landed property places between labour and the land is socially necessary to the perpetuation of capitalism. But in creating landed property as a barrier to labour, capital also creates barriers to itself. In making the reproduction of wage labour possible, the appropriation of rent also becomes possible. Herein lies one aspect to the contradictory position of landed property under capitalism.

2 Landownership and the principle of private property

Capitalists could organize the separation of labour from the land simply by ensuring that the 'land should not be common property, that it should confront the working class as a condition of production not belonging to it, and this purpose is completely fulfilled if it becomes state property . . . the common property of the bourgeois class, of capital' (*Theories of Surplus Value*, pt 2, p. 44). This state ownership of the land should not be confused with 'people's property', which would effectively abolish the whole basis of capitalist production (p. 104). But there is a serious barrier to state ownership of the land and the abolition of rent. Apart from the practical fact that many members of the bourgeoisie (including capitalists) are landowners, 'an attack upon one form of property . . . might cast considerable doubt on the other form' (p. 44). And the other form is ownership of the means of production from which capital derives its own legal standing and legitimacy. The preservation, and even the enhancement, of private property in land therefore performs an ideological and legitimizing function for all forms of private property; hence, some would argue, the importance of conferring privileges of home ownership (possession of a means of consumption) upon the working class. From this standpoint, we can regard rent as a side-payment allowed to landowners in order to preserve the sanctity and inviolability of private property in general. This ideological and juridical aspect to landed property has important implications, but it is not in itself sufficient to explain either the capitalist form of rent or the contradictions to which the capitalist form of landed property gives rise.

3 Landed property and capital flow

The flow of capital on to and through the land as both condition and means of production is modified in important respects by landed property and the appropriation of rent. While much is made of the 'barrier' that landed capital poses to capital flow and of the negative impacts of rental appropriations on accumulation, it turns out that landed property also has a role to play in forcing the *proper* allocation of capital to land. The difficulty is to ensure the enhancement of this positive role while restricting the negative.

In the case of both monopoly and absolute rent, landed property poses barriers that are hard to justify in relation to the basic requirements of capitalism. The appropriation of these forms of rent must therefore be regarded as a totally negative influence over the proper allocation of capital to the land and, hence, to the formation of valid market prices and the sustenance of accumulation. For this reason it is plainly in the interest of capital in general to keep absolute and monopoly rents strictly within bounds, to ensure that they remain small (as Marx insisted they must be) and of sporadic occurrence.

The most interesting problem arises in the case of the complex interaction between the two forms of differential rent which (see section III, above), can have positive, negative or neutral effects upon the formation of market prices, the concentration–dispersal of capital, and accumulation. Unfortunately, much of the polemic directed against the monopoly and absolute forms of rent and the parasitic and superfluous role of the landowner in such situations has carried over into the discussion of differential rent. The negative aspects of the interventions of landed property have therefore been stressed, while very little attention has been paid to the positive role of co-ordinating the flow of capital on to and through the land in ways broadly supportive of further accumulation. Let us consider landed property in its positive aspect.

One of the 'great achievements of the capitalist mode of production', Marx wrote, was the 'rationalising of agriculture' so that it could operate on a 'social scale' with the 'conscious scientific application of agronomy', capable of generating the surplus agricultural product so vital to the accumulation of capital through industrial production. The achievement of a proper balance in the division of labour between industry and agriculture, and of a proper allocation of the total social labour in society to different lines of production within agriculture, depends crucially on the ability of capital to flow freely on and through the land (*Capital*, vol. 3, pp. 617–18, 635). The form that landed property assumes under capitalism, in contrast to all preceeding or alternative modes of control over the land, appears a superlative set of arrangements totally adapted to capital's requirements. The fact that such arrangements entail the appropriation of ground rent makes no difference. The land is liberated and transformed into an open field for the operation of capital. Marx put it very succinctly in *The Poverty of Philosophy* (p. 159): 'Rent, instead of binding man to Nature, merely bound the exploitation of the land to competition' – and, we may add, to the accumulation of capital.

There is a sense in which the appropriation of differential rent enhances rather than limits competition. By taxing away excess profits that are relatively permanent, the landlord operates to equalize rates of profit between competing producers. To the extent that producers compete, they must do so on the basis of new methods (which, like those in industry, can quickly become general) rather than upon the basis of 'unfair' advantages which are due either to 'free gifts of Nature' or to the inherited results of human endeavours that stretch back over many centuries. When the unfair advantages are eliminated, competition forces producers into further development of the productive forces and further rationalization of production. This principle carries over, as we shall see in section VI below, to the rationalizing of the spatial organization of capitalism through competition.

The trouble is that there is no way to ensure that the appropriators of rent take their due and only their due. The brilliance of Marx's analysis of differential rent now becomes apparent. The complex interactions of DR-1 (owing plainly to the landlord) and DR-2 (at least partially due to capital) make it impossible to distinguish who should get what: the real relations are rendered opaque. The existence of land rent not only binds the use of the land to competition and all the contradictions that flow therefrom, but it also introduces a wholly new kind of difficulty into the processes of reproduction of capitalism. What at first appears as a neat rationalizing device for co-ordinating investment in and on the land becomes a source of contradiction, confusion and irrationality.[16] It is against such a background that we have to interpret the active struggle between landed proprietors and capitalists. A social process of some sort has to fix, openly and clearly, what has become opaque from the standpoint of the real social relations of production.

V   DISTRIBUTION RELATIONS AND CLASS STRUGGLE BETWEEN LANDLORD AND CAPITALIST

The total annual value produced in capitalist society is distributed in the forms of wages, rent, interest, profit of enterprise and taxes. What is the equilibrium share of rent in this total annual value, and how is that equilibrium share determined? The most obvious answer is to appeal to the relative power of the different classes and to see distribution relations as an outcome of class struggle. From the standpoint of landed property, such a struggle is multidimensional because the landowner is pitted against all users of land — capitalists (using the land as means of production or simply as space), peasants, workers, financiers, the state and various other factions of the bourgeoisie. Rent can be appropriated out of revenues (thus giving rise to many secondary forms of exploitation) as well as out of the surplus value directly produced through production. The landlord is presumably indifferent to the particular source as long as the rent keeps rolling in.

Marx's theoretical investigation of ground rent deals only with the relative shares of landlord and capitalist in surplus value produced on the land. But it invites us to look at the evident struggle over distributive shares as an expression of deeper forces which circumscribe the relative powers of the classes involved.

Take the relation between landlords and peasant producers, for example. If the latter are regarded as independent labourers in control of their own

---

[16] This explains an otherwise somewhat confusing theme in *Capital* (vol. 3, pp. 617–22), where landed property is viewed simultaneously as the great rationalizer of agricultural production and as the source of all kinds of deleterious effects.

production process, then landlords exist in a direct relation of exploitation to them and have every incentive to extort as much rent as possible in order to force labour from the peasant and to force expanding commodity production. The struggle between landlord and peasant is directly engaged. Force decides the outcome.[17] The interest of capital, all the while an adequate supply of cheap food and raw materials is achieved, is to ally with landlords and encourage ever higher levels of exploitation on the land.

The situation is very different when landlords appropriate rents from capitalists using the land as means of production. The former could, if powerful enough, appropriate much of the capitalist's profit. But here we encounter limiting circumstances which materially alter the class relations. Landlords cannot compel capitalists to invest in the same way that they can compel peasants to labour. And to the degree that maximizing the extraction of rent diminishes the flow of capital on to the land, it is plainly a self-defeating tactic on the part of the landlord. Indeed, if we look more closely, we see strong incentives for landlords to open up the land to capital flow. The use value of land to its owner, after all, is that it permits the appropriation of rent, and it is the rent per acre that matters. The use value of land to the capitalist is as a means for the production of surplus value: it is the rent in relation to capital advanced and surplus value produced that matters. The difference between the two perspectives permits a 'terrain of compromise' to exist between them. The rate of rent on land can continue to rise, for example, at the same time as the rate of rent on capital advanced remains constant or even diminishes (*Capital,* vol. 3, p. 683). Under certain conditions, the landlord has a strong incentive to remain passive and to minimize the barriers that landed property places to the flow of capital[18]

The relationship between capital and landed property is not reduced thereby to one of perpetual harmony. It is not easy to distinguish, for example, between peasant producers and independent capitalist producers, and landlords are not necessarily sophisticated enough to see the virtue of altering their strategy from maximizing the rent they extract from peasants and adjusting their sights when it comes to capital. Also, the development of social labour 'stimulates the demand for land itself', and landed property acquires thereby 'the capacity of capturing an ever-increasing portion' of the surplus value produced (*Capital,* vol. 3, pp. 637–9). Blessed with such a capacity, what landlord could resist using it? The landlord is perpetually

[17] Landlords attempt to extract the equivalent of absolute surplus value in commodity form rather than directly as labour. The analogy between the landlord–peasant struggle and the struggle over the working day is useful.

[18] The implication that landlords should maximize the extraction of rent from peasants and hold down the appropriation of rent from agricultural capitalists immediately follows. Postel-Vinay (1974) provides a mass of evidence in support of this idea. But Rey misinterprets the significance of the findings and so views them as inconsistent with Marx's theory of rent.

caught between the evident foolishness of taking too little and the penalties that accrue from taking too much.

The same tension hovers over the conditions of contract relating to permanent improvements. Though improvements may be made by the capitalist, they 'become the property of the landowner' as soon as 'the time stipulated by contract has expired'. The interest on buildings, for example, 'falls into the hands of the industrial capitalist, the building speculator, or the tenant, so long as the lease lasts', but afterwards it 'passes into the hands of the landlord together with the land, and [so] inflates his rent.' Herein 'lies one of the secrets of the increasing enrichment of the landowners, the continuous inflation of their rents, and the constantly growing money value of their estates.' But herein also lies 'one of the greatest obstacles to the rational development of agriculture', as well as all other forms of investment in the built environment, because the tenant 'avoids all improvements and outlays for which he cannot expect complete returns during the term of his lease' (*Capital*, vol. 3, pp. 619–22).

The struggle over the length and terms of tenancy and just compensation for capital investment in permanent improvements predictably becomes the central contractual issue in the relation between capital and landowner. And, like the contract over the working day (so central to the relationship between capital and labour), it is ultimately regulated by the state, either by legislation or legal precedent.

The outcome of this struggle has important implications for accumulation. If capital acquires a perpetual right to the permanent improvements capital itself creates, then excess profits become a permanent rather than transitory feature within the competition for relative surplus value. The forces that tie the exploitation of the land to competition are blunted. The allocation of social labour to activities will be distorted in comparison with balanced accumulation. The over-concentration of activities in space will almost certainly result. A variety of serious imbalances will arise within the capitalist accumulation process.

The theory of ground-rent illustrates that such consequences can be avoided only if landed property ruthlessly appropriates the excess profits to be had from any kind of permanent advantage, whether it is created by human agency or not. But if the landlord appropriates too quickly or too savagely, then the stimulus to make investments in the first place is also blunted. Is it possible to identify an equilibrium point between these two contrary requirements? The most obvious point to look is at that time when the investment has been fully amortized. But that point is hard, if not impossible, to identify because the physical lifetime of these investments is exceedingly long while the economic lifetime suffers from all the ambiguities that face the circulation of fixed capital in general (see chapter 8). To the degree that the lifetime of fixed capital is standardized according to the interest rate, and to the degree that rent is assimilated to interest on a form of fictitious capital, so the conflict is regulated by at least some kind of social process (although the interest rate, as we saw in chapters 9 and 10, is not exactly a coherent or contradiction-free regulator).

The evident tensions involved in all of this admit of a variety of possible solutions. Perhaps the most interesting, from the standpoint of the social history of capitalism, is the owner-occupied family farm. Under such a system, producers can be both capitalists and landowners so that the conflict between the two roles seems to disappear. Marx considers such a situation both exceptional and fortuitous (*Capital,* vol. 3, pp. 751–2). It is hard to deny his reasoning. Owner-occupiers are liable for the purchase price of the land, and even when the land has been handed down freehold over many generations the income forgone by virtue of the fictitious capital locked up in the 'value' of the land cannot be cavalierly thrust aside. And in many instances, nominal owner-occupancy conceals a mortgage relation (equivalent to rent) and a credit relation (equivalent to interest on capital loaned for current production), leaving the owner-occupier with profit of enterprise only. To the extent that ownership of land guarantees the circulation of interest-bearing capital, modern forms of owner-occupancy in agriculture simply achieve all that would be expected under the social relations of capitalism. Indeed, some curious forms of circulation can arise here which deserve fuller investigation. If producers grow on contract, perform much of the labour themselves and are heavily indebted to financial institutions for both mortgage payment and credit on current operations, the nominal 'owner-occupier' is probably better regarded as a manager or even a labourer who receives a kind of 'piecework' share of the total surplus value produced. It is important, as always, to penetrate beneath the surface appearance and to establish the real social relations of production that prevail.

While the struggle between capitalist and landlord occurs most obviously on the terrain of (1) the conditions of contract regulating the use of land, (2) the magnitude of rent and (3) the length of lease and compensation for improvements, there are other more general considerations that affect distributional arrangements. Landlord revenues – rents – form part of the general revenues of the bourgeoisie. These revenues can be either hoarded or thrown back into circulation. In the former case the circulation of capital in general stands to be seriously disrupted. In the latter, the revenues can continue to circulate through the purchase of services, luxury goods and so forth, or be converted into money capital, which flows into both production and consumption via the credit system. How the revenues are used has important implications.

Revenues that flow back in the purchase of luxury goods can play an important role in stimulating effective demand, though not, as we have already seen (chapter 3), in solving the 'realization' problem for capital.

Landlords in this case also operate as one of the 'consuming classes' of society whose activities are integrated into the overall dynamics of the circulation of capital. But, given their placement within this system, it is not hard to see their activities as disruptive of the necessary proportionalities between agriculture and industry, between city and countryside and between the production of basic wage goods (food, in particular) and luxury items.

The use of landlord revenues as money capital is more interesting to contemplate. It suggests a strong potential link between landed property and banking – a link that is easily observable and of great importance in capitalist history. It also indicates a powerful potential to mobilize surplus product off the land (by forcing producers into commodity exchange) while centralizing capital, albeit in the hands of landowners, through the appropriation of rent from innumerable small producers. To the degree that landlords use the capital they centralize in productive ways, rather than living off the fat of the land in conspicuous consumption, they play a vital and very central role in the history of accumulation.

Indeed, one of the triumphs of capitalism has been to force upon land-owners such a positive role as a condition for survival. But herein lies a rather more general line of class struggle, because the landed interest was by no means necessarily willing to treat the land under its command as a pure financial asset, nor was it necessarily willing to use the money power it centralized simply as money to be thrown into circulation as capital. But the social power of money was, in the end, destined to dominate over the social power of land. The use of land to acquire money had long been the goal of the most dynamic segments of the landed interest, and in the long run this meant, quite simply, the fusion of landed property with rentiers of all types.[19] The landed interest lost its autonomous and independent role and was necessarily transformed into a faction of capital itself. The historic struggles between the landed and industrial interests in nineteenth-century Britain, and the continuing struggles of like character in many other parts of the world, have to be set against the background of such a necessary transformation which assimilates both within the framework of the circulation of interest-bearing capital. In the process, the share of rent in total surplus value produced is less and less the product of overt class conflict between two quasi-independent social classes and more and more internalized within the logic that fixes the circulation of interest-bearing capital among the various forms of fictitious capital that arise within the capitalist mode of production. Which brings us more directly to how and why interest-bearing capital comes to circulate through land itself.

---

[19] Spring (1963) and Thompson (1963) document the gradual absorption of the British landed aristocracy into the ranks of the bourgeoisie as capitalists, financiers, etc.

VI THE LAND MARKET AND FICTITIOUS CAPITAL

Marx did not undertake any detailed analysis of land markets. He gave priority to constructing the theory of ground rent because this was where he considered the real theoretical challenge lay. But, in the same way that pinning the origins of money to the different forms of value embodied in the commodity does not say everything there is to say about the role of money and credit, so tying the origin of land price to a capitalized ground-rent does not exhaust all of importance that can be said about land markets under capitalism. Land markets exhibit peculiar characteristics and perform important functions. They deserve analysis in their own right.

The theory of ground-rent resolves the problem of how land, which is not a product of human labour, can have a price and exchange as a commodity. Ground-rent, capitalized as the interest on some imaginary capital, constitutes the 'value' of the land. What is bought and sold is not the land, but title to the ground-rent yielded by it. The money laid out is equivalent to an interest-bearing investment. The buyer acquires a claim upon anticipated future revenues, a claim upon the future fruits of labour. Title to the land becomes, in short, a form of *fictitious capital* (see above, pp. 266–70). 'If capital is lent out as money, as land and soil, house, etc., then it becomes a commodity as capital, or the commodity put into circulation is capital as capital' (*Grundrisse,* p. 724). This much we have already established.[20]

The basic forces regulating the price of land and its appurtenances are the rate of interest and anticipated future rental revenues. Movements in the interest rate impose strong temporal rhythms and bring land price movements within an overall framework defined by the relation between the accumulation of capital and the supply and demand for money capital (see chapters 9 and 10). Long-run tendencies towards a falling rate of interest or temporary plethoras of money capital will generally result in enhanced land values (rents remaining constant).

Changing anticipations of future rents, tied to both future capital flows and future labour, likewise affect land and property prices. For this reason even unused land can acquire a price (*Capital,* vol. 3, p. 669). The speculative element is always present in land trading. The importance of this has now to be established, though Marx in general excludes speculation from his purview. He does, however, take up one interesting example. In the case of house building in rapidly growing cities, he notes, the profit from building is extremely small and 'the main profit comes from raising the ground-rent', so

[20] The social incentives to hold land – prestige, symbolic important, tradition, etc., – are also very important in practice, but we exclude them from consideration here because they have no direct root within a pure theory of the capitalist mode of production.

that it is the 'ground-rent, and not the house, which is the actual object of building speculation' (*Capital,* vol. 3, pp. 774–6; vol. 2, p. 234). The holders of land by no means assume a passive stance in this case. They play an active role in creating conditions that permit future rents to be appropriated. The advance of capital and the application of labour in the present ensures an increase in future rents.

This case is of more general significance than Marx appears to have realized. By actively pursuing the appropriation of values, landholders can force production on the land into new configurations and even push surplus value production on a scale and with an intensity that might not otherwise occur. In so doing, of course, they condemn future labour to ever-increasing levels of exploitation in the name of the land itself. The activist role of fictitious capital operating on the land and the contradictions it engenders deserve careful scrutiny. It performs certain important co-ordinating functions and thereby legitimates and justifies the appropriation of rent within the overall logic of the capitalist mode of production.

The circulation of interest-bearing capital through land markets co-ordinates the use of land in relation to surplus value production in much the same way that it helps to co-ordinate allocations of labour power and to equalize the rate of profit across different lines of production in general. The peculiarities of land add some new wrinkles to this process. In practice there is little to force capitalists to forgo the relatively permanent advantages (of fertility or location) they enjoy on a particular plot of land in order to promote a different but higher rent-yielding use, particularly if the benefits to be had from investing in such a change are immediately drawn off in the form of higher rents. The situation changes materially if interest-bearing capital circulates through land markets perpetually in search of enhanced future ground-rents and fixes land prices accordingly. In this case, the circulation of interest-bearing capital promotes activities on the land that conform to highest and best uses, not simply in the present, but also in anticipation of future surplus value production. The landowners who treat the land as a pure financial asset perform exactly such a task. They coerce (by raising rents, for example) or co-operate with capital to ensure the creation of enhanced ground rents. In the case of an activist alliance between landowner and capitalist, the former takes on the role of developer who seeks to capture enhanced rents while the capitalist captures profit.[21] Situations of the sort that Marx notes can then all too easily arise: the enhanced rents far outweigh the profit to be had from direct investment.

By perpetually striving to put land to its 'highest and best use', landowners create a sorting device which sifts land uses and forces allocations of capital and labour that might not otherwise occur. By looking to the future, they also

[21] Lamarche (1976) provides one of the best theorizations of the role of developer from a Marxist perspective.

inject a fluidity and dynamism into the use of land that would otherwise be hard to generate. The more vigorous landowners are in this regard, the more active the land market and the more adjustable does the use of the land become in relation to social requirements – in the present instance, the accumulation of capital.

We can now bring the argument with respect to the role of landownership and rental appropriation under capitalism full circle. Not only is the appropriation of rent socially necessary, but landowners must necessarily take an active role in the pursuit of enhanced rents. There is nothing inconsistent in such behaviour, provided, of course, that the land is treated simply as a financial asset, a form of fictitious capital open to all investors. The freer interest-bearing capital is to roam the land looking for titles to future ground-rents to appropriate, the better it can fulfil its co-ordinating role.

But by the same token, the more open the land market is, the more recklessly can surplus money capital build pyramids of debt claims and seek to realize its excessive hopes through the pillaging and destruction of production on the land itself. Investment in appropriation, so necessary to the performance of these co-ordinating functions, is here, as elsewhere, the 'fountainhead of all manner of insane forms' and the source of potentially serious distortions. Speculation in land may be necessary to capitalism, but speculative orgies periodically become a quagmire of destruction for capital itself.

The significance of these powers of co-ordination, together with their negative consequences, are particularly evident when it comes the problem of spatial organization, a topic Marx also tends to exclude from his theoretical purview, except as a peripheral concern. The land market shapes the allocation of capital to land and thereby shapes the geographical structure of production, exchange and consumption, the technical division of labour in space, the socioeconomic spaces of reproduction, and so forth. Land prices form signals to which the various economic agents can respond. The land market is a powerful force making for the rationalization of geographical structures in relation to competition.

Landowners, furthermore, play an active role in the process of geographical structuring and re-structuring, provided, of course, they treat the land as a pure financial asset. Consider transportation relations. The stimulus to revolutionize these arises out of the need to diminish the circulation time of commodities, to extend markets geographically and so simultaneously to build the possibility for cheapening raw material inputs, expanding the basis for realization while accelerating the turnover time of capital. If rent depends upon relative location, and the relative location stands to be transformed by improved transportation, then transport investment stands to enhance land values in areas proximate to it. Landowners stand to gain (or lose) accordingly. They have a strong vested interest in the where and when of transportation investment. They may even be willing to promote it at a loss (preferably using other people's money or through the agency of the state) in order to benefit from enhanced ground-rents. The English landed interest learned this trick relatively early, and it has remained a basic facet of capitalism ever since.

Landowners are generally drawn to compete for that particular pattern of development, that particular bundle of investments and activities, that has the best prospect of enhancing future rents. Shaping the geographical pattern of use of land to competition depends upon competition among landholders for enhanced rents. The co-ordinations rendered possible by the existence of land markets and price signals are, in this regard, of vital importance.

But the anarachistic character of such competition can have strong negative consequences. Surplus capitals may be put to work in profligate ways; individual landholders, acting in their own immediate self-interest and seeking to maximize the ground-rent they can appropriate, may force allocations of capital to land in ways that make no sense from the standpoint of the overall requirements of accumulation. To this landed property version of the forces that create general disequilibrium under capitalism (see chapter 7) must also be added the particular problems that arise out of the complex interactions of DR-1 and DR-2. These ensure that no one landowner can confine the costs and benefits of the schemes he or she promotes to his or her own plot of land. Taken together, the forces that shape the geography of capitalism through the functioning of land markets are in perpetual danger of dissolving into a nightmare of incoherency and periodic orgies of speculation. Future labour is forced into configurations that are unsustainable (from the point of view of labour, capital or both). The problem is to prevent such a dissolution, while preserving the land market as a basic co-ordinating device.

Capital has only two lines of defence in such situations: monopolization or state control. Neither solution is free of internal contradictions. The monopolization of the land development process through large-scale concentration of landownership permits a coherent process of land development in which the various synergistic effects of investments can be orchestrated to advantage. Herein, incidentally, lies the temptation to connect landownership with high finance – a connection that stretches back over a long period and makes the landed version of 'finance capitalism' historically prior to the industrial capital version which we have already considered (chapter 10).[22] The trouble with this kind of monopolization is, of course, that it opens the possibility to appropriate monopoly rents – a form of appropriation that is in generally inimical to accumulation. The financiers can partially offset this tendency by taking charge of their own account. The credit system structures

[22] Marx considered that the 'glorious Revolution' of 1688 in Britain forged a ruling oligarchy out of a 'natural alliance' between 'the new landed aristocracy' and 'the new bankocracy, . . . the newly-hatched *haute finance*, and . . . the large manufacturers' (*Capital*, vol. 1, p. 724).

the land market to preserve the circulation of interest-bearing capital as a whole. The result is a kind of double co-ordination achieved through the interlocking of the various forms of circulation of interest-bearing capital. The trouble with this solution is that, although land markets may be better co-ordinated, they become more directly exposed to all the problems inherent within the credit system itself.

The final line of defence is the state, which can take on a variety of powers of land use regulation, land expropriation, land use planning and, finally, actual investment, to counter the incoherency and periodic speculative fevers land markets are periodically heir to. While the state can undoubtedly put its stamp on geographical structures, it does not necessarily do so in ways that effectively bind the use of land to competition or the process of geographical re-structuring to the accumulation of capital. Too great a level of state involvement also begins to call into question the whole validity of property rights over the means of production in general as well as over the land.

Capitalism cannot do without land price and land markets as basic co-ordinating devices in the allocation of land to uses. It can merely strive to constrain their operation so as to make them less incoherent and less vulnerable to speculative disorders. Two implications then derive from this general conclusion.

First, land prices could not exist without the monopoly power of private property in land and the capacity to appropriate rent which that power confers. Both rent and private property in land are socially necessary to the perpetuation of capitalism. The necessity for the social reproduction of landed property and for the appropriation of rent has been fully defined. The questions with which we began this chapter are effectively resolved.

There is an important caveat to this argument. Only that kind of land-ownership that treats the land as a pure financial asset will do. All other forms of landed property must give way. The land must become a form of fictitious capital and be treated as an open field for the circulation of interest-bearing capital. Only under such a condition does the apparent contradiction between the law of value and the existence of rent on land disappear. How far capitalist social formations have advanced down such a path is a matter for historical investigation. That the law of value under the capitalist mode of production entails such a transformation process is incontrovertible.

Secondly, land price captures simultaneously the temporality of accumulation (as registered by movements in the rate of interest) and the specificity of material use values distributed in space, and therefore unites both temporal and spatial considerations within a single framework defined by the law of value. But it does not do all this in a passive or neutral manner. Land price must be realized through future rental appropriation, which rests on future labour. The payment of land price by capital therefore condemns labour to very specific activities in particular locations over the time span fixed by the rate of interest – if, that is, the capital advanced in land purchase is not to be devalued. Here we see, once more, how the operation of the law of value constrains living labour. We will take up further implications of this result in chapter 12.

The circulation of interest-bearing capital in land titles plays an analogous role to that of fictitious capital in general. It indicates locational paths for future accumulation and acts as a catalytic forcing agent that reorganizes the spatial configuration of accumulation according to the underlying imperatives of accumulation. The fact that it sometimes forces too hard (beyond the capacity of either capital or labour to bear) or in erroneous directions (because of the inevitable distortions that arise when the circulation of money capital encounters and makes use of the monopoly privileges that attach to private property in land) simply establishes that the land market necessarily internalizes all the fundamental underlying contradictions of the capitalist mode of production. It thereby imposes those contradictions upon the very physical landscape of capitalism itself. Yet it is, at the same time, a vital co-ordinating device in the struggle to organize the use of land in ways that contribute to the production of surplus value and the structuring of capitalist social formations in general.

CHAPTER 12

The Production of Spatial Configurations: the Geographical Mobilities of Capital and Labour

The historical geography of capitalism has been nothing short of remarkable. Peoples possessed of the utmost diversity of historical experience, living in an incredible variety of physical circumstances, have been welded, sometimes greatly and cajolingly but more often through the exercise of ruthless brute force, into a complex unity under the international division of labour. Monetary relations have penetrated into every nook and cranny of the world and into almost every aspect of social, even private life. This *formal* subordination of human activity to capital, exercised through the market, has been increasingly complemented by that *real* subordination which requires the conversion of labour into the commodity labour power through primitive accumulation. This radical transformation of social relations has not progressed evenly. It has moved faster in some places than in others. It has been stongly resisted here and made more welcome there. It has penetrated relatively peaceably in one place and with genocidal violence in another.

It has also been accompanied by physical transformations that are breathtaking in scope and radical in their implications. New productive forces have been produced and distributed across the face of the earth. Vast concentrations of capital and labour have come together in metropolitan areas of incredible complexity, while transport and communications systems, stretched in far-flung nets around the globe, permit information and ideas as well as material goods and even labour power to move around with relative ease. Factories and fields, schools, churches, shopping centres and parks, roads and railways litter a landscape that has been indelibly and irreversibly carved out according to the dictates of capitalism. Again, this physical transformation has not progressed evenly. Vast concentrations of productive power here contrast with relatively empty regions there. Tight concentrations of activity in one place contrast with sprawling far-flung development in another. All of this adds up to what we call the 'uneven geographical development' of capitalism.

This surface appearance of extraordinary historical–geographical change cries out for theoretical examination. There is much to do here and unfortunately not much theoretical guidance as to how to do it.[1] The difficulty is to find a way to approach the issue that is both theoretically grounded in basic Marxian concepts and robust enough to handle the evident confusions, antagonisms and conflicts that characterize the spatial articulation of human activities under capitalism. The phenomena to be looked at are, besides, of seemingly infinite variety. They include events and processes as diverse as individual fights over jurisdictional rights to a plot of land; colonial and neocolonial policies carried out by different nation-states; residential differentiation within urban areas; fights between street gangs over 'turf'; the organization and design of space to convey social and symbolic meanings; the spatial articulation of diverse market systems (financial, commodity, etc.); regional patterns of growth within a division of labour; spatial concentrations in the distribution of the industrial reserve army; class alliances built around territorial concepts like community, region and nation; and so on.

It would be all too easy in the face of such diversity to succumb to that 'spatial fetishism' that equalizes all phenomena *sub specie spatii* and treats the geometric properties of spatial patterns as fundamental. The opposite danger is to see spatial organization as a mere reflection of the processes of accumulation and class reproduction. In what follows I shall try to steer a middle course. I view location as a fundamental material attribute of human activity but recognize that location is socially produced. The production of spatial configurations can then be treated as an 'active moment' within the overall temporal dynamic of accumulation and social reproduction.

[1] Marxist work on the problem of spatial organization has been remarkably sporadic and unsystematic. There is a vast and variegated literature on imperialism and neo-colonialism which is suffused with spatial concepts. But the terms are descriptive rather than well-grounded theoretically. Phrases like 'centre and periphery' and 'first and third world' slip easily in and out of the literature without much forethought. The forces that produce and sustain spatial configurations often get lost in the intricacies of particular historico-geographic descriptions. The literature which helps towards the construction of theory is much more limited. I have found the formulations of Palloix (1975a; 1975b) and Aydalot (1976) very suggestive. Henri Lefebvre (1972; 1974) has repeatedly drawn attention to the importance of the production of space, the politics of space and the role of space in social reproduction (mainly in the urban context). The rich literature on urbanization that has emerged since Castells, 1977, for example, is useful but by no means definitive. Studies on regional development have likewise yet to pin the whole problem down in any rigorous way (see Lipietz, 1977; the *Review of Radical Political Economics*, vol. 10, no. 3, 1978; Dulong, 1978; Santos (1979); Carney, Hudson and Lewis, 1979; and the interesting work of Massey, 1978; 1979). De Gaudemar's (1976) study is a pioneering attempt to write theoretically on the issue while Shaikh's (1979–80) study on foreign trade and the law of value is trenchant. The next two chapters have benefited immeasurably from discussions with Beatriz Nofal and Neil Smith, both of whom contributed many original ideas to these last chapters.

The theoretical basis for this was laid down in part in chapter 11. Space, we there showed, is a material attribute of all use values. But commodity production converts use values into *social* use values. We then have to consider how material spatial attributes of use values – location in particular – are converted into social spaces through commodity production. Since commodity production entails relations between use value, exchange value and value, it follows that our understanding of spatial configurations in their social aspect must likewise be built upon an understanding of how use value, exchange value and value integrate with each other in the production and use of spatial configurations. The investigation of the land market in chapter 11 provides an example of the path to take. We must now construct a more general kind of argument.

Concrete useful labour produces use values at a particular place. The different labours undertaken at different locations are brought into a relationship with each other through acts of exchange. Spatial integration – the linking of commodity production in different locations through exchange – is necessary if value is to become the social form of abstract labour. This is, presumably, what Marx had in mind when he wrote:

> Abstract wealth, value, money, hence *abstract labour*, develop in the measure that concrete labour becomes a totality of different modes of labour embracing the world market. Capitalist production rests on the *value* or the transformation of the labour embodied in the product into social labour. But this is only possible on the basis of foreign trade and of the world market. This is at once the pre-condition and the result of capitalist production. (*Theories of Surplus Value*, pt 3, p. 253)

It then follows that failure to achieve spatial integration disturbs the universality of the value form. And in some cases this may lead to exchange between different 'value systems' or unequal exchange between different trading systems:[2]

> Here the law of value undergoes essential modification. The relationships between labour days of different countries may be similar to that existing between skilled, complex labour and unskilled, simple labour within a country. In this case, the richer country exploits the poorer one, even where the latter gains by the exchange. (*Theories of Surplus Value*, pt 3, pp. 105–6)

So how is a spatial integration achieved? Exchange of commodities is a *necessary* condition, as is the availability of a 'universal equivalent' (such as gold) as the money basis of world exchange. Physical barriers to the movement of both commodities and money over space have to be reduced to a minimum. The *sufficient* conditions for spatial integration are, however,

---

[2] The theme of unequal exchange is explored by Emmanuel (1972) and the general problem of value in international exchange by Shaikh (1979–80).

given by the geographical mobilities of capital and labour power.[3] 'In capital,' after all, 'the independent existence of value is raised to a higher power than in money' (*Theories of Surplus Value*, pt 3, p. 131), while 'the tendency to create the world market is directly given in the concept of capital itself' (*Grundrisse*, p. 408). The geographical movement of money and commodities *as capital* is not the same as the movement of products and of precious metals. Capital is, after all, money used in a certain way, and is by no means identical with all money uses.

If spatial integration is achieved through the circulation of capital over space, then our attention must focus on how capital and labour power move. We cannot here appeal to common bourgeois notions of the mobility of separate 'factors of production' – 'things' that can be shunted from one point in space to another. The Marxian conception is necessarily somewhat more complicated. Capital can move as *commodities*, as *money*, or as a *labour process* employing constant and variable capital of different turnover times. Furthermore, the relation between the mobility of *variable capital* and that of the *labourers themselves* introduces another dimension into class struggle, while the problems that attach to the circulation of capital in *the built environment* also call for special attention. This disaggregation follows automatically, given Marx's depiction of the circulation of capital as:

$$M - C\left(\frac{LP}{MP}\right) \ldots P \ldots C' - M' \text{ (etc.)}.$$

The ability of capital to move depends upon which of these various states it occupies. In what follows we will consider the separate mobility potential of capital in each of these states, before integrating the separate motions into an understanding of temporal and spatial rhythms to the circulation and accumulation of capital. In this way we may hope to unravel how spatial integration is achieved through concrete material circulation processes of capital itself.

I   TRANSPORT RELATIONS AND THE MOBILITY OF CAPITAL AS COMMODITIES

The ability to move goods around defines the mobility of capital in commodity form.[4] This mobility depends upon transport relations modified by the attributes of commodities such as their weight, size fragility, perishability, etc. Marx argues that 'the spatial condition, the bringing the product to

[3] The failure to make the distinction between exchange of commodities and money, on the one hand, and the circulation of capital, on the other, mars the otherwise interesting work of Wallerstein (1974).

[4] De la Haye (1979) collects together many of the basic texts out of Marx's and Engels's writings on this topic.

market, belongs to the production process itself' (*Grundrisse*, pp. 533–4; *Capital*, vol. 2, pp. 149–51). The transport industry is therefore productive of value because it is a 'sphere of material production' that effects a material change in 'the object of labour – a spatial change, a change of place'. The transport industry 'sells change of location' as its product (*Capital*, vol. 2, p. 52; *Theories of Surplus Value*, pt 1, p. 412).

Like any other intermediate input, the value of the commodity 'change of location' enters into the cost price of other commodities. The value of all commodities is therefore inclusive of all *socially necessary* costs of transportation, defined as the average cost of getting products to their final destinations. The cost of movement is not the sole consideration. The regularity and reliability of transport flows can reduce the need for inventories of both raw materials and finished products and so release 'fallow' capital for active accumulation (*Capital*, vol. 2, p. 142). Continuity in the circulation of capital can be assured only through the creation of an efficient, spatially integrated transport system, organized around some hierarchy of urban centres (such as that represented in the location theory of Lösch, 1967, and Christaller, 1966). The speed of movement is also vital. 'Spatial distance' then reduces itself to time because 'the important thing is not the market's distance in space but the speed with which it can be reached' (*Grundrisse*, p. 538; *Capital*, vol. 2, p. 249).

Reductions in the cost and time of movement, together with improvements in the regularity and reliability of transport services, belong to the 'development of the forces of production by capital'. Marx depicts the consequent impulse to revolutionize transport relations in very general terms. Capital, he writes, must 'strive to tear down every spatial barrier to . . . exchange, and conquer the whole earth for its market', it must 'annihilate this space with time' in order to reduce the turnover time of capital to 'the twinkling of an eye'. 'The more production comes to rest on exchange value, hence on exchange, the more important do the physical conditions of exchange – the means of communication and transport – become for the costs of circulation' (*Grundrisse*, pp. 524–39). And as technological revolutions in other sectors expand the volume of commodities to be exchanged so do revolutionary changes in the means of communication and transportation become an absolute necessity (*Capital*, vol. 1, p. 384).

The effects are legion. The mobility of capital in commodity form is accomplished within a perpetually shifting framework of relative spaces since 'cost and time distances may be shifted about by the development of the means of transportation in a way that does not correspond to geographical distances' (*Capital*, vol. 2, p. 249). Falling average costs of movement directly reduce the value (and price of production) of the commodities moved. The indirect effects are no less important. Put simply, if we conceive of value as a social average taken over all locations integrated into some network of exchange, then expansion or contraction of that network through changes in transport capability alter value relations. Previously inaccessible products and resources brought into the network of exchange through new transportation arrangements can have startling effects upon values (and prices of production). The domain of locations across which 'value' is averaged depends, in short, upon the level and degree of spatial integration achieved under specific transport relations. It then follows that such crucial magnitudes as the value of labour power and the value composition of capital are highly sensitive to the productive forces brought to bear within the transport industry.

As space relations alter in response to transport investment, so do the relative fortunes of capitalists in different locations. Some suffer devaluation of labour power, their fixed capital and consumption fund (housing, etc.) while others enjoy, temporarily at least, excess profits and an upward revaluation of available means of production and consumption. An important conclusion then follows, a conclusion that necessarily modifies the general concept of overaccumulation-devaluation laid out in chapter 7: *devaluation, arising for whatever reason, is always particular to a place, is always location specific.*

We will take up the implications of this far reaching principle later. We confine attention here to its effects within the transport industry itself. Since change of location is produced and consumed at the same moment, immediate overproduction and devaluation is a technical impossibility. Only the fixed capital can be devalued. But the fixed capital required in the transport industry is extensive and a lot of it is embedded in the built environment as roads, rails, terminals, etc. Fixed capital of this sort is particularly vulnerable to the cold winds of devaluation. But the devaluation is always on a particular route or at a particular place – a terminal loses trade here, a new highway supplants traffic over a rail line there. Revolutions in productive forces within the transport industry always have location specific effects. Competition within the industry therefore acquires some peculiar characteristics. This is so in part because when fixed capital is embedded in the land, competition is between what Adam Smith called 'natural monopolies' in space. The quality of this 'natural monopoly' implies that several competing rail lines between two cities hardly make sense, whereas competition between several carriers over common routes (as in road haulage) has a stronger rationale. Since large quantities of capital are often called for to build the rail lines, docks and harbours, airports, etc., capitalists may be unwilling to invest without protection against the risk of location specific devaluation through competition. This means restriction of competition and the creation of state-regulated or even state-owned monopolies. Herein lies a dilemma. The competitive stimulus to revolutionize the productive forces within the industry is blunted. Yet we have already seen that capitalism in general requires perpetual reductions in the cost and time of movement, the elimination of all spatial barriers and the 'annihilation of space by time'.

The tension can in part be resolved if capital within the transport industry splits into fixed capital of an independent kind circulating in the built environment and other kinds of capital (trucks, ships, etc.) which are free to move in space. The place bound quality of devaluation is minimized in the latter sector and the barriers to open competition and investment are correspondingly diminished. The really serious problems of place-specific devaluation through technological change in transportation are then confined to the fixed capital which circulates independently in the built environment.

Such a split can occur only through the involvement of the credit system and the state (*Grundrisse*, pp. 523–33). The 'natural monopoly' element can then be brought under collective regulation and control, while the effects of devaluation are socialized to a corresponding degree. Furthermore, as we saw in chapters 7 and 8, investments of this sort can be organized so as to yield interest only and so diminish the overall upward pressure on the value composition of capital. The disadvantage is that the pace of technological change within this portion of the transport industry is subject to the economic power, policies and sometimes arbitrary whims of associated capitalists (a powerful cabal of financiers, for example) or of state bureaucrats. The coordination of investment strategies for the formation of new physical infrastructures within the transport industry then becomes problematic. Land price movements (of the sort discussed in chapter 11) now enter into the picture because those who organize investments in immobile transport infrastructures can often appropriate the benefits of rising land values in the areas served (this is as true for the state as it is for associated capitalists). This means that it is beneficial (from the standpoint of capital in general) to let loose land speculation and the appropriation of rents and land taxes as a means to pull, push and guide transport investments. We here find additional validation for the general thesis set out in chapter 11 – that the appropriation of rent performs vital co-ordinating functions within capitalism. The effect, however, is that the creation of transport infrastructures depends upon speculative and political mechanisms rather than upon more usual market mechanisms.

There are some major contradictions in all of this. Accumulation requires that more and more capital should shift into the production of means of transportation and communication (*Capital*, vol. 2, p. 251). But the transport industry typically has a high technical and value composition of capital and weak powers of surplus value production within its confines. This weakness has therefore to be offset by compensating advances in capacity for surplus value production in the sectors served by the transport industry if aggregate rates of profit are to be maintained.

But worst of all, we see that capitalism seeks to overcome spatial barriers through the creation of physical infrastructures that are immobile in space and highly vulnerable to place-specific devaluation. Roads, railways, canals, airports, etc., cannot be moved without the value embodied in them being lost. Value has to be immobilized in the land to an increasing degree, therefore, in order to achieve spatial integration and to eliminate spatial barriers to the circulation of capital. At some point or other, the value embodied in the produced space of the transport system becomes the barrier to be overcome. The preservation of particular values within the transport network means constraints to the further expansion of value in general. Strong devaluations and re-structurings within the transport system, with all that this implies for the shaping of spatial configurations and levels of spatial integration, then become inevitable. This is the central contradiction which modifies and circumscribes the mobility of capital in commodity form.

II THE MOBILITY OF VARIABLE CAPITAL AND LABOUR POWER

Labour power is a commodity, but the conditions that govern its mobility are very special. It is the only commodity that can bring itself to market under its own steam. The term 'mobility of labour' therefore occupies a special position in economic discourse. In bourgeois theory, and frequently in common parlance, it refers to the freedom of the labourer to sell his or her labour power whenever, wherever, for whatever purpose and to whomsoever he or she pleases. Such freedom of contract is crucial to bourgeois conceptions of human rights and civil liberties. Marx does not deny the significance of these positive freedoms, but he does insist they be seen in relation to another, darker side of things. The labourer is 'free in the double sense, that as a free man he can dispose of his labour power as his own commodity, and that on the other hand he has no other commodity for sale, is short of everything necessary for the realization of his labour power' (*Capital*, vol. 1, p. 169). 'Freed' by the process of primitive accumulation from control over the means of production (including access to the land), most labourers have no option but to sell their labour power to the capitalist in order to live.

The duality of this freedom translates into radically different ways of viewing its geographical mobility.[5] As creative subjects (see above, pp. 111–19), labourers perpetually roam the world seeking to escape the depredations of capital, shunning the worst aspects of exploitation, always struggling, often with some success, to better their lot. Capital must necessarily accommodate to this process, and to the extent that this is so labourers fashion both the history and geography of capitalism. Conceived of as an object essentially dominated by capital, however, the labourer is nothing but

---

[5] De Gaudemar (1976) has an excellent discussion and provides good summaries of Lenin's and Luxemburg's views on labour migration under capitalism.

variable capital, an aspect of capital itself. The laws that govern the movement of variable capital are embedded within those that regulate the mobility and accumulation of capital in general.

Marx emphasizes the second of these viewpoints in *Capital*. In so doing he counters prevailing bourgeois myths as to the supposed freedom of the labourer. Given the general conditions of wage labour, the freedom of the labourer to move is converted into its exact opposite. In search of employment and a living wage, the labourer is forced to follow capital wherever it flows. This implies the 'abolition of all laws preventing the labourers from transferring from one sphere of production to another and from one local centre of production to another', and the elimination of 'all the legal and traditional barriers that would prevent [capitalists] from buying this or that kind of labour power' (*Capital*, vol. 3, p. 196; *Results of the Immediate Process of Production*, p. 1013). It likewise entails the disruption and destruction of traditional ways of life and sustenance through primitive accumulation – a process that Marx considers at length. It also pushes capitalists to adopt labour processes that are not dependent upon traditional monopolizable skills. The implications for the labourer are legion. The 'indifference' of capital to the particular forms of the labour process is immediately extended to the worker, while 'free workers' must accept that 'their labour always produces [for them] the same product, money.' They must be 'in principle' always 'ready and willing to accept every possible variation in . . . [their] activity which promises higher rewards.' Wage differentials then provide the means to co-ordinate workers' moves to capital's requirements. The versatility and geographical mobility of labour power as well as the 'indifference' of workers to the content of their work are essential to the 'fluidity of capital'. 'Nowhere', Marx opines, do such conditions 'appear more vividly than in the United States' (*Results of the Immediate Process of Production*, pp. 1014, 1034). Under these conditions the 'freedom of the labourer' is in practice reduced to the 'freedom of capital' (*Capital*, vol. 1, p. 671). The more mobile the labourer, the more easily capital can adopt new labour processes and take advantage of superior locations. The free geographical mobility of labour power appears a necessary condition for the accumulation of capital.

This proposition is not free of contradiction. If the geographical mobility of labour power is to meet capital's needs, then the absolute freedom of the labourer to move must be strictly circumscribed. The reserve army of the unemployed, for example, so unceremoniously 'freed' from its means of livelihood by technological change, can create conditions favourable to further accumulation only if it remains available to capital. This often means that it must stay in place. Escape routes must be blocked off by legal requirements or other social mechanisms – land ownership and rent, for example, prevent labourers from going back to the land and so escaping from the clutches of capital. The industrial reserve army cannot be allowed to die off either, unless capital can absorb 'primitive and physically uncorrupted elements from the country' or mobilize the *latent* as opposed to the active reserve army (*Capital*, vol. 1, pp. 269, 642). Otherwise, capital must find ways to maintain a reserve army alive and in place by unemployment benefits, social security, welfare schemes and so on. Individual capitalists cannot easily assume such burdens, which typically devolve upon the state.

Various dilemmas then arise. A social support system, like factory act legislation and regulation of the working day, is inherently worth struggling for from the standpoint of the working class. The condition of the reserve army is a focus for class struggle – who is to bear the cost and how can capital sustain access to labour reserves becomes problematic. Different governments may squabble over the issue; but most important of all, from the standpoint of the present argument, the 'free' mobility of labour power is checked by capitalists' desire to keep labour reserves in place. This principle becomes even more evident when labourers possess skills or when capitalists invest in education, job-training, health care, etc. The qualities of labour power then become important. Marx notes, for example, that during the cotton famine of the 1860s in Lancashire, the 'manufacturers acted in secret agreement with the government to hinder emigration as much as possible, partly to retain in readiness the capital invested in the flesh and blood of the labourers' (*Capital*, vol. 3, p. 134). Tactics to bind preferred workers to particular firms and locations abound. Emigration and immigration policies can be manipulated at the behest of particular capitalists, while firms may themselves confer non-transferable seniority rights and pension agreements which act as barriers to movement. Even geographical mobility can be in part controlled within the internal labour market of the large corporation through promotion and incentive schemes. Thus can the social and geographical mobility of labour power be orchestrated according to particular needs. But particular needs are not necessarily compatible with the general requirements for accumulation. Individual capitalists or factions of capital can, in pursuing their own self-interest, curb the aggregate mobility of labour power in ways that may be inimical to the reproduction of the capitalist system as a whole. For these reasons, the 'free' mobility of labour dissolves into a mess of contradictory requirements even when viewed purely from the standpoint of capital.

The mobility of labour power has also to be understood in the context of the processes that govern its production and reproduction. It takes many years to raise a labourer, and ingrained skills, attitudes and values are hard to change once acquired. Labour power is, besides, the one commodity produced outside the direct capitalist relations of production. Workers raise their own families, and no matter how sophisticated the bourgeois institutions that surround them, the reproduction of labour power always remains outside of direct capitalist control. Nevertheless, long-lasting and often immovable social and physical infrastructures, difficult to build and just as difficult to dismantle or transform, are required to facilitate the production of labour power of a certain quantity and quality.[6] Such infrastructures may also absorb considerable quantities of capital (chiefly in the form of government debt).

The supply of labour power also necessarily exhibits internal differentiations. To begin with, labour power as a commodity always has a 'joint product' aspect – men, women and children, the old and the young, the weak and the strong, are all available for exploitation. Secondly, social infrastructures that help produce labour power of one sort may inhibit the creation of another. Herein lies the logic of residential differentiation in the contemporary metropolis, since neighbourhoods organized for the reproduction of professionals are necessarily different from those given over to the reproduction of blue-collar workers. When super-imposed upon historical, religious, racial and cultural differentiations, this tendency towards geographical specialization in social reproduction can take on even more emphatic form. The processes of social reproduction then crystallize into a relatively permanent patchwork quilt of local, interregional and even international specialization. This patchwork quilt may then also be associated with marked differentials in the value and value-productivity of labour power.

Capitalists can and do seize upon such differentiations and actively use them to divide and rule the working class – hence the importance of racism, sexism, nationalism, religious and ethnic prejudice to the circulation of capital. In so doing, however, capitalists support the perpetuation of barriers to free individual mobility, which is, in the long run, also vital to accumulation. Capitalists can therefore move back and forth between support and opposition for social policies that eliminate racial, sexual, religious, etc., discrimination in labour markets, depending upon the circumstance. We should also note that free individual mobility may not be consistent with the sustenance of appropriate mechanisms of social reproduction. Marx observed that it is typically destructive of traditional ways of life and that it necessarily fragments and undermines the social cohesion of the family and the community. Certain negative consequences, from the standpoint of capital, flow from this. If the qualities of labour power associated with a particular system of social reproduction are important to even a faction of capitalists, then the latter, out of pure self-interest, may seek to stabilize institutions of the family and the community, either through private philanthropy of through the state. For these reasons also, a segment of the bourgeoisie may support civic improvement, educational and urban reform,

---

[6] Donzelot (1979) and his critics provide interesting insights.

housing and health care measures and so on.[7] But in so doing, capitalists support differentiations that necessarily act as barriers to individual mobility.

Again, we can identify fundamental tensions and ambivalences on the part of capital. Free individual mobility of the labourer is an important attribute to be promoted. But capitalists also need to keep labour reserves in place, keep labour markets segmented as a means of social control and support adequate social reproduction processes for labour powers of certain qualities. Such contradictory impulses, which derive from the internal contradictions of capitalism in general, generate countervailing influences over the geographical mobility of labour power, independently of the will of the workers themselves.

But workers are more than mere objects for capital. Geographical mobility has quite a different meaning for them. It represents the possibility of escape from tyranny and oppression, including that visited on labour by capital. It represents the hope and striving for a better life, even if that striving plays into the hands of capital as workers respond to the material incentives capital offers (higher wages and improved work conditions). There is, in this, a certain irony. Capital in general relies upon this perpetual search by workers for a better life – defined in material and money terms – as means to orchestrate labour mobility to its requirements and to discipline individual capitalists to class requirements. The 'free' geographical mobility of labourers helps equilibrate, for example, the wage rate to that average value of labour power that keeps accumulation in balance (see chapter 2).

But geographical mobility also imposes burdens upon the labourer. Disruption of traditional support mechanisms and ways of life can be hard to bear. We here encounter the reverse side of the push for mobility as a means of escape. The networks of personal contacts, the support systems and elaborate coping mechanisms within family and community, institutional protections, to say nothing of the mechanisms for political mobilization, can all be built up through the creative efforts of workers and their families into islands of strength and privilege within a sea of class struggle. Protection of such islands often assumes great importance in the lives of workers. Strong loyalties to family, community, place and cultural milieu act as barriers to geographical mobility. Exclusion of other workers – on economic, social, religious, ethnic, racial, etc., grounds – may also be seen as crucial to the protection of the islands of strength already established. This was a problem that Marx encountered as he ventured into the complex politics of English and Irish workers under nineteenth-century British capitalism.[8]

---

[7] The nineteenth century urban reform movements on both sides of the Atlantic provide splendid examples of commitment to the welfare of the working classes through moral and material reform.

[8] 'Every industrial and commercial centre in England now possesses a working class *divided* into two *hostile* camps, English proletarians and Irish proletarians. The

The upshot is that labour, if it cannot escape entirely from the clutches of capital, is faced with a bitter choice. It can flee and seek the better life elsewhere, or it can stay in place and fight. The choice is not all or nothing – seasonal, periodic and even relatively long-term migrations (together with remittances to take care of families left behind) are some of the intermediate solutions. The choice, in the final analysis, belongs to labour no matter what the influence of capital. But the irony remains. Whatever path labour takes has the potential for conversion into something advantageous to capital. It follows from Marx's argument that this potential is bound to be realized (albeit with many a quirk and wrinkle) if the one fundamental condition that defines the position of the labourer in capitalist society remains intact. If labourers must sell their labour power in order to live, then there is no escape. This was, of course, the political point that Marx always sought to hammer home. The only solution to the contradictions of capitalism entails the abolition of wage labour.

Short of such a dramatic resolution, labour and capital are forced into curious patterns of struggle and compromise over the geographical mobility of labour. Both capital and labour have rights to move, and between two rights force decides. But the outcomes are not easy to interpret. In struggling to achieve their own ends – either by moving or by staying in place and fighting to improve conditions of social reproduction – workers may help, if the ends always remain limited, to stabilize capitalism rather than undermine or overthrow it. The erratic movement of capital, on the other hand, may disrupt conditions of labour reproduction and so threaten the very basis of further exploitation of labour power. Capital may then be forced back into patterns of support for family and community which may, in turn, enhance the workers' base for political struggle. The geographical mobility of both capital and labour is not an unambiguous affair from either standpoint. This is the condition that is fundamental to understanding the mobility of labour. It is the condition that will remain in place until workers no longer have to sell their labour power as a commodity in order to live.

III THE MOBILITY OF MONEY CAPITAL

Different forms of money – gold bullion, coins, notes, credits, etc. – vary according to the ease and security with which they can be moved. Gold coins, with high value-to-weight ratio, are not that costly to move physically, but time taken and the risks attached pose definite limitations. Under modern

ordinary English worker hates the Irish worker as a competitor who lowers his standard of life. . . . This antagonism is kept alive and intensified . . . by all means at the disposal of the ruling classes, (It) is the *secret of the impotence* of the English working class, despite its organization. It is the secret whereby the capitalist class maintains its power' (*Selected Correspondence* (with Engels), pp. 236–7).

conditions, credit moneys are the most mobile of all. They can move around the world as quickly as information and instructions concerning their use will allow. The only physical barrier lies in the communications system through which messages can be transmitted.

Improvements in techniques of information transfer are therefore as fundamental to accumulation as the revolutions in transportation that enhance the mobility of commodities (*Grundrisse*, p. 161).[9] Post, telegraph, telephone, radio, telex, electronic transfers, etc – all help credit money to traverse space 'in the twinkling of an eye'. Money capital of this sort can apparently roam the world with scarcely any let or hindrance, integrating and co-ordinating production and exchange with almost no regard for material spatial barriers. Since Marx argues (see above, chapter 1) that values become the regulators of commodity exchange only to the degree that a well-integrated exchange system evolves, it follows that the more freely credit moneys move, the more perfectly exchange relations reflect value relations and the more meaningful it comes to speak of a money commodity as a universal equivalent.

But we immediately encounter certain paradoxes and contradictions that impinge socially upon the free mobility of even credit moneys. The latter can function only in the context of certain firm institutional arrangements, the most important of which are those provided by the state. Marx insists that all 'ideal' forms of money posses a 'local and political character', and his chapter on 'Money' in *Capital* is strewn with allusions to the nation-state as the basic monetary unit when money is used as pure medium of circulation. Relations between the money systems of different nation-states and between monetary blocs then enter into the picture. Social barriers arise to money movement because of the different legal, institutional and political arrangements that back the money system. The drive to create a credit system as free as possible from material spatial constraints therefore rests, paradoxically, upon territorial differentiations, which can prevent the movement of money under certain conditions. We have encountered this kind of contradiction before. The spatial mobility of commodities depends upon the creation of a transport network that is immobile in space. In both cases, spatial barriers are overcome only through the creation of particular spatial structures. When the latter become the barriers, which, with time, they must, then we can see more clearly how it is that 'the universality towards which [capitalism] irresistibly strives encounters barriers in its own nature' (*Grundrisse*, p. 410).

Credit moneys could freely roam the world, of course, if they were directly tied to a money commodity, like gold. But it is the central virtue of credit money that it is liberated from being so pinned down. It must necessarily be liberated from monetary restraints during the upswing, for example, if new configurations of surplus value production and organization are to be

[9] See De la Haye (1979) who emphasizes the communications aspects in his introduction to Marx's writings on the topic.

achieved. By the same token, it stands to be devalued in relation to 'high-quality' money during a crisis. Where that high-quality money is located, and its strength as a measure of social labour, then become important. When gold still functions as the sole measure of value, then the gold reserves of the central banks form the monetary basis. When inconvertible paper money backed by the state functions as the sole measure of value within a country, then the supply and quality of central bank money is all that counts as internal backing for credit money. International exchanges then occur according to the fluctuating exchange ratios established between different national moneys. In either case, the value of social labour as registered either by the gold reserves or by the foreign exchange position of the nation state become fundamental supports of the credit system. The stronger its foreign exchange position and/or gold reserves, the more leeway a central bank has to provide a firm monetary basis for the credit system. Marx was well aware of the importance of such relations, as his writings on crisis formation and 'bullion drain' clearly illustrate (*Capital*, vol. 3, ch. 35).

The upshot is this: while credit moneys can roam the world as fast as infomation can move, they also encounter social barriers posed by the existence of different national moneys of varying quality (depending upon foreign exchange position, gold reserves, central bank policies and the like).[10] At times of crisis, credit moneys are forced to relate back to a monetary basis that is geographically differentiated. Each nation-state strives to protect its monetary basis if the viability of the credit system is to be assured. This means enhancing value and surplus value production within its borders or appropriating values produced elsewhere (through colonial or imperialist ventures). Interstate competition with respect to flows of capital (in whatever form) automatically follows. Each nation-state may then find it necessary to protect its monetary basis by restricting the movement of capital (through protective tariffs, production subsidies, foreign exchange controls, etc.). The movement of labour power may also be controlled.

But the whole logic now collapses back on to itself. In order to protect the monetary basis that forms the foundation for credit money – the most mobile form of capital – it may become necessary to restrict the spatial mobility of capital in general! Such a situation is inherently unstable and contradictory. And instability breeds uncertainty and further defensiveness on the part of monetary authorities in different nation-states. We are then well on our way to understanding how, in the absence of any supra-national agreement (of the sort negotiated at Bretton Woods in 1944), the international monetary system can dissolve into chaos as crises unfold geographically upon the world stage. We will pick up this theme later.

[10] Mandel's analysis of *The Second Slump* is an instructuve study of how such processes come together at a particular conjuncture.

IV THE LOCATION OF PRODUCTION PROCESSES

The origin of surplus value lies in a concrete labour process organized under capitalist relations of production and exchange. The material transformation of nature, the production of social use values, necessarily occurs at a particular place. With the sole exception of the transport industry (which produces change of location as its product), the production of commodities is tied to a particular location for the duration of the labour process. Locations can be changed without incurring devaluation of the capital employed only after the labour process has run its course. The duration of each labour process is fixed by the real turnover time of the capital employed. The longer these turnover times, the harder it is to shift locations unless components of that capital – machines and inventories – can be moved at nominal cost. Producers are firmly pinned down for long time periods through reliance upon fixed capital of long turnover time embedded in the land itself. They can be liberated to some degree from such constraints if the state or another faction of capital (property owners, financiers) hold such elements of fixed capital and rent them out to users on a short-term basis.

The location of production under capitalism is a very intricate affair subject to multiple determinations. The advantage of a particular location to the individual capitalist depends on the cost of constant and variable capital, of transportation to markets with sufficient effective demand, the cost of interest-bearing capital, the cost and availability of a wide range of ancillary services, as well as land price. These costs vary according to the munificence of nature (so-called 'natural' resource endowments), social, political and economic conditions which affect the value of labour power, costs of intermediate inputs, levels of effective demand, etc. Producers also engage in *spatial* competition – that is, competition for favourable sites and locations, for domination of particular market areas, and the like. These considerations are dealt with, of course, in bourgeois location theory.[11] Our task here is to interpret them from a Marxian perspective.

The 'coercive laws of competition' play an important role in Marx's theory. But he tends to ignore spatial aspects. They are briefly alluded to in the analysis of rent (see chapter 11) and receive an occasional mention elsewhere. Indeed, Marx frequently asserts that the details of how competition actually works can reasonably be left until later. He is interested in the underlying relations which prevail after competition, demand and supply, price fluctuations, and all the other surface phenomena characteristic of the market have done their work. For his purpose a crude assumption of perfect competition is

---

[11] The best survey is still that by Isard (1956) and the most intriguing work on the whole subject is still that of Lösch (1967).

sufficient. What happens, then, when we build the spatial aspects to competition more explicitly into the argument?

Under competition, relative locational advantage translates into excess profit. This excess profit, like that which accrues to capitalists who use superior technologies, may be regarded as a form of relative surplus value. It accrues to individual capitalists who sell at the social average but produce at local costs which are lower than the social average. It must be distinguished from the permanent form of relative surplus value which affects the capitalist class as a whole through the decline in the value of labour power. To keep the distinction clear I will stick to the terminology of excess profit to indicate the relative surplus value which individual capitalists can gain from technological or locational advantage. In so far as producers can re-locate at will, the excess profit from a superior location, like that from superior technology, will be ephemeral. If, on the other hand, the excess profit turns out to be relatively permanent, then it will be taxed away as land (location) rent (see chapter 11). The rate of profit to capitalist producers will tend to be equalized across locations either through the appropriation of rent or through the geographical mobility of production capital.

Our focus here, however, is upon spatial competition and the consequent geographical mobility of capitalist production. In order to get some sense of where the argument is headed, we begin with a highly simplified model. Assume that all capitalists turn over all elements of their capital on an annual basis and that they are free to change location without incurring any devaluation at the end of each year. Imagine, also, a closed plain upon which competing capitalists with identical technologies accumulate capital through the production and exchange of a homogeneous product. Assume, finally, that all capitalists have perfect information about profit opportunities on the plain. At the end of each year capitalists can shift into a spatial configuration of production locations which equalize the profit rate. But what, then, do they do with their accumulated capital? If one capitalist expands output and shifts location to maximize the prospects of realizing values (in both production and exchange), then other capitalists are forced to follow suit in order to defend their competetive position.[12] The aggregate long-run effect on a closed plain is that the search for individual excess profits from location forces the average profit rate closer and closer to zero. This is an extraordinary result. It means that competition for relative locational advantage on a closed plain under conditions of accumulation tends to produce a landscape of production that is antithetical to further accumulation. Individual capitalists, acting in their own self-interest and striving to maximize their profits under the

[12] The bourgeois literature on location theory is full of all manner of intricate discussions on the different forms of spatial competition. For purposes of argument I adopt a highly simplified version here. The problem is not to describe the processes of competition but to get to the social relationships that underlie its results.

coercive pressures of competition, tend to expand production and shift locations up to the point where the capacity to produce further surplus value disappears. There is, it seems, a spatial version of Marx's falling rate of profit thesis.[13]

This model is not particularly realistic but it does help identify some useful working hypotheses. First, the processes making for 'spatial equilibrium' – broadly spelled out in bourgeois location theory – are, from the Marxian perspective to be seen as part and parcel of the processes which lead to crises of accumulation. Conversely, those countervailing forces (including those unleashed in the course of crises) which push the space economy of production into some seeming state of chronic disequilibrium, have a potentially important role to play in staving off, limiting or resolving aggregate spatial crises of accumulation. The general import of these hypotheses is to confirm that location is an active moment within the overall circulation and accumulation of capital, that what we will later call 'uneven geographical development' together with radical re-structurings of the space economy of capitalism play a vital role in the processes of crisis formation and resolution, and that there may even be a 'spatial fix' (as we call it) to the internal contradictions of capitalism. In what follows we will strive to put flesh on the bare bones of these ideas.

But is there a spatial crisis? If so, what is it like?

1 *Technology versus location as sources of relative surplus value*

Capitalists can individually hope to acquire relative surplus value for themselves – excess profits – by adopting superior technologies or seeking out superior locations. A direct trade off exists, therefore, between changing technology or location in the competitive search for excess profits. Producers in disadvantaged locations, for example, could compensate for that disadvantage by adopting a superior technology, and vice versa. The relations between these two potential sources of excess profit therefore deserve close consideration.

We first note that in both cases the excess profit which accrues to individual capitalists is in principle temporary. It disappears as soon as other capitalists adopt the same technology or shift to equally advantageous locations. Under

[13] It should then follow that the spatial equilibrium set out in Lösch's *Economics of Location*, with its neat hexagonal networks of market areas and its hierarchies of central places, is a landscape of zero accumulation, totally inconsistent with the capitalist mode of production. Hardly surprisingly, such landscapes are not observed and Lösch himself had the greatest difficulty injecting dynamics into his argument. Technological change is treated as an externally given, unexplained phenomena when what we really have to show is how and why technological change is induced *within* a locational system by competitive pressures. A closer investigation of this point suggests that 'spatial equilibrium' in the bourgeois sense is an impossibility under the social relations of capitalism for deeply structural reasons.

conditions of instantaneous and costless re-location, the excess profit due to location would be negligible except in the case of monopolizable and special resources of the sort that give rise to rental appropriation. To the degree that barriers exist to re-location (through cost, the time taken to complete a given labour process, etc.). islands of relative locational advantage could be produced through the action of capital. The analogy with the case of differential rent of the second sort (see chapter 11) is exact. Relatively permanent spatial configurations of excess profits would dull the incentive of capitalists to engage in technological change in those advantaged locations, unless the excess profit is taxed away as land rent. We here re-affirm the thesis explored in chapter 11, that the appropriation of rent plays an important role in equalizing the rate of profit to producers across locations, thus forcing individual capitalists back onto the straight and narrow path of seeking excess profits through technological change.

Consider, now, a situation in which the mobility of production capital and rental appropriation have equalized the rate of profit across all locations within a bounded plain on which there is a finite supply of labour power. Accumulation will proceed unchecked all the time there are surpluses of labour power. As the labour surpluses are absorbed, more and more capitalists, in pursuit of excess profits, will be forced to adopt new technologies. These disturb and alter the conditions under which the preceding spatial equilibrium (defined as equalization of the profit rate) was achieved. Spatial competition is reactivated in a variety of ways:

First, producers with superior technologies may extend their market areas at the expense of others who are then forced to respond either by shifting locations or adopting the new technology. If the new technology effects economies of scale and is neutral with respect to the value of labour power (i.e., it does not give rise to the permanent form of relative surplus value), then the surplus value produced on the plain remains constant. It is merely redistributed. If the new technology requires an increase in the capital advanced, then the average rate of profit declines, although advantaged individual capitalists still stand to gain excess profits. Here again we see the spatial aspect of the falling profit rate in action. If the profit rate is to be stabilized then some of the competitors must be driven out of business – and that means place-specific devaluation.

Secondly, when producers increase the technical and value compositions of capitals they employ then three related effects follow:

(1) The demand for labour power in the vicinity of the innovators may drop triggering unemployment, falling wages and extra opportunities to acquire relative surplus value on the basis of local labour market conditions favourable to expansion (we presume, for the moment, no mobility of labour).

(2) The market for wage goods in that vicinity declines and local suppliers of wage goods are at least temporarily disadvantaged. They can innovate or re-locate in response.

(3) The demand for means of production will rise locally and suppliers will be temporarily advantaged.

The total interaction effects are, evidently, legion and the economy will take some time to 'shake down' into some kind of 'spatial equilibrium' in which profit rates are again equalized.

Thirdly, substitutions within the categories of constant and variable capital through technological change will also play a role in altering the calculus of locational advantage:

(1) The shift from skilled to unskilled labour (or vice versa) consequent upon changes in the labour process will alter the significance of access to different kinds of labour supply (quantity and quality), while the separation of design from execution may even allow split locational decisions for different phases of an otherwise integrated labour process.

(2) The substitution of one kind of raw material for another has direct locational consequences depending upon the availability of such materials 'in nature'.

(3) Changing techniques alter the sensitivity to overall spatial constraints – water power permits small-scale, spatially constrained but dispersed locations, the steam engine liberated production from such constraints but tied location more closely to convenient transport nodes, while electric power permits relatively unconstrained dispersal or concentration of production as the case may require (cf. *Capital*, vol. 1, pp. 377–8).

Fourthly, technological and organizational change – co-operation, the detail division of labour and the employment of machinery – all tend to promote the increased spatial concentration of production activities. Economies of scale reinforce a trend that may also be promoted by the increasing centralization of capital (see chapter 5). Growing interdependency within the division of labour (as opposed to competition for control over spatially distinct markets) means that technological and organizational changes may well lead to the agglomeration of activities within large urban centers. Marx frequently alludes to such processes but he also points out that co-operation 'allows of the work being carried on over an extended space' while the social division of labour and the opening of new product lines stimulates the territorial division of labour and geographical dispersal (*Capital*, vol. 1, pp. 328–9, 388). The tension between geographical concentration of production on the one hand and territorial specialization and dispersal on the other is very evident and cannot be understood independently of the technological dynamism associated with the accumulation of capital. Such geographical effects in turn create opportunities for individual capitalists to acquire excess profits (temporarily) through locational moves.

The general conclusion to be drawn from all of the above points is that the search for excess profits through technological change is not independent of the search for excess profits through re-location. To the degree that opportunities for excess profits from location are eliminated (by the mobility of production or through the appropriation of rent), individual capitalists are forced to seek excess profit through technological changes. The latter typically create new openings to acquire excess profits from location. Put another way, the closer production approaches some spatial equilibrium condition (the equalization of profit rates across locations, for example), the greater the competitive incentive for individual capitalists to disrupt the basis of that equilibrium through technological change. And this is so independently of any other forces – such as the mobility of labour or changes in transportation – which will also alter the basis of spatial equilibrium. Competition, we may conclude, simultaneously promotes shifts in spatial configurations of production, changes in technological mixes, the re-structuring of value relations and temporal shifts in the overall dynamic of accumulation. The spatial aspect to competition is an active ingredient in this volatile mix of forces. In the absence of any restraining of countervailing forces, the individual search for excess profits would keep the space economy of capitalist production in a state that resembles an incoherent and frenetic game of musical chairs.[14]

This conclusion is modified to the degree that the initial assumptions of a fixed labour supply and a bounded plain are relaxed. Under conditions of labour surplus (and a high rate of exploitation) the competetive incentive towards technological change or re-location is much reduced, while on an unbounded plain the conditions prevailing at capitalism's geographical frontier become important. There are, in addition, other influences at work which tend to stabilize location patterns. We now turn to consider them.

2 The turnover time of capital in production – geographical and temporal inertia and the problem of devaluation

The different elements of capital employed in production turn over at different rates within different industries. The longer these turnover times the greater the geographical and temporal inertia within the space economy of

[14] This parallels the bourgeois thesis, first advanced by Koopmans and Beckman, that there is no set of prices which will assure the optimal assignment of activities to locations under conditions of decentralized profit maximization when the facilities being located are indivisible and interlinked in any way. The failure of the price system here makes any location pattern unstable.

capitalist production. The inertia is imposed specifically by the threat of devaluation.

Individual capitalists can move without incurring devaluation only under the unlikely circumstance of a simultaneous closing out of all turnover times and working periods of the capital (variable, constant, fixed, etc.) they employ. Lack of simultaneity means some degree of devaluation always attaches to a move. The only question is how much and with what effect? A 'rational' re-location rule would simply have the gain in surplus value from the move outweigh the devaluation incurred. But what social processes guarantee that capitalism can come close to implementing such a rational rule?

The threat of devaluation imposes restraints upon both the pace of technological change and the speed of locational adjustment. The longer the turnover times the greater the geographical and temporal inertia within the space economy of production. The effect is to stabilize the landscape of production – a not altogether undesirable countervailing influence to the tendency towards frenetic instability identified in the preceding section. But problems of another sort then emerge.

Industries employing large quantities of fixed capital cannot re-locate easily. In a production system characterized by both interdependency and competition, differentials in turnover times as between industries, specific structures of agglomeration and dispersal, and the like, problems of co-ordination abound and barriers to the spatial reorganization of production multiply to corresponding degree. Space and location then appear as active sources of surplus value to individual capitalists. By the same token, the threat of devaluation through spatial reorganization looms ever larger. The effect may be to tip the scales from chronic instability towards locational stagnation. We here encounter an even deeper version of that contradiction which plagues the circulation of fixed capital. Capitalism increasingly relies upon fixed capital (including that embedded in a specific landscape of production) to revolutionize the value productivity of labour, only to find that its fixity (the specific geographical distribution) becomes the barrier to be overcome. The tension between the instability generated by newly forming capital and the stagnation associated with past investments, is ever-present within the geography of capitalist production.

Herein lies a basis for understanding the processes of crisis formation and resolution within the space economy of capitalist production. A break with past technological mixes and spatial configurations often entails massive devaluation. But failure to 'rationalize' technological mixes and spatial configurations underlies crises of overaccumulation in the first place. The general devaluation which occurs in the course of the crisis 'liberates' capital to establish new technologies and new spatial structures simultaneously.[15] But

[15] This theme has been explored in recent works by Massey (1979) and Walker and Storper (1981).

we now have to add a further wrinkle to this already complex picture. The devaluation is always, we have shown, place-specific. It does not have to be spread evenly across the plain. Indeed, the very nature of spatial competition assures that excess profits at one place will be gained at the expense of devaluation losses elsewhere. Crises therefore unfold with differential effects across the surface of the plain.

V THE SPATIAL CONFIGURATION OF BUILT ENVIRONMENTS

If production capitalists can purchase the use values which attach to the capital embedded in the land on a 'fee for service' or annual basis, then they can more easily shift locations without incurring massive penalties of devaluation. It is therefore advantageous to them if the capital embedded in the land is owned by somebody else. This advantage – which applies to all other economic agents (merchants, financiers, and even labourers) – is realized when a portion of the total capital circulates through the built environment as 'fixed capital of an independent kind' (see chapter 8). The general principle at work is this: both capital and labour can become more geographically mobile at the price of freezing a portion of the total social capital in place.

Such a condition is inherently conflictual. If the portion of capital free to move takes full advantage of its potential mobility, then that portion of the capital locked in place will surely suffer from all manner of uncertain revaluations (both increase and decline). If the capital locked into the built environment is owned by a separate faction of capital, then the stage is also set for inter-factional conflict. We now consider the underpinnings of this.

The peculiar necessities of circulation of capital through built environments has meant to evolution of a special kind of production-realization system which defines new roles for economic agents. *Landowners* receive *rent, developers* receive *increments in rent* on the basis of improvements, *builders* earn *profit of enterprise, financiers* provide money capital in return for *interest* at the same time as they can capitalize any form of revenue acruing from use of the built environment into a *fictitious capital* (property price), and the *state* can use *taxes* (present or anticipated) as backing for investments which capital cannot or will not undertake but which nevertheless expand the basis for local circulation of capital. These roles exist no matter who fills them. When capitalists buy land, develop and build upon it using their own money, then they assume multiple roles. But the more capital they advance into this kind of activity, the less they have to put directly into production. For this reason, the production and maintenance of built environments often crystallizes out into a highly specialized system linking economic agents who perform each role separately or in limited combinations.[16]

[16] Topalov (1974) and Lamarche (1976) provide analyses of this system for production of built environments.

How this system works cannot be understood without invoking the facts of distribution – rent, interest and taxes. Rent (see chapter 11) is the basis of land price and operates to allocate capital and labour to land, guides the location of future production, exchange and consumption, fashions the geographical division of labour and the spatial organization of social reproduction. This is true only to the degree that land becomes a pure form of fictitious capital. Property titles to land must be freely traded as a pure financial asset. Rent is then assimilated as a form of interest identified specifically with locational attributes. Money capital, for its part, can also be converted into a material use value and lent out as such in return for an interest payment (see chapter 8). Interest-bearing capital can therefore circulate directly through the built environment and the revenues so generated can be capitalized and property titles traded. The state can also facilitate the circulation of capital in the built environment by issuing bonds against future tax revenues. The latter can be capitalized and converted into forms of fictitious capital also.

Within this whole system, the circulation of interest-bearing capital plays a hegemonic role. The power of money capital is continuously exerted over all facets of production and realization at the same time as spatial allocations are brought within its orbit. The credit system affects land and property markets and the circulation of state debt. Pressure is thereby brought to bear on landowners, developers, builders, the state, and users. The formation of fictitious capital, furthermore, permits interest-bearing money capital to flow on a continuous basis in relation to the daily use of fixed, long-lived and immobile use values. The titles to such revenues can even circulate on the world market though the assets themselves are immobile. The advantage of this are legion. The gap between production need and realization possibilities can be continuously monitored through fluctuations in rents, interest rates and taxes, while markets for land, property and government debt provide elaborate signals for investment and disinvestment from one place to another. Major one-shot devaluations can be avoided by allowing multiple and minor price adjustments over the lifetime of some fixed and immobile asset. Investors can push money capital in or take it out at any time (sometimes with a gain and sometimes at a loss). The omnipresent risk of devaluation can also be partially socialized because a serious loss here may be more than offset by a particular gain there. And if massive localized devaluations do occur, they can be partially absorbed within the credit system or by the state.

The intricate mediations of diverse economic agents appropriating revenues of different types are brought within a common framework – that of the credit system performing fundamental co-ordinating functions (see chapter 9). The effect is to reduce time and space to a common socially determined metric – the rate of interest, itself a representation of value in motion. Temporal and geographical horizons of capital flow are simultaneously defined. Resources are taken from the earth and land taken up at the periphery, for example, at rates dictated by the prevailing rate of interest rather than in accord with some other conception of current or future well-being. And as the rates of interest – themselves a product of accumulation through the exploitation of labour power (see above, pp. 296–305) – fluctuate, so the temporal and geographical horizons of capital flow pulse outwards or contract.

Within this general system a wide variety of special kinds of institutional arrangements spring up to deal with the day-to-day problems of co-ordination in the production, use, transformation and abandonment of particular elements within the built environment.[17] For example, 'red-lining' by financial institutions and urban renewal often entail organized abandonment. The state also establishes urban and regional planning strategies and channels both public and private investments accordingly. Legal and administrative regulations arise to control and promote interactive benefits and costs of different kinds of proximate land uses. Arrangements of this sort modify the basic land and property market mechanisms, founded on trading in fictitious capitals. The effect is the creation of a hierarchy of means – market, institutional and state – for the production, modification and transformation of spatial configurations to the built environment.

The general purpose of such intricate arrangements is to establish independent means and independent forms of circulation which can shape the spatial configurations of the built environment to the variegated requirements of both capital and labour in general. This grand objective is achieved, however, at tremendous cost. The appropriation of rent, for example, fosters the fetishistic illusion that land and even location are directly productive of value. Similar illusions surround property markets and the circulation of government debt. Fictitious capitals are, after all, fictitious. The circulation of titles to claims on future labour is inherently speculative. The whole system of relations upon which the production of spatial configurations in the built environment is based, tends to facilitate and, on occasion, to exacerbate the insane bouts of speculation to which the credit system is in any case prone. In addition, factional struggles over distributive shares – between landowners, developers, financiers, builders, and the state – can easily degenerate into vicious blood-lettings with material outcomes that often have little or nothing to do with the real needs of capital and labour in general. There is, it seems, something perverse in trying to create physical conditions favourable to accumulation by giving free reign to the *appropriation* of surplus value by landlords, developers, financiers, and the like (none of whom, with the exception of builders, organize the real production of surplus value). In particular, it opens the question: how much appropriation is appropriate? To this there is no clear answer and even if there were there is no guarantee that

[17] See Dear and Scott (1981) and Scott (1980).

the forces at work under capitalism could ever achieve it. Hence arises the persistent worry that too much capital might circulate in 'unproductive' land and property speculation, or in state debt, at the expense of actual surplus value production.

So why tolerate the existence of that army of real estate speculators, land jobbers, and the like? The answer should by now be clear: speculation in land and property markets and in government debt are necessary evils. Too much speculation, to be sure, diverts capital away from real production and meets its fate of devaluation as a consequence. But curtailment of speculation has equally invidious results from the standpoint of capitalism. The transformation of spatial configurations in the built environment would be held in check and the physical landscape necessary to future accumulation could not hope to materialize. It would be nice is there were some middle path between these two extremes. But this cannot be. Rampant speculation and unchecked appropriation, costly as these are for capital and life-sapping as they may be for labour, generate the chaotic ferment out of which new spatial configurations can grow. Speculative re-structurings achieved in phases of easy credit and expansion, stand to be rationalized in the course of the subsequent crises. Waves of speculation in the creation of new spatial configurations are as vital to the survival of capitalism as other forms of speculation. And given their form, there can be no doubt that the processes we have here considered can all too easily add their bit to the height of insanity periodically manifest within the credit system. The creation of spatial configurations and the circulation of capital in built environment is, we can firmly conclude, a highly active moment in the general processes of crisis formation and resolution.

VI   THE TERRITORIALITY OF SOCIAL INFRASTRUCTURES

The social infrastructures which support life and work under capitalism are not created overnight and require a certain depth and stability if they are to be effective. They are also geographically differentiated. How and why they got that way is a problem for history. But there are powerful forces at work within the logic of capitalism which keep them that way. These forces deserve some elucidation.

The social infrastructures and institutions of capitalism are incredibly diverse and fulfil an immense variety of functions. They regulate contracts, exchange, money and credit, as well as inter-capitalist competition, the centralization of capitals, the conditions of labour (such as the working day) and various other aspects of the capital–labour relation. They often define particular frameworks for class struggle. They provide means to produce scientific and technical knowledge, new managerial techniques and new means to facilitate the collection, storage and communication of information. They also embrace the wide variety of institutions which contribute to the reproduction of labour power (health, education, social services, etc.) and cultural life in all of its variegated aspects (including that of the bourgeoisie). They offer means of ideological control as well as forums for ideological debate. More sinister are the means of surveillance and repression, always the last resort when society is plunged into the cauldron of fierce class conflict.

An immense army of people is employed in the preservation and enhancement of such social infrastructures and institutions, which coalesce, sometimes tightly and sometimes loosely, into a system of social relations of a particular sort at a particular time and place. A proper dissection of these social relations (and of their internal contradictions) requires far more consideration than we can here afford to give. Yet something must be ventured if the principal forces governing their spatial evolution are to be identified. Though by no means as easy to pin down, and on that account more nebulous, social infrastructures and built environments exhibit certain parallels in the relations they bear to the circulation of capital. That idea will be much elaborated upon in what follows.

The different elements of social infrastructure meld together to form a kind of 'human resource complex', greater than the mere sum of its parts. Such a resource complex is hard to change if only because of the strong bonding of seemingly different elements within it – the strong links between religion and education form a good example. On this account alone, the 'human resource complex' is by no means instantly adjustable to capital's requirements. It forms a part of the human geographical environment to which capital must, to some degree, adapt. It is, furthermore, deeply sensitive to every nuance in cultural, racial, ethnic, religious and linguistic history. The social relations of capitalism, for example, either incubated within the womb of some pre-existing society or were forcibly imposed from outside in later years. Already differentiated social infrastructures were the 'raw materials' out of which new human resource complexes had to be fashioned. The quality of the initial raw materials are readily discernible in the results. And the organizational form and history of the elements of social infrastructure ensures that political power centers and territorial arrangements exist that are by no means direct expressions of the social relations of capitalism. This is particularly true for the state apparatus, administration, organized religion, and so on.

Our thesis, however, is that the circulation of capital transforms, creates, sustains, and even resurrects, certain social infrastructures at the expense of others. It is hard to get a handle on exactly how. But the general line of interconnection is clear enough. Social infrastructures have to be supported out of surpluses, and under capitalism that means out of surplus value production. From this standpoint they can be interpreted in no other way than as superstructures erected upon an economic base.[18] The circulation of

[18] I have seen estimates to the effect that capitalism reproduces the *whole* of its total wealth every seven years.

value to the support of social infrastructures and the people employed therein therefore integrates the material processes of surplus value production in the workplace with the perpetuation of social infrastructures.

How to conceptualize this relation is a problem. At one extreme there are those who insist on the independent power and relative autonomy of social infrastructural organization in relation to the economic base (which implies the power to tax surplus value without restraint). At the other, are those who view social infrastructures as mere reflections of the requirements of accumulation (which denies the intricate interlocks and the significance of history and tradition).[19] Under the latter conception the problem of geographical organization would become largely moot — the territoriality of social infrastructures would simply reflect the needs of the geographical division of labour and other facets of spatial organization required by capital. Neither conception is satisfactory. We need some way to break the impasse.

The circulation of capital, we have argued throughout this work, has to be considered as a continuous process of expansion of value. The circulation of values through social infrastructures is but a moment in this total process. We must now discover the significance of that moment in relation to the overall process.

Values taxed from capital which flow to support social infrastrcutures return to capital in the form of an effective demand for the commodities which capitalists produce. There is, in this, no loss to capital. Those employed then appear as pure 'consuming classes' and as such can occasionally play a role in countering problems of disproportionality, etc. (see chapter 3). But time absorbed by the circulation of value in social infrastructures is lost time for surplus value production. The aggregate turnover time of capital is extended through the expansion of this sphere of circulation, to the detriment of the expansion of values. Moreover all kinds of geographical redistributions are possible, The 'tax' on surplus value produced in one place can re-emerge as an effective demand on the other side of the world — this is as true for organizations like the Roman Catholic Church as it is for the Bank of America. Consumption centers can arise that have no basis in local surplus value production. Populated predominantly by 'consuming classes', such centres can become identified mainly with ideological, administrative, research and other social infrastructural functions. The principles governing such geographical redistributions of value flows through social infrastructures are hard to establish. Apart from the general restraint of turnover time (itself malleable as ease of geographical movement improves), the geographical redistributions appear at worst as arbitrary and accidental and at best as the outcome of power struggles between factions of the bourgeoisie (including the 'consuming classes' who have specific interests of their own), some of

[19] For a sample of opinion see Althusser and Balibar (1970); Cohen (1978); Poulantzas (1975; 1978) and Thompson (1978).

whom may also define themselves geographically in the name of a city, region, or nation state. We will return to this issue in the next chapter.

The circulation of value through social infrastructures can also have direct and indirect impacts upon surplus value production. Though hard to pin down with precision, the concept of the 'productivity' of flows of value into social infrastructures is by no means redundant (the parallel to public invest-ment in physical infrastructures comes immediately to mind). Improvements in the social conditions for surplus value production can have important long-term effects. Improvements in the quality of quantity of labour power through health care and education, as well as through a host of intangible means which affect discipline, the work ethic, respect for authority, con-sciousness, and the like, can have a salutary effect upon surplus value produc-tion. And if workers are proving recalcitrant and rumbustious, then why not preach to them from press or pulpit, or intimidate them through the deploy-ment of moral sanctions, or legal or repressive power? Some of the flows into the social infrastructure can therefore be viewed as investments designed to enhance the social conditions for the production of surplus value. The same principle applies when flows into administration and regulation help main-tain the security and smoothness of an accelerating turnover process of capital. Flows to support scientific and technical research, to cite yet another instance, can also return directly to the sphere of production as a material force (new technologies). The immense significance of the social infra-structural 'moment' in the total circulation process of capital cannot be denied.

Value flows of this sort do not produce surplus value in themselves. They simply enhance the conditions for surplus value production. The problem – which besets the capitalists as well as us – is to identify the conditions, means and circumstances which allow this potentiality to be realized. To the degree that individual capitalists stand to benefit, they may attempt limited invest-ment in social infrastructures and so promote research and development, improvement in the qualities of labour power (health care, job-training, etc.). But since many of the benefits are as uncertain as they are diffuse, capatalists have to constitute themselves as a class – usually through the agency of the state – and thereby find collective means to satisfy their needs. Since the state is a general field of class struggle, it becomes impossible to discern directly which flows of value under its aegis represent the immediate needs of capital and which result from pressures exerted by other classes. Many of the flows into social infrastructures have no relation to improving value productivity and everything to do with the circulation of revenues. Capitalists may be forced to contribute surplus value by the 'consuming classes' which have somehow acquired the political power to tax. The working classes may also force them to it. Investment in ideological control and repression, for example, is related to the threat of organized working class resistance, while the need to integrate and co-opt workers through social expenditures arises only when workers have accumulated sufficient power to require co-optation.

Viewed from the standpoint of accumulation, however, investment in social infrastructures is no loss to capital provided the increase in surplus value production achieved as a consequence of improvements in social conditions more than offsets the increase in the turnover time of capital. This provides a useful rule upon which to base some assessment of the role of this particular 'moment' in the overall circulation of value.

Improvements in social conditions are often a long time in the making. They absorb value over a period of time and generate benefits often much later and for extended periods (it takes many years to socialize and educate a labourer, for example). This makes investment in social infrastructures an ideal field for the absorbtion of surplus, overaccumulated capital, thereby staving off devaluation since, during the period of investment, there is no diminution of effective demand. Since different kinds of social investment have different pay-off times, appropriate fiscal management by the state holds out the prospect for the stabilization of the accumulation process over extended periods.

But in the final analysis exactly the same dilemmas arise here as with investment in the built environment. In so far as improved social conditions give rise to increased surplus value production, the underlying problem of overaccumulation is exacerbated. On the other hand, if improved social conditions do not lead to such an increase, then the investment must be judged unproductive and the value absorbed therein is effectively lost. The devaluation of capital through unproductive circulation through social infrastructures therefore becomes a very real prospect. Whether or not the investments are productive depends, however, not on their inherent qualities, but upon the ability of capitalists to take advantage of them – the education of a skilled work force goes for nought if the labour process alters so as to demand unskilled labour power. For this reason, what initially appears as an easy device for the stabilization of accumulation, becomes a quagmire of uncertainty, rendered real enough by periodic fiscal crises in state social expenditures.[20]

Investments of this sort exhibit an additional peculiarity. They do not wear out through use (like machines) but, like improvements in soil fertility, can be built up incrementally over time as renewable rather than exhaustible assets. Gains in scientific knowledge do not wear out, nor do gains in legal sophistication, educational tactics, technical expertise in management and administration, and the like. Attitudes in the labour force may also evolve incrementally in ways more favourable to accumulation. The circulation of

---

[20] O'Connor (1973) provides a stimulating analysis.

value through social infrastructures can produce geographical concentration of high quality conditions. Such regions then appear 'naturally' advantaged for accumulation by virtue of the 'human and social resources' that have been built up there. Production capital will likely be attracted to these regions on such a basis.

But countervailing tendencies are also at work. Relatively permanent social infrastructural advantages can form a basis for the extraction of location rents. More importantly, the maintenance of social infrastructures impose costs — either directly or indirectly because their preservation is contingent upon 'restrained' forms of use by capital (the parallel with soil fertility maintenance is evident). If costs of maintenance rise (relative to competing regions), then the locational advantage to capitalists will diminish. Tired of paying heavy taxes or restraining their thirst for exploitation, capitalists may move (often with the aid of new labour processes adapted to unskilled labour) to new social environments where the 'human resources' are poorer but much less costly to maintain. The assets accumulated in the previously privileged regions are thereby destroyed and the value absorbed in their creation is thereby lost.

This brings us more directly to the geographical aspects of the problem. The uneven geographical development of social infrastructures is, in the final analysis, reproduced through the circulation of capital. Capital produces and reproduces, albeit through all manner of subtle mediations and transformations, its social as well as its physical environment. Even the pre-capitalist elements that persist must be reproduced, in the end, out of surplus value production. The social geography which evolves is not, however, a mere mirror reflection of capital's needs, but the locus of powerful and potentially disruptive contradictions. The social geography shaped to capital's needs at one moment in history is not necessarily consistent with later requirements. Since that geography is hard to change and often the focus of heavy long-term investment, it then becomes the barrier to be overcome. New social geographies have to be produced, often at great cost to capital and usually accompanied by not a little human suffering. The periodic re-structuring of the geography of social infrastructures is, for this reason, usually accomplished in the course of a crisis. Place-specific devaluation of the capital embodied in social infrastructures, to say nothing of the destruction of traditional ways of life and all forms of localism built around social and human institutions, then becomes one of the central elements of crisis formation and resolution under capitalism.[21]

This general picture must be modified to the degree that various aspects of social infrastructure, or the advantages they generate for accumulation, are themselves geographically mobile. Transfers of value of the sort already

[21] The trauma of New York City's 'fiscal crisis' of the 1970s is an excellent case in point.

noted can put research and development functions in places far distant from production, for example. The advantages of agglomeration and of access to the highly skilled labour power required often pulls many such functions together into a few major centres which, in turn, become the breeding grounds for starting up totally new product lines (the silicon chip industry around Palo Alto is a recent case in point). The 'products' of such social infrastructural investment can also be moved. Knowledge and highly skilled labour, both achieved at great expense, are geographically mobile so that 'technology transfer' and the 'brain drain' are two very important aspects within the general process of geographical redistribution. The cross-currents of movement are far too complicated to yield easily to theoretical analysis. And the signification of such movements for different industries with different labour processes varies greatly. Their importance has, however, to be acknowledged in any consideration of the evolution of spatial configurations under capitalism.

One overwhelming feature does cry out for special attention. The state provides the single most important channel for flows of value into social infrastructures. Herein lies the significance of taxes as a form of revenue allocated to the maintenance and enhancement of social infrastructures. And in so far as state debt is the vehicle for investment in social infrastructures, the co-ordinating and monitoring powers of capital markets and the rate of interest are brought to bear. State involvement arises in part because collective means have to be found to do what individual capitalists cannot reasonably do and in part because class struggle requires the mediations of the state apparatus if any kind of investment is to be made at all in socially sensitive areas. The involvement took on a new shape when it was recognized that such investments could be both productive (in the sense of improving the social conditions for surplus value creation) and stabilizing (in the sense of managing effective demand over a long period). State fiscal policy thereby became a vital tool in the arsenal of the bourgeoisie for managing the accumulation process (the use of military expenditures in this way is a good example). The limits to such managerial practices are by now self-evident (see also chapter 10).

The significance of state involvement from the standpoint of our present topic deserves brief elucidation. In so far as the state takes on the role of overall manager of the production and reproduction of social infrastructures (including itself), the hierarchical form of organization of the state is deployed to discriminate between local, regional, national and supra-national aspects of value flows. The territorial organization of the state – and the boundaries of the nation state are by far the most important – then becomes *the* geographical configuration within which the dynamics of the investment process is worked out. This territorial organization is not, of course, immutable and from time to time radical reorganizations are called for on the grounds of improved efficiency of administration, and so on.[22] Nevertheless, at any particular moment, the territorial organization of state powers forms the fixed geographical environment within which investment processes operate. States are then forced to compete with each other for the provision of social infrastructural conditions which are attractive to capital. They are also forced to compete for money capital to fund their debt. The state, as a consequence, loses its power to dominate capital politically and is forced into a subservient, competetive posture. And in so far as devalution and destruction of human resource complexes becomes necessary in the course of a crisis, state is pitted against state in vigorous competition as to who is to bear the cost of that devaluation and that social destruction. The general principle of place-specific devaluation is then converted, at least in this particular realm, into the question of state-specific devaluations and social destruction. How this works out at the local, regional, and national levels will be taken up again in chapter 13.

VII THE MOBILITIES OF CAPITAL AND LABOUR TAKEN AS A WHOLE

The historical geography of the capitalist mode of production is constructed, we have so far implied, out of the intersecting motions of the different kinds of capital and labour power. We must now see if there is any underlying unity to seemingly diverse and incoherent movements and, if so, uncover the contradictions contained therein.

The necessary basis to explore such questions is given in the concept of unity and contradiction within the circulation of capital (see chapter 3). Capital in each of the states contained in the process

$$M - C \begin{pmatrix} LP \\ MP \end{pmatrix} \dots P \dots C' - M',$$

has a special and uniquely defined capacity for geographical movement. Since capital is defined as value in motion, it must necessarily pass from one state to another which means that two or more forms of capital (and labour power) must necessarily be in the same place at the same time at the moment of transition. Each transition constitutes, therefore, a mutually restraining intersection of different capacities for spatial movement. The circulation process as a whole comprises several such mutually restraining intersections, each with its own peculiar problems. As a general rule, it is far easier, for example, to go from $M - C$ than from $C - M$ not only because money is social power incarnate but also because it is easier to move around geographically.

---

[22] The re-organization of local and regional governments, the striving to build common markets, and so on, are examples of this kind of process at work.

The mutual restraints, we can conclude, necessarily limit the overall geographical mobility of both capital and labour power.

The constraints are tightened even further when we recall that crisis-free accumulation requires that the circulation of capital be completed within a certain time-span – the socially necessary turnover time considered in chapter 4. Capital that does not circulate in this time-span is devalued. But spatial movement requires that capital be held in a particular state – as money or commodities, for example – while it moves. This increases the turnover time. The significance of Marx's phrase 'the annihilation of space with time' now strikes home with redoubled force. The temporal requirements of circulation of capital limit the time available for spatial movement within each state. The unity of production and realization of values keeps the geographical movement of capital within strictly circumscribed bounds.

This conclusion is modified by two important considerations. First of all, it applies in the strict sense to an individual capital undergoing its standard process of self-expansion. The aggregate circulation in society is made up of innumerable individual processes of this type, each beginning and ending at different time points. The opportunity arises, therefore, for myriad spatial substitutions between different temporal processes. Individual capitalists can receive money on account for production processes not yet completed, a commodity not yet sold. Capitalists in an industrial region can lend the money they earn in the first part of the year to farmers in another region who pay them back after harvest time. What appears as very tight constraints to spatial movement at the individual level are much reduced when the circulation process is viewed as a whole. The credit system, in particular, facilitates long distance transfers and substitutions between highly divergent temporal processes. But the importance of substitutions also helps explain agglomeration. The likelihood of finding the right kind of labour power, raw materials, replacement parts, etc., improves the more individual capitalists and labourers cluster together – substitutions minimize the possibility of breakdowns in the circulation processes of individual capitalists. There is a tension here between the dispersal made possible by the credit system and the agglomeration which appears desirable at other transition points.

The temporal discipline to spatial movement is even more deeply disturbed, however, when we consider the circulation of capital (or simply of values) through physical and social infrastructures. Such forms of circulation have a double effect. First, in so far as many aspects of physical and social infrastructure are fixed in space, the problem of geographical mobility is converted into one of transformation of the social and physical environment within which other forms of capital circulate. Given the lengthy turnover time and the complexity of the task, this transformation process is necessarily slow. Secondly, the length of turnover times involved allows substitutions over much longer time-spans. Consider the matter from the standpoint of money capital. Several potential paths for circulation exist. Down the standard path, capital is put into a production process, converted into a commodity and sold upon the market under the tight discipline of socially necessary turnover time. But money can also flow into fixed capital and consumption fund formation, including the formation of physical infrastructures. It can also flow into science and technology, improved administration, or into the creation and maintenances of a variety of social infrastructures which enhance the conditions for surplus value production. The temporal discipline down each of these paths is much relaxed because the turnover times are much longer. This explains how physical and social infrastructural provision can move way out ahead of the other mobilities if need be – plenty of time is available for other forms of capital and labour power to catch up. Yet, in the long run, all these different forms of circulation have to relate to each other. Fictional relationships can be established via the credit system and through the standardization of all turnover times against the interest rate (see chapter 9). This is money itself, seeking to impose a common discipline on the different paths it can take. But real value creation, as opposed to fictitious value movements, depends upon the continuity of all flows in relation to actual production. The different circulation processes must therefore flow into each other directly, in the manner portrayed in figure 12.1. Each path has different temporal requirements and, by inference, spells out radically different opportunities for spatial movement. Yet the underlying unity of production and realization must be preserved, forcibly be crises if necessary. It is, we can conclude, this unity which, in the final analysis, subjects the divergent geographical mobilities within such a temporally disjointed system of flows to a common discipline.

1 Complementarity

Disaggregation of the circulation process into many seemingly independent systems creates tensions within the unity of production and realization. But it also admirably adapts capitalism to the task of shaping spatial organization and flows to long-run aggregative requirements. Different kinds of capital can move so as to complement each other in the search for a new spatial order. If capital cannot penetrate spatial barriers in one guise it may readily do so in another. Here the movement of money capital may pioneer the way, there it may be merchants bearing commodities. Even labourers, seeking freedom at some frontier, can play a role. The transformation of spatial configurations occurs through the continuous leap-frogging of different kinds of capital and labour power blessed with very different powers of mobility. And there is, in this, no danger provided that complementarity is achieved within a requisite time-span.

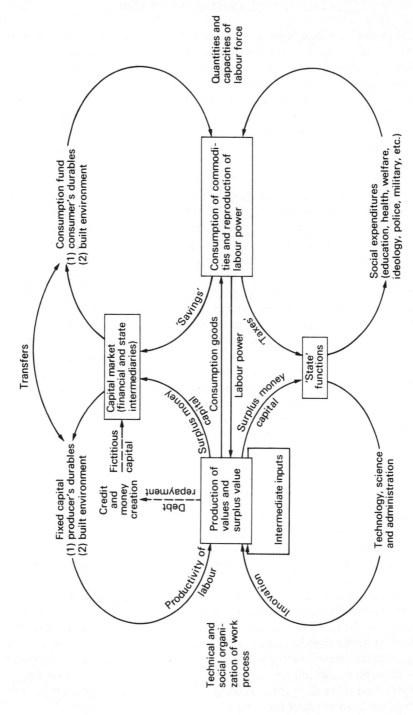

Figure 12.1 The Paths of Capital Flow

As conditions change, however, so different kinds of capital tend to take on a leading role. The movement of commodities and gold, once the cutting edge of the internationalization of capital, was steadily supplanted during the late nineteenth century by the movement of money capital as credit – a shift that testified to the growing sophistication of credit arrangements as well as to the rise of 'finance capital' (of whatever sort) as the ministering angel of economic imperialism. The interventions of fictitious capital and the state also tended more and more to liberate production capital from the tighter constraints which it had previously experienced – direct investment became more feasible, accompanied, of course, by the rise of new organizational forms such as the multinational corporation to ensure the complementarity of money, commodity, production, and labour movements. The relative significance of merchants, financiers, industrialists, and labourers, in the transformation of spatial configurations has varied in the course of the history of capitalism.

Investment in physical and social infrastructures calls for some special consideration. Released from the strict constraints of socially necessary turnover time, much longer leads and lags are possible here. Whether such possibilities will be realized and with what effects depends upon certain conditions. There must be surplus capital and a form of organization – usually the state but sometimes a powerful group of financiers – capable of centralizing the surplus capital, putting it into the creation of certain use values, and waiting several years before reaping any reward. This also implies a conscious recognition and anticipation of capitalism's future needs. Conversely, it is also possible to see such investments as the cutting edge of future capital flows and therefore as the principal instrument of geographical transformation, structuring future labour. It is, however, a peculiarly exposed cutting edge, a necessary rather than sufficient condition for future geographical configurations of capital flows. Production, labour power and commerce do not necessarily follow the paths beaten out by infrastructural investments. In which case, of course, such investments are effectively devalued.

This brings us to the edge of some very interesting theoretical insights and historical controversies. While merchant capitalists can trade pretty much wherever and how they want – even engaging in barter if they have to – capitalist production is far more demanding with respect to infrastructural requirements. Geographical expansion entails the prior establishment of property rights, law, administration, and basic physical infrastructures such as transportation. Most important of all, the commodity character of labour power has to be assured. In all of this, the agency of the state is vital. And it must necessarily move out ahead of production. But the productivity of state expenditures of this sort cannot be guaranteed. The creation of favourable physical and social conditions may lure other forms of capital into complementary configurations of investment which more than pay back the initial outlay. Or the state may try to force other elements of capital and labour to conform in order to guarantee the productivity of its own investments. But the risk of devaluation always looms large.

The political history of colonialism and imperialism provides an interesting illustration of the problem. Military conquest establishes state control. Surveyors establish private property in land (the labourer can then be excluded from the land by rent), transport and communications links are built, legal systems (conducive to exchange, of course) are established, and pre-capitalist populations proletarianized and disciplined (by force and repression, if necessary, but also through law, education, missionary activity, and the like). All of this costs vast sums of money. Beneath its surface ideological justifications, therefore, the politics of capitalist imperialism amount to a vast, long-run speculative investment which may or may not pay off. The debate over how much capitalists benefited from imperialism is really a debate over whether this investment paid off or was effectively devalued. The destruction wrought on pre-capitalist populations and the high rate of exploitation achieved does not guarantee that colonial ventures were paying propositions. Nor does their failure prove that they were set in motion out of some benevolent attempt to bring enlightenment and development to 'backward' regions of the world. They were simply caught up in the capitalist dynamic of accumulation and devaluation. The investments were, in short, necessary but not sufficient conditions for the perpetuation of accumulation.[23]

The dynamic is not, however, without its pattern. The temporal and spatial horizons of capitalism are, we have shown, increasingly reduced to a manifestation of the rate of interest, itself a reflection of conditions of accumulation. Overaccumulation usually depresses the interest rate and so extends temporal and spatial horizons. Capitalists can then afford, indeed are impelled, to explore geographical frontiers or look to the production of use values that will pay off further and further into the future. In so doing, capital ultimately encounters those barriers within its own nature which precipitate crises – crises often characterized by soaring interest rates that restrict temporal and spatial horizons once more. In so far as all forms of capital are sensitive to the rate of interest, they tend to operate under a common discipline. This goes far to explain the pulsating rhythms of capitalism's development in space.[24] The downswings and contractions in this process are marked by rupture of the unity of production and realization and, contemporaneously, by a disruption of the complementarity in the highly differentiated movement of capital. We now consider the basis for such disruptions.

[23] The debate over whether the railroads led or lagged nineteenth century development in the United States and Britain is also very instructive in this regard.

[24] Brinley Thomas's (1973) study of the Atlantic economy in the nineteenth century describes the phenomenon well, as does Walker's (1977) study on suburbanization.

2 Contradictions and conflict

The highly differentiated forms of circulation and spatial mobility may enable capitalism to shape its historical geography in accordance with the dictates of accumulation. But they also increase immeasurably the possibilities for crisis formation. The separation of sales and purchases in time and space, recall, forms the basis for Marx's attack on Say's Law (see chapter 3). We now encounter circumstances in which the separations in space and time are necessarily much attenuated. To the degree that complementarity between the different circulation processes is more difficult to ensure, the possibilities for crisis formation proliferate. We here seek a purely technical basis for understanding spatial aspects to crisis formation.

Devaluation is, we saw in chapter 3, a normal facet of circulation. Losses which cannot be fully recovered through a resumption of the circulation of capital are what really concern us. To be sure, innumerable 'accidental' and individual devaluations occur simply because the requisite forms and quantities of capital and labour power are not in exactly the right place at the right time. Miscalculation, lack of foresight, poor information, unreliable transport systems, etc., typically lie behind such devaluations. They are not necessarily part of some grander process within the logic of capitalism, but part of the normal cost of doing business, of exploring new spatial configurations, defining new geographical opportunities. The striving to minimize such risks is not inconsequential in its effects, however. Agglomeration, transport improvements, and other kinds of geographical organization can much reduce these normal costs.

The tensions associated with the prospects of even minor devaluations spark strong competitive currents which can spill over, on occasion into factional conflicts. Antagonisms can breed when the different kinds of capital are separately owned. Money capitalists may be at loggerheads with merchants and both may conflict with producers, while those with a stake in preserving the values sunk in physical and social infrastructures are threatened by the fluid motion of credit money, runaway shops, and the like. The mobility of capital of one sort can constitute a threat to the value of capital of another sort. And when general crises of devaluation break out, the struggle of each faction to foist the costs of devaluation onto another frequently means the invocation of threats to move if not actual moves. The social significance of Marx's analysis of differentiations within the overall unity of the circulation of capital now becomes more apparent. It sets the stage for dissecting the contradictions as well as the complementarities between the different kinds of mobility, We will consider in chapter 13 how all of this can crystallize into inter-territorial rivalries.

The threat and counter-threat of movement also becomes a major weapon in the war between capital and labour. We hardly need to elaborate on the variety of tactics and methods employed – these have already been partially uncovered. But there is something interesting to note about the outcomes. If workers engage in unlimited individual migration within the confines of the wage-labour system, the best they can hope to achieve is equalization in living standards and work conditions from place to place, at an average level consistent with the perpetuation of accumulation. If they stay in place and fight collectively they may do better than this within that territory. It is not always easy for capital to move in response. Though the mobility of credit money and runaway shops are formidable weapons, they cannot always be employed without destroying the values which other factions of capital have embedded in physical and social infrastructures.

Unrestrained mobility on the part of capital does not, however, produce the same results as the unrestrained mobility of workers. Capitalists are sensitive to the value of labour power and surplus value productivity (represented by profit rates). The equalization of profit rates does not necessarily produce an equalization in material living standards and work conditions for the labourers. Indeed, capitalists stand to gain, as a general rule, if differentials in the value of labour power and conditions of work are maintained. The unrestrained mobility of capital is therefore more appropriate to accumulation than the unrestrained mobility of labour – which may account for the twentieth century trend to restrict the mobility of labour power relative to that of capital.

The idea of unity and contradiction within the production and realization of values is fundamental to Marx's dissection of the crises in the circulation of capital. We have seen, in this chapter, how that idea carries over into the analysis of the intersections between highly differentiated forms of geographical mobility. Within such a framework we can better understand how different factions of capital can just as frequently bar each other's way as complement each other in the search for a more profitable spatial order, how capital and labour can use space as a weapon in class struggle. All of this leaves its imprint upon the growth of productive forces and the evolution of social relations within the concrete geography of the history of capitalism. It is, therefore, out of the concrete materiality of that geography that the forces making for crises must arise.

CHAPTER 13

Crises in the Space Economy of Capitalism: the Dialectics of Imperialism

The final chapter of volume 1 of *Capital* deals with 'The Modern Theory of Colonization'. At first sight, its placement is somewhat odd. Throughout most of *Capital*, Marx explicitly excludes questions of foreign and colonial trade on the grounds that consideration of them merely serves 'to confuse without contributing any new element of the problem [of accumulation], or of its solution'. Marx generally theorizes about capitalism as a 'closed' economic system (*Capital*, vol. 1, p. 591; vol. 2, p. 470). So why open up such questions at the end of a work that appeared to reach its natural culmination in the preceding chapter, where Marx announces, with a grand rhetorical flourish, the death-knell of capitalist private property and the inevitable 'expropriation of a few usurpers by the mass of the people'?

Marx's overt purpose in the chapter is to expose the contradictions in the bourgeois account of 'primitive accumulation' and so to reaffirm the coherence of his own analysis. According to bourgeois accounts, capital had its origins historically in the fruitful exercise of the producer's own capacity to labour, while labour power originated as a social contract, freely entered into, between those who accumulated wealth through diligence and frugality and those who chose not to do so. 'This pretty fancy', as Marx calls it, is 'torn asunder' in the colonies. There, the bourgeois ideologists are forced to discover 'the truth as to the conditions of production in the mother country'. So long as the labourer 'can accumulate for himself – and this he can do as long as he remains possessor of his means of production – capitalist accumulation and the capitalistic mode of production are impossible.' Capital is not a physical product but a social relation, which rests on 'the annihilation of self-earned private property; in other words, the expropriation of the labourer.' This was the secret that the bourgeoisie, in promoting colonization schemes, was forced to discover in the new world (*Capital*, Vol. 1, ch. 33).

The chapter is a neat coda to the theme broached earlier: that original accumulation was anything but 'idyllic' and 'written in the annals of mankind in letters of blood and fire' (*Capital*, vol. 1, pp. 714–15). That the bourgeoisie came to power, and preserves its power through appropriation of the labour of others, also conveniently legitimizes the struggle of the mass of the people to turn the tables and 'expropriate the expropriators'. But the placement of the chapter suggests that Marx had something broader in mind.

A clue to Marx's intent lies, perhaps, in a curious parallel between his presentation and a problematic identified in Hegel's *Philosophy of Right* (Hegel, 1967, pp. 149–52). Hegel examines the internal expansion of population and industry within civil society and, like Marx, spots an 'inner dialectic' which produces an increasing accumulation of wealth at one pole and an increasing accumulation of misery at the other. Bourgeois society appears unable to stop this increasing polarization and its concomitant, the creation of a penurious rabble, through any *internal* transformation of itself. It is therefore forced to seek *external* relief. 'This inner dialectic of civil society thus drives it . . . to push beyond its own limits and seek markets, and so its necessary means of subsistence, in other lands which are either deficient in the goods it has overproduced, or else generally backward in industry.' More particularly, a 'mature' civil society is driven to found colonies to supply its population with new opportunities and to supply 'itself with a new demand and field for industry'. Hegel proposes, in short, imperialist and colonial solutions to the inner contradictions of a civil society founded on the accumulation of capital.

Somewhat uncharacteristically, Hegel leaves open the exact relation between the processes of *inner* and *outer* transformation and fails to indicate whether or not civil society can permanently resolve its internal problems through spatial expansion.[1] Intended or not, this is the open question that Marx's chapter on colonization addresses. The 'outer transformation' can supply new markets and new fields for industry only at the price of re-creating capitalist relations of private property and a capacity to appropriate the surplus labour of others. The conditions that gave rise to the problems in the first place are simply replicated anew. Marx draws the same conclusion with respect to the expansion of foreign trade. Its increase merely 'transfers the contradictions to a wider sphere and gives them greater latitude' (*Capital*, vol. 2, p. 408). There is, in the long run, no *outer* resolution to the internal contradictions of capitalism. The only solution is an 'internal transformation' that forcibly weans society away from accumulation for accumulation's sake and looks to mobilize natural and human capacities in quest of the freedom which begins only when 'the realm of necessity' is left behind (*Capital*, vol. 3, p. 820).

[1] Avineri (1972, ch. 7) summarizes the general argument while Hirschman (1976) juxtaposes an interpretation of Hegel's argument against a somewhat wayward interpretation of Marx.

Brahms / Variations of a theme by paganini

Given Marx's penchant for jousting with Hegel's ghost, it is difficult to believe he did not have all of this in mind in closing out his only major finished published work in this way.[2] His logic, as usual, is impeccable, and his critique of bourgeois ideology devestating. Yet the chapter does not entirely resolve the issue. It merely affirms that 'outer transformations' entail first the formal and then the real subjugation of labour to capital wherever capital moves to. The outer limit to this process lies at the point where every person in every nook and cranny of the world is caught within the orbit of capital. Until that limit is reached, 'outer' resolutions to the inner contradictions of capitalism appear entirely feasible. Marx comes close to admitting as much in his brief remarks on the role of foreign trade in counteracting the supposed law of falling profits. Foreign trade (and the export of capital) can certainly increase the rate of profit in a variety of ways. But in so far as this means 'an expansion of the scale of production' at home, which in turn 'hastens the process of accumulation', it merely ends up exacerbating those processes that gave rise to the falling rate of profit in the first place. What looks like a solution turns into its opposite in the long run. But Marx is also forced to conclude that the law of falling profits 'acts only as a tendency', and that 'it is only under certain circumstances and only after long periods that its effects become strikingly pronounced' (*Capital*, vol. 3, pp. 237–9). So what are these 'circumstances' and how long is the long run? Marx's final chapter, evidently intended as a subtle response to Hegel, ends up posing the question anew.

The role of imperialism and colonialism, of geographical expansion and territorial domination, in the overall stabilization of capitalism is unresolved in Marxian theory. Indeed, it continues to be the focus of intense controversy and often bitter debate.[3] A comprehensive and irrefutable answer to the problem Hegel so neatly posed so many years ago has yet to be constructed. Is there, then, a 'spatial fix' to capital's problems? And if not, what role does geography play in the processes of crisis formation and resolution?

I UNEVEN GEOGRAPHICAL DEVELOPMENT

Capitalism does not develop upon a flat plain surface endowed with ubiquitous raw materials and homogeneous labour supply with equal transport facility in all directions. It is inserted, grows and spreads within a richly

---

[2] When Marx argued in one of the Afterwords to *Capital* (vol. 1, p. 19) that he had come to terms with Hegel 'nearly thirty years ago' it was his *Critique of Hegel's Philosophy of Right* that he has in mind. O'Malley's 'Introduction' to the latter work is very useful. He argues that Marx's reading of Hegel's *Philosophy of Right* lived with Marx for much of his subsequent intellectual life.

[3] The literature on imperialism is immense. For surveys see Barratt-Brown (1974), Kemp (1967) and Amin (1980).

variegated geographical environment which encompasses great diversity in the munificence of nature and in labour productivity, which is 'a gift, not of Nature, but of a history embracing thousands of centuries' (*Capital*, vol. 1, pp. 512–14). The forces unleashed under capitalism attack, erode, dissolve and transform much of the pre-capitalist economy and culture. Commodity and money exchanges, the formation of wage labour through primitive accumulation, massive labour migrations, the rise of a distinctly capitalist form of the labour process and, finally, the integrating motion of the circulation of capital as a whole, drive 'beyond national barriers and prejudices as much as beyond nature worship, as well as all traditional, confined, complacent, encrusted satisfactions of present needs, and reproduction of old ways of life'. Capitalism 'is destructive towards all of this, and constantly revolutionizes it, tearing down all the barriers which hem in the development of the forces of production, the expansion of needs, the all-sided development of production, and the exploitation and exchange of natural and mental forces' (*Grundrisse*, p. 410).

But capitalism also 'encounters barriers within its own nature', which force it to produce new forms of geographical differentiation. The different forms of geographical mobility described in chapter 12 interact in the context of accumulation and so build, fragment and carve out spatial configurations in the distribution of productive forces and generate similar differentiations in social relations, institutional arrangements and so on. In so doing, capitalism frequently supports the creation of new distinctions in old guises. Pre-capitalist prejudices, cultures and institutions are revolutionized only in the sense that they are given new functions and meanings rather than being destroyed. This is as true of prejudices like racism, sexism and tribalism as it is of institutions like the church and the law. Geographical differentiations then frequently appear to be what they truly are not: mere historical residuals rather than actively reconstituted features within the capitalist mode of production.

It is important to recognize, then, that the territorial and regional coherence that it is at least partially discernible within capitalism is actively produced rather than passively received as a concession to 'nature' or 'history'. The coherence, such as it is, arises out of the conversion of temporal into spatial restraints to accumulation. Surplus value must be produced and realized within a certain timespan. If time is needed to overcome space, surplus value must also be produced and realized within a certain geographical domain.

Follow that idea through for a moment and the basis for uneven geographical development under capitalism becomes more readily apparent. If surplus value has to be produced and realized within a 'closed' region, then the technology of production, structures of distribution, modes and forms of consumption, the value, quantities and qualities of labour power, as well as all necessary physical and social infrastructures must all be consistent with each other within that region. Each change in the labour process would have to be matched by changes in distribution, consumption, etc., if a stable basis for accumulation is to be maintained.[4] Each region would tend to evolve a law of value unto itself, associated with particular material living standards, forms of the labour process, institutional and infrastructural arrangements, etc.

Such a developmental process is totally inconsistent with the universalism towards which capitalism always strives. Regional boundaries are invariably fuzzy and subject to perpetual modification because relative distances alter with improvement in transportation and communication. But regional economies are never closed. The temptation for capitalists to engage in interregional trade, to lever profits out of unequal exchange and to place surplus capitals wherever the rate of profit is highest is in the long run irresistable. And workers will surely be tempted to move to wherever the material living standards are highest. Besides the tendency towards overaccumulation and the threat of devaluation will force capitalists within a region to extend its frontiers or simply to move their capital to greener pastures.

The upshot is that the development of the space economy of capitalism is beset by counterposed and contradictory tendencies. On the one hand spatial barriers and regional distinctions must be broken down. Yet the means to achieve that end entail the production of new geographical differentiations which form new spatial barriers to be overcome. The geographical organization of capitalism internalizes the contradictions within the value form. This is what is meant by the concept of the inevitable uneven development of capitalism.

II GEOGRAPHICAL CONCENTRATION AND DISPERSAL

Uneven geographical development is expressed partially in terms of an opposition between countervailing forces, making for geographical concentration or dispersal in the circulation of capital. Marx's considerations on this point, though fragmentary, are interesting. He is primarily preoccupied in *Capital*, for example, with explaining the incredible concentration of productive forces in urban centres and in correlated changes in social relations of production and living. He captures the interaction effects that led to the rapid agglomeration of production within cities that became, in effect, the collective workshops of capitalist production (*Capital*, vol. 1, p. 352; *Grundrisse*, p. 587). He also shows how the forces making for agglomeration can build cumulatively upon each other, drawing new transport investments and consumer goods industries to already established locations (*Capital*, vol. 2, pp.

[4] This idea is strongly present in Aydalot's (1976) work.

250–1). All of this requires an increasing concentration and expansion of the proletariat in large urban centres, which means either radical changes in the social conditions of reproduction of labour power within urban centres, or 'the constant absorption of primitive and physically uncorrupted elements from the country' (*Capital*, vol. 1, pp. 269, 488, 581, 642). The emergence of a 'floating' industrial reserve army in the main urban centres is, furthermore, a necessary condition for sustained accumulation. The crowding together of labourers in the midst of an 'accumulation of misery, agony of toil, slavery, ignorance, brutality, mental degradation', all exacerbated by various secondary forms of the exploitation (such as rent on housing), became the hallmark of the capitalist form of industrialism. The accumulation of capital and misery go hand in hand, concentrated in space.

These tendencies towards agglomeration obviously encounter both physical and social limits. Congestion costs, increasing rigidity in the use of physical infrastructures, rising rents and sheer lack of space more than offset agglomeration economies. Concentrations of misery form a breeding ground for class consciousness and social unrest. Spatial dispersal begins to look increasingly attractive.

We here invoke all of those forces at work under capitalism that tend to produce 'a constantly widening sphere of circulation', to integrate the world into a single system characterized by an international territorial division of labour. The mobility of credit money and the tendency to eliminate spatial barriers become the key to understanding the rapid dispersal of the circulation of capital across the face of the earth. The prospects of high profits lure capitalists to search and explore in all directions (*Capital*, vol. 3, p. 256). Accumulation spreads its net in ever-widening circles across the world, untimately enmeshing everyone and everything within the circulation process of capital.

But dispersal also encounters powerful limiting constraints. The large quantities of capital embedded in the land itself, the social infrastructures that play such an important role in the reproduction of both capital and labour power, restrictions on the mobility of capital tied down in concrete labour processes, all tend to keep capital in place. And the provision of costly physical and social infrastructures is highly sensitive to economies of scale through concentration.

Opposed tendencies towards geographical concentration and dispersal run up against each other. And there is no guarantee of a stable equilibrium between them. The forces making for agglomeration can easily build cumulatively upon each other and produce an excessive concentration inimical to further accumulation. The forces making for dispersal can likewise easily get out of hand. And revolutions in technology, in means of communication and transport, in the centralization and decentralization of capital (including the degree of vertical integration), in monetary and credit arrangements, in social and physical infrastructures materially affect the balance of forces at work. Capital is thereby impelled sometimes towards simultaneous and sometimes towards successive phases of deepening and widening in the spatial configurations of productive forces and social relations.

It is through such a theorization that we can better understand the accelerated development of the productive forces in one place and their relative retardation in another, the rapid transformation of social relations here and their relative rigidity there. Phenomena like urbanization and regional and international development find their natural place within the Marxian scheme of things.[5] But they are understood in terms of oppositions rather than simply one-sidedly. The antagonisms between town and country, between centre and periphery, between development and the development of underdevelopment, are not accidental or exogenously imposed. They are the coherent product of diverse intersecting forces operating within the overall unity of the circulation process of capital.

III THE REGIONALIZATION OF CLASS AND FACTIONAL STRUGGLE

That class struggle and factional conflict assume a spatial, often territorial, aspect under capitalism is undeniable. Phenomena of this sort are often explained away as the product of deep-seated human sentiments – loyalties to place, 'the land', community and nation that spawn civic pride, regionalism, nationalism, etc. – or of equally deep-seated antipathies between human groups founded in race, language, religion, nationality, etc. But the preceeding analysis allows us to explain the regionalization of class and factional struggle independently of such sentiments. I do not mean to imply by this that human sentiments play no role in interregional conflict, or that conflicts cannot autonomously arise on such bases, I simply want to assert that a material basis exists, within the circulation process of capital itself, for interregional manifestations of class and factional struggle.[6]

The basis rests on that conflictual condition that arises because a portion of the total social capital has to be rendered immobile in order to give the remaining capital greater flexibility of movement. The value of capital, once it

[5] See Dear and Scott (1981); Carney, Hudson and Lewis (1979).

[6] The question of how national, regional and local bourgeoisies form and act has never been clearly analysed from a Marxist perspective except from a purely political and strategic standpoint within some overall conception of class struggle. The issue is deep and riddled with controversy. Recent contributions by Nairn (1977), Davis (1978) and Amin (1980) have broached the question more fully and provoked vigorous criticism. I do not pretend to identify a full answer to the problems posed. I simply want to reveal the material basis within the logic of accumulation for certain kinds of factionalization along regional lines.

is locked into immobile physical and social infrastructures, has to be defended if it is not to be devalued. At the very minimum this means securing the future labour that such investments anticipate by confining the circulation process of the remaining capital within a certain territory over a certain period of time.

Some factions of capital are more committed to immobile investment than others. Land and property owners, developers and builders, the local state and those who hold the mortgage debt have everything to gain from forging a local alliance to protect and promote local interests and to ward off the threat of localized, place-specific devaluation. Production capital which cannot easily move may support the alliance and be tempted to buy local labour peace and skills through compromises over wages and work conditions – thereby gaining the benefits of co-operation from labour and a rising effective demand for wage goods in local markets. Factions of labour that have, through struggle or historical accident, managed to create islands of privilege within a sea of exploitation may also rally to the cause of the alliance. Furthermore, if a local compromise between capital and labour is helpful to local accumulation, then the bourgeoisie as a whole may support it. The basis is laid for the rise of a territorially based alliance between various factions of capital, the local state and even whole classes, in defence of social reproduction processes (both accumulation and the reproduction of labour power) within a particular territory. The basis for the alliance rests, it must be stressed, on the need to make a certain portion of capital immobile in order to give the remainder freedom to move.

The alliance typically engages in community boosterism and strives for community or national solidarity as means to defend the various factional and class interests. Spatial competition between localities, cities, regions and nations takes on a new meaning as each alliance seeks to capture and contain the benefits to be had from flows of capital and labour power through territories under their effective control. And at times of more general crisis, bitter struggles erupt over which locale is to bear the brunt of the devaluation that must surely come. Such objective material conditions provide abundant nourishment to notions of community harmony and national solidarity. Such notions are as meaningful to factions of labour as they are to factions of capital, and the pursuit or territorially based interests is frequently convenient to both. Capital can hope, thereby, to prevail through compromise over a geographically fragmented working class, but in so doing divides and weakens itself. Labour, for its part, may enhance its local position, but at the cost of dropping more revolutionary demands and opening up territorial divisions within its ranks. Global class struggle then dissolves into a variety of territorially based conflicts which support, sustain and in some cases even reconstitute all manner of local prejudices and encrusted traditions.

The stability and coherence of each territorially based alliance is threatened, however, by powerful forces of disruption. Some factions of capital – money capitalists in particular – are more susceptible to the lure of high profits, and production capital can hardly afford to ignore the relative surplus value to be garnered from moves to superior locations. Factions of capital break from the local alliance and seek higher returns elsewhere. And while capital and labour may ally on certain issues (such as tarriff barriers to cheap imports) and compromise on others, the antagonism between them never disappears. To the degree that class struggle sharpens, factions of capital may be increasingly tempted to flee the territory or to strike back at the organized power of labour through such means as open immigration policies. The coherency of the local alliance is always under challenge, both from within and without.

Different factions of capital and labour power have different stakes within a territory depending upon the nature of the assets they own and the privileges they command. Some are more solid partners in a local alliance than others. But all factions feel some sense of tension between the virtues of local commitment and the temptation to move. Landowners, for example, might appear to be the 'natural' backbone of any local alliance by virtue of the asset they hold. But if land is treated as a pure financial asset, then the speculative action of land companies can be as disruptive of a local alliance as anything else. At the other end of the spectrum, we find money capitalists beset by similar dilemmas even though the asset they control is highly mobile. If a powerful bank holds the mortgage debt on much of the infrastructural investment within a territory, then it undermines the quality of its own debt if it syphons off all surplus money capital and sends it to wherever the rate of profit is highest. In order to realize the value of the debt it already holds, the bank may be forced to make additional investments within a territory at a lower rate of profit than could be commanded elsewhere. The capitalists engaged in production likewise have a choice. They can improve their competetive position by supporting local infrastructural improvement through participation in a local alliance, or they can move to another place where conditions are known to be better. They can also use the threat of a move to blackmail concessions (tax-breaks, for example) from more vulnerable partners. And labour is not immune from such pressures either. It may refrain from pushing its demands in revolutionary directions for fear of sparking capital flight, which will undermine the privileges it has already won.

Class and factional struggle are not abrogated thereby. They simply assume a territorial aspect which operates jointly with other forms of struggle. In exactly the same way that the search for relative surplus value invokes technology and location jointly, so class and factional struggles necessarily unfold in space and time. The historical geography of capitalism is a social process which rests on the evolution of productive forces and social relations which exist as particular spatial configurations. Countervailing forces are at work which put the spatial mobility of capital and labour power into a tension-packed and contradiction-prone geography. Territorial-based conflicts then become part of the means whereby class struggle around accumulation and its contradictions search out new bases for, or alternatives to, accumulation. These new bases simultaneously embrace the creation of new spatial configurations as well as new labour processes. Territorial alliances and inter-territorial conflicts are to be construed as active moments, rather than aberrations, within the general history of class struggle.

IV HIERARCHICAL ARRANGEMENTS AND THE INTERNATIONALIZATION OF CAPITAL

The tensions between fixity and motion in the circulation of capital, between concentration and dispersal, between local commitment and global concerns, put immense strains upon the organizational capacities of capitalism. The history of capitalism has, as a consequence, been marked by continuous exploration and modification of organizational arrangements that can assuage and contain such tensions. The result has been the creation of nested hierarchical structures of organization which can link the local and particular with the achievement of abstract labour on the world stage. Crises are articulated, and class and factional struggles unfold within such organizational forms while the forms themselves often require dramatic transformation in the face of crises of accumulation.

We have already encountered an example of such a nested hierarchical structure. We showed in chapter 9 that a hierarchy of moneys of different qualities is necessary for accumulation to proceed. Only in this way can the local need for medium of circulation be related to the universal equivalent as a measure of value. Local and particular events, such as the creation of money through a credit transaction at a particular place and time, can be integrated into world monetary arrangements through the hierarchy of institutions within the monetary system. We also argued that contradictions exist within this hierarchical system and that what happens at one level is not necessarily consistent with what ought to happen at another. The ultimate expression of crises, for example, is as a contradiction between the financial system and its monetary base. The preservation of the quality of money as a measure of value is a task that falls to the lot of those international institutions that occupy the commanding heights of the hierarchy. It follows that crises are invariably manifest as conflicts between various levels within this hierarchy of monetary arrangements.

Other hierarchical forms of organization abound and exhibit similar tensions within themselves. Multinational firms, for example, have a global perspective but have to integrate with local circumstances in a variety of

what is the historical standing of contradictions? how unstable are these formations in reality?

places.[7] They may rely heavily on patterns of local sub-contracting and may therefore participate, to limited degree, in support of a local territorial alliance. The centralization of capital within their organization is invariably accompanied (see chapter 5) by spatial decentralization, and that means some degree of local commitment and accountability, which goes along with the capacity to wield a great deal of local power by direct or indirect threats. The local integration of multinational firms makes the decision to stay put or close down a branch plant in a particular place a difficult one. And within the hierarchy of the multinational firm, what makes sense at one level does not necessarily make sense at another. The same dilemmas confront multinational merchant capital. Global strategies bridge the tension between local commitment and the struggle to appropriate surplus value wherever it can be had. While it always appears as if the power lies at the top of these hierarchical structures, it is production in particular locales that is always the ultimate source of that power. Multinational firms internalize the tensions between fixity and movement, between local commitment and global concerns. Their only advantage is that they can organize their occupation of space and the history of their own geography according to conscious plan. The only problem is that these plans are conceived in an environment of accumulation plagued by uncertainty and riddled with contradictions.

The political system is organized along similar hierarchical lines for similar reasons.[8] While the nation-state occupies a key position in this hierarchy, supra-national organizations reflect the need for global co-ordinations, and regional, city, and neighbourhood governmental arrangements links universal with purely local concerns. Conflict abounds between levels within this hierarchical structure, making a mockery of any theory of the state as a monolithic, unitary phenomenon. And even though much of the power may be located at the national level, the problem of integrating local with global requirements always remains a thorny problem for any administration. The conflict becomes particularly acute for any nation that aspires to the role of world banker. Should it, in the name of global prospects for accumulation, accede to and even orchestrate the destruction of certain local economies within its borders? Or should it seek to protect them and pursue parochial and even isolationist policies which in the end spell autarky and the death-knell to open global patterns of accumulation?

These various hierarchically organized structures in the spheres of finance, production, the state, etc., together with the urban hierarchies structured to ensure efficient movement of commodities mesh awkwardly with each other to define a variety of scales — local, regional, national and international (to use common categories that roughly reflect our meaning). Territorially based

[7] Radice (1975); Palloix (1973; 1975a).

[8] Dulong's (1978) discussion of the organization of regional power in France is very interesting.

Diller: a disney education: analyse & critique d'un entertainment corporation

alliances can form at any of these scales. But the nature and politics of the alliance tend to alter, sometimes quite dramatically, from one scale to another. Patterns of class and factional struggle and of inter-territorial competition shift also. Issues that appear fundamental at one scale disappear entirely from view at another; factions that are active participants at one scale can fade from the scene or even change at another. Between the particular and the universal lies a whole mess of untidy organizational arrangements which mediate the dynamics of capital flow within the space economy of capitalism and provide multiple and diverse forums in which class and factional struggle can unfold.

The untidy intricacy of such arrangements often obscures their importance as transmission devices which relate particular concrete action to the global effects of abstract labour and thereby confirm the political economy that integrates the individual into the complex totality of civil society. When workers, for example, buy a house at a particular place and time, they may do so on the basis of a mortgage arrangement sanctioned by traditions of contract, supported by government policies and promoted by bourgeois ideology. Their monthly payments to the bank reflect a time of amortization and an interest rate reflective of global conditions of accumulation, mediated by the strength and security of particular institutions within the financial system and the strength of the national economy in relation to world trade. All of these mediations are captured and reduced, in the final analysis, to a monthly payment to the bank (or parallel financial institution). At the other extreme, when international bankers struggle to bring stability to a world economy that seems on the brink of chaos, they do so in the context of myriad individual decisions and the chaotic intersection of inter-territorial struggles, class and factional alliances, etc. Sensing their powerlessness, they may set out to create institutions, such as the International Monetary Fund, that have the power to discipline and cajole nation-states and so force through policies that effect the individual's daily life in vital and sometimes traumatic ways. We must now consider how mediations of this sort affect the formation and resolution of crises within the space economy of capitalism.

V   THE 'THIRD CUT' AT CRISIS THEORY: GEOGRAPHICAL ASPECTS

Capitalists behave like capitalists wherever they are. They pursue the expansion of value through exploitation without regard to the social consequences. They overaccumulate capital and in the end create the conditions that lead to the devaluation of individual capitals and labour power through crisis. This happens, however, within a framework of uneven geographical development produced by differential mobilities of various kinds of capital and labour power, all linked together within temporal constraints imposed by the circulation process of capital itself. These mobilities fashion individualized concrete labour processes into 'a totality of different modes of labour embracing the world market' and so define abstract labour as value.

Our task is to construct a 'third-cut' theory of crisis formation which specifically acknowledges the material qualities of social space as defined under capitalist relations of production and exchange. The 'first-cut' theory of crisis, recall, dealt with the underlying source of capitalism's internal contradictions. The 'second-cut' theory examined temporal dynamics as these are shaped and mediated through financial and monetary arrangements. The 'third-cut' theory, with which we are here concerned, has to integrate the geography of uneven development into the theory of crisis. The task is not easy. We have to deal somehow with multiple, simultaneous and joint determinations. The trade-off between relative surplus value from locational or technological advantage, for example, often gives capitalists considerable latitude in confronting their competitors. This lack of unique determinations makes theorization difficult. In what follows, therefore, we will employ some drastic simplifying assumptions in order to capture the essence of crisis formation within the geography of uneven development.

1 Particular, individual and place-specific devaluation

If capital in whatever guise and labour power of whatever sort happen, for whatever reason, not to be in the right place at the right time, then they will likely suffer devaluation. Myriad speculative movements make proper and exact co-ordinations in space and time a matter of accident, unless conscious planning powers are exercised via the financial system or the state. In the normal course of events, some individuals will suffer devaluation of their capital or labour power while others will profit handsomely or find well remunerated jobs. The myriad particular and place-specific devaluations that result do not have to coalesce into any grander pattern. They are simply part of the normal human cost, the social wear and tear, of accumulation through competition.

This conception has a two-fold significance. First, devaluation is a social determination. It is not that a particular labour process absolutely cannot work in a particular place, but that it cannot generate at least the average rate of profit. Devaluations always fuse the particular and the individual (concrete labour) with the universal and the social (abstract labour). And the devaluation is *always* specific to a particular place and time. Secondly, more general forms of crisis rest upon and arise out of this confusion of local, particular and individual events. In the same way that Marx broke open the identity presupposed in Say's Law into so many *possibilities* of crises (by considering the separation of sales and purchases in space and time), so do innumerable, particular and place-specific devaluations create openings within which more general possibilities for crises can fester. We have now to show how festering sores are converted into gaping wounds by social processes unique to capitalism.

Revolutions in value are sparked by the search for relative surplus value through technological change or locational shifts. The effect is to devalue the capitals employed under inferior technologies or in inferior locations. This process is complicated because the drive to accelerate turnover time through improvements in transport and communications alters relative spaces and so transforms superior into inferior locations and vice versa. The movement of individual labourers in search of higher material living standards and better work conditions adds to the confusion – the advantage to capital of access to cheap pools of surplus labour in certain locations may be whittled away through labour migration. The total effect is that place-specific devaluations become more than just a random, accidental affair. Spatial competition leads to a plant closure here, the loss of a rail link there. Associated losses of jobs and the diminuation of local effective demand for wage goods or constant capital spark adjustments within the space economy that entail further devaluations. The devaluations are systematized into a certain spatial configuration through the rationalizing power of class conflict and competition over absolute and relative forms of surplus value. The continuous re-structuring of spatial configurations through revolutions in value must again be seen, however, as a normal feature of capitalist development.[9]

2   Crisis formation within regions

Overaccumulation stems from contradictions between the productive forces and social relations within the process of circulation of capital. These contradictions break the desired unity between the production and realization of surplus value. The unity can be restored only forcibly through crises of devaluation. Production and realization have to be accomplished within a given turnover time, however, and we earlier showed that this translates, under certain conditions, into production and realization of surplus value within the confines of a definite space. The aggregate effect is hard to describe because each individual capital, operating from a particular location, has its own specific conditions of production, exchange (including transportation) and realization.

To simplify, we initially assume that all production and realization of interdependent capitals occurs within a closed region. Accumulation proceeds within that region at rates dependent upon the local expansion of the proletariat, that state of class struggle, the pace of innovation, the growth in aggregate effective demand, etc. But since capitalists will be capitalists, overaccumulation is bound to arise. The threat of massive devaluation looms

[9] Massey (1981) explores this idea in depth with reference to the UK electronics and electrical engineering industries.

large and civil society appears destined to experience the social distress, disruption and unrest that accompany the forcible restoration of conditions favourable to accumulation.

This is, of course, exactly the kind of 'inner dialectic' that forces society to seek relief through some sort of 'spatial fix'. The frontiers of the region can be rolled back or relief gained by exports of money capital, commodities or productive capacities or imports of fresh labour powers from other regions. The tendency towards overaccumulation within the region remains unchecked, but devaluation is avoided by successive and ever grander 'outer transformations'. This process can presumably continue until all external possibilities are exhausted or because other regions resist being treated as mere convenient appendages.

But as soon as a region opens its borders to flows of capital and labour, the value relations within the region begin to reflect the 'totality of different modes of labour embracing the world market'. Value revolutions can equally well be imposed on the region from without. The competitive position of the region as a whole can be eroded because other regions have gone through the discomfort and tragedy of internal re-structuring of their productive apparatus, social relations, distributive arrangements, and so on. The region, far from resolving its problems of overaccumulation through the creation of external relations, may be forced into even more savage devaluation through outside pressure. Interregional competition becomes the order of the day. And the relative strengths of different territorially based alliances become an important factor.

Matters now become more than a little confused. The distinction between 'inner' and 'outer transformations' becomes hard to isolate. Regional 'boundaries', if they exist at all, are highly porous to capital and labour movements; local alliances are notoriously shakey on certain issues; and hierarchical forms of organization, operating at a variety of scales, offer different possibilities for co-ordination. The degree to which overaccumulation problems arising in one place can be relieved by further development or devaluation in another place depends upon the intersection of all manner of diverse and conflicting forces.

But the upshot is that some regions boom while others decline. This need not augur a global crisis of capitalism, however. The different regional rythms of accumulation may be but loosely co-ordinated because the co-ordinations rest on the variegated and often conflicting mobilities of different forms of capital and labour.[10] The timing of upturns and downturns in the accumulation cycle can then vary from one region to another with interesting interaction effects. The unity to the accumulation process presupposed in earlier versions of the crisis theory fragments into different regional rhythms

[10] See Carney, Hudson and Lewis (1979) and the special issue of the *Journal of the Union of Radical Political Economics*, vol. 10, no. 3 (1978).

that can just as easily compensate each other as build into some vast global crash. The very real possibility exists that the global pace of accumulation can be sustained through compensating oscillations within the parts. The geography of uneven development helps convert the crisis tendencies of capitalism into compensating regional configurations of rapid accumulation and devaluation.

3 Switching crises

The smooth switching of surpluses of capital and labour from one region to another create a pattern of compensating oscillations within the whole encounters strong barriers. Frontiers may become closed, pre-capitalist societies may resist primitive accumulation, revolutionary movements may spring up, and so on. But barriers also arise out of the whole contradictory logic of capital accumulation itself. We now consider these more carefully.

The more open the world is to geographical re-structuring, the more easily temporary resolutions to problems of overaccumulation can be found. Geographical expansion, like increase of population (see above, p. 163), provides a strong basis for sustained accumulation. Crises are reduced to minor switching crises as flows and capital and labour switch from one region to another, or even reverse themselves, and spark regional devaluations (which can sometimes be intense) as well as major adjustments in the spatial structures (such as the transport system) designed to facilitate spatial flows.

The problem, of course, is that the more capitalism develops, the more it tends to succumb to forces making for geographical inertia. We here encounter a version of that contradiction that Marx described as the domination of dead over living labour. The circulation of capital is increasingly imprisoned withim immobile physical and social infrastructures which are crafted to support certain kinds of production, certain kinds of labour processes, distributional arrangements, consumption patterns, and so on. Increasing quantities of fixed capital and longer turnover times on production check uninhibited mobility. The growth of productive forces, in short, acts as a barrier to rapid geographical re-structuring in exactly the same way as it hinders the dynamic of future accumulation by the imposition of the dead weight of past investments. Territorial alliances, which often became increasingly powerful and more deeply entrenched, arise to protect and enhance the value of capital already committed within the region.

All of these forces interlock, strengthen the trend towards geographical inertia and so prevent rapid re-structurings in the space economy of capitalism. Worse still, under pressure of devaluation, the forces of inertia may strengthen rather than loosen their grip and so exacerbate the problem — a local alliance may act to conserve privileges already won, to sustain investments already made, to keep a local compromise intact, and to protect itself from the chill winds of spatial competition through import and export controls, foreign exchange controls and immigration laws. New spatial configurations cannot be achieved because regional devaluations are not allowed to run their course. The uneven geographical development of capitalism then assumes a form that is totally inconsistent with sustained accumulation either within the region or on a global scale.

The more the forces of geographical inertia prevail, the deeper will the aggregate crises of capitalism become and the more savage will switching crises have to be to restore the disturbed equilibrium. Local alliances will have to be dramatically reorganized (the rise of fascism being the most horrible example), technological mixes suddenly altered (incurring massive devaluation of old plant), physical and social infrastructures totally reconstituted (often through a crisis in state expenditures) and the space economy of capitalist production, distribution and consumption totally transformed. The cost of devaluation to both individual capitalists and labourers becomes substantial. Capitalism reaps the savage harvest of its own internal contradictions.

But savage though such switching crises can be, the total re-structuring of the space economy of capitalism on a global scale still holds out the prospect for a restoration of equilibrium through a reorganization of the regional parts. The contradictions of capitalism are still contained within the global structures of uneven geographical development.

4 Building new arrangements to co-ordinate spatial integration and geographical uneven development

Not all forms of geographical uneven development and spatial expansion diminish problems of overaccumulation. Indeed, spatial configurations are as likely to contribute to the problem as resolve it. This focuses our attention upon the co-ordinating mechanisms that shape spatial configurations and capital flows. We showed in chapter 12, for example, that the geographical mobility of money, commodities, production capital and labour power depend upon the creation of fixed and immobile physical and social infrastructures. How can the latter be changed to accommodate the expanding volumes of capital in motion?

New transport and communications systems can be built, we saw in chapter 8, using overaccumulated capital, albeit at the cost of some devaluation of capital embodied in time past. The new investments stand to be devalued only if the anticipated expansions fail to materialize in the expected spatial configuration, or if further competing investments are piled too rapidly on top of each other. The pace of transformation in transport and communications systems is constrained by such considerations. They cannot necessarily expand fast enough to accommodate the needs of continuously accelerating quantities of commodity movement into new regions. The fixed spatial structures required to overcome space themselves become the spatial barriers to be overcome.

The same observation applies to those social and organizational infrastructural arrangements which, we earlier saw, tend to exhibit a nested hierarchical structure, characterized by all kinds of untidy overlaps and discontinuities, but which can link the local and particular with the global and universal aspects of labour under capitalism. Indeed, much of the seeming untidiness of these arrangements reflects the fact that they are continuously in process of transformation. The dramatic increase in the volume of world trade and capital flow put immense pressure upon the international monetary and financial system, for example. Whole new levels have been created within the hierarchy (central banks and international monetary institutions) and new power relations between the levels have come into being. Multinational companies have similarly fumbled towards new forms of organization to cope with continuously changing circumstances. Political and administrative systems are likewise always under pressure to aapt.

Such hierarchical structures do not instantaneously adapt to capitalism's needs, however. To begin with, each set of institutions adjusts in the light of the particular interests of those that run them as well as in response to external pressure. Multinational corporations act to secure access to raw materials, markets and labour power; seek to cover space and exclude competition; and are as much interested in monopolization as they are in co-ordinating particular with global requirements. Once in a position to manage scarcity, they may simply organize international trade and even whole patterns of uneven geographical development in their own narrowly defined interest. They are likely to use their power to thieve, appropriate and cajole as much surplus value as possible from others. The same is true for bankers (at whatever level in the hierarchy), politicians, administrators, and so on. Appropriation of this sort disrupts the co-ordinations and may necessitate the creation of ever newer layers within the hierarchy to discipline the others.

Even when not succumbing to pure venality, the managers within this hierarchical system possess enough power often to influence both the pace and direction of geographical expansion. This is particularly true of vast enterprises, the major financial institutions and the state, which has the nominal power to control flows of capital and labour power in accordance with the interests of the territorial alliance that rules it. Competition between states (or other units) or power struggles between levels within the hierarchy have marked effects upon patterns of uneven development. Furthermore, the hierarchical structures are not independent of each other: the evolution of multinational corporations depended upon new international monetary arrangements and new forms of state intervention, for example. The integrations imply that power struggles over who is to exercise what co-ordinating function are endemic. And such power struggles are often fought out with total disregard for the needs of capitalism in general.

But even if the abuses were not there, the underlying tension between fixity and mobility – which spawned the hierarchical arrangements in the first place – would remain unresolved. The stability of co-ordinating arrangements is, after all, a vital attribute in the face of perpetual and incoherent dynamism. At some point the tension between the two is bound to snap.

At such points a crisis in the co-ordinating mechanisms ensues. The nested hierarchical structures have to be reorganized, rationalized and reformed. New monetary systems, new political structures, new organizational forms for capital have to be brought into being. The birth pangs are often painful. But only in this way can institutional arrangements grown profligate and fat be brought into tighter relation to the underlying requirements of accumulation. If the reforms turn out well, then co-ordinations that absorb overaccumulation through uneven geographical development at least appear possible. If they fail, then the uneven development that results exacerbates rather than resolves the difficulties. A global crisis ensues. The only solution is a total re-structuring of the relations within the capitalist mode of production, including the hierarchical co-ordinating arrangements.

VI BUILDING TOWARDS GLOBAL CRISES

Uneven geographical development and expansion cannot possibly cure the internal contradictions to which capitalism is heir. The problems of capitalism cannot, therefore, be resolved through the instant magic of some 'spatial fix'. Yet it is important to recognize that more general crises arise out of the chaos and confusion of local, particular events. They build upwards on the basis of concrete individual labour processes and market exchanges into global crises in the qualities of abstract labour, in the value form. The temporal and spatial constraints on turnover time ensure that a variety of regional differentiations are produced *en route*. Crises build, therefore, through uneven geographical development, co-ordinated through hierarchical organizational forms. And the same observation applies to the impacts of devaluation. They are always felt at particular places and times and are built into distinctive regional, sectoral and organizational configurations. The impacts can be spread and to some degree mitigated through switching of flows of capital and labour between sectors and regions (often simultaneously) or into a radical reconstruction of physical and social infrastructures. Global crises build up through the impact of less traumatic switching crises.

Global crises form, then, as 'violent fusions of disconnected factors operating independently of one another yet correlated' (*Theories of Surplus Value,* pt 3, p. 120). To explore this process of fusion more concretely, we adopt some rather drastic simplifying assumptions. Assume that the globe is divided into regional economies 'operating independently yet correlated'. The regions are connected by flows of capital and labour power under the aegis of hierarchically structured organizational arrangements which are neutral as to their effects. Rhythms of accumulation vary from one region to another. The tendency towards overaccumulation and devaluation is, however, universal to all regions. Each region is therefore periodically forced to seek some transformation in its external relations which will alleviate the discomfort of crises of devaluation within itself.

Marx was fully aware of the existence of such situations. He notes, for example, that under conditions of overaccumulation the English 'are forced to lend their capital to other countries in order to create a market for their commodities', that capital has 'to put on seven league boots', break through spatial barriers, and so to reach a 'development of the productive forces which could only be achieved very slowly within its own limits' (*Theories of Surplus Value*, pt 3, p. 122; *Grundrisse*, p. 416). Whether or not crises dissipate or build through such mechanisms becomes the problem to be solved. And the answers are as various as the means open to capitalists in one region to dispose of their overaccumulated capital in another. We take up each possibility in turn.

1 *External markets and underconsumption*

If overaccumulated capital in Britain is lent as means of payment to Argentina to buy up the excess commodities produced in Britain, then the relief to overaccumulation is at best short-lived and the general prospects for avoiding devaluation negligible. Pursuit of such a strategy assumes that the crises of capitalism, which are partially manifest as an apparent lack of effective demand, are entirely attributable to underconsumption. Marx is as firm in his rejection of the interregional version of this argument as he is of the original. All that happens, he suggests, is that the effects of overaccumulation proliferate over space during the credit-fuelled phase of the upswing and are registered as a growing gap between the balance of trade and the balance of payments between regions. When the credit system collapses back onto its monetary basis, as Marx insists it must, then the sequence of events is modified by these interregional balances. He describes a typical sequence this way:

> The crisis may first break out in England, the country which advances most of the credit and takes the least, because the balance of payments ... which must be settled immediately, is *infavourable*, even though the general balance of trade is *favourable*. . . . The crash in England,

initiated and accompanied by a gold drain, settles England's balance of payments. . . . Now comes the turn of some other country. . . .

The balance of payments is in times of crisis unfavourable to every nation . . . but always to each country in succession, as in volley-firing. . . . It then becomes evident that all these nations have simultaneously over-exported (thus over-produced) and over-imported (thus over-traded), that prices were inflated in all of them, and credit stretched too far. And the same break-down takes place in all of them.

The costs of devaluation are then forced back on to the initiating region by:

first shipping away precious metals; then selling consigned commodities at low prices; exporting commodities to dispose of them or obtain money advances on them at home; increasing the rate of interest, recalling credit, depreciating securities, disposing of foreign securities, attracting foreign capital for investment in these depreciated securities, and finally bankruptcy, which settles a mass of claims. (*Capital*, vol. 3, pp. 491–2, 517))

The sequence sounds dismally familiar. No prospect here, evidently, of a 'spatial fix' to capitalism's contradictions. Yet the world is manifestly a complicated place, so that even here possibilities arise that can at least postpone the inevitability of crises. If, for example, Argentina has abundant gold reserves but England none, then excess commodities produced in the latter country can be paid for with specie. Balances are maintained through interregional transfers of specie. This can attenuate the process of crisis formation. But in the long run it can have no more effect than invoking the gold producers as the grand stabilizers of the circulation process of capital as a whole (see above, pp. 93–6).

A more intriguing possibility arises when capitalism becomes highly dependent upon trade with non-capitalist social formations. Circumstances can indeed arise, Marx concedes, in which 'the capitalist mode of production is conditional on modes of production lying outside of its own stage of development' (*Capital*, vol. 2, p. 110). The degree of relief afforded thereby depends on the nature of the non-capitalist society and its capacity to integrate into the capitalist system through commodity and money exchanges. But crisis formation is checked only if the non-capitalist countries 'consume and produce at a rate that suits the countries with capitalist production' (*Capital*, vol. 3, p. 257). And how can that be done without engaging in the politics and economics of imperialist domination? And even then, there are contradictions involved which make such a resolution temporary. 'You cannot continue to inundate a country with your manufactures, unless you enable it to give you some produce in return.' Hence, 'the more the [British] industrial interest become dependent on the Indian market, the more it felt the necessity of creating fresh productive powers in India, after having ruined her native industry' (*On Colonialism*, with Engels, p. 52). It is no longer a matter of seeking external relief through trade, but of forging new systems of production based on new social relations in new regions. We now take up that prospect directly.

2 The export of capital for production

Surplus capital lent abroad as means of purchase (rather than as means of payment) contributes to the formation of new productive forces in other regions. An external move of this sort has an entirely different relation to the general process of overaccumulation. It accords with Marx's argument that the realization problem can be resolved only through an expansion of production. But it then simply transfers the dilemmas of 'accumulation for accumulation's sake, production for production's sake' to other regions at the same time as it intensifies overaccumulation at home. 'If capital is sent abroad,' Marx argues, 'this is not done because it absolutely could not be applied at home, but because it can be employed at a higher rate of profit in a foreign country' (*Capital*, vol. 3, p. 256). The effect is to increase the average rate of profit (*Theories of Surplus Value* pt 2, pp. 436–7) and hasten the tendency towards falling profits in the long run (*Capital*, vol. 3, p. 237). The same result is achieved if expanding production abroad cheapens the elements of constant capital and wage goods in the home market. The value composition of capital temporarily declines and the rate of exploitation increases. Even more capital is produced as a result.

The implication is that overaccumulation at home can be relieved only if surplus money capital (or its equivalent in commodities) is sent abroad to create fresh productive forces in new regions on a continuously accelerating basis. Furthermore, the productive forces have to be used in a certain way if capital is to be reproduced. The social relations appropriate to capitalism – wage labour – have to be in place and capable of a parallel expansion. Geographical expansion of the productive forces therefore means expansion of the proletariat on a global basis. We arrive back at the proposition (see above, p. 163) that crises of capitalism are less intense under conditions of rapid increase in the labour force, through either primitive accumulation or natural increase. We will take up the deeper implications of that shortly.

Export of the productive forces means export of the whole package of the capitalist mode of production which includes modes of distribution and consumption. This appears to be the only way to resolve the overaccumulation problem of capitalism. It spawns a variety of regional effects, depending upon the relations between regions and the conditions prevailing in each.

The destruction of pre-capitalist forms of economy and industry through competition of machine manufactures (aided by cheap transport costs) 'forcibly converts' countries into raw material suppliers. 'A new and international division of labour, a division suited to the requirements of the chief centres of modern industry, springs up, and converts one part of the globe into a chiefly agricultural field of production, for supplying the other part which remains a chiefly industrial field' (*Capital*, vol. 1, p. 451). If the territorial division of labour remains constant, however, then the circulation of capital will almost certainly generate deeper and deeper switching crises in flows of capital and labour between them. The only solution is a further transformation in the territorial division of labour based upon an intensification of the capitalist mode of production within the new region. Marx expected such a transformation in India:

> when you have introduced machinery into the locomotion of a country, which posseses iron and coals, you are unable to withold it from its fabrication. . . . The railways system will therefore become, in India, truly the forerunner of modern industry . . . [which] will dissolve the hereditary divisions of labour, upon which rest the Indian castes, those decisive impediments to Indian progress and Indian power. . . . The bourgeois period of history has to create the material basis of the new world. . . . Bourgeois industry and commerce create these material conditions of a new world in the same way that geological revolutions have created the surface of the earth. (*On Colonialism*, with Engels) pp. 85–7)

The anticipated transition was long delayed in India by a mixture of internal resistance to capitalist penetration and imperialist policies imposed by the British. The theoretical point, however, is that, if such transitions are blocked for whatever reasons, then the capacity of the home country to dispose of further overaccumulated capital is also in the long run blocked. The spatial fix is negated and global crises are inevitable. The unconstrained growth of capitalism within new regions – the United States and Japan immediately spring to mind – is, therefore, an absolute necessity for the survival of capitalism. These are the fields in which excess overaccumulated capitals can most easily be absorbed in ways that create further market openings and further opportunities for profitable investment. But we here encounter dilemmas of another sort. The new productive forces in new regions pose a competitive threat to home-based industry. Furthermore, capital tends to overaccumulate in the new region, which is forced to look to its own spatial fix in order to avoid internal devaluations.

Devaluation is the end result, no matter what. The home country is faced with a 'catch-22'. The unconstrained development of capitalism in new regions caused by capital exports brings devaluation at home through international competition. Constrained development abroad limits international competition but blocks off opportunities for further capital export and so sparks internally generated devaluations. Small wonder, then, that the major imperialist powers have vacillated in their policies between 'open door', free trade, and autarky within a closed empire.[11]

Nevertheless, within these constraints all kinds of options exist. The 'historical mission' of the bourgeoisie is not accomplished overnight, nor are the 'material conditions of a new world' created in a day. The intensification and spread of capitalism is a long drawn-out revolutionary transformation accomplished over successive generations. While local, regional and switching crises are normal grist for the working out of that process through uneven geographical development, the building of global crises – usually experienced initially as switching crises of increasing intensity – depends upon the exhaustion of possibilities for further revolutionary transformation along capitalist lines. And that depends not upon the propagation of new productive forces across the face of the earth, but upon the supply of fresh labour power. It is to that prospect that we now turn.

3 The expansion of the proletariat and primitive accumulation

Beneath all of the nuanced shifts in the international division of labour, in technology and organization and in the distribution of productive forces, lies a basic Marxian proposition: the accumulation of capital *is* increase of the proletariat (*Capital*, vol. 1, p. 614). The central point of Marx's implied disagreement with Hegel, for example, is not that colonization can afford *no* temporary relief to the contradictions of capitalism, but that it can only do so if it is accompanied by primitive accumulation. The significance of that last chapter to the first volume of *Capital* now strikes home with redoubled force. The accumulation of capital is increase of the proletariat, and that means primitive accumulation of some sort or another.

But primitive accumulation comes in many guises. The penetrations of money forms and commerce exercise a 'more or less dissolving influence everywhere on the producing organization which it finds at hand and whose different forms are mainly carried on with a view to use value' (*Capital*, vol. 3, pp. 331–2; *Grundrisse*, pp. 224–5). But the form of labour process and the social relations of production that result vary considerably depending upon the initial conditions. The 'classical' account of primitive accumulation that Marx sets out in *Capital* is open to repetition elsewhere only to the degree that roughly parallel conditions are encountered. Marx himself recognized some of the possible variations. Plantation colonies, run by capitalists on the basis of slave labour, produced for the world market and were formally integrated into capitalism without being based on wage labour.

> No matter how large the surplus product [extracted] from the surplus labour of their slaves in the simple form of cotton or corn, they can

[11] Gardner's (1964) study of 'New Deal' diplomacy on the part of the United States captures the essence of this conflict very well.

adhere to this simple undifferentiated labour because foreign trade enables them to convert these simple products into any kind of use value. (*Theories of Surplus Value*, pt 2, pp. 302–3; pt 3, p. 243)

Modes of exploitation in traditional peasant-based societies can also be converted into realms of formal rather than real subsumption under capital. The whole debate, which Marx in part presaged, over the Asiatic mode of production and the direct conversion of state powers into forms of state capitalism poses a similar problem. Even what Marx called 'the colonies proper' – such as 'the United States, Australia, etc.' – do not escape from subtle nuances within the general framework of primitive accumulation. 'Here', says Marx,

> the mass of the farming colonists, although they bring with them a larger or smaller amount of capital from the motherland, are not *capitalists*, nor do they carry on *capitalist* production. They are more or less peasants who work themselves and whose main object . . . is to produce *their own livelihood.* . . . They are, and continue for a long time to be, competitors of the farmers who are already producing more or less capitalistically. (*Theories of Surplus Value*, pt 2, pp. 202–3)

> There the capitalist regime everywhere comes into collision with the resistance of the producer, who, as owner of his own conditions of labour, employs that labour to enrich himself, instead of the capitalist. The contradictions of these two diametrically opposed economic systems, manifests itself here practically in the struggle between them. Where the capitalist has at his back the power of the mother-country, he tries to clear out of his way by force, the modes of production and appropriation, based on the independent labour of the producer. (*Capital*, vol. 1, p. 765)

It takes many generations before the labourer is ultimately made 'free' as a pure wage labourer. There are many intermediate steps on that road, many intermediate forms the social relations of production can acquire. And each pays its due to capital in the form of at least a surplus product. But as the revolutionary power of capitalism gathers strength, so the intermediate forms give way to wage labour pure and simple. New rounds of primitive accumulation attack and erode social relations of production achieved through preceding rounds. The uneven geographical development of that process is etched in the annals of human history 'in letters of blood and fire'. Violent and episodic guerilla struggle, fought on a highly varied terrain and under all manner of social conditions, periodically erupt into major confrontations between the representatives of opposed economic systems. Thus is the social and human geography of the new world created to match the new material conditions laid down there.

But as capitalism exhausts the possibilities for primitive accumulation at the expense of pre-capitalist and intermediate social formations, so it has to look elsewhere for fresh sources of labour power. In the end it has only one place to go. It has to cannibalize itself. Some capitalists, while remaining nominally in control of their own means of production, become formally subordinate to other capitalists – chiefly via the credit system but also through patterns of tied sub-contracting to larger firms or dependency upon monopoly sources of supply. Others are forced into the proletariat directly, sometimes on a part-time and sometimes on a full-time basis, through heightened competition and bankruptcy. Other layers within the bourgeoisie likewise lose their former independence and become mere wage labourers, albeit within a finely graded hierarchical system. *this influence was much constrained*

Marx was well aware, of course, that capitalists stood to be pro-*84* letarianized, but mainly confined attention to phases of devaluation that are *though* always, to some degree or other, phases of primitive accumulation at the expense of already existing capitalists (*Capital*, vol. 1, p. 626). The deepening and widening of crises into global configurations transforms the cannibalistic tendencies of capitalism into so many modes of mutually assured destruction, to be periodically unleashed as the ultimate form of devaluation.

4 The export of devaluation

At times of savage devaluation, interregional rivalries typically degenerate into struggles over who is to bear the burden of devaluation. The export of unemployment, of inflation, of idle productive capacity become the stakes in the game. Trade wars, dumping, interest rate wars, restrictions on capital flow and foreign exchange, immigration policies, colonial conquest, the subjugation and domination of tributary economies, the forced reorganization of the division of labour within economic empires, and, finally, the physical destruction and forced devaluation of a rival's capital through war are some of the methods at hand. Each entails the aggressive manipulation of some aspect of economic, financial or state power. The politics of imperialism, the sense that the contradictions of capitalism can be cured through world domination by some omnipotent power, surges to the forefront. The ills of capitalism cannot so easily be contained. Yet the degeneration of economic into political struggles plays its part in the long-run stabilization of capitalism, provided enough capital is destroyed *en route*. Patriotism and nationalism have many functions in the contemporary world and may arise for diverse reasons; but they frequently provide a most convenient cover for the devaluation of both capital and labour. We will shortly return to this aspect of matters since it is, I believe, by far the most serious threat, not only to the survival of capitalism (which matters not a jot), but to the survival of the human race.

VII IMPERIALISM

Marx never proposed a theory of imperialism. He presumably would have confronted the subject in proposed books on the state, foreign trade and the world market (*Selected Correspondence*, with Engels, pp. 112–13). In the absence of such works we are left to speculate as to how he might have integrated the themes of imperialism, writ so large in the history of capitalism, with the theory of accumulation.

Studies of imperialism since Marx have contributed much to our understanding of history but have been hard put to ground their findings in Marx's own theoretical framework. The result has been the construction of not one theory of imperialism but a whole host of representations on the matter.[12] When directly grounded in Marx's thought at all, they tend to appeal to one or other aspect only – the quest for foreign markets, the export of surplus capitals, primitive accumulation, uneven geographical development or whatever – rather than to theory as a whole. In other cases they claim to go beyond Marx and to rectify omissions and supposed errors. Much of this literature is both powerful and pursuasive. It constitutes a moving testimony to the depredations wrought in the name of human progress by a rapacious capitalism. It also captures the immense complexity and richness of human interaction as diverse peoples of the world with equally diverse histories, cultures and modes of production are forged into an akward and oppressive unity under the banner of the capitalist law of value.

The dominant imagery within this literature dramatically unifies themes of exploitation and 'the spatial fix'. Centres exploit peripheries, metropoli exploit hinterlands, the first world subjugates and mercilessly exploits the third, underdevelopment is imposed from without, and so on. Class struggle is resolved into the struggle of peripheral social formations against the central source of oppression. The countryside revolts against the city, the periphery against the centre, the third world against the first. So powerful is this spatial imagery that it flows back freely into the interpretation of the structures even in the heart of capitalism. Regional underdevelopment in advanced capitalist countries is seen as a coherent process of exploitation of regions by a dominant metropolis which itself maintains ghettos as 'internal neo-colonies'. The language of *Capital* appears to be displaced by an equally compelling imagery of exploitation of people in one place by those in another.

The challenge is to reconstitute what sometimes appear as antagonistic lines of thought and to integrate them into a single theoretical frame of reference. As things stand, the links are either founded in emotion, founded through appeal to the facts of exploitation, or else are projected on to the highest possible planes of abstraction by conceiving of imperialism as the

[12] See the surveys by Barratt-Brown (1974), Kemp (1967) and Amin (1980).

violent confrontation between capitalism and other modes of production (or social formations), which then become 'articulated' one upon another in particular configurations at different places and times, depending upon the outcome of the struggles waged. The third approach, which both Luxemburg and Lenin share, is to see imperialism as the *external* expression, dominant at a particular stage in capitalism's history and achieved under the aegis of finance capitalism, of the *internal* contradictions to which capitalism is systematically prone. Such writers appeal directly to the idea of 'the spatial fix' but explain Marx's neglect of the topic simply as a matter of history out-dating the master. None of these approaches is very satisfactory. Imperialism was alive and well in Marx's own time and was frequently commented upon in his popular writings (see *On Colonialism*, with Engels), while the idea of intersecting and conflicting modes of production is launched, albeit in preliminary fashion, in the *Grundrisse*. It remains, then, to extend Marx's theory of accumulation to embrace the diverse theories of those who seek to represent the historical experience of exploitation through imperialism. I cannot take up this challenge here in all of its fullness. But the somewhat more nuanced account of the spatial dynamics of capitalism, as presented in these last chapters, can help define a material basis within the theory of accumulation for much of what passes for imperialism.

The central point I have sought to hammer home in the last two chapters is that the production of spatial configurations in necessarily an active constitutive moment in the dynamics of accumulation. The shape of spatial configurations and the means for the annihilation of space with time are as important for understanding these dynamics as are improved methods of co-operation, the more extended use of machinery, etc. All of these features have to be assimilated within a broad conception of technological and organizational change. Since the latter is the pivot upon which accumulation turns as well as the nexus from which the contradictions of capitalism flow, then it follows that spatial and temporal expressions of this contradictory dynamic are of equal import.[13]

We have seen that spatial configurations are produced and transformed through the variegated mobilities of different kinds of capital and labour power (including the motion of capital through immobile social and physical infrastructures). The complementarities and antagonisms within the necessary unity of these mobilities produce an uneven, unstable and tension-packed geographical landscape for production, exchange and consumption.

---

[13] Writings on crises, such as those surveyed by Wright (1978) and Shaikh (1978) often neglect the geographical dimension altogether, or treat it as an appendage, while writings on imperialism are often curiously naive in their conception as to how crises form and proliferate within a framework of uneven development. Mandel's (1975) *Late Capitalism* and Amin's (1974) *Accumulation on a World Scale*, though far from perfect, have the virtue of keeping geographical aspects broadly in view.

Forces of concentration counter those of dispersal and produce centres and peripheries which the forces of inertia can turn into relatively permanent features within the space economy of capitalism. The division of labour assumes a territorial form and the circulation of capital under spatial constraints assumes regionally confined configurations. These provide a material basis for class and factional alliances to defend and enhance the value in motion within a region. In so far as class struggle yields a terrain of compromise between capital and labour within a region, organized labour may rally in support of such alliances in order to protect jobs and privileges already won. The regionalization of the circulation of capital is accompanied and reinforced, therefore, by the regionalization of class and factional conflict.

The homogeneity towards which the law of value tends contains its own negation in increasing regional differentiation. All kinds of opportunities then arise for competition and unequal exchange between regions. Massive concentrations of economic and political power within one region can become a basis for the domination and exploitation of others. Under threat of devaluation, each regional alliance seeks to use others as a means to alleviate its internal problems. The struggle over devaluation takes a regional turn. But the regional differentiations are rendered unstable thereby. Furthermore, the variegated mobilities of capital and labour power tend to undermine the very regional structures they help create. Regional alliances founder on the rock of international competition and the impulsion to equalize the rate of profit (particularly on money capital). The struggle to reduce turnover time reorders relative distances and makes nonsense of regional boundaries, which are highly porous anyway (even when patrolled by customs and immigration officers). And when devaluation threatens, individual elements of both capital and labour can just as easily run for the safest havens as stay in place and fight to export the costs to other regions.

The result is a chaos of confused and disordered motions towards both homogeneity and regional differentiation. Hierarchically structured organizations – of the financial and political system in particular – are essential if the disorder is to be contained. Such organizations, though lacking entirely in direct creative effect, typically concentrate immense repressive power – financial, political and military – in their upper echelons. These powers can be used to increase the rate of exploitation directly (chiefly by deployment of the repressive arm of the state apparatus) or to redistribute surplus value already produced among factions or regions. The struggle for control over strategic centres within the state, the international monetary system, the institutions of finance capital and so on are vital preparation if any faction or region is to visit the costs of devaluation on another.

There is more to imperialism than this, of course. Yet much of what passes for imperialism rests on the reality of exploitation of the peoples in one region by those in another under the aegis of some superior, dominant and repressive power. We have now shown that such a reality is contained in the very notion of capital itself. There is, then, a material basis for the perpetuation and reconstitution of traditional prejudices, of regional and national rivalries within an evolving framework of uneven geographical development. We can likewise understand the formation of alliances within regions, the struggle for control of hierarchically ordered institutions and periodic violent confrontations between nations and regions. To say, however, that there is a 'material basis' within the circulation of capital for such phenomena is not to claim that everything there is can be so understood. Nor does it mean that such phenomena — even when they achieve some rough equilibrium between homogeneity and regional differentiation, between geographical concentration and dispersal — provide a firm basis for future capital accumulation. Indeed, it is not hard to spot a central contradiction. The processes described allow the geographical production of surplus value to diverge from its geographical distribution, in much the same way that production and social distribution separate. Since, as we have seen, the disjunction between production and distribution is one of the rocks upon which the continuous circulation of capital founders, we can safely conclude, with both Marx and Lenin, that the basis for crisis formation is broadened and deepened by the processes we have here described. There is, in short, no 'spatial fix' that can contain the contradictions of capitalism in the long run.

VIII   INTER-IMPERIALIST RIVALRIES: GLOBAL WAR AS THE ULTIMATE FORM OF DEVALUATION

Twice in the twentieth century, the world has been plunged into global war through inter-imperialist rivalries. Twice in the space of a generation, the world experienced the massive devaluation of capital through physical destruction, the ultimate consumption of labour power as cannon fodder. Class warfare, of course, has taken its toll in life and limb, mainly through the violence daily visited by capital upon labour in the work place and through the violence of primitive accumulation (including imperialist wars fought against other social formations in the name of capitalist 'freedoms'). But the vast losses incurred in two world wars were provoked by inter-imperialist rivalries. How can this be explained on the basis of a theory that appeals to the class relation between capital and labour as fundamental to the interpretation of history?

This was, of course, the problem with which Lenin wrestled in his essay on imperialism. But his argument, as we saw in chapter 10, is plagued by ambiguity. Is finance capital national or international? What is the relation, then, between the military and political deployment of state power and the undoubted trend within capitalism to create multinational forms and to forge global spatial integration? And if monopolies and finance capital were so powerful and prone in any case to collusion, then why could they not contain capitalism's contradictions short of destroying each other? What is it, then, that makes inter-imperialist wars necessary to the survival of capitalism?

The 'third cut' at crisis theory suggests an interpretation of inter-imperialist wars as constitutive moments in the dynamics of accumulation, rather than as abberations, accidents or the simple product of excessive greed. Let us see how this is so.

When the 'inner dialectic' at work within a region drives it to seek external resolutions to its problems, then it must search out new markets, new opportunities for capital export, cheap raw materials, low-cost labour power, etc. All such measures, if they are to be anything other than a temporary palliative, either put a claim on future labour or else directly entail an expansion of the proletariat. This expansion can be accomplished through population growth, the mobilization of latent sectors of the reserve army, or primitive accumulation.

The insatiable thirst of capitalism for fresh supplies of labour accounts for the vigour with which it has pursued primitive accumulation, destroying, transforming and absorbing pre-capitalist populations wherever it finds them. When surpluses of labour are there for the taking, and capitalists have not, through competition, erroneously pinned their fates to a technological mix which cannot absorb that labour, then crises are typically of short duration, mere hiccups on a general trajectory of sustained global accumulation, and usually manifest as mild switching crises within an evolving structure of uneven geographical development. This was standard fare for nineteenth-century capitalism. The real troubles begin when capitalists, facing shortages of labour supply and as ever urged on by competition, induce unemployment through technological innovations which disturb the equilibrium between production and realization, between the productive forces and their accompanying social relations. The closing of the frontiers to primitive accumulation, through sheer exhaustion of possibilities, increasing resistance on the part of pre-capitalist populations, or monopolization by some dominant power, has, therefore, a tremendous significance for the long-run stability of capitalism. This was the sea-change that began to be felt increasingly as capitalism moved into the twentieth century. It was the sea-change that, far more than the rise of monopoly or finance forms of capitalism, played the crucial role in pushing capitalism deeper into the mire of global crises and led, inexorably, to the kinds of primitive accumulation and devaluation jointly wrought through inter-capitalist wars.

The mechanisms, as always, are intricate in their details and greatly confused in actual historical conjunctures by innumerable cross-currents of conflicting forces. But we can construct a simple line of argument to illustrate the important points. Any regional alliance, if it is to continue the process of accumulation, must maintain access to reserves of labour as well as to those 'forces of nature' (such as key mineral resources) that are otherwise capable of monopolization. Few problems arise if reserves of both exist in the region wherein most local capital circulates. When internal frontiers close, capital has to look elsewhere or risk devaluation. The regional alliance feels the stress between capital embedded in place and capital that moves to create new and permanent centres of accumulation elsewhere. Conflict between different regional and national capitals over access to labour reserves and natural resources begins to be felt. The themes of internationalism and multilaterialism run hard up against the desire for autarky as the means to preserve the position of some particular region in the face of internal contradictions and external pressures – autarky of the sort that prevailed in the 1930s, as Britain sealed in its Commonwealth trade and Japan expanded into Manchuria and mainland Asia, Germany into eastern Europe and Italy into Africa, pitting different regions against each other, each pursuing its own 'spatial fix'. Only the United States found it appropriate to pursue an 'open door' policy founded on internationalism and multilateral trading. In the end the war was fought to contain autarky and to open up the whole world to the potentialities of geographical expansion and unlimited uneven development. That solution, pursued single-mindedly under United States's hegemony after 1945, had the advantage of being super-imposed upon one of the most savage bouts of devaluation and destruction ever recorded in capitalism's violent history. And signal benefits accrued not simply from the immense destruction of capital, but also from the uneven geographical distribution of that destruction. The world was saved from the terrors of the great depression not by some glorious 'new deal' or the magic touch of Keynesian economics in the treasuries of the world, but by the destruction and death of global war.

The internationalism and multilateralism of the postwar world appears, on the surface, to be very different. Global freedom for the movement of capital (in all forms) has allowed instant access to the 'spatial fix' through geographical expansion within a framework of uneven geographical destruction. The rapid accumulation of capital on this basis led to the creation and in some cases the re-creation of independent regional centres of accumulation – Germany, Japan, Brazil, Mexico, South-East Asia, etc. Regional alliances build once more and compete for shrinking profit opportunities. The threat of autarky looms again. And with it comes the renewed threat of global war, this time waged with weapons of immense and insane destructive power, and oriented towards primitive accumulation at the expense of the socialist bloc.

Marxists, ever since Luxemburg first wrote on the subject, have long been attracted to the idea of military expenditures as a convenient means to absorb surpluses of capital and labour power. The instantaneous obsolescence of military hardware, and the easy manipulation of international tensions into a political demand for the increase in defence expenditures, adds lustre to the idea. Capitalism, it is sometimes held, is stabilized through the defence budget, albeit in ways that rob society of more humane and socially worthwhile programmes. This line of thinking is cast, unfortunately, in the underconsumptionist mould. I say 'unfortunately' not so much because that interpretation is wrong, but because the present theory suggests a rather more sinister and terrifying interpretation of military expenditures: not only must weapons be bought and paid for out of surpluses of capital and labour, but they must also be put to use. For this is the only means that capitalism has at its disposal to achieve the levels of devaluation now required. The idea is dreadful in its implications. What better reason could there be to declare that it is time for capitalism to be gone, to give way to some saner mode of production?

Afterword

A work of this sort admits no conclusion. The dialectical mode of thinking, at least as I construe it, precludes closure of the argument at any particular point. The intriguing configurations of internal and external contradiction, which I commented upon in the *Introduction,* force the argument to spin onwards and outwards to all manner of new terrain. The opening of new questions to be answered, new paths for enquiry to take, provokes simultaneously the re-evaluation of basic concepts – such as value – and the perpetual re-casting of the conceptual apparatus used to describe the world. Perhaps the most extraordinary insight to be gained from a careful study of Marx is the intricate fluidity of thought, the perpetual creation of new openings within the corpus of his writings. Strange, then, that bourgeois philosophers frequently depict Marxist science as a closed system, not amenable to the verification procedures with which they seek to close out their own hypotheses into universal and unchallengeable truths. Strange, also, that many Marxists convert deeply held and passionately felt commitments into doctrinaire dogmatism, as closed to new openings as traditional bourgeois modes of thought, when Marx's own work totally belies such closure.

Each ending should, in truth, be viewed as but a new beginning. It is hard for mere mortals to accept that truth, let alone to struggle and play with its implications in creative ways. Unfortunately, there is, as Marx himself observed, 'no royal road to science', and it is indeed a 'fatiguing climb' to reach the 'luminous summits' of knowledge. Though potentially endless, it is not, however, a seamless web of argument we seek to spin. Dim forms emerge from initial shadows of mystification, take firmer shape as different features are illumined from new vantage points, studied from new conceptual 'windows' opened up. It is a far from formless set of relationships that we come to discern. But if each end is but a beginning, then the efforts of preceding pages should lead us to consider new paths to take, new concepts to construct, new relationships to explore. The purpose of this Afterword is to take up such questions.

this is "open" marxism

The crucial commodity for the production of surplus value, labour power, is itself produced and reproduced under social relations over which capitalists have no direct control. It is odd that Marx did not pay closer attention to this paradox in all its multiple dimensions. There is more to it, of course, than a simple exploration of the relations between temporal rhythms of demographic growth in different regions and the spatial dynamics of accumulation, though this would be a useful point to start, since long-run accumulation always presupposes an expansion of the proletariat. We should never forget, however, that though labour power is a commodity the labourer is not. And though capitalists may view them as 'hands' possessed of stomachs, 'like some lowly creature on the sea-shore', as Dickens once put it, the labourers themselves are human beings possessed of all manner of sentiments, hopes and fears, struggling to fashion a life for themselves that contains at least minimal satisfactions. The conditions of production and reproduction of labour powers of different quantity and quality exist at the very centre of that life. And though susceptible of all manner of influence through bourgeois institutions and culture, nothing can in the end subvert the control workers exercise over certain very basic processes of their own reproduction. Their lives, their culture and, above all, their children are for them to reproduce.

Historians, both Marxist and other, have paid great attention to these themes in recent years, while Marxist students of the urban process are fond of viewing the city as the locus of reproduction of labour power. Studies of the working-class family, community, culture, stratification and social life in all its manifest complexity now abound. And the emergence of a strong feminist critique has made for new insights and contributions. Such studies are in desperate need of synthesis: indeed this is perhaps the most urgent task Marxian theory faces. It is, furthermore, a task that must be undertaken in the clear knowledge that the reproduction of labour power through the lived life of the working classes is a quite different dimension to the analysis of the capitalist mode of production. It is not a mere addendum to what we already know, but constitutes a fundamentally different point of departure to that upon which the theory of *Capital* is based. The starting point is not the commodity, but a simple event – the birth of a working-class child. The subsequent processes of socialization and instruction, of learning and being disciplined, may transform that human being into someone who has a certain capacity to labour and who is willing to sell that capacity as a commodity. Such processes deserve the closest possible study.

How the reproduction of capital through surplus value production meshes and intertwines with the reproduction of the lived life of the labourer becomes problematic. The two dimensions capture, in their opposition, the central tension between the richness of variegated culture and the arid realities of profit seeking. Some sort of unity must exist between the two if

but there are tensions unlikely to become revolutiona[?]
e.g. need for food... is labor tension like that?

448   AFTERWORD

capitalist society is to achieve even the semblance of social stability, and
major disjunctions must surely be the signal for crises marked by serious civil
strife. Yet neither process can easily or directly dominate the other, despite
their mutual interdependence. Means of co-ordination must be found, so many
mechanisms of mutual restraint, that somehow keep society in sufficient
equilibrium in its separate parts to prevent any total social collapse. This
theme has also been explored elsewhere, largely in terms of the relations
between work-based struggles and those struggles waged in the living space,
over housing, health, education and so on. That there is some sort of underlying unity to all such struggles is obvious. And both sides know it. Workers
know that monopolizable skills learned in the community can pay off handsomely both in wage rates and work conditions. And capitalists have long
been aware that if they are to dominate workers at the point of production
they must exercise a signal influence over them at their point of reproduction.
But the connections are far-flung, and the modes of countervailing influence
of extraordinary complexity. Crises of devaluation, which strike at capital
and labour alike, necessarily send reverberations through work place and
community which may rock civil society to its very foundations.

The chief channel whereby co-ordinating and mutually restraining functions can be exercised is through the variegated institutions of the modern
state. I have not considered the Marxist theory of the capitalist state in the
present work, in part because I felt that a full treatment of this controversial
subject ought to await a careful analysis of the processes of reproduction of
the labourer and of labour power. Yet the capitalist state has not been totally
neglected in preceding pages. Indeed, it has been omnipresent as the
guarantor of contracts and the freedoms of juridical individuals, and as the
repressive power that both forges and maintains labour power as a commodity. The state puts a floor under inter-capitalist competition and regulates
conditions of employment. It can facilitate the centralization of capital but
may also play a role in searching out the balance between centralization and
decentralization that preserves stability to the value composition of capital. It
undertakes the production of commodities (chiefly in the built environment)
which individual capitalists are unable or unwilling to furnish, however vital
they may be as conditions of further accumulation. It uses its planning powers
to shape the space economy of capitalism directly and thereby can even
regulate the pervasive tension between geographical concentration and dispersal. Through the aegis of a central bank, it plays hegemonic role in the
supply of money of a certain quality. Consideration of the fiscal and monetary functions of the state indicates the wide latitude of its potential intervention in both the temporal and spatial dynamics of accumulation within the
territory under its jurisdiction. The state system thereby becomes a vital part
of that battery of hierarchically ordered organizations linking individual
labours into the totality expressed as abstract labour. Occupying such a

but people accept the state!
idea: critique richard, maybe ask for more ↑ ambition
/s work

strategic position, and blessed as it is with the ultimate weapons of political and military power, the state becomes the central institution around which class alliances form. The fiscal and monetary powers can then be pressed into the service of such an alliance. Distributional arrangements can be modified, investment in appropriation controlled, fictitious capitals created and tendencies to devaluation thereby converted into inflation. The state becomes the central institution through which interregional conflicts are worked out, and the base from which each regional alliance seeks its 'spatial fix'.

The state, in short, plays a vital role in almost every aspect of the reproduction of capital. Furthermore, when government intervenes to stabilize accumulation in the face of multiple contradictions, it succeeds only at the price of internalizing these contradictions. It acquires the dubious task of administering the necessary doses of devaluation. But it has some choice as to how and where it does so. It can locate the costs within its territory through tough labour legislation and fiscal and monetary restraints. Or it can seek external relief through trade wars, combative fiscal and monetary policies on the world stage, backed in the end by appeal to military force. The ultimate form of devaluation is military confrontation and global war.

We have considered all these aspects to the modern state in the preceding text. Yet they do not form an adequate basis for a comprehensive theory of the state. Too many elements are left out. The reproduction of the labourer and of labour power, the production and use of knowledge as both a material force in production and as a weapon for domination and ideological control, must all be integrated into the argument. And as we strive to complete this task, two things become apparent. First, the institutions so fundamental to the reproduction of capital (such as the central bank) are to some degree kept quite separate from those that deal with the reproduction of the labourer and labour power. But secondly, some kind of unity has to prevail among diverse institutions, some balance struck, if society as a working whole is to be reproduced. This raises questions of the allocation of powers, of legitimacy, democracy and ideology, which Marxists have confronted directly in an immense and controversial literature. Above all, our attention must then focus upon the political struggle for control over the state apparatus and the powers that reside therein. Class struggle is displaced from the point of production into the political arena.

But an additional problem then arises. The relation between capital and labour has by now become transformed into multiple and conflicting configurations. We have already identified certain features within this process, as capital and labour split into different factions and sometimes reconstitute themelves around some regional alliance. And as soon as we take other aspects of capitalist life into account – the formation of a scientific and technical elite, the growth of management functions, of bureaucracy and so *in what sense?*

on – it often becomes almost impossible to discern the single capital–labour relation underneath. In this regard I think it symbolic that the last chapter of the third volume of *Capital* deals with the problem of classes under capitalism. The position of the chapter is important, though its content cannot be taken that seriously. It suggests that class configurations that actually exist under capitalism have to be interpreted as the product of forces ranged in support of both the accumulation of capital and the reproduction of the labourer as bearer of the commodity labour power. Class configurations cannot, therefore, be assumed *a priori*. They are actively produced. The class relation between capital and labour – a relation which simply acknowledges the centrality of buying and selling of labour power to economic life under capitalism – is merely a starting point from which to analyse the production of far more complicated class configurations unique to capitalism. The flux of forces at work within the dynamic of capitalist history – a flux we have sought at least partially to capture in preceding pages – creates pressures towards the formation of new class structures and alliances (including those based on territory). But class allegiances, identity and consciousness are by no means instantaneously malleable. The tension which results deserves the closest possible scrutiny. Class struggle cannot be properly understood, after all, without understanding how class configurations and alliances are forged and maintained in the first place.

Such an approach can help bridge what often appears as a most serious disjunction between the theorists of a purely capitalist mode of production and those seeking to reconstruct the actual historical geographies of capitalist social formations in all their rich complexity. Theorists may seek to spin and weave their arguments so as to 'locate and describe the concrete forms which grow out of the movements of capital as a whole', and so 'approach step by step' the concrete forms which capital 'assumes on the surface of society' (*Capital*, vol. 3, p. 25). In this way 'the life of the subject matter' may be 'ideally reflected as in a mirror' (*Capital*, vol. 1, p. 19). But the conceptual apparatus embedded in such a theoretical reconstruction is by no means an idea*list* abstraction. It is built up out of categories and relationships, like labour power, surplus value (absolute and relative) and capital as process, forged through actual historical transformations – through primitive accumulation, the rise of money forms and market exchange, the fierce struggle for capitalist control within the realm of production. The categories themselves are born out of an actual historical experience.

Theory begins when we put these historically-grounded categories to work to forge new interpretations. We cannot, by this means, hope to explain everything there is, nor even procure a full understanding of singular events. These are not the tasks which theory should address. The aim is, rather, to create frameworks for understanding, an elaborated conceptual apparatus, with which to grasp the most significant relationships at work within the

mx als social constructivist

intricate dynamics of social transformation. We can explain as general propositions why technological and organizational change and geographical reorganizations within the spatial division of labour are socially necessary to the survival of capitalism. We can understand the contradictions embedded in such processes and show how the contradictions are manifest within the crisis-prone historical geography of capitalist development. We can understand how new class configurations and alliances form, how they can be expressed as territorial configurations and degenerate into inter-imperialist rivalries. These are the kinds of insights that theory can yield.

But theory that cannot shed light on history or political practice is surely redundant. Worse still, erroneous theorizing – by no means an exclusive prerogative of the bourgeoisie – can mislead and mystify. And no theorist can claim omniscience. At some point or other tangible connections must be made between the weft of theory and the woof of historical geography. The persuasive power of the first volume of *Capital* derives precisely from the way in which the conceptual apparatus for theorizing supports and is supported by historical evidence. This is the kind of unity we must continually strive to maintain and improve upon.

Yet the separation within this unity, properly construed, has its place. It can be the locus of a creative tension, a point of leverage for the construction of new insights and understandings. Premature insistence upon the unity of theory and historical practice can lead to paralysis and stasis, sometimes to totally erroneous formulations. We either strive to stuff a recalcitrant historical geography into a dynamic described by a few simplistic categories, or else we create new categories, historically-grounded in such particular events that they can capture only the surface appearance, never the inner social meaning.

There is, then, a certain virtue in accepting and even pursuing to its utmost limits the separation between theory and historical practice, if only because their uneven development opens up new perspectives on the unity which necessarily must prevail between them. Running on two legs is faster than hopping along, both legs bound together.

But, in the final analysis, it is the unity which is important. The mutual development of theory and of historical and geographical reconstruction, all projected into the fires of political practice, forms the intellectual crucible out of which new strategies for the sane reconstruction of society can emerge. The urgency of that task, in a world beset by all manner of insane dangers – including the threat of all-out nuclear war (an inglorious form of devaluation, that) – surely needs no demonstration. If capitalism has reached such limits, then it is for us to find ways to transcend the limits to capital itself.

note: read marx in english,
then in german

References

WORKS BY MARX

Capital, International Publishers, New York: 1967.
A Contribution to the Critique of Political Economy, International Publishers, New York: 1970.
Critique of the Gotha Programme, International Publishers, New York: 1970.
Critique of Hegel's Philosophy of Right (ed. A. O'Malley), Cambridge University Press, London: 1970.
Early Texts (ed. D. McClellan), Basil Blackwell, Oxford: 1972.
Economic and Philosophic Manuscripts of 1844, International Publishers, New York: 1964.
The Eighteenth Brumaire of Louis Bonaparte, International Publishers, New York: 1963.
Grundrisse, Penguin, Harmondsworth, Middlesex: 1973.
Notes on Adolph Wagner, in *Value: Studies by Marx* (ed. A. Dragstedt), New Park Publications, London: 1976.
The Poverty of Philosophy, International Publishers, New York: 1963.
Results of the Immediate Process of Production (Appendix to *Capital,* vol. 1), Penguin, Harmondsworth, Middlesex: 1976.
Texts on Method (ed. Terrell Carver), Barnes and Noble, New York and Basil Blackwell, Oxford: 1975.
Theories of Surplus Value, Lawrence and Wishart, London: part 1 and 2, 1969; part 3, 1972.
Wage Labour and Capital, Foreign Languages Press, Peking: 1978.
Wages, Price and Profit, Foreign Languages Press, Peking: 1965.

WORKS BY MARX AND ENGELS

Collected Works, International Publishers, New York: volumes 1–12, 1975–80.

The German Ideology, International Publishers, New York: 1970.
Ireland and the Irish Question, International Publishers, New York: 1972.
Manifesto of the Communist Party, Progress Publishers, Moscow: 1952.
On Colonialism, International Publishers, New York: 1972.
Selected Correspondence, Progress Publishers, Moscow: 1955.

WORKS BY ENGELS

Anti-Dühring, Progress Publishers, Moscow: 1947.
The Condition of the Working Class in England in 1844, Allen and Unwin, London: 1962.
The Housing Question, International Publishers, New York: 1935.
The Origin of the Family, Private Property and the State, International Publishers, New York: 1942.

OTHER WORKS CITED

Aglietta, M. (1979), *A Theory of Capitalist Regulation,* London.
Althusser, L. (1969), *For Marx,* Harmondsworth, Middlesex.
Althusser, L. and Balibar, E. (1970), *Reading 'Capital',* London.
Altvater, E. (1973), 'Notes on some problems of state interventionism', *Kapitalistate,* vol. 1, 96–108; vol. 2, 76–83.
Amin, S. (1974), *Accumulation on a World Scale,* New York.
Amin, S. (1976), *Unequal Development,* New York.
Amin, S. (1980), *Class and Nation, Historically and in the Current Crisis,* New York.
Anderson, P. (1974), *Lineages of the Absolutist State,* London.
Anderson, P. (1980), *Arguments within English Marxism,* London.
Arrighi, G. (1978), *The Geometry of Imperialism,* London.
Arthur, C. J. (1976), 'The concept of "abstract labor" ', *Bulletin of the Conference of Socialist Economists,* vol. 5, no. 2.
Avineri, S. (1972), *Hegel's Theory of the Modern State,* Cambridge.
Aydalot, P. (1976), *Dynamique Spatiale et développement inégal,* Paris.
Ball, M. (1977), 'Differential rent and the role of landed property', *International Journal of Urban and Regional Research,* vol. 1, 380–403.
Banaji, J. (1976), 'Summary of selected parts of Kautsky's *The Agrarian Question',* *Economy and Society,* vol. 5, 1–49.
Baran, P. (1957), *The Political Economy of Growth,* New York.
Baran, P. and Sweezy, P. (1966), *Monopoly Capital,* New York.
Barker, C. (1978), 'The state as capital', *International Socialism,* series 2, no. 1, 16–42.

Barratt-Brown, M. (1974), *The Economics of Imperialism,* Harmondsworth, Middlesex.

Barrère, C. (1977), *Crise du système de crédit et capitalisme monopoliste d'Etat,* Paris.

Bassett, K. and Short, J. (1980), *Housing and Residential Structure: Alternative Approaches,* London.

Baumol, W. J. (1974), 'The transformation of values: what Marx "really" meant (an interpretation)', *Journal of Economic Literature,* vol. 12, 51–62.

Baumol, W. (1976), 'Review of *Introduction au Capital de Karl Marx* by G. Maarek', *Journal of Economic Literature,* vol. 14, 82–7.

Becker, J. F. (1977), *Marxian Political Economy,* London.

Benetti, C. (1976), *Valeur et répartition,* Grenoble.

Benetti, C., Berthomieu, C. and Cartelier, J. (1975), *Economie classique, économie vulgaire,* Grenoble.

Bernal, J. D. (1969 edn), *Science in History* (4 vols), Cambridge, Mass.

Berthoud, A. (1974), *Travail productif et productivité du travail chez Marx,* Paris.

Blaug, M. (1968), 'Technical change and Marxian economics', in D. Horowitz (ed.), *Marx and Modern Economics,* New York.

Blaug, M. (1978 edn), *Economic Theory in Retrospect,* London.

Bleaney, M. (1976), *Underconsumption Theories,* London.

Boccara, P. (1974), *Etudes sur le capitalisme monopoliste d'Etat, sa crise et son issue,* Paris.

Boddy, R. and Crotty, J. (1975), 'Class conflict and macro-policy: the political business cycle', *Review of Radical Political Economics,* vol. 7, no. 1, 1–19.

Böhm-Bawerk, E. von (1949), *Karl Marx and the Close of his System* (ed. P. Sweezy), New York.

Bouvier, J., Furet, F. and Gillet, M. (1965), *Le Mouvement du profit en France au XIXe siècle,* Paris.

Braverman, H. (1974), *Labor and Monopoly Capital,* New York.

Brighton Labour Process Group (1977), 'The capitalist labour process', *Capital and Class,* vol. 1, 3–26.

Bronfenbrenner, M. (1968), ' "Das Kapital" for the Modern Man', in D. Horowicz (ed.), *Marx and Modern Economics,* New York.

Bukharin, N. (1972a), *Imperialism and the World Economy,* London.

Bukharin, N. (1972b), 'Imperialism and the accumulation of capital', in R. Luxemburg and N. Bukharin, *Imperialism and the Accumulation of Capital,* New York.

Burawoy, M. (1978), 'Toward a Marxist theory of the labor process: Braverman and beyond', *Politics and Society,* vol. 8, 247–312.

Burawoy, M. (1979), *Manufacturing Consent: Changes in the Labor Process under Monopoly Capitalism,* Chicago.

Carney, J. G., Hudson, R. and Lewis, J. R. (1979), *Regions in Crisis,* London.

Castells, M. (1977), *The Urban Question,* London.

Chandler, A. (1962), *Strategy and Structure,* Cambridge, Mass.

Chandler, A. (1977), *The Visible Hand: the Managerial Revolution in American Business,* Cambridge, Mass.

Cheape, C. W. (1980), *Moving the Masses,* Cambridge, Mass.

Christaller, W. (1966), *Central Places in Southern Germany,* Englewood Cliffs, N.J.

Churchward, L. G. (1959), 'Towards the understanding of Lenin's Imperialism', *Australian Journal of Politics and History,* vol. 5, no. 1, 76–83.

Clarke, S. (1980), 'The value of value', *Capital and Class,* vol. 10, 1–17.

Cogoy, M. (1973), 'The fall in the rate of profit and the theory of accumulation: a reply to Paul Sweezy', *Conference of Socialist Economists Bulletin,* vol. 2, no. 7.

Cohen, G. A. (1978), *Karl Marx's Theory of History – a Defense,* Princeton, New Jersey.

Conference of Socialist Economists (1976), *On the Political Economy of Women* (CSE Pamphlet no. 2).

Coutière, A. (1976), *Le Système Monétaire Français,* Paris.

Crouzet, F. (1972), *Capital Formation in the Industrial Revolution,* London.

Cutler, A., Hindess, B., Hirst, P. and Hussain, A. (1978), *Marx's Capital and Capitalism Today* (2 vols), London.

Davis, H. (1978), *Toward a Marxist Theory of Nationalism,* New York.

de Brunhoff, S. (1971), *L'Offre de monnaie,* Paris.

de Brunhoff, S. (1976), *Marx on Money,* New York.

de Brunhoff, S. (1978), *The State, Capital and Economic Policy,* London.

de Brunhoff, S. (1979), *Les rapports d'argent,* Grenoble.

de Gaudemar, J. P. (1976), *Mobilité du travail et accumulation du capital,* Paris.

de la Haye, Y. (1979), *Marx and Engels on the Means of Communication,* New York.

Deane, P. and Cole, W. (1962), *British Economic Growth: 1688–1959,* London.

Dear, M. and Scott, A. (eds.) (1981), *Urbanization and Urban Planning in Capitalist Society,* London.

Desai, M. (1979), *Marxian Economics,* Oxford.

Dichervois, M. and Theret, B. (1979), *Contribution a l'étude de la rente foncière urbaine,* The Hague.

Dobb, M. (1940), *Political Economy and Capitalism,* London.

Dobb, M. (1963), *The Economic Development of Capitalism,* New York.

Dobb, M. (1973), *Theories of Value and Distribution since Adam Smith: Ideology and Economic Theory,* New York.

Dobb, M. (1975–6), 'A note on the Ricardo–Marx–Sraffa discussion', *Science and Society,* vol. 39, 468–70.

Domhoff, W. G. (1978), *The Powers That Be: Processes of Ruling-Class Domination in America,* New York.

Donzelot, J. (1979), *The Policing of the Families: Welfare versus the State,* London.

Dostaler, G. (1978a), *Valeur et prix: histoire d'un débat,* Paris.

Dostaler, G. (1978b), *Marx: la valeur et l'économie politique,* Paris.

Draper, H. (1977), *Karl Marx's Theory of Revolution,* Part 1; *State and Bureaucracy,* New York.

Dulong, R. (1978), *Les régions, l'Etat et la société locale,* Paris.

Dumenil, G. (1975), 'L'expression du taux de profit dans "Le Capital" ', *Revue économique,* vol. 26, 198–219.

Dumenil, G. (1977), *Marx et Keynes face à la crise,* Paris.

Edel, M. (1976), 'Marx's theory of rent: urban applications', *Kapitalistate,* vol. 4/5, 100–25.

Edwards, R. (1979), *Contested Terrain: the Transformation of the Workplace in the Twentieth Century,* New York.

Eisenstein, Z., (ed.) (1979), *Capitalist Patriarchy and the Case for Socialist Feminism,* New York.

Elbaum, B., Lazonick, W., Wilkinson, F. and Zeitlin, J. (1979), 'The labour process, market structure and Marxist theory', *Cambridge Journal of Economics,* vol. 3, 227–30.

Elbaum, B. and Wilkinson, F. (1979), 'Industrial relations and uneven development: a comparative study of the American and British steel industries', *Cambridge Journal of Economics,* vol. 3, 275–303.

Elger, T. (1979), 'Valorization and "deskilling"; a critique of Braverman', *Capital and Class,* vol. 7, 58–99.

Elson, D. (ed.) (1979), *Value: the Representation of Labour in Capitalism,* London.

Elster, J. (1978), 'The labor theory of value: a reinterpretation of Marxist economics', *Marxist perspectives,* vol. 1, no. 3, 70–101.

Emmanuel, A. (1972), *Unequal Exchange: a Study of the Imperialism of Trade,* New York.

Erlich, A. (1978), 'Dobb and the Marx–Feldman model: a problem in Soviet economic strategy', *Cambridge Journal of Economics,* vol. 2, 203–14.

Fairley, J. (1980), 'French developments in the theory of state monopoly capitalism', *Science and Society,* vol. 44, 305–25.

Fine, B. (1979a), 'World economic crisis and inflation', in F. Green and P. Nore (eds.), *Issues in Political Economy: a Critical Approach,* London.

Fine, B. (1979b), 'On Marx's theory of agricultural rent', *Economy and Society,* vol. 8, 241–78.

Fine, B. (1980), *Economic Theory and Ideology,* London.

Fine, B. and Harris, L. (1979), *Re-Reading Capital,* London.

Fitch, R. and Openheimer, M. (1970), 'Who rules the corporations?' *Socialist Revolution,* vol. 1, no. 4, 73–107; no. 5, 61–114; no. 6, 33–94.

Foster, J. (1975), *Class struggle in the Industrial Revolution,* New York.

Frank, A. (1969), *Capitalism and Underdevelopment in Latin America,* New York.

Freyssenet, M. (1971), *Les rapports de production: travail productif et travail improductif,* Paris.

Freyssenet, M. (1977), *La division capitaliste du travail,* Paris.

Friedman, A. (1977a), *Industry and Labour,* London.

Friedman, A. (1977b), 'Responsible autonomy versus direct control over the labour process', *Capital and Class,* vol. 1, 43–57.

Gardner, L. C. (1964), *Economic Aspects of New Deal Diplomacy,* Boston.

Gerdes, C. (1977), 'The fundamental contradiction in the neoclassical theory of income distribution', *Review of Radical Political Economics,* vol. 9, no. 2, 39–64.

Gerstein, I. (1976), 'Production, circulation and value: the significance of the "transformation problem" in Marx's critique of political economy', *Economy and Society,* vol. 3, 243–91.

Gillman, J. (1957), *The Falling Rate of Profit,* London.

Glyn, A. and Sutcliffe, R. (1972), *British Capitalism, Workers and the Profit Squeeze,* Harmondsworth, Middlesex.

Godelier, M. (1972), *Rationality and Irrationality in Economics,* London.

Goldsmith, R. W. (1969), *Financial Structure and Development,* New Haven, Conn.

Gough, I. (1972), 'Productive and unproductive labour in Marx', *New Left Review,* vol. 76, 47–72.

Gramsci, A. (1971), *Prison Notebooks,* London.

Grossman, H., (1977), 'Archive: Marx, classical political economy and the problem of dynamics', *Capital and Class,* vol. 2, 32–55; vol. 3, 67–89.

Gurley, J. G. and Shaw, E. S. (1960), *Money in a Theory of Finance,* Washington, DC.

Hannah, L. (1976), *The Rise of the Corporate Economy,* London.

Harris, L. (1976), 'On interest, credit and capital', *Economy and Society,* vol. 5, 145–77.

Harris, L. (1978), 'The science of the economy', *Economy and Society,* vol. 7, 284–320.

Harris, L. (1979), 'The role of money in the economy', in F. Green and P. Nore (eds.), *Issues in Political Economy: a Critical Approach,* London.

Hartmann, H. (1979), 'The unhappy marriage of Marxism and feminism: towards a more progressive union', *Capital and Class,* vol. 8, 1–33.

Harvey, D. (1969), *Explanation in Geography,* London.

Harvey, D. (1973), *Social Justice and the City,* London.

Harvey, D. (1975), 'The geography of capitalist accumulation: a reconstruction of the Marxian theory', *Antipode,* vol. 7, no. 2, 9–21.

Harvey, D. (1977), 'Labor, capital and class struggle around the built environment in advanced capitalist societies', *Politics and Society,* vol. 6, 265–95.

Harvey, D. (1978), 'Urbanization under capitalism: a framework for analysis', *International Journal of Urban and Regional Research,* vol. 2, 101–31.

Harvey, J. (1977), 'Theories of inflation', *Marxism Today,* January.

Heertje, A. (1972), 'Essay on Marxian economics', *Schweizerisches Zeitschrift für Volkwirtschaft und Statistik,* vol. 108, 33–45.

Heertje, A. (1977), *Economics and Technical Change,* New York.

Hegel, G. W. (1952 edn), *Philosophy of Right,* Oxford.

Hendrick, B. J. (1907), 'Great American fortunes and their making: street railway financiers', *McClures Magazine,* vol. 30, 33–48.

Herman, E. S. (1973), 'Do bankers control corporations?' *Monthly Review,* vol. 25, no. 1, 12–29.

Herman, E. S. (1979), 'Kotz on banker control', *Monthly Review,* vol. 31, no. 4, 46–57.

Hilferding, R. (1970 edn), *Le Capital financier,* Paris.

Hilton, R. (ed.) (1976), *The Transition from Feudalism to Capitalism,* London.

Himmelweit, S. and Mohun, S. (1977), 'Domestic labour and capital', *Cambridge Journal of Economics,* vol. 1, 15–31.

Hindess, B. and Hirst, P. (1975), *Pre-Capitalist Modes of Production,* London.

Hindess, B. and Hirst, P. (1976), *Mode of Production and Social Formation,* London.

Hirschman, A. O. (1976), 'On Hegel, imperialism, and structural stagnation', *Journal of Development Economics,* 3, 1–8.

Hobson, J. A. (1965), *Imperialism,* Ann Arbor, Michigan.

Hodgson, G. (1974), 'The theory of the falling rate of profit', *New Left Review,* vol. 84, 55–82.

Hodgson, G. (1980), 'A theory of exploitation without the labor theory of value', *Science and Society,* vol. 44, 257–73.

Holloway, J. and Picciotto, S. (1978), *State and Capital: a Marxist Debate,* London.

Hook, S. (1933), *Towards the Understanding of Karl Marx: a Revolutionary Interpretation,* New York.

Howard, M. C. and King, J. E. (1975), *The Political Economy of Marx*, London.

Humphries, J. (1977), 'Class struggle and the persistence of the working-class family', *Cambridge Journal of Economics*, vol. 1, 241–58.

Hunt Commission Report (1971), *Financial Structure and Regulation*, Washington, DC.

Hunt, E. K. (1979), 'The categories of productive and unproductive labor in Marxist economic theory', *Science and Society*, vol. 43, 303–25.

Hymer, S. (1972), 'The multinational corporation and the law of uneven development', in J. Bhagwati (ed.), *Economics and World Order from the 1970s to the 1990s*, New York.

Isard, W. (1956), *Location and Space Economy*, Cambridge, Mass.

Itoh, M. (1976), 'A study of Marx's theory of value', *Science and Society*, vol. 40, 307–40.

Itoh, M. (1978a), 'The formation of Marx's theory of crisis', *Science and Society*, vol. 42, 129–55.

Itoh, M. (1978b), 'The inflational crisis of capitalism', *Capital and Class*, vol. 4, 1–10.

Jacobi, O., Bergmann, J. and Mueller-Jentsch, W. (1975), 'Problems in Marxist theories of inflation', *Kapitalistate*, vol. 3, 107–25.

Jacot, J-H. (1976), *Croissance économique et fluctuations conjuncturelles*, Lyons.

Kalecki, M. (1971), *Selected Essays on the Dynamics of the Capitalist Economy*, London.

Kautsky, K. (1970 edn), *La question agraire*, Paris.

Keiper, J.S., Kurnow, E., Clark, C.D. and Segal, H.H. (1961), *Theory and Measurement of Rent*, New York.

Kemp, T. (1967), *Theories of Imperialism*, London.

Keynes, J. M. (1936),*The General Theory of Employment, Interest and Money*, New York.

Koeppel, B. (1978), 'The new sweatshops', *The Progressive*, vol. 42, no. 11, 22–6.

Kolko, G. (1977), *The Triumph of Conservatism: a Reinterpretation of American History*, New York.

Kotz, D. (1978), *Bank Control of Large Corporations in the United States*, Berkeley, Calif.

Krelle, W. (1971), 'Marx as a growth theorist', *German Economic Review*, vol. 9, 122–33.

Kühne, K. (1979), *Economics and Marxism* (2 vols), London.

Laclau, E. (1977), *Politics and Ideology in Marxist Theory: Capitalism Fascism, Populism*, London.

Laibman, D. (1973–4), 'Values and prices of production: the political economy of the transformation problem', *Science and Society*, vol. 37, 404–36.

Lamarche, F. (1976), 'Property development and the economic foundations of the urban question', in C. Pickvance (ed.), *Urban Sociology: Critical Essays,* London.

Lazonick, W. (1979), 'Industrial relations and technical change: the case of the self-acting mule', *Cambridge Journal of Economics,* vol. 3, 231–62.

Lebowitz, M. A. (1977–8), 'Capital and the production of needs', *Science and Society,* vol. 41, 430–47.

Lefebvre, H. (1972), *La droit à la ville: suivi d'espace et politique,* Paris.

Lefebvre, H. (1974), *La production de l'espace,* Paris.

Lenin, V. I. (1956 edn), *The Development of Capitalism in Russia,* Moscow.

Lenin, V. I. (1970 edn), *Selected Works* (3 vols.), Moscow.

Levine, D. (1978), *Economic Theory,* London.

Lipietz, A. (1974), *Le tribut foncier urbain,* Paris.

Lipietz, A. (1977), *Le capital et son espace,* Paris.

Lösch, A. (1967), *The Economics of Location,* New York.

Luxemburg, R. (1951), *The Accumulation of Capital,* London.

Luxemburg, R. and Bukharin, N. (1972 edn), *Imperialism and the Accumulation of Capital,* New York.

Maarek, G. (1979), *An Introduction to Karl Marx's Capital: a Study in Formalization,* Oxford.

Macfarlane, A. (1978), *The Origins of English Individualism: The Family, Property and Social Transition,* Oxford.

MacPherson, C. B. (1962), *The Political Theory of Possessive Individualism,* Oxford.

Magaline, A. D. (1975), *Lutte de classes et dévalorisation du capital,* Paris.

Malos, E. (1980), *The Politics of Housework,* London.

Mandel, E. (1968), *Marxist Economic Theory,* London.

Mandel, E. (1971), *The Formation of the Economic Thought of Karl Marx,* London.

Mandel, E. (1975), *Late Capitalism,* London.

Mandel, E. (1978), *The Second Slump,* London.

Massey, D. (1978), 'Regionalism: some current issues', *Capital and Class,* vol. 6, 106–25.

Massey, D. (1979), 'In what sense a regional problem?' *Regional Studies,* vol. 13, 233–44.

Massey, D. (1981), 'The U.K. electrical engineering and electronics industries: the implications of the crisis for the restructuring of capital and locational change', in M. Dear and A. Scott (eds.), *Urbanization and Urban Planning in Capitalist Society,* pp. 199–230.

Massey, D. and Catelano, A. (1978), *Capital and Land: Landownership by Capital in Great Britain,* London.

Mathias, P. (1973), 'Capital, credit and enterprise in the industrial revolution', *Journal of European Economic History,* vol. 2, 121–44.

Mattick, P. (1969), *Marx and Keynes,* London.

Mattick, P. (1980), *Economics, Politics and the Age of Inflation,* London.

McKinnon, R. (1973), *Money and Capital in Economic Development,* Washington, DC.

Meek, R. L. (1973), *Studies in the Labour Theory of Value,* London.

Meek, R. L. (1977), *Smith, Marx and After,* London.

Meillassoux, C. (1981), *Maidens, Meal and Money,* London.

Merignas, M. (1978), 'Travail social et structures de classe', *Critiques de l'économie politique,* New Series, no. 3, 24–56.

Montgomery, D. (1979), *Worker's Control in America,* London.

Morin, F. (1974), *La Structure financière du capitalisme français,* Paris.

Morishima, M. (1973), *Marx's Economics,* London.

Morishima, M. and Catephores, G. (1978), *Value, Exploitation and Growth,* Maidenhead, Berks.

Morris, J. and Lewin, H. (1973–4), 'The skilled labor reduction problem', *Science and Society,* vol. 37, 454–72.

Nabudere, D. (1977), *The Political Economy of Imperialism,* London.

Nagels, J. (1974), *Travail collectif et travail production,* Brussels.

Nairn, T. (1977), *The Break-up of Britain: Crisis and Neo-Nationalism,* London.

Niehans, J. (1978), *The Theory of Money,* Baltimore.

Noble, D. (1977), *America by Design: Science, Technology and the Rise of Corporate Capitalism,* New York.

O'Connor, J. (1973), *The Fiscal Crisis of the State,* New York.

O'Connor, J. (1975), 'Productive and unproductive labor', *Politics and Society,* vol. 4, 297–336.

Okishio, N. (1961), 'Technical change and the rate of profit', *Kobe University Economic Review,* vol. 7, 85–99.

Ollman, B. (1971), *Alienation: Marx's Conception of Man in Capitalist Society,* London.

Ollman, B. (1973), 'Marxism and political science: a prologomenon to a debate on Marx's method', *Politics and Society,* vol. 3, 491–510.

Osadchaya, I. (1974), *From Keynes to Neo-Classical Synthesis: a Critical Analysis,* Moscow.

Palloix, C. (1973), *Les firmes multinationales et le procès d'internationalisation,* Paris.

Palloix, C. (1975a), *L'internationalisation du capital,* Paris.

Palloix, C. (1975b), 'The internationalization of capital and circuit of social capital', in H. Radice (ed.), *International Firms and Modern Imperialism,* Harmondsworth, Middlesex.

Palloix, C. (1976), 'The labour-process: from Fordism to neo-Fordism', in Conference of Socialist Economists, *The Labour Process and Class Strategies,* London.

Palmer, B. (1975), 'Class, conception and conflict: the thrust for efficiency, managerial views of labour, and the working class rebellion, 1903–1922', *Review of Radical Political Economics*, vol. 7, no. 2, 31–49.

Pannakoek, A. (1977), 'The theory of the collapse of capitalism', *Capital and Class*, vol. 1, 59–81.

Peet, R. (1981), 'Spatial dialectics and Marxist geography', *Progress in Human Geography*, vol. 5, 105–10.

Pilling, G. (1972), 'The law of value in Ricardo and Marx', *Economy and Society*, vol. 1, 281–307.

Pinkney, D. H. (1958), *Napoleon III and the Rebuilding of Paris*, Princeton, New Jersey.

Portes, A. (1980), 'The informal sector and the capital accumulation process in Latin America', in A. Portes and J. Walton (eds.), *The Political Economy of Development*, New York.

Postel-Vinay, G. (1974), *La rente foncière dans le capitalisme agricole*, Paris.

Poulantzas, N. (1975), *Classes in Contemporary Capitalism*, London.

Poulantzas, N. (1978), *State, Power, Socialism*, London.

Radice, H., (ed.) (1975), *International Firms and Modern Imperialism*, Harmondsworth, Middlesex.

Report of the Commission on Money and Credit (1961), *Money and Credit, Their Influence on Jobs, Prices, and Growth*, Englewood Cliffs, New Jersey.

Revell, J. (1973), *The British Financial System*, New York.

Rey, P-P. (1973), *Les alliances de classes*, Paris.

Ricardo, D. (1970 edn), *The Works and Correspondence of David Ricardo*, London.

Roberts, S., (1961), 'Portrait of a robber baron: Charles T. Yerkes', *Business History Review*, vol. 35, 344–71.

Robinson, J. (1967), *An Essay on Marxian Economics*, London.

Robinson, J. (1968), 'Marx and Keynes', in D. Horowicz (ed.), *Marx and Modern Economics*, New York.

Robinson, J. (1977), 'The labor theory of value', *Monthly Review*, vol. 29, no. 7, 50–9.

Robinson, J. (1978), 'The organic composition of capital', *Kyklos*, vol. 31, 5–20.

Roemer, J. (1977), 'Technical change and the "tendency of the rate of profit to fall" ', *Journal of Economic Theory*, vol. 16, 403–24.

Roemer, J. (1978), 'The effect of technological change on the real wage and Marx's falling rate of profit', *Australian Economic Papers*, vol. 17, 152–66

Roemer, J. (1979), 'Continuing controversy on the falling rate of profit: fixed capital and other issues', *Cambridge Journal of Economics*, vol. 3, 379–98.

Roemer, J. (1980), 'A general equilibrium approach to Marxian economics', *Econometrica,* vol. 48, 505–30.

Roncaglia, R. (1974), 'The reduction of complex labour to simple labour', *Bulletin of the Conference of Socialist Economists,* Autumn.

Rosdolsky, R. (1977), *The Making of Marx's 'Capital',* London.

Rostow, W. W. (1960), *The Stages of Economic Growth: a Non-Communist Manifesto,* London.

Rowthorn, B. (1980), *Capitalism, Conflict and Inflation,* London.

Rubin, I. (1972 edn), *Essays on Marx's Theory of Value,* Detroit.

Samuelson, P. (1957), 'Wages and prices: a modern dissection of Marxian economic models', *American Economic Review,* vol. 47, 884–912.

Samuelson, P. (1971), 'Understanding the Marxian notion of exploitation: a summary of the so-called transformation problem between Marxian values and competitive prices', *Journal of Economic Literature,* vol. 9, 399–431.

Santos, M. (1979), *The Shared Space: the Two Circuits of the Urban Economy in Underdeveloped Countries,* London.

Schefold, B. (1977), 'Fixed capital as a joint product', *Jahrbucher für National Ökonomie und Statistik.*

Schmidt, A. (1971), *The Concept of Nature in Marx,* London.

Schumpeter, J. (1934), *The Theory of Economic Development,* Cambridge, Mass.

Schumpeter, J. (1939), *Business Cycles,* New York.

Scott, A. (1980), *The Urban Land Nexus and the State,* London.

Scott, J. (1979), *Corporations, Classes, Capitalism,* London.

Seccombe, W. (1974), 'The housewife and her labour under capitalism', *New Left Review,* vol. 83, 3–24.

Shaikh, A. (1977), 'Marx's theory of value and the "transformation problem" ', in J. Schwarts (ed.), *The Subtle Anatomy of Capitalism,* Santa Monica, Calif.

Shaikh, (1978), 'An introduction to the history of crisis theories', in Union of Radical Political Economics, *U.S. Capitalism in Crisis,* New York.

Shaikh, A. (1979–80), 'Foreign trade and the law of value', *Science and Society,* vol. 43, 281–302; vol. 44, 27–57.

Sherman, H. (1967), 'Marx and the business cycle', *Science and Society,* vol. 31, 486–504.

Sherman, H. (1971), 'Marxist models of cyclical growth', *History of Political Economy,* vol. 3, 28–55.

Sherman, H. (1976), *Stagflation: a Radical Theory of Unemployment and Inflation,* New York.

Smith, A. (1937 edn), *An Inquiry into the Nature and Causes of the Wealth of Nations,* New York.

Smith, H. (1937), 'Marx and the trade cycle', *Review of Economic Studies,* vol. 4, 192–205.

Smith, N. (1980) 'The production of nature' (unpublished ms.).

Smith, N. (1981), 'Degeneracy in theory and practice: spatial interactionism and radical eclecticism', *Progress in Human Geography,* vol. 5, 111–18.

Soja, E. (1980), 'The socio-capital dialectic', *Annals of the Association of American Geographers,* vol. 70, 207–25.

Sowell, T. (1972), *Say's Law: an Historical Analysis,* Princeton, New Jersey.

Spring, D. (1963), *The English Landed Estate in the Nineteenth Century,* Baltimore.

Sraffa, P. (1960), *The Production of Commodities by Means of Commodities,* London.

Steedman, I. (1977), *Marx after Sraffa,* London.

Stone, K. (1974), 'The origin of job structures in the steel industry', *The Review of Radical Political Economics,* vol. 6, no. 2, 113–73.

Studenski, P. and Kroos, H. E. (1952), *Financial History of the United States,* New York.

Sweezy, P. (1968 edn), *The Theory of Capitalist Development,* New York.

Sweezy, P. (1971), 'The resurgence of financial control: fact or fancy?' *Monthly Review,* vol. 23, no. 6, 1–33.

Sweezy, P. (1979), 'Marxian value theory', *Monthly Review,* vol. 31, no. 3, 1–17.

Sweezy, P. and Magdoff, H. (1972), *The Dynamics of U.S. Capitalism,* New York.

Taylor, J. G. (1979), *From Modernization to Modes of Production,* London.

Therborn, G. (1976), *Science, Class and Society,* London.

Théret, B. and Wievorka, M. (1978), *Critique de la théorie du capitalisme monopoliste d'Etat,* Paris.

Thomas, B. (1973), *Migration and Economic Growth,* London.

Thompson, E. P. (1968), *The Making of the English Working Class,* Harmondsworth, Middlesex.

Thompson, E. P. (1978), *The Poverty of Theory and Other Essays,* London.

Thompson, F. M. L. (1963), *English Landed Society in the Nineteenth Century,* London.

Thompson, G. (1977), 'The relationship between the financial and industrial sector in the United Kingdom economy', *Economy and Society,* vol. 6, 235–83.

Tilly, L. A. and Scott, J. (1978), *Women, Work and Family,* New York.

Topalov, C. (1974), *Les promoteurs immobiliers,* The Hague.

Tortajada, R. (1977), 'A note on the reduction of complex labour to simple labour', *Capital and Class,* vol. 1, 106–16.

Tribe, K. (1977), 'Economic property and the theorization of ground rent', *Economy and Society,* vol. 6, 69–88.

Tribe, K. (1978), *Land, Labour and Economic Discourse,* London.

Tsuru, S. (1968), 'Keynes versus Marx: the methodology of aggregates', in D. Horowicz (ed.), *Marx and Modern Economics,* New York.

Tucker, R. (1970), *The Marxian Revolutionary Idea,* London.

Uno, K. (1980), *Principles of Political Economy: Theory of a Purely Capitalist Society,* Brighton.

Vilar, P. (1976), *A History of Gold and Money,* London.

van Parijs, P. (1980), 'The falling-rate-of-profit theory of crisis: a rational reconstruction by way of obituary', *Review of Radical Political Economics,* vol. 12, 1–16.

von Bortkiewicz, L. (1952), 'Value and price in the Marxian system', *International Economic Papers,* vol. 2, 5–60.

von Thunen, J. H. (1960 edn), *The Frontier Wage,* (trans. and ed. B. Dempsey), Chicago.

von Weizsäcker (1977), 'Organic composition of capital and average period of production', *Revue d'économie politique,* vol. 87, no. 2, 198–231.

Walker, R. A. (1977), 'The suburban solution: urban reform and urban geography in the capitalist development of the United States', Doctoral Dissertation, The Johns Hopkins University, Baltimore.

Walker, R. A. and Storper, N. (1981), 'Capital and industrial location', *Progress in Human Geography,* (forthcoming). vol. 5, 473–509.

Wallerstein, I. (1974), *The Modern World System,* New York.

Weeks, J. (1979), 'The process of accumulation and the "profit-squeeze" hypothesis', *Science and Society,* vol. 43, 259–80.

Weisskopf, T. (1978), 'Marxist perspectives on cyclical crises', in Union of Radical Political Economics, *U.S. Capitalism in Crisis,* New York.

Wilson, J. C. (1938), 'A note on Marx and the trade cycle', *Review of Economic Studies,* vol. 5, 107–13.

Wolfstetter, E. (1972), 'Surplus labour, synchronized labour costs and Marx's labour theory of value', *Economic Journal,* vol. 83, 787–809.

Wright, E. J. (1978), *Class, Crisis and the State,* London.

Yaffe, D. (1973), 'The Marxian theory of crisis, capital and the state', *Economy and Society,* vol. 2, 186–232.

Zaretsky, E. (1976), *Capitalism, the Family and Personal Life,* London.

Zeitlin, J. (1979), 'Craft control and the division of labour: engineers and compositors in Britain, 1890–1930', *Cambridge Journal of Economics,* vol. 3, 263–74.

Zeitlin, M. (1974), 'Corporate ownership and control: the large corporation and the capitalist class', *American Journal of Sociology,* vol.79, 1073–119.

Name Index

Note: This index does not include the authors of works cited in footnotes – see References. Marx is also excluded.

Subject Index

get thru explication quickly and spin ⊙ out on clothing industry

idea: gute e'o burostende, aber sprich nur 1v2 malonklasse